ADMINISTRATIVE LAW

by

J. F. GARNER, LL.D. (Lond.)

Solicitor; Professor of Public Law,
University of Nottingham

FOURTH EDITION

LONDON
BUTTERWORTHS
1974

ENGLAND:	BUTTERWORTH & CO. (PUBLISHERS) LTD. LONDON: 88 KINGSWAY, WC2B 6AB
AUSTRALIA:	BUTTERWORTH & CO. (AUSTRALIA) LTD. SYDNEY: 586 PACIFIC HIGHWAY, CHATSWOOD, NSW 206 MELBOURNE: 343 LITTLE COLLINS STREET, 3000 BRISBANE: 240 QUEEN STREET, 4000
CANADA:	BUTTERWORTH & CO. (CANADA) LTD. TORONTO: 14 CURITY AVENUE, 374
NEW ZEALAND:	BUTTERWORTH & CO. (NEW ZEALAND) LTD. WELLINGTON: 26/28 WARING TAYLOR STREET
SOUTH AFRICA:	BUTTERWORTH & CO. (SOUTH AFRICA) (PTY.) LTD. DURBAN: 152/154 GALE STREET

First Edition	..	..	*May* 1963
Second Edition	..	..	*April* 1967
Reprinted..	..	..	*January* 1969
Third Edition	..	..	*July* 1970
Reprinted	..	..	*November* 1971
Fourth Edition	..	..	*March* 1974

ISBN – Casebound: 0 406 58794 9
Limp: 0 406 58795 7

Made and printed in Great Britain by
William Clowes & Sons, Limited
London, Beccles and Colchester

PREFACE TO THE FOURTH EDITION

More changes have had to be made to the text of the previous edition on this occasion than ever before. Apart from the reorganisation of local government, of the national health service and of water supply and distribution, Parliament has created a number of new public corporations and reorganised some existing ones, and there has also been a major consolidation of the law of town and country planning, and a (mercifully) shorter statute on Tribunals and Inquiries. All these statutory changes together with the creation of new tribunals have had to be taken into account, and the Local Government Act, 1972, in particular has made necessary a major re-writing of several chapters in the book.

The entry of the United Kingdom into the European Communities has not yet had any direct effect on our administrative law, but its potential significance cannot be ignored. There has also been a considerable volume of case law, in particular on the subject of natural justice, and the developing notion of "fairness". Notice has been taken of helpful observations made by reviewers of previous editions, and the text has been modified in places to meet comments by colleagues and students, to all of whom the author is sincerely thankful.

The law is ever changing, and the Working Paper of the Law Commission on "Remedies in Administrative Law" is particularly welcome in presaging future desirable changes. All lawyers in this country, practitioners and academics alike, would surely prefer the Commission's proposed single "petition for review", to the complicated and unsatisfactory tangle of remedies at present available. But it is to be hoped that a similar careful examination of substantive administrative law, from which the Law Commission were precluded by their terms of reference, will be undertaken by them before long; *Justice* has blazed the trail (in its report *Administration under Law* (issued in 1971); see *post*, p. 108).

In this edition the law is intended to be stated as it was on 1st January, 1974, but the text assumes that the Local Government Act, 1972, the National Health Service Reorganisation Act, 1973, and the Water Act, 1973, all due to come into force on that fateful day—1st April, 1974—are already in operation. In appropriate places references have been made to the Local Government Bill, the Protection of the Environment Bill and the Consumer Credit Bill, all of which were on their way through Parliament when this edition went to press. The changes made in Mr. Heath's Government in January, 1974, were announced too late to be taken into account in the text (particularly p. 33) and it should be read with this in mind.

J.F.G.

Nottingham.

PREFACE TO THE FIRST EDITION

No excuse is advanced for a new book on administrative law, as most writers on the subject have confined their attention to particular branches or facets of this modern section of our jurisprudence. In particular, local government law and the law relating to the public corporations have often been dealt with as though they formed separate and somewhat esoteric parts of our legal system; on the contrary, it is one of the features of English law that the same general principles apply to all the various agencies of government, and that there is no clear distinction between administrative law, and private, or "civil" law.

The first book to be published in this country bearing the title *Administrative Law*, seems to have been that written by Dr. F. J. Port in 1929; this was almost exclusively concerned with the judicial review of "quasi-judicial" and legislative acts of administrative agencies of the central government, and together with Lord Hewart's famous *The New Despotism*, it prepared the way for the Donoughmore Report of 1932. We have now—after the Franks Report—travelled a long way, and today administrative law is concerned with a much wider field. Most university law faculties recognise the subject as a separate course in their syllabus, although the even greater importance it assumes in practice has not yet been adequately reflected in the syllabuses for the professional examinations.

I would like to express my most sincere gratitude to my friend, Mr. C. E. P. Davies, M.A., B.C.L., Barrister-at-Law, of King's College, University of London, who has read and commented on the entire manuscript, and has given me the benefit of his years of teaching experience; he is not, of course, responsible for any errors or mis-statements that may have crept into the text. I am also grateful for the assistance I have had on points of detail from many of my present and former colleagues, in academic life and in local government. My thanks are due to my publishers and in particular to Mr. H. Kay Jones who has always been ready with helpful suggestions and general guidance; also to my long-suffering wife, who has painstakingly deciphered and typed an untidy manuscript.

The law is stated in this book as it was on 1st January, 1963, but it has also been assumed that the consolidating Town and Country Planning Act, 1962, is actually in force.

J.F.G.

Birmingham.

TABLE OF CONTENTS

PAGE

CHAPTER VI—REDRESS THROUGH THE COURTS

CHAPTER VII—REDRESS THROUGH THE ADMINISTRATION—TRIBUNALS AND INQUIRIES GENERALLY

CHAPTER VIII—REDRESS THROUGH THE ADMINISTRATION—PARTICULAR TRIBUNALS AND INQUIRIES

CHAPTER IX—ADMINISTRATIVE AUTHORITIES IN LITIGATION

CHAPTER X—THE PUBLIC CORPORATIONS

CHAPTER XI—LOCAL AUTHORITIES

PAGE

CHAPTER XII—THE MEMBERS AND OFFICERS OF LOCAL AUTHORITIES

CHAPTER XIII—THE ORGANISATION OF LOCAL AUTHORITIES

CHAPTER XIV—LOCAL GOVERNMENT FINANCE

CHAPTER XV—CONTROLS OVER LOCAL AUTHORITIES

CHAPTER XVI—LOCAL AUTHORITY SERVICES

APPENDIX I

APPENDIX II

INDEX

TABLE OF STATUTES

In the following Table references to *"Statutes"* are to Halsbury's Statutes of England, Third Edition, showing the volume and page where the annotated text of the Act will be found.

TABLE OF STATUTES

NEW ZEALAND

TABLE OF CASES

In the following Table references are given where applicable to the English and Empire Digest where a digest of the case will be found.

A

B

E

PAGE

I

J

K

PAGE

L

N

O

P

Q

R

T

U

V

W

[illegible]

Wilson v. [illegible] 120 J.P. [illegible] (Supp.) [illegible]

Wilson, Walker [illegible] Public Authority [illegible] Digest Cont. Vol. C 1056 [illegible]

Wirral Estates, Ltd. [illegible] L.J.K.B. 370 [illegible] L.G.R. 171, C.A.; 31 (2) Digest (Reissue) 679 [illegible]

Wiseman v. Borneman [illegible] All E.R. [illegible] W.L.R. 706; 113 Sol. Jo. 838; 45 Tax Cas. [illegible] T.R. 359; [illegible] H.L.; 28 (1) Digest (Reissue) 492

Wolverhampton Borough Council's Aldermanic Election, Re, [1961] [illegible] All E.R. [illegible] L.R. 1159; 125 J.P. 613 [illegible] L.G.R. [illegible] 33 Digest (Supp.) 77 [illegible]

Wong Yung [illegible] Grath (1950), 339 U.S. 33 [illegible]

Woods v. [illegible] Hemsley R.D.C., [1957] Adm. L.R. [illegible]

Woollett v. Minister of Agriculture and Fisheries, [1955] [illegible] All E.R. 502; [illegible] Q.B. 103; [1954] 3 W.L.R. 776; 98 Sol. Jo. 804; 53 L.G.R. [illegible] C.A.; Digest Cont. Vol. A 214 [illegible]

Wright (Ad [illegible]) [illegible] v. Bedford Corpn. [1956] 1 All E.R. [illegible] Q.B. 431; [1956] 2 W.L.R. [illegible] 120 J.P. [illegible] Digest (Supp.) [illegible]

Yabbicom v. [illegible] [1899] 1 Q.B. [illegible] L.J.Q.B. [illegible] L.T. 159; 63 J.P. [illegible] 47 W.R. [illegible] Sol. [illegible] Digest (Repl.) 236 [illegible]

Young v. Ladies Imperial Club, [1920] 2 K.B. [illegible] [1920] All E.R. Rep. 223; 89 L.J.K.B. [illegible] L.J. [illegible] 36 T.L.R. 392; 64 Sol. Jo. 374, C.A.; 8 Digest (Repl.) 653 [illegible]

CHAPTER I

INTRODUCTION

1. ADMINISTRATIVE LAW

At the outset of the study of any branch of law, it is desirable to endeavour to define and delimit the field of study; administrative law or the law relating to the administration, however, defies almost any precise definition or limitation. Dicey[1] in the last century went so far as to say that there was no administrative law in this country; in the sense that there is no concise and separate system of administrative law[2] as it is to be found in many Continental countries,[3] he was, and still is, right, but it is certainly not true to say there is no administration in this country, or that there is no law relating to the administration.

Law itself also defies definition, but perhaps the most satisfactory description of law (in the lawyer's, and not the scientist's, sense) is that body of rules which are recognised by the courts of the country as law. Logically, of course, this is not a valid definition, for "courts" can themselves be defined only by reference to law, and so we have a *circulus inextricabilis*. As a description, however, the theories of the realist school,[4] are perhaps the most acceptable for the English legal system. Can then "administrative law" be described as those rules which are recognised by the courts as law, and which relate to and regulate the administration of government? Before the value of this description can be assessed, three matters must be clarified:—

(a) *The distinction between administrative law and constitutional law.*—This distinction, important when delimiting the subject, is not essential or fundamental; constitutional law does not differ in essence from administrative law, or indeed from other branches of law. The sources of both are the same and both are concerned with the functions of government. Both are part of what is sometimes known as "public law"; but perhaps the happiest description of the borderline between the two is that constitutional law is concerned with the organisation and functions of government *at rest*, whilst administrative law is concerned with that organisation and those

---

1 "The words 'administrative law', which are its [*droit administratif*] most natural rendering, are unknown to English judges and counsel, and are in themselves hardly intelligible without further explanation": Dicey, *Law of the Constitution*, 10th Edn., p. 330.

2 "We do not have a developed system of administrative law—perhaps because until fairly recently we did not need it": *per* Lord Reid, in *Ridge* v. *Baldwin*, [1963] 2 All E.R. 66, at p. 76; [1964] A.C. 40. Some jurists are now, however, prepared to contend that we have achieved such a system; see for example the remark of the present Master of the Rolls in *Breen* v. *Amalgamated Engineering Union*, [1971] 1 All E.R. 1148, at p. 1153. How far such a contention is justified, we will leave our readers to judge.

3 In particular, in France: see Chapter V, *post*, p. 90.

4 *E.g.*, "for any particular lay person, the law, with respect to any particular set of facts, is a decision of a court with respect to those facts so far as that decision affects that particular person": Jerome Frank, *Law and the Modern Mind*, at p. 46.

functions *in motion.*[5] Even this is not entirely true, as the law relating to the electoral system, and the organisation of certain administrative bodies at a level below the central government, such as local authorities and independent statutory corporations, is commonly regarded as being within the scope of administrative law. The distinction between the two, we are forced therefore to concede, is one rather of convenience and custom than logic. Administrative law and constitutional law together may be said to amount to the *ius publicum* or public law of a modern state, although modern lawyers recognise specialised branches of public law, such as the law of taxation and military law, which are not considered under either main heading.

Dr. F. J. Port, the writer of the first book to be published in this country with the title *Administrative Law,*[6] gave up all attempts at a definition and contented himself with the following description[7]:

> "Administrative Law then is made up of all those legal rules—either formally expressed by statutes or implied in the prerogative[8]—which have as their ultimate object the fulfilment of public law. It touches first the legislature, in that the formally expressed rules are usually laid down by that body; it touches secondly the judiciary in that (a) there are rules (both statutory and prerogative) which govern the judicial actions that may be brought by or against administrative persons, and (b) administrative bodies are sometimes permitted to exercise judicial powers; thirdly it is, of course, essentially concerned with the practical application of the law."

(b) *Administrative law is not concerned only with law.*—Other subjects in the law, such as tort, industrial law, the law of property, etc., are concerned solely with "lawyers' law"—with law as understood by the realist school, and the sources of all these branches of law will be found exclusively in statutes, in judicial precedent, and perhaps in custom. When studying administrative law, however, the student —and even more the practitioner—is concerned with these[9] and also with rules which are strictly not law at all. Administrative "law" is concerned also with Ministerial circulars and memoranda, decisions of local authorities or public corporations, or "*la jurisprudence constante*" (in the French sense[10]) of the several administrative tribunals, none of which would be recognised or applied by the "ordinary" courts as law. Even the internal structure of the various government agencies is of interest to the administrative lawyer and

---

[5] Hood Phillips, *Constitutional and Administrative Law*, 4th Edn., p. 12, citing Holland on *Jurisprudence*. Robson on the other hand points out that, whilst constitutional law emphasises individual rights, administrative law lays equal stress on public needs (*Justice and Administrative Law*, 3rd Edn., at p. 429).

[6] Longman's, 1929, now out of print.

[7] *Ibid.*, at p. 13.

[8] Port does not mention the influence of precedent, the other important modern source of law, but this should not be overlooked.

[9] Custom is not relevant, so far as administrative law is concerned, but of course delegated legislation is very important.

[10] The general effect or trend of a series of decisions; in French law this is the only extent to which decided cases become a definitive source of law, the English doctrine of precedent and the binding effect of the *ratio decidendi* of a single case being unknown. The decisions of administrative tribunals in this country do not have the weight of precedents, but a series of decisions to the same effect tend to establish a practice to be followed in future cases. This tendency is strengthened in some cases where "reports" of decided cases are published by the Department responsible for the particular tribunal (see *post*, p. 25).

it has been suggested that there are common practices observed by local authorities which would seem in some respects comparable with the conventions of the Constitution.[11]

(c) *The meaning of administration.*—Administrative law is concerned with administration; what then is meant by this concept or expression? "*The* Administration" is something quite different, in that it is used to signify the government of the day or the body of persons who for the time being carry on that government. Finer[12] has defined administration as being "the governmental machine by which policy is implemented". Unfortunately this at once introduces another difficulty of definition, as a distinction has to be made between administration and "policy". By policy is meant formation of a general line or course of action—the idea of leadership, and the taking of a major decision on a matter of discretion; administration involves the execution or implementation of that policy so formulated in accordance with general principles.

It seems then that we are dealing with rules, most but not all of which are rules of law in the strict sense, that are concerned with the conduct of the general business of the government of the country, within the broad principles laid down by the policy-makers (who are in most instances the politicians). Nearer than this it is probably impossible to approach a precise definition of administrative law. Its content, at least as it seems to English lawyers, will appear from the subjects considered in this book. It is concerned with various kinds of government agencies, both at the centre and locally, with the interplay of ideas and control between these several agencies, and the relationship between the several agencies and the general public or the private citizen. It is concerned with the preservation of order, the welfare of the citizen and the rights of the individual as against the government of the country, and also with the machinery by which such matters are protected.[13]

2. THE ADMINISTRATIVE PROCESS

To understand the administrative process, with which administrative law is vitally concerned, it is necessary to return to the distinction between administration and policy, as that distinction works out in practice. Policy lays down a general principle; the administrative process involves applications of that general principle to particular facts or sets of circumstances, and at times also requires the taking of minor discretionary decisions within the framework of the general policy. Thus, the central government may, as a matter of policy, decide that all cab drivers shall be required to obtain a licence as a condition of carrying on that activity. It then becomes a matter of administration to draft the necessary law (either an Act of Parliament

---

[11] As to the "sources" of administrative law, see *post*, p. 23.

[12] *The Theory and Practice of Modern Government.* In his *English Local Government*, the same writer describes government as being "the system of functions and machinery established by any society for the supreme and ultimate control of all individuals and groups within its territory": see p. 3 thereof.

[13] On this point, see further "The Purpose of Administrative Law", *post*, p. 22.

or some form of subordinate legislation[14]), and to apply that law in particular cases, to draft any necessary application forms and licences, to arrange for and carry out any driving tests considered necessary, to collect and account for any fees payable, to issue and record the licences, to give advice to applicants, etc. There is of course no clear line between policy and administration in theory as distinct from practice, for at any time a particular aspect of administration may be taken out of the hands of administrators by the policy-makers, and a new or additional policy laid down. For instance, in the case of cab drivers' licences, it may be decided as a matter of policy that in future no fee shall be charged for the issue of a licence, whereas previously the charging of a reasonable fee may have been left to the administrators. The borderline between policy and administration may also be different in different types or sizes of government agencies and the borderline may even shift within the same agency. Thus, a civil servant may be empowered by his Minister to issue or withhold licences for additional petrol in a time of petrol rationing, in accordance with general principles laid down by the Minister himself or possibly by a senior civil servant. The town clerk of a small local authority would, however, normally expect to be required to obtain the approval of his authority (or at least of a committee thereof) to the issue of each licence, say, for the storage of petroleum.[15] A large local authority on the other hand may lay down general principles for the issue of such licences, leaving the imposition of appropriate conditions in each particular case to the discretion of the administrative officials, whilst a small authority may wish to be informed of and be given the opportunity of approving, or rejecting, the conditions proposed by the officials in each case. Again, if a dispute arises over a particular case, either because of an official's error or a cantankerous attitude adopted by some prominent citizen affected, the local authority may reduce the amount of discretion previously entrusted to their officials—or in other circumstances, increase it. The line between administration and policy is never precisely defined, and it will vary from agency to agency and from instance to instance, or even in individual cases.[16]

Although the distinction between policy and administration is thus often not clear, the distinction between the policy-maker and the administrator is much more obvious. In this country, policy is habitually entrusted to amateurs—the representatives of the people or the "man in the street"—whilst the administrator is normally a professional with a career. Members of Parliament and Ministers of the Crown are concerned with formulation of the policy of the central government, and elected Councillors are concerned with formulation of the policy of their various local authorities; even in the public corporations, the managerial body responsible for formulating general policy often consists of amateurs—persons who will have been nominated rather than elected, but most of whom will have been deliberately chosen for

---

[14] See Chapter IV, *post*, p. 51.

[15] Under the Petroleum (Consolidation) Act, 1928.

[16] On this subject, see Headrick, *The Town Clerk in English Local Government*, pp. 72–7.

reasons other than their special knowledge of the particular industry or activity. On the other hand the administrators—civil servants and local government officers, secretaries and technical officers to public corporations—are concerned only with advising on the formulation of policy, and once that policy has been formulated, with its implementation in practice. This amateur-professional partnership, with the amateur responsible to the public and having the last word in government, is an essential feature of administration and government in England[17], and is to be found at all levels; the jury system and the lay justices are but further examples in another sphere of the same suspicion of the unrestrained professional.

"Lay" assessors are to be found in the Restrictive Practices Court, and the Trinity Brethren sit as assessors in the Court of Admiralty. Here the lay element are experienced men in their own field but, again, the same distrust of lawyers unguided by "common sense" is apparent. The seventeenth century's almost deliberate misunderstanding of Cap. 29 of Magna Carta[18]—"that judgment by his peers" meant that every man was entitled to a trial by his equals—has been at the origin of much of our judicial and administrative procedure.

3. THE PURPOSES OF GOVERNMENT

The administrative process consists of carrying on the business of government—or regulating the affairs of individuals in the particular community in the interests of all. What then are the purposes of government? Traditionally these have been said to consist of preservation of order at home and protection of the community from attack by alien enemies, and these remain, of course, primarily important. Indeed it can perhaps be said that the atomic age and the possibilities of space travel have made the question of defence of supreme importance. Nevertheless these two objectives are not generally considered sufficient in the modern world. *Laissez faire* died with the dawn of the twentieth century, and today the State has to concern itself with the welfare of its individual members.

In *Pfizer Corpn.* v. *Ministry of Health*[19] the question arose whether the administration of medicines to patients in National Health Service hospitals was a use of those medicines "for the services of the Crown", within s. 46 (1) of the Patents Act, 1949. In giving judgment in the Court of Appeal, which answered the question in the affirmative, WILLMER, L. J., said (at p. 785):

> "It is no doubt true that in mid-Victorian times the treatment of patients in hospitals would have been regarded as something quite foreign to the functions of government. But in the years that have elapsed since then there has been a revolution in political thought, and a totally different conception prevails today as to what is and what is not within the functions of government".

---

17 The Local Government Act, 1972, allows a local authority to delegate to an officer (or officers) the power to take decisions in specified fields; to the extent this section (101) may be used, the permanent official becomes a policy maker, but it is not anticipated that the delegation power will be used in important matters; see *post*, p. 385.

18 Of the issue of 1225; cap. 39 in the original version of 1215; see J. C. Holt, *Magna Carta*, pp. 1 and 9 *et seq.*

19 [1963] 3 All E.R. 779, C.A.; upheld by H.L. at [1965] 1 All E.R. 450; [1965] A.C. 512; and *cf.* the judgment of LORD EVERSHED in the House of Lords, at p. 460.

Pensions, allowances, hospitals and a state medical service, free legal aid, environmental hygiene with its emphasis on housing, sanitation, clean food, water and air, the optimum use of the country's natural resources and in particular its land (the justification for the vast body of law dealing with town and country planning) the protection of agriculture[20] and the education of the country's children and even its adult citizens, are all considered proper subjects for the concern of the State. These and many others are included among the purposes of modern government. To carry out such complicated tasks government has to utilise all its functions, which have traditionally been divided into three main groups, executive, legislative and judicial.

4. THE FUNCTIONS OF GOVERNMENT

(a) The Executive.—The executive function consists primarily of initiating, formulating and directing general policy. It also includes administration which, as we have seen, involves the implementation and application of policy. This is the function of government with which administrative law is most concerned, and it is desirable to describe the several methods by which the administrative process operates.

(i) *Taking decisions.*—The taking of decisions within existing policy as laid down by law or in Ministerial or other directions (*e.g.*, resolutions of the Cabinet, which in themselves have no legal effect), on matters where the policy so formulated may often leave some measure of discretion to the administrator. For instance, in our cab drivers' example, it may be a matter for the administrators to decide how many drivers shall be licensed for a particular area or, within a more detailed field, it will almost certainly be left for them to decide on the form that the licence shall take.[21]

(ii) *Inspection.*—In many branches of government provision is made for the appointment of inspectors who are responsible for checking the manner in which a particular activity is being carried on by private individuals or, more often, by other administrative authorities. Thus, Her Majesty's Inspectors of Schools and of Constabulary respectively, inspect schools and police forces administered by local authorities on behalf of the central government, so as to ensure the maximum exchange of technical information and the maintenance of a certain minimum level of efficiency throughout the country. Similarly, inspectors of factories, officers of the central government, have local offices and enforce the standards of the Factories Acts in the interests of persons employed in all factories. Local authorities also appoint

---

[20] See *Cartwright* v. *Post Office*, [1969] 1 All E.R. 421; [1969] 2 Q.B. 62.

[21] Sometimes even the form that the particular government agency is to use is prescribed in a statute. In the last century, when Parliament was feeling its way in giving powers to the executive, this was commoner than it is at the present day (see *e.g.*, the conveyancing forms scheduled to the Lands Clauses Consolidation Act, 1845), but even today forms are often prescribed by Ministerial Regulations when they are to be used by a subordinate agency such as a local authority (see, *e.g.*, the forms that have to be used under the Housing Act, 1957).

inspectors for multifarious tasks, such as public health inspectors,[22] weights and measures inspectors, school attendance officers, etc. These inspectors are responsible for reporting on the condition of sewers, food exposed for sale, houses, weights and measures or whatever it may be, and the local authority will then, on the information so obtained, decide what action, if any, should be taken either generally or in the particular case. Similarly a central department, on receiving information from their inspectors may take action to enforce a particular standard.[1]

(iii) *Inquiries.*—Many different kinds of government agencies hold inquiries into a variety of events and circumstances; some of these, such as an inquiry into the objections made to a compulsory purchase order, are expressly provided for by the law, in that the government agency concerned is required to convene the inquiry when objections to the order are made and not withdrawn. In other cases, such as an inquiry into an aircraft or railway accident or one involving a privately owned pipe-line,[2] the holding of the inquiry is an optional power given by the law to the government agency concerned; in yet other circumstances a Minister may decide to convene a departmental inquiry having no legal status whatever, or Parliament may set up a special tribunal to inquire into some special matter of grave public concern.[3] The object of all these different inquiries is virtually the same; to obtain information required by the government agency so that they may as a matter of policy (not law) decide whether to take action in the circumstances, and if so, what the nature of that action shall be, and also incidentally, to satisfy the public that what should be done is being fully investigated. We shall see later[4] that these inquiries should be distinguished in law from administrative tribunals, but both inquiries and tribunals must themselves be distinguished from the courts of law, in that while decisions arrived at by the latter may reflect some aspects of policy, the agency responsible for the conduct of an inquiry or tribunal is not normally confined to principles of law either in matters of procedure or in the process of arriving at a decision.[5]

(iv) *Licensing.*—In the modern state it is often found desirable to subject specified activities to some form of governmental control. The purposes of such controls will vary. Sometimes a control is imposed for the purpose of collecting revenue; sometimes the type of activity may be such that it is desirable in the public interest to restrict the number of persons who exercise it, or control may be considered desirable so as to ensure that the activity is carried on in a particular manner in the interests of public health, safety or the preservation of local amenities. In practice one of the commonest methods whereby controls can be imposed is the licence. The individual who desires to carry

[22] Formerly known as sanitary inspectors, but in 1956 Parliament was persuaded to change their name: Sanitary Inspectors (Change of Designation) Act, 1956.

[1] Sometimes this may take the form of default action, *mandamus*, or the withholding of a grant to a local authority or other government agency; see *post*, p. 10.

[2] Pipe-lines Act, 1962, s. 34.

[3] Under the Tribunals of Enquiry (Evidence) Act, 1921; see Chapter VII, *post*, p. 199.

[4] Chapter VII, *post*, p. 195.

[5] There are exceptions here; some administrative tribunals, such as the National Insurance Commissioner and the Lands Tribunal, work within almost as closely defined a legal framework as do the courts of law; see Chapter VII, *post*, p. 193.

on the particular activity—start a business as a cab driver or as a pawnbroker, open a betting shop, sell milk, either generally or of specified designations,[6] or carry out development on his land—may be required to obtain a licence from the relevant local or central government agency. In circumstances where the legislature consider such a control should be imposed the need to obtain a licence is provided for in a statute, but the form of the licence and the conditions on which a licence may or may not be issued in the particular instance, are either settled by the government agency concerned or laid down as a matter of policy by the legislature, often in some form of subordinate legislation. Conditions to which the licence is subject may themselves amount to a standard which must be met before the licence can be granted (*e.g.*, in the case of a licence to drive a motor vehicle, that the applicant has not been disqualified), or they may regulate the manner in which the particular activity may be carried on under the terms of the licence (*e.g.*, in a licence to sell pasteurised milk, it is made a condition that the words "Pasteurised" shall appear on the cap of the bottle), and the statute may give to the government agency a wide discretion in the matter of the imposition of conditions in particular instances (as for example, in the case of licensing milk dealers and distributors). As a general rule, a government agency may not require any payment as a condition precedent to the issue of a licence, without express statutory sanction,[7] even in a case where the statute empowers the authority to impose such conditions as they think fit.[8] Express provision may be made in the statute for an appeal against a refusal of a licence, to a court of law,[9] to an administrative tribunal[10] or to a superior government agency such as the Minister himself or an inspector or tribunal appointed by him.[11] Such an appeal may be provided for where an applicant for a licence is aggrieved by a refusal of a licence, or by the conditions imposed in such a licence; in certain circumstances the courts will intervene to review errors of law made in such matters.[12] Where a licensing power is conferred by or under statute, the licensing authority must consider each case on its merits and the courts may intervene to ensure that this is done.[13]

In some cases an activity is controlled by the device of *registration*. Here the person carrying on the particular activity, or desiring to do so, is required (by statute) to apply to a specified government agency for a certificate of registration. If his case complies with the rules laid

[6] There is a different licensing control for each of these activities.

[7] This is because of the presumption against a statute conferring a taxation power in the absence of clear words to that effect: see Chapter III, *post*, p. 49, and *A.-G.* v. *Wilts United Dairies, Ltd.* (1922), 127 L.T. 822. See also in the special context of town and country planning, *Hall & Co., Ltd.* v. *Shoreham-by-Sea U.D.C.*, [1964] 1 All E.R. 1; [1964] 1 W.L.R. 240.

[8] As in *Liverpool Corpn.* v. *Arthur Maiden, Ltd.*, [1938] 4 All E.R. 200.

[9] Usually to the magistrates, as under s. 290 of the Public Health Act, 1936, but in some cases direct to the Crown Court, as under the Pawnbrokers Act, 1872.

[10] As is the case under the Milk and Dairies Regulations, 1959.

[11] For example, an appeal lies to the Secretary of State for the Environment against a refusal to grant planning permission, under s. 36 of the Town and Country Planning Act, 1971.

[12] See Chapter V, *post*, p. 94 *et seq*.

[13] *R.* v. *London County Council, ex parte Corrie*, [1918] 1 K.B. 68.

down in or by the enabling statute, the agency are required to register him forthwith; sometimes a mere notification of the applicant's name and place of business is sufficient (as in the case of the registration of scrap metal dealers under the Scrap Metal Dealers Act, 1964). Again, a fee may not be charged without statutory authority, but in cases of registration it is more usual for the statute to provide for a fee,[14] and normally the government agency has no discretion but to issue a certificate of registration once all the terms of the statute have been complied with.[15] The courts will review any breach of the terms of the statute by the government agency concerned at the instance of a party aggrieved, but it is not normally necessary for provision to be made for any express system of appeals, as in the case of licensing, owing to the absence of any discretion vested in the registration authority.

Administrative control by means of licensing or registration is a fertile source of litigation. Appeals against refusals or conditions are common, particularly in town and country planning where a planning permission may be a valuable asset. It also frequently becomes necessary for a member of the public to be able to ascertain what licences (or certificates of registration) have been issued, and so in several cases the relevant statutes make provision for registers of consents, refusals and conditions to be maintained and to be made available for inspection by interested persons.[16]

(v) *Enforcement of standards.*—Government agencies are often concerned with the enforcement or application of a standard—in the public interest—laid down in legislation. "Fitness for human habitation", "fitness for consumption", "satisfactory provision for drainage", "suitable and sufficient sanitary accommodation", and many other phrases contained in statutes have to be applied by the relevant government agencies, usually in this context by local authorities. This enforcement of standards is effected partly by the devices of licensing or registration, as described above, and partly by inspection. In both cases, there will be an element of compulsion, and statute will usually empower the agency concerned to take proceedings in the courts against any recalcitrant person who may refuse to comply with the prescribed standards, fail to apply for a specified licence or certificate before carrying on some controlled activity, or fail to comply with conditions laid down in a licence. A central department of the government will often possess powers to enforce observance of standards of administration by a subordinate government agency, and those powers may

---

[14] For example, under the Rag Flock and Other Filling Materials Act, 1951. Sometimes the device of registration is introduced solely, or mainly, for the purpose of obtaining revenue. This seems to be the true reason behind the so-called control imposed by the Small Lotteries and Gaming Act, 1956, (see now Betting, Gaming and Lotteries Act, 1963) which brings in useful revenue for local authorities, but serves very little other purpose. Under s. 35(2) of the Local Government Act, 1966, a number of these fees may be varied by statutory instruments made by the appropriate Minister; the Local Government Bill will in many cases permit a local authority to determine the amount of the fee.

[15] If the licensing authority have no discretion and must issue a "licence" on application (or on payment of a fee), the process is correctly classified, it is submitted, as "registration", and *not* "licensing", whatever term may be used in the statute.

[16] See for example, Town and Country Planning Act, 1971, s. 34; Water Resources Act, 1963, s. 53; Hairdressers (Registration) Act, 1964, s. 7 (1).

take the form of *mandamus*[17] proceedings in the courts, the appropriate Minister may be able to exercise "default powers"[18] conferred on him by statute, or the Minister may be empowered to withdraw or withhold some financial grant otherwise payable to the subordinate agency.[19]

(vi) *Subordinate legislation.*—Legislation is clearly not part of the executive power; but the formulation and drafting of various forms of subordinate legislation—regulations, byelaws, orders, directions and schemes—is the responsibility of the executive, and in any modern State this forms an important means whereby the policy of the Government of the day may be implemented. Allied to such drafting, is the process of consultation with interested bodies, both public and private,[20] which often precedes the making of important subordinate legislation. Confirmation of draft legislation initiated by subordinate administrative agencies also provides a means of control by the central government over the activities of subordinate bodies.

(vii) *Appeals.*—As the drafting of subordinate legislation trenches on the legislative power, so does the hearing of appeals by members of the executive trench on the judicial power. In another sense, appeals against decisions of the executive are an aspect of the rights of the subject rather than part of the machinery of government, but the two ideas tend to get entangled in practice. Strictly speaking, inquiries into objections to some administrative order, such as a compulsory purchase order, where the Minister is to some extent acting as a judge, are different from the type of inquiry that is convened by some government agency for the purpose of ascertaining facts, and there may also be a distinction between administrative tribunals and administrative courts.

> "What are generally termed administrative tribunals in common law countries are institutions set up within the administration itself to decide questions which come within the statutory competence of a particular branch of the administration."[1]

Such distinction as there may be between administrative tribunals and administrative courts cannot be clearly drawn, and it has no precise legal significance in the English system, but it can perhaps be said that bodies staffed by judges and having an administrative jurisdiction with a procedure similar to that of an ordinary court of law, such as the Restrictive Practices Court or the Family Division acting in matters related to the guardianship of infants, are administrative courts. The difference between these bodies and tribunals in permanent session, such as the Lands Tribunal or the Transport Tribunal,[2] is not always logical, but can be drawn in practice and as a matter of convenient classification.

---

17 Chapter VI, *post*, p. 183. 18 Chapter XV, *post*, p. 435.

19 This may be either a specific grant, or a general grant payable towards the expenses of the authority by statute (see, *e.g.*, Local Government Act, 1966, s. 4, and Chapter XIV, *post*, p. 414).

20 Under modern conditions this is becoming more commonplace, and such consultation takes place at all stages of the legislative process; see Chapter III, *post*, p. 48.

1 Brian Chapman, *The Profession of Government*, at p. 185.

2 See Chapter VIII, *post*, p. 259.

As with inquiries, the decision of an administrative tribunal (but not that of an "administrative court") is not necessarily taken with reference only to the law or to "abstract justice", for the tribunal may also properly concern itself with policy.[3]

(b) The Legislative.—The legislative function of government consists of enacting rules binding on the citizens of the particular State generally, and any such rule made in due form, will be accepted as law by the courts of a unitary State without question. Even this statement needs qualification, as the element of generality may relate to all persons and to all places in the given State, or only to all persons within a certain limited area or areas, as in the case of a local Act, or only to persons falling within a specified category. Because Parliament is omnicompetent[4] it may even pass a statute which directly concerns one person only,[5] but all organs of the State will nonetheless recognise such a statute as law. The legislative process is not concerned solely with the actual making of new laws; it also involves the *travaux préparatoires*,[6] the parliamentary process of debate, inter-departmental consultation and discussion, and also consultation with "outside" interested bodies, such as local authorities, trade unions or professional associations[7]; and in some countries the legislative process may also involve the subsequent promulgation of the legislation when made.[8] Much of this process is the concern of the executive, although the legislation itself is the result and creation of the legislature—the general rule or expression of policy as determined and enacted by them. In this country legislation takes the form of an Act of Parliament, or of some subordinate instrument enacted by a government agency under the express authority of an Act of Parliament, known as subordinate legislation, because it derives its authority and status from an agency subordinate to and limited by the supreme legislature.

(c) The Judicial.—The judicial function of government includes interpretation, definition and arbitration. The nature of the judicial process or function has been the subject of much discussion and at times even decision in the courts,[9] but it is usually said that the essential characteristics are that:

---

[3] The courts of law therefore cannot always effectively review the decisions of such a tribunal, for this very reason, that the tribunal does not consider itself concerned with the law alone: see *Franklin* v. *Minister of Town and Country Planning*, [1947] 2 All E.R. 289; [1948] A.C. 87, and Chapter VI, *post*, p. 125.

[4] See Chapter III, *post*, p. 43.

[5] See, *e.g.* the Honourable Lady Hylton-Foster's Annuity Act, 1965.

[6] The debates in the House itself, the Reports of Royal Commissioners, etc., that inspired the legislation, and possibly even the public speeches of Ministers.

[7] Chapter III, *post*, p. 48.

[8] Promulgation is no problem in this country, so far as statute law is concerned, and probably has not been since before the Conquest, for every man is presumed to know the law. This convenient theory cannot be taken too far, however, and even a lawyer is not presumed to know the law contained in a new statutory instrument before it has been printed and published: Chapter IV, *post*, p. 65.

[9] Under a written constitution, such as that of the Australian Commonwealth, it may be necessary to decide whether an *ad hoc* tribunal set up by statute was exercising any part of the judicial power entrusted by the statute to the courts, for if so, the statute might be held to be unconstitutional and void. This point was discussed in *Shell*

(i) there must be a *lis inter partes*, or a dispute between two or more parties;

(ii) the proceedings in the *lis* must have been initiated by one (or more) of the parties to the *lis*, but not by the tribunal itself or by some government agency or other body not being a party to the *lis*;

(iii) as a general rule, the deciding judge, having found the facts and applied the appropriate principles of law thereto, has little discretion in coming to his decision[10]; he may not be influenced by preconceived principles of policy, but must apply prescribed rules of law so as to reach a decision.

The distinction between judicial and "quasi-judicial" functions (if any exists) has also greatly exercised certain writers; fortunately in this country at least, where the constitution is not written,[11] the question is not very important. What is more important is the distinction between judicial and administrative functions; but this can now be left until we come to the remedies that may be available to review the decisions of administrative bodies.[12]

5. THE SEPARATION OF POWERS

This discussion of the three functions or powers of government leads to the famous doctrine of the Separation of Powers ascribed to the French jurist Montesquieu in his *L'Esprit des Lois*, written in the middle of the eighteenth century. This doctrine has been interpreted to mean that the three powers of government (executive, legislative and judicial) must, in a free democracy (such as England), always be kept separate and never become exercisable by the same organs of government. This principle, "raised to the rank of a new and universal constitutional principle to which the English people owed their liberty",[13] was applied strictly by the Founding Fathers when the constitution of the U.S.A. was drafted in 1787; in that constitution there is such a system of "checks and balances" that no one organ of

---

Co. of Australia v. *Federal Commissioner of Taxation*, [1931] A.C. 275, and see Robson, *Justice and Administrative Law*, 3rd Edn., at pp. 7 *et seq.* The meaning of the closely related expression, a "judicial office" has often occurred in the context of a written constitution; see, for example, *United Engineering Workers Union* v. *Devanayagam*, [1967] 2 All E.R. 367; [1968] A.C. 356, a case from Ceylon. One of the difficulties of any judicial discussion of the meaning of a "judicial" function is that the explanation has to be given in the context of a particular constitution or statute, and consequently such explanation is rarely completely valid for another context: see Dussault, *Le Controle Judiciaire de l'Administration au Québec*, at pp. 208 *et seq.*; a very useful commentary on this subject.

[10] In such matters as the guardianship of infants and the administration of trusts, a judge certainly has a discretion in a legal sense, but that discretion is to some extent regulated by the law, and if he exceeds it the judge will be liable to be over-ruled on appeal.

[11] See note 9, *ante*, p. 11; many other examples could be given from the U.S.A.

[12] Chapter VI, *post*, p. 171.

[13] Committee on Ministers' Powers (*The Donoughmore Report*) 1932, Cmd., 4060, at p. 8.

government can ever alone become supreme. The President as the executive, alone can exercise any or all of the powers of the executive, the two Houses of Congress alone can legislate,[14] and the Supreme Court and the lower judiciary have a monopoly of the judicial power; no one organ of government can trench on the powers of another.[15]

In England there is no such "sharing out" of the powers of government; the three powers still exist, and each have their own peculiar features, but we cannot say that one particular function is the sole province of any specific institution or organ of government. Thus, the Lord Chancellor is the head of the Judiciary, Chairman of one of the Houses of the Legislature, and a prominent member of the Executive, and is also often (but not necessarily) a member of the Cabinet. The judges have executive functions when administering the control of the supply of intoxicating liquor, when supervising wards of court, and when exercising the powers given by the Variation of Trusts Act, 1958, and they even exercise legislative functions, when making Rules of Court regulating their own procedure. Ministers of the Crown are members of the Legislature, and may be given power to make subordinate legislation, and also to exercise judicial powers in many different forms of administrative tribunals. Even the House of Commons, the more important part of the Legislature, is not exclusively concerned with legislation, for it exercises judicial powers when it investigates complaints of infringements of its own privileges.

The Executive indeed, has a considerable part to play in legislation. The initiative in introducing prospective new legislation, and in settling many of the details of a Bill before it is presented to either House of Parliament, must rest with the Executive.[16] Bills introducing changes in major policy must be found a place in the legislative timetable—no easy task under modern conditions—and so must consolidation and law reform Bills. Here Whitehall—the permanent civil service—may have as considerable an influence as the politicians in Westminster, for much of the work in a consolidation or law reform Bill takes place in the offices of Parliamentary Counsel, and they must find time and energy for such tasks, without the incentive of firm instructions from their political masters.[17]

At the present time, therefore, the separation of powers, as understood by Montesquieu, does not obtain in this country. Probably it is not desirable that it should exist; it is not easy to draw the line between one power and another, and the process of drawing that line is itself somewhat fruitless of any profitable results. Parliament cannot afford to be too practical, and it must delegate some of its legislative powers, especially in matters of detail, to the executive; there are not enough

---

[14] This has led to very considerable difficulties in recent years, as the principle strictly means that the President cannot make or authorise any Departmental regulations of the type so common in modern government.

[15] There is a similar rigid separation of powers in the unitary state of Ceylon: see *Liyanage* v. *R.*, [1966] 1 All E.R. 650, especially at p. 659.

[16] On this important topic of the initiative taken by the executive in legislation, see J. T. Craig, "The Reluctant Executive", at [1961] P.L. 45.

[17] This is still true since the passing of the Law Commissions Act, 1965, except that there is now a warmer climate in favour of law reform in Westminster (and therefore also in Whitehall).

judges, nor are the present judges really suited for adjudicating over all the thousands of disputes that regularly come before the many and varied administrative tribunals of the modern state. To attempt to separate the powers of government is today futile and almost certainly undesirable; it should be recognised that in some measure the administration of a modern state must exercise all three traditional powers, and there is a specialisation rather than a separation of powers.

6. THE ORGANS OF GOVERNMENT

In a modern state, it is quite impossible for all the powers of government to be exercised individually by the central authority. Outside the few remaining city states, such as San Marino and Monaco, some of the powers of government must be entrusted to subordinate central or local agencies of government. In this country, much of the detail of internal public order is entrusted to autonomous local authorities, who are subject to the general law and some administrative and judicial control from the centre, but are in other respects sovereign within their own powers; in most continental countries those same (or similar) functions of maintaining public order are entrusted to local agencies of the central government, established by law and having a certain measure of separate existence, but being little more than the servants of the central government.

In recent years, other functions of government have been entrusted to special agencies having country-wide responsibilities, but not directly responsible in matters of detail to the central government. These bodies, known in this country as public corporations,[18] are often organised in a manner similar to ordinary private law trading companies, and are particularly suited for carrying on a nationalised industry, such as the supply of gas or electricity or the development of atomic energy, or some social service such as the hospitals, on behalf of the state; yet other public corporations are entrusted with the supervision of some particular governmental activity, such as the Federal Trade Commission and the Inter-State Commerce Commission of the U.S.A., or the Countryside Commission or Decimal Currency Board in this country.

There is no pre-determined characteristic which decides whether a particular government activity shall be entrusted to a central agency or whether it should be entrusted to a local or subordinate agency, although some activities (such as foreign affairs, trunk roads and air lines) are clearly best suited for a centralised form of administration, and others[19] are more commonly left to local agencies. Sometimes

---

[18] See Chapter X, *post*, p. 317.

[19] It is more difficult to identify precisely those functions which must be performed locally. Lighting streets and emptying dustbins are functions that come readily to mind, but both functions could be organised by a centralised service having regional or local offices and depots. The extent to which a particular country will entrust governmental functions to the lower local levels of administration depends very largely on the traditions of government in the particular country. There is also the further problem of the distribution of functions as between the several types of local authorities; even when it has been decided to entrust a particular function to local government, the subsidiary problem must be answered as to which class or classes of authorities shall be made responsible; see further, Chapter XIII, *post*, p. 400.

railroads are directly administered by a central department, as in Switzerland and in Austria, while other countries entrust this activity to a public corporation or corporations, as in this country and in Canada; and the administration of the other public utilities similarly does not follow any universal pattern in all countries.

The central executive agency may itself be split in some cases; in many branches of central administration the Scottish Office in Edinburgh is independent of Whitehall, and the same tendency can be seen in the establishment of a Secretary of State for Wales.

Not only the executive powers of government may be split between two or more classes of agencies. In this country there is a unitary legislature, except for the special case of Northern Ireland, but in other countries there may be a federal constitution, where no one legislature can legislate on all subjects. In the U.S.A., for example, the constitution gives certain powers to the federal legislature, and others to the legislatures of the several States, while any residuary powers to legislate on subjects not so specifically mentioned are left to the State legislatures. The same is true of the federal constitution of Australia, but in Canada the residuary legislative power is entrusted by the British North America Acts to the Dominion Parliament.

The judicial power also has to be entrusted to a number of separate courts organised throughout the country, but the system is usually pyramidial in structure, there being an ultimate court of appeal, in this country the House of Lords, which enforces and applies a uniform system of law throughout the country. Under a federal constitution such as the U.S.A. there may be several pyramids of courts; one in each State, with a final bridge over all the pyramids, consisting of the Supreme Court but having jurisdiction in a limited range of cases only. In France there are several pyramids, separated not according to geography, but according to function; the two most important of these pyramids administer respectively the Code Civil and the Droit Administratif.

7. SOVEREIGNTY

In any state there must be some ultimate power capable of altering and declaring the law; in Nazi Germany the sovereign was Hitler, the Führer, whose whim was law; in this country the sovereign is the Queen in Parliament, which can pass any law it likes with the reasonable certainty that its every edict will be recognised and enforced by the courts as law. The courts may, and in practice are required to, construe the terms of a statute and apply them in a particular manner in a given factual situation, but they may never ignore the terms of a statute. The supremacy of Parliament has the following consequences in practice:

(a) There is no higher legal authority than the Queen in Parliament, and the Queen in Parliament alone can change the law. An edict of the Crown acting alone can call attention to existing law, and in so far as the Royal Prerogative[20] has not been limited by statute, the Crown can, acting by and with the advice of its Ministers, make war

[20] The residue of the Royal Power left to the Crown unregulated by statute; *post*, p. 41.

or peace, confer honours, and convene or dissolve Parliament, without the prior sanction of Parliament, but the Crown alone cannot change the law, a principle established as long ago as the time of James I.[1] Nor can the House of Commons alone alter the law, as Mr. Bowles proved in 1913.[2]

(b) It is generally said that it is not legally possible for any body or power in the State to question the enactments of the Queen in Parliament; even the House of Lords, as the highest court of law in the country, cannot refuse to enforce an Act of Parliament on the ground that it is "unconstitutional". This may happen in a federal state or other country having a written constitution, where a Supreme Court is empowered to declare that some enactment of the legislature is contrary to the fundamental principles of the constitution, and is therefore invalid. In the ordinary sense, England has no written constitution against which can be measured the validity of legislation. However, it has been suggested that legislation by the U.K. Parliament which contravened the provisions of the treaty that preceded the Act of Union of the realms of England and Scotland in 1706 could be declared unconstitutional and void[3]; it has also been argued that no Parliament has legal power to repeal section 6 (4) of the Indian Independence Act, 1947, and legislate for India, without the concurrence of the Indian Parliament.[4] To such extent, it seems to be true to say that even the otherwise omnicompetent United Kingdom Parliament is only "sovereign within its powers", although it does not seem likely that these constitutional limitations on its powers will ever be raised in practice. It is, moreover, quite clear that no Act of Parliament can be held to be invalid because it is absurd or has become obsolete.[5]

The European Communities Act, 1972, may seem to have limited in some measure the supremacy of the United Kingdom Parliament; section 2 of that Act confers wide powers on the institutions of the Community to legislate in accordance with the Treaties, and provides that all such legislative instruments shall without further enactment be recognised and available in this country, and that they shall "be enforced, allowed and followed accordingly." However, this provision really amounts to little more than a widely drawn power to make

---

[1] *The Case of Proclamations* (1610), 12 Co. Rep. 74.

[2] *Bowles* v. *Bank of England*, [1913] 1 Ch. 57, but see now the Provisional Collection of Taxes Act, 1968. A similar power to legislate by resolution of the House of Commons is conferred by s. 5 of the House of Commons Disqualification Act, 1957, which enables the House by resolution to amend the list of offices which disqualify a holder thereof from being a member of the House. These are really, however, specialised examples of delegated legislation, as such resolutions take effect under the express authority of statute.

[3] *British Justice: The Scottish Contribution*, by Professor T. B. Smith (Hamlyn Lectures) at p. 210.

[4] *Constitutional Structure of the Commonwealth*, by K. C. Wheare, at pp. 30–2.

[5] *A.-G.* v. *H.R.H. Prince Ernest Augustus of Hanover*, [1957] 1 All E.R. 49; [1957] A.C. 436. On the general subject, see Mitchell, "Sovereignty of Parliament—Yet Again", (1963), 79 L.Q.R. 196.

"subordinate legislation",[6] and there is no attempt in the statute to restrict the power of a future Parliament to repeal the Act of 1972, or to inhibit it from enacting legislation which is inconsistent with the provisions of the Treaties or of Community legislation. When asked, the Court of Appeal refused to answer the question whether, once this country had entered the Community it could subsequently withdraw,[7] but so far as English law is concerned (whatever the implications of international law may be) there seems to be no reason why the Act of 1972 should not be repealed if a subsequent Parliament so decided.

(c) There is no limit on the legislative powers of the Queen in Parliament (subject, possibly, as above mentioned); it can lengthen (or shorten) its own life,[8] change the religion of the country,[9] or declare an individual to be a traitor without trial, and to have forfeited his life.[10] One Parliament could presumably provide that a particular statute was not to be amended except after the observance of a special procedure (*e.g.*, a referendum); there is no authority, however, in this country showing how in such circumstances the courts would construe a statute purporting to amend an earlier statute prescribing some such special procedure, without observing that procedure[11]; whichever view was adopted in such a case, it would seem that the decision would in some measure limit the sovereignty of Parliament.[12]

8. THE RULE OF LAW

Some writers would urge that the sovereignty of Parliament is an illustration of the Rule of Law as it applies in this country, and it is true, of course, that the Rule of Law can be explained as meaning no more than that law and order—the same law—is observed throughout

---

[6] Admittedly of a special kind, as the law-making power is delegated to authority *outside* the U.K., and also the *vires* of Community legislation can be determined, in the final resort, not by the English courts, but only by the Court of the European Communities at Luxembourg: Treaty of Rome, art. 177.

[7] *Blackburn* v. *A.-G.*, [1971] 2 All E.R. 1380, *per* Lord DENNING, M.R., at p. 1383.

[8] *E.g.*, the Septennial Act, 1715.

[9] Act of Supremacy, 1558.

[10] E.g., as was done in the several Acts of Attainder that disgraced English history.

[11] In *A.-G. for N.S.W.* v. *Trethowan*, [1932] A.C. 526, this question was raised within the context of a subordinate legislature, and there it was held that the first (the procedural) statute had to be complied with. The courts of the Union of South Africa in *Ndlwana* v. *Hofmeyer*, [1937] A.D. 229, held that the legislature of the Union, being a sovereign legislature by virtue of the Statute of Westminster, was not bound by the special procedure required by the Union Act of 1909 (of the U.K. Parliament) for revoking the "entrenched clauses" of the constitution protecting coloured voters. However, this decision was not followed by the Supreme Court of South Africa in *Harris* v. *Minister of the Interior* 1952 (2) S.A. 428, in which it was pointed out that the fact that a specified procedure must be followed by the legislature of a State, did not make that state any the less a sovereign independent country. This seems now to be the view that is most likely to be adopted should the question ever arise in this country: see the judgment of the Privy Council in *Bribery Commissioner* v. *Ranasinghe*, [1964] 2 All E.R. 785; [1965] A.C. 172 (a case from Ceylon).

[12] Professor Heuston argues (in *Oxford Essays in Jurisprudence*, at pp. 198 *et seq.*) that the courts are entitled to examine the circumstances surrounding the making of a statute to ascertain whether or not the machinery prescribed by law for the law making process for the time being in force has been complied with. This does not, he suggests, in any measure impair the sovereignty of the legislature, but merely indicates how the sovereign power is to be exercised.

the territory of a State, and that in this sense every state having a reasonably competent and efficient police force is subject to the Rule of Law.[13] The Rule of Law is, however, usually understood to signify something more than this, namely, that in the particular state there are adequate safeguards for the reasonable interests of the individual. Professor Dicey, writing at the end of the Victorian age of *laissez faire*, elaborated and popularised the concept, saying that the Rule of Law existed in this country by virtue of the three following features:

(a) No man can be arrested in this or in other countries enjoying the Rule of Law, such as the U.S.A., except by due process of law, thereby showing that the state recognises a distinction and a contrast between regular and arbitrary power. In England (said Dicey) all men are equal in the eyes of the law, and they can be proceeded against only in the ordinary courts and in accordance with the ordinary law. But the law does not really ensure that this fortunate state of affairs shall continue; as we saw during two world wars, in time of emergency there is nothing to stop the legislature from empowering the executive to imprison individuals suspected of having enemy associations.[14] The trade unions have for a long time exercised wide powers of control over their members, and by exiling a person from membership or by refusing him permission to join,[15] a union could make it impossible for him to earn his living in the only calling for which he had been trained[16]; until recently this was controlled by the law only to the extent that the principles of natural justice were relevant. Even under the Industrial Relations Act, 1971, registered trade unions are in some measure in a specially favoured position so far as the law is concerned. The Official Secrets Act, 1911 makes it an offence to enter a prohibited place for a "purpose prejudicial to the safety or interests of the state." In *Chandler* v. *Director of Public Prosecutions*,[17] the House of Lords held that what was or was not such a purpose was a matter for the exclusive discretion of the Crown.

(b) The rule of law guarantees equality before the law—all persons are subject to the same law and (in particular) officials of the state have no special privileges not possessed by ordinary individuals, nor are they exempt from the jurisdiction of the ordinary courts. In this aspect of his version of the rule of law, Dicey was criticising the French system of *droit administratif*, in which all questions involving the administration fall within the purview of a special hierarchy of administrative courts, headed by the Conseil d'État. If a private individual wishes to sue the administration in France in

---

[13] "The business of keeping the peace is an industry which everyone agrees should be nationalised": Robson, *Justice and Administrative Law*, 3rd Edn., at p. 2.

[14] *Liversidge* v. *Anderson*, [1941] 3 All E.R. 338; [1942] A.C. 206; *post*, p. 162.

[15] See Chapter VIII, *post*, p. 269.

[16] This was mitigated somewhat by *Bonsor* v. *Musicians' Union*, [1955] 3 All E.R. 518; [1956] A.C. 104; where the House of Lords held that a trade union could be sued for damages where it had expelled one of its members, and such expulsion amounted to a breach of a contract with the member. On this subject see Lord Macdermott, *Protection from Power*, (*Hamlyn Lectures*), Chapter 7.

[17] [1962] 3 All E.R. 142; [1964] A.C. at p. 777.

respect of a *faute de service*[18] he does so, not in the "ordinary" courts as he would in this country, but in the Conseil d'État or in one of the local administrative courts. Dicey viewed this feature of the French constitution with alarm and dislike, contending that administrative courts were a direct threat to the liberty of the individual. The control of the over-mighty subject, the administration itself, in the interests of the individual is the main problem and object of administrative law, but this is no place to consider whether the controls over the administration exercisable at the initiative of the individual in this country are more or less effective than those available under *droit administratif*. Suffice it here to point out that even in Dicey's time in this country many officials had special powers and immunities; thus, police officers were (and are) protected by the Constables Protection Act, 1750, and many specialist officers, such as public health inspectors are given powers of entry on privately owned property by the Public Health Acts.[19] Judges and members of the diplomatic corps are given special immunity by the law, and Parliament has from time to time relieved individuals from the consequences of venial or inadvertent breaches of the law (see, *e.g.*, the William Preston Indemnity Act, 1925).

(c) The constitution is part of the ordinary law of the land; Dicey regarded this feature of the English constitution also as an essential safeguard of individual liberty. Because the constitution is part of the "ordinary" law, the constitution can be changed, in deference to the wishes of the people, as easily and by precisely the same machinery, as that by which any other law can be enacted. Thus, the powers of the House of Lords were trimmed in 1911 and 1949 by the Parliament Acts of those years as easily as the same Parliaments passed the annual Finance and Army Acts. The elaborate machinery customarily required under a written constitution to effect a constitutional amendment as, for example, in the U.S.A.,[20] is unknown in our system and public opinion can therefore the more readily be expressed in terms of changes in the law. This feature of the constitution need not, however, operate exclusively in favour of the liberty of the subject, for an unscrupulous government possessing a majority in the House of Commons could use that very simplicity of legislative machinery to repeal fundamental safeguards of personal liberty, such as the Habeas Corpus Acts (which were suspended in one day in 1939), or other characteristics of the constitution of equal importance. As there are no fundamental principles

[18] The distinction between "*fautes de service*", and "*fautes personelles*" turns upon nice points of jurisdiction. Suffice it here to say that Dicey's strictures based on the exclusive jurisdiction of the French administrative courts to hear complaints against the administration were never completely justified, and since his day, by the extension of the concept of the *faute personelle* and the doctrine of *cumul*, proceedings may in an appreciable number of cases be properly taken by a citizen against the administration in the "ordinary" civil courts: see Waline, *Droit Administratif*, 9th Edn., Part V, Chapter 4.

[19] Almost every session of Parliament adds to the number of these statutory powers of entry.

[20] See Article V of the Constitution. An amendment can be proposed only by a two-thirds majority of both Houses of Congress, and the amendment must then be ratified by the legislatures (or a convention) in at least three-fourths of the several States.

clearly expressed in the constitution and no entrenched clauses,[21] no outside body would be able to exercise any control over such a reforming government. The only real safeguard against personal dictatorship, Fascist or Communist, in this country lies in public opinion. Even paper constitutions can be and are torn up on occasion, but certainly the absence of such a piece of paper is no safeguard of liberty.

Is then the Rule of Law now meaningless in this country? Man has throughout the ages appealed to something higher than the law of his own invention, be it the *jus naturale* of the Romans, the law of God of the mediaevalists, or the social contract and natural law of Hobbes, Locke and Rousseau, and in our own day we try to state the "rule of law" as a norm or ideal which the laws of each state should seek to achieve or fulfil. The idea that law must be certain and known to all and not dependent on the whim of an individual, is part of this ideal concept [22] but the rule of law is something more than that. Clearly the ideal could never override the positive law of the state in that it could become a higher norm or principle to which appeal might be made in a court, asking the judge to invalidate the internal law for that reason, but in the modern world, especially in a developing country, it seems that some principle is required against which proposals for new legislation can be measured and existing rules tested for essential validity or "rightness". Presumably it is in this sense that the Law Reform Commission understood the expression when in their First Programme (1965) they said (Note, para. 5):

> "English law, in its history and substance, exhibits a great respect for both the concept and the application of the rule of law".

This idea of the Rule of Law, as a modern form of the law of nature, was formulated in some detail by the International Commission of Jurists,[1] in their Declaration of Delhi, made at that city in January, 1959.[2] This Declaration may be summarised as follows:

(a) The function of the *legislature* in a free society under the Rule of Law is to create and maintain the conditions which will uphold the dignity of man as an individual. This dignity requires not only certain recognition of his civil and political rights but also establishment of the social, economic, educational and cultural conditions which are essential to the full development of his personality. In

---

[21] That is to say clauses (as in the constitution of the Union of South Africa, at least in theory; see note 11 on p. 17, *ante*) which require some special machinery to be implemented before they may be amended. A "Bill of Rights" is a popular feature of the constitutions of many of the newly independent countries in Africa and Asia: see de Smith, *The New Commonwealth and its Constitutions*, Chapter 5.

[22] "The rule of law stands for the view that decisions should be made by the application of known principles or laws": *Franks Report*, para. 29. In other words, "Palm-tree justice" is not justice at all; justice according to law is always to be preferred.

[1] A voluntary body of lawyers, not associated with any governments, drawn from over fifty different countries.

[2] See Vol. 2, No. 1 of the Journal of the International Commission of Jurists, Spring-Summer, 1959, and *The Rule of Law in a Free Society*, published by the International Commission in 1960. See also N. S. Marsh, in *Oxford Essays in Jurisprudence*, at p. 223. This Declaration has been since further elaborated in the "Law of Lagos" (*post*), 1961, the "Resolution of Rio", 1962, and the "Declaration of Bangkok", 1965, all passed at conferences convened by the International Commission.

other words, guarantees of civil rights, obviously desirable in themselves, are not enough if the ordinary people are living below the level of subsistence, as may be the case in the under-developed countries of Asia and Africa.

(b) The Rule of Law depends not only on the provision of adequate safeguards against abuse of power by the Executive, but also on the existence of effective government capable of maintaining law and order and of ensuring adequate social and economic conditions of life for the society. Again the emphasis is on the need for government to pay heed to the welfare of the individual; in the context of a westernised state this aspect of the Rule of Law can be read as justifying a complete code of social legislation in the interests of the individual. Thus it becomes part of the Rule of Law that a code of national health insurance and social security should be established, that the courts should be readily available to all and not only to those who can afford to litigate, that the right to earn one's living should be recognised and protected by the law. Indeed this aspect of the Rule of Law may be interpreted in the terms of the late President Roosevelt's famous Four Freedoms; freedom of speech and religion, freedom from want and freedom from fear.

(c) An independent judiciary and a free legal profession are indispensable requisites of a free society under the Rule of Law. To an Englishman a free judiciary seems self-evident and does not need elaboration, but an independent legal profession is almost as important. Every lawyer must feel himself able to make the best case he can for his client without fear of state intervention or loss of income, status or reputation.

These three general principles were worked out in considerable detail in the Declaration of Delhi, and most lawyers in the Western world are agreed that they represent the underlying principles of government which should be followed in a free society. They were again applied, in the special context of Africa, at a Congress held in Lagos in January, 1961, and re-formulated in a document called the "Law of Lagos".

> "The Rule of Law on a supra-national plane may on examination appear to lack at its edges the sharpness of definition which we expect of legal concepts. But this does not mean that there is no agreement on the basic values which it represents. . . ."[3]

The concept in its modern dress meets a need that has been felt throughout the history of civilisation; law is not sufficient in itself and it must serve some purpose. Man is a social animal, but to live in society he has had to fashion for himself, and in his own interest, the law and other instruments of government, and as a consequence those must to some extent limit his personal liberties. The problem is how to control those instruments of government in accordance with the Rule of Law and in the interests of the governed.[4]

---

[3] Marsh, *op. cit.*, at p. 260.

[4] Other writers suggest that the "Rule of Law" is of political significance only, of no concern to the lawyer or jurist. In the Fourth Edition of his *Machinery of Justice in England*, however, Dr. R. M. Jackson recognises that the "rule of law" is dynamic though lacking in precision. "The Rule of Law, which is a fine sonorous phrase, can now be put alongside the Brotherhood of Man, Human Rights and all the other slogans of mankind on the march" (at p. 373).

9. THE PURPOSE OF ADMINISTRATIVE LAW

It is the object and purpose of administrative law to answer that question; how and by what means is government itself within a given society to be brought under effective control? Wide powers must be given to the executive to combat criminals equipped with the inventions of science; conscription for military service may be necessary in time of peace, and limitations on freedom of speech and of association may be justifiable in an atmosphere of a "cold war" of ideologies. The citizens of a State in their fear of enemies within and without are compelled to create a powerful executive to protect them. Yet that Executive must not itself be allowed to become all powerful, like the King Stork of the fable. The problem may be elaborated in this form:

(a) How can the machinery of the modern state be so operated as to leave the maximum personal liberty to the governed? If that machinery becomes so complicated that individual liberty is swamped, the rule of law ceases to exist;

(b) How can the decisions of the administration be subjected to control by the courts? Can justice ever be allowed to triumph over policy, or must the politicians always have the last word?

(c) How should the function of government be divided between the several governmental agencies? Is local independence of administration to be preferred to national uniformity and is either inconsistent with efficiency? Should the police forces be under local or central control?[5]

(d) Where a monopoly business has to be established in the public interest, how and to what extent should it be subjected to control by politicians or by administrators, or by the courts?

Where these questions involve civil rights, as many of them do, there is in modern international law, sometimes a supra-national remedy. Thus, if the State concerned is a party to the European Convention of Human Rights, and has recognised as compulsory the jurisdiction of the European Court of Human Rights (as the U.K. Government did on January 14, 1966), a national of that State may have a right to appeal to the Court[6] if he can show that there has been a breach of the convention in his case. This is, however, in essence a residuary procedure; the citizens of a State are entitled to fair treatment by their own government, and in default of such treatment to have adequate means of redress within their own legal system.

It is surely the purpose of administrative law in any country to endeavour to provide some answer to these and related problems. The law must regulate the legislature, describing how legislation and subordinate legislation must be made, and it must control the activities of the administration and the executive itself. There may be many different approaches to the problem—the Ombudsman of Scandinavia[7] or the

[5] Discussed in the Report of the Royal Commission on the police issued in 1962.

[6] The procedure before the Court is complicated: see, for example, the *Lawless Case*, the judgment in which was published by the Court on July 1, 1961.

[7] Chapter V, *post*, p. 98.

doctrine of socialist legality in Communist countries—but we are primarily concerned with the system of the common law. As we have said, in this country there is no separate *corpus* of administrative law, for this, like the constitution itself, is part of the "ordinary" law. Nevertheless, one cannot say of administrative law in England that "elle n'existe point". The principles of administrative law in this country are fundamentally the same principles that apply to any other field of law; they are not a separate code or system like the principles of equity before the Judicature Acts, but are applied in the same courts as the law generally, and can be distinguished or characterised only by reference to their subject matter.

It is therefore intended to describe the content of English administrative law and discuss how and to what extent the administration in this country is subjected to the control of law. It is not our purpose to list all the many powers of the administration, but to discuss and explain the extent to which and the means by which those powers are subject to some measure of control. Where there is no rule of law there is either anarchy or a police state, as has been proved only too often in the modern history of Europe.[8] Before dealing with the substance of the subject, however, we must say something about the sources of administrative law.

10. THE SOURCES OF ADMINISTRATIVE LAW

Administrative law in the private lawyer's sense has, *ex hypothesi*, the same sources as any other branch of English law; as we have already said, there is no *droit administratif* in this country in the sense of there being a different or separate *system*, and administrative law is part of the "ordinary law" of the land. We are therefore concerned primarily in this subject with statute, with subordinate legislation and with precedent or case law. However, administrative law is very closely allied to the extra-legal subject of political science, or the study of government, and therefore an account of legal principles and rules alone cannot hope fully to explain the subject as it is today or as it may develop in the future. Ideas about government and law change and have their influence on law and practice. In a more formal sense, we may be concerned in a study of this subject with documents, orders and decisions which are neither true sources of law in the Austinian sense nor are they similar to Dicey's "constitutional conventions", in the sense that there would be a breach of law "properly so called", if they were ignored. We should therefore at this stage discuss briefly the kinds of these documents that we have in mind, and indicate the extent to which they are of importance.

(a) Reports of committees.—Since the end of the First World War the importance of administrative law has been brought more and more into public notice. A former Lord Chief Justice, Lord HEWART,

[8] "The great problem, as we now see it: how far is power to be controlled by law": Professor H. W. R. Wade at (1962), 78 L.Q.R. 189. See also the very interesting article by Professor Gelinas, "Judicial Control of Administrative Action: Great Britain and Canada", at [1963] P.L. 140.

published a famous book, *The New Despotism*, in 1929, which purported to expose the extent to which the Civil Service and "bureaucracy" were then alleged to be the true rulers of the country. Two particular evils were singled out for attack, the extent to which the executive was given freedom by Parliament to make delegated legislation, and the complementary evil of freedom from control by the courts over the exercise of executive discretions, by reason of the extremely wide powers given by the legislature. The response to the publication of Lord HEWART'S book was the setting up of the "Committee on Ministers' Powers", which issued a Report in 1932, usually known by the name of its first[9] Chairman, as the Donoughmore Report.[10] This called attention to three main defects in administrative law as it then existed, namely (1) the inadequate provision made for publication and control of subordinate legislation; (2) the *lacuna* in the law caused by the inability of a subject to sue the Crown in tort; and (3) the extent to which the control and supervision of administrative decisions were passing out of the hands of the courts and were being entrusted by Parliament to specialist tribunals and enquiries. The rules regulating subordinate legislation were tidied up to some extent by the Statutory Instruments Act, 1946, and when the subject was again reviewed by the Davies Committee in 1953,[11] no further substantial improvements were recommended. The Crown Proceedings Act, 1947, revolutionised the law relating to civil proceedings against the Crown, and the subject who has a legal cause of action against the Crown or a Crown servant, should now be able to obtain justice from the ordinary courts.[12] The third subject considered by the Donoughmore Report, however, had to wait longer before action was taken. In 1955[13] a new Committee was set up to consider the question of tribunals and inquiries generally; their report, known as the Franks Report,[14] was issued in July 1957. As a result of this Report, and with commendable expedition, the Tribunals and Inquiries Act, 1958, was passed, which statute set up a permanent Council on Tribunals and laid down certain general procedural principles to be applied to most administrative tribunals and inquiries, and also provided for their supervision by the courts of law. The Annual and

---

[9] Lord Donoughmore resigned as Chairman before the Report was published and Sir Leslie Scott was appointed Chairman in his place.

[10] Cmd. No. 4060.

[11] *Report of the Select Committee on Delegated Legislation*, dated 27th October, 1953.

[12] As to Crown privilege in litigation, see Chapter IX, pp. 289 *et seq.*

[13] Largely as a result of the scandal in 1954 known as the "Crichel Down Affair". In this case certain land in Dorset had been acquired compulsorily on behalf of a Crown Department early in the Second World War, an undertaking being given to the owners from whom it was purchased that they would be offered a chance to buy it back if the Crown should subsequently have no use for the land. Eventually the Ministry of Agriculture, in whom the land had by then vested, disposed of it without offering it to the successor in title of the original owner, and when he protested, the complaints were somewhat cursorily brushed aside. However, the complainant persisted, and the matter was debated in the House of Commons, the civil servants concerned were reprimanded, and the Minister resigned. It was recognised, however, that there was no formal machinery by which such a grievance could be ventilated, and if the complainant in the Crichel Down Affair had not been of some substance and pertinacity the case would never have been heard of and the grievance would never have been redressed.

[14] Report of the Committee on Tribunals and Enquiries, Cmd. 218; the Chairman of the Committee was Sir Oliver Franks.

special Reports[15] of the Council on Tribunals have contributed to changes in public opinion and in some respects have been instrumental in bringing about changes in law, more particularly in the procedural rules governing administrative tribunals. The appointment of a Parliamentary Commissioner for Administration[16] has given the citizen suffering from a sense of injustice an opportunity of ventilating his grievance, not met by the 1958 Act.

(b) Quasi-Law.—In the Chapter in this book on Subordinate Legislation a paragraph has been included[17] on the subject of Ministry regulations, but most government agencies also issue circulars and memoranda that virtually have the effect of law, but which would certainly not be recognised as such by the Courts. An example of this is the Circular (64/69) of the former Ministry of Housing and Local Government explaining how the system of making grants by local authorities to private owners for the improvement of dwellinghouses under the scheme as revised by the Housing Act, 1969, is to be administered. Advice is given on points of interpretation of the statute, and forms are recommended for use by local authorities and applicants for grant.

Akin to this "near legislation", are the "near precedents", which are established in several jurisdictions of Ministers or administrative tribunals. The decisions of the Secretary of State for the Environment on appeals to him against refusals by local planning authorities to grant planning permission under the Town and Country Planning Act, 1971 (and its predecessors), are from time to time reported in an official publication known as the "Bulletin of Selected Appeal Decisions", wherein the subjects are classified and decisions on related matters are grouped together. From a study of these decisions and others appearing in professional journals, some indication can be obtained as to how the Secretary of State is likely to decide a subsequent appeal, which planning "principles" will most probably be applied, and which arguments are likely to have the most weight. In this fashion a system something like English "case law" is growing up, although it cannot be said that one decision standing alone, however important it may be, can have the force of a binding precedent. No Minister can ever decide entirely in accordance with former decisions, as he always has some element of "policy" to consider. The influence of such decisions can nevertheless be of particular importance where the questions in issue are essentially questions of law, and where there are few policy or "general planning" principles to be applied, such as is normally the case with appeals against enforcement notices,[18] or decisions of the local planning authority under section 53 of the Town and Country Planning Act, 1971.[19] A similar tendency towards the establishment of a system

---

[15] See especially Cmd. Paper 1787 on the "Chalkpit affair", discussed in Chapter VII, *post*, p. 221.

[16] Parliamentary Commissioner Act, 1967; the Local Government Bill makes provision for similar Commissioners for local government; see Chapter V, *post*, p. 104.

[17] Chapter IV, *post*, p. 56.

[18] Under s. 88 of the Town and Country Planning Act, 1971.

[19] On application for a determination whether planning permission is necessary or whether a proposal amounts to "development" in a particular case.

of "jurisprudence" (in the French sense) can also be detected in other administrative fields; for example, Her Majesty's Stationery Office publishes a series of reports of decisions of the Industrial Tribunal, and the decisions of the National Insurance Commissioner on national insurance and industrial injuries are published by the Department of Social Security; the value of a lost limb or eye can now be computed in advance of an inquiry with some mathematical accuracy by reference to previous decisions of the Commissioner and the earnings of the complainant.[20] Tribunals also tend to follow "precedents", examples are to be seen more clearly in those tribunals from whose decisions an appeal lies to the Court of Appeal on a point of law, but even the most independent tribunals of all, those established under the Tribunals of Enquiry (Evidence) Act, 1921,[21] follow established practices at least in such matters as the procedure to be observed, the class of persons entitled to give evidence or to be represented, etc.[1] Departments of Government naturally develop house rules for the exercise of any discretion vested in them, as do (for example) senior police officers charged with the decision whether or not to prosecute in particular circumstances.[2]

Administrative agencies, such as local authorities and the several public utilities, also follow a standard pattern in exercising their functions. Especially is this true of those local authorities where the range of functions is the same or similar, and even more so with those statutory corporations, such as the health authorities, which, though nominally and legally independent bodies,[3] are subject to general directions (the Secretary of State or a health authority of higher status) and are in some respects little more than regional offices of a central department. Practices among local authorities tend to become uniform; for example, there are three or four standard methods for the selection of a Mayor, adopted by many Boroughs prior in time to the legal process of electing an individual at the annual meeting of the Council[4]; it is generally accepted that a lady Mayor should be addressed as "Mr. Mayor"[5]; it is customary in local authorities to delegate a

---

[20] Chapter VIII, *post*, p. 247.

[21] Chapter VII, *post*, p. 199.

[1] *Trial by Tribunal*, by Professor G. W. Keeton, see p. 200 *et seq*. Tribunals and other administrative bodies must consider a matter on its merits when exercising a discretion, and must not normally decide according to pre-conceived rules: see *R.* v. *Port of London Authority, ex parte Kynoch, Ltd.*, [1919] 1 K.B. 176. DEVLIN, L.J., puts the matter clearly in *Merchandise Transport, Ltd.* v. *British Transport Commission*, [1961] 3 All E.R. 495, at p. 507: "In my opinion a series of reasoned judgments such as the [Transport] Tribunal gives is bound to disclose the general principles on which it proceeds. I think that that is not only inevitable but also desirable. It makes for uniformity of treatment and it is helpful to the industry and to its advisers to know in a general way how particular classes of applications are to be treated; but the Tribunal may not in my opinion make rules which prevent or excuse either itself or the licensing authorities [from whom appeals lie to the Tribunal] from examining each case on its merits." On this topic, see Chapter VI, *post*, p. 140.

[2] Review of the Parliamentary Commissioner over the "bad rule" is discussed in Chapter V, *post*, p. 105. The whole question of administrative discretion is discussed (from an American angle) by Professor K. C. Davis in his *Discretionary Justice*.

[3] See National Health Service Reorganisation Act, 1973, Part I.

[4] *Cf. Civic Ceremonial* by the present writer, 2nd Edn., at p. 12.

[5] *Ibid.*, at p. 44. This is not universal.

large measure of discretionary power to committees,[6] and most local authorities take the advice of their finance committee before striking a rate. These common practices are not conventions in the constitutional sense, but the practical working of the administrative agencies to which they relate can scarcely be understood if those practices are ignored.[7]

11. ARRANGEMENT OF SUBJECT-MATTER

In the Chapters that follow we shall discuss the following main subjects of administrative law:

(a) The central government and the legislature (Chapters II–IV);

(b) The redress of the grievances of a citizen, through the courts and by other means (Chapters V–IX);

(c) The independent public corporations (Chapter X);

(d) The administration of local government and the general legal principles applying to local authorities (Chapters XI–XVI).

Readers of this Chapter will by now be aware of the writer's view that administrative law is primarily concerned with the rules and restrictions binding on the various organs of the executive, and with the extent to which those rules and restrictions may be used by a citizen to obtain redress from the courts. Logically perhaps it could be argued that administrative law is also concerned with the several powers conferred on the organs of the Executive by the common law and by statute. A catalogue of these powers would, however, fill many volumes and would not evidence any, or many general principles. These are, it is suggested, best left for discussion in practice books on the various branches of government, such as housing, public health, customs and excise, liquor licensing, etc.

---

[6] See Maddick & Pritchard, "The Conventions of Local Authorities in the West Midlands", Public Administration for Summer 1958 and 1959. Practices of this kind will probably be more widely followed in future as a consequence of the passing of the Local Government Act, 1972 as there are now fewer and larger local authorities; see Chapter XI, *post*, p. 358.

[7] Local authorities are often influenced by the practice adopted by the Secretary of State of issuing Model Standing Orders. As such orders (unlike byelaws) do not have to be confirmed by the Secretary of State there is, however, no obligation or pressure on authorities to adopt the Model.

CHAPTER II

THE CENTRAL GOVERNMENT

1. INTRODUCTION

Administrative law is not greatly concerned with the structure of the central government, this normally being considered the concern of constitutional law. The difference between the law and the conventions of the constitution, the conventions under which the Cabinet system operates, and the relationship between the Crown and the Cabinet will therefore not be discussed here,[1] but we must examine in outline the processes by which the central government of the country is carried on.

2. THE CABINET

This ill-defined body of advisers of the Sovereign, "the mainspring of all the mechanism of government",[2] the members of which owe political allegiance to the political party (or coalition of parties) at the time capable of commanding the support of a majority in the House of Commons, and whose members are jointly and severally responsible for all decisions of policy, is as such unknown to the law. A Cabinet Minister may be entitled to a salary, but is so entitled by virtue of the statutory office he holds under the Crown and not because he is a member of the Cabinet.

The figure-head of the executive—the governing body as it were—is in law the Sovereign, assisted and advised by Her Privy Council, or rather, by such members of Her Privy Council as she may (on the advice of Her Prime Minister) decide to consult. Decisions of the Cabinet are of themselves of no legal effect; if it is desired to implement a Cabinet decision which involves a change in the law, the government must introduce a Bill in one or other of the Houses of Parliament and secure (by use of its majority) its passage into law through the ordinary Parliamentary process. In other cases it may be necessary only to obtain ratification of the Cabinet decision at a meeting of the Privy Council. This latter course will be effective in that range of subjects where there is no need to "change" existing statute law or to introduce new law, but where the Crown has previously obtained a power to enact subordinate legislation under statutory authority or where it can act of the Royal Prerogative,[3] it can so act by signifying its pleasure in the Privy

---

[1] See, for example, Hood Phillips, *Constitutional and Administrative Law*, 5th Edn. (1973).

[2] Machinery of Government Committee Report, 1918 (Cmd. 9230).

[3] Or where the Crown is given specific power to act by means of an Order in Council, under the authority of a statute. The Royal prerogative may be described as those executive powers allowed to the Sovereign by the common law, unrestricted and un-

Council. The government of the day will find no difficulty in practice in obtaining a decision of the Privy Council which is in accord with their wishes, although there may be many more members of the Privy Council who are politically opposed to the existing government than there are supporters of it. Membership of the Privy Council is normally for life,[4] but it is customary to summon to any particular meeting of the Council only a few Privy Councillors, all of whom are supporters of the Government in power; these, with the Sovereign (or her personal representative)[5] constitute a meeting of the Council and may execute the formal Orders in Council implementing the decisions, in theory of the Sovereign taken on the advice of the Council, but in fact of the Cabinet or possibly, in less important matters, of an individual Minister. This process has been described as a "constitutional disguise for legislation by the executive".[6] All Cabinet Ministers, and some other Ministers, are sworn of the Privy Council, the total membership of which is usually about 300—including many privy councillors who are not Ministers. The courts recognise the formal acts of the Privy Council as law, provided they are *intra vires* the Prerogative or some statute delegating legislative power to the Council.

In yet other circumstances, a decision of the Cabinet may amount to a mere executive direction, instructing a Minister of the Crown how he is to use his existing powers. Such a decision then attaches political (not legal) responsibility on all members of the Cabinet for the action taken.

Membership of the Cabinet is not decided by any pre-determined rules, and the identity of those Ministers who are invited by the Prime Minister to become members of the Cabinet may vary from government to government. Since the last war there have usually been about twenty members of the Cabinet. In recent administrations it has become the practice to recognise an informal "inner cabinet" consisting of a few Ministers who assist the Prime Minister in all more important or urgent matters; these are such Ministers as the Chancellor of the Exchequer, the Lord Privy Seal or some other Minister without portfolio or with

---

controlled by statute. The largest field of government in which the Royal Prerogative can operate at the present time is that of foreign affairs, but it should be remembered that a statutory power will always take the place of a prerogative power dealing with the same subject matter: *A.-G.* v. *De Keyser's Royal Hotel*, [1920] A.C. 508. See, *post*, p. 42.

[4] There is nothing in law to prevent the Crown from cancelling an individual's membership of the Privy Council but this is very rarely done. Anson (*Law and Custom of the Constitution*, 4th Edn., Vol. II, Pt. I., p. 154) suggests there are three forms of membership of the Privy Council:

(a) Politicians—Ministers of the Government of the day, Dominion Prime Ministers and former Ministers.

(b) Great officers of State who are not politicians (such as Lords of Appeal in Ordinary and the Archbishops of the Established Church).

(c) Those who have been made members of the Privy Council as an honour, and who play no part in government or politics.

The whole Privy Council meets in modern times only at an Accession of the Crown (Hood Phillips, *Constitutional and Administrative Law*, 5th Edn., at p. 255).

[5] Under the Regency Acts, 1937–1953, or Letters Patent (issued, for example, when the Sovereign is out of the country). The quorum of members of a Privy Council for a meeting is three.

[6] Sir Carleton Allen, *Law in the Making*, 6th Edn., at p. 523; and see *post*, p. 41.

slight Departmental duties (such as the Chancellor of the Duchy of Lancaster), the Foreign Secretary, and the Secretary of State for Defence (who is responsible for the co-ordination of the work of the three Service Departments). However, the identity of the "inner cabinet"—if indeed there be one in any particular administration—will depend rather on the personalities of the individual Ministers than the offices which they may hold. This kind of "inner committee" or pressure group—the few who "really matter"—is to be found at practically any level of administration, public or private. It is most noticeable in local government. Thus, in one town it may be the chairman of the Finance Committee, the Mayor and the chief executive officer who effectively make the decisions, or in another town the leader of the majority political party and one or two of the senior members may be the inner "Cabal". So it is with the central government; there must be a few individuals "at the top" with a broad enough vision and freedom from concern with daily routine who have the time to form policy, and the energy and persuasive powers to ensure that the policy is tested, accepted and finally implemented.

The regular Cabinet may be augmented on occasion (and often is) by the presence of other Ministers attending by invitation of the Prime Minister when matters concerning their Departments are to be discussed, or where their advice on a particular matter coming before the Cabinet would be relevant.

There are therefore three "ranks" of Ministers in modern Government:

(a) the inner cabinet;
(b) other Cabinet Ministers;
(c) Ministers not in the Cabinet.

This last class will include junior Ministers subordinate to departmental Ministers. All of these posts will carry salaries,[7] as they will all be established under the authority of statute, and most of the Ministers will be sworn of the Privy Council. The official duties of each individual Minister may be laid down more or less precisely by statute,[8] but those duties may now be transferred from one Minister to another by the comparatively simple machinery of an Order in Council,[9] and the same procedure may be used to change the title of a Minister.[10] Statutory authority will have to be obtained, however, for the creation of a new Minister, so that he may receive a salary; it may also be necessary[11] to increase the number of holders of Ministerial Offices in the House of Commons.

---

[7] See the Ministerial Salaries Consolidation Act 1965.

[8] See, *e.g.*, the Minister of Town and Country Planning Act, 1943, which by s. 1 thereof provided that the Minister of Town and Country Planning shall be "charged with the duty of securing consistency and continuity in the framing and execution of a national policy with respect to the use and development of land throughout England and Wales".

[9] Under the Ministers of the Crown (Transfer of Functions) Act, 1946.

[10] As was done, for example, in 1951, when the then Minister of Town and Country Planning was given some of the functions of the Minister of Health and re-designated the Minister of Local Government and Planning, and then later his title was changed again and he became the Minister of Housing and Local Government (now the Secretary of State for the Environment).

[11] As it was when the Labour administration took office in the autumn of 1964; see the Ministers of the Crown Act, 1964.

During the present century the proceedings of the Cabinet have gradually become more formalised. Since the First World War there has been a Cabinet Secretariat and decisions are recorded, although discussion is not minuted, and occasionally a minute may not be taken even of a decision. The Secretariat forms a link between the Cabinet and the Ministers who are not members of the Cabinet, both by obtaining information from the Departments prior to a Cabinet meeting and by informing them of the Cabinet "conclusions".[12] The whole system, however, still depends on fundamental conventions of the constitution, such as:

(a) the collective and individual responsibility of Ministers;
(b) the Cabinet must have the support of the House of Commons;
(c) members of the Cabinet must be members of one or other of the Houses of Parliament;
(d) the Sovereign is entitled to information from the Cabinet but must act on the advice of her Ministers.

Although Ministers cannot possibly themselves make all the decisions taken in their name in their respective departments—indeed, decisions on appeals "to the Secretary of State" in planning matters are openly given over the signature of a civil servant—the doctrine of Ministerial responsibility is by no means non-existent in our modern constitution. The Minister of Agriculture and Fisheries accepted responsibility for the mistakes made by civil servants in his Department over the "Crichel Down affair" in 1954, and the Secretary of State for the Environment (or one of his subordinate Ministers) will answer questions in the House on planning appeals or compulsory purchase inquiries.

In the Haldane Report on the "Machinery of Government Committee" (1918),[13] it was said that the main functions of the Cabinet may be described as:

(1) the final determination of the policy to be submitted to Parliament;
(2) the supreme control of the national executive in accordance with the policy prescribed by Parliament;
(3) the continuous co-ordination and delimitation of the activities of the several Departments of State.

3. THE CENTRAL DEPARTMENTS

The structure of the central departments is provided for by statute, although historically most of the major departments have developed from the departments of the two original Secretaries of State (for Home Affairs and for Foreign Affairs respectively). There must be a statutory framework for the departments because of the need to pay salaries to the Ministers and their civil servants, and also so that the several functions of Government may be distributed among Departments[14];

---

[12] As the decisions of the Cabinet are termed: Jennings, *Cabinet Government*, 3rd Edn., at p. 272.

[13] Cmd. Paper 9230, at para. 6.

[14] Although this may now be done by Order in Council under the Ministers of the Crown (Transfer of Functions) Act, 1946: *ante*.

moreover, when the office of a new Minister is created it is desirable to decide whether although he holds an "office of profit" under the Crown, he should be prevented legally from being a member of the House of Commons. Only those office-holders which are specified in the House of Commons Disqualification Act, 1957, are now disqualified from sitting in the Commons, although the list may be amended by Order in Council under section 5 of that Act, and has also been added to by subsequent statutes.[15] Not more than ninety-one persons holding Ministerial office (of senior or junior rank) are entitled to sit and vote in the House of Commons at any one time.[16]

At the present time the more important departments include the following:

(a) The Home Office.—The Home Office is headed by the Secretary of State for Home Affairs. He has been described as the "residuary legatee"—the Minister responsible for the conduct of all functions of central government not specifically entrusted to some other Minister. As such he provides the official means of communication between a subject and the Sovereign and he advises the Sovereign on the exercise of the prerogative of mercy in cases arising within the United Kingdom. He is also specifically responsible for the keeping of the "Queen's peace", and as such is directly responsible for the administration of the Metropolitan Police Force and supervises and advises the other police forces in the country,[17] and he is also responsible for the activities of the Prison Commission, the administration of magistrates' courts and the probation service. Other matters with which the Home Secretary is concerned include the control of aliens, the welfare of children, extradition, and the supervision of local authority fire brigades and other services, including the control of explosives and firearms and the administration of the Factories Acts.

(b) The Treasury.—The Treasury is a department which has been in commission for over 200 years.[18] The Board (which has not sat for over 100 years) consists of the First Lord (since 1902 a post always held by the Prime Minister), the Chancellor of the Exchequer and five Junior Lords. In common with most other Central Departments, there is a Parliamentary Secretary who is virtually a junior Minister, and also another politician holding the office of Chief Secretary. The Junior Lords assist the Chief Whip in marshalling the Government majority in the House of Commons and have virtually no Treasury functions.[19] The main functions of the Treasury may be summarised under the following:

(i) Collection of revenues due to the Crown. In collecting the Crown Revenues the Treasury has the assistance of the Revenue

---

[15] See, for example, adjudicators and members of the Immigration Appeal Tribunal; Immigration Act, 1971, Schedule 5, paras. 4 and 10.

[16] Ministers of the Crown Act 1964, s. 3 (2), amending s. 2 of the Act of 1957.

[17] Chapter XVI, *post*, p. 441.

[18] "The last Lord Treasurer, the Earl of Shrewsbury, resigned in 1714": Lord Bridges, "The Treasury", at p. 18.

[19] *Ibid.*, p. 161.

Departments—the Commissioners of Inland Revenue and the Commissioners of Customs and Excise.

(ii) Control of expenditure by other central departments.

Parliamentary Counsel and the Treasury Solicitor, the chief legal advisers to the Government on matters of detail, The Stationery Office and the Central Office of Information are also under the general supervision of the Treasury.

(c) **The Ministries.**—Until comparatively recently other Ministries were organised exclusively on vertical lines for particular sectors, such as agriculture, industry, the armed services, etc. More recently the need for a horizontal approach has been appreciated in some measure, and "super Ministries", with a broad range of interests and subordinate vertical departments have been established. The first group of Ministries to be so organised was the three Service Departments of the Navy, Army and Air Force, now and for several years past grouped under the Secretary of State for Defence. In the Government of Mr. Edward Heath (as re-organised in November, 1972) the Secretary of State for the Environment has subordinate to him the Ministers for Local Government and Development, for Housing and Construction and for Transport Industries, while the Secretary of State for Trade and Industry has subordinate to him the Ministers for Industry, for Trade, for Industrial Development and for Aerospace, but the (new) Minister for Trade and Consumer Affairs* is in charge of a separate Department. The Prime Minister,* historically always holding also the portfolio of First Lord of the Treasury, is now also Minister for the Civil Service[20] being here assisted by the Lord Privy Seal* (who is himself also Leader of H.M. Government in the House of Lords). Another organisational change has become apparent in Mr. Heath's Government; traditionally there were only two Secretaries of State (for Home* and Foreign Affairs* respectively), but these were soon joined by the Secretary of State for Scotland,* and one or two more followed in various twentieth century governments. Today, however, in addition to the three named, we have no less than eight Secretaries of State, namely, for Social Services,* Defence,* Employment,* Education and Science,* Wales,* Trade and Industry,* Environment,* and Northern Ireland.*

Other Ministers in addition to the Home Secretary, the Treasury Ministers and those mentioned, are the Lord Chancellor* and the other Law Officers (The Attorney-General, the Lord Advocate, the Solicitor-General and the Solicitor-General for Scotland), the Lord President of the Council* (who is Leader of H.M. Government in the House of Commons), the Chancellor of the Duchy of Lancaster,* the Minister of Agriculture, Fisheries and Food;* the Minister of Posts and Telecommunications, and the Paymaster-General.

---

* The Secretaries of State and Ministers starred, with the Chancellor of the Exchequer constituted Mr. Heath's cabinet in November, 1972 [a total of 19]. The Foreign Secretary is now known as the Secretary of State for Foreign and Commonwealth Affairs.

[20] The Civil Service Department is responsible for personnel management, training and manpower requirements. The Civil Service Commission (see, *post*, p. 35) is part of the Civil Service Department, but it retains a considerable measure of independence and impartiality for the selection of recruits for the Civil Service generally.

The organisation of the various Departments may vary in detail, but the general pattern is that there should be a Secretary of State or Minister at the head, with one or more Parliamentary Secretaries or junior Ministers[1] who are also politicians, and as we have seen, the Minister may or may not be a member of the Cabinet, but either he or his parliamentary secretary will be a member of the House of Commons and both will of course be supporters of the Government in power. To assist the Minister, to advise him, and to implement his decisions and carry out his instructions, there is invariably a body of civil servants headed by a permanent secretary or under-secretary; the number of civil servants in any particular department will vary considerably, according to the range of the functions of the particular Department.

There are also many departments subordinate to the "Departments of State" and "Ministries", which enjoy greater or less degrees of independence. Thus, the Chief Land Registrar has closely defined statutory functions, but is virtually independent of his nominal "overlord", the Lord Chancellor, and apart from this general responsibility no politician is in any way concerned with the conduct of the department. In some matters the Board of Inland Revenue may make their own decisions; but in other respects they will be able to act only on the instructions or with the authority of the Treasury. These and many other subordinate departments are agencies of the central government and it will be found that some Minister is ultimately responsible to Parliament for their activities. In this respect they are distinguishable from the independent statutory corporations in respect of whose detailed administration no Minister is responsible, although a Minister may be charged by statute with the power of giving them "general directions" within certain more or less precisely defined limits.[2] Local authorities—also in a sense agencies of government—are on the other hand autonomous bodies in their own right and no Minister is responsible for their decisions or the manner in which they conduct their affairs. A Minister may be called to account in Parliament in respect of an exercise of his statutory powers to control the activities of a local authority, but he is in no way responsible for the manner in which the authority have themselves acted.

In the present century it has become common practice for Parliament (or the government of the day) to set up advisory committees of one kind or another, by way of supplementing the ordinary Ministries and subordinate departments. These bodies are staffed by Civil Servants but the members are usually persons taken from business life or some other sphere outside public administration; their functions consist of advising the Minister to whose department they may be attached, either as to the nature or scope of new legislation that may be required, or as to the working of existing legislation, or so as to provide expert information and advice. The members are often amateurs in government, though

---

[1] Known as "Ministers of State", a title of recent origin. There may also be further junior Ministers, known as Parliamentary or Under-Secretaries.

[2] Chapter X, *post*, p. 329.

experts in their particular field. They will often be engaged in other work and usually will receive no remuneration. Advisory Committees of this kind differ from Royal Commissions and Departmental Committees only in that the latter are set up *ad hoc* to study or report on a particular problem or incident; Advisory Committees are normally permanent bodies in constant (though perhaps occasional) session. Such are the Building Regulations Advisory Committee,[3] the Clean Air Council,[4] and the Allotments Advisory Committee. It was said in the House of Commons in 1958 that there were then "about 850 advisory bodies of a central or national character",[5] and in 1965 the Prime Minister gave a list of some 250 permanent standing advisory committees advising him or other Ministers on "various aspects of policy".[6]

4. THE CIVIL SERVICE

In order that decisions of politicians at Cabinet level or in a particular Department may be first formulated and then implemented a corps of permanent officials is essential. In this country this is the function of the civil service, so called in contra-distinction to the Armed Forces of the Crown and to the exclusion of political servants of the Crown.[7] The chief adviser of each Minister is his permanent secretary, the head of the Civil Service in his department, who is not (except by accident) a specialist in anything, but rather the general adviser of the Minister, with the ultimate responsibility to the Minister for all the activities of the department (and of its officials).[8]

> "The civil servants' function is thus to advise, to warn, to draft memoranda and speeches in which the Government's policy is expressed and explained, to take the consequential decisions which flow from a decision on policy, to draw attention to difficulties which are arising or are likely to arise through the execution of policy, and generally to see that the process of government is carried on in conformity with the policy laid down."[9]

The civil servant owes loyalty to the government of the day, and he must and normally does serve efficiently governments of any political persuasion.

There were formerly three grades of established civil servants—administrative, executive and clerical—none of which specialised in any particular profession or calling. But as a result of the recommendations of the Report of the Fulton Committee on the Civil Service[10] members of the executive and clerical classes have been merged with the administrative class and the whole Civil Service Department placed under the direct supervision of the Minister for the Civil Service (the Prime Minister; see *ante*, p. 33); in addition there are professional and technical

---

[3] Set up under Part II of the Public Health Act, 1961.
[4] Set up under the Clean Air Act, 1956.
[5] Marshall and Moodie, *Some Problems of the Constitution* (1959), at p. 107.
[6] *Hansard*, 23rd February, 1965, col. 70.
[7] The expression "civil service" originated in the use of the expression in its modern sense in the East India Company: *Shorter Oxford English Dictionary*.
[8] Royal Commission on the Civil Service (1929), quoted by Sir Ivor Jennings in *Cabinet Government*, *op. cit.*, at p. 122.
[9] Jennings, *op. cit.*, p. 126.
[10] Cmnd. 3638 of 1968.

civil servants appointed for particular purposes,[11] In a central government department the senior permanent civil servant is an administrative officer; there is never any question of a practising lawyer as such being the head of the administration, as was until recently the normal practice in local government.[12] Recruitment to the permanent civil service is by competitive examination, although some professional appointments are made on interview alone. These examinations and interviews are conducted by a body known as the Civil Service Commissioners (constituted in 1855 when competitive examinations were introduced), now part of the Civil Service Department. Matters of establishment, conditions of service, promotion, pay, pensions and dismissal[13] are the concern of the Civil Service Department and are not a matter for the individual civil servant's own Minister or Departmental chief officer. In each Department there is an Establishments branch responsible for these matters, the staff of which are answerable not to the Department but to the Civil Service Department. The civil service is regulated not by statute but by Orders in Council issued under the Royal Prerogative, but these are in practice supplemented by Treasury (now Departmental) regulations and circulars.

In law the civil servant is in a precarious position. Whereas he seems to be in a contractual relationship with his employer, the Crown, it is clear that he may be dismissed at pleasure and that no clause in the contract of employment purporting to fetter the right of the Crown to bring to an end the employment of a civil servant (whether with or without cause) is binding on the Crown. This seems to be the result of a number of decided cases, some of which, however, contain conflicting *dicta*.[14]

In *Reilly* v. *R.*[15] a barrister employed by the Canadian Government was dismissed after his office had been abolished by statute, and he sued the Crown for damages for wrongful dismissal. In the course of his judgment in the House of Lords, Lord ATKIN said[16]:

> "A power to determine a contract at will is not inconsistent with the existence of a contract until so determined."

This case is not altogether satisfactory as a precedent because of the complicating feature of the statute; any contract will be determined if a statute so provides. In the leading case of *Terrell* v. *Secretary of State for the Colonies*,[17] the plaintiff was a judge in Malaya and would normally

---

[11] Professor Hood Phillips (*Constitutional and Administrative Law*, 3rd Edn., at p. 314) said in 1961 that there were then about 4,500 in the administrative grade, 80,000 professional, technical and scientific officers, about 60,000 in the executive grade, about 300,000 in the clerical grade, and also some 600,000 in the manipulative and industrial groups, including post office sorters and workers in dockyards and ordnance factories.

[12] Chapter XII, *post*, p. 381.

[13] As to the rights of a civil servant to appeal, etc.

[14] In *Riordan* v. *War Office*, [1959] 3 All E.R. 552; [1959] 1 W.L.R. 1046, the learned judge had apparently been asked not to add to the existing conflicting views on the topic. On this subject generally, see Marshall, "The Legal Relationship between the State and its servants in the Commonwealth", (1966) 15 I.C.L.Q. 150.

[15] [1934] A.C. 176.

[16] At p. 180.

[17] [1953] 2 All E.R. 490; [1953] 2 Q.B. 482.

have retired on pension in 1942. In 1940 Malaya was overrun by the Japanese, but the plaintiff managed to escape and get back to Great Britain. He was told that there was no more work for him and his contract with the Crown was thereupon determined. He then sued the Crown under the Crown Proceedings Act, 1947,[18] for a declaration and damages for loss of the salary he would have earned if he had been retained in employment until his normal retirement age. The claim was not allowed, it being said by Lord GODDARD, C.J.[19]:

> "... even if the Secretary of State purported to contract with the claimant, he could not in my opinion, limit the power of the Crown to dismiss at pleasure."

Terrell's case was followed in *Inland Revenue Commissioners* v. *Hambrook*,[20] an action by the Crown to recover damages in an action *per quod servitium amisit* in respect of a road accident which caused a civil servant to be away from his duties for several months. The action was dismissed by the Court of Appeal because it was held that this type of action was limited to cases where the lost services were of a domestic nature, but at first instance[21] Lord GODDARD, C.J., had referred to his own earlier decision in *Terrell's case* (*supra*) and suggested *obiter* that there was no contractual relationship between the civil servant and the Crown. In *Riordan* v. *War Office*,[1] the plaintiff was a temporary employee of the War Department appointed under the terms of a contract which incorporated a Royal warrant issued under the authority of the Army Council (but which did not have the force of law as it was not issued under the authority of the prerogative or of statute), and which provided that he could be dismissed for misconduct without notice but was otherwise entitled to one week's notice. The plaintiff was dismissed without notice in circumstances where no misconduct was alleged. He thereupon sued the War Office for damages for wrongful dismissal. It was held that the plaintiff had no cause of action arising out of the termination of his employment because the Crown's right to terminate employment at pleasure (without notice) could be taken away only by statute[2]; any clause in a contract, otherwise than one made under express statutory authority which purported to take away this right, would be *ultra vires*.

It seems therefore to be reasonably clear from these cases that there is a contract of employment between the Crown and a civil servant, but that any such contract is subject to the implied condition that the civil servant may be dismissed at pleasure as above mentioned.[3] It must follow that the civil servant cannot sue for damages for unlawful dismissal,[4] but it now seems established that he can sue for arrears of

---

[18] See Chapter IX, *post*, p. 275.
[19] At p. 496.
[20] [1956] 3 All E.R. 338; [1956] 2 Q.B. 641.
[21] [1956] 1 All E.R. 807, at p. 811.
[1] [1959] 3 All E.R. 552; [1959] 1 W.L.R. 1046. Until the decision in this case, *Rodwell* v. *Thomas*, [1944] 1 All E.R. 700; [1944] 1 K.B. 596 was sometimes cited in support of the argument that there was no contract between the Crown and the civil servant that was enforceable by the Crown, but see below.
[2] As in *Gould* v. *Stuart*, [1896] A.C. 575.
[3] The Contracts of Employment Act, 1972 does not bind the Crown.
[4] But he may have a remedy under the Industrial Relations Act, 1971 (see below).

salary due before his dismissal; if there is a contract between the employer and the employee the employee must be able to enforce it to this extent.[5] As to a civil servant's conditions of service (as distinct from the liability to be dismissed at pleasure) it has been argued from *Rodwell* v. *Thomas*[6] that these are not enforceable by the civil servant, but that decision could be explained on the ground that it was an action for wrongful dismissal, and it is submitted that terms in the contract of service, such as those relating to his pay or allowances, are enforceable.[7] Superannuation rights, given to a civil servant by statute, are not enforceable in the courts of law.[8]

Since the passing of the Industrial Relations Act, 1971, however, civil servants have been in a somewhat more secure position, legally; the Act expressly applies to "Crown employment".[9] When the employment of a civil servant is terminated,[10] he will still not be able to sue for breach of contract (as explained above), but he will now be able to take proceedings before an industrial tribunal[11] if he contends that he was unfairly dismissed[12] by his employer, the Crown, and in such a case the Crown may be ordered to pay him compensation.[13] A civil servant may also complain of some other "unfair industrial practice", in this case to the Industrial Court, as can any other employee,[14] but in that event the court could not make a mandatory order against the Crown.[15]

In practice, it is not likely that this Act will be widely used by civil servants, as they can rely on the practice of the Civil Service Department, in particular that no civil servant will be summarily dismissed

---

5 This must follow, it is suggested, from the unequivocal acceptance in *Riordan* v. *War Office* (*ante*) of the existence of a contract. *Lucas* v. *Lucas and the High Commissioner for India*, [1943] 2 All E.R. 110; [1943] P. 68, doubts this, but the reasoning adopted in *Lucas* was said by the Privy Council in *Kodeeswaren* v. *A.-G. of Ceylon*, [1970] 2 W.L.R. 456, at p. 465, to be defective. Although this case was decided on appeal from Ceylon, it is clear that their Lordships supported the view expressed in the text above. See also Logan, "A Civil Servant and his Pay", (1945) 61 L.Q.R. 240, and Blair, "The Civil Servant—Political Reality and Legal Myth", [1958] P.L. 32, at p. 39). *Lucas* seems, however, to be authority for the contention that a civil servant cannot charge or assign future salary and wages which he has not then earned. A member of the Armed Forces of the Crown cannot sue even for pay that he has already earned: *Leaman* v. *R.*, [1920] 3 K.B. 663.

6 [1944] 1 All E.R. 700; [1944] 1 K.B. 596.

7 This question was raised in *Dudfield* v. *Ministry of Works* (1964), *The Times* January 24, but not decided. See also *Sutton* v. *A.-G.* (1923), 39 T.L.R. 294, discussed by Blair, at [1958] P.L. 43 (*ante*) and see also " 'Contracts' with the Crown", by Miss Cowan, in 1965 *Current Legal Problems*, at p. 153.

8 Because of the terms of the statutes; see Superannuation Act, 1834, s. 30; Superannuation Act, 1859, s. 2, and *Nixon* v. *A.-G.*, [1931] A.C. 184.

9 Act of 1971, s. 162. Where an individual civil servant's employment is of a kind that it should be excepted from the Act "for the purpose of safeguarding national security", it may be so certified by a Minister of the Crown (s. 162 (7)), and in such a case the common law will apply without modification.

10 *Ibid.*, s. 162 (3) (b).

11 *Ibid.*, s. 106; for the industrial tribunals, see *post*, p. 262.

12 Section 22, *ibid.*, provides that every employee has a right not to be" unfairly dismissed" by his employer, and s. 24 explains what is meant by an unfair dismissal.

13 *Ibid.*, s. 24; but this is limited in amount by the Act.

14 *Ibid.*, ss. 101 and 102.

15 *Ibid.*, s. 162 (4).

except for really serious misconduct. Pay and conditions of service are negotiated in "Whitley Councils"[16]—bodies representing the employers (the Department) and the employees (the other civil servants) in equal numbers. Civil servants are allowed to join a trade union, and they are not now legally prohibited from taking part in a strike[17]; the very influential and powerful Civil Servants Clerical Association is a member of the Trades Union Congress. If a Minister forms the opinion that a civil servant is a security risk because he is a Communist, the civil servant may be sent on special leave, and he can ask for his case to be referred to the Three Advisers, a tribunal appointed by the Government. Eventually the employee may be transferred to non-secret work, or dismissed. Further, in the case of work of a special nature, an employee may be subjected to the Positive Vetting System, as a preliminary to being so employed.[18]

Civil servants can exercise all the normal civil rights of the subject and they are not disfranchised.[19] However, they may not play a full part in party politics, a rule which is embodied in civil service regulations agreed by the Whitley Councils. Thus, the administrative and professional grades may not take an active part in national politics, but an individual may be able to obtain permission to become a member of a local authority. Civil servants in the minor grades may stand for election as members of Parliament, but must resign if elected.[20] All civil servants are subject to penalties under the Official Secrets Acts if they offend against the provisions of these statutes, and an alien may not normally be appointed to "any office or place in the Civil Service of the State", unless he is appointed in a country outside the United Kingdom or a certificate issued by a Minister with the consent of the Civil Service Department is in force in respect of the case: see Aliens Restriction (Amendment) Act, 1919, as modified by section 1 of the Aliens' Employment Act, 1955.

A civil servant is not normally personally liable on a contract that he has entered into on the Crown's behalf,[1] nor can he be sued for breach of warranty of authority.[2] If he commits a tort in the course of his employment, this will now in most circumstances make his employer, the Crown, liable,[3] but he will not normally himself thereby escape liability, and he will not be able to plead superior orders or Act of State as a defence, except where the tort complained of is committed outside the Queen's allegiance and where the plaintiff is not a British subject.[4]

---

[16] First established in 1919.

[17] Civil servants were denied the right to strike by the Trade Disputes and Trade Unions Act, 1927, but that statute was repealed in 1947.

[18] On this subject, see Joelson, "The Dismissal of Civil Servants in the Interests of National Security", [1963] P.L. 51, and Williams, *Not in the Public Interest* (1966).

[19] This rule is common in West European countries; see *The Profession of Government*, by Brian Chapman, at p. 287.

[20] Servants of the Crown (Parliamentary Candidature) Order, 1950, and the Civil Service Order in Council, 1956, made under the Royal Prerogative.

[1] Chapter IX, *post*, p. 262.

[2] *Dunn* v. *Macdonald*, [1897] 1 Q.B. 555.

[3] Chapter IX, *post*, p. 265; Crown Proceedings Act, 1947, s. 2 (6).

[4] *Musgrave* v. *Pulido* (1879), 5 App. Cas. 102; *Buron* v. *Denman* (1848), 2 Exch. 167. These observations do not apply to members of the Armed Forces of the Crown.

5. CONTROLS OVER THE CENTRAL GOVERNMENT

The central government being what it is in our constitution, and there being no strict "separation of powers" with a corresponding system of checks and balances, there are few effective controls over its activities, except such as exist naturally by virtue of the good sense of politicians and civil servants and their awareness of public opinion. The rule of law and the personal freedom of the individual may, however, be at stake, and a certain amount of machinery has been devised or developed whereby Westminster and Whitehall can be kept in check. These controls may be summarised as follows:

(a) Financial control.—All revenue received by any central department on behalf of the Crown must be paid into the Bank of England, where it is credited to Exchequer account under the title of the "Consolidated Fund". No money may be expended out of the Consolidated Fund except on the authority of Parliament, which may be either permanent in respect of what are known as the Consolidated Fund Services (The Queen's Civil List and the salaries of Judges of the Supreme Court, etc.), or be given annually in the Appropriations Act, which authorises expenditure on the Armed Forces and other "Supply Services". If the Appropriation Act were not passed in any particular year, the government of the country would come to a halt for lack of funds. This is an outline of the financial machinery; this machinery is watched over by a senior official known as the Comptroller and Auditor-General, whose salary is charged direct on the Consolidated Fund and who is therefore above periodic criticism in Parliament.[5] He has the duty of authorising all withdrawals of credit from the Consolidated Fund from the Bank of England, which he will do only if each item is covered by statutory authority, and he is also responsible for auditing all Government accounts. To assist him in his duties he has a small number of civil servants known as the Exchequer and Audit Department, and he is free from responsibility to any Minister, but he reports annually (or specially as required) to the Public Accounts Committee of the House of Commons, calling attention to any irregularities of expenditure or malservation or misapplication of public funds. He is a highly respected official, and his reports are invariably scrutinised with the greatest care by members of Parliament and press publicity is often given to them. The Public Accounts Committee cannot, however, exert as much control over the finances of the government as might seem desirable, owing to the period of time which often elapses before particular accounts can be examined and a report thereon presented to the Committee.

(b) Parliamentary control.—In theory at least Parliament is the supreme arbiter and has absolute control over the activities of the

---

[5] As in the case of a Judge of the High Court, he may be removed from office only by an address moved in both Houses of Parliament.

executive. However, the effectiveness of the modern party political machine and the lack of parliamentary time, means that this control is at best spasmodic and haphazard. Nonetheless the device of parliamentary questions and the Adjournment Debate (though the latter may not be pressed to a division), in the hands of an experienced Parliamentarian, may be used to embarrass and hamper the most efficient of Governments enjoying a large majority.

(c) Judicial control.—The extent to which the courts may review —for their control can but be retrospective in effect[6]—the activities of central or local government agencies is of course the subject of primary interest to the administrative lawyer and therefore the one which will be of greatest importance in this book. Indeed one might describe administrative law as a commentary on the extent to which the courts may control the administration, were it not for the fact that in order to assess this, one must first appreciate the nature and something of the working of the administration. This subject is therefore left for later chapters.

6. THE PREROGATIVE

The Royal Prerogative may be described as that residuum of power left vested in the Crown not dependent on and not regulated by statute. There are still a number of powers vested in the Crown which, however, can be exercised only on the advice of the Ministers of the Sovereign. Such matters as the making of treaties with foreign powers, the prerogative of mercy, the conferment of honours, the government of dependent colonies,[7] the physical extension of the sovereignty of the Crown,[8] the management of the Armed Forces and even the declaration of war and of peace, and the waging of war,[9] can be effected by and through the prerogative, without recourse to Parliamentary legislation. The implementation of decisions in this field of administration is not open to discussion or question in the courts, and when a prerogative decision has to be expressed formally, the machinery of an Order in Council is used,[10] which is as much legislation, within the limits of the prerogative accepted by the common law and statute, as is an Act of Parliament.

---

[6] Even if an order of prohibition is sought, it must be shown that the court or tribunal against which the order is sought, has given some indication that it is likely to exceed its jurisdiction.

[7] See *Sabally* v. *A.-G.*, [1964] 3 All E.R. 377; [1965] 1 Q.B. 273. An unusual use of the prerogative in recent years has been the establishment of the Criminal Injuries Compensation Board (see Chapter VIII, *post*, p. 250).

[8] "It still lies within the prerogative power of the Crown to extend its sovereignty and jurisdiction to areas of land or sea over which it has not previously claimed or exercised sovereignty or jurisdiction": *per* DIPLOCK, L.J., in *Post Office* v. *Estuary Radio, Ltd.*, [1967] 3 All E.R. 663, at p. 680.

[9] See *Burmah Oil Co. (Burma Trading), Ltd.* v. *Lord Advocate*, [1964] 2 All E.R. 348; [1965] A.C. 75; in this case it was held that if a subject was deprived of his property for the benefit of the State in exercise of the royal prerogative, the subject was normally entitled to compensation).

[10] *Ante*, p. 20.

The Sovereign also has certain powers which can be exercised personally, without necessarily taking and acting on Ministerial advice. These are now few in number, consisting mainly of the conferment of certain personal honours, but it seems that the Sovereign may be entitled to act independently of Ministerial advice when selecting a new Prime Minister. On the retirement, on the grounds of ill-health, of Sir Anthony Eden (as he then was) in 1957, Her Majesty consulted the Marquis of Salisbury and Sir Winston Churchill (who did not then hold any Ministerial post), as well as the retiring Prime Minister[11]; however, the situation was somewhat unusual, as there was no change of political power in the Commons, and the Conservative Party in power had not themselves selected a leader to follow Sir Anthony. In 1965, the Conservative Party revised their practice for the choice of a leader and as a consequence the events of 1957 are not likely to recur. Nevertheless, it is probably true that no one is in a position to give Her Majesty "advice" in the constitutional sense that she must follow it.[12]

It is of course a constitutional convention that in the exercise of the Royal Prerogative the Sovereign shall consult with and act on the advice of her Ministers (except in the matters still left to her personal decision as above mentioned). As the Ministers are themselves answerable to the House of Commons in accordance with the convention of Ministerial responsibility, an effective political control may on occasion be exercised over the prerogative. The prerogative is however, free from any legal controls. This is not to say that Parliament is powerless in this context. The prerogative may always be reduced in its scope (and once it has been reduced in a particular manner, it cannot be revived, for the power will thenceforth depend on statute), either expressly or by necessary implication, by the medium of an Act of Parliament. Although there is a maxim of statute law construction to the effect that a statute shall be deemed not to bind the Crown unless the contrary intention clearly appears, nevertheless a prerogative power will not be exercisable where a corresponding power has been conferred by statute on the[13] same or some other government agency.[14] If a statute deals with or regulates a matter hitherto regarded as being part of the prerogative, the prerogative is treated as having been abrogated *pro tanto*.[15]

---

[11] See Marshall and Moodie, *Some Problems of the Constitution* (1959), p. 61.

[12] See *The Times*, October 14, 1963, p. 9.

[13] *A.-G.* v. *De Keyser's Royal Hotel*, [1920] A.C. 508; *Oxford University and Cambridge University* v. *Eyre and Spottiswoode, Ltd.*, [1963] 3 All E.R. 289.

[14] As in *Re Baker*, [1961] 2 All E.R. 250; [1961] Ch. 303, where the court declined to exercise the royal prerogative jurisdiction in respect of infants, in a case where the Education Act, 1944 (without referring in any way to the Prerogative power) had conferred a similar jurisdiction on the local education authority, and see also *Re M. (an infant)*, [1961] 1 All E.R. 788; [1961] Ch. 328.

[15] *Food Controller* v. *Cork*, [1923] A.C. 647.

CHAPTER III

LEGISLATION

1. INTRODUCTION

Having outlined the organisation of the central government, it is now time we considered the legislative or law-making power. This divides naturally into two parts, namely, legislation by Parliament, and legislation by other, subordinate law-making bodies, known as delegated or subordinate legislation. In this Chapter we propose to discuss briefly the powers of the Central Legislature, and such controls as there may be over it; we deal with the more complicated subject of subordinate legislation in the next Chapter.

2. PARLIAMENTARY LEGISLATION

To infer that the legislation of Parliament is a less complicated subject than that of subordinate legislation is not to suggest, of course, that the parent is less important than the child. Because of their importance, and the absence of any rules controlling their extent such as are to be found in a "written" constitution of the American or Australian pattern,[1] the legislative powers of Parliament in this country are capable of fairly simple statement. Apart from a few somewhat vague jurisdictional restrictions (see page 15 *ante*), which have themselves only become apparent in recent years, Parliament is supreme and can effect, in due form,[2] any changes in the law that it may consider desirable. As was said in an earlier Chapter,[3] there are virtually no legal restrictions on the sovereignty of the Queen in Parliament, although it may prove politically impracticable to obtain the necessary majority in the House of Commons at any one moment of time in order to secure the passing of some measure, however desirable this may seem to its protagonists.[4] Many things may be legally possible, but legal sovereignty has to yield to political reality.

Until recently the only other kind of legislation in this country, which does not owe its origin and authority to the Queen in Parliament, was

[1] Although the French constitution is embodied in a formal "written" constitution, legislation passed in due form in accordance with the terms of the Constitution is not capable of being declared unconstitutional by the Courts.

[2] This form may itself be changed by Parliament, as was done in the Parliament Acts of 1911 and 1949; and see Chapter I, *ante*, p. 17.

[3] Chapter I, *ante*, p. 15.

[4] In *Law and Opinion in England in the Nineteenth Century*, Dicey showed how far "behind" public opinion changes in legislation may be. On the other hand, where the exigencies of war or some other emergency so dictate, legislation of a fundamental and sweeping kind may be enacted in a very short time; the Emergency Powers (Defence) Act, 1939, was passed through all its stages in the House of Commons in less than 24 hours.

legislation by virtue of the Royal Prerogative, described in an earlier Chapter.[5] In addition, regulations of the institutions of the European Communities are self-executing in this country and have legal effect, although they have not been enacted by the Queen in Parliament or under the Royal Prerogative; they are given this effect by the terms of the Treaties, but these are themselves recognised in English law by virtue of the European Communities Act, 1972, and therefore the whole subject of European Community legislation is left to be considered as a specialised form of subordinate or delegated legislation (see *post*, p. 87). The Prerogative, however, can legislate by its own authority, recognised by the common law, and it is in no sense subordinate, although in practice the formal organ of the Prerogative, the Privy Council, may often be given powers to make subordinate legislation under the authority of some specific statute.[6]

3. THE LEGISLATIVE PROCESS

It is a commonplace to state that there are three elements in the legislature in this country, the Sovereign, the House of Lords and the House of Commons, and we will leave to the constitutional lawyers a detailed discussion of these several elements of the central legislature. It is, however, of consequence for our purposes to observe that there are two classes of Bills, public and private Bills. Public Bills are so classified by virtue of their subject matter; they are sponsored by the Government of the day or by a private member of either House, and they are of general public import.[7] Private Bills, on the other hand, will have been "promoted" by some "private" interest, such as a local authority, a statutory corporation or possibly a private individual or company[8] and they will be of some "private", local, or otherwise restricted concern. A private Bill, when it becomes an Act, is as much law as is a statute which started life as a public Bill, and it will be recognised by the courts as such[9] and enforced (if appropriate) against all Her Majesty's subjects; nevertheless it is restricted in scope or in the area over which it is operative, and for that reason the standing orders of both Houses of the legislature make provision for a special procedure to be followed in this form of law making.

Of particular interest to the administrative lawyer is the special kind of private Bill promoted by a local authority. Any of the Queen's subjects may promote or oppose a local Bill, subject to compliance with the standing orders of both Houses of Parliament, and this rule applies also to local authorities. However, local authorities are regulated in

[5] Chapter II, *ante*, p. 41.

[6] Chapter IV, *post*, p. 57.

[7] There are also "Hybrid Bills", which are Bills introduced as public Bills but which affect private interests. The procedure regulating the passage of such Bills through Parliament ensures that the private individuals concerned have an opportunity of petitioning against the Bill (see Hood Phillips, *Constitutional and Administrative Law*, 5th Edn. at p. 176).

[8] The Divorce Acts of the eighteenth century are examples of private Bills promoted at great expense by private individuals.

[9] The courts are, however, prepared to go behind a *private* Act (but not a public Act) and investigate whether it has been improperly obtained: *Pickin* v. *British Railways Board*, [1972] 3 All E.R. 923; [1973] Q.B. 219.

this matter by the Local Government Act, 1972. This gives an express power to promote or oppose a local or personal[10] Bill in Parliament to any local authority (except a parish or community council)[11] where they are satisfied that it is "expedient" so to do.[12] Before a Bill is deposited in Parliament under this provision, however, the local authority must have followed certain preliminary procedure.

The local authority must first pass a resolution in favour of (or opposing) the proposed Bill, by a majority of the whole number of the members of the authority (not just a majority of those actually present) at a meeting held after 30 clear days' notice[13] of the meeting and the purpose thereof[14] has been given by advertisement in one or more local newspapers. Formerly this resolution then had to be submitted to the Secretary of State for the Environment for his approval, but this is no longer necessary. This change in the law is part of the greater administrative freedom given to local authorities by the 1972 Act. Once the first resolution has "been passed", the Bill may be deposited in Parliament.

In a case of promotion of, but *not* opposition to, a Bill, a second meeting of the authority must be convened in the same manner, "as soon as may be after the expiration of 14 days after the Bill has been deposited in Parliament", and a second resolution to the same effect and with the same majority, must be passed. If this second resolution is not passed, the Bill must be withdrawn; if it is passed, the Bill may proceed in accordance with Parliamentary procedure.[15] The requirements of town's meetings and polls contained in earlier legislation have been abolished by the 1972 Act.

The Examiners of Private Bills (one appointed by the House of Lords and the other by the Speaker of the House of Commons) will have to be satisfied that the procedure of the 1972 Act and of both Houses has been complied with. The further proceedings on the Bill in the two Houses will then be governed by Standing Orders. In the Commons if the Bill is opposed by any one Member there must be a debate on Second Reading; the promoters will then have to brief Members who are prepared to support the Bill. The Committee stage in both Houses will be quasi-judicial in character.[16]

The practice of promoting private Bills by local authorities has during the last 100 years been regarded as the traditional means by

---

[10] This is a reference to the classification adopted in the House of Lords of private Bills. "Local" Bills deal either with the construction or alteration of works or other local authority or public utility matters, while personal Bills deal with such matters as estates, naturalisation, peerages, etc. Local Bills may be initiated in either House, but "Personal" Bills (*i.e.*, those private Bills that are not local) must be introduced first in the House of Lords.

[11] As to parish and community councils, see Chapter XI, *post*.

[12] Local Government Act, 1972, s. 239.

[13] The usual period of notice for the summoning of a meeting of a local authority is *three* clear days: Local Government Act, 1972, Schedule 12, para. 4.

[14] 10 days is sufficient in a case of opposition.

[15] Local Government Act, 1972, s. 239.

[16] For a description of this procedure, see Hood Phillips, *Constitutional and Administrative Law*, 5th Edn., at p. 182. An interesting account of the proceedings on the Leeds Bill in 1956, will be found in *Parliament at Work* (1962), by A. H. Hanson and H. V. Wiseman, at pp. 192 *et seq*.

which new local government services or new legal powers have been "tried out" on a limited scale. Municipal gas and electricity undertakings were originally launched by this means; district heating for council estates was experimented with under the authority of local Acts by a few local councils shortly after the Second World War, and many local authorities have obtained new statutory powers on a variety of detailed subjects. In more recent times it became popular for a county council to promote a Bill which gave new powers, not only to the county council itself, but also to the district councils in the county. The propriety of this practice was questioned in Parliament, but a Joint Committee of both Houses reported to the effect that no principle was thereby infringed and indeed it was to be welcomed where the matter involved was of general convenience, and where private legislation was required by several of the district councils in the county.[17]

Local authorities and statutory undertakers may also acquire new powers by the devices of "provisional orders" and "special orders". Provisional orders are made by a Minister of the Crown under the authority of a statute, and they are therefore sometimes described as a form of delegated or subordinate legislation, but they have no legal force until they have been included (usually by way of reference in a schedule) in a Provisional Orders Confirmation Act. In the case of a provisional order conferring powers on a local authority, the procedure is now governed by section 240 of the Local Government Act, 1972. Before the order is made, notice of the purport of an application by a local authority for an order must be published in the London Gazette and one or more local newspapers. The Secretary of State for the Environment is then obliged to consider any objects received, and unless he considers an inquiry to be unnecessary for "special reasons", he must hold a local inquiry. If the Secretary of State decides to proceed, he then makes the order and submits it to Parliament for confirmation; if any person petitions either House while the Bill is awaiting confirmation, the petitioner will be allowed to appear before the Select Committee to which the Bill is referred, and the proceedings then follow those applicable to a private Bill. When the Bill has been passed, the Provisional Order then is itself the equivalent of a statute.[18]

Until recently provisional order procedure was rarely used, but it now applies to orders made by the Secretary of State for the Environment under section 303 of the Public Health Act, 1875, which gives him wide powers to amend specific provisions in local Acts so as to bring them into line with modern legislation.[19]

The other procedure, more commonly applied by enabling statutes in cases where a Minister is empowered to confer new powers on local authorities or statutory undertakings, is that known as "special parliamentary procedure", invented by the Statutory Orders (Special Procedure) Act, 1945. These orders are true examples of subordinate

---

[17] See "Report of Joint Committee on Promotion of Private Bills" (H.L. 176; H.C. 262, of 1958–9), noted at [1960] P.L. 99.

[18] *Bessemer & Co. Ltd.* v. *Gould* (1912), 107 L.T. 298.

[19] Statutory Orders (Special Procedure) Order, 1962, S.I. 1962 No. 409.

legislation, as they become law once they have been made and all the procedure has been followed, without any express confirmation in an Act of Parliament; for convenience, however, it is proposed to deal with them briefly in this Chapter.

Under the Act of 1945 which, like the procedure by way of provisional order, needs an enabling Act to bring it into operation, an order is made by the local authority or statutory undertakers and submitted for approval by the appropriate Government Department; if it is an order authorising the compulsory acquisition of some special parcel of land,[20] the normal procedure[1] of advertisement and local inquiry must be followed. When the order has been approved by the Secretary of State, it must be laid before Parliament; if no petitions are submitted for its amendment and the order has not been annulled by resolution of either House, the order will come into effect at the end of a prescribed period. If, however, a petition is presented against the order within 21 days, this is referred to the Lord Chairman of Committees in the House of Lords and the Chairman of Ways and Means in the House of Commons; they then report thereon to their respective Houses.

Within twenty-one days[2] of such report a resolution of annulment may be passed in either House. If there are no such resolutions, the petition is referred to a Joint Committee of both Houses, who hear evidence on the matter in manner similar to the proceedings on a Private Bill, and report to both Houses. If a special order is not opposed the procedure is of course much simpler than that by way of provisional order,[3] from the point of view of the authority acquiring powers by the order in question, for in the latter case affirmative action has in any event to be taken in each House, whereas in the case of a special order the promoters of the order merely have to meet such opposition as may be raised.

4. CONTROL OVER PARLIAMENTARY LEGISLATION

Parliament is supreme, and can legislate as it likes; it is difficult therefore to appreciate how the machinery of administrative law could ever impose any effective control over the activities of Parliament. However, there are a few factors in the Parliamentary and administrative process that possess some measure of controlling effect, which should be considered here.

(a) Parliamentary machinery.—In theory the members of the House of Commons have absolute control over the nature and form of legislation. In practice, however, the party political machine and the programme of legislation will allow only a certain amount of discussion,

[20] Especially applicable to cases of compulsory acquisition of a common or land owned by another local authority, statutory undertakers or the National Trust: Acquisition of Land (Authorisation Procedure) Act, 1946.

[1] Chapter VIII, *post*, p. 228.

[2] Statutory Orders (Special Procedure) Act 1965, amending the Act of 1945 by substituting a period of 21 days for the original period of 14 days, thereby giving Parliament a longer time within which to consider these Orders.

[3] There is not much saving in time where the order is contested: see *Parliament at Work*, at p. 218.

and on controversial matters, such devices as the guillotine[4] and the kangaroo[5] may seriously cut short discussion. Many of the details of administrative statutes are not, however, controversial and the Government may bow to criticism on points of detail or agree to amendments, especially in the course of debates in Committee in the Commons, or at any stage in the Lords.[6] Such detailed control as is in practice exercised, operates most effectively in Committee, especially in the case of private Bills, where the entire policy of the Bill may be questioned at this stage.

(b) Consultation.—It has become modern practice for a Government Department proposing to introduce a Bill on an administrative subject[7] to discuss the details that it is intended to include in the Bill, with interested bodies outside the central administration. This is usually done informally, behind the scenes as it were, but it can prove most useful in practice. Many of the clauses included in local government Bills in recent times (such as the Public Health Act, 1961) have been initially suggested to the government departments concerned by local government associations of various kinds, such as the Association of Municipal Corporations, the Royal Society for the Promotion of Health or the Society of Town Clerks. It has also become customary for the Council on Tribunals to be consulted at an early stage in the drafting of a Bill wherever proposals are included for the creation of a new tribunal or tribunals, or an extension of the jurisdiction of existing tribunals.[8] At a later stage, when the Bill has been introduced in Parliament, the sponsoring government department may be agreeable to discussing possible amendments in matters of detail with these interested bodies; if those bodies are unable to convince the civil servants or the Minister concerned of the need for amendments, they may then take up the matters in which they are interested with individual members of Parliament, in the hope that such matters may be raised in committee or on the floor of the House.[9] Such informal consultation and lobbying is an important part of the modern legislative process and to the extent to which it is effective in practice it

---

[4] This cuts short any further discussion on a clause or a whole Bill by resolution put and carried by use of the Government's majority.

[5] This is a similar device whereby a clause or clauses in a Bill as presented are "jumped over" and all discussion thereon is excluded. This device is sometimes employed when the early sections of a Bill have been heavily contested; as a consequence the later clauses of a Bill are often not discussed or examined in detail.

[6] A good example of this can be seen in the House of Lords second reading debate on the Bill that became the Public Health Act, 1961. Lord Chorley, an opposition Peer, strenuously attacked clause 49 in the Bill as presented (H.L. Deb., Vol. 226, No. 13, Col. 889), and as a consequence the clause was quietly dropped from the Bill by the Government.

[7] This phrase is not here used in any precise or technical sense, but merely to indicate that a major Bill implementing some change of government policy is not so treated, as in such a case it would be considered a breach of the privileges of Parliament to divulge the contents of a proposed Bill before it had been introduced in Parliament.

[8] See, for example, the Annual Report of the Council for 1971/72, paras. 24–44. There could never be a legal requirement that there should be consultation over legislative proposals, as contrasted with delegated legislation (see p. 74). As to the Council on Tribunals, see *post*, p. 201.

[9] In such a case Parliament may be a "sort of umpire" between the executive and vested interests: see Lord Chorley, at 7 M.L.R. 144.

may be regarded as providing some measure of outside control over the "freedom" of Parliament. At this level[10] however, consultation can only be informal and extra-statutory.

(c) Judicial control.—The courts can have no direct control over the content of Parliamentary legislation; there is no written constitution in this country and therefore no Act of Parliament can ever be declared to be void on the grounds of unconstitutionality. Indeed the courts exhibit a very great respect for the *ipsissima verba* of the Legislature. Nevertheless, there are certain "canons of construction" evolved by the common law, which will be applied by the Courts when construing the terms of a Statute. Space does not admit of more than the briefest summary of the more important rules of statutory interpretation, but the application by the Courts of these rules may at times operate so as to modify the apparent or strict meaning of the words used by Parliament. The fundamental rule of interpretation, to which all others are subordinate, is that a statute is to be expounded "according to the intent of them that made it".[11] Nevertheless, in the absence of clear words to the contrary, the following general principles of construction will, *inter alia,*[12] be applied by the Courts:

(i) There is a presumption against any alteration of the existing law beyond the specific extent of the statute being construed.

(ii) A statute will, if possible, be construed in practice in such a manner as to prevent evasion of its plain terms and so as to prevent an abuse of powers thereby conferred.

(iii) A statute will be presumed not to bind the Crown unless the contrary intention is made clear.[13]

(iv) A construction will if possible be applied which will not have the effect of giving the statute retrospective operation, of causing injustice[14] or absurdity, or of causing some unreasonable result.

(v) Penal laws will be construed strictly in favour of the accused; byelaws will be presumed to be reasonable, but if shown to be unreasonable they will be liable to be quashed on that ground.[15]

(vi) A statute will not be construed so as to confer a power to impose a tax unless the intention is clear. This is of particular importance in connection with a statute conferring a power to make subordinate legislation.[16]

---

[10] Contrast the position in connection with the making of subordinate legislation; Chapter IV, *post*, p. 74.

[11] Maxwell, *The Interpretation of Statutes*, 12th Edn., at p. 1.

[12] See Maxwell, *op. cit.*, *passim*, from which standard work the principles stated in the text are taken.

[13] This rule of statutory interpretation has been expressly saved by statute: Crown Proceedings Act, 1947, s. 40 (2) (f), and Chapter IX, *post*, p. 288.

[14] It is under this heading that the courts will in appropriate circumstances read into the statute a requirement that the principles of natural justice should be observed; see Chapter VI, *post*, p. 115.

[15] Chapter IV, *post*, p. 84.

[16] Chapter IV, *post*, p. 79. Where a local authority was empowered to impose conditions on the grant of a licence, it was held that conditions could not be imposed which would have had the effect of depriving the licensee of his land without compensation, in the absence of a precise statutory authorisation to that effect: *Hall & Co., Ltd.* v. *Shoreham-by-Sea U.D.C.*, [1964] 1 All E.R. 1; [1964] 1 W.L.R. 240.

These are but a few of the leading principles; it should be emphasised that any and all of these principles of construction may be excluded by the precise words of the statute in a particular case, but within those limits they enable the Courts to control the effect of parliamentary legislation. If Parliament wishes in a particular case to legislate (for example) with retrospective effect, it must explicitly so provide in unmistakable terms.[17] Parliament is supreme and it can always expressly exclude these established canons of construction. On the other hand, the Courts can interpret and apply only the words used by Parliament; they cannot have regard to what has been said in Parliament while the Bill was in process of becoming an Act. What the legislators had intended or wanted to do by way of legislation is not material when the Courts have to consider what has actually been provided in the statute. *Travaux préparatoires*, as they are called in France, cannot at present be used by a Court to assist in the construction of a statute[18]; the Law Commission are however, currently considering amendments in the law to enable the Courts in future to take notice of the *travaux préparatoires* when construing a statute. "But, the modern rule is clear: the Parliamentary history of legislation is not a permissible aid in construing a statute."[19]

In this limited sense, the Courts in the course of interpreting statutes and applying them to particular factual situations (not all of which may have been foreseen by the Legislature) exercise some measure of control over the activities of Parliament. In every other sense Parliament in this country is in law supreme; where *de facto* or political sovereignty resides in our constitution is not a question an administrative lawyer is called upon to answer.

The extent to which an individual may be able to obtain redress of his grievances[20] must therefore ultimately depend on Parliament, but at least the courts are watchful to ensure that Parliament does not inadvertently contravene the general principles here discussed.

---

[17] As in the War Damage Act, 1965, which reversed the effect of *Burmah Oil Co. (Burma Trading), Ltd.* v. *Lord Advocate* (*ante*, p. 41).

[18] Even the report of a Royal Commission or of a Departmental Committee, which preceded and recommended the passing of the particular statute, cannot be admitted to assist in construction: *Assam Rlys. and Trading Co.* v. *Central Indian Rly.*, [1935] A.C. 445.

[19] Maxwell, *The Interpretation of Statutes*, 12th Edn., at p. 50.

[20] See Chapters V–IX, *post*.

CHAPTER IV

SUBORDINATE LEGISLATION

1. INTRODUCTION

In the ideal State the legislative power would presumably be reserved exclusively for legislators directly responsible to the electorate. In theory this is true of the modern English constitution, but in practice, Parliament has to entrust some of its legislative power to subordinate law-making bodies. Ministers of the Crown, local authorities, independent statutory corporations, the Church of England, private companies[1] and the Commission and the Council of the European Communities,[2] are all given power by Parliament to make laws in many different circumstances. The legal sovereignty of Parliament still holds good, for none of these lesser bodies can legislate except by and with the authority of Parliament. Subordinate legislation is, however, a feature of modern civilisation in any State; it has been said to be the result of "collectivism", but it is widely used in countries with differing political and constitutional systems, including France, the U.S.A., and the U.S.S.R.

In England the power to legislate by way of administrative regulation was freely exercised in the sixteenth and seventeenth centuries by the Sovereign in his Privy Council, by virtue of the Royal Prerogative. After the "glorious Revolution" of 1688 the Whig Parliament assumed this power into their own hands. It was almost an article of political faith to deny the Executive discretionary powers, and such legislation as was necessary was kept firmly within the powers of Parliament itself. As a consequence in the eighteenth century, though a time when there was not much government in a modern sense, the statute book rapidly became choked with Divorce Acts, Enclosure Acts and Customs and Excise legislation, while the control of local government was handed over to Quarter Sessions to be exercised by legal process.[3] As all legislation, even the most restricted in effect, had to be formulated and passed at Westminster, detailed administration of the country was almost at a standstill. During the nineteenth century when the aftermath of the industrial revolution brought the period of *laissez faire* to an end, Parliament was obliged to surrender a power to make

---

[1] The "legislation" of a private company or club is law only in the sense that it will be enforced by the courts as between the shareholders of the company or members of the club in question: the courts will merely expect ordinary members of society outside the company or club to accept rights thereby created. This has been described by Sir C. K. Allen as "autonomic legislation" (*Law in the Making*, 7th Edn., at pp. 542 *et seq.*) and it is not directly the concern of this book as it is a matter primarily of private law.

[2] *Post*, p. 87.

[3] *The History of Local Government in England*, by Redlich & Hirst, ed. Keith-Lucas, at p. 38.

detailed administrative rules to the newly created central government departments,[4] setting the pattern for the intense activity, especially in the social field, of the twentieth century. Two world wars gave yet further impetus to the general trend, as it proved essential in the interests of national security and for the efficient prosecution of any war, for Parliament to give even wider powers of legislative discretion to the Executive. The introduction of the Welfare State after the Second World War yet further accelerated and increased this process. It was quite impossible for Parliament itself to attend to all the details of national health insurance, the National Health Service, controls over the economy, town and country planning, road traffic control, and the legal aid scheme.

This chapter is concerned with the various methods by which this subordinate law-making power may be exercised, and the means by and the extent to which the resulting subordinate legislation may be controlled by the courts or other external agencies. First, however, we must discuss the sort of circumstances in which Parliament may consider itself justified in delegating its legislative power, and also comment on some of the criticisms that may be made of the practice.

2. THE JUSTIFICATION OF SUBORDINATE LEGISLATION

The very summary historical remarks made in the last paragraph merely offer some explanation of the extensive use of this phenomenon of subordinate legislation in modern government; they cannot justify it. The arguments commonly put forward[5] in favour of subordinate legislation, by way of extenuation and starting from the assumption that Parliament should be directly responsible for all legislation,[6] may be summarised as follows:

(1) In a modern State the bulk of legislation is so great that Parliament has not sufficient time or energy, or even desire, to concern itself with details. Therefore the general policy of a major measure such as the Town and Country Planning Act, 1971, or the Road Traffic Act, 1960, or of an emergency measure such as the Counter Inflation (Temporary Provisions) Act, 1972, is settled in Parliament, the Act being issued often as a mere skeleton, and the appropriate Minister is empowered to fill in the details—to give flesh and blood to the skeleton so that it may live—in the form of regulations and orders made under the authority of the parent Act.

(2) Sometimes the subject matter on which legislation is required is of a technical nature, too technical it may be for the issues to be fully

---

[4] As long ago as 1888 Maitland called attention to the "subordinate legislative powers of the great officers" (*Constitutional History*, p. 506), and in 1910 Professor Ramsay Muir was able to say that "Parliament now passes Acts of a general character, and entrusts to one or another department of State very large powers of giving effect to these general provisions by specific regulations": *Peers and Bureaucrats*, at p. 20.

[5] As in, for example, the Donoughmore Committee Report.

[6] This idea has been very considerably influenced by the theory of the separation of powers (Chapter I, *ante*, p. 12) to the existence of which subordinate legislation is a complete denial.

appreciated in Parliament. Even if the technicalities involved are not such as to be beyond the grasp of any but experts in the particular subject, details are rarely appropriate for discussion in Parliament.[7] Here the result is that the legislative power is handed over to scientific or other experts. This argument may be important in connection with such matters as the control of atomic energy or in exchange or other economic controls.

(3) Provision may have to be made for unforeseen contingencies; these may occur at any time, whether Parliament is sitting or not, and it may be desirable or necessary that prohibitive or regulatory action should be taken in relation to particular conduct forthwith. Police regulations and certain economic matters such as the level of the bank rate and exchange control may fall into this class. The device of subordinate legislation enables a Minister to manipulate controls of various kinds with a flexibility greater than could ever be possible if he had to obtain a new statute every time he wished to make a change of detail.[8]

(4) The power to make "sub-laws" that may themselves, if necessary, be readily revoked, enables a Minister to permit executive organs of government, or even independent bodies, to experiment. Parking meters and other road traffic devices have been "tried out" under the authority of Ministerial Regulations from time to time; if the experiment has been thought to have been proved successful, the regulations may then easily be extended or made permanent, with or without any desirable modifications.

(5) Finally there is the necessity for the Executive to be given special powers in time of war or other national emergency. In these circumstances subordinate law-making powers are often extremely wide. By section 1 of the Emergency Powers (Defence) Act, 1939, His Majesty was empowered by Order in Council to

> "make such Regulations as appear to him [*i.e.*, to His Majesty's advisers, the Cabinet] to be necessary or expedient for securing the public safety, the defence of the realm, the maintenance of public order, and the efficient prosecution of any war in which His Majesty may be engaged, and for maintaining supplies and services essential to the life of the community."

Every year those orders and regulations that are published by H.M. Stationery Office (and we shall see that some forms of subordinate legislation are not required to be so published) greatly exceed in bulk the statutes passed by Parliament during the same period.

> "It is impossible to pass an Act of Parliament to control an epidemic of measles or an outbreak of foot-and-mouth disease as and when it occurs, and such

[7] For example, such matters as "patents, copyrights, trade marks, designs, poisons, the pattern of miners' safety lamps, wireless telegraphy, the heating and lighting values of gas, legal proceedings and the intricacies of finance": Donoughmore Committee's Report, at p. 23, quoting from Sir Cecil Carr's *Delegated Legislation* (1921).

[8] Difficulties may often arise in practice where Parliament has attended to details and circumstances have changed since the original enactment. A special case of this is to be found in the many examples of maximum fines that may be imposed on the commission of offences, that for many years were too low, having been fixed at a time when social conditions and the value of money was different, and which had to be increased by the Criminal Justice Act, 1967.

measures as the Public Health Acts must be differently applied in different parts of the country. . . . The truth is that if Parliament were not willing to delegate law-making power, Parliament would be unable to pass the kind and quantity of legislation which modern public opinion requires."[9]

This is not to say, however, that the bulk of subordinate legislation is ever growing; as Sir Cecil Carr has shown,[10] the annual output has decreased since the last war; the bulk is nonetheless still considerable.

3. CRITICISMS OF SUBORDINATE LEGISLATION

Why then, and on what ground, have political scientists, lawyers and others criticised the practice whereby Parliament delegates some portion of its legislative power to subordinate government agencies? The tidy and readily intelligible theory of the separation of powers is of course thereby shaken; but this in itself is immaterial. The more fundamental criticisms have been aimed

"rather against the volume and character of delegated legislation than against the practice of delegation itself".[11]

They have been summarised as follows[11]:

(1) We have seen that statutes are often passed in skeleton form only, leaving the details to be filled in by Ministerial regulations. In practice the regulations as to matters of detail are often the very ones that are of most concern to the "man in the street". The system of planning control introduced by the Town and Country Planning Act, 1947 and now contained in the Act of 1971 (as amended in 1972), was intended to be far-reaching and comprehensive, but the manner in which it might affect the ordinary citizens has been considerably modified by such forms of subordinate legislation as the General Development Order, 1973 (exempting particular kinds of development from the need to obtain express planning permission) and the Town and Country Planning (Structure and Local Plans) Regulations, 1972 (prescribing the detailed contents of the new type of development plants and limiting and regulating the rights of persons interested to object to the contents of such plans). It is no doubt convenient but perhaps undesirable that legislation of such importance should be made in Whitehall and not by the elected representatives of the nation in Parliament itself.

(2) Controls over subordinate legislation are inadequate; Parliament has neither the time nor the opportunity to keep a watch on what its delegates, the Ministers, are doing under the authority of Parliament, and the control of the courts is often either excluded, because of the sweeping terms of the delegation, or is made ineffective because those terms are drafted in vague or loosely defined words. Judicial control over delegated legislation is also (it may be argued) bound to be to some extent unsatisfactory, in that by its nature it will be invoked too late, after harm has been done, while in many cases it will not be invoked at

---

[9] Donoughmore Committee Report, p. 23.
[10] See his article ," Parliamentary Control of Delegated Legislation", [1956] P.L. 200.
[11] Donoughmore Committee Report, p. 53.

all because of the expense, or owing to inanition, ignorance or indifference on the part of the persons affected. Controls over subordinate legislation have in some respects been improved since the Report of the Donoughmore Committee was published; the extent to which complaints about lack of control may be justified, and the need for any further kinds of control will be considered later in this Chapter.

(3) It is not always possible or practicable for adequate publicity to be given to subordinate legislation, and the actual process of law-making is not altogether satisfactory. Complaints of this kind were almost certainly justified at the time when the Donoughmore Committee reported. Since 1932, however, this matter has received the attention of Parliament in the Statutory Instruments Act, 1946, to be considered later[12]; nevertheless even at the present time, criticisms on this score are not always ill-founded.[13]

(4) A further criticism that is often advanced of subordinate legislation is that the process leads to legislation by reference.[14] The legislative process is comparatively simple, and therefore the draftsmen in the Departments concerned rarely take the care over an amending regulation that they would over a Parliamentary Bill that has to stand up to the scrutiny of Members in the Commons. It is also always easier to amend piecemeal, rather than to revoke the old regulations and replace with new. Although this criticism is often valid, it does not really amount to a condemnation of the practice of subordinate legislation, for legislation by reference can be avoided, and if indulged in too freely is rather an abuse of the practice than a necessary feature of it.

4. CLASSIFICATION OF SUBORDINATE LEGISLATION

It is now time we considered the different forms of subordinate legislation. These may be considered informally, according to the objects they are designed to achieve, and then formally according to the process followed in their making and the type of agency which is entrusted by Parliament with the law-making power.[15] H.M. Stationery Office adopts a third system of classification, according to the subject matter dealt with by the several regulations or orders, but this would be of little value for our present purpose.

(1) Classification according to objects.—Subordinate legislation may be classified according to its content or purpose. Most instruments will fall within one or other of the following:

(i) Certain regulations are made for the purpose of bringing a statute into operation. It is common practice for a statute to provide that it shall not come into operation until such date as the appropriate

---

[12] *Post*, p. 64.
[13] See, for example, the observations of STREATFEILD, J., in *Patchett* v. *Leathem* (1949) 65 T.L.R. 69; *post*, p. 67.
[14] See the examples given by Sir Carleton Allen in *Law in the Making* 7th Edn., at p. 551, and in *Law and Orders*, 3rd. Edn., at pp. 172 *et seq*.
[15] European "secondary" legislation is considered separately: see *post*, p. 87.

Minister may appoint. This device allows the Government Departments concerned any "breathing space" they may require to set up the administrative machinery necessary to implement the new statute, and to draft any subordinate legislation required; it also enables adequate steps to be taken to bring the provisions of the new statute to the notice of any members of the public who may be particularly concerned. Sometimes this device may be used to bring different portions of the Act into force on different days.[16]

(ii) Some forms of subordinate legislation adopt or modify existing Acts of Parliament, under the authority of the enabling Act. This is a common practice where a general statute has dealt with a subject on which a number of local authorities had previously obtained a local Act containing similar (but not identical) provisions to those now proposed. In the new statute the appropriate Minister will then be given power to revoke or modify the provisions of such local Acts in so far as they may conflict with the new Act.[17] Sometimes the enabling statute goes even further and empowers a Minister to modify the provisions of the enabling Act itself, "so far as may appear to him to be necessary" for the purpose of bringing the Act into operation. This is the provision that has been called "the Henry VIII clause", because that King is regarded popularly as "the impersonation of executive autocracy."[18] It is this particular example of wide legislative discretion conferred on a Minister that became the target of most of the criticism aimed at subordinate legislation generally.[19] As a consequence of this criticism this clause has not appeared in recent Acts; if it is necessary to amend existing Acts so as to make a new statute operate, it should not be beyond the skill of the Parliamentary draftsman to include all the necessary provisions within the Act itself. In a few cases the enabling statute may empower the Minister to make regulations for particular purposes which, when made "shall be of the same force as if enacted in this Act".[20] On the face of it, such a power seems little better than the Henry VIII clause, but at least it may be exercised only for the specified purposes.

(iii) Regulations may provide, explain or add to lists of objects or substances, or define terms, referred to in the parent statute. Standards

---

[16] As was done, for instance, with the Road Traffic Act, 1956. The Offices Act, 1960, which was virtually "forced" onto a reluctant government by pressure from back-benchers, had not been brought into force until it was repealed by the Offices, Shops and Railway Premises Act 1963. Commencement orders may also be used to bring parts of an Act into force on different dates in different parts of the country, as is being done with Part I of the Town and Country Planning Act, 1971 (the new development plan procedure).

[17] For good examples of this device, see s. 35 (4) of the Clean Air Act, 1956, and s. 82 of the Public Health Act, 1961.

[18] With particular reference to the Statute of Proclamations, 1539; see Donoughmore Committee Report, p. 36, and *post*, p. 160.

[19] In particular Lord HEWART's famous book *The New Despotism*, published in 1929.

[20] A good example of this type of clause will be found in the Land Registration Act, 1925, s. 114 (2). The Land Registration Rules, 1925, made under this subsection were said by DIPLOCK, L.J., in *Re Freehold Land in Dances Way*, [1962] 2 All E.R. 42, at p. 51; [1962] 1 Ch. 490, not to be "subordinate legislation", because of the nature of the power under which they were made. Under the Local Government Act, 1972, extensive powers are given to adapt existing legislation by subordinate instruments, but in the more important cases this may be effected only by Order in Council subject to the "affirmative resolution" procedure (see *post*, p. 69): s. 252; but contrast s. 253, *ibid.*

also may sometimes be prescribed in general terms in the parent statute, and a Minister be empowered to provide by regulations that the standard shall or may be satisfied in particular detailed cases. Poisons regulations, regulations under the Diseases of Animals Acts, and many other statutes fall within this category.

(iv) Regulations are often required to "clothe" the statute. This is of course the class into which most forms of subordinate legislation fall. General principles, more or less widely drawn, are expounded in the statute, and then it is left to the delegate law-making authority to fill in the details.

(2) Classification according to procedure.—Subordinate legislation classified according to the process adopted by way of implementation of the law-making power, may be discussed under the following headings:

(i) *Orders in Council.*—It has become customary in modern statutes to confer the more important law-making powers on the Sovereign in Council; as we have seen[1] this means that the executive, usually the Cabinet, will make the decision, but any such decision will have to be put into the solemn form of an Order of the Privy Council. Some orders of the Council are, however, not subordinate legislation at all; the Privy Council can still legislate in its own right on matters within the Royal Prerogative, in so far as this has not been taken away or restricted by statute.[2] Except where an order of the Privy Council is made by virtue of the prerogative, it can, like all forms of subordinate legislation, have the force of law only so far as such authority has been conferred on it by Parliament in a statute.

(ii) *Regulations.*—There are an infinity of examples of these, and there is no limit to the identity or kind of administrative agency that may be authorised by Parliament to make subordinate legislation. By far the commonest agency is a Minister of the Crown or other head of a Central Department, but the Rules Committee of the Supreme Court may make Rules regulating High Court procedure which fall within this class of subordinate legislation.[3] Sometimes a Minister is required to provide by "order", sometimes by "regulation". Apart from any different provisions as to "laying" which may be applicable in the one case and not in another (see below), there is really no jurisprudential distinction between "orders", "regulations", "directions", and other terms that may be used in particular contexts; see *post*, p. 59.

(iii) *Provisional orders.*—Here a Minister makes an order in draft or provisionally and then obtains Parliamentary approval thereto (or more often to a batch of such orders), by means of a Provisional Orders Confirmation Bill. This is really only a device to save Parliamentary

---

[1] Chapter II, *ante*, p. 29.

[2] Chapter II, *ante*, p. 41, and *A.-G.* v. *De Keyser's Royal Hotel*, [1920] A.C. 508.

[3] Supreme Court Rules are made under the authority of s. 99 of the Supreme Court of Judicature (Consolidation) Act, 1925; they must be laid before Parliament, but there are no other special procedural provisions to be observed. Similar Rules of procedure may be made in respect of county courts under s. 102 of the County Courts Act, 1959; these are subject to allowance and/or alteration by the Lord Chancellor, and must be embodied in a statutory instrument to which the provisions of the Statutory Instruments Act, 1946 (see *post*) will apply.

time, and is not a true example of subordinate legislation; it is not widely used at the present day.[4]

(iv) *Special procedure orders.*—These are regulations or orders of a Minister to which the enabling Act has specifically applied the provisions of the Statutory Orders (Special Procedure) Act, 1945.[5]

(v) *Orders of local authorities.*—In many different circumstances a statute may authorise a local authority to acquire privately owned land without the owner's consent,[6] to make an order for public access to open country,[7] to prepare a development plan showing the optimum use of all land in the authority area[8] or to take a number of other steps which will have legal consequences on the rights of private individuals. These orders are of no effect until they have been confirmed by a named Minister[9]; they will then become for all intents and purposes subordinate legislation.

(vi) *Byelaws.*—Byelaws are made by local authorities or other independent government agencies (such as the four Transport Boards), or even by specially favoured independent bodies, such as the National Trust. Byelaws, which are subject to certain exceptional judicial tests as to their validity, will be considered in more detail later in this Chapter.[10]

(vii) *Sub-delegated legislation.*—In some cases the enabling statute may provide that the subordinate law-maker shall have power, not only to make substantive laws itself, but also to delegate the law-making power to yet another government agency or other body. The standard example of this device is the Emergency Powers Defence Act, 1939, s. 1, which empowered His Majesty to make Defence Regulations in the very widest terms (see *ante*, p. 53). The Defence Regulations themselves then authorised Ministers to make "orders", which in turn authorised Ministers or other agencies to give "directions". Sub-delegated legislation must not, however, offend the principle, originating in private law and which has been generally adopted into public law, known as *delegatus non potest delegare*. In other words, a government agency entrusted by Parliament with a subordinate law-making power cannot delegate that power to another agency, except in so far as such delegation may itself, expressly or by necessary implication, have been authorised by Parliament. We shall return to this topic later in this Chapter.

(viii) *Measures of the Church of England.*—Under the Church of England Assembly (Powers) Act, 1919, the National Assembly may make Measures dealing with any matter "concerning the Church of

---

4 See Chapter III, *ante*, p. 46.
5 *Ibid.*
6 See, for example, Housing Act, 1957, s. 97; in almost all cases the procedure is now standardised by the Acquisition of Land (Authorisation Procedure) Act, 1946; Chapter VIII, *post*, p. 228.
7 National Parks and Access to the Countryside Act, 1949, s. 65.
8 Town and Country Planning Act, 1971, Part II.
9 In accordance with the appropriate prescribed statutory procedure; normally provision is made for the holding of an inquiry into any objections or representations.
10 See *post*, p. 80.

England," and these Measures have the force of law, subject to confirmation by resolution of each House of Parliament (which resolutions are in practice rarely debated) and the Royal Assent. The Measures so passed are printed by H.M. Stationery Office, and included in the annual volumes of the Statutes; logically it could perhaps be argued that Measures are not subordinate legislation, but are true legislation in their own right.

(ix) *Budget resolutions.*—Under the Provisional Collection of Taxes Act, 1968, resolutions of the House of Commons have the effect of law for a period of not more than four months, pending the passing of the annual Finance Act.

(3) Classification according to nomenclature.—It may have been considered that the various forms of delegated legislation should be classified according to their names: there are, it is true, Orders in Council, Orders of Ministers or Departments, regulations, rules, directions and byelaws. Unfortunately, however, only the first and the last in this list are terms which are used with any precision. The Donoughmore Committee Report (p. 64) had recommended that:

> "the expressions 'regulation', 'rule' and 'order' should not be used indiscriminately in statutes to describe the instruments by which the law-making power conferred on Ministers by Parliament is exercised. The expression 'regulation' should be used to describe the instrument by which the power to make substantive law is exercised, and the expression 'rule' to describe the instrument by which the power to make law about procedure is exercised. The expression 'order' should be used to describe the instrument of the exercise of (a) executive power, (b) the power to take judicial and quasi-judicial decisions."

Although this recommendation was endorsed in the Report of the Davies Committee (p. vii), it has not been generally adopted, and any classification of delegated legislation on these lines would be misleading. The expression "rules" is used in connection with Supreme Court procedure, but the procedure for the making of development plans in the law of town and country planning (for example) is contained in "Regulations". All that can be said is that in general the relative order of importance of the particular form of delegated legislation approximately follows that given in the text above.

5. PROCEDURE FOR THE MAKING OF SUBORDINATE LEGISLATION

Originally the only provisions regulating the methods by which a law-making power could be exercised by the Minister or other body to whom the power had been entrusted by Parliament were those, if any, contained in the enabling statute itself, as for example, where the notorious Statute of Proclamations, 1539, empowered the King to legislate by proclamation. The Rules Publication Act, 1893, eventually made provision for certain kinds of subordinate legislation to be printed by the Queen's Printer, while other kinds were not required to be so printed, but the provisions of this statute[11] did not go far enough

[11] The statute itself, and the Treasury Regulations made thereunder was scheduled to the Donoughmore Report (see p. 119 thereof).

and were in other respects unsatisfactory. The 1893 Act was repealed by the Statutory Instruments Act, 1946, which purports to enact a comprehensive procedural code for the making of subordinate legislation. The scheme of the 1946 Act is first to define the newly-invented expression "statutory instrument", then to formulate rules for the publication of statutory instruments as so defined, and finally to regulate the procedure whereby Parliament is given some measure of control over the making of statutory instruments.

(1) The meaning of "statutory instrument".—Section 1 of the Act of 1946 provides as follows:

"1—(1) Where by this Act or any Act passed after the commencement of this Act[12] power to make, confirm or approve orders, rules, regulations or other subordinate legislation is conferred on His Majesty in Council or on any Minister of the Crown then, if the power is expressed—

(a) in the case of a power conferred on His Majesty, to be exercisable by Order in Council;

(b) in the case of a power conferred on a Minister of the Crown, to be exercisable by statutory instrument,

any document by which that power is exercised shall be known as a 'statutory instrument' and the provisions of this Act shall apply thereto accordingly.

(2) Where by any Act passed before the commencement of this Act[12] power to make statutory rules within the meaning of the Rules Publication Act, 1893, was conferred on any rule-making authority within the meaning of that Act,[13] any document by which that power is exercised after the commencement of this Act shall, save as is otherwise provided by regulations made under this Act,[14] be known as a 'statutory instrument' and the provisions of this Act shall apply thereto accordingly."

The section thus differentiates between subordinate legislation made after 1947 under statutes passed before 1st January 1948, and that made under statutes passed after that date. The Act does not apply at all to Orders in Council made by virtue of the Prerogative, and therefore such Orders are not published by H.M.S.O. as Statutory Instruments.[15] Any *statutory* power[16] to legislate by Order in Council must, however, be

---

[12] January 1 1948; Statutory Instruments Act, 1946 (Commencement) Order, 1948 (S.I. 1948 No. 3).

[13] "Rule-making authority" was defined in the 1893 Act (see s. 4 thereof) as including "every authority authorised to make any statutory rules", and "statutory rules" was defined in its turn as meaning "rules, regulations, or byelaws made under any Act of Parliament which (a) relate to any court in the U.K., or to the procedure, practice, costs or fees therein, or to any fees or matters applying generally throughout England, Scotland, or Ireland; or (b) are made by Her Majesty in Council, the Judicial Committee, the Treasury, the Lord Chancellor of Great Britain, or the Lord Lieutenant or the Lord Chancellor of Ireland, or a Secretary of State, the Admiralty, the Board of Trade, the Local Government Board for England or Ireland, the Chief Secretary for Ireland, or any other Government Department."

[14] See the Statutory Instruments Regulations, 1947 (S.I. 1948 No. 1), *post*.

[15] For example, the Civil Service Order in Council, 1956, is not so published. A reference will be found to this Order in the H.M.S.O. *Index to Statutory Rules and Orders* (*sub. tit. Civil Service*), where the person desiring to ascertain the law on this topic is referred to the Commissioners or the Department. The Malta (Letters Patent) Act, 1959, apparently had the effect of conferring on Her Majesty a statutory power to make subordinate legislation which is, however, to be treated as if it were a prerogative power (exercisable by Letters Patent) and so is not to be treated as if it were a statutory instrument.

[16] Whenever conferred, and irrespective of the date of the Statute.

exercised by way of statutory instrument, as must any power which in the enabling statute is required to be exercised by way of statutory instrument; but this section of the 1946 Act applies only where the rule-making power is conferred on a "Minister of the Crown" (a term defined widely enough to cover any government department).[17] In most statutes passed since 1947 it is provided that any power thereby conferred to make regulations or orders shall be exercisable by statutory instrument, either generally[18] or in relation to specific powers only.[19] It by no means follows, however, that necessarily or invariably the enabling statute passed after 1947 will require any exercise of a subordinate law-making power to be by way of statutory instrument,[1] and the 1946 Act will not apply where such a requirement does not appear. It is a comparatively simple matter in the case of subordinate legislation made under a power contained in a post-1947 statute, to ascertain whether the power is exercisable by statutory instrument; the statute itself is conclusive.[2]

In the case of subordinate legislation made (after 1947) under a power contained in a statute passed before 1948, however, the position is not so simple. There are three different types of "rules" (used in a general sense) contained in pre-1948 statutes, which must be considered in this context:

(a) Rules which fell within the definition of "statutory rules" in the Rules Publication Act, 1893,[3] and which are not expressly excepted therefrom under section 1 (2) of the 1946 Act. These if made after 1947 must be made by way of statutory instrument.

(b) Rules made after 1947, which would have been statutory rules under the 1893 Act, but which are *excepted* by regulations made (by statutory instrument) under section 1 (2) of the 1946 Act. The Statutory Instruments Regulations, 1947,[4] have the effect of including as statutory rules for this purpose, all such rules which are of "a legislative and *not* of an executive character". There is no guidance whatever in either the Regulations themselves or the statute as to the meaning of

---

[17] Section 11 of the 1946 Act.

[18] See, for example, Housing Act, 1957, s. 178; Town and Country Planning Act, 1959, s. 55 (4); Road Traffic Act, 1960, s. 260 (1).

[19] For example, Public Health Act, 1961, s. 82 (5).

[1] For example, by a variety of statutes a Minister (usually the Secretary of State for the Environment) is empowered to confirm a compulsory purchase order or other order made by a local authority, and until such confirmation the order will be of no legal effect. Any such confirmation (which in some cases is expressly termed an "order": National Parks and Access to the Countryside Act, 1949, First Schedule, para. 1 (2) relating to National Parks) is not normally required to be by way of statutory instrument. In the Housing Act, 1957 (s. 178, *supra*) it is only "regulations" that are required to be made by way of statutory instrument. Orders made under s. 17 (2) of the Clean Air Act, 1956 (now replaced by s.11 of the Clean Act Act, 1968) are not required to be made by statutory instrument, and therefore it is the view of the Department that they cannot be so made. Their existence can be discovered on enquiry of the Department but the orders are not sold by H.M.S.O.

[2] In his article "The Reluctant Executive", at [1961] P.L. 45, Mr. J. T. Craig points out how unsatisfactory this really is, in that the application of the 1946 Act depends in practice on the parliamentary draftsman remembering to insert the appropriate clause in a new Bill.

[3] See footnote 13, p. 60, *ante*.

[4] S.I. 1948 No. 1, reg. 2 (1) (a).

this expression, and it is the only context in which this "separation of powers" is of consequence in our legal system. Although the statute does not help, there is no shortage of advice on this subject from academic lawyers,[5] but this is not always directed to the regulations in question. Thus, the Donoughmore Committee Report observed[6]:

> "It is indeed difficult in theory and impossible in practice to draw a precise dividing line between the legislative on the one hand and the purely administrative on the other; administrative action so often partakes of both legislative and executive characteristics."

In some circumstances it would be easy to conclude that a rule was of a "legislative" character; for example, the Rules prescribing the Statutory Form of Conditions of Sale under section 46 of the Law of Property Act, 1925,[7] or the Motor Vehicles (Construction and Use) Regulations made under the Road Traffic Acts.[8] If, however, the Secretary of State gives "directions" to a particular local authority as to the method of service of notices in connection with the making of a compulsory purchase order,[9] the document (possibly only a letter) by which the Secretary of State exercises his powers is not customarily regarded as being of a "legislative" character, and therefore is not treated as being a statutory instrument.

Regulation 2 of the Statutory Instruments Regulations, 1947, goes on to provide that any document which, "although of a legislative character, applies only to a named person or premises . . ." shall not be a statutory rule; from this it seems clear that the test whether a particular document is of a "legislative" or of an "executive" character, cannot be determined entirely by the question whether it affects one or more persons. The confirmation by a Minister of a scheme or order made by a local or other similar authority is also to be deemed not to constitute the making of a statutory rule (except as below mentioned). There is no clear answer to the question, which rules are executive and which legislative in character, except the one of expediency,[10] that those documents which it is thought *ought* to be published are treated as being legislative, and so are published.

To sum up this paragraph therefore, rules applying to a named person or persons only, and rules which are not of a "legislative character", made under pre-1948 Acts, are *not* statutory instruments, although they may have been entitled to be called "statutory rules" under the 1893 Act.[11]

---

[5] See literature cited in Griffith and Street, *Principles of Administrative Law*, 5th Edn., at p. 48.

[6] At p. 19.

[7] S.R.& O. 1925, No. 779/L.14.

[8] The current series are those of 1973 (S.I. 1973 No. 24).

[9] Under art. 3 (1) (b) of the First Schedule to the Acquisition of Land (Authorisation Procedure) Act, 1946.

[10] See Sir Carleton Allen, "Statutory Instruments Today", (1955) 71 L.Q.R. 490, at p. 493.

[11] There are two other special exceptions provided for in regulation 2 (3) of the 1948 Regulations, namely Orders in Council approving subordinate legislation in the nature of a local and personal or private Act (*e.g.*, University schemes, etc.) and special documents listed in the Schedule to the Regulations, which includes certain forms of subordinate legislation relating to the armed forces of the Crown.

(c) Special treatment is given to certain orders of Ministers passed in confirmation of orders made by a subordinate government agency (such as a local authority) which was not a "rule-making authority" for the purposes of the Act of 1893.[12] Where any such order is required by the enabling statute to be laid before Parliament or the House of Commons[13] and it is of a legislative and not an executive character, then it is to be treated as a statutory instrument, by virtue of an Order in Council made under section 9 of the Act of 1946.[14] The need for this provision, accepting the desire to bring such orders within the definition of "statutory instruments", arises from the definition of "statutory rules" in the 1893 Act, which is confined to rules made by a "rule-making authority" and would not include orders confirming orders or rules made by some other agency. As we have already seen[15] confirmatory orders made under statutes passed after 1947 are not regarded as being statutory instruments unless Parliament expressly so provides.

(d) Parliament may of course subsequently intervene, and provide that a pre-1948 statutory power shall be exercisable only by statutory instrument.[16]

Where the definitions of the 1946 Act apply, whether the subordinate legislation is made under a pre-1948 statute or under one made after 1947, the document is to be regarded as a statutory instrument and in any such case the substantive provisions of the 1946 Act will apply thereto.

(2) The "making" of subordinate legislation.—It is contemplated in the 1946 Act that any exercise of a subordinate legislative power must be by way of a document; there is no question of an oral "ukase" of a Minister. Although, presumably, there is no reason why Parliament should not, if it chose to do so, authorise a Minister to legislate orally, there has been no case to date where such power has been expressly conferred, and it is always assumed that the intention is that there shall be a document. Apart, however, from this requirement, there is not necessarily any other formal requirement for the actual making of subordinate legislation. In practice the document is always signed by the Minister or by some person in his department who has been duly authorised[17] to sign that particular document (or all documents of a class comprising the one in question) on behalf of the Minister: this signing is necessary as evidence that the document in question is the official act of the Minister. If the document is also sealed, as is often the case, the courts will in most cases take judicial

---

[12] See footnote 13, p. 60, *ante*.

[13] As to the "laying" of documents before the House, see *post*, p. 68.

[14] Statutory Instruments (Confirmatory Powers) Order, 1947 (S.I. 1948 No. 2) made under s. 9 (1) of the Act of 1946.

[15] *Ante*, p. 61, footnote 1.

[16] This was done by s. 1 (1) of the New Towns (No. 2) Act, 1964; see now s. 53 (4) of the New Towns Act, 1965.

[17] Such authority will normally be conferred by the Minister under seal, although this is probably not necessary; see *Carltona, Ltd.* v. *Commissioners of Works*, [1943] 2 All E.R. 560, and the case from the European court, *Imperial Chemical Industries, Ltd.* v. *European Communities Commission*, [1972] C.M.L.R. 557.

notice of the seal.[18] In some cases the enabling statute may lay down special rules to be observed in the course of making a statutory instrument or other subordinate legislation; in particular the statute may require the instrument or other document[19] to be "laid" before Parliament;[20] until it has been so laid in accordance with the terms of the enabling statute the instrument will not be "made", whenever it may become effective.[1] In cases where an order is originally drafted and sealed by a local authority, and is then subject to confirmation by a Minister, it is only "made", in the sense of being effectively made, when it is so confirmed.[2] The 1946 Act has otherwise no provisions on this subject of the making of any form of subordinate legislation, and therefore these observations apply to statutory instruments as they do to such legislation that is not a statutory instrument.

(3) The publication of statutory instruments.—The 1946 Act makes specific provision for publication of statutory instruments—a process which must be distinguished from the "making" thereof.[3] Thus, by section 2 (1) of the Act it is provided that:

> "Immediately after the making of any statutory instrument, it shall be sent to the King's printer of Acts of Parliament and numbered in accordance with regulations made under this Act,[4] and except in such cases as may be provided by any Act passed after the commencement of this Act or prescribed by regulations made under this Act, copies thereof shall as soon as possible be printed and sold by the King's printer of Acts of Parliament."

Further, every statutory instrument must bear on its face a statement showing the date on which the instrument came or will come into operation.[5] There are, however, certain exceptions from the need for a particular instrument to be printed and put on sale, as follows:

---

[18] Under a special statute applying to the particular Ministry: see, *e.g.*, Ministry of Health Act, 1919, s. 7; Minister of Town and Country Planning Act, 1943, s. 5 (2).

[19] Where a document is required to be "laid" before Parliament the enabling statute will also almost invariably require the law-making power to be exercised by way of statutory instrument.

[20] As to "laying" before Parliament, see *post*, p. 68.

[1] In other cases the Minister on whom the law-making power is conferred, may be required to "consult" with certain specified interests before actually making an instrument. In these cases consultation (on which see *post*, p. 74) or "laying" before Parliament, may be regarded as part of the formal law-making process.

[2] *Per* Lord DENNING, M.R., in *Earl Iveagh* v. *Minister of Housing and Local Government*, [1963] 3 All E.R. 817, at p. 819, [1964] 1 Q.B. 395.

[3] "The making of an instrument is one thing and the issue of it is another": *per* STREATFEILD, J., in *R.* v. *Sheer Metalcraft, Ltd.*, [1954] 1 All E.R. 542, at p. 545; [1954] 1 Q.B. 586, and *post*, p. 67.

[4] Statutory Instruments Regulations, 1947, S.I. 1947 No. 1.

[5] 1946 Act, s. 4 (2). It is now also customary for a statutory instrument to give the date when it was laid before Parliament, if the statute had required this to be done. The opening words of the instrument refer to the statutory power under which it is made, giving the section or sections as well as the title of the statute, and if the statute requires any other procedure to have been followed, this also will be stated. Thus, the Town and Country Planning Appeals (Inquiries Procedure) Rules, 1962, S.I. 1962 No. 1425, stated as follows:

Made 9th July 1962
Laid before Parliament 13th July 1962
Coming into operation 1st October 1962

The opening words read: "I, David, Viscount Kilmuir, Lord High Chancellor of Great Britain, in exercise of the powers conferred upon me by section 7A of the Tribunals and Inquiries Act, 1958 and of all other powers enabling me in this behalf and after consultation with the Council on Tribunals, hereby make the following Rules. . . ."

(a) Any "local" instrument, *i.e.*, one which is "in the nature of a local and personal or private Act", and certified by the "responsible authority" (*i.e.*, the Minister by whom the instrument is made or, in the case of an Order in Council, the Sovereign in Council) to be such, and which the Reference Committee[6] have not directed to be otherwise classified.[7]

(b) Any "general" instrument (*i.e.*, one "in the nature of a Public General Act", subject to reclassification by the Reference Committee) certified by the responsible authority (above) to be

> "of a class of documents which is or will be otherwise printed as a series and made available to persons affected thereby".[8]

(c) Any instrument which the responsible authority (above) consider to be temporary in nature,

> "having regard to the brevity of the period during which that instrument will remain in force and to any other steps taken or to be taken for bringing its substance to the notice of the public,"

and which the Reference Committee have not directed shall be published.[9]

(d) Bulky schedules or other documents referred to or identified in a statutory instrument need not be printed if the responsible authority (para (a) above) certifies this to be unnecessary or undesirable, and the Reference Committee do not direct otherwise.[10]

(e) Also if the responsible authority (above) considers that printing and sale of copies of any particular instrument would be "contrary to the public interest", the authority may so certify[11]; there is no power in the Regulations for any such certificate to be overruled by the Reference Committee or otherwise.

In all of these exceptional cases, it should be appreciated that the document in question, though not printed by H.M. Stationery Office, is still a statutory instrument. Where these exceptions do not apply, the Act imposes a procedural penalty on the Crown, if a statutory instrument is not printed and put on sale reasonably soon after it is made. This is contained in section 3 (2) of the 1946 Act, which provides as follows:—

> "(2) In any proceedings against any person for an offence consisting of a contravention of any such[12] statutory instrument, it shall be a defence to prove that the instrument had not been issued by His Majesty's Stationery Office at the date of the alleged contravention unless it is proved that at that date reasonable steps had been taken for the purpose of bringing the purport of the instrument to the notice of the public, or of persons likely to be affected by it, or of the person charged."

---

[6] Consisting of such two or more persons as the Lord Chancellor and the Speaker of the House of Commons may nominate for the purpose: Statutory Instruments Regulations, 1947, reg. 11.

[7] *Ibid.*, reg. 4.

[8] Statutory Instruments Regulations, 1947, reg. 5.

[9] *Ibid.*, reg. 6.

[10] *Ibid.*, reg. 7.

[11] *Ibid.*, reg. 8.

[12] The inclusion of the word "such" here seems to relate the defence only to those instruments that have been printed and sold by H.M.S.O., (by reference back to s. 3 (1)) or to those which are liable to be printed and sold, and so excludes those instruments which are exempted under the 1947 Regulations (above).

Thus, a person charged with an offence against a statutory instrument may have a special defence available to him if he can show that at the date of the offence the instrument had not been issued. If the case cannot be brought within one or other of the exemptions above mentioned (because, for example, of the want of the appropriate certificate[13]), the instrument is none the less valid,[14] but the onus is then thrown on the Crown to establish that the effect of the instrument has been made known to the public, or to the defendant, or that at least reasonable steps have been taken to that effect.

(4) The publication of other forms of subordinate legislation.—Except for the case of byelaws, to which special rules apply,[15] there are no general provisions regulating the form in which the various kinds of subordinate legislation, other than statutory instruments, are required to be made or published. This is particularly true of "sub-delegated" legislation; legislation made under a power reserved or granted in an instrument which itself exercises a law-making power conferred by Parliament or by virtue of the royal prerogative.[16] As we have seen, sub-delegated legislation may otherwise be indulged in by a subordinate law-making authority only when Parliament has expressly or by implication[17] authorised such delegation. In practice, especially under wartime or "emergency" conditions, sub-delegated legislation is very common. Ministers, under powers reserved to them in Regulations, may give directions having legislative effect by means of circular letters issued only to local authorities or other government agencies, although those letters may have important legal consequences to the rights of members of the public. Sub-delegated legislation will always be construed strictly by the courts and they jealously ensure that all the steps in the legislative procedure have been followed. On several occasions the courts have made adverse comment on this general practice; the *locus classicus* is perhaps *Blackpool Corpn.* v. *Locker*,[18] in which SCOTT, L.J., observed:

> "Of such secondary or 'sub-delegated' legislation, as I call it for clarity, neither the general public, of which the defendant in this case is typical, nor the legal adviser of an affected member of the public, however directly he may be affected, has any source of information about his rights to which he can turn as of right and automatically. The modern extent of sub-delegated legislation is almost boundless, and it seems to me vital to the whole English theory of the liberty of the subject that the affected person should be able at

---

[13] *Defiant Cycle Co.* v. *Newell*, [1953] 2 All E.R. 38; this was a case which it was sought to bring within the "bulky schedules" exception, but the necessary certificate of the responsible authority could not be produced.

[14] *R.* v. *Sheer Metalcraft, Ltd.*, [1954] 1 All E.R. 542; [1954] 1 Q.B. 586, arising out of the same order as *Newell's case*.

[15] See *post*, p. 80.

[16] See, for example, the Civil Service Order in Council, 1956. By art. 6, the Treasury are authorised from time to time to make regulations or give instructions "for controlling the conduct of Her Majesty's Home Civil Service . . .".

[17] As in the case, for example, of s. 1 of the Emergency Powers (Defence) Act, 1939, see *ante*, p. 53.

[18] [1948] 1 All E.R. 85; [1948] 1 K.B. 349; see also *Jackson Stansfield & Sons* v. *Butterworth*, [1948] 2 All E.R. 558, and *Howell* v. *Falmouth Boat Construction Co.*, [1951] 2 All E.R. 279; [1951] A.C. 837.

any time to ascertain what legislation affecting his rights has been passed under sub-delegated powers."[19]

Again, in *Patchett* v. *Leathem*,[20] STREATFEILD, J., castigated a particular circular made under a sub-delegated power as being

> "at least four times cursed. First, it has seen neither House of Parliament; secondly it is unpublished and is inaccessible even to those whose valuable rights of property may be affected; thirdly it is a jumble of provisions, legislative, administrative or directive in character,[1] and sometimes difficult to disentangle one from the other; and, fourthly, it is expressed not in the precise language of an Act of Parliament or an Order in Council but in the more colloquial language of correspondence, which is not always susceptible of the ordinary canons of construction."[2]

However, it is not only sub-delegated legislation that is open to the charge that it is not readily available to members of the public. Statutory Instruments excepted from the publication provisions of the 1946 Act as above mentioned,[3] Orders in Council issued pursuant to the prerogative and not arising out of the exercise of a statutory power, and also subordinate legislation issued pursuant to a statute passed after 1947 that is not expressly made exercisable only by statutory instrument, are all similarly open to criticism. For example, the Civil Service Order in Council, 1956, being a prerogative order, is not printed in the volumes of statutory instruments,[4] and "directions" issued by the Secretary of State for the Environment (formerly the Minister of Housing and Local Government) under provisions of the town and country planning legislation,[5] are published only as appendices to Ministry Circulars issued to local authorities. Similar treatment is given to such matters as the standards prescribed by the Secretary of State for houses in order to attract an improvement grant[6] or for caravan sites.[7] These and many other examples are forms of legislation which may be of very considerable importance in particular factual situations, yet there is no standard procedure for the publication or printing of any such documents.

---

19 *Blackpool Corpn.* v. *Locker*, [1948] 1 All E. R. 85, at p. 92.

20 (1949), 65 T.L.R. 69, at p. 70.

1 Of course this is not necessarily a characteristic of all examples of sub-delegated legislation.

2 See below as to the operation of the doctrine of *ultra vires*.

3 *Ante*, p. 65.

4 See footnote 15, on p. 60, *ante*.

5 For example, the Town and Country Planning (Housing Accommodation) Direction, 1952, made under art. 9 (3) of the Town and Country Planning General Development Order, 1950 (since revoked) and s. 15 of the 1947 Act; and also the Town and Country Planning (Development Plans) Direction, 1965, made under the Town and Country Planning General Development Order, 1963. "Directions" issued under art. 4 of the General Development Order 1973, excluding prescribed development from "permitted development" under the Order, are normally not "published" generally at all, but are sent in typewritten form to the local planning authority concerned.

6 Under s. 3 (2) of the Housing Act, 1969; *see* Circular 64/69 of the Ministry of Housing and Local Government.

7 Under s. 5 (6) of the Caravan Sites and Control of Development Act, 1960: see *Model Standards*, enclosed with Circular 42/60 of the Ministry of Housing and Local Government. Several powers exercisable by the Secretary of State to prescribed standards, periods, etc., under the Housing Act, 1969, have been exercised by Circular; see especially Circ. 64/69 (of the Ministry of Housing and Local Government).

6. CONTROLS OVER SUBORDINATE LEGISLATION—I—PARLIAMENTARY

It is now necessary to consider the extent to which Parliament has—or may have—control over any particular exercise of a subordinate law-making power. In the first place, it must be pointed out that enabling statutes may require instruments made under the powers conferred, to be "laid" before Parliament, and in the second place it will be necessary to consider the procedural or other controls exercisable by Parliament as a body, or by any individual member of Parliament, over the contents of particular instruments, whether or not they have been required to be "laid" before Parliament. These matters must be considered separately.

(1) "Laying" before Parliament.—Laying before Parliament, *i.e.*, a procedure whereby the particular instrument in question has to be laid on the table of either House of Parliament for a prescribed time,[8] so that it may then be subject to either the "affirmative" or "negative" procedure as explained below, may be required by the enabling statute[9] to be adopted in relation to subordinate legislation made thereunder with the object of bringing the provisions of the particular instrument to the notice of Members of Parliament. "Laying" is only a technical expression without any precise meaning, and if a document has been presented to the House of Commons it has been *laid*.[10] "Presented to" means that the paper in question must have been delivered to the Votes and Proceedings Office of the House.[11] Laying in this sense may be required to be of several different kinds, according to the consequences that may follow, as may be provided for in the particular enabling statute:

(a) Cases where the statute merely requires the instrument to be laid before Parliament before it comes into operation. This practice, which merely calls attention to the existence of the regulation in question, was used in the nineteenth century in relation to certain rules of pleading and court procedure, but is not as often used at the present time.[12]

(b) Cases where the instrument is required to be laid before Parliament and then made subject to the "negative resolution" procedure. This means that the instrument must be so laid *before* it comes into

[8] In accordance with Standing Orders for the time being in force in either House, and see the Laying of Documents before Parliament (Interpretation) Act, 1948, s. 1. The courts may regard such a provision as directory only, and if an instrument is not "laid" as specified, it may not be void for that reason: (1950), 66 L.Q.R. 229, and 28 C.B. Rev. 791, referring to an unreported case from Barbados.

[9] Or by a subsequent statute amending the enabling statute, as in s. 1 (2) of the New Towns (No. 2) Act, 1964, now replaced by s. 53 (5) of the New Towns Act, 1965.

[10] *R.* v. *Immigration Appeal Tribunal*, [1972] 3 All E. R. 213; [1972] 1 W.L.R. 1390.

[11] *Ibid.*, and S.O. of the House of Commons, No. 119. There is a similar provision in the House of Lords: see Erskine May's *Parliamentary Practice*, 18th Edn., at p. 566.

[12] *Parliamentary Supervision of Delegated Legislation*, by John E. Kersell, a comparative study on the subject, of very considerable value.

operation,[13] unless it is essential that it shall come into operation at an earlier date, in which event notification of the fact and an explanation of the urgency must "forthwith" be sent to the Lord Chancellor and the Speaker of the House of Commons.[14] When the instrument has been so laid, any Member may in either House, within a period of 40 days[15] move that an Address be presented to Her Majesty praying that the instrument be annulled; if any such resolution is carried, the instrument must then be revoked by Order in Council.[16] This is the procedure most commonly applied by enabling statutes to the making of statutory instruments; it is a useful device, but not without its defects, one of which is the rule that debates on annulment resolutions are now cut short in the Commons at 11.30 p.m.,[17] and also because it is not possible for a resolution to be moved seeking to amend a particular instrument or to quash it in part; the instrument must be revoked or allowed as a whole.

(c) Cases where the enabling statute requires an instrument to be laid before Parliament, and then to be made subject to an affirmative resolution in each House. This of course provides a most effective control by Parliament, as the instrument cannot come into effect until the resolution has been passed, but the value of subordinate legislation is impaired in that the practice may take some Parliamentary time that could have been saved by the "negative resolution" procedure being adopted. This "affirmative resolution" procedure, moreover, is comparatively rarely applied by an enabling statute.[18] Variants of it are sometimes employed, which require that the instrument shall be laid with immediate effect, but that it shall remain in force after a specified time only if an affirmative resolution is passed. Similarly, an instrument may be required to be laid with its operation deferred until approval is given by affirmative resolution.[19]

(d) Cases where the statute requires a draft of the instrument to be laid before Parliament. This may then be subject to an affirmative resolution, or to a negative resolution, according to the provisions of the enabling statute. Where the instrument is subject to a negative resolution, the final instrument of which the draft has been laid, may not be made until the expiration of 40 days from the date of such laying.[20]

---

[13] The date when the instrument has been laid before Parliament and when it will come into operation must appear on every copy of the instrument sold to the public: Statutory Instruments Act, 1946, s. 4 (2).

[14] *Ibid.*, s. 4 (1), proviso. Where there is a vacancy in either office, the procedure is governed by s. 2 of the Laying of Documents before Parliament (Interpretation) Act, 1948.

[15] The instrument may come into operation before the end of that 40 days although in the normal case it may not come into operation before it is "laid". The period of 40 days is to be computed without regard to any period during which Parliament is dissolved or prorogued, or during which both Houses are adjourned for more than four days: Statutory Instruments Act, 1946, s. 7 (1).

[16] Statutory Instruments Act, 1946, s. 5. Note that the resolution does not of itself automatically "kill" the instrument.

[17] Kersell, *op. cit.*, p. 18.

[18] For a recent example, see s. 252 of the Local Government Act, 1972.

[19] *Ibid.*, p. 16.

[20] Statutory Instruments Act, 1946, s. 6; as to the calculation of the 40 days, see note 15, *ante*.

In a considerable number of cases[1] the statute conferring powers to make subordinate legislation makes no provision whatever as to "laying" for instruments made under the power: in these cases, there being no general provisions applicable, Parliament has no means of knowing of the existence of such instruments, although members of both Houses regularly receive lists of instruments that are subject to the negative resolution procedure. It seems to be quite fortuitous as to which—if any—"laying" procedure is written into any particular enabling statute, and this is not a matter which usually arouses attention when the statute is itself passing through Parliament.

(2) The obtaining of information.—Publication and the device of "laying" in some form or another, are the means by which Members of Parliament may be informed of the making of particular instruments. As we have seen, neither of these means is completely satisfactory. They are, however, supplemented by special committees, one in each House, set up to "watch" over the exercise of subordinate law-making powers, and to report accordingly. These committees are described below.

(a) *The House of Lords Special Orders Committee.*—This was first set up as long ago as 1925. Its terms of reference require the committee to consider the following matters related to subordinate legislation:

- (i) whether the provisions of a particular instrument raise important questions of policy or principle;
- (ii) how far those provisions are founded on precedent (as has been observed by other writers, the significance of this point is not obvious);
- (iii) whether there should be any further inquiry, and
- (iv) whether there is any doubt as to the *vires* of the instrument (*i.e.*, whether the instrument is within the powers of the enabling statute).

The terms of reference of the committee are, however, confined to those instruments which are subject to the "affirmative resolution" procedure; as there are now comparatively few of these, and they are the instruments to which the members of the House are compelled to pay some attention in any event, this committee is not of very great importance. This is unfortunate, as it would seem that the Lords is the more appropriate part of the Legislature to keep a revisionary check on all instruments: a few Life Peers and one or two of the Law Lords, with some Lords who had had political experience in the Commons, would seem to be ideally suited to form such a committee with wide terms of reference. However, the Special Orders Committee as at present constituted had, during the period 1925–1960, "scrutinised and reported upon almost 1,000 pieces of subordinate legislation".[2]

(b) *The House of Commons Scrutiny Committee.*—This committee was established in 1945, as a result of the recommendation in the Donoughmore Committee's Report to the effect that a small Standing Committee

---

[1] See Kersell, *op. cit.*, p. 19.
[2] Kersell, *op. cit.*, p. 30.

should be set up in each House for the purpose of considering legislation and subordinate legislation.[3] The terms of reference of this Committee require[4] them to consider every instrument laid or laid in draft before the House (and the Committee *may* now consider other instruments) with a view to determining whether the special attention of the House should be drawn to it on any of the following grounds:

(i) that it imposes a tax or charge;
(ii) that by virtue of the enabling statute it is excluded from challenge in the Courts;
(iii) that it appears to make some unusual or unexpected use of the delegated power;
(iv) that it purports to have retrospective effect, where no such express authority was conferred by the parent statute;
(v) that there appears to have been some unjustified delay in the publication or laying of the instrument;
(vi) that the instrument has come into operation prior to "laying" and the Speaker of the House has not been promptly notified thereof (as required by section 4 (1) of the Statutory Instruments Act, 1946, as explained above);
(vii) that for any special reason its form or purport requires elucidation.; or
(viii) that the drafting appears to be defective.

Counsel to the Speaker looks at all instruments that are within the terms of reference of the Committee, and suggests those instruments that should be examined by the Committee; the Committee may then make a special report on any instrument to the House, and it also makes a general report annually. It is not concerned with the "merits" of, or the policy behind any particular statutory instrument, except in so far as may concern questions of *vires;* in particular, it may not even give its view as to whether the instrument is in fact a proper use of the power delegated to the executive.[5]

"In its reports to the end of the 1958–9 session the Scrutiny Committee has drawn the attention of the House to 120 instruments of the 10,000 odd instruments it has examined."[6]

The Committee itself takes no action in the House of Commons if it finds some instrument falling within one or more of its terms of reference; it will call for an explanation or observations from Government departments concerned, but having done this it will then report to the House, leaving the matter to be followed up by a Member or Members, as mentioned below.

In an article in *The Times* newspaper of March 16, 1964, the Committee was described in the following terms:

"The eleven [members] are the real guard-dogs whose barking sounds a general alarm that the law- and therefore individual liberty- may have been put under threat."

---

[3] Report, para. 14, p. 63.
[4] Kersell, *op. cit.*, p. 47.
[5] For a criticism of this restriction, see Andrew Shonfield's "*Modern Capitalism*", at p. 394.
[6] Kersell, *op. cit.*, p. 58.

In view of the restricted terms of reference of the Committee, this may be a somewhat roseate view of its importance in practice.

(c) *Suggested Reforms.*—In a report issued in 1972[7] a Committee of both Houses recommended the setting up of a Joint Committee of both Houses having all the functions of the existing Special Orders and Scrutiny Committees. It would also become the duty of the new Committee to consider delegated legislation passed in accordance with directives issued by the authorities of the European Communities,[8] and in particular to examine whether the regulations so made (under the European Communities Act, 1972) would in fact give effect to the terms of any such directives. This Report had been preceded by a Report of the Davies Committee[9] issued in 1952 which made no substantial recommendations for alterations in procedure.

In substance, therefore, subject to the recommendation as to fusion of the two Committees, it seems that Members of Parliament generally are satisfied with the degree of control they are able to exercise over delegated legislation.

(3) The Controls themselves.—Members may obtain information about delegated legislation from the lists of those instruments which are subject to the "negative resolution" procedure, by the fact of publication of the several instruments by H.M. Stationery Office, and from the Reports of the Commons' Scrutiny Committee (which may not in practice be issued within the period of 40 days during which the instrument reported on may be subject to the "negative resolution" procedure[10]). It now remains to discuss the procedures whereby Members of Parliament may actually exercise control over statutory instruments. These procedures apply also to other forms of delegated legislation, and to sub-delegated legislation, subject to the important proviso that the Member raising the matter must first have been aware of the existence of the legislation in question. These methods may be classified as follows:

(a) Where an instrument is subject to the "affirmative resolution" procedure,[11] the problem of control provides no difficulty; the Government must find Parliamentary time for the passing of the resolution if they want the instrument to become (or to remain) law.

---

[7] *Report of the Joint Committee on Delegated Legislation*, H.L. 184, H.C. 475, 1971–2.

[8] Directives issued by the Commission or by the Council are addressed to a Member State and by the terms of the Treaty must be implemented by the State (and see *post*, p. 88).

[9] *Report from the Select Committee on Delegated Legislation*; October 27, 1953.

[10] Some extension of the time was recommended by the Davies Committee in any case where the Scrutiny Committee issue a report on an instrument, but this would require an amendment to the Statutory Instruments Act, 1946, and the recommendation has not yet been implemented.

[11] In the Davies Committee Report (p. xix), it was said there were three types of cases where the affirmative resolution procedure was normally preferred, namely, where the exercise of the power would substantially affect the provisions of an Act of Parliament, where the power was to impose a financial charge, or where the parent Act fixes the purpose and the whole substance of the law is left to be dealt with by subordinate legislation. The abortive Offices Act, 1960, s. 1 (5) provided a good example of the third of these classes.

(b) If the instrument is subject to the "negative resolution" procedure, it can be questioned in the House of Commons only if a Member (usually a private Member) puts down a prayer to annul (not to amend[12]) the instrument. He must "seek an opportunity upon which to move the prayer. That opportunity will not occur until Government business is disposed of and this usually means that the opportunity will not occur until after 10 p.m."[13] The Member must ensure there is a quorum in the House, and because as a consequence of the adoption of a recommendation of the Davies Committee, any debate on a prayer is in normal circumstances concluded at 11.30 p.m., the time of this business is therefore very short. Even if a Member is successful in securing a vote against a particular instrument, which must then be annulled, there is nothing to prevent the Minister introducing a fresh instrument in the same terms on another occasion.

(c) A Member may at any time and on any matter within the Minister's responsibilities, put a Question to a Minister. This means of control, which is not restricted to subordinate legislation, may be most effective if there has been an error of drafting, mistake or unintentional hardship caused by a particular instrument.

(d) A motion of censure may be moved on the Minister responsible for the statutory instrument; this is too unwieldy a process for most purposes connected with subordinate legislation, but it could be used on occasion.

(e) There could be a debate, and possibly a motion, relating to subordinate legislation, when the House is in Committee of Supply. Other opportunities for debate may arise on the Address in reply to the Speech from the Throne at the opening of Parliament, on the continuance in force of the relevant enabling legislation, on Private Members' Bills, and on motions to adjourn.[14]

(f) Finally, there is the control over subordinate legislation exercisable in advance, over the contents of the parent Act itself. Such matters as the extent of the legislative powers to be given to a Minister, the inclusion of a requirement that every exercise of a delegated (or subdelegated) power shall be by statutory instrument, and that the instrument when made shall be "laid" before Parliament and be subject to either the affirmative or the negative resolution procedure, the inclusion of a requirement for consultation with interested bodies, etc., are all matters to which Members of the Legislature may give attention while the Bill is passing through the House. In practice, however, Parliamentary time can rarely be found for any extensive discussion of such matters, and this control therefore is often reduced to a reliance on the good sense and skill of the original draftsman of the Bill.

---

12 *Ante*, p. 68.
13 Davies Report, p. xx.
14 See Kersell, *op. cit.*, p. 97.

7. CONTROLS OVER SUBORDINATE LEGISLATION—II—CONSULTATION

In recent years a practice has grown up of including in an enabling statute a requirement to the effect that the Minister shall "consult" with certain bodies, either those named specifically, or those described in general terms, before he exercises a power to make subordinate legislation.[15] Often the body with whom he is required to consult is an Advisory Committee specially constituted for the purpose and the members of which are appointed by the Minister himself. Thus, the Secretary of State for the Environment is required to consult with the Building Regulations Advisory Committee, "and such other bodies as appear to him to be representative of the interests concerned", before he makes building regulations under Part II of the Public Health Act, 1961,[16] and the same Minister, before making an order varying the payments of rate support grants to local authorities, is required to consult with "such associations of local authorities as appear to him to be concerned and with any local authority with whom consultations appear to him to be desirable".[17] Again, no power to make procedural rules for a tribunal listed in the First Schedule to the Tribunals and Inquiries Act, 1971, may be exercised by any Minister, except after consultation with the Council on Tribunals.[18]

This requirement of consultation before the making of delegated legislation seems to be growing in popularity in Whitehall and Westminster, but it has not yet attained the importance given to it in the United States. By section 4 of the (American) Administrative Procedure Act, 1946,[19] any governmental agency that has (as required by the Act) given notice in the Federal Register of some proposed rule-making, must afford interested persons "an opportunity to participate in the rule-making", and the agency must consider all relevant matter presented; it is contemplated that in certain circumstances the agency may give the interested persons an opportunity to appear at a hearing held by the agency.[20] "Consultation" in this country does not yet extend as of right to any persons who may consider themselves to be interested; the persons who are consulted are either specified in the enabling Act, or they are confined to persons whom the Minister considers to be interested. In section 19 (3) of the Agriculture (Miscellaneous Provisions) Act, 1972, for example, when prescribing poisons for use in the destruction of grey squirrels or coypus, the Minister of Agriculture, etc., must undertake "such consultation as he thinks appropriate with such organisations as appear to him to represent the

---

15 On this topic generally, see article by the present author, "Consultation in Subordinate Legislation", at [1964] P. 105.

16 See s. 9 of that Act and S.I. 1972, No. 317.

17 Local Government Act 1966, s. 1 (3).

18 Tribunals and Inquiries Act, 1971, s. 10 (1); *post*, p. 210.

19 Appendix I, *post*, p. 460.

20 In a few cases, in particular in connection with "special regulations" under the Factories Act, 1961, general regulations under the Mines and Quarries Act, 1954, and Orders in Council under the Merchandise Marks Act, 1926, there must be an inquiry into any objections before the regulations or order is made.

interests concerned."[1] In *Gallagher* v. *Post Office*,[2] the Post Office Act, 1969, provided that in certain circumstances the Post Office must consult with "any organisation appearing to it to be appropriate". It was said by BRIGHTMAN, J.,[3] that in such a case the Post Office "has an absolute discretion as to organisations which it will consult". "Consultation" in this context is not of course a precise word, nor can the process of consultation be given any exact formality. Under the New Towns Act, 1965, section 1 (1), the Minister, before he makes an order designating an area as the site of a proposed new town, must consult "with any local authorities who appear to him to be concerned". In *Rollo* v. *Minister of Town and Country Planning*,[4] the view was expressed by BUCKNILL, L.J.,[5] that in that section consultation means that:

> "on the one side the Minister must supply sufficient information to the local authority to enable them to tender advice, and on the other hand, a sufficient opportunity must be given to the local authority to tender that advice".

Where it is required by the statute consultation must be genuine, and if it is not adequate, it seems that any delegated legislation subsequently made would be invalid as having been made in a manner contrary to that provided for in the enabling statute,[6] but this does not mean that those parties who have been consulted can complain or challenge the validity of the order if their views, expressed in the course of such consultation, are not accepted by the Minister. The direct control effected by this device of consultation may therefore be worthless, but in practice few Ministers will be so regardless of public opinion as to ignore serious views carefully advanced in the course of statutory consultations of this kind.

There are also many examples at the present day of Ministers—or their Departments—voluntarily "consulting" with outside interests before exercising powers of subordinate legislation. Under the complicated conditions of modern civilisation, even the large departments of Central Government do not contain experts on every branch of human activity. In some cases the central department's officials are in almost daily contact with representatives of specialist outside bodies and prior consultation is part of the normal law-making process. This is particularly so in local government matters, in education, road transport and public health. In many cases where a Minister has power to legislate, he has also voluntarily appointed an Advisory Committee, such as the Clean Air Council or the Housing Advisory Committee under powers conferred on him by statute, and their opinion would normally

---

[1] This almost certainly means that if he undertook no consultation at all, the Minister's regulations would be void; *cf.* the reasoning in *Padfield* v. *Minister of Agriculture, Fisheries and Food*, [1968] 1 All E.R. 694; [1968] A.C. 997, *post*, p. 136. See also *Agricultural, Horticultural and Forestry Industry Training Board* v. *Aylesbury Mushrooms, Ltd.*, [1972] 1 All E.R. 280; [1972] 1 W.L.R. 190.

[2] [1970] 3 All E.R. 712.

[3] *Ibid.*, at p. 720.

[4] [1948] 1 All E.R. 13. This case was followed in the ecclesiastical case of *Re Union of the Beneficiaries of Whippingham and East Cowes*, [1954] 2 All E.R. 22; [1954] A.C. 245.

[5] At p. 17.

[6] See *Port Louis Corpn.* v. *A.-G. of Mauritius*, [1965] A.C. 1111, P.C.

be sought before new subordinate legislation were made; a similar process often also takes place before a Government Bill is introduced on any particular subject, although there will be no statutory obligation to undertake any such consultation.

8. CONTROLS OVER SUBORDINATE LEGISLATION—III—JUDICIAL

Any form of subordinate legislation is liable to question in the Courts on the ground that it is *ultra vires*, that it goes beyond the powers conferred by the enabling statute on the rule-making agency. This question of *ultra vires* may be raised by way of a defence if proceedings are taken for an offence against the provisions of the particular instrument; it may be raised in any proceedings where the validity of the instrument is material,[7] or proceedings may be initiated by way of an action for a declaration to establish the invalidity of the order.[8] In *Harper* v. *Secretary of State*[9] proceedings were brought for an injunction prohibiting the Home Secretary from proceeding any further under an order that was alleged to be *ultra vires*, but which in the circumstances was ultimately held to be valid.

The doctrine that subordinate legislation is invalid if it is *ultra vires*, is based on the principle that a Minister or other subordinate agency has no power to legislate, other than such as may have expressly been conferred by the Legislature. It has three distinct applications in practice, namely procedural, substantive, and its effect on the construction of an instrument.

(1) Procedural *ultra vires*.—If the procedure laid down in the enabling statute for the making of an instrument is not observed, the instrument will be declared void by the Courts. Thus, if the rules of the Statutory Instruments Act, 1946, in so far as they have been applied by the parent Act in the particular case, are not observed, if the instrument has not been signed by or on behalf of the Minister,[10] or if there has been

---

[7] As in *Jackson Stansfield & Sons* v. *Butterworth*, [1948] 2 All E.R. 558. Here the plaintiff company, a firm of builders, who brought an action for the recovery of moneys due under a building contract, were met with the defence that the contract was illegal as it had been carried out without any licence having been obtained under the Defence Regulations (then in force), it being further contended that a purported oral licence was *ultra vires* and void.

[8] Chapter VI, *post*, p. 188.

[9] [1955] 1 All E.R. 331; [1955] Ch. 238.

[10] It appears from a decision of the Court of Appeal for Eastern Africa that the courts would probably not treat as delegation the entrusting of the act of signing a legislative instrument to a subordinate by a Minister. "In my view, such a formal signification may properly be effected by a subordinate of the person whose consent under delegated powers from the Governor has been properly given. It is not a question of powers being sub-delegated by the latter to a subordinate for the subordinate had no discretion in the giving or withholding of consent, but was no more than a piece of administrative machinery": *per* WINDHAM, J.A., in *Samuel Kenneth Odendaal* v. *Richard Gray*, [1960] E.A. 263, cited by J. P. W. B. McAuslan, in "Administrative Law in Kenya—a General Survey" (a very informative article), to be found in *East African Law To-day*, published by the British Institute of International and Comparative Law. See also note 14, *post*.

no "consultation" where this is required by statute, the instrument will be *ultra vires* and void.[11] In practice these cases occur seldom, but there are a few examples where an instrument made under a sub-delegated power has been held to be void on these grounds. In all cases involving delegated legislation, the courts are anxious to ensure that the appropriate steps in the relevant law-making process have been rigidly observed. Thus, in *Patchett* v. *Leathem*,[12] a requisitioning notice served by a town clerk was held to be void because the notice did not exclude furniture in the house from the effect of the notice, while the power delegated to the town clerk by the Minister (under powers conferred on him under the Defence Regulations, which had in turn been made under the Emergency Powers (Defence) Act, 1939) included a requirement that requisitioning should not be extended to furniture. In *Lewisham Corporation* v. *Roberts*,[13] a similar exercise of sub-delegated power was attacked, though unsuccessfully, on the ground that the Ministry circular (issued again under the authority of Defence Regulations) was not signed personally by the Minister but by an officer in his department.[14] In a case from Ceylon, statutory power to hold an inquiry was conferred on the Governor-General in relation to any matter which would in his opinion be in the interests of public welfare. The Governor-General instructed a commissioner to hold an inquiry under the Act, but left the scope of the inquiry to the commissioner's discretion. It was held by the Privy Council that as the power of selection of the ambit of the inquiry had been delegated to the commissioner, his appointment was *ultra vires*.[15]

In this context of sub-delegated legislation, the courts will quash any purported delegation of a legislative power unless and in so far as Parliament has authorised the particular delegation. This principle of *delegatus non potest delegare* is of wide application in administrative law. In countries such as the U.S.A., having a federal constitution, it is customary for the legislative power to be entrusted expressly by the constitution to the supreme legislature. Any delegation of that power to the executive (for example, in times of emergency) will therefore

---

[11] Similarly, if subordinate legislation is not made by statutory instrument when it should have been so made: *Simms Motor Units, Ltd.* v. *Minister of Labour*, [1946] 2 All E.R. 201. Certain national insurance consolidating regulations were made in 1967, and the procedural requirement to consult the Council on Tribunals before the regulations were made was overlooked. When this came to light, a fresh set of regulations were made after such consultation: Annual Report of the Council on Tribunals for 1967, para. 43 and Chapter VIII, *post*, p. 248. In a case where a particular organisation was not consulted and should have been consulted, it was held that the regulations in question were void *pro tanto*, *i.e.*, as against that organisation alone: *Agricultural, Horticultural and Forestry Industry Training Board* v. *Aylesbury Mushrooms, Ltd.*, [1972] 1 All E.R. 280; [1972] 1 W.L.R. 190.

[12] (1949), 65 T.L.R. 69.

[13] [1949] 1 All E.R. 815; [1949] 2 K.B. 608.

[14] "The mere act of instructing or permitting an officer of the Ministry to authorise a town clerk to exercise a requisitioning power in the Minister's name, is an administrative, not a legislative act, and therefore there is no question of delegation involved" (*per* DENNING, L. J., *ibid.*, at p. 824; and see note 10, *ante*). Thus, a local authority's committee, acting under delegated powers, can instruct an officer to seal a byelaw, but they could not authorise him, or even a sub-committee of their number, to take the decision whether or not the byelaw should be made.

[15] *Rajah Ratnagopal* v. *A.-G.*, [1970] A.C. 974; [1969] 3 W.L.R. 1056.

be *prima facie* void as offending against the general principle.[16] In local government in this country, we shall see[17] that it is customary for a local authority to delegate functions to committees of their members, or in certain circumstances to another local authority, but in all these cases there must be express and precise statutory sanction for the delegation; the same principle is also justification for the rule that a discretionary function of a governmental agency may not without statutory authority be delegated to an officer of that agency.[18]

(2) Substantive *ultra vires*.—In other circumstances subordinate legislation may be *ultra vires* simply because the subordinate law-making authority has gone outside or beyond the powers conferred on him by the enabling statute. The operation of the *ultra vires* doctrine is discussed more fully in this book in its relationship to the judicial control of the executive, and there are not many modern cases relating exclusively to the avoidance of subordinate legislation on this ground.[19] The courts will examine subordinate legislation strictly and confine it precisely within the limits of the enabling legislation.[20] Thus, the courts will not readily imply a power to legislate by regulation in a manner which may impair the liberty of the subject,[1] or to impose some form of taxation,[2] or which would have retrospective effect. Even where the enabling power is widely drawn the subordinate act must be, it was said,[3] "capable of being related to the prescribed purposes" of the enabling Act. However, even in a case affecting the liberty of the subject, the House of Lords has recently said[4] that a wide power to make regulations for the preservation of peace and the maintenance of order (in Northern Ireland) is one with which the Courts will not lightly interfere. Following *Carltona, Ltd.* v. *Commissioners of Works*,[5] it was held by the majority in the House of Lords that "the Court will only interfere if the Minister is shown to have gone outside the four corners of the Act or has acted in bad faith".[6]

---

[16] See E. S. Corwin, *The Constitution and What it means To-day*, 11th Edn., at p. 4, and such cases as *Hampton* v. *U.S.* 276 U.S. 394 (1928).

[17] Chapter XIII, *post*, p. 393.

[18] *Allingham* v. *Minister of Agriculture and Fisheries*, [1948] 1 All E.R. 780, where an executive officer of a county agricultural committee purported to exercise a function which had been delegated by the Minister to the committee.

[19] But see *Customs and Excise Commissioners* v. *Cure and Deeley, Ltd.*, [1961] 3 All E.R. 641; [1962] 1 Q.B. 340.

[20] Just how strictly the enabling statute and regulations made thereunder will be construed may be seen in the Privy Council case of *Utah Construction and Engineering Pty., Ltd.* v. *Pataky*, [1965] 3 All E.R. 650.

[1] *Chester* v. *Bateson*, [1920] 1 K.B. 829.

[2] *Institute of Patent Agents* v. *Lockwood*, [1894] A.C. 347; *A.-G.* v. *Wilts United Dairies, Ltd.* (1922), 91 L.J.K.B. 897; *Hall & Co., Ltd.* v. *Shoreham-by-Sea U.D.C.*, [1964] 1 All E.R. 1; [1964] 1 W.L.R. 240.

[3] *Carltona, Ltd.* v. *Commissioners of Works*, [1943] 2 All E.R. 560, at p. 564, *per* Lord GREENE, M.R.

[4] In *McEldowney* v. *Forde*, [1969] 2 All E.R. 1039.

[5] [1943] 2 All E.R. 560; "Parliament, which authorises this regulation, commits to the executive the discretion to decide and with that discretion, if *bona fide* exercised, no court can interfere." (At p. 564.)

[6] As to bad faith, see Chapter VI, *post*, p. 147.

Where subordinate legislation is *ultra vires*, the court will if possible separate those provisions which are *intra vires* from those which are *ultra vires*, and will uphold the validity of the former.[7] Where, however, the good is inextricably mingled with the bad, there will be no course open to the court other than to hold the whole instrument void on the ground of *ultra vires*.[8] The doctrine of *ultra vires* has also a special application to byelaws, considered below.[9]

(3) The construction of delegated legislation.—The courts will always construe a statutory instrument or other subordinate legislative document within the context of the enabling legislation.[10] If the parent Act provides that regulations may be made for a specified purpose, and the regulations are clearly made for some other purpose, then obviously those regulations will be to that extent (or possibly totally) void. But if the regulations are not said to be made for any particular purpose, then the courts will assume them to have been made for the purpose or purposes stated in the parent Act, and will construe them accordingly. Thus, in *MacFisheries, Ltd.* v. *Coventry Corpn.*,[11] the Food Hygiene Regulations, 1955, had been made under section 13 of the Food and Drugs Act, 1955, which empowered regulations to be made "for the protection of the public health". Regulation 8 of these Regulations prohibited any person engaging in the handling of food from placing any food, or permitting it to be so placed "as to involve any risk of contamination". The appellants in this case had been charged with an offence against this Regulation because they had placed some fish in such a situation that there was risk of contamination to the food. It was not, however, established that the contamination was of such a nature as to be injurious to health, and the appeal was therefore allowed and the appellants were held not guilty of an offence; the regulations had to be read in the context of the Act, and it was an essential ingredient of any offence against the regulation to show that there was risk of contamination which was injurious to health. There was no question of the regulations themselves being *ultra vires*, but the regulations could not be construed on their own without reference to the parent statute.

The ordinary rules for the construction of statutes will be applied also to delegated legislation,[12] and the courts will give full force and effect to delegated legislation that cannot be shown to be *ultra vires* the parent legislation. There is no question of a statutory instrument being declared to be void because it is unreasonable or uncertain in operation, although the courts will (as they would with a statute) endeavour to give it such a construction that it will not have that effect.

---

[7] *Fielding* v. *Thomas*, [1896] A.C. 600, a Privy Council case on appeal from Canada.

[8] Two further Canadian cases, *Re Initiative and Referendum Act*, [1919] A.C. 935, and *reat West Saddlery Co.* v. *R.*, [1921] 2 A.C. 91, illustrate this point.

[9] *Post*, p. 83.

[10] See, *e.g.*, Interpretation Act, 1889, s. 31. Regulations or byelaws made under the authority of statute are to be assumed (subject to the contrary intention appearing) to use words in the same meanings as those ascribed to them in the parent statute.

[11] [1957] 3 All E.R. 299.

[12] Chapter III, *ante*, p. 49.

9. BYELAWS

Byelaws[13] are a special form of delegated legislation, which have several peculiar features which do not apply to other forms of delegated legislation. Thus:

(a) they are made by some governmental agency, such as a local authority or independent statutory corporation, *other* than the central government;
(b) before becoming effective they need to be confirmed by some central government department;
(c) they are general in operation, although restricted to the locality or special area[14] over which they are intended to apply;
(d) as well as the *ultra vires* doctrine, their validity as law can be questioned in the courts on several general grounds, as hereafter described.

In this last respect byelaws are a unique form of subordinate legislation. All other "sub-laws" must be shown to be within the terms of the enabling statute and to have been made in due form, but are not liable to be declared invalid on any other grounds.

Byelaws cannot be dispensed with or ignored, even by the byelaw-making authority themselves,[15] although any byelaw may be amended or repealed by a new byelaw made in due form, or by statute. If the statute conferring the power to make byelaws is itself repealed, any byelaws made thereunder will automatically cease to have effect.[16] Byelaws may be of any length and complexity but they will usually deal with one series of matters on a particular topic, such as the behaviour of the public on a particular railway system, the suppression of nuisances or the maintenance of "good rule and government" in the whole of the area of the byelaw-making local authority, or in one or all of their parks and pleasure grounds, or the preservation of order and public decency at an open space belonging to the National Trust. The term "byelaw" as understood in this country, should not be confused with the same expression used in many other jurisdictions in common law countries, where the term is often used to signify a resolution of a government agency acting under statutory powers, and embodying a decision or giving an order in a particular case, which may or may not need central (or provincial) government confirmation. We must now consider the detailed provisions of the law on this subject.

---

[13] This is the spelling adopted in statutes (see, *e.g.*, Local Government Act, 1972, s. 235, or Railways Clauses Act, 1863, s. 32), although the spelling "by-law" will often be found in law reports and elsewhere. The word probably means in origin, "town" laws, from the Scandinavian meaning of "by".

[14] Such as a railway system or a dock in the case of byelaws made by the British Railways Board (or its predecessors), or a docks undertaking respectively.

[15] *Yabbicom* v. *King,* [1899] 1 Q.B. 444; a case concerning byelaws made by a local authority.

[16] As occurred when the Building Regulations, 1965 came into effect; the relevant provisions of the Public Health Act, 1961 authorising the making of these Regulations were brought into effect on February 1, 1966, and the power conferred on local authorities by the Public Health Act, 1936 to make building byelaws was thereupon revoked.

(1) Byelaw-making procedure.—Parliament may lay down a different procedure for the making of byelaws on each occasion when it confers a byelaw-making power, and the procedure that has to be followed by a statutory corporation such as the British Railways Board or a body like the National Trust is different in detail from that applicable to a local authority. However, in the case of byelaws made by local authorities, the procedure applicable to the making of any byelaws, whatever may be the origin of the byelaw-making power, has now been standardised,[17] and it is therefore here intended to describe this common procedure.

(a) *Making of the byelaws.*—The byelaws must be made "under the common seal of the authority",[18] and they will be ineffective unless and until they have been confirmed by the appropriate Minister of the Central Government (normally the Secretary of State for the Environment but in some cases the Home Secretary).[19] The actual byelaws should therefore be adopted by the local authority by resolution duly recorded in their minutes.

(b) *Advertisement and confirmation.*—After the byelaws have been made, but at least one month before application for confirmation thereof is submitted to the Secretary of State, the local authority must give notice of their intention to apply for confirmation, in one or more local newspapers circulating in the area,[20] and a copy of the byelaws must be put on deposit at the local authority's offices and made available to public inspection without charge,[1] and the authority must also supply a copy of the byelaws when made (for which they may make a charge)[2] to any person on application. In practice, before the byelaws are formally made, they will have been submitted in draft for the observations of the confirming authority, and informal discussions on the draft will probably have taken place between Departmental officials and officers of the local authority. Where the Department has issued a "model" series of byelaws on the particular topic, confirmation will not lightly be given to byelaws which depart substantially from the model, and strong local reasons will have to be advanced to justify variations.[3]

When the byelaws are formally submitted, the Department concerned will consider any representations made in response to the local authority's advertisement, although they are not expressly required by the statute to do so. In some cases the Secretary of State may hold a local inquiry into such representations, but this is very rare in practice.[4]

---

[17] Local Government Act, 1972, ss. 235–238, replacing similar provisions in the Local Government Act, 1933.

[18] Local Government Act, 1972, s. 236 (3).

[19] The identity of the confirming authority will depend on the terms of the authorising statute.

[20] *Ibid.*, s. 236 (4).

[1] *Ibid.*, s. 236 (5).

[2] *Ibid.*, s. 236 (6).

[3] As to this indirect means of exercising administrative control over the discretionary powers of local authorities, see Chapter XV, *post*, p. 432.

[4] The procedure of s. 250 of the Local Government Act, 1972, will then apply.

The byelaws as submitted may or may not be confirmed, but apparently they cannot be confirmed in a form different from that in which they are submitted.[5] The confirming authority will normally fix a date on which the byelaws are to come into operation, but if no date is so fixed, the byelaws will come into operation on the expiration of one month from the date of confirmation.[6]

(c) *Promulgation and proof.*—When the byelaws have been confirmed a copy must be printed and placed on deposit at the authority's offices and made available without charge for inspection by members of the public; copies must also be available for purchase at a charge not exceeding 20p each.[7] A copy of any byelaws made by a district council, and confirmed, must be sent to the proper officer of every parish or community council (or the chairman of any parish not having a parish council) in the district, a copy of byelaws made by a county council, and confirmed, must be sent to the council of every district in the county, and a copy of byelaws made by a district, and confirmed, must be sent to the county council concerned.[8] These requirements are mandatory, but failure to comply with them would not seem to affect the validity of the byelaws in question. A printed copy of byelaws made by a local authority is *prima facie* evidence in court proceedings of the fact that the byelaws were made by the authority, that the copy is a true copy, that the byelaws were duly confirmed or has not been disallowed, and that they came into effect on the date stated, provided a certificate to that effect is endorsed thereon which purports to be signed by the proper officer to the authority.[9] Byelaws generally, whether made by local authorities or other bodies, are not statutory instruments, and are not published as such, nor are they printed by the Queen's Printer. There is no central record of their existence, although each Government Department will keep a copy (*not* available for public inspection) of all byelaws confirmed in the Department.

(2) Validity of byelaws.—Byelaws are commonly drafted as orders or prohibitions, breach of which will amount to an offence punishable on summary conviction. In order that they may be enforceable, the empowering statute must of course include a provision to the effect that the byelaws themselves may provide that breach of their substantive provisions shall be an offence.[10] When proceedings are taken for alleged offences against the byelaws, the defendant will be entitled to attack the validity of the byelaw,[11] as well as to raise

---

5 There is no express power to "modify". The informal procedure for the consideration of the byelaws in draft is therefore all the more important.

6 Local Government Act, 1972, s. 236 (7).

7 *Ibid.*, s. 236 (8).

8 Local Government Act, 1972, s. 236 (9) and (10).

9 *Ibid.*, s. 238.

10 As for example, s. 237 of the Local Government Act, 1972, which is of wide application.

11 The existence of the byelaw will have to be proved by the prosecution, as the courts will not take judicial notice of local byelaws. In practice an attack on byelaws in the course of a defence is the most common means by which their validity is raised.

substantive defences by way of denial of the offence. The validity of the byelaw may be called so in question on any one or more of the following grounds:

(a) *Lack of form.*—If the statutory procedure prescribed for the making of a byelaw has not been followed (whether that described above for local authorities or some other procedure laid down in the particular enabling statute) the byelaw will it seems, be invalid *ab initio*. This does not mean that all the steps in the procedure must be established by a prosecutor relying on a byelaw in every case, for the court will assume the byelaw has been properly made until the contrary is proved,[12] but the onus of proving otherwise will rest on the defence, although proceedings taken in respect of a breach of a byelaw are criminal in nature and form. Failure to comply with the publication procedure *after* the byelaws has been made (under section 236 (8)–(10) of the 1972 Act; *supra*) may not affect the validity of the byelaw, there being no provision to this effect in the statute.[13]

(b) *Ultra vires.*—If the terms of a byelaw exceed the powers contained in the enabling statute, the byelaw will be void. Byelaws imposing obligations on private persons enforceable by criminal sanctions, are rigidly construed in the light of the terms of the enabling statute. Thus, a byelaw providing that no dwelling-house should be erected without having at the rear or side thereof a good and sufficient roadway for the purpose of affording access to the privy or ashpit, was held to be *ultra vires* a statute enabling byelaws to be made with respect to the drainage of buildings and to waterclosets, privies, etc., used in connection with buildings, and was therefore void.[14] This does not mean, however, that a perverted construction will be given so as to enable the accused to circumvent the purpose of the byelaw. It was said by Lord GODDARD, C.J., in *McQuade* v. *Barnes*[15]:

> "We must so construe a byelaw as to give effect to the intention of the authority which made it just as we must construe a statute so as to give effect to the wishes of Parliament, . . . "

This was a case where a shopkeeper standing on a private forecourt outside his shop was held guilty of an offence against a byelaw prohibiting the importuning of customers *in* a street.

The general question of *ultra vires* is discussed elsewhere in this book, and in different contexts; it does not really have any special or peculiar significance in the present circumstances.

(c) *Uncertainty.*—A byelaw can be attacked and may be declared void on the ground that it is vague in its terms, or uncertain in operation or application. This is not, however, to say that the court will think up fanciful arguments, for if a byelaw is capable of reasonable interpreta-

---

[12] *Omnia praesumuntur rite esse acta;* and see Local Government Act, 1972, s. 238 (*ante*).

[13] *Duncan* v. *Knill* (1907), 96 L.T. 911.

[14] *Waite* v. *Garston Local Board* (1867), 32 J.P. 228.

[15] [1949] 1 All E.R. 154 at p. 155.

tion within the terms of the enabling statute, the court will be prepared to give it that interpretation.[1]

(d) *Repugnancy.*—A byelaw will also be void if it can be shown to be repugnant to a provision of some other statute or, it seems, to some express rule of the common law, beyond that contemplated in or authorised by the enabling statute. If a statute of general application, for example, expressly permits a certain activity, a byelaw cannot be made prohibiting that same activity or attempting to control exercise of the activity by imposing conditions.[2]

> "It is conceded and no one doubts that if the statute deals with precisely the same matter the byelaw would be ultra vires, because a byelaw cannot, in effect, cross the t's and dot the i's of a statute."[3]

A statute enabling byelaws to be made for a certain purpose, will not be so narrowly construed that the purpose cannot be achieved, just because the byelaw offends some principle of the common law.[4] "Repugnancy" will, however, prevent a byelaw being so construed as to defeat a rule of the common law, if it could (whilst still being *intra vires*) be construed in some other manner.[5]

(e) *Reasonableness.*—It has been said that a byelaw must be reasonable, but this rule is applied by the courts in the sense that they will declare an unreasonable byelaw to be invalid. There are no definite standards against which this test of "unreasonableness" may be measured. In the leading case of *Kruse* v. *Johnson*, Lord RUSSELL, C.J., said[6]:

> "Unreasonable in what sense? If, for instance, they [the byelaws] were found to be partial and unequal in their operation as between different classes; if they were manifestly unjust; if they disclosed bad faith; if they involved such oppressive or gratuitous interference with the rights of those subject to them as could find no justification in the minds of reasonable men, the court might well say 'Parliament never intended to give authority to make such rules; they are

---

[1] In *Nash* v. *Finlay* (1901), 66 J.P. 183, a byelaw providing that "no person shall wilfully annoy passengers in the streets", was held void for uncertainty, and see *Townsends (Builders), Ltd.* v. *Cinema News and Property Management, Ltd.*, [1959] 1 All E.R. 7.

[2] *Powell* v. *May*, [1946] 1 All E.R. 444; [1946] K.B. 330: *Gentel* v. *Rapps*, [1902] 1 K.B. 160.

[3] *Per* LORD GODDARD, C.J., in *Galer* v. *Morrissey*, [1955] 1 All E.R. 380, at p. 381.

[4] In *Collman* v. *Mills*, [1897] 1 Q.B. 396, the statute conferred a power to make byelaws for the purpose of regulating conduct at slaughterhouses. The byelaw in question made the proprietor liable criminally for the acts of his servants committed in the course of carrying on the slaughterhouse business, in so far as these contravened the substantive provisions of the byelaws. Although the byelaws appeared to contravene the common law principle that "a man is not criminally responsible for things done by his servants without his knowledge", it was held by WILLS and WRIGHT, JJ., that the statute was widely enough drawn to cover this case, and the byelaws were therefore valid.

[5] The only cases in support of this proposition come from countries outside England. Thus, in New Brunswick, it was held that a statutory power to make byelaws could not be exercised in such a manner as to result in discrimination in exemptions from local taxes (*Carleton Woollen Co.* v. *Woodstock*, [1905] 3 N.B. Eq. Rep. 138), and in South Africa it has been held that a subordinate lawmaking body may not, without express power, legislate in a manner which would interfere with the ordinary principles applicable to the administration of justice: *Germiston Municipality* v. *Angehrn and Piel*, [1913] T.P.D. 135, discussed in *S.* v. *Schoenfeld*, 1963 (4) S.A. 77.

[6] [1898] 2 Q.B. 91 at p. 99.

unreasonable and *ultra vires*.' But it is in this sense, and in this sense only, as I conceive, that the question of unreasonableness can properly be regarded. A byelaw is not unreasonable merely because particular judges may think that it goes further than is prudent or necessary or convenient, or because it is not accompanied by a qualification or an exception which some judges may think ought to be there."

Applying this reasoning, a byelaw prohibiting any person from playing music or singing in any place within 50 yards of a dwelling-house after having been required to desist, was held not to be unreasonable, and therefore valid.

It might be thought from these observations that reasonableness is not really a separate test of validity, being but a special application of the *ultra vires* doctrine, but the doctrine of *ultra vires* could not in some circumstances be applied to invalidate byelaws palpably unreasonable, owing to the wide terms of the enabling statute, such as the power to make byelaws, for "good rule and government" in the district of the byelaw-making local authority.[7] Thus, a byelaw made under a statutory power to regulate the selling of articles on a beach, was held to be unreasonable and therefore invalid, because it prohibited certain sales "except in pursuance of an agreement" with the byelaw-making authority.[8] A byelaw which applied to both new buildings and extensions to existing buildings and which required that any such buildings or extensions should be provided with an open space of a certain size at the rear of the building was held to be unreasonable, for it might be quite impracticable and unnecessary to provide such an open space in the case of an extension.[9]

Whereas each byelaw in a series of byelaws may be tested for unreasonableness, and one void byelaw will not invalidate the whole series, this does not mean that the unreasonable portions of a byelaw can be struck out and the remainder of the byelaw enforced. A byelaw must be valid as it stands or else the whole byelaw will be invalidated; in *Parker* v. *Bournemouth Corporation*,[10] for instance, there was no question of deleting the offending words relating to agreements and enforcing the remainder of the byelaw.

In the case of byelaws made by local authorities the onus of establishing their invalidity on the grounds of unreasonableness is, as above mentioned, on the defence, but in the case of byelaws made by other public bodies it has been suggested that the onus rests on the party arguing their validity.[11] This argument originates, however, in relation to byelaws made by railway companies, which were formerly commercial bodies though invested with special statutory powers; at the present time there seems to be no logic in distinguishing between one class of public body, such as the British Railways Board or an Area Electricity Board, and another, the local authorities. It is submitted that this is

---

[7] Local Government Act 1972, s. 235, giving this power to the council of every district and London borough. A similar power is often given by the instrument of government (issued under the Royal Prerogative) to the legislature of a Crown Colony.

[8] *Parker* v. *Bournemouth Corpn.* (1902), 66 J.P. 440.

[9] *Repton School* v. *Repton R.D.C.*, [1918] 2 K.B. 133.

[10] See note 8, *ante*.

[11] See *per* Lord RUSSELL in *Kruse* v. *Johnson*, [1898] 2 Q.B. 91 at p. 99.

not a distinction which would be applied by the courts at the present time. It should perhaps be emphasised that whether or not there is a difference between local authority and other byelaws in this matter of the application of the "unreasonableness" test, it is clear that all byelaws, by whomsoever made, are subject to the judicial tests herein discussed.

(3) Enforcement of byelaws.—The normal method of enforcement of byelaws is for the appropriate authority to take criminal proceedings for a penalty, if these are provided for in the byelaws themselves. The "appropriate authority" will normally be the byelaw-making authority, and it is customarily provided[12] that such authority alone (except with the consent of the Attorney-General) may institute proceedings for a breach of the byelaws. It may also be possible in a particular case to obtain an injunction from the High Court restraining the defendant from committing further breaches of the byelaw in question, or (in an appropriate case) to require him to pull down work which he has constructed in contravention of the byelaw.[13] The grant of an injunction is, however, a discretionary proceeding and the court will need to be satisfied that all other available remedies have been exhausted or would not be satisfactory in the circumstances[14]; also a local authority or member of the public applying for an injunction will first have to obtain the consent of the Attorney-General to the proceedings being taken in his name in the form of a "relator" action.[15]

Byelaws will remain in force until revoked or amended, unless a limit has been set to their life by the enabling statute.[16]

(4) Byelaw-making authorities.—All local authorities have powers—some more limited than others—to make byelaws for the particular purposes specified in the enabling statutes. The four Transport Boards, the Universities (their byelaws are more usually known as "statutes") and a few privileged bodies such as the Countryside Commission, and the National Trust (the latter under the authority of private Acts of Parliament) also have byelaw-making powers.

---

[12] See, so far as concerns byelaws made under the Public Health Act, 1936, s. 298 of that Act.

[13] See s. 65 (5) of the Public Health Act, 1936 (now repealed) where special provision was made in relation to the former building byelaws, now replaced by the Building Regulations, 1972, made under the Public Health Act, 1961. Continuing and deliberate breaches of byelaws, where it can be shown that the penalties provided for in the byelaws themselves are insufficient to prevent such conduct, may be made the subject of proceedings by the Attorney-General (at the relation of a local authority or interested member of the public), as was done in *A.-G.* v. *Harris*, [1960] 3 All E.R. 207; [1961] 1 Q.B. 74; *post*, p. 187. Such a remedy is, however, a matter of discretion for the court and will not be granted as of right: *A.-G.* v. *Kerr and Ball* (1914), 79 J.P. 51.

[14] *A.-G. ex rel. Hornchurch U.D.C.* v. *Bastow*, [1957] 1 All E.R. 497; [1957] 1 Q.B. 514.

[15] The Attorney-General has a discretion whether he will agree to be a party to such proceedings; see, *e.g.*, *London County Council* v. *A.-G.*, [1902] A.C. 165 and *A.-G.* v. *Harris* (*ante*).

[16] As is done in the case of byelaws in relation to offensive trades by s. 108 (4) of the Public Health Act, 1936, which restricts their normal "life" to ten years.

10. THE PROOF OF SUBORDINATE LEGISLATION

Judicial notice is taken of all public statutes, whenever they were passed, and also of all kinds of statutes (*i.e.*, including private and local Acts) passed since 1850.[17] Judicial notice will also be taken of Rules of the Supreme Court made under section 99 of the Supreme Court of Judicature (Consolidation) Act, 1925,[18] but in general Orders in Council and Ministerial Regulations are not so noticed, and so have to be proved before the courts. This is done quite simply, by the production of a copy of the statutory instrument in question, as issued by Her Majesty's Stationery Office, and the same rule applies also to any other regulation so issued.[19] In the case of a regulation or other form of subordinate legislation (for example, the type of sub-delegated legislation considered in *Blackpool Corporation* v. *Locker*[20]) which has not been printed by H.M. Stationery Office, a copy either printed or written (or partly printed and partly written), certified by the appropriate certifying officer in the Department concerned, will be receivable in evidence in any court.[21] If it is necessary to prove, for the purpose of criminal proceedings, that a Minister has "approved" some object, this must be done strictly; thus, a circular from the Home Office stating that the Secretary of State had approved a particular device for the purpose of carrying out the "breath test" authorised under the Road Safety Act, 1967, was held not to be admissible as evidence of approval by the Secretary of a particular piece of equipment used in a specific case.[1] If the regulations in issue are well known, it seems that a criminal court should not dismiss a prosecution simply because a proper copy of those regulations has not been produced, but, if pressed by the defence, the court should adjourn the case for a reasonable time to afford the prosecution the opportunity of obtaining a copy, and the defence may be ordered to pay the costs of any such adjournment.[2] The special position regulating the proof of local or other byelaws has been outlined above.[3]

11. LEGISLATION OF THE EUROPEAN COMMUNITIES

Legislation of the European Communities may be recognised as law in England and Wales, by virtue of the European Communities Act,

---

[17] Interpretation Act, 1889, s. 9.

[18] See Phipson, *Law of Evidence*, 10th edn., para. 50.

[19] By the Crown Debts Act, 1801, s. 9, a King's Printer's copy of a statute was made receivable in evidence in any court, and a similar copy of a Regulation was made receivable by s. 2 of the Documentary Evidence Act, 1868 (see also Schedule thereto, and the many regulations made thereunder extending the operation of the statute to Government Departments other than those originally listed). By the Documentary Evidence Act, 1882, any copy of a document which purports to have been issued by Her Majesty's Stationery Office is receivable in evidence to the same extent as is a copy printed by the Queen's Printer.

[20] *Ante*, p. 66.

[21] Documentary Evidence Act, 1868, *ante*.

[1] *Scott* v. *Baker*, [1968] 2 All E.R. 993; [1969] 1 Q.B. 659; but in *R.* v. *Clarke*, [1969] 1 All E.R. 924; [1969] 2 Q.B. 91, a Stationery Office copy of an order (*not* a statutory instrument) made by the Minister was accepted in evidence under the 1882 Act.

[2] *Palastanga* v. *Solman* (1962), 106 Sol. Jo. 176.

[3] See *ante*, p. 82.

1972; this legislation is not, however, really "subordinate", as the institutions of the Communities are by no means subordinate to the U.K. Parliament, and only some of the legislation may properly be called "delegated", as a considerable quantity was passed by the institutions before Britain's accession to the Treaty of Rome, but this is none the less recognisable as part of English law. It may therefore be more correct to term community legislation which is "self-executing", (*i.e.*, that which will be recognised by the courts of a country as law, without further action being taken by or under the authority of the legislature of that country) as being "secondary" legislation.[4]

Legislation of the communities which by the European Communities Act, 1972 and the Treaty, is so self-executing in England, normally takes the form of *regulations*. The E.E.C. Treaty provides that "a regulation shall have general application. It shall be binding in its entirety and directly applicable in all Member States."[5] In addition, the Council or the Commission may give a *directive* to a Member State, and this is then binding "as to the result to be achieved", but "shall leave to the national authorities the choice of form and methods".[6] There also may be *recommendations* and *opinions* which have no binding force, and *decisions*, which are binding only upon those to whom they are addressed.[7] From the point of view of English law, the only true secondary legislation capable of being passed by the E.E.C. institutions are therefore regulations.

Regulations are part of the law of England[8] by virtue of s. 2 (1) of the 1972 Act, which provides as follows:

> "All such rights, powers, liabilities, obligations and restrictions from time to time created or arising by or under the Treaties,[9] and all such remedies and procedures from time to time provided for by or under the Treaties as in accordance with the Treaties are without further enactment to be given legal effect or used in the United Kingdom shall be recognised and available in law, and be forced, allowed and followed accordingly . . ."

Any questions concerning the interpretation of the E.E.C. Treaty, the validity and interpretation of acts of institutions of the E.E.C. (including regulations) or the interpretation of statutes of bodies established by an act of the Council of the E.E.C., which arise in the course of legal proceedings (civil or criminal), may be referred by the court or tribunal of trial to the European Court of Justice at Luxembourg for a ruling thereon. If such a question is raised in a case pending

---

[4] This is the expression used by Professor Mathijsen in his *Guide to European Community Law* (1972), at p. 184.

[5] E.E.C. Treaty, art. 189.

[6] *Ibid.* Directives also may in some circumstances be self-executing: see *Grad* v. *Finanzamt Traunstein*, [1971] C.M.L.R. 1 (a decision of the European Court).

[7] *Ibid.*

[8] Except in so far as their effect in the U.K. may be postponed by the Accession Treaty.

[9] *I.e.* the Accession Treaty, the Treaty of Rome (E.E.C.), the European Coal and Steel Community Treaty, the Treaty establishing the European Atomic Energy Community, and the subsequent amending Treaties (see s. 1 (2) and Part I to Schedule I of the 1972 Act).

before a court or tribunal[10] against whose decisions there is no judicial remedy under national law, the question must be referred to the European Court.[11] That court will therefore have ultimate exclusive jurisdiction on such questions of validity and interpretation, and the duty is put clearly on an appellate court so to refer a question, whether or not a party has requested such a reference. It is also reasonably clear that rulings of the European Court so given are binding on the courts of the Member State concerned, and probably of other Member States as well.[12] So far as such questions of interpretation are concerned, therefore, the case law of the European Court, like regulations, has become part of English law[13] and judicial controls over Community secondary legislation are ultimately exercisable by the European Court alone.

Regulations may be made by the Council or the Commission of the E.E.C.; they must be published in the Official Journal of the Community (which is issued in all the official Community languages) and they will enter into force on the date specified in the Regulation, or failing such specification, on the twentieth day following publication.[14] No other promulgation or publication in any of the Member States is necessary, but of course in this country copies of the Official Journal are available for purchase at H.M. Stationery Office, and will be found in a number of libraries; the Official Journal does not have to be strictly proved, as judicial notice must be given of its contents, and a copy of any Community instrument purporting to be printed by the Queen's printer is admissible in evidence in legal proceedings.[15]

---

[10] "Tribunal" is not defined for the purposes of the Treaty, but it is presumably wide enough to include an English administrative tribunal, although the French word "tribunal" is normally used with reference to what an English lawyer would call a "court". It would seem that a tribunal whose decisions are "final" (such, for example, as the National Insurance Commissioner: see *post*, p. 248) is nevertheless *not* a tribunal of "last report" if its decisions are susceptible to *certiorari* or to a statutory appeal on a point of law.

[11] E.E.C. Treaty, art. 177.

[12] See the leading case of *Costa* v. *ENEL*, [1964] C.M.L.R. 425.

[13] And see European Communities Act, 1972, s. 3 (1).

[14] E.E.C. Treaty, art. 191.

[15] European Communities Act, 1972, s. 3 (2) and (4).

CHAPTER V

THE REDRESS OF GRIEVANCES

1. INTRODUCTION

We have already pointed out that it is the special concern of administrative law to consider the extent to which the several organs of the Executive can be brought under control in the interests of the governed. Put in another way, this involves an examination of the circumstances in which and the methods by which an individual member of the public can effectively obtain redress of a grievance sustained by him at the hands of some agency of the executive power in the State. An applicant for some form of government aid or permission, such as a new telephone service, a hackney carriage licence, the tenancy of a Council house, or a pension or social security benefit, may be unable to obtain what he wants, and to which he may consider he is entitled, when he first asks for it. Alternatively, the complainant may be the victim of the exercise of some power by the executive not of his own choosing; thus, his land may be compulsorily acquired by a central government agency, an area electricity board or by a local authority, or he may be refused a right to vote in an election. In these and many other kinds of factual situation, a member of the public will have a sense of grievance if he cannot obtain from the administration a decision which appears to him to be just and one which seems to have been arrived at in a proper manner. Administrative law is concerned with precisely these situations, and with analysing the circumstances in which a citizen is to be allowed to obtain satisfaction in some kind of an "appeal" machinery, either to the courts or to some superior administrative agency. First, the legal system must seek to categorise the types of grievances that shall be recognised as being worthy of being provided with a remedy, then it must provide means whereby redress may be made available in each particular class of case.

The second of these two questions has a standard answer in some countries; in France, for example, if the citizen is suffering under a recognised grievance at the hands of the administration, his remedy (except in a few cases where he may be obliged to take proceedings in the civil courts) will be provided by *droit administratif*, a separate body of law, through the medium of the local administrative courts and the Conseil d'Etat. In this country, however, having no separate system of administrative law, the answer is more complicated; sometimes the citizen may have to seek his remedy in the ordinary courts of law, sometimes before an administrative tribunal or by means of an appeal to a Minister of the Crown, and in some cases he may be left to a political or extra-legal remedy, possibly by way of a complaint to an "Ombudsman" (see below, p. 98). This may mean in effect that in a number of circumstances where in other countries the citizen would almost certainly have open to him some means of pursuing his grievance, in this country he will be without any effective remedy.

It is also a feature of this fundamental part of our administrative law that until recently there have been comparatively few general principles; such as there were had been worked out by the courts rather than enacted by Parliament. The Tribunals and Inquiries Act, 1958, passed as a result of the Franks Report, and the Parliamentary Commissioner Act, 1967, are notable exceptions to this statement, but even now there is no comprehensive code comparable with the American Administrative Procedure Act of 1946.[2]

In this Chapter we shall discuss the topic in general terms only, giving a more detailed consideration to the problems that may arise, in later Chapters.

2. THE COURTS

Recourse to the courts of law is the normal remedy for the citizen in this country who suffers from a grievance at the hands of some other person. It is therefore the course of action that he might expect to be open to him in a case where the source of a grievance is some act of the executive.

Ubi ius ibi remedium has long been a fundamental concept in our legal system,[3] and the complainant who has a grievance cognisable by the law may be assured of a remedy through the courts. The *ius* or right must, however, be one accepted by the courts as giving rise to a cause of action, and the complainant must be able to bring the terms of his complaint into such a form. The forms of action may be dead, but, as Maitland said,[4] "they still rule us from their graves", and an allegation that a complainant has been unfairly treated, or has suffered financial loss at the hands of the executive, will not of itself assure him of success in proceedings before the courts of law.[5] Though the common law has been traditionally the guardian of our liberties, it is not sufficiently flexible to provide a new remedy in all kinds of novel circumstances. Provided the executive strictly observes the terms of a power conferred on it by statute, and does not exceed the limits set by the common law and by Parliament to the powers of the Royal Prerogative,[6] the courts cannot question or interfere with an exercise

---

[2] See Appendix I, *post*, p. 460.

[3] See, for example, Broom, *Legal Maxims*, 10th Edn., at p. 118.

[4] *Forms of Action*, Lecture 1, at p. 296 (1932 Edn.).

[5] This is partly a consequence of the absence of any formal constitution in this country. A plaintiff cannot invoke the fundamental rights of the subject, or claim that he has been deprived of his property, without "due process of law". Even his right to personal liberty depends on the availability of a writ of Habeas Corpus, and if that remedy has been removed or suspended under statutory authority, as has happened on occasion throughout our history, the citizen will be unable to obtain redress, the courts being powerless to question the legality of either his imprisonment or the statute in question. On this topic, see Dicey, *Law of the Constitution*, at pp. 229 *et seq.*

[6] The prerogative is not, of course, above the law; it is part of it, and the prerogative may be cut down or regulated by statute (Chapter II, *ante*, p. 42).

of that statutory or prerogative power.[7] There is no natural or fundamental law to which a litigant can appeal in the courts where he alleges that the exercise of an executive power has caused him injustice or hardship.

However, when the grievance amounts to a cause of action recognised by the courts of law, such as an action in tort or for a breach of contract, or a claim in quasi-contract, the plaintiff will be able to invoke the jurisdiction of the courts against any agency of the executive, in the same manner and on the same grounds as would be applicable to similar proceedings commenced by him against any other defendant. Local authorities and public corporations are liable to be sued before the courts, and proceedings can now be brought against the Crown for breach of contract or in tort in almost all cases[8] where an action would lie against a subject. In proceedings against the Crown, the plaintiff may find himself bound by a few special procedural rules, but apart from the privileges that may be claimed in connection with the production of documents and the giving of evidence[9] the plaintiff will not normally find himself at any special disadvantage, just because the defendant is the Crown.

In circumstances where the gravamen of the complaint cannot be brought within the terms of a common law cause of action, the citizen may still have a remedy before the courts in two different kinds of circumstances:

(a) where a statute expressly confers a right to appeal to a named court on one or more specified grounds; or

(b) where he can invoke the inherent jurisdiction of the Supreme Court to supervise or review, within certain ill-defined limits, the decisions of inferior courts and administrative agencies.

We will now say a little about each of these two different kinds of remedy.

(a) Statutory appeals.—Statutory rights of appeal follow no set pattern; they depend for their existence on the terms of the particular statute, and there are comparatively few common features. There are for example, no rules as to the kinds of circumstances in which there shall be such a right of appeal, the forum given jurisdiction to hear the appeal may vary from one statute to another (even when dealing with similar subject matter), and the grounds on which an appeal may be brought will depend on the precise words of the statute in question.

Thus, an appeal will lie to the county court against the decision of the local housing authority to make a demolition or a closing order in respect of an unfit house,[10] but in the case of a similar decision in relation to a house "in multiple occupation", an appeal will lie to the local magistrates.[11] Where the local housing authority deal with several

[7] Except in circumstances where the statute itself has given a right of appeal to the courts (see *post*).

[8] Chapter IX, *post*, pp. 276 *et seq.*

[9] *Ibid.*, p. 289.

[10] Housing Act, 1957, s. 20.

[11] Housing Act, 1961, ss. 12 (4) and 14 (5); this is in spite of the fact that this Part of the 1961 Act is to be "construed as one with" the 1957 Act: 1961 Act, s. 28 (2).

houses at one and the same time by way of making a clearance order (which has an effect very similar to that of a demolition order), the remedy open to the landowner is to appeal, not to any court, but to the Secretary of State for the Environment.[12] In other circumstances, statute makes provision for an appeal to lie direct to the Crown Court (formerly a local court of quarter sessions),[13] although the court most commonly used for statutory appeals from the decisions of administrative agencies is undoubtedly the local magistrates.[14]

The grounds on which a statutory appeal may be brought also vary considerably. Sometimes the jurisdiction of the court is precisely defined by reference to a number of grounds of appeal,[15] and in some cases a list of this kind is concluded with words to the effect that "in any other case" the court shall dismiss the appeal.[16] A common ground for a statutory right of appeal is that the administrative agency against whose decision the appeal is brought, has acted *ultra vires* or otherwise than in accordance with the procedure of the statute.[17] In the former case, the observations we shall make later[18] in relation to the *ultra vires* principle will apply equally to these statutory appeals. In yet other cases, the right of appeal may be "at large"; in other words, the appellant will be able to ask the appropriate court to investigate the merits of the matter and to substitute their decision for that of the administrative agency against which the appeal has been brought.[19]

On a statutory appeal the appellant must therefore bring his claim within the terms of the statute, both as to procedure (within any specified time limit, in writing, on any specified form, etc.), and within any grounds specified. He will also normally have to show that under the terms of the statute in question he is entitled to be an appellant. This may mean that he must show he is an owner of certain land, or possibly an occupier[20]; but in very many cases he will have to be able to show that he is a "person aggrieved" (or a "party aggrieved"). The meaning of this expression is discussed in a subsequent Chapter.[1] A statutory appeal is thus often technical and limited in scope to the precise terms of the statute; in practice the courts are almost over-

[12] Housing Act, 1957, s. 44 and Schedule V.

[13] For example, under the Highways Act, 1959, s. 74 (2), as amended by the Courts Act, 1971, s. 56 (2).

[14] See in particular s. 290 of the Public Health Act, 1936.

[15] As is done, for example, by s. 174 of the Highways Act, 1959, specifying the grounds on which a frontager may appeal to the magistrates against a decision of the local authority to make up a private street under the "code of 1892".

[16] See s. 23 (4) of the Town and Country Planning Act, 1947 providing for appeals against enforcement notices, in the form in which it was originally drafted, before the passing of the Caravan Sites and Control of Development Act, 1960 (see now Town and Country Planning Act, 1971, s. 88). This provision was the cause of much unsatisfactory litigation before it was repealed.

[17] See, for example, para. 16 of the First Schedule to the Acquisition of Land (Authorisation Procedure) Act, 1946, under which an appeal lies to the High Court on certain specified grounds, within six weeks of the confirmation by the Secretary of State of a local authority's compulsory purchase order.

[18] Chapter VI, *post*, p. 133.

[19] See, for example, s. 75 (1) of the Public Health Act, 1936 (notice requiring an owner or occupier of premises to provide a dustbin).

[20] Sometimes, as in the case of enforcement notices under the Town and Country Planning Act, 1971, the notice must be served on both the owner and the occupier: see s. 87 (4) thereof.

[1] Chapter VI, *post*, p. 175.

zealous in this context not to assume jurisdiction where it has not been clearly conferred by the statute. The courts in this respect regard themselves bound by the same principles of *ultra vires* which they apply to restrict the activities of government agencies.

(b) The supervisory jurisdiction.—As we said above, apart from cases where the statute provides a specific remedy, the complainant may be able to invoke the supervisory jurisdiction of the court, a jurisdiction which has a respectable history and has always been vested in the superior courts at Westminster. This jurisdiction stems from the common law; the King's Courts are, in the name of the sovereign, concerned to ensure that inferior bodies are observing the law, and their powers in this respect, though regulated in some measure by statute, are not based on statute. The "person aggrieved" (and we are here not using the expression in the context of any statute[2]) by the action of an administrative agency may, by means of one of the orders in the nature of the former prerogative writs,[3] ask the court to review the decision of which he complains; if a question of personal liberty is involved, the complainant may be able to apply for a writ of *habeas corpus*. In some cases he may commence proceedings for an equitable remedy, commonly by way of an action for a declaration to the effect that the administrative decision in question was for some reason invalid, or possibly for an injunction. The respective grounds on which the remedies afforded by the prerogative orders may be sought, and the circumstances in which they will lie, will be considered in a subsequent Chapter. It should also be remembered here, however, that a complainant may have certain remedies by way of "self help", available to him against some legal step taken to his disadvantage by an administrative agency. Thus, if the officers or agents of a local authority enter on his land to enforce the provisions of (for example) a compulsory purchase order which he contends is for some reason invalid, he may decide to obstruct such an invasion of his private property. If he is subsequently prosecuted under some statutory provision, he may use as a defence the argument that the local authority's order was *ab initio* invalid, and that therefore the entry was a trespass and the obstruction justified.[4]

Alternatively, the complainant in such circumstances may decide to bring proceedings against the local (or other) authority in trespass, contending that the entry on his land was illegal. In yet other circumstances, an individual may be prosecuted for an infringement of the terms of some administrative order[5] or act of a subordinate law-making authority,[6] and it will then be open to him to impeach the validity of the order or regulation in question. An individual may be sued by an

---

[2] *Post*, p. 175.

[3] Of *certiorari*, prohibition and *mandamus*: Chapter VI, *post*, p. 177. By the Administration of Justice (Miscellaneous Provisions) Act, 1938, the former writs were abolished and orders substituted therefor, the change being one of procedure, *ibid.*

[4] *Stroud* v. *Bradbury*, [1952] 2 All E.R. 76; Chapter VI, *post*, p. 190.

[5] Such as, for example, an order made by the Secretary of State under the Water Act, 1958, prohibiting the taking of water from a "specified source".

[6] For example, a byelaw for "good rule and government", made by a London borough or a district council under s. 235 of the Local Government Act, 1972.

administrative agency for the recovery of expenses incurred by them in the execution of works carried out under statutory authority in default of compliance by the defendant (or, possibly, by his predecessors in title of the land affected[7]) with the terms of a notice served on him by the agency under the provisions of some statute.[8] In all these circumstances, the agency may be met by the same argument, namely that the initial exercise of statutory power by the agency was illegal or that there was some material error at some stage of the statutory process.

3. TRIBUNALS AND INQUIRIES

In some circumstances, Parliament has made provision for an appeal to lie from the decision of an administrative agency, such as a local authority or a single civil servant,[9] an *ad hoc* local committee[10] or an inferior tribunal,[11] to a specially constituted tribunal charged with the duty of hearing and determining such appeals. In some cases these statutory tribunals, which are outside the normal hierarchy of the ordinary courts of law and are not subject to their procedural rules, are given a wide jurisdiction over a number of different kinds of appeal,[12] but in most instances they have an extremely limited jurisdiction, sometimes indeed being specially constituted for each appeal. In other instances a statute may provide for an appeal to lie from a decision of an inferior administrative agency to a Minister of the Crown, at the instance of a person "aggrieved". In these cases[13] it is customary for the statute to provide that the Minister shall arrange for an "inquiry" or hearing to be convened before a person appointed by him (usually *ad hoc*), to hear the arguments presented by and on behalf of the appellant and the administrative agency respectively. In other cases, action taken by an administrative agency may require confirmation by a Minister before it can acquire any legal effect; for example, compulsory purchase orders made by a local authority,[14] development plans under town and country planning legislation,[15] clearance orders under the Housing Acts[16] and orders providing for public access to open country,[17] are all dependent on Ministerial confirmation for their legal

---

[7] Expenses incurred under private street works legislation may be recovered by the local authority from the "owner for the time being" of premises affected: Highways Act, 1959, s. 181 (1).

[8] See, for example, Highways Act, 1959, s. 189, or Housing Act, 1957, s. 9; many other examples could be given.

[9] For example, the valuation officer in connection with valuation for rating (General Rate Act, 1967).

[10] Such as the area legal aid committees.

[11] Such as local valuation courts (for rating), from which appeals may be taken to the Lands Tribunal.

[12] The Lands Tribunal again is an example of this type of tribunal: see Chapter VIII, *post*, p. 234.

[13] For example, against a refusal of a local planning authority to grant planning permission for specified development: an appeal will lie to the Secretary of State for the Environment under s. 36 of the Town and Country Planning Act, 1971.

[14] Under the Acquisition of Land (Authorisation Procedure) Act, 1946.

[15] Town and Country Planning Act, 1971, Part II.

[16] Housing Act, 1957, s. 44 and Schedule V.

[17] National Parks and Access to the Countryside Act, 1949, s. 65 and Schedule 1.

validity. The statute usually provides in these cases for any person "interested" or "aggrieved"[18] to make observations or representations about the order in question to the confirming Minister; that Minister is then normally required to convene a local inquiry or hearing before a person appointed by him. In yet other circumstances, a Minister may be empowered to convene an inquiry *proprio motu*, so that he may be informed as to the facts affecting a particular matter, before he comes to a decision thereon.

This last mentioned case brings out the essential difference between a tribunal and an inquiry.[19] A tribunal is convened to hear and determine once and for all time (subject, of course, to any possible appeal), the matter in dispute or the gravamen of the complaint. An inquiry on the other hand is essentially a fact-finding agent, convened to ascertain what the facts may be relating to the matters in issue, with the object of so informing the Minister or other person who may have convened the inquiry, in order that he may the better be able to come to a decision on the questions before him. A tribunal is expected to come to a decision on the subject matter presented before it, although in coming to its decision it may be entitled, or required, to take into consideration matters of policy or general considerations that would not be the concern of a court of law. In most cases, however, any such rules of policy or other considerations will have been laid down beforehand, and will be known to the parties before the tribunal.[20] An inquiry, on the other hand, does not come to any decisions; the conclusion is that of the convening Minister, and while it is often provided in the regulating statute[1] that the Minister shall "have regard to" (or words to a like effect) the report of the person presiding at the inquiry, this does not mean that he is not entitled in the course of arriving at his decision to take into consideration matters which were not raised at the inquiry,[2] including questions of national policy.

In later Chapters,[3] we shall have to consider in some detail the constitution and procedure of the several tribunals and inquiries, and the extent to which they themselves may be subject to control by the courts of law.

4. PARLIAMENTARY REMEDIES

The Parliamentary responsibility of Ministers of the Crown for all policy pursued—a responsibility which is both joint, being shared by all of Her Majesty's Ministers, and several—is a cardinal principle of the unwritten constitution of this country. Therefore, as Lord KILMUIR, L.C., said,[4] "criticizing a Minister's policy is a matter for Parliament",

[18] Chapter VI, *post*, p. 175.

[19] There are other distinctions, and several kinds of both tribunals and inquiries: see Chapter VII, *post*, p. 195.

[20] See, for example, the matters which the Traffic Commissioners are required to take into account when considering whether to grant a road service licence under s. 135 of the Road Traffic Act, 1960.

[1] See, for example, Housing Act, 1957, Schedule 5, para. 5 (2), relating to clearance orders made by local authorities under s. 44 of that Act.

[2] Chapter VII, *post*, p. 220.

[3] *Post*, Chapters VII and VIII.

[4] In the House of Lords, on December 7, 1961: *The Times*, December 8, 1961.

and the "natural" remedy open to a subject aggrieved as a consequence of a policy decision taken by an agency of Government, is for him to write to his Member of Parliament in an attempt to obtain redress. The Member may then raise the matter informally with the Minister concerned, or formally in the House of Commons, usually by question or exceptionally on a motion for the adjournment of the House, or in the course of a Supply Debate. Where the grievance is considered to be of sufficient public importance, the Member may press for a special court of inquiry to be set up to investigate the matter, under the Tribunals of Inquiry (Evidence) Act, 1921, but this is an exceptional and expensive process, not often resorted to.[5]

Parliamentary action may, however, be of uncertain effect. It depends for its effectiveness on far too many uncertain elements, so far as the original complainant is concerned. Thus:

(a) The initiative in pursuing a remedy is taken out of the hands of the complainant and the result depends very largely on the persistence, ability and status of the particular Member whose constituent the complainant happens to be. A Member of the Opposition may be prepared to "attack" a Minister vigorously, but the Minister would probably be more prepared to yield to reasoned criticism if it came from a member of his own party. Again, pressure from a Member who happened to be a Minister or a member of the Opposition's "Shadow Cabinet", is more likely to achieve substantial results than is the same criticism coming from a new Member or a comparatively obscure back-bencher.

(b) In the course of discussion of the particular grievance in the Commons, political considerations may well affect the issue to such an extent that the personal element in the original complaint may be forgotten, and it may not necessarily follow that the complainant will obtain satisfaction, even if his case is fully debated in the House.

(c) There is a wide area of administrative activity within which no Minister will accept responsibility, and in respect of which therefore no Question can be set down in the Commons or motion be debated. The detailed decisions of local authorities or of the independent public corporations (for example) are not the responsibility of any Minister of the Crown,[6] and no adequate redress of grievances can be obtained through the Parliamentary machinery in such cases.

(d) Even where the particular ground of complaint falls within the sphere of responsibility of a specific Minister, and where the Member who has undertaken to investigate the matter is conscientious and pertinacious, the process of obtaining an effective remedy may be

---

[5] The procedure has now been used on 18 occasions; the most recent example, under a corresponding Northern Ireland statute, is the enquiry into the disturbances between Catholics and Protestants in Northern Ireland in 1969. The procedure has been most frequently invoked in cases of alleged or suspected public scandal (as, for example, when a Minister of the Crown was suspected of having some financial advantage), but it has also been used where there has been an accusation of mismanagement or abuse of executive power. Thus, in the *Waters case* in 1959, a tribunal was convened under the Act to investigate a complaint by a youth against two police officers in Scotland. See Keeton, *Trial by Tribunal* and the Report of the Royal Commission on Tribunals of Inquiry, 1966 (Cmnd. 3121).

[6] See Chapter X, *post*, p. 333.

slow and cumbersome. The Member of Parliament who desires to obtain proper redress for his constituents may have to be prepared to follow up the ministerial answer to his question with supplementaries, and to press for a precise and unequivocal promise of an effective remedy. Many Members are too busy or preoccupied with other interests, to be able to spare the time to pursue a matter of this kind to any considerable extent. There are of course, many exceptions to this observation, but it is certainly no fault of the original complainant if his Member is not one of the exceptions.

5. THE "OMBUDSMAN" REMEDY

There is, therefore, a considerable area within which complaints against the administration may arise, for which until recently there has been no very effective machinery for the securing of redress to the person aggrieved. Among other instances, this area of administrative action may include such matters as exchange control, the Home Office power to deport aliens, the Foreign Office power to grant "political asylum", and also the following[7]:

(i) The selection of a school for a child; the parent has no right of appeal against the decision of the local education authority if, as the result of the "11 plus" examination, the child is not admitted to a selective school for secondary education. Similarly, at a later stage in the child's academic career, even if he reaches an adequate standard in the General Certificate of Education examinations, the child (or the parent) has no redress if he cannot persuade the University of his choice to accept him for a degree course.[8]

(ii) "Marginal benefits" under the National Health Service may be granted to or withheld from individuals, at the discretion of civil servants in the Department of Health and Social Security, and there is no formal machinery for a review of their decisions.

(iii) If the local Telephone Manager refuses to allocate a new telephone service to a particular would-be subscriber, the applicant has no remedy except to appeal to a higher official within the Post Office organisation.

(iv) The War Office has power to make *ex gratia* payments when claims are made for compensation (and possibly in circumstances where no action would lie in tort under section 10 of the Crown Proceedings Act, 1947[9]), in circumstances where it is considered, within the Department, that it should "assume some moral responsibility for loss or injury",[10] but there is no remedy if the War Office refuses to make such a payment.

---

[7] Most of these examples are taken from the *Justice* Report mentioned below.

[8] Technically, of course, the Universities are independent bodies, rightly jealous of their academic freedom from State control, but an applicant will not always be prepared to see the matter in this light where he is refused a place, especially in circumstances where he has been awarded a grant from the State or the local education authority.

[9] Chapter IX, *post*, p. 282.

[10] *Justice* Report, p. 20.

Normal parliamentary action may in some circumstances merely result in a discussion of the burden of the complaint; it may merely amount to a "ventilation", rather than a "redress" of the grievance. Moreover, in practice a complainant may have one of two different types of grievance. In the first place, he may merely want the administrative decision reversed, and has no complaint about the manner in which the administrative agency that made the decision against him considered his application. Here he wants the matter reviewed "on the merits"; it is a matter of considerable consequence to him, and he wants to be assured that the decision is taken at a high level, that his case is fully and properly considered, and that, if the eventual decision cannot be favourable, he will at least have the satisfaction of expressing his views; he wants to have "his day in court". In the second class of case, however, the complaint is based on some allegation of maladministration or abuse of power. Here the contention will be that the decision has been arrived at for the wrong motive, or that an official responsible for the decision had a personal interest in the matter, that there has been inordinate delay in coming to the decision, or possibly that a promise given on a previous occasion, on which the complainant had relied, had been broken.[11]

The first class of cases where there is no remedy could be met simply enough by an extension (which would of course need legislation) of the existing process of allowing statutory appeals, to either the courts of law or a special tribunal. For the other class of case, where it is not simply a question of reviewing an administrative decision, some novel machinery had to be devised, if complainants were not to be left to rely on their Members of Parliament.

It was an appreciation of this position which led a committee of *Justice*, the all-party organisation of lawyers, to arrange for an investigation into the Scandinavian institution of the "Ombudsman", or "grievance man", with a view to considering whether some similar institution should be established in this country. A Report (the *Whyatt Report*) under the Chairmanship of Sir John Whyatt was published in November, 1961.[12] After a careful survey of the present position in this country, and an examination of Scandinavian practice, the Report made a number of interesting and important recommendations.

The Scandinavian Ombudsman is an officer of Parliament, having as his primary function the duty of acting as an agent for Parliament, "for the purpose of safeguarding citizens against abuse or misuse of administrative power by the Executive".[13]

> "He is not a super-administrator to whom an individual can appeal when he is dissatisfied with the discretionary decision of a public official in the hope that he may obtain a more favourable decision. His primary function . . . is to investigate allegations of maladministration."[14]

This he does in an informal manner; he inquires into the matter of the complaint fully, having access to the departmental files, and he then issues his report, which is published in the national newspapers (in

[11] As, for example, occurred in the Crichel Down affair, *ante*, p. 24.
[12] *The Citizen and the Administration*, Stevens.
[13] *Justice* Report, para. 2.
[14] *Ibid.*, para. 18.

Denmark these reports are invariably given the maximum coverage). If the report is adverse to the administration, the mere fact of publication will normally prove to be sufficient to ensure remedial action being taken by the department concerned.[15] In practice, however, we are assured that a very large proportion of the Danish Ombudsman's early reports were favourable to the administration, a feature which rapidly overcame initial opposition among administrators to the setting up of the office. Friendly relations between the Ombudsman and the administration is an essential feature of the institution in all the three Scandinavian countries where the office has been operating, as this enables the Ombudsman to achieve many positive results "behind the scenes" and in an informal manner.

In recent years the "Ombudsman idea" has been adopted or recommended in a number of countries. Apart from Scandinavia, its original home, the first was New Zealand where an Ombudsman was appointed in 1962; one has been appointed in Guyana (formerly British Guiana), on the recommendation of a report by the International Commission of Jurists, and there is also an Ombudsman in each of the Canadian provinces of Alberta and New Brunswick. The Northern Ireland Parliament adopted its own Parliamentary Commissioner in 1970 (before "rule from Westminister"), and there is also a separate "Commissioner for Complaints" for local authorities and corporations. The institution was also recommended in general terms in a resolution passed by the Ceylon Section of the I.C.J. in January, 1966.[16]

So far as this country is concerned, the recommendations in the *Whyatt Report* were, firstly, that the present provisions for appeals should be extended.[17] Secondly, the Report emphasised that

> "Parliament is and must remain the most important channel for making representations",

regarding complaints of maladministration against the executive. Parliamentary procedure would, however, it is suggested, be more effective if it were

[15] There is a very good description of the work of the Danish Ombudsman, by Professor Hurwitz at [1958] P.L. 236, and see other articles at [1959] P.L. 115, [1962] P.L. 15, 24, 34 and 43 and *Journal of the International Commission of Jurists*, Vol. IV, No. 1, pp. 150 and 151. The Scandinavian "Ombudsmen" are fully examined in a masterly work (in French), *L'Ombudsman Scandinave*, by André Legrand (1970). For a more general account, see Chapter 12 in Brian Chapman's *The Profession of Government*, and for comparative accounts of various ombudsmen throughout the world, see *The Ombudsman* 2nd Edn. 1968 (ed. Professor D. C. Rowat) and *When Americans Complain*, by Professor W. Gellhorn. *The British Ombudsman*, by Frank Stacey (1971) is principally an interesting account of the establishment of the British Parliamentary Commissioner.

[16] Bulletin No. 26 of the International Commission of Jurists (June 1966), at p. 7.

[17] Persons who are aggrieved by discretionary decisions of the administration should be provided with "a right of appeal to an independent authority, unless there are overriding considerations which make it necessary, in the public interest, for the final decision to be left with the Executive": Report, para. 165. In order that this recommendation might be implemented, the Report suggested that the functions of the Council on Tribunals (established by the Tribunals and Inquiries Act, 1958, Chapter VII, *post*, p. 201) should be extended, so as to enable them to make proposals to bring administrative discretions at present outside the "tribunal system", within that system, "wherever it is appropriate to do so". This part of the *Whyatt* Report has not been implemented, but a similar "Administrative Review Tribunal" has recently been suggested for Australia (1971) Parl. Pap. No. 144, and article by Professor Whitmore at (1972) 5 Fed. L. Rev. 7.

"supplemented by machinery which would enable such complaints to be investigated by an impartial authority if the Member requested it."[18]

The Report therefore came to the second conclusion that an Ombudsman type of institution should be established in this country. After some delay this recommendation was adopted by the Government, and the Parliamentary Commissioner Act, 1967 was passed, the first Commissioner taking office in April 1967.[19]

Under the Act, the "Parliamentary Commissioner for Administration", to give him his full title, has a status similar to that of the Comptroller and Auditor-General,[1] his salary being similarly charged direct on the Consolidated Fund, and he is not removable from his office except on an address from both Houses of Parliament. Unlike the Scandinavian Ombudsman, the Commissioner does not receive complaints direct from members of the public, but complaints must be directed to him through a Member of Parliament. The complainant may choose any one of the 630 Members, and may indeed try each Member in turn. The Member is expected to act as a filter and pass on to the Commissioner complaints which he considers worthy of investigation. Where a complaint concerns a particular Government Department, which will of course be normally the case, the Commissioner is required to notify the Minister concerned and give him an opportunity of commenting on any allegations in the complaint.[2]

The Parliamentary Commissioner is an *ex officio* member of the Council on Tribunals, and Crown privilege in respect of documents cannot be claimed against him, except that he has no right of access to Cabinet documents. Also the Commissioner may be expressly precluded by a Minister from publishing the contents of particular specified documents (s. 11 (3)).

Only specified Government Departments and other bodies fall within the Commissioner's jurisdiction; this is, however, a long list (see Schedule 2 to the Act), and it may be amended by Order in Council subject to the negative resolution procedure.[3] A complaint must be formulated in writing at the instance of a member of the public who "claims to have sustained injustice in consequence of maladministration", in connection with action taken by a Department within the Commissioner's jurisdiction; no fee is payable on the lodging of the complaint.[4] The com-

---

[18] Report, para. 166.

[19] For literature on the U.K. Parliamentary Commissioner, see notes on the Act by the present author in *Current Law Statutes* for 1967, and article in University of Toronto Law Journal, 1968, at p. 158; also article by Sir Edmund Compton in [1968] X J.S.P.T.L. at p. 101.

[1] The first Commissioner, Sir Edmund Compton, was a former Comptroller and Auditor-General.

[2] Fortunately, a proposal in the *Whyatt Report* that complaints should be subject to Ministerial veto was dropped.

[3] It has been added to by the Parliamentary Commissioner (Departments and Authorities) Order, 1968 (S.I. 1968, No. 1859), to include the Decimal Currency Board, established by the Decimal Currency Act, 1967, by the Parliamentary Commissioner Order, 1970 (S.I. 1970 No. 1535), to include the Department of Employment and the Office of Population Censuses and by the Parliamentary Commissioner Order, 1972 (S.I. 1972, No. 1716), to include the Intervention Board for Agricultural Produce (a new public Corporation made necessary by the entry of the United Kingdom into the European Economic Community) and also the Northern Ireland Office.

[4] A fee of £1 is payable in respect of each case in New Zealand.

plaint must be made to a member of the House of Commons (not necessarily the member for the constituency in which the complainant resides), and it will be referred by the member to the Commissioner at the former's discretion, and with the consent of the complainant.[5] It will then be a matter for the Commissioner to decide at his discretion, which is not subject to control by the courts,[6] whether to initiate, continue or discontinue an investigation.[7]

The following possible sources of complaint are excluded by the Act:

(a) where the complainant ("person aggrieved") had a right of appeal or review before a tribunal or court of law, unless the Commissioner considers it was not reasonable to expect the complainant to resort or have resorted to such a remedy (s. 5 (2));

(b) matters listed in the Third Schedule to the Act (*inter alia*, foreign affairs, investigation of crime, contractual or commercial transactions, etc.);

(c) stale complaints (s. 6 (3), imposing a 12 month time limit with power to the Commissioner to extend the time);

(d) complaints by persons not resident in the U.K., unless the act complained of relates to action taken in relation to him while he was present in the U.K. (s. 6 (4)).

When the Commissioner has concluded an investigation or decides not to conduct an investigation, he is required to send a report to the member of the House of Commons concerned, and in addition the Commissioner may report specially to both Houses of Parliament (s. 10).

One of the arguments most frequently heard in opposition to the office of Parliamentary Commissioner is based on the factor that the Scandinavian counterpart works well only in countries that have much smaller populations than our own. The success of the institution in Denmark, for example, owes a great deal to the personality of the first Ombudsman, Professor Hurwitz, and to the fact that he investigates his cases personally, and is assisted only by a very small staff. The same observation is true in respect of New Zealand, where a Commissioner[8] was appointed on October 1, 1962. Prestige and personal contact would be lost, it is suggested, if there were a number of Commissioners, or if the single Commissioner were obliged to build up a large staff to assist him in his work. The *Justice* Report answers this criticism by pointing out that the Commissioner is expected to deal only with the comparatively limited field of administration where there is no other means of obtaining redress; some at least of the probable frivolous or vexatious complaints are answered or otherwise dealt with by Members, and do not get through to the Commissioner at all.

[5] 1967 Act, s. 5 (1).
[6] *Re Fletcher's Application*, [1970] 2 All E.R. 527.
[7] 1967 Act, s. 5 (5). For an interesting account of the Parliamentary Commissioner's discretion, see an article by D. Foulkes at (1971) 34 M.L.R. 377.
[8] Under the (N.Z.) Parliamentary Commissioner (Ombudsman) Act, 1962; the Commissioner was given the title "Ombudsman", when the Bill was passing through the New Zealand Parliament.

Since the office of Commissioner has been established, he has investigated many complaints. In the first nine months to 31st December 1967, he received 1,069 complaints through Members of Parliament, of which 561 were outside his jurisdiction. Of the 188 cases then investigated the Commissioner found that in 19 cases there had been "some elements of maladministration", but in none of these cases had he any criticism of the action taken by the Department concerned "to remedy any injustice caused by maladministration".[9] During the first full year of the operation of the Office (ending 31.12.68), 1,120 complaints were received through Members of Parliament, of which 727 were found to be outside the Commissioner's jurisdiction. Of the 374 cases investigated during that year, the Commissioner found there had been elements of maladministration which led to some measure of injustice in 38 cases.[10]

So much for the law and the statistics concerning this institution in British (for the Act applies to Scotland as well as to England and Wales) administrative law. The whole concept of an "ombudsman" has been criticised by several writers, notably by Professor J. D. B. Mitchell,[11] who suggests that this is a mere palliative, which fails to deal with the central problem in our "system", namely, a lack of any comprehensive body of administrative law. So often the citizen has to rely on private law remedies, which do not always result in substantial justice in a public law situation.[12] A similar argument is made by Andrew Shonfield, in his "Modern Capitalism", where he says[13] that "the Ombudsman is not a substitute for a system of administrative law; he is a powerful supplement to it".

What then are the strengths and weaknesses of our British Commissioner, who is not, according to Mr. Richard Crossman,[14] an "ombudsman"? First, the *weaknesses*:

(a) Complaints have to be filtered through Members of Parliament, and the Commissioner may not act *proprio motu*, as may the New Zealand ombudsman. This is not proving a serious defect in practice; a complainant has 630 Members he can approach, and a complaint can

---

[9] Annual Report of the Commissioner for 1967, para. 9.

[10] See Annual Report of the Commissioner for 1968. By the time the Report for 1971 was published, however, the number of complaints received through members for the year had shrunk to 548. During the year (after allowing for the cases found to be outside the Commissioner's jurisdiction) 182 cases were investigated, and there were found to be elements of maladministration in 67 (37 per cent.), most of which, however, could be described as "a mistake or human error rather than serious maladministration" (Report, para. 26).

[11] See in particular [1962] P.L. 24, (1966) 15 I.C.L.Q. 133, and [1968] P.L. 201; also the articles he cites at [1968] P.L. 203, footnote 8.

[12] As, for example, in *Southend-on-Sea Corpn.* v. *Hodgson (Wickford), Ltd.*, [1961] 2 All E.R. 46; [1962] 1 Q.B. 416, referred to on p. 294. Often when a would-be developer is refused planning permission and then appeals to the Courts on some legal ground, and is successful in those proceedings, he does not really come out at the end of the day with what he wants, namely planning permission for his development, but he is merely told by the court that the Minister's order upholding the original decision of the local planning authority was wrong; he then has to start again at the beginning of the process and again may or may not be successful.

[13] At p. 427; the whole of Part 4 of this book merits reading by administrative lawyers.

[14] When moving the Second Reading of the Parliamentary Commissioner Bill in the House of Commons.

always be "inspired" in a serious case where there is any considerable body of opinion that it should be investigated[15];

(b) The Commissioner's jurisdiction is limited to the government departments listed in the second schedule to the Act, and he is excluded from investigating matters listed in the third schedule. Public Corporations do not appear in the second schedule, but this has been met in some measure by the Health Service Commissioners.[16] This leaves other public corporations[17] and local authorities outside the Commissioner's jurisdiction. So far as local authorities are concerned, a second *Justice* Report[18] was published in November 1969, recommending that Commissioners for Local Administration should be established having a wide jurisdiction over local authorities with functions similar to those of the Parliamentary Commissioner in relation to the central government.

The idea was accepted in principle by H.M. Government, and under the Local Government Bill which is expected to become law on April 1, 1974, two Commissions for Local Administration (which will have corporate status) are to be established, one for England, one for Wales. The Commissions will allocate members of their body to particular areas, and these Commissioners will investigate complaints of "injustice" suffered as a consequence of maladministration in connection with the exercise of administrative functions by a local authority, a police authority, a water authority or a joint board of local authorities. The complaint must normally be forwarded by a member of the authority concerned, but this requirement may be dispensed with by the Commissioner. After investigation of a complaint the Commissioner will make a report to the authority, and this must then be made available to public inspection; if the Commissioner finds injustice, the report must be considered by the authority and they in turn must inform the Commissioner as to the action they have taken or propose to take.

The expenses of the Commissions will be payable by all the county councils on a proportionate basis, and the Commissions will report annually to a body representative of local authorities, appointed by the Secretary of State for the Environment. The individual Commissioners will be appointed by Her Majesty on the recommendation of the Secretary of State, and they will have security of tenure. The Parliamentary Commissioner is to be a member of each of the Commissions; he has also been appointed Health Service Commissioner for England, Wales and Scotland (see *post*, p. 107).

Even after the establishment of these new Commissioners there will remain the matters excluded by the third schedule to the 1967 Act, and it is to be hoped that these matters will be reduced in number; it seems particularly unfortunate that all matters concerned with government contracts are excluded from the Commissioner's investigation. The

---

[15] This was in fact done over the investigation into noise at Heathrow Airport (see Second Report of the Commissioner for session 1967–68). As to the "filter", see article by L. H. Cohen at [1972] P.L. 204.

[16] National Health Service Reorganisation Act, 1973, Part III, and see *post*, p. 107.

[17] As to these, see Chapter X, *post*, p. 317.

[18] *The Citizen and his Council: Ombudsmen for Local Government?*; Stevens. 1969.

Parliamentary Select Committee set up by the House of Commons to exercise a general "watching brief" over the activities of the P.C.A., have twice recommended that his functions should be extended to include personnel matters relating to Crown Servants, but this has not been accepted by H.M. Government.[19]

(c) Then there is the fact that the Parliamentary Commissioner (and the local commissioners) is confined to investigating complaints of injustice resulting from "maladministration". This term was deliberately not defined in the statute, and section 12 (3) "declares" that

> "nothing in this Act authorises or requires the Commissioner to question the merits of a decision taken without maladministration by a government department or other authority in the exercise of a discretion vested in that department or authority."

Therefore the Commissioner may not be concerned with policy, but it is also clear that the extent of his jurisdiction is a matter for his own discretion (see s. 5 (5)). In the House of Commons,[20] Mr. Crossman attempted a definition of "maladministration", in what is sometimes called "the Crossman catalogue",[1] as "bias, neglect, inattention, delay, incompetence, ineptitude, perversity, turpitude, arbitrariness and so on", but clearly this in itself is not precise. At first the Commissioner considered that in a case where a department had laid down a rule of practice for its own guidance, he was confined to considering whether that rule had been applied fairly and properly in the particular case. However, consequent on a Report of the Select Committee of the House of Commons,[2] he agreed[3] to consider cases where such a rule of practice, though properly applied, has worked injustice; in other words he is now prepared to consider whether the "bad rule" may amount to maladministration. He still cannot consider cases of "bad law", where a statute or regulation made under statutory authority works injustice in practice.[4]

(d) Some criticism can also be levied at the Parliamentary Commissioner's Office itself. He is assisted by a staff with an establishment of 63, which seems to take the institution rather far from the personal approach of its Scandinavian forbears; and also there are no legal officers on the staff. The Commissioner says he does not need lawyers,

[19] See White Paper (Cmnd. 5766) dated Dec. 1972, and entitled "Area Excluded from Parliamentary Commissioner's investigation".

[20] On October 18, 1966 (see *Hansard*, col. 51).

[1] See an article by Sir Edmund Compton (the Commissioner) at (1968), X J.S.P.T.L. 101; and see also Marshall, "Maladministration", [1973] P.L. 32.

[2] Second Report, Session 1967–68 (H.C. 350). This is a Committee of the House of Commons appointed to examine the reports laid before the House by the Commissioner and matters in connection therewith. They are constituted not by the statute, but by Resolution of the House and they do not in any sense act as a court of appeal from the decisions of the Commissioner, but as he is an officer of the House, they consider themselves competent to give him general advice as to the exercise of his discretions under the Act. In view of the importance of the Sachsenhausen affair (see *post*, p. 106) the Select Committee made a separate report on it (First Report, Session 1967–68, H.C. 258).

[3] Annual Report of the Commissioner for 1968 (H.C. 129), at p. 6: "I now feel entitled, before deciding the terms of my report to the Member who has referred such a complaint, to enquire whether the department have reviewed the rule in the light of the hardship sustained by the complainant." See also First Report of the Commissioner for 1968–69 (H.C. 9).

[4] This is done by the New Zealand Ombudsman. It is suggested that cases of the bad rule should be within the jurisdiction of Commissioners for Local Administration.

as he can always obtain a legal opinion from the Treasury solicitor, but it should be appreciated that the Treasury solicitor's principal client is H.M. Government, and therefore a semblance of impartiality is not unequivocally maintained.

(e) It is also perhaps worthy of comment, that the Commissioner has no sanction available to him; if a government department were to take no notice of adverse comment in a report, the Commissioner would not be able to take any positive action, except possibly to include a statement in his next annual (or special) report to the Select Committee of the House of Commons. The New Zealand Ombudsman on the other hand has a statutory power to send a copy of his report and recommendation to the Prime Minister in such circumstances; this power he used on one occasion in 1968–69 (see Report for year ended March 31, 1969, at page 11), with satisfactory results. In the case of the Northern Ireland Commissioner for Complaints,[5] a finding that a person has sustained injustice as a consequence of maladministration may provide grounds for an action for damages in the county court.[6]

On the other hand, the institution of Parliamentary Commissioner has obvious *advantages*. His very existence must ensure a higher standard of administration in those Departments that are within the Commissioner's jurisdiction.[7] There is perhaps not as much publicity for the Commissioner's work as one would wish—it is a pity the reports on particular cases do not go to the press as soon as they are issued[8]—but most M.P.s are aware of the assistance the Commissioner can give them in investigating (if not always satisfying) the complaints of their constituents, and we are told that 542 Members of Parliament had referred complaints to him by 31st December 1968.[9] The outstanding example of an investigation by the Commissioner where maladministration was found to have existed, was undoubtedly the Sachsenhausen concentration camp affair, where former serving officers in H.M. Forces who had been imprisoned by the Germans during the 1939–45 war complained that, owing to an error made by the Foreign Office, they had been denied compensation in circumstances where this had been paid to other former prisoners who had (it was contended, and as the Commissioner found, proved) been in a similar situation.[10]

---

[5] Not to be confused with the Northern Ireland P.C.A. The Commissioner for Complaints is concerned only with local authorities and similar bodies.

[6] Commissioner for Complaints Act (Northern Ireland), 1969, and see article by the present writer at 21 N.I.L.Q. 353.

[7] This point is made in the Report of the Select Committee for 1968–69 (H.C. 385).

[8] As is the custom in Scandinavia. Under the 1967 Act, the Commissioner reports to the M.P., and possibly to both Houses. The latter course is rare in practice, and it is only those cases that are released to the press at the time; publicity otherwise depends on the action of the M.P., and if he should inform the press of the contents of a Commissioner's report, he will not be specially protected against the possibility of proceedings in defamation. The practice started in 1972, of issuing quarterly, instead of annual, reports may assist in this respect.

[9] Annual Report of the Commissioner for 1968 (H. C. 129), at p. 3. But in 1971 there were only 367 Members: Annual Report, para. 2.

[10] Third Report of the Commissioner for 1967–68 (H.C. 54); First Report from the Select Committee, Session 1967–68 (H.C. 258). The Foreign Secretary subsequently agreed to meet the complaints and pay the compensation asked for. More recently, the Commissioner reported to the Committee on maladministration in the Inland Revenue Department, which was discussed in the Committee's Report for 1968–69 (H.C. 385).

It is clear that from time to time there is maladministration resulting in injustice to individuals, and whereas the Commissioner cannot be the panacea for all administrative ills, nor can he replace the need for a reform of our administrative law, there is no doubt that his office fulfils a most useful function. Commissioners for Local Administration are even more necessary in view of the increased size of local authorities,[11] and the consequent greater remoteness of officials and members of the public.

Under the National Health Service Reorganisation Act, 1973, there is now a Health Service Commissioner for England and one for Wales; separate provision to a similar effect was made for Scotland by the National Health Service (Scotland) Act, 1972. All these three offices are held by the Parliamentary Commissioner in plurality.[12] The Health Service Commissioner(s) has the same status as the P.C.A. and it is his duty to investigate an alleged failure in a service provided by a health authority, an alleged failure to provide a service which it is a function of such an authority to provide, or any other action taken by or on behalf of such an authority, in any case where there is a complaint of injustice in consequence of the failure, or in consequence of maladministration.[13] The functions of the Commissioner under this provision are therefore somewhat wider than those of the P.C.A., under the 1967 Act; moreover, complaints may be made direct to a Health Service Commissioner without going through a Member of Parliament but the complaint must first have been brought to the notice of the relevant body. In other respects the procedure under these statutes is much the same as it is under the 1967 Act; in particular the Commissioners may not question the merits of a decision taken without maladministration,[14] and certain matters (*e.g.*, matters connected with the diagnosis of illness) are specifically excluded from their jurisdiction.[15] Provision has been made for consultation between Health Commissioners, the Local Commissions and the Parliamentary Commissioner, by clause 32 of the Local Government Bill.

The nationalised industries (gas, electricity, coal, transport, atomic energy and the Post Office) perhaps need a different treatment in the form of the existing Consumer Councils, but with both real and apparent independence of their parent corporations.[16]

6. THE FUTURE

The problem remains, what more needs to be done in the interests of the citizen? We have no real system of administrative law; there is no one simple procedure whereby a citizen can ask for redress before a court, and there is no assurance that when he gets before the court the

[11] On the re-organisation of local government, see Chapter XIII, *post*, p. 400.
[12] See Annual Report of the P.C.A. for 1972, at para. 42.
[13] National Health Service Reorganisation Act, 1973, s. 34 (3). The Scottish Act also includes a reference to "unfair or unreasonable treatment"; see s. 45 (2).
[14] 1973 Act, s. 38 (2); there is no parallel provision in the Scottish Act.
[15] 1973 Act, Sched. 3; Scottish Act, Sched. 5.
[16] New Zealand extended the jurisdiction of their Ombudsman to include education and hospital boards, by the Parliamentary Commissioner (Ombudsman) (Amendment) Act, 1968.

remedy or remedies that the court is empowered to give will be able to do justice in the particular case. The proposals in the *Whyatt* Report for the extension of the existing tribunal "system" (see p. 100, *supra*) would meet shortcomings to some extent, but this would be only another piecemeal reform. Some writers suggest the establishment of an English *Conseil d'Etat* on the French model, and Professor J. D. B. Mitchell has suggested[17] the Judicial Committee of the Privy Council as being well suited for this function, partly because it would be able to handle cases from Scotland as well as those from England and Wales. But the *Conseil d'Etat* enjoys its high prestige in the country of its origin,[18] partly because of its history and traditions, and also because of the fact that its members are experienced administrators and trained lawyers. Such an institution is not, as it seems to the present writer, one appropriate for importation.

A few years ago the Law Commission published a submission to the Lord Chancellor[19] on administrative law. In this interesting document, it was recommended that a Royal Commission should be constituted to carry out a thorough going investigation into our administrative law. In a preliminary working paper, five questions had been formulated; as a result of observations received in response to that Working Paper, the Law Commission had formed the opinion that all these five questions should be within the terms of reference of the Royal Commission. These questions were as follows:

"(A) How far are changes desirable with regard to the form and procedures of existing judicial remedies for the control of administrative acts and omissions?

(B) How far should any such changes be accompanied by changes in the scope of those remedies,

(i) to cover administrative acts and omissions which are not at present subject to judicial control, and

(ii) to render judicial control more effective, *e.g.*, with regard to the factual basis of an administrative decision?

(C) How far should remedies controlling administrative acts or omissions include the right to damages?

(D) How far, if at all, should special principles govern

(i) contracts made by the administration,

(ii) the tortious liability of the administration?

(E) How far should changes be made in the organisation and personnel of the courts in which proceedings may be brought against the administration?"

As a consequence of this submission, the Law Commission were requested to make a further study of the question of remedies alone, the proposal for a Royal Commission not being accepted.[20] This study resulted in a Working Paper[1] wherein the Law Commission recommended that there should be a single petition for review available

---

[17] See his "The Causes and Consequences of the Absence of a System of Public Law", [1965] P.L. 95.

[18] See Brown and Garner, *French Administrative Law*, 2nd Edn., especially Chapters 4 and 11.

[19] Cmnd. 4059, dated May 1969.

[20] Statement by the then Lord Chancellor in *Hansard* No. 744 (H.L.), p. 190.

[1] "Remedies in Administrative Law", working Paper No. 40, published 11 October 1971.

generally for the redress of grievances, whilst leaving available the existing remedies. Unfortunately, by reason of their restricted terms of reference, the Commission did not consider the closely related subject of the grounds on which these remedies should be available. None of these proposals, important as they are, have at the time of writing been implemented; they have been supplemented by a further *Justice* Report[2] which goes much further than the Working Paper of the Law Commission. Here it is suggested that there should be an Administrative Division of the High Court to which would be transferred all existing jurisdiction of the courts to supervise subordinate administrative bodies, and also to determine statutory appeals from Ministers, tribunals or inferior courts in administrative matters.[3] The proposal for a simple and single form of originating process applicable to all administrative proceedings is of great importance; the nature of the remedy that could be ordered by the court would be at large, be it an order to quash or modify, an award of damages or an injunction. It would also be necessary, it is suggested in the Report, to devise a code of principles of good administration, any breach of which would entitle a person aggrieved to commence legal proceedings before the Administrative Division (or some inferior tribunal) for a remedy.[4] Consideration should also be given in any further proposals for reform, to the grounds on which the courts may in future be entitled to review an administrative decision; certainly "bad faith" should be one of those grounds.[5] Reform of the law of contract and tort in administrative matters is perhaps subsidiary, but still important.

An Administrative Division would seem to be preferable to the establishment of a new court, principally because this would make the least break with tradition and would retain the high prestige at present attaching in the public mind to the High Court.

A separate Division would allow for a high degree of specialisation, and it is to be preferred to a mere "Administrative List" within, say, the existing Queen's Bench Division, as it would allow special procedural rules to be prepared, providing for (for example) greater use of documentary evidence and affidavits, the inspection of Government files by the Court, etc.

It is proposed in the State of Victoria[6] that there should be an administrative tribunal separate from the ordinary courts, but from which a right of appeal would lie to the courts on points of law. This seems similar to the *Whyatt* Report's general tribunal (*ante*, p. 100), and it will be interesting to see how this works in practice.

---

[2] *Administration under Law*, Stevens, 1971.

[3] A start has been made in New Zealand by the establishment of such a Division: see (1969) 3 N.Z.U.L.R. 351, 4 Recent Law 1949, and the Judicature Amendment Act 1968 (N.Z.).

[4] The Public and Administrative Law Reform Committee in New Zealand are making similar recommendations as to general rules that should be taken into account when detailed procedural rules are prepared for tribunals in New Zealand (which seem to be even more numerous than in England): see the Committeee's Sixth Report, paras. 23 *et seq.*

[5] Thereby clearing up the uncertainty in the existing law; see Chapter VI, *post*, p. 147.

[6] (1968) 42 A.L.T. 38.

In the chapters that follow, the existing law is discussed, indicating the several different kinds of machinery whereby an aggrieved citizen may at present obtain redress from the courts or from tribunals or a Government Department after the holding of an inquiry. It has recently been suggested[7] that there is nothing inherently at fault with English administrative law and that the courts are fully capable of evolving new principles to meet the problems of the modern Welfare State. Certainly some recent decisions[8] have shown that the House of Lords in particular is prepared to apply fundamental ideas of "fair play" and natural justice; but it is the present writer's view[9] that this is not a consistent attitude; as soon as a "liberal" decision is given, another decision appears showing a reversion to the more usual attitude of English courts, namely a strict construction of the words of the statute.[10] This brings out one of the major difficulties in the way of the introduction of any comprehensive system of administrative law; the supremacy of Parliament and the consequential doctrine of *ultra vires*. Any enactment of general principles would always be subject to modification in subsequent statutes, either by express provision or by implication. This should not, however, prevent or frustrate any attempt at reform.[11] Reform by the inventive genius of the common law alone is too slow for modern conditions; it amounts at present to little more than a fumbling towards principles, and at best it depends on the accidents of litigation.[12]

---

[7] See Jaffe, "Research and Reform in English Administrative Law", [1968] P.L. 119; Wade, "Crossroads in Administrative Law" (1968) Current Legal Problems, at p. 75, and counter arguments by Professor J. D. B. Mitchell and the present author at [1968] P.L. 201 and 212, with a further reply at [1969] P.L. 15.

[8] Such as *Conway* v. *Rimmer*, [1968] 1 All E.R. 874, [1968] A.C. 910 (*post*, p. 291) and, more noticeably, *Padfield* v. *Minister of Agriculture, Fisheries and Food*, [1968] 1 All E.R. 694; [1968] A.C. 997 (*post*, p. 136).

[9] See [1968] P.L. 212.

[10] Contrast with the cases in footnote 8, such cases as *Durayappah* v. *Fernando*, [1967] 2 All E.R. 152; [1967] 2 A.C. 337 and *Westminster Bank, Ltd.* v. *Minister of Housing and Local Government*, [1970] 1 All E.R. 734; [1971] A.C. 508, H.L. (*post*, p. 137). *Anisminic* v. *Foreign Compensation Commission*, [1969] 1 All E.R. 208; [1969] 2 A.C. 147 (*post*, p. 144) may also perhaps be categorised as falling within this group.

[11] The same theory of Parliamentary supremacy has not prevented the Canadian Federal Parliament from legislating in a similar field, when it passed the Bill of Rights in 1960.

[12] Thus, the unsatisfactory decision in *Pett* v. *Greyhound Racing Association* (*No. 2*), [1969] 2 All E.R. 221; [1970] 1 Q.B. 46 (*post*, p. 121) will remain where it was left by the decision of Lyell, J., as the Association changed their rules so as to permit legal representation before their domestic tribunal, an appeal against the decision has been settled out of court (see [1970] 1 All E.R. 243).

CHAPTER VI

REDRESS THROUGH THE COURTS

1. INTRODUCTION

As we have seen in an earlier Chapter, one of the main objects of administrative law is to provide a control over the administration by an outside agency strong enough to prevent injustice to the individual while leaving the administration adequate freedom to enable it to carry on efficient government. Traditionally the place of this "outside agency" has been filled in this country by the courts of law. This does not mean that the courts have had a roving commission to scrutinise and reverse or approve any and every decision of an administrative agency whenever a member of the public may claim that he is aggrieved thereby. Judicial review and the redress of grievances can be sought under the English legal system only in circumstances recognised by the law, and it is the purpose of this Chapter to examine those circumstances and the kinds of remedies offered to a subject aggrieved by some administrative act. First, however, it should be appreciated that those administrative acts which may give rise to complaints may be of different kinds.

An act of an administrative agency may be purely administrative or executive in character, or it may be of a legislative or a judicial nature or it may be a mixture of all three. Review by the courts of an act may be available on a number of different grounds, all of which may not be relevant to the facts of any particular case or within the terms of a particular statute. The nature of the remedy available and also the grounds on which that remedy may be granted, may well depend on the nature of the governmental function the particular exercise of which the court is asked to review. Thus, some remedies (especially *certiorari*[1]) are available only if the function in question is a judicial or "quasi-judicial" one. The essential nature of a judicial decision has been outlined in an earlier Chapter[2];

> "The word 'quasi', when prefixed to a legal term, generally means that the thing which is described by the word, has some of the legal attributes denoted and connoted by the legal term, but that it has not all of them".[3]

A quasi-judicial decision has therefore been described by the Donoughmore Committee as one where there is a dispute and a process involving the ascertainment of facts and possibly also legal argument, but where administrative action takes the place of the normal determination based on the evidence adduced and the relevant legal rules. A judicial

---

[1] *Post*, p. 178.
[2] Chapter I, *ante*, p. 12.
[3] Donoughmore Report, at p. 73.

decision may be the result of a hearing before a court or before a tribunal,[4] but if administrative policy is material in the decision process, the resulting decision cannot be a judicial one. Fortunately, substantial consequences rarely flow from this somewhat artificial distinction between "judicial" and "quasi-judicial"[5]; *certiorari*, or an action for a declaration, will lie in respect of either if there has been a breach of the *ultra vires* doctrine, or, as we shall see, a failure to observe the principles of "natural justice".[6] Professor Wade has pointed out[7] that a quasi-judicial decision is essentially a part of the administrative process; the real difficulty is to distinguish such a decision from one which is purely administrative.[8] A true administrative decision will be subject to review on more restricted grounds than a judicial one; if the decision is "quasi-judicial", the principles of natural justice will be applied only to the judicial part of that decision. However, as we shall see, in recent decisions the distinction between "quasi-judicial" and "administrative" has also become indistinct.

The kind of review that may be available, and the nature of the remedy provided by the courts, will also vary according to the facts of the case and the terms of the appropriate statutory provisions. The statute within the framework of which the administrative agency is for the time being operating may, for instance, make express provision for an appeal to lie against the agency's decisions. Apart from such provisions, however, the High Court may be prepared to offer some remedy in the particular case. This Chapter will therefore be concerned first with the general principles on which such judicial review may be obtained, and second, with the various kinds of remedies that may be available. The whole subject operates within a statutory framework, but statutes are construed in accordance with recognised principles of the common law. In particular, if a remedy exists at common law, that remedy will be deemed to have been taken away only where the statute clearly and expressly so provides.

2. JUSTIFICATION OF INTERVENTION BY THE COURTS

Apart from express statutory provisions, review by the courts of a decision of an administrative agency has always been based, in our legal system, on an allegation that the agency has exceeded its powers, has acted *ultra vires*. This is fundamentally a simple doctrine, based on the common law. All government power must be recognised by the law, especially where that power is exercised in some manner which affects

[4] As to the distinction between a court and a tribunal, see Chapter VII, *post*, p. 195.

[5] An appeal may in almost all cases be brought against a judicial decision, but statute may also provide for an appeal of some kind (possibly to some other kind of administrative agency; see *post*, p. 172) to lie from an administrative decision.

[6] *Post*, p. 115.

[7] "'Quasi-judicial' and its Background" (1949), 10 C.L.J. 216, at p. 227.

[8] A discretion whether or not to make a special development order vested in the Minister by s. 14 of the Town and Country Planning Act, 1962, was "an administrative, legislative power for the exercise of which the Minister was responsible to nobody but Parliament": *Essex County Council* v. *Minister of Housing and Local Government* (1967), 111 Sol. Jo. 635. A similar case, taken from housing legislation, is *Aristides* v. *Minister of Housing and Local Government*, [1970] 1 All E.R. 195.

adversely the property or the liberty of a subject, and that recognition is given only to power that emanates from a single source, the Queen in Parliament.[9] Breach of "natural justice" (as understood by the common law and to be hereafter explained), lack of jurisdiction, faulty procedure, bad faith, have all been put forward in certain contexts as justifications for judicial intervention, but all of these, in so far as they may be recognised by the courts, are really but specialised applications of the *ultra vires* doctrine; Parliament did not, and could not have intended to, confer power that could be exercised in such a manner as to flout "natural justice".[10] The various aspects of *ultra vires* can nevertheless be conveniently considered in this manner, if for no other reason than that this traditional treatment enables the principles established in the many decisions of the courts to be considered in an orderly fashion. It is in this field of the extent of the powers of government that the courts have a traditional and important part to play in the control of administrative agencies.

> "Their task is to contain administrative activity within the bounds of delegated power: to apply to administrative action the test of 'legality'."[11]

It must first be appreciated that the decisions of an administrative agency in respect of which judicial review is sought may themselves be of various kinds. Thus, a local authority, a Minister or an independent public corporation, may have made a formal order, such as a compulsory purchase order, have granted or refused a licence or certificate, or imposed conditions in a licence, or they may have decided to expend public money on some project to which exception is taken. The decision questioned may be one of a large number of petty administrative acts, from the writing of a letter or the publication of minutes containing allegedly defamatory material,[12] to the alleged breach of a contract involving high Government policy.[13] Again, the act in question may be administrative in nature, or it may be "quasi-judicial"[14], it may be a judicial decision of an administrative tribunal such as a furnished houses rent tribunal,[15] or a legislative act such as the making of a byelaw by a local authority or a statutory corporation, or the giving of general or particular instructions to local authorities in Ministerial circulars or memoranda, which may themselves be a form of delegated or sub-delegated legislation.[16]

The principles according to which the courts are prepared to apply the *ultra vires* doctrine and review the exercise of the administrative,

---

[9] The prerogative is the only exception but this is now very considerably reduced in extent by statute (Chapter II), *ante*, p. 41.

[10] "The justice of the Common law will supply the omission of the legislature" said BYLES, J., in *Cooper* v. *Wandsworth Board of Works* (1863), 14 C.B. N.S. 180, at p. 194.

[11] "Judicial Review and the Rule of Law", a historical account by L. L. Jaffe and Edith G. Henderson, at (1956), 72 L.Q.R. 345 (see p. 346).

[12] As in *De Buse* v. *McCarty*, [1942] 1 All E.R. 19; [1942] 1 K.B. 156.

[13] See, for example, *Rederiaktiebolaget Amphitrite* v. *R.*, [1921] 3 K.B. 500.

[14] *Ante*, p. 111. This will depend on the characterisation ascribed to the administrative act by the reviewing court. Thus, a decision of an interim development authority under the Town Planning Act, 1925, was held to be "quasi-judicial", in *R.* v. *Hendon R.D.C., ex parte Chorley*, [1933] 1 K.B. 696 (and see *post*, p. 122).

[15] Under Part VII of the Rent Act, 1968; see Chapter VIII, *post*, p. 243.

[16] Chapter IV, *ante*, p. 77.

judicial or legislative acts of an administrative agency may be classified as follows[17]:

(a) Breach of the principles of "natural justice";
(b) Excess of powers (or "substantive" *ultra vires*);
(c) Errors of procedure (or "procedural" *ultra vires*);
(d) Errors of law;
(e) Failure to perform a duty;
(f) Bad faith or abuse of power, in the sense of using a power in a meaning other than that contemplated in the enabling statute.

There is no general heading, it may be noted, to the effect that an act of the administration will be avoided if it is within the power granted by the statute, but none the less unreasonable. In France the organ of review of administrative decisions is itself part of the administration, as the work is undertaken by the Conseil d'Etat, assisted since 1954 by the local administrative courts.[18] In spite of, or perhaps because of,[19] this intimate link between the supervising or reviewing tribunal and the administration, the onus of proof in the French system is always on the administration. *"L'Etat, c'est un honnête homme"*; and *"l'administré"* is presumed to be in the right until the contrary has been established; the agencies must be prepared to justify their acts. In England, however, the procedure of judicial review follows the ordinary pattern of civil proceedings; the person contesting the validity of the administrative act is a plaintiff, and therefore the burden of establishing a case against the administration rests on him. For the same reason, he will have to bring his case within the terms of an accepted cause of action and ask for a remedy provided by the law.

There is also in this country no positive constitutional justification for judicial review. The citizen cannot appeal to any fundamental law other than such remedies as may be granted or recognised by statute or the common law. If Parliament provides that a citizen's property rights are to be taken away or that his liberty is to be infringed "without due process of law", he has no legal cause for complaint. In the United States of America, however, it is a basic principle of the federal constitution that no person shall

> "be deprived of life, liberty or property without due process of law,"

and also no State in the Federation may

> "deprive any person of life, liberty or property, without due process of law."[20]

In this country there is also no general statutory code as there is in some other countries, affording rights of judicial review in certain well

[17] Compare the scope of judicial review provided for in s. 10 (c) of the American Administrative Procedure Act, 1946 (Appendix, *post*, p. 460). Delay on the part of an agency is the only ground that does not feature in English law; this may, however, amount to "maladministration" and so come within the purview of the Parliamentary Commissioner for Administration; Chapter V, *ante*, p. 98.

[18] As to the local courts, see "The Reform of the French Administrative Courts", by L. Neville Brown, at (1959), 22 M.L.R. 357.

[19] Hamson, *Executive Discretion and Judicial Control* (Hamlyn Lectures), particularly at pp. 45 *et seq.*, and Brown and Garner, *French Administrative Law*, 2nd Edn., Chapter 9.

[20] See the Fifth and Fourteenth Amendments to the Constitution.

defined circumstances.[21] If, for example, it can be shown that an inferior tribunal or inquiry has come to its conclusions otherwise than in accordance with "substantial evidence", section 7 (c) of the American Administrative Procedure Act, 1946, accords a right to judicial review of the decision to any person aggrieved. However, as in the U.S.A., it can be said in this country that

> "the silence of [the legislature] is not to be construed as indicating a legislative intent to preclude review."[22]

There is no "Bill of Rights" as in Canada in the light of which subsequent statutes must be construed[23]; the courts in this country have to be content with the principles of construction spelt out from previous cases.[1]

We must now consider the circumstances mentioned above in which *ultra vires* will be recognised in this country as justifying judicial review of an administrative decision.

3. THE SCOPE OF JUDICIAL REVIEW

(a) The principles of natural justice.—"Natural justice" has meant many things to many writers, lawyers and systems of law, including an approximate synonym for divine law, and also a form of the *ius gentium* or the common law of nations.[2] The common lawyers, however, have used the expression "natural justice" with surprising precision of meaning, as referring to two important but narrow principles only, namely *audi alteram partem* ("hear both sides"), and *nemo judex in causa sua potest* ("no one can be judge in his own cause").

> "The phrase ['natural justice'] is of course used only in a popular sense and must not be taken to mean there is any justice natural among men. Among most savages there is no such thing as justice in the modern sense."[3]

The common law, moreover, originally applied these principles only in the comparatively narrow context of the decision-making process of a court of law.[4] Lord HALDANE, L.C., said in the famous case of *Local Government Board* v. *Arlidge*,[5] to which we will return later:

> "When the duty of deciding an appeal is imposed, those whose duty it is to decide it must act judicially. They must deal with the question referred to them without bias, and they must give to each of the parties the opportunity of adequately presenting the case made. The decision must be come to in the spirit and with the sense of responsibility of a tribunal whose duty it is to mete out justice."

---

[21] The Administrative Procedure Act, 1946 of the Federal legislature (as amended) goes some way towards providing such a code in the U.S.A. (see Appendix, I. *post*, p. 460).

[22] Schwarz, *An Introduction to American Administrative Law*, at p. 163.

[23] See Laskin, "*Canada's Bill of Rights*", (1962) 11 I.C.L.Q. 519.

[1] *Ante*, Chapter III, p. 49.

[2] Dowrick, *Justice according to the English Common Lawyers* (1961), Chapter 4.

[3] *Per* MAUGHAM, J., in *Maclean* v. *Workers' Union*, [1929] 1 Ch. 602, at p. 624.

[4] *Natural Justice*, by H. H. Marshall (1959), Chapters 2 and 3.

[5] [1915] A.C. 120, at p. 132, and see *post*, p. 118.

Later in the development of the common law these principles came to be applied also to the decisions of administrative bodies acting judicially[6] whereby the royal courts exercised a supervisory jurisdiction over them, primarily by means of the former prerogative writs.[7]

The justification for the application of the natural justice principles to administrative bodies is based on the *ultra vires* doctrine; the court will not readily believe that Parliament intends an administrative agency to come to a decision in such a manner as would flout natural justice; therefore if a particular body does so act, it must be exceeding the powers conferred on it by Parliament; as such the concept of "natural justice" is virtually an invention of the common law.[8] The only circumstances, it is submitted, in which the courts have recognised that the rules of natural justice need not be observed, are themselves situations where there can be no question of any excess of statutory powers.[9] It has been suggested,[10] that the idea of natural justice, as understood in this sense, "contains the very kernel of the problem of administrative justice"; it is this practice of insisting on observance of the principles of natural justice that has been used by the courts to exercise such inherent control as there may be over administrative agencies. Moreover, it has been pointed out[11] that whenever a litigant is asking for a review of an administrative decision because of an alleged failure to observe the principles of natural justice, he can establish his case by any reliable evidence, and he is not confined to the face of the record.

We shall now consider the meaning of each of these two principles, as understood and applied by the common law, and discuss the kind of administrative agencies that must apply the principles, the circumstances in which they must be observed, and the situations to which they do not apply.

(1) *The audi alteram partem principle.*—This aspect of natural justice, to the effect that the "judge" must hear both sides, must give each party a chance to state his case, and that any person who will or may be affected by an administrative decision has a right to his "day in court", is an essential characteristic of any legal process. One of the earliest cases in which the principle was expressly formulated is *R.* v. *Cambridge University*[12] where the Court of King's Bench declared a decision of the University of Cambridge to be a nullity, because in depriving Dr. Bentley of his degrees, they had not first given him an opportunity of appearing before them and stating his case, although Dr. Bentley had first contemptuously put aside originating process and

6 See Donoughmore Report, p. 73; "a quasi-judicial decision is one which has some of the attributes of a judicial decision but not all", and *ante*, p. 111.

7 *Post*, p. 177.

8 Parliament has recently recognised its existence: see Foreign Compensation Act 1969, s. 3 (10).

9 *Post*, p. 125.

10 Professor H. W. R. Wade, in *Administrative Law*, 3rd Edn., at p. 172, who suggests that the rules of natural justice rest on a wider basis than *ultra vires*, being dependent on the ideas of the common law.

11 *Per* Lord PEARCE, in *Maradana Mosque* (*Board of Trustees*) v. *Badi-ud-Din* ***Mahmud***, [1966] 1 All E.R. 545, at p. 550.

12 (1723), 1 Str. 557.

then accused the Vice-Chancellor of the University of foolish behaviour (*stulte egit*). The general principle is not usually applied in an administrative context so as to require a full investigation by the deciding body, but rather that the decision must not be arrived at until the "judge" has heard *both* sides; he must not be content to consider, as did Cambridge University, only one point of view before coming to a decision.

The "judge" must

> "hear both sides and must not hear one side in the absence of the other"

said GREER, L.J., in *Errington* v. *Minister of Health*[13]; therefore once an order made by a local authority has been submitted to a Minister for confirmation in accordance with statutory procedure, the Minister will be offending against the rules of natural justice if at that stage[14] he discusses the matter informally with representatives of the local authority and in the absence of the objectors.

The nature of the principle of *audi alteram partem* may thus be explained as a "right to a hearing", but this also includes a right to be informed of the case one is to meet at the hearing. Thus, in *Kanda* v. *Government of the Federation of Malaya*,[15] a police officer whose conduct was being investigated, was held to be entitled to see a copy of a report of proceedings before a preliminary inquiry. The right to have notice of the case and of the time and place of the hearing includes a requirement that the notice given must be reasonable.[16]

In the United States, the requirement of a fair hearing in Federal matters is stated with some particularity in section 7 (c) of the Administrative Procedure Act, 1946,[17] which provides that

> "every party shall have the right to present his case or defense by oral or documentary evidence, to submit rebuttal evidence, and to conduct such cross-examination as may be required for a full and true disclosure of the facts."

In this country, however, the nature of the right to a hearing is not so precisely defined. It is on the one hand clear that an administrative agency, whether it be a local authority, a tribunal or a statutory inquiry, when formulating a decision in circumstances to which the principles of natural justice are applied, need not observe the strict procedure of a court of justice. In a leading case,[18] where the Board of Education had determined a dispute between a board of school managers and the local education authority, LORD LOREBURN, L.C., stated:

> "In such cases the Board of Education will have to ascertain the law and also to ascertain the facts. I need not add that in doing either they must act in good faith and fairly listen to both sides, for that is a duty lying upon every one who decides anything. But I do not think they are bound to treat such a question as though it were a trial. They have no power to administer an oath, and need not examine witnesses. They can obtain information in any way they

---

[13] [1935] 1 K.B. 249, at p. 268.

[14] He is at liberty to discuss a draft order before the local authority have made it, as he is then acting administratively, not judicially: *Frost* v. *Minister of Health*, [1935] 1 K.B. 286, and *cf. post*, p. 121.

[15] [1962] A.C. 322.

[16] A mere five days was "wholly unreasonable", said DONALDSON, J., in *Lee* v. *Secretary of State* (1967), 111 Sol. Jo. 756.

[17] Appendix, I, *post*, p. 460.

[18] *Board of Education* v. *Rice*, [1911] A.C. 179, at p. 182.

think best, always giving a fair opportunity to those who are parties in the controversy for correcting or contradicting any relevant statement prejudicial to their view."

Thus, where a member of the public has a statutory right to appeal to a particular Minister, that Minister is not bound to see the appellant personally, and the Minister is entitled to determine the appeal in such manner as he sees fit, provided he observes the principles of natural justice. Proceedings before an administrative body need not follow in all respects those before a court of law, and even if the "judge" questions witnesses in the absence of the "accused", this does not necessarily involve a breach of the principles of natural justice.[19] In the leading case of *Local Government Board* v. *Arlidge,*[20] Viscount HALDANE, L.C., whilst referring to the passage from *Board of Education* v. *Rice,* above cited, said:[21]

> "I concur in this view of the position of an administrative body to which the decision of a question in dispute between parties has been entrusted. The result of its inquiry must, as I have said, be taken, in the absence of directions in the statute to the contrary, to be intended to be reached by its ordinary procedure . . . to insist that he [the Minister] and other members of the Board should do everything personally, would be to impair his efficiency. Unlike a judge in a court, he is not only at liberty but is compelled to rely on the assistance of his staff."

Again, in the same case[22] Lord SHAW OF DUNFERMLINE observed that although an administrative agency must reach

> "just ends by just means, . . . it must be the master of its own procedure."

This point was followed in *Miller* v. *Minister of Housing and Local Government,*[23] a case concerning a town planning inquiry, where the inspector admitted in evidence a letter from a person who did not attend the inquiry and which was not verified on oath. Lord DENNING, M.R. said[24]:

> "Hearsay is clearly admissible before a tribunal. No doubt in admitting it, the tribunal must observe the rules of natural justice, but this does not mean that it must be tested by cross-examination. It only means that the tribunal must give the other side a fair opportunity of commenting on it and of contradicting it . . . the inspector here did that."

Therefore the court refused to interfere with the Minister's decision.

It is then clear that a right to a hearing is not necessarily a right to a personal hearing before the person who is to make the decision. Sometimes the "appellant" may not have a right to any oral hearing; this will depend on the terms of the statute and the circumstances of the case. The complaint in *Cooper* v. *Wandsworth Board of Works*[25] was that the defendant local authority had commenced demolishing the plaintiff's building under a statutory power vested in them without

[19] *Ceylon University* v. *Fernando,* [1960] 1 All E.R. 631.
[20] [1915] A.C. 120.
[21] *Ibid.,* at p. 133.
[22] *Ibid.,* at p. 138.
[23] [1968] 2 All E.R. 633; [1968] 1 W.L.R. 992.
[24] [1968] 2 All E.R. at p. 634.
[25] (1863), 14 C.B.N.S. 180.

first affording him an opportunity of giving his views on the matter, but this did not necessarily mean that the plaintiff was entitled to an oral hearing. A similar decision was arrived at in *R.* v. *Housing Appeal Tribunal*;[26] because the statute did not entitle the appellant to insist on an oral hearing, this did not mean he was not entitled to any hearing.

In *Ridge* v. *Baldwin*[1] the plaintiff, a former Chief Constable of Brighton, had been prosecuted but acquitted on certain charges of conspiracy. In the course of that trial the presiding judge had made certain observations animadverting against the plaintiff's character as a senior police officer, and a number of damaging facts had been admitted by him in the course of the trial, all of which had been fully reported in the national newspapers. Immediately after the trial, the local watch committee summarily dismissed the plaintiff from his post as Chief Constable. He appealed to the Home Secretary under the Police Regulations, and his appeal was dismissed. In proceedings for a declaration he claimed that his dismissal was wrongful, in that the watch committee had not given him an opportunity of appearing before them. STREATFEILD, J., at first instance held that the committee were bound to observe the principles of natural justice, but that there was here no need for any further hearing, as the committee had been made fully aware of all the facts from the newspapers reports. This argument was not accepted by the higher courts, as there was no evidence before the court whether the members of the committee had read the newspaper reports, whether these reports contained such arguments as the plaintiff might have been able to adduce in support of his conduct, or indeed whether they were substantially accurate. In the Court of Appeal it was held[2] that in the circumstances of the case, there was no need to comply with the principles of natural justice; under the powers vested in the watch committee by the Municipal Corporations Act, 1882, they were acting administratively or taking executive action. However, in the House of Lords,[3] the decision of the Court of Appeal was reversed and a declaration was granted, to the effect that the dismissal of the plaintiff by the watch committee was a nullity, as the *audi alteram partem* principle had not been observed.[4] In the course of a long and important judgment Lord REID observed[5]:

> "The principle *audi alteram partem* goes back many centuries in our law and appears in a multitude of judgments of judges of the highest authority. In modern times opinions have sometimes been expressed to the effect that natural justice is so vague as to be practically meaningless. But I would regard these as tainted by the perennial fallacy that because something cannot be cut and dried or nicely weighed or measured therefore it does not exist."

Dealing with the same difficulty, the "certain vagueness" about natural justice, Lord HODSON said in the same case[6]:

---

[26] [1920] 3 K.B. 334.
[1] [1961] 2 All E.R. 523.
[2] [1962] 1 All E.R. 834.
[3] [1963] 2 All E.R. 66.
[4] *Per* Lords REID, MORRIS of BORTH-Y-GEST, HODSON and DEVLIN, Lord EVERSHED dissenting.
[5] At p. 71.
[6] At p. 114.

"No one, I think, disputes that three features of natural justice stand out—(1) the right to be heard by an unbiassed tribunal, (2) the right to have notice of charges of misconduct, (3) the right to be heard in answer to those charges."

The American system, dependent on the Constitution and the Act of 1946, is more precise than these features of the *audi alteram partem* principle in our law. Thus, it has been said in the U.S. Supreme Court, that:

"Adjudicatory action cannot be validly taken by any tribunal, whether judicial or administrative, except upon a hearing wherein each party shall have opportunity to know of the claims of his opponent, to hear the evidence introduced against him, to cross-examine witnesses, to introduce evidence in his own behalf, and to make argument. This is a requirement of the due process clause of the Fifth Amendment of the Constitution."[7]

It can now, however, be confidently stated that even in our legal system the party concerned must be timely informed of the substance of the case he has to meet which must be reasonably clearly formulated,[8] and he must be given a reasonable opportunity of presenting his case,[9] either orally, or possibly (as we have seen above) by written representations. In *General Medical Council* v. *Spackman*[10] the appellant Council had struck the respondent off the medical register, because he had been found by the Divorce Court to have committed adultery with a woman with whom he stood in a professional relationship. When the Council considered the matter in proceedings under section 29 of the Medical Act, 1858 (in the course of which they were required to make "due inquiry"), they refused the respondent leave to call evidence that had not been before the Divorce Court. In proceedings for *certiorari* to quash the decision of the Council, Lord WRIGHT in the House of Lords observed[11].

"The question of a failure of 'natural justice' is what is to be considered in this appeal, but before considering the meaning of these words, I must first observe that they can in this case be properly taken as a description of what the council has to do, namely, to make 'due inquiry', which under the statute is the governing criterion, that is an independent inquiry by the council as the body responsible for its own decision."

In *Arlidge's case* (*supra*), HAMILTON, L.J., in the Court of Appeal[12] had described "contrary to natural justice" as being an expression "sadly lacking in precision". Commenting on this remark, Lord WRIGHT said in *Spackman's case*[13]:

"So it may be, and perhaps, it is not desirable to attempt to force it into any procrustean bed, but the statements which I have quoted may, at least, be taken to emphasize the essential requirements that the tribunal should be impartial and that the medical practitioner who is impugned should be given a full and fair opportunity of being heard."

---

7 *Philadelphia Co.* v. *Securities and Exchange Commission* 175 Fed. 2d. 808 (1948), at p. 817, cited by Schwartz in *An Introduction to American Administrative Law*, at p. 109.

8 *Sloan* v. *General Medical Council*, [1970] 2 All E.R. 686; [1970] 1 W.L.R. 1130, n.

9 See, for example, Lord HODSON in *Ridge* v. *Baldwin*, [1964] A.C. 40 and *Kanda* v. *Government of Federation of Malaya*, [1962] A.C. 322; [1962] 2 W.L.R. 1153. These points are commonly covered now in procedural rules made for administrative tribunals; see Chapter VII, *post*, p. 206.

10 [1943] 2 All E.R. 337; [1943] A.C. 627.

11 At p. 640.

12 [1914] 1 K.B. 160, at p. 199.

13 At p. 644.

Therefore in this case, the application for *certiorari* was granted and the decision of the General Medical Council quashed, there having been a breach of the principles of natural justice.[14]

As a general principle also one party should be given an opportunity, if not to cross-examine the other, at least to comment on the material put forward by his opponents,[15] and to know what they have to say.[16] Normally, in any serious case the parties should be allowed legal representation by the tribunal if they wish,[17] but if rules of procedure regulating the conduct of hearings before the tribunal expressly exclude a right to legal representation, this would apparently be invalid in the absence of express statutory authority. In the absence of such express provisions the tribunal should have a discretion whether or not to allow representation.[18] If the tribunal, exercising its discretion, then denies legal representation, this may be acceptable, depending in some measure on the degree of sophistication shown by the tribunal.[19] A refusal to grant an adjournment so that the person concerned may attend the hearing amounts to a breach of natural justice,[20] and a first hearing where natural justice is not observed is not cured by a properly conducted hearing on appeal.[1]

There is no general requirement for any judicial or quasi-judicial decision to be accompanied by adequate reasons, although in many cases the statutory requirement of section 12 of the Tribunals and Inquiries Act, 1971 will apply.[2] Where reasons are given, it should be clear that the material on which the "judge" comes to his conclusion has *some* probative value,[3] although our courts are not yet, apparently, prepared to go so far as section 10 (b) of the American Administrative Procedure Act, 1946, which entitles the court to review a decision if it was unsupported by substantial evidence. Whereas an American federal court of review is prepared to examine the whole record of the proceedings before the administrative tribunal to ascertain whether the

---

[14] This case still provides, it is submitted, an instructive application of the principles of natural justice, although under s. 33 (2) of the Medical Act, 1956, the Disciplinary Committee would be bound by a finding of fact in previous matrimonial proceedings.

[15] *Hoggard* v. *Worsbrough U.D.C.*, [1962] 1 All E.R. 468; [1962] 2 Q.B. 93. The old case of *Osgood* v. *Nelson* (1872), L.R. 5 H.L. 636, had held that where opportunities for cross-examination were in fact given, the reviewing court would not interfere with the decision of the tribunal.

[16] This was really the point in *Ceylon University* v. *Fernando*, [1960] 1 All E.R. 631; [1960] 1 W.L.R. 223, where the accused was informed of the substance of the evidence given by his "opponent".

[17] *Pett* v. *Greyhound Racing Assn.* (*No. 1*), [1968] 2 All E.R. 545; [1968] 2 W.L.R. 1471 (C.A.).

[18] *Enderby Town Football Club* v. *Football Association, Ltd.*, [1971] 1 All E.R. 215; [1971] Ch. 591. On legal representation "before tribunals generally", see Alder, "Representation before Tribunals" [1972] P.L. 278.

[19] *Pett* v. *Greyhound Racing Assn.* (*No. 2*), [1969] 2 All E.R. 221; [1969] 2 W.L.R. 1228.

[20] *Rose* v. *Humbles*, [1972] 1 All E.R. 314; [1972] 1 W.L.R. 33.

[1] *Leary* v. *National Union of Vehicle Builders*, [1970] 2 All E.R. 713; [1971] Ch. 34; but contrast *Furnell* v. *Whangarei Schools Board*, [1973] 1 All E.R. 400; [1973] 2 W.L.R. 92.

[2] *Post*, p. 146.

[3] *R.* v. *Deputy Industrial Injuries Commissioner, ex parte Moore*, [1965] 1 All E.R. 81, at p. 87; [1965] 1 Q.B. 456, at p. 476, *per* WILLMER, L.J., and see also *Armah* v. *Government of Ghana*, [1966] 3 All E.R. 177; [1968] A.C. 192.

findings of fact support the decision, the English courts will merely satisfy itself that there was *some* evidence that tended towards that result. If there was no evidence at all which could have supported the decision, the court, even in England, is obliged to quash the decision.[4]

(2) *Freedom from bias.*—Not only is a person affected by an administrative decision entitled to have his case heard by the agency seised with its determination, but he may also insist on his case being heard by a fair judge, one free from "bias". Bias in this context has usually meant that the adjudicator must have no financial interest in the matter under dispute, but it is not necessarily so limited, and allegations of bias have been upheld in circumstances where there was no question of any financial interest.[5]

One of the earliest decisions recognising this principle is the famous *Dr. Bonham's case.*[6] Here a doctor of medicine was summoned before a Board of the College of Physicians, and fined and imprisoned for contempt because he had failed to take out a licence to practise from the College. Coke, when the case came before him on an action for false imprisonment, held that the Board had no power to fine Dr. Bonham, because the Board was a judge in its own cause (as half the fine would be payable to the Board) and this would be

> "against common right and reason, repugnant or impossible to be performed; the common law will control it, and adjudge such act to be void".[7]

As Professor de Smith has shown[8] the rule that a judge must be free from bias was developed in our legal system through the supervisory jurisdiction of the High Court over inferior judges. By the present century it had become clear that an administrative tribunal or other authority (for example a Ministry inspector at an inquiry) acting judicially[9] must be free from bias and must not be a judge in his own cause.

Thus, in *R.* v. *Hendon R.D.C., ex parte Chorley,*[10] an application was considered by the town planning interim development authority under the Town Planning Act, 1925, for permission to carry out certain development. One of the members of the council was an estate agent acting for the applicants, and although it does not appear that he took part in the discussion, he was present at the meeting when it was decided to approve the application. As a grant of permission would have safeguarded the right of the applicants to claim compensation under the statutory provisions then in force in certain circumstances, and

---

[4] *Coleen Properties, Ltd.* v. *Minister of Housing and Local Government,* [1971] 1 All E.R. 1049; [1971] 1 W.L.R. 433.

[5] *R.* v. *Sunderland Justices,* [1901] 2 K.B. 357; and see *R.* v. *Abingdon Justices, ex parte Cousins* (1964), 108 Sol. Jo. 840, where it was held that a magistrate should not have adjudicated in a case where the defendant was one of his former pupils at a school of which he was headmaster.

[6] (1610), 8 Co. Rep. 107.

[7] Mr. Treitel has pointed out in a helpful review of an earlier edition of this book ([1969] P.L. at p. 185) that by "act" here, Coke meant that an Act of Parliament which allowed the Board so to behave would be void; a view that would not be adopted by a modern Court.

[8] *Judicial Review of Administrative Action,* 3rd Edn., at pp. 215–218.

[9] *I.e.,* in a manner "like" a judge; see Donoughmore Report, at p. 73.

[10] [1933] 2 K.B. 696.

the councillor was not free from apparent bias, the High Court granted a *certiorari* on the application of a neighbouring landowner, and quashed the decision.[11] It should be noticed that the *appearance* of bias is regarded as seriously by the supervising court as is actual bias; the judge who appears to have or who has a bias may have the most excellent and upright motives and may not in fact allow his judicial discretion to be impaired in any way by the vitiating "interest", but the courts will still find there has been a breach of natural justice:

> "it is of fundamental importance that justice should not only be done but should manifestly and undoubtedly be seen to be done"

said Lord HEWART, C.J., in *R.* v. *Sussex Justices, ex parte McCarthy*.[12] Thus, a decision of a rent tribunal was quashed by *certiorari* when it appeared that the chairman of the tribunal was a solicitor who lived with his father, the father being a tenant of a flat owned by landlords who were an associate company of the landlords in the case heard by the tribunal.[13] The chairman's firm had also acted for tenants who had been in dispute with their landlords on matters similar to those in question before the tribunal.

> "In considering whether there was a real likelihood of bias, the court does not look at the mind of the justice himself or at the mind of the chairman of the tribunal, or whoever it may be, who sits in a judicial capacity. It does not look to see if there was a real likelihood that he would, or did, in fact favour one side at the expense of the other. The court looks at the impression which would be given to other people. Even if he was as impartial as could be, nevertheless if right-minded persons would think that, in the circumstances, there was a real likelihood of bias on his part, then he should not sit."[14]

In *Dimes* v. *Grand Junction Canal*[15] the House of Lords set aside a decision of the former Lord Chancellor, Lord COTTENHAM, when it appeared that he was a substantial shareholder in a company which was a party before the court. The decision was on an appeal upholding a judgment of the Vice-Chancellor; the House of Lords agreed with

---

[11] There are a number of difficulties about this case that do not all appear in the report. In the first place, s. 22 of the Municipal Corporations Act, 1882 (the predecessor of ss. 93–98 of the Local Government Act, 1972), in such a case required a councillor to disclose any pecuniary interest and to refrain from voting; this was apparently here ignored (see *post*, p. 378). Secondly, as there was a question of compensation involved, it was apparently taken for granted that a decision of an interim development authority was sufficiently "quasi-judicial" in nature to be reviewable by *certiorari* (see *post*, p. 179). It is by no means clear that a similar attitude would be taken by the courts at the present time towards a decision of a local planning authority on an application for planning permission under the Town and Country Planning Act, 1971. Thirdly, it is not clear what was the interest of the plaintiff in this case (Lord Chorley) which was sufficient to give him adequate *locus standi* to take *certiorari* proceedings (*post*, p. 181). He would certainly not have been a "person aggrieved" such as would entitle him to appeal to the Minister if the decision had been taken under the Town and Country Planning Act, 1971, (contrast the declaration case of *Gregory* v. *London Borough of Camden*, [1966] 2 All E.R. 196; [1966] 1 W.L.R. 899, where *Chorley's case* was not followed, and see also the "Chalk-pit affair", Chapter VII, *post*, p. 221).

[12] [1924] 1 K.B. 256, at p. 259.

[13] *Metropolitan Properties Co. (F.G.C.), Ltd.* v. *Lannon*, [1968] 3 All E.R. 304; [1969] 1 Q.B. 577. See also Professor H. W. R. Wade at (1969), 85 L.Q.R. 23.

[14] [1968] 3 All E.R. at p. 310, *per* Lord DENNING, M.R.

[15] (1852), 3 H.L.C. 759.

the Vice-Chancellor and so the result was the same, but they nevertheless quashed Lord COTTENHAM'S decision, although as Lord CAMPBELL said:

> "No one can suppose that Lord COTTENHAM could be, in the remotest degree, influenced by the interest that he had in this concern."

A person acting as a "judge" must not take part in the "prosecution" of the case. Therefore, when a police officer's conduct was being investigated by a watch committee, he was entitled to a declaration that the decision was arrived at in a manner contrary to natural justice when it was established that the chief constable of the force (who had preferred complaints against the plaintiff) was sitting with members of the watch committee throughout the hearing.[16]

In certain circumstances statutory provisions require some specified action to be taken when bias is present. Thus, a justice of the peace may not act in connection with intoxicating liquor licences in any matter in which he has a pecuniary interest, but failure to comply with this rule does not affect the validity of any proceedings in which an interested "justice may have taken part".[17] Where a statutory provision of this kind is applicable, the common law rule that enables the decision to be impeached if there has been apparent bias, is excluded by the terms of the statute.[18] Nevertheless, the courts will not refuse to quash a decision where the licensing justices are shown to have had actual bias in the particular matter coming before them.[19] Somewhat similarly, a member of a local authority is required to disclose any pecuniary interest he may have in any matter which comes before a meeting of a council or committee at which he is present; he must also leave the meeting unless he is invited by the other members to remain, and in any event he may not take part in the discussion or vote on the matter in which he is interested. The statute provides neither that a decision arrived at in contravention of this section shall be invalidated, nor that such a decision shall not be so invalidated.[20] This does not, however, mean that the common law freedom from bias rule applies to every decision of the local authority and that whenever there is a breach of the statute the decision is thereby invalidated. Such an interpretation would widen the application of the common law rule, and it is submitted that the rule can apply only to those local authority decisions which are of a judicial nature and which affect the rights of third parties.

The freedom from bias principle seems to be particularly vulnerable to statutory exclusion of judicial review (*post*, p. 154). Thus, in *Wilkinson* v. *Barking Corporation*[1] the Local Government (Superannuation) Acts provided that questions as to the entitlement of an

---

[16] *Cooper* v. *Wilson*, [1937] 2 All E.R. 726; [1937] 2 K.B. 309, and compare *Taylor* v. *National Union of Seamen*, [1967] 1 All E.R. 767. The same doctor should not be used twice at different stages of disciplinary proceedings, where his opinion is a vital factor: *Re Godden*, [1971] 3 All E.R. 20; [1971] 2 Q.B. 662. See also *Hannam* v. *Bradford Corporation*, [1970] 2 All E.R. 690; [1970] 1 W.L.R. 937.

[17] Licensing Act, 1953, s. 48 (5).

[18] *R.* v. *Barnsley Licensing Justices*, [1959] 2 All E.R. 635; [1959] 2 Q.B. 276.

[19] *R.* v. *Tempest* (1902), 86 L.T. 585.

[20] On this point, see Chapter XII, p. 381.

[1] [1948] 1 All E.R. 564; [1948] 1 K.B. 721.

employee of a local authority to a superannuation allowance were to be determined initially by the local authority, and on appeal by the Minister of Health. An action was brought asking for a declaration that decisions of the local authority and the Minister were void, as they had acted as judges in their own cause, both these bodies being required under the statute to make contributions to the superannuation fund out of which any allowance granted to the employee would be payable. The Court of Appeal were impressed with this argument, but decided that as the statute had made provision for this method of adjudication in the circumstances the courts were powerless to interfere with the Minister's decision. Again, in *Franklin* v. *Minister of Town and Country Planning*,[2] an attempt was made to quash a decision of the Minister to establish a new town at Stevenage under the New Towns Act, 1946, on the ground that the Minister had, in confirming his own order made under section 1 of the Act, acted as judge in his own cause and therefore contrary to the principles of natural justice. The House of Lords drew a line between the judicial and administrative functions of the Minister, holding that in deciding (after receiving a report on a local inquiry) to confirm his own order the Minister was not acting judicially but administratively and was taking a *policy* decision; therefore there was no question of his having to observe the principles of natural justice in the course of that process. As pointed out by Professor H. W. R. Wade,[3] however, the reasons given by the Court of Appeal for coming to the same decision in this case,[4] are greatly to be preferred, for they accepted the argument that the statute conferred the power of decision on the Minister, and that he had followed the prescribed procedure; therefore his action was in no sense open to criticism in the courts. This interpretation of the situation in *Franklin's case* follows the reasoning in *Wilkinson* v. *Barking Corporation* (*supra*) and is in accordance with general principle, in that it emphasises that the need to comply with the principles of natural justice depends upon the doctrine of *ultra vires*. However, there is no doubt that (apart from statutes above mentioned) "bias" or "interest" applies as a vitiating element only to a judicial decision, and where the decision process involves an element of application to policy, this principle of natural justice has no relevance to that element.[5]

The situation where by the terms of the statute a Minister is put into a position in which he becomes judge in his own cause, has been regarded with distaste in the United States. In the Administrative Procedure Act, 1946, an attempt has been made, in federal matters, to separate physically the process of adjudication on objections or representations made against some proposed policy, from the process of

---

[2] [1947] 2 All E.R. 289; [1948] A.C. 87.

[3] *Administrative Law*, 3rd Edn., pp. 182–185.

[4] [1947] 1 All E. R. 612. The procedure of the New Towns Act, 1946, in this respect is by no means exceptional; see, for example, the provisions of Part II of the First Schedule to the Acquisition of Land (Authorisation Procedure) Act, 1946, dealing with the confirmation of a compulsory purchase order made by a Minister. See also the Privy Council case of *Jeffs* v. *New Zealand Dairy Production and Marketing Board*, [1966] 3 All E.R. 863.

[5] See, for example, *Darlassis* v. *Minister of Education* (1954), 118 J.P. 452.

taking the policy decision itself. Where an objector or other interested party is entitled to a hearing, that hearing must be held before a "hearing officer" of the administrative agency concerned, who must be an individual different from the official responsible for formulating the policy appealed against. The hearing officer must himself propound a draft decision on the results of the hearing, which must be notified to the parties, and the final policy decision must take this draft into consideration.[6] In the outcome the final decision process rests in the same hands as it does in England, and in most corresponding cases the result may prove similar in both countries, but at least in the U.S.A. there is a greater appearance of justice.[7]

As with the *audi alteram partem*[8] principle, freedom from bias is a requirement applying to an authority acting in a judicial manner,[9] but compliance may be excluded by clear statutory provisions to that effect. Statutes may, as explained above, make provision for a special form of freedom from bias to be observed by other bodies or agencies acting administratively.

It is sometimes said that the "bias" rule may be waived by the person affected; he may agree to be judged by a prejudiced judge. The *audi alteram partem* rule, however, cannot be waived, in the sense that consent can never confer on a Court power to act outside its jurisdiction. But clearly a man who has a right to be heard need not exercise his right, and cannot complain if he has been afforded a proper opportunity of a hearing which he has chosen not to use;[10] similarly the man who agrees, knowing all the circumstances, to be heard by a prejudiced judge, cannot complain of a breach of natural justice.[11]

It should also be appreciated that a man may be judge in "his own cause" in many different circumstances. The most obvious case arises when the cause is also the judges' pecuniary interest[12] but the "interest" may merely amount to a real or apparent desire to further a particular policy,[13] or the interest may be a matter of family relationship or nepotism.[14] Prejudging the issue and deciding the matter in accordance with preconceived ideas may be described as a form of bias, but it would seem more logical to discuss this vitiating element under procedural *ultra vires* (see *post*, p. 138). The bias principle will also apply in the special context of elections, so that no candidate may be his

---

6 See American Administrative Procedure Act, 1946, ss. 7 and 8, Appendix I, *post* p. 460.

7 See also Schwartz & Wade, *Legal Control of Government*, at p. 247.

8 *Ante*, p. 116.

9 Subject only to exceptional statutory provisions applicable to particular administrative authorities, such as local authorities: Chapter XII, *post*, p. 381), and licensing, justices (*ante*, p. 124). These provisions, however, subsist in addition to and by way of supplementation of the common law principle.

10 Lack of notice may be waived by appearance at the hearing: *Re Carnao Exploration, Ltd.* (1964), 43 D.L.R. 3d. 755 (Can.).

11 See Professor H. W. R. Wade, at (1968), 84 L.Q.R. 108.

12 As in Lord COTTENHAM's case (*ante*), p. 123.

13 For example, a member of a local authority adjudicating as magistrate in a case where the local authority is responsible for the conduct of the prosecution. Other examples include the Minister in *Franklin* v. *Minister of Town and Country Planning* (*ante*).

14 See, *e.g.*, *R.* v. *Rand* (1866), L.R. 1 Q.B. 230.

own returning officer.[15] On the other hand, mere association or friendship with a party to proceedings in which the judge is adjudicating, will not normally be held to be sufficient to amount to bias, unless the circumstances show that bias was actually present.[16]

(3) *When must natural justice be observed?*—One answer to this important question may be phrased in the form "when the administration is required to act in a quasi-judicial manner". But so stated, the answer merely re-phrases the question; it has been said that the distinction between "administrative" and "judicial" is as elusive as the Scarlet Pimpernel.[17] It is clear—in so far as any principles in this branch of the law are clearly established—that judicial review on the grounds of a breach of natural justice will not apply if the decision is "purely" administrative. This aspect of the problem is discussed later;[18] here we will concentrate on the question at the head of this paragraph. Perhaps the answer should be phrased, "when the rights of an individual are involved". But even this is not totally satisfactory, for what is meant by "rights" in this context? It is clear that natural justice need not be observed in the course of the legislative process,[19] and it is also clear that if property rights are at stake, natural justice must be observed, as in the housing and slum clearance cases.[20] An alien, however, has no *right* to enter this country and therefore he cannot complain if he is deported by the Home Secretary without first being given a hearing[21]; on the other hand, it seems that a man has a "right to work", and therefore, when Mrs. Nagle was refused a licence by the Jockey Club on account of her sex and it was established that this meant she would be unable to follow her chosen occupation as a trainer of racehorses, the Court of Appeal held that this amounted to a breach of natural justice.[1]

Special difficulties arise in the employment situation. It seems reasonably clear that an employee may be dismissed by his employer without any prior observance of natural justice. If the dismissal was contrary to the terms of the contract, the appropriate remedy is an action for damages for unlawful dismissal, and the court will not review the decision to dismiss, or quash the decision on the ground that natural justice has not been observed. This seems to apply to private and public contracts of employment alike, for English law, unlike many Continental systems, has no special law of administrative contracts.[2]

---

[15] *Re Wolverhampton Borough Council's Aldermanic Election*, [1961] 3 All E.R. 446.
[16] *R.* v. *Barnsley Licensing Justices*, [1959] 2 All E.R. 635; [1959] 2 Q.B. 276.
[17] By PENNEL, J., in the Canadian case of *Voyager Explorations, Ltd.* v. *Ontario Securities Commission*, [1970] 1 Q. R. 237, at p. 242.
[18] *Post*, p. 165.
[19] *Bates* v. *Lord Hailsham of St. Marylebone*, [1972] 3 All E.R. 1019; [1972] 1 W.L.R. 1373; but in private bill legislation it seems that the process must be fair: *Pickin* v. *British Railways Board*, [1972] 2 All E.R. 923; [1973] Q.B. 219.
[20] *Errington* v. *Minister of Health*, [1935] 1 K.B. 249, *ante*, p. 117, is a good example.
[21] *Schmidt* v. *Home Office*, [1968] 3 All E.R. 795, *post*, and see *post*, p. 167.
[1] *Nagle* v. *Fielden*, [1966] 1 All E.R. 689; [1966] 2 W.L.R. 1027, *post*, p. 272. A case where the concept of natural justice was extended to include sexual discrimination.
[2] *Cf.* French *droit administratif*: see Brown and Garner, *French Administrative Law*, 2nd Edn., Chapter 8.

Thus in *Vidyodaya University of Ceylon* v. *Silva*,[3] a university professor was dismissed from his post without having been given an opportunity of being heard. *Certiorari* to quash the decision was refused by the Privy Council, as the case was treated as one of ordinary contract between master and servant.

Where there is some special feature in the employment contract, however, the courts may be able to arrive at a different result. Thus in *Ridge* v. *Baldwin*,[4] the dismissal of Mr. Ridge was effected not by the employer but by the watch committee, "a third" party to the contract of employment between the Crown and the police officer. Therefore the watch committee were in the position of a "judge" and had to observe natural justice. Similarly in *Fisher* v. *Jackson*,[5] the decision to dismiss a schoolmaster was entrusted to three vicars, who were required to act together and to observe natural justice.

In line with these authorities, *Malloch* v. *Aberdeen Corpn.*[6] also required natural justice to be observed. Here it was provided by the Public Schools (Scotland) Teachers Act, 1882 that when the local education authority were considering a complaint about the conduct of a schoolmaster employed by them, they must give at least three weeks notice to him of the meeting when it was proposed to take the matter into consideration. Due notice had been accordingly given to Mr. Malloch but he was not allowed to attend the meeting. The House of Lords declared that the consequent dismissal of Mr. Malloch was illegal because, in a case of this kind where the contractual power to dismiss was "reinforced" by a statutory provision of the present kind, it was clearly the intention of the state that a hearing should have been given; why else should there have been a requirement that Mr. Malloch had to be given notice?

Since the coming into operation of the Industrial Relations Act, 1971, an employee who is unfairly dismissed may appeal to an industrial tribunal, but this does not preclude the possibility of proceedings of the kind here described.[7]

Recent decisions seem to suggest that there is a category of situations in which natural justice does not apply, but where the courts will require the administration to be "fair". It is not yet entirely clear whether this "mini-natural justice" is a separate principle in itself, or whether it is in truth merely an example of requiring a lower standard of natural justice in these "administrative" decisions. Generally the language used in the decisions seems to suggest the former, but, in *Machin* v. *Football Association*,[8] Lord DENNING suggested that in the context of a domestic tribunal such as the disciplinary committee of the Football Association, the requirements of natural justice meant no more than that the committee must "act fairly".

---

[3] [1964] 3 All E.R. 865; [1965] 1 W.L.R. 77.

[4] [1963] 2 All E.R. 66; [1964] A.C. 40, *ante*, p. 119.

[5] [1891] 2 Ch. 84.

[6] [1971] 2 All E.R. 1278; [1971] 1 W.L.R. 1578.

[7] The industrial tribunal has no power to quash the "unfair" decision to dismiss, and the amount of compensation that may be awarded is limited. Moreover, proceedings before the tribunal must be commenced within four weeks.

[8] (1973), *The Times*, July 21.

In *Re K.* (*H*) (*an infant*),[9] the plaintiff, was not entitled to a hearing before he was made the subject of a deportation order, but the court said the immigration officer must act "fairly" and should have checked the plaintiff's story before rejecting it out of hand. Even where a tribunal could make only a preliminary decision, and where the plaintiff had a right to a full hearing at a later stage, nevertheless the tribunal at that preliminary stage had to be "fair" and at least let the plaintiff know an outline of the case he had to meet.[10] Even if a magistrate, when condemning food as being unfit for human consumption, was acting "administratively" he had to be "fair" and must not hear part of the case in the absence of the owner of the food being condemned.[11]

In *Re Liverpool Taxi Owners' Association*[12] the local authority had convened a meeting of taxi owners in the city, and after discussion promised that they would not increase the number of taxis licensed to operate in the city, until the City Council had obtained a local Act of Parliament enabling them to exercise a similar control over private cars operating for hire. The authority changed their mind six months later without giving a further hearing to the taxi owners, and decided substantially to increase the number of licensed taxis, although the local Act had not been obtained. The Court of Appeal granted an order of prohibition; in the course of his judgment Lord DENNING, M.R., expressly disagreed with the categorisation of decisions into administrative and judicial or quasi-judicial, and based his judgment on the "unfairness" of the local authority's behaviour.

Again, in *Breen* v. *Amalgamated Engineering Union*,[13] although all the members of the Court of Appeal did not go so far as Lord DENNING, the court held that a committee of a trade union who had refused to confirm the election by his workmates of the plaintiff as a shop steward, were obliged to act "fairly", although their Lordships were not all prepared to overrule the findings of fact of the trial judge.

Perhaps the last words, so far as we are here concerned, should be taken from the most famous of all our judicial protagonists for natural justice, Lord DENNING, M.R.[14] In *R.* v. *Gaming Board for Great Britain, ex parte Benaim*, he said[15]:

> "It is not possible to lay down rigid rules as to when the principles of natural justice are to apply; nor as to their scope and extent. Everything depends on the subject matter. At one time it was said that the principles only apply to judicial proceedings and not to administrative proceedings. That heresy

---

[9] [1967] 1 All E.R. 226; [1967] 2 Q.B. 617.

[10] *Wiseman* v. *Bornemann*, [1969] 3 All E.R. 275; [1971] A.C. 297. See also *Pearlberg* v. *Varty*, [1972] 2 All E.R. 6; [1972] 1 W.L.R. 534.

[11] *R.* v. *Birmingham City Justice, ex parte Chris Foreign Foods* (*Wholesalers*), *Ltd.*, [1970] 3 All E.R. 945; [1970] 1 W.L.R. 1248.

[12] [1972] 2 All E.R. 589; [1972] 2 Q.B. 299.

[13] [1971] 1 All E.R. 1148; [1971] 2 Q.B. 175.

[14] He is not, however, alone in these views. See, for example, Megarry J., in *Gaiman* v. *National Association for Mental Health*, [1970] 2 All E.R. 362, at p. 376; EDMUND DAVIES, L.J., in *Breen*'s case (*ante*) at p. 1158; Lord GUEST in *Sloan* v. *General Medical Council*, [1970] 2 All E.R. 686, at p. 688, and SACHS, L.J., in *Re Pergamon Press, Ltd.*, [1970] 3 All E.R. 535; [1971] Ch. 388. In *Pearlberg* v. *Varty*, (*ante*), Lord CROSS said (at p. 16), "the function was administrative; no doubt this involved a duty to act fairly."

[15] [1970] 2 All E.R. 528, at p. 533.

was scotched by *Ridge* v. *Baldwin.*[16] At another time it was said that the principles do not apply to the grant or revocation of licences. That too is wrong. *R.* v. *Metropolitan Police Commissioner, ex parte Parker*[17] and *Nakkuda Ali* v. *Jayaratne*[18] are no longer of authority for any such proposition."

In *Breen* v. *Amalgamated Engineering Union* (*ante*) Lord DENNING (dissenting) picked up the thread[19]:

> "It is now well settled that a statutory body which is entrusted by statute with a discretion must act fairly. It does not matter whether its functions are described as judicial or quasi-judicial on the one hand, or as administrative on the other hand, or what you will. Still it must act fairly. It must in a proper case give a party a chance to be heard."

Again, in the *Liverpool* case, *ante*[1]:

> "It is perhaps putting it a little too high to say they [the local authority] are exercising judicial functions. They may be said to be exercising an administrative function. But even so, in our modern approach, they must act fairly, and the court will see that they do so."

If this principle is applied to all decisions of administrative agencies that may affect the "interests" of members of the public (as was suggested in the *Liverpool* case), there may be very far-reaching results which may cramp the initiative of local authorities in particular. In the past authorities have always been free to make—or unmake—policy decisions even if particular members of the public might consider themselves harmed thereby.

(4) *Effects of a failure to observe natural justice.*—It is not at all clear whether a decision that has been arrived at in circumstances in which the twin principles of natural justice have not, but should have been, observed, is void or only voidable. If the decision is voidable only, it will stand until it has been challenged before a competent court, whereas if the decision is void it is a nullity *ab initio*, as is an order made without jurisdiction. Professor de Smith suggests[2] that the courts approach this question differently according to whether the case concerns a breach of *audi alteram partem*, or whether there was bias; he also points out that the question whether a decision will be declared void or voidable will often as a "rough guide" depend on the seriousness of the defect.

(i) "Right to a hearing" cases.—In *General Medical Council* v. *Spackman*,[3] Lord WRIGHT said[4]:

> "If the principles of natural justice are violated in respect of any decision, it is, indeed, immaterial whether the same decision would have been arrived at in the absence of the departure from the essential principles of justice. The decision must be declared to be no decision".

---

[16] In which passage? His Lordship does not specify.
[17] [1953] 2 All E.R. 717; *post*, p. 165.
[18] [1951] A.C. 66; *post*, p. 165.
[19] [1971] 1 All E.R. 1148, at p. 1153.
[1] [1972] 2 All E.R. 589, at p. 594.
[2] *Judicial Review of Administrative Action*, 3rd Edn., pp. 131, 209 and 241.
[3] [1943] 2 All E.R. 337; [1943] A.C. 627.
[4] At p. 345.

In *Annamunthudo* v. *Oilfield Workers' Trade Union*,[5] it was held by the Privy Council that an objector did not have to show that he had been prejudiced by a lack of a proper hearing where he was claiming before the courts that the decision should be set aside, but in *Malloch* v. *Aberdeen Corporation*[6] both Lord REID and Lord WILBERFORCE expressed the view that a remedy would not be granted for a failure to observe natural justice unless there is something of substance which has been lost by the failure."[7] This, in spite of Lord REID's earlier observation in *Ridge* v. *Baldwin*[8]:

> "Time and again in the cases I have cited it has been stated that a decision given without regard to the principles of natural justice is void".

In a dissenting judgment in the same case, Lord EVERSHED said[9]:

> "I have come to the conclusion that in a case where a body is acting within its jurisdiction but of which the courts will say that it has failed to do substantial justice in accordance with the principles of natural justice, then the decision is only voidable and cannot properly be described as a nullity."

It seems therefore that a denial of a hearing may be as destructive on the effect of a decision as is lack of jurisdiction, and the courts will be ready to avoid the decision on this ground when asked. Dr. Rubinstein suggests[10] that the difference in the approach to be detected in some of the decisions may depend on the kind of remedy sought; a voidable act will be impeached by a direct challenge (*e.g.*, by *certiorari*), but a void act can be called into question in any proceedings. Where there has not been a proper hearing it has been suggested that the other party to the proceedings is not entitled to treat them as nugatory, and one conclusion therefore is that such a defect makes the proceedings voidable and not void.[11] Professor H. W. R. Wade, however, suggests that the correct view is that such a decision is void, a nullity[12]; this seems to be the better view if it is understood that by "void" in such a context is meant void as between the parties. A third party (for instance) in the *Ridge* v. *Baldwin* situation could not, it is suggested, have tested the validity of Mr. Ridge's dismissal or alleged the invalidity of any acts done by his successor in office before Mr. Ridge's dismissal had been declared to have been unlawful on his application. But Mr. Ridge himself could attack the invalid decision by any type of proceedings.

(ii) Cases of bias.—In this instance, the effect of a failure to observe natural justice is somewhat clearer. Proof of bias must be established by the party alleging it, although "bias" here may mean actual bias or

---

[5] [1961] 3 All E.R. 621; [1961] A.C. 945.
[6] [1971] 2 All E.R. 1278; *ante*, p. 128.
[7] At p. 1294.
[8] [1963] 2 All E.R. 66, at p. 81; [1964] A.C. 40, at p. 80.
[9] *Ibid.*, at p. 85.
[10] In his excellent book, *Jurisdiction and Illegality* (1965); see also *Durayappah* v. *Fernando*, [1967] 2 All E.R. 152.
[11] Rubinstein, *op. cit.*, at p. 221.
[12] *See* (1967), 83 L.Q.R. 526 and (1968), 84 L.Q.R. 95.

a real appearance of bias (see p. 123, *ante*). Bias cannot go to jurisdiction, but a decision tainted by bias will be capable of being invalidated in proceedings taken to challenge the decision.[13] Professor de Smith suggests that such a decision is voidable because it cannot be impeached in collateral proceedings; but he also agrees that the courts will on the application of an aggrieved person declare a tainted decision to be void.[14]

This argument about whether in relation to administrative decisions that are defective in some respect (because there has been a breach of natural justice or otherwise *ultra vires*, or because they are wrong in law, etc.) there is properly a distinction to be drawn between those that are void and those that are voidable only—and the subsidiary dispute as to which class or classes of defective decisions are void and which are voidable—is interesting but somewhat sterile.

As MEGARRY, J., has said:

> "A decision reached by a tribunal wholly outside its jurisdiction and in complete defiance of natural justice is about as void as anything can be; but if nobody who is entitled to challenge or question it chooses to do so, it remains in being. Yet to describe such a decision as being 'voidable' is to use that word in a sense that is not only very special but liable to mislead."[15]

In practice the problem to be solved is most frequently raised in the following way:

(a) Was natural justice observed in the particular case?

(b) If not, was this a case where natural justice should have been observed?

(c) If yes, is this a case where the court will grant a remedy to the plaintiff?

(d) If yes, has the plaintiff chosen the appropriate remedy (*certiorari*, action for a declaration, etc.)?

Where the last is the question to be answered, it may be that declaration[16] will not lie if the decision is merely bad in law and the Court has acted within its jurisdiction without any breach of natural justice.

Finally, it should be noted that the principles of natural justice are concerned with procedural matters and not matters of substance. The fact that a tribunal has come to a wrong decision, or that a Minister, after observing the proper procedure, has come to the wrong conclusions, is not of itself a justification for quashing the decision on the grounds of breach of natural justice (or otherwise) and *certiorari*, in particular, would not lie in such circumstances.[17]

---

[13] Rubinstein, at p. 203. Professor Wade again suggests that such a decision should be categorised as "void", not voidable (*ibid.*).

[14] *Op. cit.*, at p. 260.

[15] In *Hounslow London Borough* v. *Twickenham Garden Developments, Ltd.*, [1970] 3 All E.R. 326, at p. 347. See also Akehurst, "Void or Voidable—Natural Justice and unnatural meanings" (1968), 31 M.L.R. 2 and 138.

[16] *Post*, p. 188. The same observation probably applies to other challenges to validity such as an action for damages or "self help"; these remedies lie only if the decision has previously been avoided. A void decision, on the other hand (*i.e.*, one which was arrived at contrary to natural justice or otherwise made in excess of jurisdiction) can be impeached either by a direct or by an indirect challenge.

[17] *R.* v. *Minister of Transport, ex parte W. H. Beech-Allen, Ltd.* (1963), 62 L.G.R. 76.

(b) Substantive *ultra vires*.—We now come to the major ground on which the courts in this country will review the decision of an administrative agency, namely, because the agency has exceeded its statutory powers. Every administrative agency, whether it is a government department, a local authority, an independent statutory corporation or an administrative tribunal, owes its powers exclusively to Parliament (with the sole exception of an agency operating under and by virtue of the royal prerogative[18]) and it will be acting *ultra vires* in so far as it may purport to step outside or exceed those powers; any such purported exercise of power will therefore be void. As we have said, any ground on which judicial review may be justified can logically be classified as a branch of the *ultra vires* doctrine; here we shall deal with straightforward cases where *ultra vires* was the solitary or principal justification for judicial review. Thus, in *R.* v. *Minister of Transport, ex parte Upminster Services, Ltd.*[19] it was held that the Minister had no power to revoke contingently a road service licence granted by the Traffic Commissioners under the Road Traffic Act, 1930, although a person who had been refused a licence by the Commissioners was given a statutory right to appeal to the Minister.

Some writers[20] express this principle of substantive *ultra vires* in terms of "jurisdictional facts". If a statute confers jurisdiction on an administrative body in certain defined factual situations, and if one of the essential elements of those factual situations is absent in the particular case, the body will be without jurisdiction and any decisions taken in purported exercise thereof will be *ultra vires*. In *White and Collins* v. *Minister of Health*[21] a local authority had statutory powers to acquire compulsorily any land that did not form part of a private "park". An order was made and confirmed by the Minister but the validity of the order was questioned in the High Court on the ground that the land which was the subject of the order was in fact part of a park. It was held that the court was entitled to investigate this question and review confirmation of the order by the Minister, when he had decided that the land did *not* form part of the park; on the facts the court accepted the argument of the objector and quashed the order as being *ultra vires*. In a similar more recent case, SALMON, L.J., said that whether a tenement house is a house within the meaning of the appropriate section is a "pure question of law".[1] Again, under the

---

[18] Chapter II, *ante*, p. 41.

[19] [1934] 1 K.B. 277.

[20] See, for example, Griffith and Street, *Principles of Administrative Law*, 5th edn., at p. 212. For a comparative account of English and American attitudes to these problems, see the article by Professor H. W. R. Wade, "Anglo-American Administrative Law: More Reflections", at (1966), 82 L.Q.R. 226.

[21] [1939] 3 All E.R. 548; a different line was taken, in a similar context, in the more recent case of *Ashbridge Investments* v. *Minister of Housing and Local Government*, [1965] 3 All E.R. 371; [1965] 1 W.L.R. 1320. The change of approach was due to the change in inquiry procedure; since 1959, inspector's reports have been made available to the parties. This does not, however, it is submitted, mean that the courts will not examine whether the inferior tribunal has outstepped its jurisdiction (*Anisminic* v. *Foreign Compensation Commission*, *post*, p. 144 is surely sufficient answer to such an argument), but it is merely a question as to where the court will draw the line.

[1] *Quillotex Co.* v. *Minister of Housing and Local Government*, [1965] 2 All E.R. 913, at p. 915.

Aliens Order, 1919, made under the Aliens Restriction Act, 1914, the Home Secretary was given power to order the deportation of aliens "if he deems it to be conducive to the public good". The order did not provide for any appeal from his decision in any particular case, but this did not mean that the courts would not review his decision on the preliminary question, whether a particular individual was or was not an alien; if he were in fact not an alien any deportation order would have been made without jurisdiction and be *ultra vires* and void.[2] In *Re Camberwell (Wingfield Mews) No. 2 Clearance Order, 1936*[3] the High Court considered itself entitled to review the confirmation of a clearance order by the Minister of Health, on the question whether or not certain buildings were "houses", as the term was used in the Housing Act, 1936. Sir WILFRED GREENE, M.R. (as he then was) said[4]:

> "It seems to me that these buildings properly fall under the word 'houses' in the section. Whether or not a particular building falls under that word is a mixed question of law and of fact; fact in so far as it is necessary to ascertain all the relevant facts relating to the building, and law in so far as the application of the word 'houses' to those facts involves the construction of the Act."

Similarly, a local authority which was empowered to make a "new street order" under section 159 of the Highways Act, 1959 in respect of other than "existing streets" was confined in its "jurisdiction" or power to new streets, and the reviewing court was concerned with the question whether or not the street was an "existing street".[5]

Even if the statute appears to leave a decision on a jurisdictional matter to the discretion of the inferior tribunal or a local authority, it is clear that the reviewing court will reverse that decision if there is no evidence at all to support it. Thus, in *Coleen Properties, Ltd.* v. *Minister of Housing and Local Government*,[6] a local authority had power[7] to make a compulsory purchase order to acquire land "the acquisition of which is reasonably necessary for the development or use of the [adjoining] clearance area". The acquiring authority certified by resolution that it was reasonably necessary for this purpose to acquire the premises in question, but no evidence was presented at the enquiry into objections to the order, supporting this resolution. The court therefore quashed the Minister's confirmation of the order.

The reviewing court is thus entitled to use its own judgment in relation to the application of the terms of the statute to the particular factual situation in issue, with a view to ascertaining whether the administrative agency has acted *ultra vires*. In other words, it is for the reviewing court to decide whether the inferior tribunal or agency was acting within its jurisdiction, but it is frequently difficult to decide which precisely are the factors that go to jurisdiction, and which are the factors that the inferior tribunal may be allowed to decide for itself.[8]

If an essential fact on which the deciding authority's jurisdiction

---

[2] See argument in *R.* v. *Home Secretary, ex parte Venicoff*, [1920] 3 K.B. 72.
[3] [1939] 1 All E.R. 590.
[4] *Ibid.*, at p. 597.
[5] *Relton & Sons (Contracts)* v. *Whitstable U.D.C.* (1967), 201 E.G. 955.
[6] [1971] 1 All E.R. 1049; [1971] 1 W.L.R. 433.
[7] Under s. 43 (2) of the Housing Act, 1957.
[8] This is the main point considered in *Anisminic, Ltd.* v. *Foreign Compensation Commission*, [1969] 1 All E.R. 208; [1969] 2 W.L.R. 163, *post*, p. 144.

depends is absent, then any purported exercise of that jurisdiction will be void. In *R.* v. *Agricultural Land Tribunal for Wales and Monmouth Area, ex parte Davies*[9] the Minister of Agriculture and Fisheries had given his consent to the operation of a notice to quit an agricultural holding under section 25 of the Agricultural Holdings Act, 1948. Under this Act, the Minister's consent could be granted, so that the tenant could be ejected, where certain conditions existed, but where those conditions were not satisfied, the Minister had no power to grant consent. In this case, those conditions were not satisfied, and therefore an order of *certiorari* was granted to quash the decision of the Agricultural Land Tribunal upholding the Minister's consent on appeal. It follows that:

> "If a certain state of facts has to exist before an inferior tribunal has jurisdiction, it [*i.e.*, the tribunal] can inquire into the facts in order to decide whether or not it has jurisdiction, but it cannot give itself jurisdiction by a wrong decision on them."[10]

Sometimes the decision of an administrative agency may be *ultra vires* if the agency has taken the wrong matters into consideration in arriving at its decision. Thus, when a rent tribunal requested to fix the standard rent for a dwelling under section 1 of the Landlord and Tenant (Rent Control) Act, 1949, (see now Rent Act, 1968 Part VI), took into consideration in assessing that rent certain amounts paid by way of premiums, their decision was quashed because the Act provided that premiums were to be ignored when this jurisdiction was being exercised.[11] A notice purporting to be served under statutory authority will similarly be void if it was issued on a false basis of fact. In *Francis* v. *Yiewsley and West Drayton U.D.C.*[12] an enforcement notice served under section 23 of the Town and Country Planning Act, 1947,[13] was held to be void because it stated that the development complained of had been carried out without planning permission, whereas in fact permission had been granted, but for a limited time only.

Whether or not the decision of a Minister or other body is *ultra vires*, will of course depend on the interpretation put on the statute by the reviewing court. Presumptions will be applied to assist the court in interpreting the statute,[14] and as we have seen,[15] the courts will supplement the deficiencies of the statute in a case where they think natural

---

[9] [1953] 1 All E.R. 1182.

[10] *Per* Lord GODDARD, C.J., in *R.* v. *Fulham Rent Tribunal, ex parte Zerek*, [1951] 1 All E.R. 482, at p. 485; [1951] 2 K.B. 1; and see also *Re Purkiss' Application*, [1962] 2 All E.R. 690; [1962] 1 W.L.R. 902; a case concerning the jurisdiction of the Lands Tribunal in relation to restrictive covenants, under s. 84 of the Law of Property Act, 1925.

[11] *R.* v. *Fulham Rent Tribunal, ex parte Philippe*, [1950] 2 All E.R. 211. In a somewhat similar case involving this legislation, EDMUND DAVIES, L.J., said "the demonstration that they [the local authority, in referring a case to the tribunal] have taken irrelevant factors into account may be of the greatest assistance, but that latter aspect is not conclusive" (*R.* v. *Barnet and Camden Rent Tribunal, ex parte Frey Investments, Ltd.*, [1972] 1 All E.R. 1185, at p. 1195).

[12] [1957] 3 All E.R. 529; [1958] 1 Q.B. 478. See also the earlier case of *R.* v. *Minister of Health, ex parte Davis*, [1929] 1 K.B. 619, where a slum clearance scheme under the Housing Acts was quashed because it purported to confer powers on the local authority in excess of those granted by the parent statute.

[13] See now s. 87 of the Town and Country Planning Act, 1971.

[14] Chapter III, *ante*, p. 49.

[15] *Ante*, p. 116.

justice ought to have been observed. On the other hand, the courts have often in the past shown themselves as reluctant to construe a statute in a "liberal" sense; "the golden rule is that the words of a statute must *prima facie* be given their ordinary meaning".[16] It is therefore refreshing to find in the House of Lords decision of *Padfield* v. *Minister of Agriculture, Fisheries and Food*,[17] a desire to go behind the precise expression used in the statute, and to construe that expression in the context of the whole statute.

In this case, the statute had established a scheme for the marketing of milk, and had provided that milk producers aggrieved by action taken by the Milk Marketing Board under the scheme, could complain to the Minister. Section 19 of the Agricultural Marketing Act, 1958, then set up a "committee of investigation" charged with the duty of considering and reporting to the Minister on any such complaint, "*if the Minister in any case so directs*". In spite of the apparently unlimited discretion conferred on the Minister by the words italicised, the House of Lords held that the discretion was nevertheless limited to the extent that it must not be so used as to frustrate the objects of the statute. When, therefore, the Minister refused to refer a complaint to the investigation committee, because, as was alleged, the complaint was so substantial that it would affect the milk marketing price structure as a whole, an order of mandamus was granted directing the Minister to refer the complaint to the committee pursuant to section 19, as he had not exercised his discretion in accordance with the intention of the Act. If this kind of complaint were not to be referred to the committee, why should Parliament have constituted the committee at all? This did not mean there was no discretion left in the Minister; he could still refuse to refer complaints which he considered trivial or vexatious. Lord REID said in *Padfield*[18]:

> "In a matter of this kind it is not possible to draw a hard and fast line, but if the Minister, by reason of his having misconstrued the Act or for any other reason, so uses his discretion as to thwart or to run counter to the policy and objects of the Act, then our law would be very defective if persons aggrieved were not entitled to the protection of the Court."

But this reasoning does not help if there is no general policy to be deduced from the Act. In the subsequent case of *British Oxygen Co.* v. *Minister of Technology*,[19] the Minister of Technology was given power by statute to make investment grants towards capital expenditure incurred in the provision of new machinery or plant. British Oxygen had developed a new type of storage cylinder for liquid gases, which could be supplied to customers as returnable containers. These cylinders cost £20 each, and as the Ministry had a policy rule that they would not pay grants in respect of new plant costing less than £25, they refused to make a grant in this case. The House of Lords refused to make a declaration that the plaintiffs were entitled to a grant, as they

---

[16] *Nokes* v. *Doncaster Amalgamated Colliers, Ltd.*, [1940] A.C. 1014, at p. 1022, *per* Viscount SIMON, L.C.

[17] [1968] 1 All E.R. 694; [1968] A.C. 997.

[18] [1968] 1 All E.R., at p. 699.

[19] [1970] 3 All E.R. 165; [1971] A.C. 610.

were of the opinion that the statute conferred an unqualified discretion on the Minister. Referring to *Padfield*, Lord REID said[20]:

> "One generally expects to find that Parliament has given some indication how public money is to be distributed. In this Act Parliament has clearly laid down the conditions for eligibility for grants and it has clearly given to the Board [predecessor of the Minister] a discretion so that the Board is not bound to pay to every person who is eligible to receive a grant. But I can find nothing to guide the Board as to the circumstances in which they should pay or the circumstances in which they should not pay grants to such persons."

It is the *Padfield* type of decision, most welcome as it is,[1] which reinforces the arguments of those who contend that this country has a developed, or developing, system of administrative law,[2] and that the courts are prepared always to look behind the *ipssissima verba* of the statute and apply principles of "good administration", similar to the *principes généraux du droit*, developed over the last 20 years or so by the French *Conseil d'Etat.*[3] It is the view of the present writer that this seems to be too rosy a view of the English "system", and that statutory assistance must be called in to establish some basic principles of "administrative morality".[4] *Westminister Bank* v. *Minister of Housing and Local Government*,[5] may be cited as a counterbalance to *Padfield*'s case. In the *Westminster Bank* case, a local authority had refused planning permission to the Bank when they proposed to bring forward an extension to their building nearer to the centre line of a highway. DONALDSON, J. at first instance,[6] was prepared to quash this decision because the authority had proceeded under planning powers which gave the Bank no opportunity of claiming compensation, whereas if the authority had used powers contained in the Highways Act, 1959 to achieve the same object, the Bank would have been able to claim compensation. The Court of Appeal and House of Lords, however, would have none of this; the planning decision was within the authority's statutory discretion given them by the Town and Country Planning Act, 1962, and therefore it could not be interfered with by the Court, regardless of the consequences to the Bank.

The substantive doctrine of *ultra vires* does not apply only to the judicial acts of a Minister, tribunal or other administrative agency. It applies to all the three functions of government. Thus, subordinate legislation of any kind, including the byelaws of a local authority or a statutory corporation or the regulations of a Minister, will be declared void if and in so far as they exceed the powers conferred by the parent statute.[7] The principle applies also to any exercise of executive power. Thus, where a statute required the occupier of land to

---

[20] *Ibid.*, at. p. 169.

[1] See (1968) 31 M.L.R. 446.

[2] "Research and Reform in English Administrative Law", by Professor L. L. Jaffe at [1968] P.L. 119; *contra* [1968] P.L. 201 (Professor Mitchell) and 212 (Professor Garner), and a riposte from Professor Jaffe at [1969] P.L. 15.

[3] Brown and Garner, *French Administrative Law*, 2nd Edn., Chapter 9.

[4] As suggested in the *Justice* Report *Administration under Law*; Chapter V, *ante*, p. 109.

[5] [1970] 1 All E.R. 734; [1971] A.C. 508, H.L.

[6] [1968] 2 All E.R. 104; [1968] 2 W.L.R. 1080; see [1968] P.L. 5.

[7] Chapter IV, *ante*, p. 78.

obtain a licence before he used his land as a caravan site, and in granting such a licence the authority were empowered to impose conditions, it was held that these conditions must be confined within the general purpose of the Act, and in so far as they exceeded this, they were void.[8] It has also been applied to avoid executive acts of local authorities; if an authority cannot point to precise statutory authority for any particular course of action (*e.g.*, the granting of concessionary fares to old age pensioners by a municipal corporation operating a public transport undertaking),[9] the action will be declared *ultra vires* by the courts and therefore void. This is because local authorities are creatures of statute, and therefore possess only such powers as may have been conferred on them by Parliament.[10] Moreover, the principle of *ultra vires* cannot be circumvented by any operation of an estoppel. If a local authority or other agency have alleged they possess a statutory power which they do not possess, the authority will not be estopped subsequently from pleading the absence of that power, even if the other party has relied on the original allegation and has possibly been prejudiced as a consequence. Any other answer to such a case would mean that an administrative agency could clothe itself with powers not given by statute by making use of the doctrine of estoppel.[11] Estoppel cannot in general operate in manner contrary to the provisions of a statute.[12]

To summarise, if powers conferred by statute are exceeded, the purported exercise is to that extent *ultra vires* and void. This may affect subordinate legislation, the decision of a judicial body, or the executive act of any government agency, including a contract, but will not normally affect questions of liability in tort.[13]

(c) Procedural *ultra vires*.—As administrative agencies are subject to the substantive rule of *ultra vires*, so they must exercise those powers that the legislature may have given them in the manner and in accordance with the procedure (if any) that may have been specified by the legislature. This is clearly true of subordinate legislation (including the making of byelaws) and it applies also to executive and judicial acts. So far as judicial acts are concerned, we have already seen that the superior courts will assume that the legislature intended an inferior tribunal to observe the principles of natural justice, unless the statute clearly expresses the contrary intention,[14] and that an administrative body will not be expected to observe all the principles of ordinary judicial procedure. Considerations of natural justice apart, however, a supervising court will insist on due observance by the inferior tribunal of such procedural rules as may have been laid down by any relevant statute. Thus, where a local authority was empowered by statute to refer to a rent tribunal the question of the rent that ought to be charged for any furnished dwelling, and they referred

---

[8] *Chertsey U.D.C.* v. *Mixnam's Properties, Ltd.*, [1964] 2 All E.R. 627.
[9] *Prescott* v. *Birmingham Corpn.*, [1954] 3 All E.R. 698; [1955] Ch. 210.
[10] Chapter XV, *post*, p. 422.
[11] *Rhyl U.D.C.* v. *Rhyl Amusements, Ltd.*, [1959] 1 All E.R. 257; [1959] 1 W.L.R. 465.
[12] But see Andrews, "Estoppels against Statutes", (1966) 29 M.L.R. 1.
[13] See Chapter IX, *post*, p. 296.
[14] *Ante*, p. 125.

the question of the rents to be charged for a large block of flats without considering each flat separately, the eventual decisions by the rent tribunal were quashed in proceedings for *certiorari*, because the local authority had not initially followed the correct procedure.[15]

Similarly, where a local authority were required to serve a notice as a preliminary to the taking of slum clearance action in relation to a particular house, and the notice did not give particulars of the recipient's right to appeal to the courts, as required by the statute, the notice was held to be void and the whole of the subsequent proceedings *ultra vires*.[16] Where the statute required a town planning enforcement notice to specify the date on which it would come into effect and also a time limit within which the notice was to be complied with, a notice which specified one date only was held to be void.[17] In a case where a statute conferred a compulsory purchase power provided the acquiring authority were satisfied that the land in question could not be acquired by agreement, the order was quashed because the court was not satisfied that the authority had adequately considered acquiring the land by agreement.[18]

A special example of procedural *ultra vires* is provided by those cases where a Minister is required to hold an inquiry into a certain matter; usually it is a question of informing himself of the nature and burden of objections to or representations against some proposed administrative action, such as a compulsory purchase order or clearance order (in the case of slum clearance). If the Minister makes his decision (to confirm, modify or quash the proposed order) without taking into consideration the report of his officer who conducted the hearing, it would be quashed by the courts, as he would be held to have failed to observe the full statutory procedure,[19] but on the other hand he is not obliged to accept or act on any recommendations contained in the report,[20] nor indeed will the courts compel him to disclose the contents of the report,[1] although since the recommendations of the Franks Committee have been published, Ministers have as a matter of normal departmental practice customarily provided for the publication of inspectors' reports.[2]

Naturally the supervising court will, in an appropriate case, ensure that the inferior tribunal is correctly constituted and will declare its decision void if it has in a particular case been taken by the wrong individual. This was the point at issue in *Woollett* v. *Minister of*

---

15 *R.* v. *Paddington and St. Marylebone Rent Tribunal, ex parte Bell London and Provincial Properties, Ltd.*, [1949] 1 All E.R. 720; [1949] 1 K.B. 666; *R.* v. *Barnet and Camden Rent Tribunal, ex parte Frey Investments, Ltd.*, [1972] 1 All E.R. 1185; [1972] 2 Q.B. at p. 354.

16 *Rayner* v. *Stepney Corpn.*, [1911] 2 Ch. 312.

17 *Burgess* v. *Jarvis and Sevenoaks U.D.C.*, [1952] 1 All E.R. 592; [1952] 2 Q.B. 41.

18 *Webb* v. *Minister of Housing and Local Government*, [1965] 2 All E.R. 193; [1965] 1 W.L.R. 755.

19 This is of course difficult to establish in practice; there does not seem to be any reported decision on the point.

20 *Franklin* v. *Minister of Town and Country Planning*, [1947] 2 All E.R. 289; [1948] A.C. 87, and *Nelsovil, Ltd.* v. *Minister of Housing and Local Government*, [1962] 1 All E.R. 423.

1 *Denby (William) & Sons*, Ltd. v. *Minister of Health*, [1936] 1 K.B. 337; *Re Falmouth Order*, [1937] 3 All E.R. 308.

2 Chapter VII, *post*, p. 220.

Agriculture and Fisheries,[3] although it could not there be established, and in *R.* v. *Nat Bell Liquors*[4] it was inferred in the course of a long judgment by Lord SUMNER, that a decision of an inferior tribunal could be set aside if it were shown that the tribunal had not been correctly constituted.

A tribunal or administrative body acting judicially must approach the matter they have to determine in a "judicial" manner, without any preconceived fetter on their discretion. Thus, a local planning authority were held to have acted illegally when they had agreed with an outside body that all applications for permission to develop within a certain area, would be rejected.[5] Decisions must not be arrived at without due consideration of the particular case[6]; but this does not mean that a Ministry[7] or a local authority[8] may not formulate a policy as to how it will determine a particular type of application, provided it is prepared to consider any special circumstances applicable to an individual case.

The courts will also insist that a discretion entrusted by Parliament to a particular administrative agency is exercised by that agency itself, unless the enabling statute has also expressly conferred on the agency a power to delegate the right to come to a decision. Where a power to delegate exists, any exercise of that power by the delegating authority and any exercise of the right to decide by the delegate, must be exercised strictly in accordance with the terms of the statute. The leading case on this aspect of the *ultra vires* principle is *Vine* v. *National Dock Labour Board*,[9] where the House of Lords declared that a decision of a disciplinary committee of a local dock labour board, purporting to act on behalf of the National Board, was *ultra vires* and void. By the terms of a statutory scheme made under the Dock Workers (Regulation of Employment) Order, 1947, which had itself been made under the Dock Workers (Regulation of Employment) Act, 1946, the National Board were required to delegate as many as possible of their functions to local boards. The National Board approved the delegation of their functions to committees of the local board, including the further delegation of powers to disciplinary committees. In purported exercise of that sub-delegated power the local disciplinary committee, after hearing the appellant in the present action, ordered that he should be dismissed from his employment by the National Board. The fatal

---

[3] [1954] 3 All E.R. 529; [1955] 1 Q.B. 103; see also *Howard* v. *Borneman* (*No. 2*), [1973] 3 All E.R. 641.

[4] [1922] 2 A.C. 128.

[5] *Stringer* v. *Minister of Housing and Local Government*, [1971] 1 All E.R. 65; [1970] 1 W.L.R. 1281.

[6] See *R.* v. *Port of London Authority, ex parte Kynoch, Ltd.*, [1919] 1 K.B. 176; *ante*, p. 26.

[7] *Lavender* v. *Minister of Housing and Local Government*, [1970] 3 All E.R. 871; [1970] 1 W.L.R. 1231.; *British Oxygen Co.* v. *Minister of Technology*, [1970] 3 All E.R. 165; [1971] A.C. 610 (*ante*, p. 36).

[8] *Sagnata Investments, Ltd.* v. *Norwich Corporation*, [1971] 2 All E.R. 1441; [1971] 2 Q.B. 614.

[9] [1956] 3 All E.R. 939; [1957] A.C. 488, and see also *Jeffs* v. *New Zealand Dairy Production and Marketing Board*, [1966] 3 All E.R. 863; [1967] 2 W.L.R. 136; and *Barnard* v. *National Dock Labour Board*, [1953] 1 All E.R. 1113; [1953] 2 Q.B. 18; cf. the earlier case (which does not deal with the authorities) of *General Medical Council* v. *United Kingdom Dental Board*, [1936] Ch. 41.

error lay in the delegation of disciplinary functions to the committee, for there was statutory sanction for delegation to the local board, but no further. In the judgments their Lordships made some references to the distinction between "judicial" and "administrative" acts, Lord SOMERVELL observing[10] that judicial authority normally cannot, of course, be delegated, but he also went on to observe that there are, on the other hand, many administrative duties which cannot be delegated. In an interesting case from Israel,[11] the Supreme Court in that jurisdiction held that a town council could properly delegate to its Mayor the power to designate particular parking places (already chosen by the Council) as "regulated parking places" for the purposes of certain regulations, but that they could not delegate to the Mayor the duty of determining a scale of parking fees. In *Allingham* v. *Minister of Agriculture and Fisheries*,[12] it was held that a statutory power delegated by a Minister to a local agricultural executive committee could not be delegated to an officer responsible to that committee, and a similar principle has been applied in a local government context.[13] However, although it may not be permissible to delegate a power to an officer, if he acts on his own initiative, the authority having the right to exercise that power may subsequently adopt his action as their own decision.[14] The principle *Delegatus non potest delegare*, and indeed procedural *ultra vires* generally, applies to.[15]

(a) an authority empowered to lay down general rules by way of legislation;
(b) an authority empowered to decide a particular issue affecting the rights of an individual;
(c) an authority empowered to determine whether legal proceedings shall or shall not be initiated[16];
(d) an authority empowered to do an act involving the exercise of any discretion, even if it may be one where the discretion is not wide, such as in the service of a distress warrant.

"It applies, in short, to all persons who are empowered by statute to do anything,"[17]

and the prohibition on delegation of a discretionary power even applies in a case where the delegating authority simply agrees to abide by some other person's decision.[18]

---

[10] At p. 951.
[11] *A.-G.* v. *Hornstein*, Selected Judgments of the Supreme Court of Israel, Vol. III, p. 71.
[12] [1948] 1 All E.R. 780.
[13] *St. Leonard's Vestry* v. *Holmes* (1885), 50 J.P. 132.
[14] *Firth* v. *Staines*, [1897] 2 Q.B. 70; *Warwick R.D.C.* v. *Miller-Mead*, [1962] 1 All E.R. 212. The principles here discussed have not been affected by the Local Government Act, 1972, although in practice delegation to officers is widely permissible under s. 101 of that Act (see Chapter XI, *post*, p. 370.
[15] See Willis, *Delegatus non potest Delegare*, at (1943), 21 C.B. Rev. 257.
[16] As in, *e.g.*, *Bob Keats, Ltd.* v. *Tarrant*, [1951] 1 All E.R. 899.
[17] Willis, *op. cit.*, at p. 257, and note at (1971), 34 M.L.R. 335 discussing *Lever (Finance), Ltd.* v. *Westminster Corporation*, [1970] 3 All E.R. 496; [1971] 1 Q.B. 222.
[18] See, for example, *Ellis* v. *Dubowski*, [1921] 3 K.B. 621, where a county council empowered by statute to license cinemas, issued a licence subject to a condition that all the films exhibited should be approved by the British Board of Film Censors; it was held that this amounted to an illegal delegation of discretion and that, therefore, the condition was void.

(d) Error of law.—In some cases a statute may make provision for an appeal to lie from a decision of an administrative agency, where the decision is susceptible of review on the "merits", *i.e.*, the reviewing court will be entitled to put itself in the shoes of the agency as it were, and decide the matter afresh, taking both facts and law into account. This is, however, exceptional and exists only where a statute has expressly so provided.[19] In other cases a statute may make express provision for an appeal to lie to the courts on a "point of law".[20] As a general principle the courts will, apart from these instances, review an administrative decision of a judicial nature only where there has been an error of law "on the face of the record", or where such an error is clear and obvious. This does not mean that the error must be a flagrant one, or relate to a simple or clearly established principle of law, but that the error must be readily ascertainable by the supervising court, and not one that can be ascertained only by a detailed examination of all the evidence that was before the deciding agency or which needs the assistance of technical experts to explain it.[1]

This ground of judicial review has been recognised in our legal system for some time,[2] but it was brought to the fore by the Court of Appeal decision of *R.* v. *Northumberland Compensation Appeal Tribunal, ex parte Shaw.*[3] In the course of his judgment in this case, DENNING, L.J. said[4]:

> "... the Court of King's Bench has an inherent jurisdiction to control all inferior tribunals, not in an appellate capacity, but in a supervisory capacity. This control extends not only to seeing that the inferior tribunals keep within their jurisdiction, but also to seeing that they observe the law. The control is exercised by means of a power to quash any determination by the tribunal which, on the face of it, offends against the law. The King's Bench does not substitute its own views for those of the tribunal, as a court of appeal would do. It leaves it to the tribunal to hear the case again, and in a proper case may command it to do so. When the King's Bench exercises its control over tribunals in this way, it is not usurping a jurisdiction which does not belong to it. It is only exercising a jurisdiction which it has always had."

This decision was followed and applied in *R.* v. *Westminster Compensation Appeal Tribunal, ex parte Road Haulage Executive*[5], where error of law was again detected in the inferior tribunal's record by the Court of Appeal (although the Queen's Bench Divisional Court[6] had failed to appreciate that there was any such error).

The decision of the inferior court will be quashed if it can be shown

---

[19] Examples will be found in a number of local government contexts; for example, an appeal lies to the Crown Court against a refusal by a local authority to grant a permit for the provision of "an amusement with prizes", under the Fifth Schedule to the Betting, Gaming and Lotteries Act, 1963, as amended by the Betting, Gaming and Lotteries (Amendment) Act, 1969, and the statute places no restrictions on the matters that may be in issue on such an appeal. The court is then entitled to decide the case *de novo*: *Sagnata Investments* v. *Norwich Corporation*, [1971] 2 All E.R. 1441; [1971] 2 Q.B. 614.

[20] See, for example, s. 13 (1) of the Tribunals and Inquiries Act, 1971, and *post*, p. 173.

[1] *Baldwin and Francis, Ltd.* v. *Patents Tribunal*, [1959] 2 All E.R. 433, [1959] A.C. 663.

[2] See *Bunbury* v. *Fuller* (1853), 9 Ex. 111, at p. 140, *per* COLERIDGE, C.J., and the leading Privy Council decision in *R.* v. *Nat Bell Liquors*, [1922] 2 A.C. 128.

[3] [1952] 1 All E.R. 122; [1952] 1 K.B. 338.

[4] At p. 127.

[5] [1953] 1 All E.R. 687.

[6] [1952] 2 All E.R. 764.

to be wrong in law in accordance with this principle, even if the error is a comparatively minor technicality, as in *R.* v. *Industrial Disputes Tribunal, ex parte Kigass*,[7] where the only error established was that the tribunal had directed that an award on a dispute should be effective as from 23rd November, 1951, whereas the earliest date permissible in law was 18th January, 1952. No amendment was possible because of the nature of the jurisdiction of the reviewing court; as it is supervisory in nature and exercisable by way of *certiorari*, there is no power to amend or modify a decision of the inferior tribunal, only to quash.[8]

The error of law must be "on the face of the record"; as PARKER, L.J. (as he then was), said in *Davies* v. *Price*[9]:

> "The matter was properly referred to the tribunal; it clearly had jurisdiction to decide whether to give or withhold consent, and if it misconstrued the statute or acted on no evidence, it merely erred in law and unless that error is manifest on the face of the award, the decision cannot be challenged on proceedings for an order of *certiorari*."

This raises the related question: what is meant by "the record", on the face of which the error must appear? The words used in giving an oral decision are apparently part of the record,[10] and there

> "should be included in the record, not only the formal order, but all those documents which appear therefrom to be the basis of the decision".[11]

If there are no grounds at all for the decision disclosed by the record, or if the evidence clearly does not support the findings, there will be an error of law. As Lord WIDGERY, C.J., said[12]:

> "I must first examine the Minister's decision to see whether it contains a false proposition of law *ex facie* . . . it is next relevant to consider whether the decision reached by the Minister is one which is supported by no evidence in which event of course his decision would be wrong in law.[13] Then finally I must consider . . . whether the facts found are such that no person acting judicially and properly instructed as to the relevant law could have come to the determination under appeal."

Acting within jurisdiction may or may not be an error of law; acting outside jurisdiction is an excess of power, or *ultra vires*, and therefore is always an error of law. As was said in *R.* v. *Nat Bell Liquors*[14] (cited in *Davies* v. *Price*) *per* LORD SUMNER[15]:

> "A justice who convicts without evidence is doing something that he ought not to do, but he is doing it as a judge, and if his jurisdiction to entertain the charge is not open to impeachment, his subsequent error, however grave, is a wrong exercise of a jurisdiction which he has, and not a usurpation of a jurisdiction which he has not."

---

[7] [1953] 1 All E.R. 593.

[8] As to the remedy of *certiorari*, see *post*, p. 178.

[9] [1958] 1 All E.R. 671, at p. 676; a decision which was doubted in *Anisminic* (below).

[10] *Post*, p. 180.

[11] *Per* Lord DENNING in *Baldwin & Francis, Ltd.* v. *Patents Appeal Tribunal*, [1959] 2 All E.R. 433, at p. 445. In another patents case, in an application for *certiorari*, the Queen's Bench Division considered that they were entitled to look not only at the actual decision of the Patents Appeal Tribunal but also at the application and specification which was the very basis of the Tribunal's decision: *R.* v. *Patents Appeal Tribunal, ex parte Swift*, [1962] 1 All E.R. 610.

[12] In *Global Plant, Ltd.* v. *Secretary of State for Health and Social Security*, [1971] 3 All E.R. 385, at p. 393. See also the judgment of Lord REID in *Anisminic* (below).

[13] As in *Coleen Properties, Ltd.* v. *Minister of Housing and Local Government*, [1971] 1 All E.R. 1049.; *ante*, p. 134.

[14] [1922] 2 A.C. 128.

[15] At p. 151.

The difficulty is to appreciate which kinds of error are errors of law and which of fact, and also which errors are within jurisdiction and which outside; an inferior tribunal cannot be allowed to determine the extent of its own jurisdiction. This latter problem was examined in *Anisminic, Ltd.* v. *Foreign Compensation Commission.*[16] In this interesting case, the appellants were a British company which owned property in Egypt which had been sequestrated by the Egyptian government after the Suez crisis. A sum of money was subsequently made available by the Egyptian government for distribution by the British government at their discretion. Determination of claims to this money was referred by the statute to the Foreign Compensation Commission,[17] any such determination being final and not capable of being called into question in any court of law.[18] The Commission heard the appellants' case and held that they were not entitled to compensation, under the terms of the relevant Order in Council made under the Foreign Compensation Act, 1950. The Order provided that a claim by an applicant was to be treated as having been established if the applicant was a person named in the treaty with the Egyptian Government as owner of property, or was a successor in title of such a person, provided that the person so named and the successor in title were British nationals at specified dates. The appellants here were persons named in the treaty but they had since (while reserving the benefit of any claim to compensation) transferred the property to a successor who was not a British subject. The Commission dismissed the appellants' claim for compensation holding that they were not entitled under the terms of the Order in Council. In this decision they had, as the House of Lords so found, made an error of law. Of course, if it were a "mere" error of law on the face of the record (and this certainly was "on the face"), the court would be powerless to review it, in view of the exclusion clause in the statute. But this error was in the opinion of the House of Lords, one which went to jurisdiction—it was a decision outside the power of the Commission to make, and therefore it was *ultra vires* and void. It was therefore not a "determination", and it was open for the courts to say so. An inferior tribunal cannot determine the extent of its own jurisdiction; as Lord REID said,[19]

> "if they [the Commission] reach a wrong conclusion as to the width of their powers, the court must be able to correct that—not because the tribunal has made an error of law, but because as a result of making an error of law they have dealt with and based their decision on a matter with which, on a true construction of their powers, they had no right to deal."

Much the same reasoning was applied in *Armah* v. *Government of Ghana,*[20] where Lord REID said (at p. 187):

---

[16] [1969] 1 All E.R. 208; [1969] 3 W.L.R. 163; see also *Jones* v. *Secretary of State* [1972] 1 All E.R. 145; [1972] A.C. 944; and comment at [1973] P.L. 80.

[17] A tribunal constituted by the Foreign Compensation Act, 1950.

[18] By virtue of s. 4 of the Act of 1950, a section which was expressly exempted from the provision in s. 11 of the Tribunals and Inquiries Act, 1958, now replaced by s. 3 (9) of the Foreign Compensation Act, 1969, although s. 3 (10) of that Act preserves the right of any person to question a determination of the Commission on the ground that it "is contrary to natural justice" (One of the few contexts where this expression is given statutory significance). The exemption from s. 11 of the 1958 Act has not been repeated in the corresponding section (14) of the 1971 Act (see *post*, p. 158).

[19] *Ibid.*, at page 216.

[20] [1966] 3 All E.R. 177; [1968] A.C. 192.

"Whether or not there is evidence to support a particular decision is always a question of law, but it is not a question of jurisdiction."

In most of the reported cases in which the courts have reviewed the decision of an inferior tribunal on the ground here discussed, the remedy sought has been an order of *certiorari*, discussed later in this Chapter,[1] but this is not to say that "error on the face of the record" will be taken into consideration only in *certiorari* proceedings. From *Taylor* v. *National Assistance Board*,[2] and more clearly the decision of the House of Lords in *Pyx Granite Co.* v. *Ministry of Housing and Local Government*,[3] it seems that an action for a declaration also can be brought successfully on this ground,[4] but not in cases where the decision of the tribunal is "final", and a contrary decision on a declaration would leave two contradictory opinions both apparently valid.[5]

It remains true to say that error of law on the face of the record is a ground for review by a supervising court only in respect of a decision by an inferior tribunal or authority acting judicially. Indeed this ground is not relevant in the case of an administrative or legislative act, as a straightforward allegation of substantive *ultra vires* would then normally be adequate to secure effective review. Judicial review on the grounds of an "error on the face of the record" is not likely to be made available where the inferior tribunal refuses to give, or refrains from giving reasons for its decision. This was recognised in *Davies* v. *Price*,[6] where an order of *certiorari* was refused because there was no error on the face of the record, on which the jurisdiction of the supervising court could be founded.

It is not always easy to recognise an "error of law on the face of the record"; apart from the question whether an error of law "goes to jurisdiction", there is the further question, what is an error of law as distinct from an error of fact?[7] This second question seems to amount to asking whether the tribunal could, on a correct statement of law, have reasonably come to the decision it did. If the answer is in the affirmative, there can be no review on this ground.[8] Review will not be granted simply because it can be shown that the inferior tribunal came to the wrong decision; it must have come to that decision for wrong reasons. Moreover, in the past it was rarely the practice of administrative statutes to require reasons to be given by inferior

---

1 *Post*, p. 178. 2 [1956] 2 All E.R. 455; [1956] P. 470.

3 [1959] 3 All E.R. 1; [1960] A.C. 260.

4 And see Zamir, *The Declaratory Judgment*.

5 *Punton* v. *Ministry of Pensions* (*No. 2*), [1964] 1 All E.R. 448; [1964] 1 W.L.R. 226, *post*, p. 190.

6 [1958] 1 All E.R. 671. *Davies* v. *Price* was criticised adversely by the majority of their Lordships in *Anisminic* v. *Foreign Compensation Commission* (*ante*) because "the enquiry under review was in effect directed to the wrong question" (see Lord PEARCE at p. 237); in other words, it was an error going to jurisdiction, and not a mere error of law within jurisdiction.

7 Also, what is "the record"? See *post*, p. 180. The difficulty of distinguishing between an "error of law" in respect of which *certiorari* will be granted, and an "error of fact", in respect of which the only remedy is an appeal on the merits where the relevant statute has made provision therefor, is well brought out by *R.* v. *Industrial Injuries Commissioner, ex parte Amalgamated Engineering Union*, [1966] 1 All E.R. 97; [1966] 2 Q.B. 21.

8 *R.* v. *Patents Appeal Tribunal, ex parte Swift*, [1962] 1 All E.R. 610, and see the *Global Plant* case (*ante*, p. 143).

tribunals. The Franks Committee recognised this as a defect in administrative tribunal procedure, and as a consequence of their recommendations,[9] section 12 of the Tribunals and Inquiries Act, 1958, provided that any tribunal specified in the First Schedule,[10] and also a Minister when notifying a decision he has arrived at after the holding of a statutory inquiry, must

> "furnish a statement, either written or oral, of the reasons for the decision if requested, on or before the giving or notification of the decision, to state the reasons".

In practice it does not often prove necessary, since the coming into operation of this section, formally to require reasons to be stated,[11] but the section is not of universal application, and it may not always be very valuable where the reasons given in purported compliance therewith, are scanty, uninformative or unintelligible.[12] The section will not apply:

(a) to decisions of tribunals to which the Act does not apply, and of those inquiries that are not "statutory inquiries";
(b) on the grounds of "national security"[13];
(c) in a case where the tribunal or Minister refuses to furnish a statement as to reasons to a "person not primarily concerned with the decision, if of opinion that to furnish it would be contrary to the interests of any person primarily concerned"[14];
(d) where it is expressly excluded by order of the Lord Chancellor, made under s. 12 (6) of the 1971 Act or its predecessor in the 1958 Act.[15]

The section also provides that any statement of reasons given by a tribunal or Minister to which the section applies must be taken to form part of the decision and accordingly to be incorporated in the record[16]; therefore there is no doubt but that if the statement of reasons discloses that the tribunal or Minister has made an error of law, *certiorari* will lie.[17]

In a case where the requirement to state reasons applies, *mandamus* could normally be obtained to enforce the requirement. This is certainly so in the case of an agricultural arbitrator,[18] but the requirement to state reasons for a planning decision by a planning authority has been

---

9 Report, para. 98.

10 See now Tribunals and Inquiries Act, 1971, s. 12 (1).

11 Administrative arrangements have been made by most government departments to comply with the recommendations: see, for example, Circular 9/58 of the Ministry of Housing and Local Government, and the regulations relating to compulsory purchase and planning inquiries. The Council on Tribunals when consulted on the making of procedural rules for tribunals, normally ensure that an express requirement to this effect is included in the rules. On the subject of reasons generally, see Akehurst, "Statements of Reasons for Judicial and Administrative Decisions", (1970) 33 M.L.R. 154.

12 For an example, see *Givaudan* v. *Minister of Housing and Local Government*, [1966] 3 All E.R. 696; [1967] 1 W.L.R. 250. On appeal the decision was quashed on this ground.

13 1971 Act, s. 12 (1), proviso.

14 *Ibid.*

15 See, for example, the Tribunals and Inquiries (Revenue Tribunals) Order, 1959, S.I. 1959 No. 452.

16 1971 Act, s. 12 (3).

17 *Post*, p. 178.

18 *Re Poyser and Mills' Arbitration*, [1963] 1 All E.R. 612; [1964] 2 Q.B. 467, and see note by Professor Wade at (1963), 79 L.Q.R. 344.

held to be directory only.[19] Normally failure to give reasons of itself will not justify quashing the decision, unless the insufficiency of reasons gives rise to a proper inference that there had been an error of law in arriving at the decision.[20]

(e) Failure to perform a duty.—Failure to carry out a duty imposed by statute on an administrative agency may also afford grounds for interference by the courts, though this is not precisely a case of "review" for, *ex hypothesi*, the agency has done nothing. Failure to perform a duty may take a number of forms. Thus, an agency having a statutory discretion is failing to exercise its duty if it establishes a firm rule beforehand and does not consider each case on its merits[1]; a police officer has a duty to enforce the law of the land,[2] and a Minister has a duty to observe the terms of a taxation statute and not grant extra-statutory concessions therefrom.[3] The remedies provided are of two kinds; an action for damages on the statute, and proceedings for an order of *mandamus*, ordering the agency to carry out the duty. These are discussed later in this book.[4]

(f) Bad faith.—Many writers have urged that the courts will also review an administrative[5] act if the decision has been arrived at in "bad faith". In a case in the Supreme Court of Canada damages were awarded in respect of the cancellation of a liquour permit, when it appeared that a Provincial Attorney-General had directed a local licensing commission to cancel the permit because, it was alleged, the plaintiff had acted as bondsman for persons accused of distributing seditious literature. In the course of his judgment RAND, J., said[6]:

> "In public regulation of this sort there is no such thing as absolute and untrammelled 'discretion', that is that action can be taken on any ground or for any reason that can be suggested to the mind of the administrator; no legislative Act can, without express language, be taken to contemplate an unlimited arbitrary power, exercisable for any purpose, however capricious or irrelevant, regardless of the nature or purpose of the statute. Fraud and corruption in the Commission may not be mentioned in such statutes but they are always implied as exceptions. 'Discretion' necessarily implies good faith in discharging public duty; there is always a perspective within which a statute is intended to operate; and any clear departure from its lines or objects is just as objectionable as fraud or corruption. Could an applicant be refused

---

[19] *Brayhead (Ascot), Ltd.* v. *Berkshire C.C.*, [1964] 1 All E.R. 149, at p. 154; [1964] 2 Q.B. 303, at p. 314, *per* WINN, J.

[20] *Mountview Court Properties, Ltd.* v. *Devlin* (1970), 21 P. & C.R. 689, *per* Lord PARKER, C.J., at p. 695.

[1] *R.* v. *London County Council, ex parte Corrie*, [1918] 1 K.B. 68, and *ante*, pp. 26 & 140.

[2] *R.* v. *Metropolitan Police Commissioner, ex parte Blackburn*, [1968] 1 All E.R. 763; [1968] 2 Q.B. 118.

[3] *R.* v. *Commissioners of Customs and Excise, ex parte Cook*, [1970] 1 W.L.R. 450.

[4] *Post*, p. 171.

[5] The argument applies logically only to administrative acts. "Bad faith" in connection with a judicial act will normally involve a breach of natural justice, and no form of subordinate legislation has hitherto been found void on any ground other than substantive or procedural *ultra vires*, although it seems to be suggested by Lord Hodson (at p. 1056) and Lord GUEST (at p. 1061) in *McEldowney* v. *Forde*, [1969] 2 All E.R. 1039, that, had bad faith been established, they would have been prepared to hold certain regulations made under statutory authority to have been void. The Court of Appeal were apparently prepared to take a similar line, in *Pickin* v. *British Railways Board*, [1972] 3 All E.R. 923; [1973] Q.B. 219, in relation to a private Act of Parliament. The courts will also hold byelaws of local authorities or statutory corporations void on the grounds of unreasonableness (see Chapter IV, *ante*, p. 84).

[6] *Roncarelli* v. *Duplessis* (1959), 16 D.L.R. (2d) 689, at p. 705.

a permit because he had been born in another Province, or because of the colour of his hair? The ordinary language of the Legislature cannot be so distorted."

It is by no means clear that an English Court would be prepared to go so far as this; "bad faith" in this country is recognised as a vitiating element in an administrative decision only, it seems, as a special facet of the *ultra vires* doctrine. This attitude is perhaps due to the great respect shown to the *ipsissima verba* of a statute, which itself comes from the doctrine of the supremacy of Parliament. Another, and what appears to be more appropriate, name for this variety of *ultra vires*, is "wrong motive"; it is sometimes described as "abuse of power", but if the inferior administrative authority is acting completely *within* its powers, there seems to be no question of its decision being excluded on the ground of that power having been abused.

We will first outline some of the leading cases relevant to this topic and then endeavour to ascertain such general principles as may be capable of being deduced.

In *Westminster Corpn.* v. *London and North Western Rail. Co.*[7] the Corporation had used a statutory power to construct public conveniences under a street to provide also a subway from one side of the street to the other. Their action was held not to be *ultra vires* because there was no breach of the terms of the statute. Lord HALSBURY, L.C., said[8]:

> "Assuming the thing done to be within the discretion of the local authority, no Court has power to interfere with the mode in which it has exercised it."

Then, in *Roberts* v. *Hopwood*[9] the Poplar Borough Council, being empowered by statute to pay such wages "as they may think fit", paid considerably higher wages than the general level prevailing in the district, as they did not consider that that general level amounted to a reasonable living wage. The district auditor disallowed these payments and surcharged them on members of the council; on appeal, the House of Lords agreed with the district auditor and said that the council stood

"somewhat in the position of trustees or managers of the property of others".

In *Associated Provincial Picture Houses* v. *Wednesbury Corporation*,[10] Lord GREENE, M.R., said[11] that the *ratio decidendi* of *Roberts* v. *Hopwood*, was that the council had, in fixing the wages, done so

> "by reference to something which they ought not to have entertained and to the exclusion of those elements which they ought to have taken into consideration in fixing a sum which could fairly be called a wage".

Roberts v. *Hopwood* was also referred to in *Taylor* v. *Munrow*[12] (another district audit case), where Lord PARKER, C.J., said[13] that in *Roberts* v. *Hopwood* it was held in the House of Lords,

> "that the discretion conferred on the council by the statute must be exercised reasonably . . . it was also held that an expenditure on a lawful object might be so excessive as to be unlawful".

---

[7] [1905] A.C. 426.
[8] At p. 427.
[9] [1925] A.C. 578.
[10] [1947] 2 All E.R. 680; [1948] 1 K.B. 223.
[11] At p. 684.
[12] [1960] 1 All E.R. 455.
[13] *Ibid.*, at p. 460.

In *Taylor* v. *Munrow*[14] itself, a local authority was empowered by statute to restrict the rent payable by a tenant of premises formerly held under requisition by the council under emergency powers, and to make payments to the landlord equivalent to such rents as he would otherwise have lost in consequence. The St. Pancras Borough Council resolved to use this power in all cases of derequisitioned property in their borough, from political motives. The consequent payments made from the general rate fund to landlords were eventually disallowed by the district auditor and surcharged[15] on those councillors who had voted for the resolution. The court agreed with the District Auditor's view that the payments were *ultra vires*, because—

(a) the Council should have preserved a balance between their duty to the general body of ratepayers and their duty to the particular ratepayers (the landlords) in respect of whom the payments were to be made; *and*

(b) the statute had put the Council under a duty periodically to review the position ("as the local authority may from time to time determine") which they had not carried out.

It is suggested that *Roberts* v. *Hopwood* really goes no further than to establish the proposition that a local authority or other administrative agency may not exercise its discretion unreasonably, and that such a requirement is little different from saying that an inferior tribunal is guilty of an error of law if it takes extraneous considerations into account.[16] In considering what is reasonable in the context, the court may have regard only to the terms of the particular statute. This idea is to be seen also in the decision of the House of Lords in *Westminster Corpn.* v. *London and North Western Rail. Co.* (*ante*). Lord MACNAGHTEN said[17]:

> "It is well settled that a public body invested with statutory powers such as those conferred upon the corporation must take care not to exceed or abuse its powers. It must keep within the limits of the authority committed to it. It must act in good faith. And it must act reasonably. The last proposition is involved in the second, if not in the first",

Taylor v. *Munrow* was but another application of the same principle, and so was *London and Westcliff Properties, Ltd.* v. *Minister of Housing and Local Government*.[1] In the latter case the London County Council had made a compulsory purchase order in relation to certain property subject to a long lease of which there were still some 20 years to run. Both the freeholder and the leaseholder objected to the making of the order, but the freeholder withdrew his objections when the council agreed to transfer the balance of the leasehold reversion to him after it had been acquired by the council. The court quashed the compulsory

---

[14] [1960] 1 All E.R. 455.

[15] For the functions of district auditors, see Chapter XV, *post*, p. 428.

[16] These two arguments come together in *Kennedy* v. *Birmingham Licensing Planning Committee*, [1972] 2 All E.R. 305; [1972] 2 Q.B. 140.

[17] At p. 430.

[1] [1961] 1 All E.R. 610; [1961] 1 W.L.R. 519, see also *Grice* v. *Dudley Corpn.*, [1957] 2 All E.R. 673; [1958] Ch. 329, and the judgment of MEGAW, J., in *Hanks* v. *Minister of Housing and Local Government*, [1963] 1 All E.R. 47, especially at p. 55.

purchase order as the council had originally not made the order for the purpose of vesting the reversion of the lease in the freeholders; this would have been a contravention of the statutory powers under which the order was purported to be made. Thus, the council were guilty of an "abuse" of their statutory powers and they were acting *ultra vires;* the order was therefore declared void.

Sometimes the enabling statute clearly delimits the purposes for which a particular power may be exercised. Thus, in *Sydney Municipal Council* v. *Campbell*[2] the council had purported to use a statutory power conferred on them to acquire land compulsorily for the purpose of effecting improvements in the city, not for that purpose but so as to ensure that the enhanced value that would accrue to the land as a consequence of improvements being carried out on adjoining land, would be enjoyed by the council on behalf of the city. The action of the council was therefore declared void, although it was admitted that they were acting *bona fide* in the interests of their residents. Again, in *Earl Fitzwilliam's Wentworth Estates Co.* v. *Minister of Town and Country Planning*[3] the former Central Land Board were authorised to acquire land "for any purpose connected with the performance of their functions" under the [specified] provisions of the Town and Country Planning Act, 1947. In view of these specific words, it is perhaps not surprising that no one argued in this case that the applicants were not entitled to challenge a compulsory purchase order made under the section on the grounds that it had been made for an improper purpose; the decision turned on the terms of the statute itself. An Act of the Albertan legislature taxing banks in the Province was in a sense a measure providing for "the raising of revenue for Provincial purposes", and so within the apparent competence of the Albertan legislature under section 92 (2) of the British North America Act, 1867, but when it had been shown that the true motive of the Act was not the raising of Provincial revenue, but the introduction of Social Credit in the Province, the statute was declared *ultra vires.*[4]

Where, on the other hand, a discretion is vested in an administrative agency and no restrictions whatever are imposed on the exercise of that discretion by the terms of the statute, it seems that the court will not be able to interfere with the exercise of that discretion. But a statute having apparent general operation may be subject to restriction implied from a particular context. If the court is to exercise a power of review, the restrictions need not be imposed expressly in the statute, but there must be some general context or restricting field of action within which the court can expect the agency to act. Thus, in *Roberts* v. *Hopwood,* it was a generally accepted principle of local government law that a local authority should be treated as being in a special fiduciary relationship in respect of general rate fund moneys for the benefit of

---

[2] [1925] A.C. 338, a Privy Council decision.
[3] [1952] 1 All E.R. 509; [1952] A.C. 362.
[4] *A.-G. for Alberta* v. *A.-G. for Canada,* [1939] 1 All E.R. 423; [1939] A.C. 117. *Hanks* v. *Minister of Housing and Local Government,* (*ante*) is another example of statutory purposes, and see an article by the present writer at (1963) L.J.N. for May 31, 1963.

their ratepayers,[5] and in *Taylor* v. *Munrow* the statute had provided that payments and rents should be reviewed from time to time. On the other hand, in *Associated Provincial Picture Houses* v. *Wednesbury Corpn.*,[6] where a local authority were empowered to grant licences for the Sunday opening of cinemas subject to such conditions as the authority might think fit to impose, the court would not inquire whether the local authority had acted reasonably in imposing conditions restricting the admission to cinemas that were permitted to open, of children under the age of fourteen; as there was no context within which the authority were required to act; their discretion was unfettered. Again, in *Shelley* v. *London County Council*[7] the House of Lords declined to inquire into the reasons for which a local housing authority might require possession of a house provided by them under the Housing Acts, provided they required that possession in the course of "housing management", a function expressly vested in them by the statute. In *Short* v. *Poole Corporation*[8] the local education authority had dismissed the plaintiff school teacher because she was a married woman. It was argued that the authority were actuated by motives and had pursued aims wholly outside their province as a local education authority, although by the appropriate statutory provision they were empowered to appoint and dismiss teachers, without any qualification. But the Court of Appeal refused to grant a declaration that the local authority had acted *ultra vires*, POLLOCK, M.R., observing[9]:

> "Where a discretion is given to the local authority, it is for that authority to exercise it, provided that its action is not *ultra vires*, nor its powers exercised corruptly or *mala fide*. Where the exercise of the discretion is challenged, it is for the plaintiff to prove that there is a duty in the courts to interfere upon the grounds already stated. . . . The authority may appear to be right or may appear to be wrong in the course they have adopted, according as that course may be subjected to criticism from one point of view or another. Upon such discussion and criticism it is not for the courts to pronounce. So long as the discretion has been exercised and the limits of discretion are not passed the decision rests with the local authority."

However, in *Chertsey U.D.C.* v. *Mixnam's Properties, Ltd.*,[10] a widely drawn statutory power to impose conditions in a licence for a caravan site was construed restrictively within the general intention of the statute, and conditions purporting to regulate the rents at which caravans on the site might be let, were held to be *ultra vires*, as not being concerned with the use of the land as a caravan site.

The difficulty in these cases is, of course, to determine where the courts will find "limits" to the discretion vested by statute in the administrative agency, or in which cases they will treat the discretion as absolute. If limits are set by the statute, the problem is simple; in other cases the courts are prepared to look at the surrounding circumstances, and whereas they will not go so far as to put themselves in the shoes of

---

5 See, for example, *A.-G.* v. *Aspinall* (1837), 2 My. & Cr. 613; and *per* JENKINS, L.J., in *Prescott* v. *Birmingham Corpn.*, [1954] 3 All E.R. 698, at p. 700.

6 [1947] 2 All E.R. 680.

7 [1948] 2 All E.R. 898; [1949] A.C. 56.

8 [1926] Ch. 66.

9 At p. 88.

10 [1964] 2 All E.R. 627; [1965] A.C. 735.

the agency and consider whether the particular decision was reasonable, it seems that they will reverse a decision that is so palpably unreasonable that no reasonable local authority or other administrative agency could have come to that decision without contravening the purposes (and therefore exceeding the powers) of the statute.[11] The attitude of the courts is thus similar to that adopted towards the exercise of a power given to a Minister to act if he is "satisfied" as to some specified matter.[12]

Sometimes it is argued that "bad faith" is itself sufficient justification for judicial review, even when the decision is within the statutory powers conferred on the agency in question.[13] There is no decision of the courts in this country clearly supporting such a proposition,[14] and *Smith* v. *East Elloe R.D.C.*[15] suggested that an allegation of bad faith would not be sufficient to overcome a statutory provision expressly excluding any possibility of judicial review.[16] In *Lazarus Estates, Ltd.* v. *Beasley*,[17] a landlord and tenant case arising out of the terms of a notice served under the Housing Repairs and Rents Act, 1954, DENNING, L.J., said[18]:

> "No court in this land will allow a person to keep an advantage which he has obtained by fraud. No judgment of a court, no order of a Minister, can be allowed to stand if it has been obtained by fraud. Fraud unravels everything. The court is careful not to find fraud unless it is distinctly pleaded and proved; but once it is proved it vitiates judgments, contracts and all transactions whatsoever."

This was a case where the fraud concerned was so gross that the party relying on the fraudulent statement in the notice could have been prosecuted in the criminal courts; there is a real distinction, it would seem, between fraud in this sense and "bad faith" on the part of an administrative authority. If such a complaint of extreme fraud arose in an administrative case, it seems that the court would review the decision on the ground that Parliament could never have contemplated that the power should be so exercised. "Wrong motive" must be capable of being attached to some "peg" or indication in the statute of the motive which Parliament expected the agency to follow; "bad

---

[11] See Professor de Smith, *Judicial Review of Administrative Action*, 3rd Edn., at p. 260, where he discusses recent cases dealing with conditions in planning permissions.

[12] *Post*, p. 161.

[13] See, *e.g.*, *Roncarelli* v. *Duplessis* (*ante*).

[14] Certain remarks of the House of Lords in the Scottish case of *Demetriades* v. *Glasgow Corpn.*, [1951] 1 All E.R. 457, perhaps go the farthest.

[15] [1956] 1 All E.R. 855; [1956] A.C. 736; *post*, p. 159.

[16] This case really turned on the interpretation of a statutory expression (*post*, p. 159). The decision was a majority one (3–2), and Lord REID in particular (at p. 868) was of the opinion that "general words", in a statute should be read so as not to deprive the court of jurisdiction where bad faith is involved. The decision was called into question in the House of Lords in *Anisminic* v. *Foreign Compensation Commission*, [1969] 1 All E.R. 208; [1969] 2 A.C. 147. Lord REID in that case pointed out (at p. 213) that only fraud on the part of the local authority would have affected the validity of the order in *East Elloe*, whereas the court were considering alleged fraud on the part of the clerk to the local authority; Lord PEARCE in *Anisminic* suggested that *East Elloe* referred only to an administrative, not a judicial decision (see p. 159).

[17] [1956] 1 All E.R. 341; [1956] 1 Q.B. 702.

[18] At p. 345.

faith" comes somewhere between wrong motive and a clear case of *ultra vires*, and there are no firm principles showing precisely when the courts will agree to intervene.

(g) Other grounds.—The question then arises, whether there are any other grounds on which the courts will entertain review of some administrative act. First, is there any hope to be derived from the equitable jurisdiction of the court, or is equity of "such an age as to be past child-bearing"?[19] Equity was put forward as a ground for review in *Simpsons Motor Sales (London), Ltd.* v. *Hendon Corpn.*,[20] where the validity of action threatened pursuant to a notice to treat served six years previously, was challenged. During the six years, the law relating to the assessment of compensation on compulsory acquisition had been changed, so that the plaintiffs were entitled to a much smaller sum based on the date when the notice to treat had been served, than they would have been entitled to had the corporation been obliged to start again and serve a fresh notice to treat. The House of Lords held, however, that in the absence of evidence showing an intention to abandon the original notice to treat[21], mere unfairness or hardship was not enough to justify the courts' interference. Lord EVERSHED said (at p. 494):

> [Such a course] "would, in my opinion, be no more than palm tree justice. I cannot think that this can suffice for the establishment and enforcement of an equity. If such an equitable right is to be found then it must, as I conceive, be based on the view that to permit the corporation to continue to enforce their rights under the original compulsory purchase order must in some real sense be against good conscience."

However, as may be seen, the possibility of a "new equity" was not completely ruled out; maybe a subsequent litigant will be more fortunate with this line of argument than were Simpsons Motor Sales Ltd.

Another case[1] suggested that the courts in this country might entertain an action for damages (where actual damage can be proved) at the suit of a person aggrieved by the refusal of a local or other government agency to grant some licence or consent under a statutory control, in circumstances where the refusal is inspired by "bad faith", spite or (possibly) wrong motive. Such a remedy had been denied by the English Court of Appeal in *Davis* v. *Bromley Corpn.*,[2] in which the view was taken that:

> "The possible indirect motives attributed to the defendants could not render the exercise of their statutory discretion the more susceptible to judicial review than it would be otherwise."

However, in *David* v. *Abdul Cader*,[3] Viscount RADCLIFFE in an important judgment said:

---

[19] This remark was invented by HARMAN, J. (as he then was); see Lord EVERSHED at [1963] 2 All E.R. 493.

[20] [1963] 2 All E.R. 484.

[21] As was the case in *Grice* v. *Dudley Corpn.*, [1957] 2 All E.R. 673; [1958] Ch. 329.

[1] *David* v. *Abdul Cader*, [1963] 3 All E.R. 579 (a Privy Council appeal from Ceylon); see also a note on this case by the present writer at [1963] P.L. 407.

[2] [1908] 1 K.B. 170.

[3] [1963] 3 All E.R. 579, at p. 582.

"*Davis's case* [*supra*] was decided in the year 1907. . . . it would not be correct to-day to treat it as establishing any wide general principle in this field: certainly it would not be correct to treat it as sufficient to found the proposition, as asserted here, that an applicant for a statutory licence can in no circumstances have a right to damages if there has been a malicious misuse of the statutory power to grant the licence. Much must turn in such cases on what may prove to be the facts of the alleged misuse and in what the malice is found to consist."

This idea of the tort of misfeasance in a public office is not really novel, although actions have been very few.[4] From a more general point of view it seems unlikely that the courts will be able to find some new ground for review not dependent ultimately on the *ultra vires* doctrine.

In France the question as to when judicial review will be available can be much more confidently answered than is the case in this country. The Conseil d'Etat (or the local administrative courts) will review the decision of an administrative agency if *détournement de pouvoir* can be established.[5] In order to prove this, it is necessary to consider whether the motives which inspired the author of an administrative act are those which, in accordance with the intentions of the legislature, ought to have inspired him. Has the administrator used his power to attain an end or objective (*but*) which was among those in the contemplation of the legislature? Moreover, in order to ascertain what was in the contemplation of the legislature, the French administrative courts will not only look at the terms of the statute, but will also consider *travaux préparatoires*, such as the speeches of sponsors of the measure when it was passing through the Legislature. It seems that in France the administrative courts will review an administrative act where there has been any of the following forms of misuse of an administrative power[6];

(a) obstruction to the course of justice;
(b) fraud on the law;
(c) some act inspired by a partisan rather than the public interest;
(d) an act done in the interests of a third party;
(e) an act inspired by political passion;
(f) an act inspired by a public interest other than that which caused the creation of the power ("wrong motive").

English law, in spite of sweeping *dicta* which can be found in some of the cases, does not yet go as far as this.

4. THE EXCLUSION OF JUDICIAL REVIEW

In some cases a statute expressly or by necessary implication purports to exclude judicial review of an administrative decision or of subordinate legislation. In this part of this Chapter we shall therefore

[4] See also *post*, p. 186.

[5] See Brown and Garner, *French Administrative Law*, 2nd. Edn., Chapter 9.

[6] Waline, *Droit Administratif*, 8th Edn., at pp. 443 *et seq.* These are not the only grounds on which a French administrative court will review a decision of an administrative authority. In general, it may be said that the Conseil d'État will grant a *recours pour excès de pouvoir* if there has been any breach of the *principes généraux du droit*; the right to a fair hearing, the equality of all citizens before the law, etc. Because of the idea of administrative morality recognised by the Conseil d'Etat, the general principles are widely interpreted in order to meet changing circumstances.

examine first some of the words that have been used in statutes, and consider their respective privative effect, and then we shall discuss cases where the courts have found themselves precluded from reviewing a decision or subordinate legislation although the relevant statute contained no clear provision to that effect.

First, however, a few general observations on the subject of statutory exclusion of judicial review are necessary. As a cardinal rule, access to the Queen's courts in circumstances where such access would otherwise lie,[7] is not to be denied, save by the clear words of a statute. Thus, in *Chester* v. *Bateson*[8] a Ministerial order which purported to prevent a landlord from having recourse to the courts in order to obtain possession of his property, and which had been made under a widely drawn power conferred by statute to legislate for the purpose of controlling munitions, was held to be *ultra vires*. Statutory provisions which exclude all possibility of judicial review are categorised by some judges and writers as being contrary to the general principles of justice and therefore undesirable. This argument, reasonable as it undoubtedly is, is not supported by legal considerations, because there is no principle by which the validity of a statutory provision may be called into question. In the United States, an appeal could be made to the "due process clause" of the fifth or fourteenth Amendment to the Constitution, and a provision in a Federal or State statute would be declared void if it purported to exclude the rights of the citizen to appeal to the courts.[9] In this country, however, some forms of words may effectively exclude review, although "privative clauses" will be construed as far as possible in favour of the citizen. As Professor de Smith has said[10]:

> "The Executive, however, has shown an understandable reluctance to offer the citizen a sporting chance of disturbing the course of administration, and has secured the passage of legislation designed to protect the exercise of its administrative and subordinate legislative powers against effective challenge in the courts."

(a) "Final."—If a statute declares that a decision of a Minister or other administrative agency is to be "final", this does not have the effect of excluding judicial review by means of *certiorari*. Thus, in *Re Gilmore's Application*,[11] DENNING, L.J., said[12]:

> "I find it very well settled that the remedy by *certiorari* is never to be taken away by any statute except by the most clear and explicit words. The word 'final' is not enough. That only means 'without appeal'. It does not mean 'without recourse to *certiorari*.' It makes the decision final on the facts but not

---

[7] In other words, where one or other of the grounds above mentioned is present.

[8] [1920] 1 K.B. 829. See also *Lee* v. *Showman's Guild of Great Britain*, [1952] 1 All E.R. 1175, [1952] 2 Q.B. 329, where ROMER, L.J., said (at p. 354), "the proper tribunals for the determination of legal disputes in this country are the courts and they are the only tribunals which, by training and experience, and assisted by properly qualified advocates, are fitted for the task".

[9] See, for example, *Johnstown Coal and Coke Co.* v. *Dishong* 84 A. 2d. 847, (1951), cited in Schwartz, *op. cit.*, at p. 166.

[10] *Judicial Review of Administrative Action*, 3rd edn., at p. 314.

[11] [1957] 1 All E.R. 796; [1957] 1 Q.B. 574. This case was followed in *Tehrani* v. *Rostron*, [1971] 3 All E.R. 790; [1972] 1 Q.B. 182.

[12] At pp. 801, 803.

final on the law. Notwithstanding that the decision is by a statute made 'final', *certiorari* can still issue for excess of jurisdiction or for error of law on the face of the record. . . . If tribunals were to be at liberty to exceed their jurisdiction without any check by the courts the rule of law would be at an end.[13] . . . I am glad to notice that modern statutes never take away in express words the right to *certiorari* without substituting an analogous remedy.[14] This is probably because the courts no longer use it to quash for technical defects, but only use it in case of a substantial miscarriage of justice."

There are many cases of statutes providing that the decision of an inferior tribunal or of a Minister shall be "final". Thus, a demolition or closing order made in respect of an unfit house under Part II of the Housing Act, 1957, is "final and conclusive" as respects any matters which could have been (but were not) raised in the course of an appeal against the order for which provision is made in the statute.[15]

"Final" usually means, in relation to a particular administrative jurisdiction, merely that the particular remedy in question cannot be taken any further; it does not deprive the disappointed litigant of such other remedies as he may have, or exclude him from recourse to the courts. Under section 35 (6) of the Town and Country Planning Act, 1971 (and its predecessors in earlier legislation), it is provided that any decision of the Secretary of State for the Environment on an appeal to him against a refusal of planning permission[16] by the local planning authority "shall be final". In *Pyx Granite Co.* v. *Minister of Housing and Local Government*[17] the House of Lords held that this provision did not exclude the right of a person aggrieved by a decision of the Minister to bring an action for a declaration to the effect that a decision of the Minister was *ultra vires*, although of course the merits of the decision could not be questioned. Viscount SIMONDS said[18]:

"It is a principle not by any means to be whittled down that the subject's recourse to Her Majesty's courts for the determination of his rights is not to be excluded except by clear words. . . . It must be asked then what is there in the Act of 1947 which bars such recourse. The answer is that there is nothing except the fact that the Act provides him with another remedy. Is it then an alternative or an exclusive remedy? There is nothing in the Act to suggest that while a new remedy, perhaps cheap and expeditious,[19] is given the old and, as we like to call it, the inalienable remedy of Her Majesty's subjects to seek redress in her courts is taken away."

His Lordship then proceeded, on a construction of the statute, to distinguish this case from that of *Barraclough* v. *Brown*[20] where the special remedy provided by the statute was clearly intended to be

---

[13] As to the "Rule of Law", see Chapter 1, *ante*, p. 17. Actually it is by no means clear in what sense his Lordship is using the expression in the present passage.

[14] In statutes passed since the Tribunals and Inquiries Act, 1958, where an appeal lies to a tribunal, there is normally also provision for a further appeal to the courts on a point of law (which is presumably a remedy "analogous" to *certiorari*), but there is often also a privative clause excluding other remedies; see, *e.g.*, Town and Country Planning Act, 1971, ss. 242 and 243.

[15] Housing Act, 1957, s. 37 (1).

[16] Or against a determination by the planning authority to the effect (on an application under s. 53 of the Act of 1971) that a particular operation or change of use amounts to development, or that planning permission is not required in the circumstances.

[17] [1959] 3 All E.R. 1; [1960] A.C. 260.

[18] [1959] 3 All E.R. at p. 6.

[19] Under s. 17 of the 1947 Act (now s. 53 of the 1971 Act; see footnote 16 above); this procedure is certainly cheap but not always expeditious in practice.

[20] [1897] A.C. 615, and *post*, p. 170.

exclusive. The *Pyx Granite case* demonstrates that the limited effect of the word "final" will not always be sufficient to exclude the remedy by way of an action for a declaration,[1] as well as that by way of *certiorari*, referred to by DENNING, L.J., in *Re Gilmore* (above). The Court of Appeal in *Ridge* v. *Baldwin*,[2] in which, apparently, no reference was made to the *Pyx Granite case*, held that a decision of the Home Secretary on an appeal under a statute which made the decision "final and binding upon all parties", was not capable of being questioned by means of an action for a declaration.[3] In the House of Lords,[4] the majority of the court took the view that the decision of the watch committee was void, and therefore everything that followed thereafter, including the appeal to the Home Secretary against that decision, was a nullity. The view of the Court of Appeal on the present point would seem therefore to be *obiter*.

It seems then that "final", appearing in a statute in this kind of context will be construed restrictively by the courts. In Canada the words "final and conclusive", or expressions even more positively exclusive, have been held not to be sufficient to exclude the remedy by way of *certiorari*.[5] This particular problem is not likely to arise frequently in future in this country, unless Parliament uses this kind of provision in future statutes, for section 14 (1) of the Tribunals and Inquiries Act, 1971 (replacing a provision in the Act of 1958), provides that:

> "As respects England and Wales or Northern Ireland, any provision in an Act passed before 1st August, 1958 that any order or determination shall not be called into question in any court, or any provision in such an Act which by similar words excludes any of the powers of the High Court, shall not have effect so as to prevent the removal of the proceedings into the High Court by order of *certiorari* or to prejudice the powers of the High Court to make orders of mandamus."

This section was included in the Act to implement a recommendation to this effect in the Franks Report, that the remedies by way of *certiorari*, prohibition and mandamus were

> "clearly necessary in cases where questions of jurisdiction are involved and in cases where no provision is made for appeals on points of law."[6]

The section is, however, of somewhat limited significance in the general field of judicial review because it does not apply to:

(i) cases where prohibition is sought, in spite of the Franks Committee recommendation; this is not, however, of any great practical importance[7];

---

1 See also the decision of the Court of Appeal in *Taylor* v. *National Assistance Board*, [1957] 1 All E.R. 183, at p. 185.

2 [1962] 1 All E.R. 834; [1963] 1 Q.B. 539, *ante*, p. 119.

3 A similar view seems to have been taken by the Court of Appeal in *Punton* v. *Ministry of Pensions and National Insurance* (*No.* 2), [1964] 1 All E.R. 448; [1964] 1 W.L.R. 226, which suggests that *certiorari* might still be granted in such a case although the court was not prepared to grant a declaration.

4 [1963] 2 All E.R. 66; [1964] A.C. 40, *ante*, p. 119.

5 Article by Professor Bora Laskin, "*Certiorari* to Labour Boards: The apparent futility of privative clauses"; (1952), 30 Can. Bar Rev. 986, and see *Toronto Newspaper Guild* v. *Globe Printing Co.*, [1953] 3 D.L.R. 561.

6 Report, para. 117.

7 As to prohibition, see *post*, p. 183.

(ii) actions for a declaration;
(iii) privative clauses contained in statutes passed subsequent to 1st August, 1958[8];
(iv) any case where an Act makes special provision for application to the High Court within a time limited by the Act.[9]
(v) Questions arising under section 26 of the British Nationality Act, 1948 or orders of a court.

Further, the section is limited to review of the decisions of inferior tribunals or agencies acting judicially. It is therefore not relevant to some of the other headings under which judicial review may be excluded by statute hereafter to be discussed.

(b) "Not to be questioned in any legal proceedings whatsoever."—This very sweeping exclusory phrase appears in several statutes of importance, usually within a context where Parliament has provided a specific though limited remedy, and has then also provided that except for the specified remedy, a person aggrieved by the administrative action in question (which itself is usually of a judicial nature) shall not be entitled to question the validity of that action in any other legal proceedings. Thus, a compulsory purchase order made by a local authority and confirmed by the Secretary of State under the procedure laid down in the Acquisition of Land (Authorisation Procedure) Act, 1946, may be questioned in the High Court within a period of six weeks from notification of the confirmation, on the ground that the interests of the applicant have been substantially prejudiced by some procedural error, or that the order is *ultra vires*; but apart from this remedy and after the expiration of that period an order

> "shall not, either before or after it has been confirmed, made or given, be questioned in any legal proceedings whatsoever".[10]

This was the provision in issue in *Smith* v. *East Elloe R.D.C.*[11] where it was argued that this provision was not effective to exclude the right of a person aggrieved by a compulsory purchase order to bring an action in the High Court for a declaration that the order was *ultra vires* after the expiration of the period of six weeks, in circumstances where it was alleged that the order had been made "wrongfully and in bad faith". In the course of his judgment in the House of Lords, Viscount SIMONDS was of the opinion that the Court was bound by the "plain words" of the statute:

> "There is nothing ambiguous about paragraph 16 [of the First Schedule of the 1946 Act]; there is no alternative construction that can be given to it; there is, in fact, no justification for the introduction of limiting words such as 'if made in good faith'; and there is the less reason for doing so when those

---

[8] The date when most of the provisions of the Tribunals and Inquiries Act, 1958, came into operation. For an example, see s. 39 (6) of the Water Resources Act, 1963.

[9] S. 14 (3). This is of course relevant to the class of case considered in *Smith* v. *East Elloe R.D.C.*, [1956] 1 All E.R. 855; [1956] A.C. 736; below.

[10] Acquisition of Land (Authorisation Procedure) Act, 1946, First Schedule, para. 16.

[11] [1956] 1 All E.R. 855; [1956] A.C. 736.

words would have the effect of depriving the express words 'in any legal proceedings whatsoever' of their full meaning and content."[12]

These words were considered by the House of Lords in *Anisminic* v. *Foreign Compensation Commission*,[13] the facts of which have been stated on p. 144. Their Lordships were satisfied that a privative clause of this kind could not oust the jurisdiction of the court to declare a determination to be a nullity where it was void *ab initio*. If the decision was *ultra vires*, contrary to natural justice or arrived at in bad faith[14] (specialised examples of *ultra vires*) it was no determination at all, and therefore the privative clause could not exclude the power of the court to say so.

Although *East Elloe* was criticised in *Anisminic* it should be noted that in the latter case the statute made no provision whatever for irregularities in a decision of the tribunal to be cured. In *East Elloe* on the other hand, a statutory procedure was provided for an illegal decision to be called into question—within a specified time limit. It is submitted, therefore, that *East Elloe* should not be treated as having been overruled.[15]

The words that were under consideration in *East Elloe* appear in the important sections 242 and 243 of the Town and Country Planning Act, 1971,[16] which provide that a number of plans and orders under the Act shall not be questioned in any legal proceedings, the Act having also made provision for appeals to lie to the High Court on a specific point of law; again the statutory right of appeal must be pursued (if at all) within a period of six weeks, and thereafter the validity of the order or decision may not be questioned.[17] Any form of judicial review of a "determination" other than that provided for in the statute is thus effectively excluded.[18] In particular, it seems that an action could not be brought asking for a declaration to the effect that conditions attached to a planning permission[19] or a refusal of planning permission[20] were *ultra vires*, where an appeal against the local planning authority's decision had been made to the Secretary of State, as this procedure would be caught by the section of the 1971 Act above referred to; on the other hand, if no appeal were made against the planning authority's decision, it seems that an action for a declaration might lie in a proper case, as the exclusory provision in question refers only to decisions by the Secretary of State.[21] It may be that the courts would also grant a *certiorari* to quash the decision of a planning authority where there

---

[12] [1956] 1 All E.R. 855, at p. 859.

[13] [1969] 1 All E.R. 208; [1969] 2 W.L.R. 163.

[14] See especially the judgment of Lord REID at p. 213.

[15] *East Elloe* was followed in the Scottish case of *Hamilton* v. *Secretary of State*, 1972 S.L.T. 233. See also *ante*, p. 152.

[16] See sub-s. (1) of each section.

[17] These sections apply to development plans, enforcement notices and decisions made by the Secretary of State on appeal to him (*inter alia*).

[18] Lord DENNING does not agree with this interpretation of *Smith* v. *East Elloe R.D.C.*; see his judgment in *Webb* v. *Minister of Housing and Local Government*, [1965] 2 All E.R. 193, at p. 201; [1965] 1 W.L.R. 755, at p. 770.

[19] As in *Fawcett Properties, Ltd.* v. *Buckinghamshire County Council*, [1960] 3 All E.R. 503; [1961] A.C. 636.

[20] As in the *Pyx Granite case* (*ante*, p. 156).

[21] A declaration is a discretionary remedy (*post*, p. 188) and it may be that the remedy would be refused on the ground that the plaintiff had a remedy under the statute by way of appeal to the Secretary of State.

was shown to be an error of law on the face of the record or there had been some breach of natural justice.[22]

This formula for the exclusion of judicial review appears in a number of other less important, contexts.[23] Where a time limit for appeal accompanies the exclusory words, section 14 of the Tribunals and Inquiries Act, 1971, expressly does not apply, as explained above.

After the decision in *Anisminic*, the position of the Foreign Compensation Commission was debated in the legislature. It was considered to be undesirable that the Commission's determinations should be subjected to review on any ground, and the Bill that became the Foreign Compensation Act, 1969 originally provided that a determination or purported determination should not be subjected to judicial review. However, this was not accepted without qualification; it does not apply to a complaint of a breach of natural justice (s. 3 (10)), and also an aggrieved person may state a case for the opinion of the Court of Appeal on a question of law relating to the jurisdiction of the Commission, or as to the construction or implementation of an Order in Council made under the Act of 1950 (s. 3 (2)).

(c) "As if enacted in this Act."—We must now deal with expressions that have been used in statutes conferring power to make subordinate legislation, and which have the effect, either expressly or by necessary implication, of excluding any opportunity on the part of the courts to review the validity of any particular exercise of the power. In other words, in these cases the power to make subordinate legislation is so widely drawn that it becomes impossible for the courts to apply the *ultra vires* doctrine to delegated legislation made in pursuance thereof; Parliament has handed over its supreme power completely to the subordinate agency.

In practice, Parliament has rarely gone as far as this.[1] The most notorious form of words having the effect of excluding judicial review completely, is the "Henry VIII clause" castigated by Lord HEWART[2] and the Donoughmore Committee.[3] That Committee gave nine examples of this clause in an annexure to their Report; the clause confers on the appropriate Minister a power to modify the provisions of the enabling Act

> "so far as may appear to him to be necessary for the purpose of bringing the Act into operation".

A clause of that kind was considered by the House of Lords as long ago as 1894, in the leading case of *Institute of Patent Agents* v. *Lockwood*,[4]

[22] *R.* v. *Hendon R.D.C., ex parte Chorley*, [1933] 2 K.B. 696, but see *ante*, p. 122.

[23] There are examples in connection with development plans made under the Town and Country Planning Act, and also certain compulsory orders made under s. 66 of the National Parks and Access to the Countryside Act, 1949.

[1] By the Emergency Powers (Defence) Acts of 1939 and 1940, the Executive were given the widest possible powers to legislate without further recourse to Parliament; and see *Ex parte Ringer* (1909), 73 J.P. 436.

[2] In *The New Despotism*, published in 1929.

[3] Report, p. 36.

[4] [1894] A.C. 347.

where it was held that the courts could not interfere to scrutinise the validity of a scheme made under a statutory provision drawn as widely as this. Since the publication of the Donoughmore Report, however, the clause has not been used in statutes, following their recommendation to that effect. There is of course no legal reason why it should not be inserted in some statute to be passed in the future but in the present climate of political opinion this seems unlikely. The device of applying a statutory provision to a different set of circumstances by a statutory instrument made under authority contained in the statute, and in the instrument modifying that provision to fit the different circumstances, is a modern (but limited) example of this kind of clause.[5]

A somewhat similar statutory expression is the phrase, "as if enacted in this Act", when a power is conferred on an administrative agency to make subordinate legislation having that effect. A clause of this kind contained in one of the Housing Acts, was considered by the House of Lords in *Minister of Health* v. *R.* (*on the prosecution of Yaffé*).[6] Here (to quote from the Donoughmore Report[7])

> "the House laid it down that while the provision makes the order speak as if it were contained in the Act, the Act in which it is contained is the Act which empowers the making of the order, and that therefore, if the order as made conflicts with the Act, it will have to give way to the Act. In other words, if in the opinion of the Court the order is inconsistent with the provisions of the Act which authorises it, the order will be bad."

Also it is clear that however widely the subordinate law-making power may be drawn in the enabling Act, procedural requirements must still be complied with, and if these are not observed any purported exercise of the power will be *ultra vires* and void.[8]

(d) "The Minister is satisfied."—We turn now to a number of expressions used in statutory provisions conferring powers to take administrative action, to make a judicial decision, or to make some form of subordinate legislation, where the intention to exclude judicial review, if indeed such intention exists at all, is not clearly expressed, but where nonetheless the courts have in fact found such intention of exclusion to exist.[9] Such expressions include "where it appears to the Minister [or to the local authority] that —— he [they] may ——", *or* "provided the Minister is satisfied that", *or,* "where in the opinion of the Minister ——, he may ——,". In cases of this kind, is it open to the courts to examine whether there were any grounds on which it could (or should) have "appeared" to the Minister or to *any* reasonable Minister, or to examine whether the Minister was really "satisfied", or whether there were grounds on which a reasonable Minister could

---

[5] Discussed in *Britt* v. *Buckinghamshire County Council*, [1963] 2 All E.R. 175; [1964] 1 Q.B. 77.

[6] [1931] A.C. 494

[7] Report, p. 40.

[8] *R.* v. *Minister of Health, ex parte Davis*, [1929] 1 K.B. 619.

[9] As is pointed out by Professor de Smith (*Judicial Review of Administrative Action*, 3rd Edn., at p. 316), it seems that if Parliament has expressly excluded judicial review the courts will do their best to construe the privative clause restrictively, so as leave them some right of review; on the other hand, if the exclusory clause is ambiguous, the courts seem to put more into the mouth of Parliament than readily appears, and abandon their claims to review.

or ought to have been "satisfied", or even whether there were any grounds on which a Minister could reasonably have formed the necessary "opinion"? If the courts are entitled to undertake any such processes, the result will be of course that they may review the particular decision taken by the Minister or other agency concerned; if not, that decision becomes virtually absolute and outside the jurisdiction of the courts. Unfortunately, no clear answer can be given to the question how the courts will approach a problem of this kind, although it is clear that in such cases the power to form an opinion or be satisfied cannot be delegated without express authority.[10]

One of the most important cases on this topic is *Liversidge* v. *Anderson,*[11] where the House of Lords had to consider the effect of a Defence Regulation made under the Emergency Powers (Defence) Act, 1939, which empowered the Home Secretary to detain without trial any person whom he, the Home Secretary, had "reasonable cause to believe to be of hostile origin or associations", and that, by reason thereof "it was necessary to exercise control over" that person. In his judgment, Viscount MAUGHAM expressed[12] the opinion that a court

> "could investigate the question whether there were grounds for a reasonable man to believe some at least of the facts"

conducing to show that the individual in question was of hostile associations, but as to the second question, namely, whether it was therefore necessary to exercise control over him, he said:

> "this is so clearly a matter for executive discretion and nothing else, that I cannot believe myself that those responsible for the Order in Council could have contemplated for a moment the possibility of the action of the Secretary of State being subject to the discussion, criticism and control of a judge in a court of law".

Lord ATKIN gave an outspoken dissenting judgment in favour of reviewing the Home Secretary's decision, but the other Law Lords, MACMILLAN, WRIGHT and ROMER, agreed with Viscount MAUGHAM that the words of the regulation gave the Home Secretary an absolute discretion, putting his action outside any control by the courts. Thus, this case, decided in the special context of emergency legislation, is

> "an authority for the proposition that the words 'if A.B. has reasonable cause to believe' are capable of meaning 'if A.B. honestly thinks that he has reasonable cause to believe', and that in the context and attendant circumstances of Defence Regulation 18B they did in fact mean just that".[13]

Therefore in *Nakkuda Ali* v. *Jayaratne,*[14] it was held that the words

> "where the Controller has reasonable grounds to believe that any dealer is unfit to be allowed to continue as a dealer"

---

[10] *Ratnagopal* v. *A.-G.*, [1970] A.C. 974; [1969] 3 W.L.R. 1056 (a Privy Council case); this should be contrasted with the local government case of *Goddard* v. *Minister of Housing and Local Government*, [1958] 3 All E.R. 482; [1958] 1 W.L.R. 1151, where a power to delegate "functions" was held to be sufficient to include the "function" of forming an opinion.

[11] [1941] 3 All E.R. 338; [1942] A.C. 206. See also the other "emergency" case; *Point-of-Ayr Collieries, Ltd.* v. *Lloyd-George*, [1945] 2 All E.R. 546.

[12] At p. 345.

[13] *Per* Lord RADCLIFFE in the Privy Council case, on appeal from Ceylon, of *Nakkuda Ali* v. *Jayaratne*, [1951] A.C. 66, at p. 76.

[14] [1951] A.C. 66.

must be construed to mean that there must in fact exist reasonable grounds, known to the Controller, before he could validly exercise the power of cancellation of a dealer's licence given to him by the relevant Regulations in force in Ceylon. In this case, this method of construction was no great assistance to the applicant seeking to set aside a decision of the Controller by *certiorari* proceedings. *Liversidge* v. *Anderson* was an action against the Home Secretary for false imprisonment and the plaintiff would therefore have succeeded, had he been able to show that the Home Secretary's action was *ultra vires*; in *Nakkuda Ali* v. *Jayaratne* however, the plaintiff also had to establish that the Controller was required to act judicially, so that *certiorari* could be granted.[15] Lord RADCLIFFE observed[16]:

> "It is not difficult to think of circumstances in which the Controller might in any ordinary sense of the words, have reasonable grounds of belief without having ever confronted the licence holder with the information which is the source of his belief. It is a long step in the argument to say that because a man is enjoined that he must not take action unless he has reasonable ground for believing something he can only arrive at that belief by a course of conduct analogous to the judicial process."

Therefore *certiorari* was not granted.

Liversidge v. *Anderson* and *Nakkuda Ali* v. *Jayaratne* have both been severely criticised, particularly in *Ridge* v. *Baldwin*,[17] and the wide discretion conferred on the executive in these cases would probably not now be applied in other than very special circumstances.[18] *Liversidge* v. *Anderson* was explained in the New Zealand case of *Reade* v. *Smith*[19] by TURNER, J., who suggested that one of the main reasons for the decision was the danger to the nation in time of war of disclosing the sources of the Minister's factual information. In *Ross-Clunis* v. *Papadopoullos*,[20] a Privy Council appeal from Cyprus, the Commissioner of Limassol was empowered by regulation to take certain action, provided he "satisfied himself" as to certain matters. The Privy Council were of the opinion that on the facts there were ample grounds on which the Commissioner could here be "satisfied", but in the course of the judgment, Lord MORTON OF HENRYTON said[21]:

> ". . . [their Lordships] . . . think that if it could be shown that there were *no* [*sic*] grounds on which the appellant could be so satisfied, a court might infer either that he did not honestly form that view or that, in forming it, he could not have applied his mind to the relevant facts."

---

15 See *post*, p. 168, as to the grounds for the grant of an order of *certiorari*.

16 [1951] A.C. 66, at p. 77.

17 [1963] 2 All E.R. 66; [1964] A.C. 40, *ante*, p. 119 and see below. In *Maradana Mosque Trustees* v. *Badi-Ud-Din Mahmoud*, [1966] 1 All E.R. 545; [1967] 1 A.C. 13, the decision of a Minister to close a school was treated as being quasi-judicial, and *certiorari* was granted when it was proved that natural justice had not been observed.

18 It has also been suggested to the writer that a more tolerant attitude is taken by the courts towards powers granted to a Minister of the Crown responsible to Parliament, than that adopted towards the same powers granted to a lesser official (such as a police officer or a District Commissioner as in *Ross-Clunis case* (*post*)). This may well be so but the argument has not been adopted in any reported cases.

19 [1959] N.Z.L.R. 996, at p. 1000.

20 [1958] 2 All E.R. 23.

21 [1958] 2 All E.R. 23, at p. 33.

In other words, the courts will apparently apply to this type of expression an objective or external test; it will not be sufficient merely for the person or administrative agency on whom the statutory power is conferred (subject to the statutory condition that he must be "satisfied" as to some state of facts), to come forward and say that he *is* so satisfied.[22]

Since *Ridge* v. *Baldwin*[1] it seems clear that the courts will not lightly accept such expressions as "the Minister is satisfied", or "final", as totally excluding review. In this case, Lord REID characterised *Liversidge* v. *Anderson* as "a very peculiar decision",[2] and went on to criticise *Nakkuda Ali* v. *Jayaratne*, saying[3]:

> "This House is not bound by decisions of the Privy Council and for my part nothing short of a decision of this House directly in point would induce me to accept the position that, although an enactment expressly requires an official to have reasonable grounds for his decision, our law is so defective that a subject cannot bring up such a decision for review however seriously he may be affected and however obvious it may be that the official acted in breach of his statutory obligation."

An objective test has also been applied to a number of statutory provisions conferring a power on a Minister or other agency to make such rules or regulations as "he may consider necessary" to achieve some specified purpose. Thus, in *A.-G. for Canada* v. *Hallett and Carey, Ltd.*, Lord RADCLIFFE said[4]:

> "Here the words that invest the Governor[5] with power are neither vague nor ambiguous: Parliament has chosen to say explicitly that he shall do whatever things he may deem necessary or advisable. That does not allow him to do whatever he may feel inclined, for what he does must be capable of being related to one of the prescribed purposes."

This passage was cited in *Reade* v. *Smith* (*ante*), where TURNER, J., went on to say, while considering a power conferred on the Governor-General of New Zealand to make such regulations as he "thinks necessary", for certain specified purposes:

> "I hold that [these words] lay upon me the duty of inquiring whether the purposes of the regulation could reasonably as a matter of law have been considered by the Governor-General to be necessary in order to secure the due administration of the Act; and if the regulation cannot pass this test it will become my duty to declare that it is *ultra vires* and void."[6]

Again, in *Ross-Clunis* v. *Papadopoullos* (*ante*), the regulation under which the Controller acted had been made under an Order in Council conferring powers on the Governor to make such regulations

> "as appeared to him to be necessary or expedient for securing the public safety,"

---

[22] But see *obiter* to the contrary, by ROMER, J., in *Land Realisation Co., Ltd.* v. *The Postmaster General*, [1950] 1 All. E.R. 1062, at p. 1067.

[1] [1963] 2 All E.R. 66; [1964] A.C. 40.

[2] *Ibid.*, at p. 76.

[3] *Ibid.*, at p. 79.

[4] [1952] A.C. 427, at p. 450.

[5] Of one of the Canadian Provinces (Manitoba).

[6] *Ibid.*, at p. 1002.

etc. The Privy Council considered that the regulation in question was clearly related to the purposes specified, and was therefore not *ultra vires*, but the implication followed that review by the courts was not excluded, in spite of the apparent wide terms of the statutory power, so as to prevent them from examining a particular exercise of that power and ensuring that it fell within the purposes of the enabling statute.

The jurisdiction of the superior courts is therefore not readily or lightly to be excluded by phrases of the kind here mentioned,[7] and the courts will be zealous to exercise their powers of judicial review. Where, however, Parliament has conferred an administrative discretion on a Minister or agency, it seems that the courts are almost equally ready to acknowledge themselves defeated, and to admit that they then have no review powers.

The difficulty here is to recognise those cases in which the courts will say Parliament has conferred an unfettered discretion on the administrative agency, and to distinguish them from the cases where the agency will be expected to exercise its discretion in accordance with standards, prescribed in the statute or implied by the court.

In *Nakkuda Ali* v. *Jayaratne*[8] as we have seen, the Privy Council refused to grant *certiorari*, because they held that the decision of the Commissioner to revoke the dealer's licence was an administrative and not a judicial act:

> "In truth when he [the Commissioner] cancels a licence he is not determining a question; he is taking executive action to withdraw a privilege because he believes, and has reasonable grounds to believe, that the holder is unfit to retain it."[9]

This was followed in *R.* v. *Metropolitan Police Commissioner, ex parte Parker*,[10] where the Commissioner had revoked a licence held by a London taxi-cab driver acting under the Metropolitan Public Carriage Act, 1869, and powers delegated to the Commissioner by the London Cab Order, 1934. The order gave powers to revoke a licence when the Commissioner was "satisfied" of the holder's unfitness; in purported exercise of this power the Commissioner gave the holder no prior opportunity of any hearing or of putting his case before him, but acted on police reports and revoked his licence. The Queen's Bench Division nevertheless refused to grant *certiorari* to quash the Commissioner's decision, holding that he acted administratively and not judicially, in that he was exercising "what I may call a disciplinary authority",[11] and that therefore the court had no jurisdiction to review his decision (even on the grounds of a breach of the *audi alteram partem* rule).

---

[7] Certainly not so far as the scrutiny of delegated legislation is concerned. See also the tax case of *Customs and Excise Commissioners* v. *Cure and Deeley, Ltd.*, [1961] 3 All E.R. 641; [1962] 1 Q.B. 340.

[8] [1951] A.C. 66.

[9] *Ibid.*, at p. 78, *per* Lord RADCLIFFE.

[10] [1953] 2 All E.R. 717, and see "The Cab-Driver's Licence Case", by D. M. Gordon, Q.C., at (1954), 70 L.Q.R. 203.

[11] *Per* Lord GODDARD, C.J., at p. 721. It is difficult to appreciate why the powers of the Commissioner to revoke a licence of a cab driver should be categorised as "disciplinary", as the Commissioner is in no sense a superior of the cab driver, there is no common employment, nor are cab drivers members of a uniformed "force".

This argument that a superior officer exercising disciplinary powers should be free from judicial review of his decisions, a notion which seems alien to ordinary ideas of justice, was also accepted in the case of *Ex parte Fry*.[12] Here a fireman sought an order of *certiorari* to quash a decision of the chief officer of his fire brigade cautioning the applicant, because he had been guilty of disobedience as he had refused to clean the uniform of a superior officer when he was ordered to do so. The grounds of the application were that the order was illegal, and that the chief officer did not afford the applicant a proper opportunity of stating his case before he came to a decision. Lord GODDARD, C.J., at first instance followed his own decision in *R.* v. *Metropolitan Police Commissioner, ex parte Parker*, and refused to grant *certiorari*. When the case came before the Court of Appeal,[13] SINGLETON, L.J., said that *Parker's case* was decided on two grounds, namely (i) that the Commissioner of Police was not sitting in a judicial or quasi-judicial capacity, and (ii) that the remedy which was sought was discretionary in the court. In *Ex parte Fry* it would have been difficult to maintain that the chief officer was not acting judicially, and therefore the Court of Appeal's decision, upholding the Divisional Court's refusal to grant a *certiorari*, was based on the discretionary argument. The fire service code provided for an appeal to the fire authority from the decision of the chief officer in any case where the punishment imposed was more severe than a caution. As a caution only was imposed in this case there was no such right of appeal, but, said SINGLETON, L.J.:

> "there are ways and means of bringing to the notice of the fire authority in a proper case the conduct of one who has to preside over a disciplinary tribunal of this kind if it is thought right and proper that that should be done".

Therefore the discretion of the court in refusing *certiorari* was held to have been correctly exercised.[14]

Parker's and *Fry's* cases were not discussed in *Ridge* v. *Baldwin*,[15] although it may be that they would not be followed to-day. *Ridge* v. *Baldwin* also did not consider the important discretions conferred on the Home Secretary in respect of the control of aliens under the Aliens Restriction Acts, 1914 and 1919, and the Aliens Order, 1953.[16] Under art. 20 of the Order the Home Secretary could, if "he thinks fit" make a deportation order requiring an alien to leave and remain out of the United Kingdom if (*inter alia*) the Home Secretary "deems it to be conducive to the public good to make a deportation order against the alien".

---

[12] [1954] 2 All E.R. 118.

[13] [1954] 2 All E. R. 118, at p. 121.

[14] This reasoning was followed by PLOWMAN, J., in *Buckoke* v. *Greater London Council*, [1970] 2 All E.R. 193; [1971] Ch. 655, also involving disciplinary matters concerning a fire brigade, where the learned judge exercised his discretion and refused to grant an injunction restraining the fire authority from continuing disciplinary proceedings against the plaintiff. But in the Scots case of *McDonald* v. *Lanarkshire Fire Brigade Joint Committee*, 1959 S.L.T. 309, the Outer House granted a reduction and interdict against the fire authority in circumstances not very different from those in *Ex parte Fry*. Lord GUTHRIE was of the opinion that "there is not a necessary distinction between disciplinary procedure and judicial or quasi-judicial procedure" (at p. 313).

[15] [1963] 2 All E.R. 66; [1964] A.C. 40; *ante*, p. 119.

[16] S.I. 1953, No. 1671. These discretions are now controlled by the Immigration Act, 1971; *post*, p. 263.

In *R.* v. *Brixton Prison (Governor), ex parte Soblen*,[17] the validity of a deportation order made under this power was challenged in proceedings on a writ of *habeas corpus*. It was alleged (*inter alia*) that the order was bad, because it had been made without the alien deportee having been given an opportunity of a hearing (*i.e.*, that the procedure was contrary to natural justice), and also because the order had been made for the wrong motive or purpose.[18] In the Court of Appeal Lord DENNING, M.R., refused to accept either of these arguments.[19] As a general rule a party aggrieved has a right to be heard:

> "But there are exceptions. A statute may expressly or by necessary implication provide that the person affected is not to be given a right to be heard. Such an exception has been held to exist in the case of deportation orders."[20]

As to the second point, his Lordship said:

> "The court cannot compel the Home Secretary to disclose the materials on which he acted, but if there is evidence on which it could reasonably be supposed that the Home Secretary was using the power of deportation for an ulterior purpose, then the court can call on the Home Secretary for an answer; and if he fails to give it, it can upset his order. But, on the facts of this case, I can find no such evidence."[21]

Therefore the application for a writ of *habeas corpus* was refused; it was for the Home Secretary to decide whether the deportation was conducive to the public good, and since rules of natural justice do not apply in such a case[22], the courts would not interfere unless it appeared that the Minister was acting improperly.

These cases are in many respects unsatisfactory, although the decision in *Ridge* v. *Baldwin* is certainly to be welcomed. It is by no means clear why the revocation of a licence should be regarded as an administrative process not subject to review in the courts, especially as there are many cases where the *grant* of a licence pursuant to some administrative control has been characterised as a quasi-judicial process susceptible to review.[23] Disciplinary action, at least in circumstances where the statute has made no provision for an alternative remedy,[1] is a topic which one might think most suitable for judicial review. The control of aliens, leaves a wide discretion in the Executive; but the Immigration Act, 1971, now provides a statutory appellate procedure against refusal of

---

[17] [1962] 3 All E.R. 641; [1963] 2 Q.B. 243.

[18] It was alleged that the deportation order had been made, not because the alien (Dr. Soblen) was an undesirable alien, but because he was wanted by the U.S. Government to face a trial on a charge of espionage. The correct procedure in such a case (said Soblen) was by way of an extradition order, which could not be granted under the treaty between the U.K. and U.S.A., because espionage is a political offence. Therefore, it was argued, it was improper to use the deportation procedure in such a case.

[19] See pp. 658 and 661.

[20] Here his Lordship cited the earlier case of *R.* v. *Leman Street Police Station Inspector, ex parte Venicoff*, [1920] 3 K.B. 72.

[21] Compare the reasoning adopted in *Ross-Clinics* v. *Papadopoullos*, *ante*, p. 164.

[22] See also *Schmidt* v. *Home Office*, [1968] 3 All E.R. 795, *per* UNGOED-THOMAS, J. (at p. 801).

[23] Specific rights of appeal are given by statute in many cases where a licence is withheld: *e.g.*, an appeal lies to the magistrates under many sections of the Public Health Act, 1936, or to a special tribunal if licences are not granted for the use of a special designation in connection with the sale of milk, under regulations made under the Food and Drugs Act, 1955.

[1] As in *Ex parte Fry* (*ante*).

permission to enter the U.K. (and as to certain other matters).[2] Professor Wade[3] has referred to several Commonwealth decisions where the courts adopted a different attitude to such matters; in this country the atmosphere created by the Franks Report, the Tribunals and Inquiries Act, 1958, the *Justice* Report,[4] the Parliamentary Commissioner Act, 1967, and the 1971 Act, have improved the position in this particular field; perhaps in the future more frequent express provision will be made either for statutory "appeals" to the courts or allowing review by the traditional methods of the prerogative orders and actions for declarations.

The attitude of the courts towards the decisions of some administrative agency other than a Minister or Government Department, such as a local authority, seems to be somewhat different. As we have seen, expressions like "such wages as they may think fit"[5] and "review from time to time"[6] do not confer on a local authority any absolute discretion; the reasonableness of their decisions will be judged by an objective test, and the courts will not be content merely to allow the authority to take such decisions as they may consider reasonable. Thus, although section 85 of the Housing Act, 1936,[7] conferred a duty on the local authority to review rents charged for houses provided by them, and also empowered them to grant such rebates from rent "as they may think fit", it was held in *Smith* v. *Cardiff Corporation* (*No.* 2),[8] that the reasonableness of such charges and rebates was open to review by the courts, because the charges must be reasonable in fact, and not merely reasonable in the opinion of the local authority. In this case, DANCKWERTS, J., said[9]:

> "It is not sufficient that the corporation have acted in an entirely *bona fide* manner, and have formed the opinion that the charges are reasonable. If the reasonableness of the charges is challenged, it is necessary for the court to examine the circumstances and to decide whether the charges are reasonable, though the onus of showing that they are not reasonable must rest on the plaintiffs."

Similar questions were raised in *Summerfield* v. *Hampstead Borough Council*,[10] where again the court was prepared to consider whether the rent scheme of the defendant local authority was a reasonable one. But provided the local authority have considered the matter fully and in accordance with the statute, it is not for the court "to substitute its view of what would be reasonable for the view of the corporation on whom this discretion has been conferred by Parliament".[11] This jurisdiction to review was open to the court in these cases because of the terms of the statute; again it is really a question of the application of

---

[2] Chapter VIII, *post*, 263.
[3] *Administrative Law*, 1st Edn., p. 164.
[4] Chapter V, *ante*, p. 95.
[5] *Roberts* v. *Hopwood*, [1925] A.C. 578, and *ante*, p. 139.
[6] *Taylor* v. *Munrow*, [1960] 1 All E.R. 455, and *ante*, p. 139.
[7] The method of fixing council house rents has since been changed drastically by the Housing Finance Act, 1972.
[8] [1955] 1 All E.R. 113; [1955] Ch. 159.
[9] At p. 121.
[10] [1957] 1 All E.R. 221.
[11] *Per* HARMAN, L. J., in *Luby* v. *Newcastle-under-Lyme Corpn.*, [1964] 3 All E.R. 169, at p. 173; [1965] 1 Q.B. 214, at p. 230 (another housing rents case).

the *ultra vires* doctrine. The whole problem of the circumstances in which the terms of a statute will be held to be so wide as to exclude any opportunity of judicial review, is an extremely difficult one, and ultimately each case must turn on the terms of the particular statute. Where a local authority are given powers to decide to impose conditions or make byelaws, "as they think fit", the discretion may well be found by the courts to be an absolute one, and capable of being questioned in a court of law only on the ground that the discretion has not really been exercised at all.[12]

(e) Where exclusive remedy provided.—In many contexts where a statute has made a specific remedy available to a person aggrieved by a decision taken under a statute by an administrative agency, the courts will decline jurisdiction to review that decision in other legal proceedings. This is based not so much on the express terms of the statute,[13] as on the situation which Parliament must have intended to result as a consequence of an express remedy being provided by the statute. Sometimes the statute expressly excludes any review other than that specifically provided,[14] but we are here concerned with the class of case where the court decides that the intention of the statute was that the specific remedy provided should be exclusive.

Thus, a local authority were put under a duty by section 14 of the Public Health Act, 1936,[15] to

> "provide such public sewers as may be necessary for effectually draining their district for the purposes of this Act".

By section 322 of the same Act, any person aggrieved by a failure of a local authority to perform this duty in a particular instance, could complain to the Secretary of State on the ground that the authority had

> "failed to discharge their functions under this Act in any case where they ought to have done so".

Therefore it was held in a case[16] arising out of the corresponding sections of earlier statutes, that no action would lie in the courts against a local authority who had failed to provide a public sewer where they ought to have done so; the plaintiff should have pursued his remedy by way of appeal to the Minister (now the Secretary of State).

In *Healey* v. *Minister of Health*,[17] the plaintiff brought an action for a declaration to the effect that he was a "mental health officer" for the purposes of the National Health Service (Superannuation) Regulations, 1950, this question having already been determined by the Minister adversely to the plaintiff by a procedure provided for in the regulations.

---

[12] See the judgment of Lord GREENE, M.R., in *Associated Provincial Picture Houses* v. *Wednesbury Corpn.*, [1947] 2 All E.R. 680, at p. 682; [1948] 1 K.B. 223.

[13] Although this may sometimes be the case, as in *Vestry of St. James and St. John Clerkenwell* v. *Feary* (1890), 24 Q.B.D. 703.

[14] As in *Smith* v. *East Elloe R.D.C.* (*ante*, p. 158).

[15] A duty now vested in the water authority under the Water Act, 1973; *post*, p. 444.

[16] *Pasmore* v. *Oswaldtwistle U.D.C.*, [1898] A.C. 387, and see also *Cutler* v. *Wandsworth Stadium*, [1949] 1 All E.R. 544; [1949] A.C. 398, for an example of the general principle from a different context. See also the present author's *Law of Sewers and Drains*, 4th Edn., at p. 32.

[17] [1954] 2 All E.R. 580; [1954] 2 Q.B. 221.

It was held that the procedure by way of declaration could not be used in this manner, which in effect amounted to an appeal against the determination of the Minister. The statute provided that the matter was to be determined by the Minister and therefore the court had no jurisdiction to review the same matter[18] of which the Minister alone had jurisdiction, and from whose decision that statute had made no provision for appeal. Similarly, in *Punton* v. *Ministry of Pensions and National Insurance* (*No.* 2)[19] a plaintiff was refused a declaration in a case where the matter to be decided was vested by statute within the jurisdiction of an administrative tribunal.

In *Barraclough* v. *Brown*,[20] a harbour undertaking was empowered by statute to recover their expenses incurred in removing a vessel sunk in a harbour under its control, from the owner of that vessel, although such expenses would not be so recoverable at common law. The statute made such expenses recoverable summarily before the local magistrates, but in this case the harbour undertaking sought to recover them by action in the High Court. In the House of Lords, Lord HERSCHELL said[21]:

> "The only right conferred [by the statute] is 'to recover such expenses from the owner of such vessel in a court of summary jurisdiction'. I do not think the appellant can claim to recover by virtue of the statute, and at the same time insist upon doing so by means other than those prescribed by the statute which alone confers the right. . . . I think it would be very mischievous to hold that when a party is compelled by statute to resort to an inferior court he can come first to the High Court to have his right to recover—the very matter relegated to the inferior court—determined."

As Lord WATSON said[1]:

> "The right and the remedy are given *uno flatu* and the one cannot be dissociated from the other."

Where, however, the plaintiff would have had another remedy apart from the statute, and that remedy is not expressly barred, it seems that the remedy (*e.g.*, by way of an order of *certiorari* or an action for a declaration) is not excluded simply because an additional remedy is provided by the statute. Thus in *Pyx Granite Co., Ltd.* v. *Ministry of Housing and Local Government*,[2] the appellants asked the court for a declaration to the effect that they were entitled to carry out certain quarrying operations on their land without the need to obtain planning permission under the Town and Country Planning Act, 1947. It was contended[3] that the court had no jurisdiction to grant such a declaration, because section 17 of the 1947 Act provided a specific procedure (by way of application to the local planning authority and a possible

---

18 It should be noted that there was no question here of challenging the Minister's decision on any grounds of *ultra vires* or breach of natural justice; it was desired to obtain a declaration on the merits of the case, to an effect opposite to that of the Minister's decision. For other examples, see *East Midlands Gas Board* v. *Doncaster Corpn.*, [1953] 1 All E.R. 54 and *Gillingham Corpn.* v. *Kent County Council*, [1952] 2 All E.R. 1107; [1953] Ch. 37.

19 [1964] 1 All E.R. 448; [1964] 1 W.L.R. 226; and *post*, p. 190.

20 [1897] A.C. 615.

21 *Ibid.*, at p. 620.

1 At p. 622.

2 [1959] 3 All E.R. 1; [1960] A.C. 260.

3 A number of other issues were raised in this case which are not here relevant.

appeal to the Minister, which was then said to be "final") whereby this same question could be determined.[4] It was held in the House of Lords that the principle of *Barraclough* v. *Brown* (*ante*) did not apply. As Lord JENKINS said[5]:

> "The appellants are not seeking to enforce statutory rights by methods other than those prescribed by the Act creating them. They are merely seeking to ascertain the extent of their statutory liabilities. It is true that section 17 itself may be said in a sense to create a statutory remedy in the shape of an application under it for the determination of any question of the kind to which it refers, but it is not a remedy for the breach of any statutory right. It is merely directed to the removal of doubts regarding the effect of the legislation in particular cases."

Therefore this special procedure did not have the effect of shutting out the general remedy by way of an action for a declaration. In *Ridge* v. *Baldwin*,[6] Lord REID said:

> "There are many cases where two remedies are open to an aggrieved person, but there is no general rule that by going to some other tribunal he puts it out of his power thereafter to assert his rights in court."

The terms of the statute must therefore be examined carefully; only if it clearly appears that the intention was to make a specific remedy exclusory will the courts refuse to exercise the normal remedies of judicial review, just because a specific remedy has been provided.

5. THE REMEDIES

We must now consider the several kinds of remedy that may be available to a citizen aggrieved by an agency decision of an executive, legislative or judicial nature, on one or more of the several grounds previously discussed. The different remedies may be classified as follows:

(a) Statutory—those for which specific provision is made by a statute or some form of subordinate legislation, and which will vary from case to case;
(b) Prerogative—the orders replacing[7] the former prerogative writs of prohibition, *certiorari* and *mandamus*, and the remaining writs of *habeas corpus* and *quo warranto*;
(c) Common Law remedies—actions in tort or for breach of contract —actions on a statute—criminal proceedings;
(d) Equitable remedies—injunctions and declarations[8];
(e) Self help—the extent to which an individual may legally be entitled to ignore, resist or obstruct some administrative action taken against him.

It is now proposed to deal with these different remedies *seriatim*.

---

[4] See now s. 53 of the Town and Country Planning Act, 1971.
[5] At p. 17.
[6] [1963] 2 All E.R. 66, at p. 81; [1964] A.C. 40, at p. 81.
[7] By virtue of the Administration of Justice (Miscellaneous Provisions) Act, 1938; *post*, p. 177.
[8] Reviewers of previous editions have criticised the designation of the action for a declaration as an "equitable" remedy, but it has always been thought of as within the jurisdiction of the Court of Chancery; see, for example, the cases referred to by Zamir in *The Declaratory Judgment*, at p. 7.

(a) Statutory remedies.—Several different kinds of remedies may be provided for in different statutes; and it is also impossible to define precisely which circumstances will be accepted by Parliament as justifying the creation of a special remedy. In general terms, however, the kinds of factual situation where an "appeal" of some kind is normally provided for in the statute, may be illustrated as follows:

(i) where an individual is prohibited from pursuing a particular kind of employment or business without obtaining a licence from an administrative agency, and where the agency are given a discretion to grant or withhold such licence, within prescribed limits[9];

(ii) where the statute empowers an agency to assess an individual's liability to taxation[10];

(iii) where the statute enables an agency to impose restrictions on property rights[11];

(iv) in cases of compulsory acquisition of estates and interests in land,[12] or of chattels.[13]

It will be noted that there is no heading here referring to interference by the executive with personal liberty. This is because the executive in this country cannot order the imprisonment or detention of an individual except under specific statutory authority, which is normally conferred only in times of emergency.[14] When under war-time conditions the executive has in the past found it necessary to obtain arbitrary powers of arrest and detention from Parliament, these have been conferred without restriction, the liberty of the subject being left entirely to the good sense of the Minister concerned, who is responsible for his actions to the House of Commons, but whose decisions have not normally in this context been open to question in the courts. In normal times the liberty of the subject is left to the protection of the courts, and statutes rarely confer powers affecting this topic on administrative agencies. The position was, until recently,[15] very different in connection with aliens, in respect of whom a very wide discretionary power is conferred by statute on the Home Secretary. The various

[9] As, for example, in the control of the use of special designations in connection with the sale of milk, or the licensing of hackney carriage proprietors outside the Metropolis (in London there is no right of appeal in the latter case; *Ex parte Parker*, above p. 155).

[10] An appeal lies against the decisions of the General or Special Commissioners under the Taxes Management Act, 1970, (*post*, p. 165), and similarly from the decisions of the local valuation officer for rating under the General Rate Act, 1967 (Chapter VIII, *post*, p. 241).

[11] In agricultural controls exercisable under the authority of the Minister of Agriculture Fisheries and Food, appeals lie to the Agricultural Land Tribunals; see also as to town and country planning, Chapter VIII, *post*, p. 235.

[12] Under the Acquisition of Land (Authorisation Procedure) Act, 1946: Chapter VIII, *post*, p. 229. Rights less than full ownership may be acquired compulsorily, as under the Pipe-lines Act, 1962.

[13] Under the Defence (General) Regulations, made under the Emergency Powers (Defence) Act, 1939, which conferred powers on various organs of the Executive to requisition chattels, appeals as to the amount of the compensation payable lay to the General Claims Tribunal.

[14] Such as the power under consideration in *Liversidge* v. *Anderson*, [1941] 3 All E.R. 338; [1942] A.C. 206, *ante*, p. 162.

[15] Above, p. 166, and *post*, p. 263.

remedies for which statutory provision may be made in particular instances can be listed as follows:

(i) *Appeals to the courts.*—Examples can be given of statutes providing for appeals to lie from the decision of an administrative agency to all the various "ordinary" courts, including the magistrates and the High Court.[16] The decisions from which such appeals lie may be those of different kinds of agency, including a local authority, or a Minister of the Crown. Similar considerations do not apply in practice to decisions of statutory corporations, because by the nature of their functions, the factual situations giving rise to a need for a right of appeal as above described, rarely if ever arise. A statutory corporation will normally be entitled to exercise monopoly rights but this will not otherwise entitle or require it to interfere with the ordinary rights of an individual.

Appeals of this kind will lie sometimes on defined grounds alone,[17] but more often the statute will say nothing about the grounds of appeal; in such a case the court will review the matter on both facts and law.[18]

Appeals from the decisions of administrative tribunals of various kinds are frequently provided for in the statutes creating the particular tribunal or tribunals. Here the appeal customarily lies either to the High Court[19] or to the Court of Appeal,[20] and the right is often restricted to points of law. The Franks Committee[1] recommended that an appeal on a point of law should lie to the courts from any tribunal decision, although they were of the opinion that special considerations applied to decisions of the National Insurance Commissioner and National Assistance Appeal Tribunals. Express provision was made for appeals to lie in a number of cases by section 9 of the Tribunals and Inquiries Act, 1958 (now s. 13 of the Act of 1971) and the principle was extended to decisions of the Minister after the holding of a statutory inquiry in a wide range of town and country planning matters by section 32 of the Town and Country Planning Act, 1959, and section 34 of the Caravan Sites and Control of Development Act, 1960.[2] In other branches of law also, since the passing of the 1958 Act, Parliament has been careful to make due provision for appeal to the courts in appropriate cases,[3]

---

[16] To the magistrates, from the decisions of local authorities, under several sections of the Public Health Act, 1936; to the county court, from similar decisions under sections of the Housing Acts of 1957 and 1961; to the Crown Court, from an order made by a local authority under s. 159 (4) of the Highways Act, 1959; to the High Court from a decision of the district auditor under s. 229 of the Local Government Act, 1933 (see now the Act of 1972, *post*, Chapter XV, p. 428). Many other examples could be given; and see Chapter V, *ante*, p. 92.

[17] See, for example, s. 290 (3) of the Public Health Act, 1936, or s. 117 (1) of the Highways Act, 1959.

[18] As in *Stepney Borough Council* v. *Joffe*, [1949] 1 All E.R. 256; [1949] 1 K.B. 599; see also *Sagnata Investments, Ltd.* v. *Norwich Corpn.*, [1971] 2 All E.R. 1441; [1971] 2 Q.B. 614.

[19] As in the case of compulsory acquisition (appeals against the decision of a Minister on a (restricted) point of law): Acquisition of Land (Authorisation Procedure) Act, 1946, First Schedule, para. 16.

[20] As in the case of the Lands Tribunal, under the Lands Tribunal Act, 1949, s. 3(4).

[1] Report, paras. 103–12.

[2] See now ss. 245–247 of the Town and Country Planning Act, 1971.

[3] As in the case of the appeal tribunals constituted under the Betting Levy Act, 1961. (see now Betting, Gaming and Lotteries Act, 1963).

or the same result has been achieved by the making of an order under section 15 (3) of the Tribunals and Inquiries Act, 1971 (or its predecessor in the 1958 Act), extending the effect of section 13 to newly created tribunals.[4]

The difficulty in this context is, of course, exactly what is meant by the expression "point of law". Failure to observe natural justice and other forms of excess of power clearly involve points of law, so does a failure to adjourn the proceedings before a tribunal which the appellant could not attend owing to adverse weather conditions.[5] Sometimes an "appeal on a point of law" comes very near to an appeal on the merits.[6]

(ii) *Appeals to a tribunal.*—In circumstances where a new statutory control or system of licensing is introduced, the statute also may create a special appellate tribunal or series of tribunals to which appeals will lie against decisions of the agency entrusted with original jurisdiction. Thus, the Betting Levy Act, 1961, (since replaced by the Betting, Gaming and Lotteries Act, 1963) made provision for the establishment of a Horserace Betting Levy Board who were given powers to assess the amount of "betting levy" that should be paid by each individual bookmaker. On receiving an assessment from the Board, a bookmaker may appeal to one of the four appeal tribunals constituted under section 29 of the 1963 Act. As is usual in this type of case, the jurisdiction of the tribunal is not restricted by any precise form of words, and any appeal may therefore be "at large", on merits as well as law.

In many cases there is a further appeal on a point of law from such a tribunal to the High Court, provided for either in the parent statute, or as a result of section 13 of the Tribunals and Inquiries Act, 1971.[7] In a few cases a new statute may make provision for an appeal to lie to an already existing tribunal. This has been done on several occasions in the case of the Lands Tribunal, statutes[8] giving the tribunal additional jurisdiction so that it now resembles an "ordinary" court of law even in the extent of its jurisdiction.[9]

(iii) *Appeals to a Minister.*—The device of providing for an appeal against an administrative decision to lie to a Minister is common in the

---

[4] As was done in the case of the Mental Health Review Tribunals set up under the Mental Health Act, 1959 (Chapter VIII, *post*, p. 254).

[5] *Priddle* v. *Fisher & Sons*, [1968] 3 All E.R. 506; [1968] 1 W.L.R. 1478.

[6] In *R.* v. *Industrial Injuries Commissioner, ex parte Amalgamated Engineering Union* [1966] 1 All E.R. 97; [1966] 2 Q.B. 21, the court refused to interfere with the Commissioner's decision as to whether an employee was acting in the course of his employment, as this was a "question of fact and degree"; a similar line is often taken in planning cases; *e.g. Marshall* v. *Nottingham Corpn.*, [1960] 1 All E.R. 659; [1960] 1 W.L.R. 707.

[7] Giving a general right of appeal on points of law: *ante.*

[8] *E.g.*, the Town and Country Planning Act, 1954, and the Rights of Light Act, 1959.

[9] See also the Redundancy Payments Act, 1965, which provided that certain questions arising thereunder should be referred to the tribunal constituted under s. 12 of the Industrial Training Act, 1964; see s. 9 and s. 56 (1) of the 1965 Act. Another example of a statutory tribunal is to be found in the Immigration Act, 1971, Chapter VII, *post*, p. 206.

local government field. Thus, an appeal lies to the Secretary of State for the Environment from a decision of a local authority under town and country planning controls.[10] Virtually the same effect is achieved by a statute which provides that a particular order or other administrative act of a local authority is not to have legal effect unless and until it has been confirmed by the Secretary of State, this being the normal provision in relation to such matters as compulsory purchase orders and clearance orders. In these cases the statute will normally provide that before the Secretary of State determines the appeal he must hold either a local inquiry or a "hearing", before some person appointed by him (that is, in the case where his confirmation is sought, assuming that some objection or representation has been lodged against the order in question). Statutory inquiries of this kind are discussed further in a subsequent Chapter.[11]

(iv) *Reference to arbitration.*—In a few instances, usually in matters where there is some question as to the amount of compensation to be paid by an administrative agency in the circumstances, a statute may make provision for an appeal against an agency decision to be determined by arbitration, in accordance with a more or less detailed procedure laid down in the statute. Before 1949 most compensation questions were determined in this manner, but now nearly all these matters are required to be referred to the Lands Tribunal. However, arbitration is still the appropriate method provided by statute for the determination of some questions, in particular for a number which may arise under the Highways Act, 1959.[12] Under this Act the parties must agree to submit to arbitration, the county court being given jurisdiction in the event of a failure to reach agreement. Under the Public Health Act, 1936, however, no alternative (where the amount involved is in excess of £50) is provided to arbitration,[13] and in this case the single arbitrator must be appointed by agreement between the parties or, in default, by the Secretary of State for the Environment.[14] Compulsory submission to arbitration is also provided for in the law of agricultural holdings.

(v) *General observations.*—In all these cases, the party seeking to take advantage of a particular statutory remedy must of course bring his case within the terms of the statute. He must also be able to satisfy the court that he is a person who, within the terms of the statute, is entitled to pursue that particular remedy. Under many statutes he will have to be able to prove that he is a "person [or a 'party'] aggrieved" by the decision against which he seeks to appeal or complain. This is an extremely difficult expression to apply in some

---

[10] Chapter VIII, *post*, p. 235.
[11] Chapter VII, *post*, pp. 218 *et seq.*
[12] See s. 267 thereof.
[13] Public Health Act, 1936, s. 278 (2).
[14] *Ibid.*, s. 303.

contexts. However, in spite of protests from the Bench,[15] it continues to be used in modern statutes, often without any explanation or definition being given in the statute. An administrative agency, such as a local authority, cannot be a "person aggrieved" merely because a court may have decided against them in proceedings taken against a decision made by the authority under statutory powers, and they therefore have no status to pursue the matter further under a right of appeal conferred by statute on a "person aggrieved"[16]; they may have been "frustrated in their legitimate purpose", but this does not make them a person aggrieved, unless the decision adverse to them has the effect of compelling them "to bear a legal burden".[17] Further, an administrative authority are not "aggrieved" in this sense even if a court of first instance has awarded costs against them.[18] "Person aggrieved" is, in the absence of any definition in the particular context, incapable of any precise explanation, but the term seems to include the following:

1. Anyone who, from the context of the particular statute, is expressly or by necessary implication, given a right of appeal to the court;
2. Anyone whose legal rights are directly affected as a consequence of the exercise of the statutory power complained of[19];
3. Any person who has been ordered to do something to which he takes exception, or who has suffered a legal grievance.[20]

If, on the other hand, the would-be appellant cannot establish to the satisfaction of the court that any legal rights of his have been infringed, or that the statute concerned contemplates him as one who should have a remedy, he will not normally be accepted as a person entitled to appeal under a right granted to "persons aggrieved". Thus, in

---

[15] See Lord PARKER, C.J., in *Ealing B.C.* v. *Jones*, [1959] 1 All E.R. 286, at p. 287; [1959] 1 Q.B. 384.

[16] "Is a person who cannot succeed in getting a conviction against another a person 'aggrieved'? He may be annoyed at finding that what he thought was a breach of the law is not a breach of the law; but is he 'aggrieved' because someone is held not to have done wrong? It is difficult to see that the section meant anything of that kind. The section does not give an appeal to anybody but a person who is by the direct act of the magistrates 'aggrieved'—that is, who has had something done or determined against him by the magistrate", said Lord COLERIDGE, C.J., in *R.* v. *Keepers of the Peace and Justices of the County of London* (1890), 25 Q.B.D. 357, at p. 361, and see also *Ealing B.C.* v. *Jones* (*ante*), where DONOVAN, J., said (at p. 289), "the word 'aggrieved' connotes some legal grievance, for example, a deprivation of something, an adverse effect on the title to something".

[17] Where, *e.g.*, they are rendered liable to bear some part (or the whole) of the expenses which they have unsuccessfully sought to recover from the respondent; see *Phillips* v. *Berkshire County Council*, [1967] 2 All E.R. 675; [1967] 2 Q.B. 991.

[18] *R.* v. *Dorset Sessions Appeals Committee, ex parte Weymouth Corpn.*, [1960] 2 All E.R. 410; [1960] 2 Q.B. 230.

[19] Thus, a local authority are not a "person aggrieved" in this sense simply because the court may have found against them in proceedings they had commenced under some administrative statute, but they could be such a person (and so entitled to exercise a statutory right of appeal) if their own property rights were concerned, as for instance where a proposal was made for an increase in the assessment for rating of a hereditament occupied by the authority: *R.* v. *Horsham and Worthing Assessment Committee, ex parte Burgess*, [1937] 2 K.B. 408.

[20] *Re Sidebotham, ex parte Sidebotham* (1880), 14 Ch.D. 458; see *per* JAMES, L.J., at p. 465.

Buxton v. *Minister of Housing and Local Government*[21] a landowner appealed to the High Court under section 31 of the Town and Country Planning Act, 1959, asking it to quash a decision of the Minister granting planning permission for certain development on land adjoining that of the appellant. The appellant, in attempting to pursue a statutory right of appeal open only to a "person aggrieved", sought to show that, although he was not the original applicant for planning permission, his land would be prejudicially affected if the development in question were allowed. In refusing to entertain the appeal, SALMON, J., said[22]:

> "In my judgment, the Minister's action which these applicants seek to challenge infringed none of their common law rights. They have no rights as individuals under the statutes. Accordingly, in my judgment, none of their legal rights has been infringed, and in these circumstances it could not, in my view, have been the intention of the legislature to enable them to challenge the Minister's decision in the courts. Ever since the judgment of JAMES, L.J., in the well-known case of *Re Sidebotham*,[1] it has been generally accepted that the words 'person aggrieved' in a statute connote the person with a legal grievance, that is to say, someone whose legal rights have been infringed."

On the other hand, in the Privy Council case of *A.-G. of Gambia* v. *N'Jie*,[2] Lord DENNING said that the definition adopted by JAMES, L.J., should not be regarded as "exhaustive".

> "The words 'person aggrieved' are of wide import and should not be subjected to a restrictive interpretation. They do not include, of course, a mere busybody who is interfering in things which do not concern him; but they do include a person who has a genuine grievance because an order has been made which prejudicially affects his interests".

It is doubtful, however, whether this view goes so far as to reverse the effect of *Buxton's* case (*ante*). A statutory remedy must therefore be carefully examined and strictly construed before a would-be appellant can be sure that the remedy will be available to him in the particular circumstances of his case.

(b) Prerogative remedies.—We come now to those traditional remedies whereby the Royal Courts have exercised supervisory jurisdiction over the inferior courts and which were originally granted by the King as the "fountain of justice", and by virtue of the royal prerogative. They were therefore known as the "prerogative writs", and have only become "orders in the nature of the former prerogative writs," since 1938.[3]

In the eighteenth century when such local government as existed outside the towns was exercised by the local justices of the peace,[4] the only supervision of their administration from any central authority was judicial in form and was exercised through the medium of the

---

[21] [1960] 3 All E.R. 408; [1961] 1 Q.B. 278; this litigation arose out of what later became known as the "Chalkpit affair"; see notes at [1961] P.L. 121, and [1962] J.P.L. 315, and Chapter VII, *post*, p. 221.

[22] *Buxton's* case, *supra*, at p. 412.

[1] (1880), 14 Ch.D. 458.

[2] [1961] 2 All E.R. 504, at p. 511.

[3] Administration of Justice (Miscellaneous Provisions) Act, 1938. As to the prerogative writs generally, see article at (1951), 11 C.L.J. 40, by Professor de Smith.

[4] See *History of Local Government in England*, by Redlich and Hirst (ed. Keith-Lucas, 1959), Chapter 2.

prerogative writs of *certiorari*, prohibition and *mandamus*.[5] With the development in the late nineteenth century of administrative tribunals and Government Departments entrusted with judicial functions, it was a short step to employ this supervisory jurisdiction once more in the field of public administration. Here of course it had a more appropriate part to play by giving some redress for a grievance, rather than, as in the eighteenth century, endeavouring to assert a somewhat uncertain central government policy by means of the accidents of litigation. The procedure of the prerogative writs was always highly technical, but we are spared from an examination of the technicalities because the three main writs were abolished by the Administration of Justice (Miscellaneous Provisions) Act, 1938, and orders of the same names were substituted therefor.[6] We will now consider each of these orders separately, and then say something of the surviving prerogative writ of *habeas corpus* and also the former proceedings for *quo warranto*.

(i) *Certiorari*.—It is virtually essential for any discussion of the order of *certiorari* to commence with a quotation from the famous judgment of ATKIN, L.J. (as he then was) in *R.* v. *Electricity Commissioners*,[7] which contains the following passage:

> "The matter comes before us [the Court of Appeal] upon rules for writs of prohibition and *certiorari* which have been discharged by the Divisional Court. Both writs are of great antiquity, forming part of the process by which the King's Courts restrained courts of inferior jurisdiction from exceeding their powers. Prohibition restrains the tribunal from proceeding further in excess of jurisdiction; *certiorari* requires the record or the order of the court to be sent up to the King's Bench Division, to have its legality inquired into, and, if necessary, to have the order quashed. It is to be noted that both writs deal with questions of excessive jurisdiction; and doubtless in their origin dealt almost exclusively with the jurisdiction of what is described in ordinary parlance as a court of justice. But the operation of the writs has extended to control the proceedings of bodies which do not claim to be, and would not be recognised as, courts of justice. Whenever any body of persons having legal authority to determine questions affecting the rights of subjects, and having the duty to act judicially, act in excess of their legal authority they are subject to the controlling jurisdiction of the King's Bench Division exercised in these writs."

The final sentence in this passage was criticised in *R.* v. *Manchester Legal Aid Committee, ex parte Brand*,[8] by PARKER, J. (as he then was), as being too wide. In this case he said (at pp. 487 and 489):

> "That the local committee was a body of persons having legal authority to determine questions affecting the rights of subjects was admitted and, indeed, is clear. The real contest in the present case is whether they also had the duty

---

[5] The absence of any centralised administrative control was in part a conscious reaction from Cromwell and his Major-Generals, and in part due to the abolition of the Star Chamber in 1640. The development of the prerogative writs as a means of judicial control may be seen in the history of the Sewer Commissioners: Jaffe and Henderson, "Judicial Review and the Rule of Law" (1956), 72 L.Q.R. 345, and de Smith, *Judicial Review of Administrative Action*, 3rd Edn., at p. 507.

[6] In the House of Commons, the then Attorney-General (Sir Donald Somervell) described the former procedure as being "encumbered by a mass of unintelligible archaic matter, much of which is disregarded at present but which cannot be got rid of without authority" (Hansard, 1937–8, Vol. 335, Col. 1328).

[7] [1924] 1 K.B. 171, at p. 204.

[8] [1952] 1 All E.R. 480; [1952] 2 Q.B. 413.

to act judicially. . . . The true view, as it seems to us, is that the duty to act judicially may arise in widely different circumstances which it would be impossible, and, indeed, inadvisable, to attempt to define exhaustively."

This is therefore one of the few areas of administrative law, or indeed of any branch of our law, where it is necessary to categorise a particular function as "judicial", for only if an inferior tribunal, a Minister, a public corporation, a local authority, or some other administrative agency are required to act "judicially", will it be possible to obtain an order of *certiorari* (or prohibition) to quash their decision. In this context it is clear that "judicial" includes "quasi-judicial", in the sense that the latter term is used by the Donoughmore Committee.[9] In *R.* v. *Electricity Commissioners* (*ante*), ATKIN, L.J.,[10] gave as examples of bodies whose decisions have been quashed by *certiorari*, licensing justices,[11] the Board of Education[12] and the Tithe Commissioners,[13] and in the case itself prohibition was granted to quash a scheme made by the Electricity Commissioners for the delegation of powers vested in the Joint Electricity Authority to Committees. *Certiorari* has also been granted to quash the decision of a local planning authority,[14] of a local legal aid committee,[15] of many furnished houses rent tribunals,[16] of an appeal tribunal whose decision was said by the statute to be "final"[17] and against the decision of a valuation officer of the Board of Inland Revenue in making a rating valuation list for a particular area.[18] It seems that it will also lie to the governing body of a University guilty of a breach of natural justice.[19] The order will not lie to a domestic tribunal, but it is not confined to statutory bodies, and it will lie to quash a decision of a body established under the prerogative.[20]

"The ambit of *certiorari* can be said to cover every case in which a body of persons, of a public as opposed to a purely private or domestic character, has to determine matters affecting[1] subjects provided always that it has a duty to act judicially."[2]

---

[9] *Ante*, p. 111.
[10] At pp. 204–5.
[11] *R.* v. *Woodhouse*, [1906] 2 K.B. 501.
[12] *Board of Education* v. *Rice*, [1911] A.C. 179, and see *ante*, p. 117.
[13] *Re Crosby-upon-Eden* (1849), 13 Q.B. 761.
[14] *R.* v. *Hendon R.D.C., ex parte Chorley*, [1933] 2 K.B. 696; this was decided on the special context of the Town Planning Act, 1925, and it is doubtful whether a similar decision would be taken in the context of the modern planning legislation (see p. 122, *ante*).
[15] *R.* v. *Manchester Legal Aid Committee, ex parte Brand*, [1952] 1 All E.R. 480; [1952] 2 Q.B. 413.
[16] *E.g.*, *R.* v. *Fulham Rent Tribunal, ex parte Zerek*, [1951] 1 All E.R. 482; [1951] 2 K.B. 1.
[17] *Re Gilmore's Appln.*, [1957] 1 All E.R. 796; [1957] 1 Q.B. 574.
[18] *R.* v. *Paddington Valuation Officer, ex parte Peachey Property Corpn., Ltd.*, [1965] 2 All E.R. 836; *certiorari* was not granted in this case, but it is clear that it would have been granted if an error of law could have been established.
[19] *R.* v. *Aston University Senate, ex parte Roffey*, [1969] 2 All E.R. 964; [1969] 2 W.L.R. 1418; see *post*, p. 272.
[20] *R.* v. *Criminal Injuries Compensation Board, ex parte Lain*, [1967] 2 All E.R. 770; [1967] 2 Q.B. 864.
[1] It is thus not confined to a consideration of a subject's legal rights.
[2] *Per* Lord PARKER, C.J., in *Lain's* case (*ante*), at p. 778.

This does not mean, however, that once the courts have allowed *certiorari* to be brought impugning a decision of a particular tribunal or agency, that all subsequent decisions of that agency will in future be categorised as "judicial" and subject to *certiorari*. One such case will establish a precedent only for similar decisions within the same jurisdiction of that particular agency. Again, an administrative agency may in some matters act administratively, and in others be required to act judicially,[3] and it is even possible for a Minister to be required to act judicially at one stage of a certain matter, and yet to be free to act administratively at a later (or earlier) stage in the same matter.[4] Only when the agency or Minister is so required to act judicially will *certiorari* lie to quash his decision. Apparently a disciplinary decision of a senior officer in a fire service is not a "judicial" decision,[5] neither is a decision of a committee of a local authority to grant or refuse a music and dancing licence,[6] nor is a preliminary decision as to whether a particular offence had been committed, or if so, whether a named individual was concerned in it.[7] A watch committee, when deciding whether to dismiss a chief constable, is acting judicially as there is no relationship of master and servant[8]; and so was a Minister in Ceylon when deciding whether a school should continue to be aided by the State.[9]

An order of *certiorari* is a judicial process whereby the order of the "court" below can be brought up before the supervising court, examined and quashed. The record cannot be amended, as the order of *certiorari* is a process of review and not of appeal. Not all the grounds of judicial review discussed earlier in this Chapter apply to procedure by way of *certiorari*; by the nature of the remedy the grounds must be those relevant to a judicial decision. As Dr. Yardley has said[10]:

> "The remedy may be obtained on the grounds of a defect in the jurisdiction of the court or tribunal below, or of a breach of the rules of natural justice in those proceedings, or an error of law on the face of the proceedings;"

the last mentioned ground being perhaps the most popular in recent years,[11] a popularity which is strengthened by the requirement of the Tribunals and Inquiries Act, 1971, that a Minister or a tribunal must give reasons for their decision.[12] In order that *certiorari* may lie, there must be a "record". It was formerly assumed that this meant the decision must have been formulated in writing, but this may not be necessary, as the supervising court may be prepared to grant *certiorari*

---

[3] *R.* v. *Registrar of Building Societies, ex parte A Building Society*, [1960] 2 All E.R. 549.

[4] *Robinson* v. *Minister of Town and Country Planning*, [1947] 2 All E.R. 851; [1947] K.B. 702; *B. Johnson & Co. (Builders), Ltd.* v. *Minister of Health*, [1947] 2 All E.R. 395. It is this class of case that is often classed as "quasi-judicial"; *ante*, p. 111.

[5] *Ex parte Fry*, [1954] 2 All E.R. 118 but this is doubtful; see p. 166.

[6] *Royal Aquarium and Summer and Winter Garden Society* v. *Parkinson*, [1892] 1 Q.B. 431, and Chapter IX, *post*, p. 285.

[7] *Jayawardane* v. *Silva*, [1970] 1 W.L.R. 1365, *per* Lord GUEST at p. 1370.

[8] *Ridge* v. *Baldwin*, [1963] 2 All E.R. 66; [1964] A.C. 40, and *ante*, p. 119.

[9] *Maradana Mosque (Board of Trustees)* v. *Badi-ud-Din Mahmud*, [1966] 1 All E.R. 545; [1967] 1 A.C. 13.

[10] "*Certiorari* and the Problem of *Locus Standi*" (1955), 71 L.Q.R. 388.

[11] As appears from such decisions as *R.* v. *Northumberland Compensation Appeal Tribunal, ex parte Shaw*, [1952] 1 All E.R. 122, *ante*, p. 142.

[12] See s. 12, and *ante*, p. 146.

where it can find an error in an oral decision.[13] The right to *certiorari* is not lightly to be excluded,[14] but it will not lie for an error of fact or because the decision of the inferior court was unreasonable; the procedural rules also must be observed and in some circumstances a plaintiff may be out of time for *certiorari* proceedings but still be able to take proceedings for a declaration.[15] *Certiorari* will not lie as a means of interfering with the legislative process,[16] nor does it lie to a domestic tribunal.[17]

Certiorari is said to be a discretionary remedy,[18] and therefore it will not normally be granted unless and until the plaintiff has exhausted other remedies reasonably available and equally appropriate, such as a statutory right of appeal.[19] Clearly where there is such a right of appeal it will normally be in the plaintiff's own interest to pursue such a remedy, as it will probably be cheaper and more expeditious than *certiorari* proceedings. Dr. Yardley has suggested[20] that *certiorari*, being a discretionary remedy, will be granted to anyone, whether he is a person aggrieved or not, the conduct and circumstances of the plaintiff being one of several factors which will be taken into consideration by the court when deciding whether to grant an order in a particular case. If, however, the plaintiff is a "person aggrieved", understanding the expression in the sense of *Re Sidebotham*,[1] and provided he has no other remedy, it seems that the court will be almost certain to grant a *certiorari* on his application.

> "But if he is not a person grieved, or if being a person grieved, he has another remedy, as, for instance, by appeal, then the discretion of the court remains intact to grant or refuse the order."[2]

---

[13] *R.* v. *Chertsey Justices, ex parte Franks,* [1961] 1 All E.R. 825; [1961] 2 Q.B. 152, and comment by D. M. Gordon at (1961), 77 L.Q.R. 322.

[14] *R.* v. *Medical Appeal Tribunal, ex parte Gilmore,* [1957] 1 All E.R. 796; [1957] 1 Q.B. 574, and *ante*, p. 155; Tribunals and Inquiries Act, 1971, s. 14.

[15] Proceedings in *certiorari* must be commenced within 6 months of the date of the decision it is desired to quash, unless a delay is accounted for to the satisfaction of the Court; R.S.C. 1965, O. 53, r. 2 (2), and see *Barnard* v. *National Dock Labour Board,* [1953] 1 All E.R. 1113; [1953] 2 Q.B. 18.

[16] *R.* v. *Legislative Committee of the Church Assembly, ex parte Haynes-Smith,* [1928] 1 K.B. 411.

[17] *Per* DENNING, L.J., in *Lee* v. *The Showman's Guild of Great Britain,* [1952] 1 All E.R. 1175; [1952] 2 Q.B. 329 at p. 346; as to domestic tribunals generally, see Chapter VIII, *post*, p. 266, and also *R.* v. *Disputes Committee of the National Joint Council for the Craft of Dental Technicians, ex parte Neate,* [1953] 1 All E.R. 327; [1953] 1 Q.B. 704.

[18] It will not be granted to an applicant whose conduct does not merit it. Thus, in the Australian case of *Permanent Trustee Co. of N.S.W.* v. *Municipality of Campbelltown* (1960), 34 A.L.J.R. 255, *certiorari* was refused to an applicant who sought to quash a decision of an inferior court given in proceedings commenced by himself, but in which the decision had been unfavourable to the applicant. *Certiorari* may also be refused to an applicant who is guilty of unreasonable delay: see, *e.g.*, *R.* v. *Stafford Justices, ex parte Stafford Corpn.*, [1940] 2 K.B. 33.

[19] The choice of remedies may in practice be determined by the nature of the grounds on which it is desired to challenge the decision of the inferior court; see Professor de Smith, *Judicial Review of Administrative Action*, 3rd. Edn., at pp. 335 *et seq.*

[20] "*Certiorari* and the Problem of *Locus Standi*" (1955), 71 L.Q.R. 388.

[1] (1880), 14 Ch.D. 458, and *ante*, p. 151.

[2] *Per* Lord DENNING in *Baldwin and Francis* v. *Patents Tribunal,* [1959] 2 All E.R. 433, at p. 448; [1959] A.C. 663 and see also *R.* v. *Patents Appeal Tribunal, ex parte J. R. Geigy, Société Anonyme,* [1963] 1 All E.R. 850; [1963] 2 Q.B. 728; *per* Lord PARKER, C.J., at p. 851.

It should also be remembered that the remedy by way of *certiorari* is not lightly to be excluded by a privative clause in a statute, in view of s. 14 of the Tribunals and Inquiries Act, 1971.[3]

In *R.* v. *Paddington Valuation Officer, ex parte Peachey Property Corpn., Ltd.*,[4] a company owning a large number of properties within the Paddington rating area sought a *certiorari* to quash the whole of the valuation list prepared for that area. In the course of his judgment in the Court of Appeal, Lord DENNING, M.R. discussed the various points that had to be established before this remedy could be granted, and these may be summarised as follows:

(1) Is *certiorari* a proper remedy in the circumstances, or is there some other remedy provided by statute for the particular case?
(2) Is the plaintiff a "party aggrieved"?
(3) Is *certiorari* available; is the respondent under a duty to act "judicially"?
(4) Are the consequences of granting *certiorari* such that the Court ought not to exercise its discretion in favour of granting the remedy?
(5) Can some ground be established on the basis of which *certiorari* can be granted? In other words, has there been some error of law? "I would say that, if a tribunal or body is guilty of an error which goes to the very root of the determination, in that it has approached the case on an entirely wrong footing, then it does exceed its jurisdiction."[5]

Questions 1–3 were answered affirmatively in favour of the applicants for *certiorari*; on question 4, it was argued that if the entire valuation list were quashed before a new one could be prepared, "chaos" would result and that therefore, as *certiorari* was a discretionary remedy, it should not be granted. Lord DENNING was prepared to avoid the chaos by suspending the operation of the *certiorari*; SALMON, L.J., however, roundly observed[6] that,

> "Whatever inconvenience or chaos might be involved in allowing the appeal, the court would not be deterred from doing so if satisfied [the valuation officer] had acted illegally."

In the outcome, the applicants lost only on question (5), in that they were unable to establish that there had been any error of law.

The remedy by way of *certiorari* is therefore not always satisfactory. First, it has to be shown that there was a duty to act judicially and that the applicant was "aggrieved". Second, there are procedural disadvantages; the 6 months time limit, the fact that discovery of documents cannot be obtained, and that *certiorari* will not lie against the Crown[7]; also the nature of the proceedings themselves, in that the

---

[3] *Ante*, p. 155.
[4] [1965] 2 All E.R. 836.
[5] At p. 842.
[6] At p. 852.
[7] But it will lie against a Minister acting as such: see, *e.g.*, *Padfield* v. *Minister of Agriculture, Fisheries and Food*, [1968] 1 All E.R. 694; [1968] A.C. 997.

"record" alone is examined and there can be no trial of disputed facts.[8] Finally (but this is a feature also of other remedies), the remedy is a discretionary one, and even a successful applicant may find difficulty in obtaining an order for costs.[9]

(ii) *Prohibition.*—An order of prohibition is in many respects similar to *certiorari*; it is granted by the High Court, on the same grounds as *certiorari* to prevent an inferior court or government agency required to act in a judicial manner, from exceeding its jurisdiction.[10] Often proceedings for prohibition are combined with proceedings for some other prerogative remedy, such as mandamus. It seems that anyone can obtain an order of prohibition, and the plaintiff does not have to show that he is a "person aggrieved", or has any personal interest in the matter,[11] but the remedy is a discretionary one, and will not be granted as of right.[12]

(iii) *Mandamus.*—This order is different in nature from prohibition and *certiorari*; it commands any person to whom it is directed to carry out a public duty imposed by law. The order is therefore not restricted in operation to orders against inferior tribunals and government agencies required to act judicially or quasi-judicially. Indeed, it is an instrument of judicial review of the discretionary acts of an inferior agency only in the sense that an order of *mandamus* can be obtained if an agency has not exercised a discretion vested in it by statute; moreover, if a discretion has been abused, it can be said that the discretion has not been exercised at all, and that therefore *mandamus* will lie ordering the agency to exercise its discretion properly. Otherwise, however, *mandamus* cannot be used as a judicial process to scrutinise or reverse the manner in which a discretion has been exercised by an agency in a particular instance.

An order of *mandamus* was granted against a rent tribunal which had wrongly held that they had no jurisdiction to hear and determine an application properly made to them, but[13] no order was granted in a case where the tribunal had correctly declined jurisdiction.[14] A *mandamus* was granted ordering the Special Commissioners of Income Tax to give a certain direction under the Finance Acts affecting the liability of the applicants to profits tax,[15] and also against a county

---

[8] Further, although more than one prerogative remedy can be sought in the same proceedings, an application for *certiorari* (or prohibition) cannot be combined with an action for damages. Exceptionally the court has jurisdiction to allow a cross-examination of deponents to affidavits in proceedings for *certiorari*: see *R.* v. *Stokesley Justices*, [1956] 1 All E.R. 563; [1956] 1 W.L.R. 254.

[9] This point was discussed in *Tysons (Contractors), Ltd.* v. *Minister of Housing and Local Government* (1965), 63 L.G.R. 375.

[10] And see the speech of ATKIN, L.J., in *R.* v. *Electricity Commissioners*, cited *ante*, p. 178.

[11] As in *R.* v. *Minister of Health, ex parte Villiers*, [1936] 1 All E.R. 817.

[12] See article by Dr. Yardley, "Prohibition and *Mandamus* and the Problem of *Locus Standi*" (1957), 73 L.Q.R. 534. For a recent example of a case in which prohibtiion was granted, see *R.* v. *Minister of Health, ex parte Ellis*, [1967] 3 All E.R. 65; [1968] 1 Q.B. 84.

[13] *R.* v. *Paddington Rent Tribunal*, [1955] 1 All E.R. 691.

[14] *R.* v. *Twickenham Rent Tribunal, ex parte Dunn*, [1953] 2 All E.R. 734; [1953] 2 Q.B. 425.

[15] *R.* v. *Special Commissioners of Income Tax*, [1957] 2 All E.R. 167.

court judge requiring him to make an order for payment of costs out of court to a legally aided litigant.[16] If an agency refuses to exercise a discretion because it has laid down a policy rule in advance, *mandamus* will lie to require the agency to hear and determine the application according to law.[17] *Mandamus* will lie to enforce any duty imposed by statute, such as the service of a notice[18] or, in a proper case, the issue of a licence.[19]

The duty which it is sought to enforce by order of *mandamus* must be of a public nature; thus, where the duty was one imposed on an officer of a university by the university's statutes to convene a meeting, this was held to be a domestic matter and one which should be settled by the visitor to the University; *mandamus* was therefore refused.[20] On the other hand, the duty need not have been imposed by statute,[1] and it certainly need not be of a judicial nature. A hackney carriage licence granted (outside London) under the Town Police Clauses Act, 1847, is granted in respect of the carriage, and not the owner, and therefore where a local authority refused—possibly for improper reasons—to give effect to a change of ownership in manner provided for in the statute, an order of *mandamus* was granted ordering them to take the appropriate action.[2] A local authority are under a duty to comply with their own standing orders as to inviting tenders for contracts,[3] and therefore *mandamus* was granted on the application of a ratepayer requiring them so to comply.[4] Where, however, a duty is by statute expressly made enforceable against a government agency, such as a local authority, by a Minister of the Crown,[5] it seems that *mandamus* will be refused to a private individual.[6] In *R.* v. *Metropolitan Police Commissioner, ex parte Blackburn,*[7] a former Member of Parliament took proceedings for a *mandamus* requiring the Commissioner to reverse a policy decision to the effect that the time of police officers would not be spent on enforcing the complicated provisions of the Betting, Gaming and Lotteries Act, 1963 in London. In the events that followed, the Commissioner agreed to change his policy decision and no *mandamus* was granted, but the case was fully argued, and it was accepted that an order would lie against the Commissioner in such a case, as it was the

---

[16] *R.* v. *Judge Fraser Harrison,* [1955] 1 All E.R. 270; [1955] 1 Q.B. 287. See also *R.* v. *Flint County Council Licensing Committee, ex parte Barrett,* [1957] 1 All E.R. 112, where *mandamus* was granted because licensing justices had refused to grant an unrestricted liquor licence, on grounds which almost amounted to allowing an appeal on the merits of the case.

[17] *R.* v. *London County Council, ex parte Corrie,* [1918] 1 K.B. 68.

[18] *R.* v. *Epsom and Ewell Corpn., ex parte R.B. Property Investments (Eastern), Ltd.,* [1964] 2 All E.R. 832; [1964] 1 W.L.R. 1060.

[19] *R.* v. *Axbridge R.D.C., ex parte Wormald,* [1964] 1 All E.R. 571; [1964] 1 W.L.R. 442.

[20] *R.* v. *Dunsheath, ex parte Meredith,* [1950] 2 All E.R. 741; [1951] 1 K.B. 127; contrast *R.* v. *Aston University Senate,* [1969] 2 All E.R. 964; [1969] 2 W.L.R. 1418, a case of *certiorari,* where no domestic remedy seems to have been available.

[1] de Smith, *Judicial Review of Administrative Action,* 3rd Edn., at p. 482.

[2] *R.* v. *Weymouth Corpn., ex parte Teletax (Weymouth), Ltd.,* [1947] 1 All E.R. 779; [1947] K.B. 583.

[3] See now Local Government Act, 1972, s. 135; *post,* p. 302.

[4] *R.* v. *Hereford Corpn., ex parte Harrower,* [1970] 3 All E.R. 460; [1970] 1 W.L.R. 1424.

[5] As for example under s. 99 of the Education Act, 1944.

[6] *Watt* v. *Kesteven County Council,* [1955] 1 All E.R. 473; [1955] 1 Q.B. 408.

[7] [1968] 1 All E.R. 763.

duty of every police officer to enforce the law. The fact that the applicant for the order had another remedy open to him, by taking private proceedings in the criminal courts, was insufficient answer to the argument that he should follow that remedy first, but the court was not satisfied that he would have had sufficient *locus standi*. In the course of his judgment, Lord DENNING, M.R. said (at p. 770)

> ". . . mandamus is a very wide remedy which has always been available against public officers to see that they do their public duty. It went in the old days against justices of the peace both in their judicial and in their administrative functions. The legal status of the Commissioner of Police is still that he is a justice of the peace, as well as a constable. No doubt the party who applies for mandamus must show that he has sufficient interest to be protected and that there is no other equally convenient remedy; but once this is shown, the remedy of mandamus is available, in case of need, even against the Commissioner of Police of the Metropolis."

Whether *mandamus* is granted to a particular plaintiff seems to be a matter of discretion for the court; if the plaintiff has no interest whatever, the court will in most circumstances exercise their discretion against him and refuse to grant a *mandamus*.[8] However, when Mr Blackburn went again to the Court of Appeal, asking them to require the Metropolitan Police Commissioner to enforce the law against the sale of pornography, the question of *locus standii* was not raised, although *mandamus* was refused on the merits.[9] A successful applicant for *mandamus* must also be able to show that he has asked the defendant authority to perform the duty and has been refused. *Mandamus* will not lie against the Crown,[10] but it will lie against a corporate body, and if continually disobeyed, it may be enforced against the members of the governing body of the corporation.[11]

Professor de Smith has pointed out[12] that a private individual could bring an action of *mandamus* under the Rules of the Supreme Court, which was similar to the order of the same name, but this was abolished in 1962.

(iv) *Habeas corpus*.—This is a special process (which is still technically a prerogative writ) whereby an individual may test the validity of any executive act restricting his personal freedom. Questions of substantive *ultra vires* may be raised if, for example, an alien is imprisoned by order of the Home Secretary in time of emergency,[13] or ordered to be deported,[14] and also in cases concerning the detention of persons of unsound mind.[15]

---

[8] See Dr. Yardley's article, "Prohibition and *Mandamus* and the Problem of *Locus Standi*" (1957), 73 L.Q.R. 534.

[9] *R.* v. *Metropolitan Police Commissioner, ex parte Blackburn*, [1973] 1 All E.R. 324; [1973] Q.B. 241, and see note by Professor Wade at (1973) 89 L.Q.R. 329.

[10] Chapter IX, *post*, p. 287; but it will lie against a Minister acting as such: *Padfield* v. *Minister of Agriculture, Fisheries and Food*, [1968] 1 All E.R. 694; [1968] A.C. 997; a case of *certiorari* and *mandamus* combined.

[11] *R.* v. *Poplar Borough Council* (*No. 2*), [1922] 1 K.B. 95.

[12] *Judicial Review of Administrative Action*, 1st Edn., at p. 551.

[13] See the judgment of Lord ATKIN in *Eshinghayi Eleko* v. *Government of Nigeria*, [1931] A.C. 662, at p. 670.

[14] *R.* v. *Brixton Prison* (*Governor*), *ex parte Soblen*, [1962] 3 All E.R. 641; [1963] 2 Q.B. 243.

[15] *R.* v. *Board of Control, ex parte Rutty*, [1956] 1 All E.R. 769; [1956] 2 Q.B. 109.

The other grounds of judicial review, such as breach of natural justice, would in a proper case support an application for *habeas corpus*, but the factual situation will not often arise.[16] The process is still by writ; it is now clear that only one application may be made for the writ by the same applicant on the same grounds,[17] and an appeal lies against an order for the release of a person restrained or against the refusal of such an order.[18]

(v) *Quo warranto*.—Proceedings by way of the former prerogative writ of *quo warranto* to challenge the right of any person to act in a public office have been abolished, but the Queen's Bench Division may now be requested to issue an injunction restraining an individual from acting in a public office in circumstances in which *quo warranto* could formerly have been brought.[19] There is no reported case of any such proceedings, partly no doubt because the Local Government Act, 1972, (and its predecessor of 1933) makes provision[20] for the validity of a local government election to be challenged by a special procedure before the courts on an election petition; the validity of a parliamentary election can be questioned only by proceedings in Parliament or by petition to the Election Court under the procedure of Part 3 of the Representation of the People Act, 1949.

(c) Common law remedies.—The courts may also be asked to review the acts of the administration by the ordinary process of litigation; the Crown, a local authority or a statutory corporation may sue or be sued for damages in breach of contract, quasi-contract or tort, in accordance with normal common law principles, subject only to a few special rules discussed in a later Chapter.[1] It may be possible to sue for damages on a breach of a statute where a duty has been imposed.[2] Damages may also be recoverable in a case where a public officer does some act which to his knowledge amounts to an abuse of his office and he thereby causes damage to the plaintiff.[3] Criminal proceedings cannot be instituted against the Crown, but there is no reason why a local authority[4] or statutory corporation,[5] should not be

---

16 See Rubinstein, *Jurisdiction and Illegality*, at pp. 105–116.

17 Administration of Justice Act, 1960, s. 14.

18 *Ibid.*, s. 15.

19 Administration of Justice (Miscellaneous Provisions) Act, 1938, s. 9.

20 See s. 92 of that Act.

1 See Chapter IX, *post*, p. 275.

2 Chapter IX, *post*, p. 298.

3 This was recognised as a tort in the inadequately reported case in the Court of Appeal of *Wood* v. *Blair and Helmsley R.D.C.*, [1957] Adm. L.R. 243; and that case was applied in the Supreme Court of Victoria (*per* SMITH, J.) in *Farrington* v. *Thomson*, [1959] V.R. 286. See also the Privy Council case of *David* v. *Abdul Cader*, [1963] 3 All E.R. 579, *ante*, p. 153. The essence of an action of this nature seems to be that the officer must "misdemean himself by any falsity . . . or otherwise misbehave himself in his Office" (*Comyn's Digest*, cited by SMITH, J. at p. 293, in the *Farrington* case, *ante*). These cases have been discussed recently in articles by B. C. Gould at (1972) 5 N.Z.U.L.R. 105 and by Miss G. Ganz at [1973] P.L. 84.

4 As for example, for a statutory nuisance: *R.* v. *Epping Justices, ex parte Burlinson*, [1947] 2 All E.R. 537.

5 See, for example, art. 32 of the Third Schedule to the Gas Act, 1948, which makes it an offence for a gas board to pollute inland water, and *National Coal Board* v. *Gamble*, [1958] 3 All E.R. 203; [1959] 1 Q.B. 11, where the N.C.B. were convicted of aiding and abetting the commission of an offence under the Motor Vehicles (Construction and Use) Regulations, 1955.

charged with a criminal offence if the facts justify it. Before the coming into operation of the Highway Act, 1959, when the inhabitants at large were liable to repair a public highway, that duty could be enforced by indictment triable at quarter sessions.

(d) Equitable remedies.—The ordinary equitable remedies of private law may also, in certain circumstances, be obtained in administrative law. Specific performance does not need any special comment; it may be obtained against an administrative agency other than the Crown on the same grounds as against any other defendant. The other remedies of injunction and declaration are, however, often used in this context and they merit more detailed treatment.

(i) *Injunction.*—Equitable remedies are given on less restricted grounds than are prerogative remedies; an injunction, like a declaration (see below) is a discretionary remedy and it can be obtained against any type of administrative agency, except the Crown, exercising any government function, whether this be judicial, administrative or legislative.

> "An injunction is an order of a court addressed to a party to proceedings before it, and requiring him to refrain from doing, or to do, a particular act."[6]

In administrative law it will most frequently be sought and granted on the grounds that what the agency proposes to do will or would be *ultra vires*.

The plaintiff in proceedings for an injunction will normally have to show himself to be in some measure in the position of a "person aggrieved",[7] and if there is some alternative remedy open to the plaintiff, such as a right of appeal under statute, the court will expect the plaintiff to pursue that remedy and may decline to grant him an injunction if he has not done so. An injunction may be granted at the instance of the Attorney-General acting *ex officio*, against a local or other public authority acting *ultra vires*,[8] but it may also prove a useful weapon to an administrative agency in a case where, for example, a member of the public persistently breaks the law and is not sufficiently deterred (possibly because of the lightness of the penalties that may be imposed) by successive criminal proceedings being taken against him.[9] In such a case a local authority may themselves take the initiative and persuade the Attorney-General to act as nominal plaintiff, with the local authority as relator, in proceedings for an injunction to restrain breaches of the authority's byelaws,[10] or the commission of a public nuisance.[11] On the other hand, even without any relator and in

---

[6] de Smith, *Judicial Review of Administrative Action*, 3rd Edn. at p. 388.

[7] *Ante*, p. 175. In *A.-G.* v. *Independent Broadcasting Authority*, [1973] 1 All E.R. 689; [1973] Q.B. 629, it was said in the Court of Appeal that in a case of an exceptional character where were was *prima facie* evidence that a public corporation was in breach of its statutory duty and where the Attorney-General had refused to act *ex officio* and also where there was no sufficient time for related proceedings, an injunction would be granted if a member of the public could establish a case.

[8] *A.-G.* v. *Manchester Corpn.*, [1906] 1 Ch. 643.

[9] *A.-G., ex rel. Manchester Corpn.* v. *Harris*, [1960] 3 All E.R. 207; [1961] 1 Q.B. 74.

[10] *A.-G.* v. *Wimbledon House Estate Co.*, [1904] 2 Ch. 34.

[11] *A.-G., ex rel. Glamorgan County Council and Pontardawe R.D.C.* v. *P.Y.A. Quarries, Ltd.*, [1957] 1 All E.R. 894; [1957] 2 Q.B. 169.

addition to the common law remedy of indictment or any specific remedy provided by the statute, the Attorney-General may at any time apply to the High Court to exercise its equitable jurisdiction of granting an injunction against the breach of a statutory duty or the infringement or threatened infringement of a public fright. There is no need to exhaust other private rights before such a remedy is pursued, as public rights are here concerned.[12] It is a matter for the absolute discretion of the Attorney-General whether he will commence such proceedings, with which discretion the courts will not interfere, but they are in no sense bound to grant an injunction in a particular case at the Attorney-General's request.[13]

Injunction is not often used in this country as a remedy in administrative proceedings, mainly because either *certiorari* or an action for a declaration will often be more appropriate. In the U.S.A., in the Federal system, an injunction is much more common. After the decision in *Degge* v. *Hitchcock*,[14] it was accepted that *certiorari* would lie only to courts of law, and there was no real alternative to the injunction, until the Federal Declaratory Judgments Act, 1936, and the simple petition for review established by section 10 (e) of the Administrative Procedure Act of 1946.[15]

(ii) *Declaration.*—By Order 15, rule 16, of the Rules of the Supreme Court 1965, a single judge of any Division of the High Court is empowered to

> "make binding declarations of right whether or not any consequential relief is or could be claimed."

This is a very wide power,[16] which has often been invoked as a means of judicial control over the acts of the administration, especially since the passing of the Crown Proceedings Act, 1947, which made it possible to obtain a declaration against the Crown.[17] A declaration is subject to the defect that it is not enforceable; in private law this is of course serious, but in public law the defect is insignificant, as no administrative agency can afford to be so irresponsible as to ignore an adverse decision of a High Court judge.

The remedy is a discretionary one, and it will be refused if the question on which the court's ruling is requested is academic and has not yet actually arisen[18]; it has been said that there must always be a "proper contradictor", or a person whose interest it is to answer

[12] *A.-G.* v. *Sharp*, [1931] 1 Ch. 121.
[13] *A.-G.* v. *Harris*, (*ante*).
[14] 229 U.S. 162 (1913).
[15] *Post*, p. 460.
[16] There is an alternative procedure by way of an originating summons under R.S.C. 1965, O. 5, r. 2 where a question arises on an instrument: see Zamir, *The Declaratory Judgment*, Chapter 9.
[17] See s. 23 (2) of that Act.
[18] *Re Bernato, Joel* v. *Sanges*, [1949] 1 All E.R. 515; [1949] Ch. 258, where trustees asked the court to say whether, if they took a certain course, the trust funds would be liable to estate duty; not surprisingly, a declaration was refused. A declaration was refused to Mr. Blackburn, when he asked the court to declare that it would be unconstitutional for Her Majesty to sign the proposed Treaty of Accession to the European Communities, as the event had not, at that time, happened: *Blackburn* v. *A.-G.*, [1971] 2 All E.R. 1380; [1971] 1 W.L.R. 1037. In *Mellstrom* v. *Garner*, [1970] 2 All E.R. 9, KARMINSKI, L.J., said, "it is not the practice to grant [a declaration] if it is embarrassing or useless for any good purpose" (at p. 12).

the argument of the plaintiff who must have *locus standi*,[19] and also there must be a justiciable issue; for example a dispute concerned merely with professional ethics is not justiciable and no declaration would be granted.[20] A declaration will lie to question the validity of any administrative agency's decision, and the decision certainly need not have been of a judicial nature, as in the case of *certiorari*.[1] An action may be brought on the ground that a decision of an administrative agency was in excess of jurisdiction,[2] that it had been arrived at in violation of the rules of natural justice,[3] or that an executive act is *ultra vires*.[4] The remedy may of course not be available, in view of the terms of an exclusory statute,[5] and it cannot be used if there is some other effective remedy provided,[6] nor can it be used as a collateral attack on a decision which was wrong in law in a case where the tribunal acted within its jurisdiction. In such a case the decision impeached must first be quashed by *certiorari*.[7] However, the remedy will not lightly be found by the courts to have been excluded,[8] and it is frequently preferred by litigants to the remedy of *certiorari*. The words of Lord DENNING on this topic have become almost classical[9]:

> "Just as the pick and shovel is no longer suitable for the winning of coal so also the procedure of *mandamus*, *certiorari* and actions on the case are not suitable for the winning of freedom in the new age. They must be replaced by new and up-to-date machinery, by declarations, injunctions, and actions for negligence."

A declaration cannot be obtained in the county court except as ancillary to some other relief.[10] A declaration may show that a judicial decision was void because it was *ultra vires* as above mentioned,[11] but

---

[19] *Russian Commercial and Industrial Bank* v. *British Bank for Foreign Trade*, [1921] 2 A.C. 438. As to *locus standi*, see article by the present author at (1968), 31 M.L.R. 512, and *Wilson, Walton International (Offshore Services), Ltd.* v. *Tees and Hartlepool Port Authority*, [1969] 1 Lloyd's Rep. 120 and also *Thorne R.D.C.* v. *Bunting*, [1972] 1 All E.R. 439.

[20] *Cox* v. *Green*, [1966] 1 All E.R. 268; [1966] Ch. 216; *Aliter* if the question in issue is concerned with restraint of trade: *Dickson* v. *Pharmaceutical Society*, [1967] 2 All E.R. 558; [1967] Ch. 708.

[1] *Ante*, p. 179.

[2] *Vine* v. *National Dock Labour Board*, [1956] 3 All E.R. 939; [1957] A.C. 488. On this subject, the author is greatly indebted to an interesting article, "Declaratory Judgment v. Prerogative Orders", at [1958] P.L. 341, by I. Zamir and the same author's book, *The Declaratory Judgment* (1962); see also Borrie, "The Advantages of the Declaratory Judgment in Administrative Law", at 18 M.L.R. 138.

[3] *Cooper* v. *Wilson*, [1937] 2 All E.R. 726.

[4] *Prescott* v. *Birmingham Corpn.*, [1954] 3 All E.R. 698; [1955] Ch. 210.

[5] *Ante*, p. 154 *et seq.*

[6] *Watt* v. *Kesteven C.C.*, [1955] 1 All E.R. 473; [1955] 1 Q.B. 408.

[7] *Healey* v. *Ministry of Health*, [1954] 3 All E.R. 449; [1955] 1 Q.B. 221; *Punton* v. *Ministry of Pensions and National Insurance (No. 2)*, [1964] 1 All E.R. 448; [1964] 1 W.L.R. 226, *Anisminic* v. *Foreign Compensation Commission*, [1969] 1 All E.R. 208; [1969] 2 A.C. 147, and *ante*, p. 144.

[8] *Pyx Granite Co.* v. *Minister of Housing and Local Government*, [1959] 3 All E.R. 1; [1960] A.C. 260. SWANWICK, J., said in *Ealing London Borough* v. *Race Relations Board*, [1971] 1 All E.R. 424; [1971] 1 Q.B. 309, "clear words are needed to oust the jurisdiction of the High Court expressly, and I would add at least as clear words to oust it by implication" (at p. 430).

[9] *Freedom under the Law* (Hamlyn Lectures), at p. 126.

[10] *De Vries* v. *Smallridge*, [1928] 1 K.B. 482.

[11] *Ante*, p. 133.

the merits of a decision that is within jurisdiction cannot be discussed on this procedure. In some circumstances a declaration may not be granted because the court may consider a *certiorari* to be a more appropriate remedy. Thus, in *Punton* v. *Ministry of Pensions and National Insurance* (*No.* 2),[12] a declaration was sought to the effect that the National Insurance Commissioner had come to a wrong decision in law. A declaration was refused, as this would have amounted to re-opening questions in a case where the commissioner's decision was declared by the statute to be "final"; moreover, the argument that the commissioner erred in law would have been "the precise issue if proceedings had been taken by way of *certiorari*".[13] *Certiorari* proceedings (as contrasted with the action for a declaration) would not usurp the function of the tribunal, and would have left the way open for the claim to be heard again and determined correctly.[14] This case perhaps shows that the procedure by way of a declaration is not quite so readily available as has been imagined in recent years, and that the would-be litigant must be careful to choose the remedy best suited to his case. The general observation of Lord DENNING in *Barnard* v. *National Dock Labour Board*,[15] should, it seems, be read with some reserve:

> "I know of no limit to the power of the court to grant a declaration except such limit as it may in its discretion impose upon itself, and the court should not, I think, tie its hands in this matter of statutory tribunals."[16]

(e) Self help.—In addition to invoking the direct assistance of the courts by an application for *certiorari*, an action for a declaration or an injunction, or proceedings for damages in tort, the citizen aggrieved by some act of the administration which he contends is illegal, is entitled to sit back, as it were, and wait for proceedings to be taken against him. Anyone prosecuted for a breach of a byelaw or Ministerial regulation has a defence if he can show that the byelaw or regulation was *ultra vires* or has not been made in due form. If a citizen is required by an administrative authority to carry out some act and is then prosecuted for failing to comply with that requirement, he is entitled to question the validity of the notice,[17] and also the legal powers of the agency to act as they have done in the circumstances. If as a result of his failure to comply with such a requirement, the administrative authority exercise a purported statutory power and enter his land, in order for example, to carry out the work in question in default, he is

---

[12] [1964] 1 All E.R. 448; [1964] 1 W.L.R. 226.

[13] *Per* SELLERS, L.J., at p. 451.

[14] However, *certiorari* and declaration are not necessarily mutually exclusive: see *per* Lord GODDARD in *Pyx Granite Co., Ltd.* v. *Ministry of Housing and Local Government*, [1959] 3 All E.R. 1, at p. 8; [1960] A.C. 260, at p. 290.

[15] [1953] 1 All E.R. 1113, at p. 1119; [1953] 2 Q.B. 18, at p. 41.

[16] The two remedies are not inter-changeable; "One has to look at the matter a little differently, because in a matter of a declaration, only the rights of the plaintiff and the defendant are involved, and not the rights of all persons who might be governed by the order made" [as in a *certiorari*]: *per* PAULL, J., in *Gregory* v. *London Borough of Camden*, [1966] 2 All E.R. 196, at p. 201.

[17] In some cases technical defences of this kind are expressly excluded by statute where the party concerned has at an earlier stage of the proceedings had an opportunity of raising the point but has failed to take advantage thereof; see, *e.g.*, Public Health Act, 1936, s. 290 (7); Housing Act, 1957, s. 37 (1).

entitled to resist such entry, or to sue the authority for trespass, if he can show that the authority have acted *ultra vires* or without due regard to the details of the procedure laid down by statute. In *Stroud* v. *Bradbury,*[18] Lord GODDARD, C.J., observed:

> "To be entitled to enter the premises to execute the works the employees of the council had to observe the provisions of the Public Health Act, 1936, section 287 (1) of which gives them that right subject to their giving proper notice of their intention. When the sanitary inspector of the council arrived, the appellant obstructed him with all the rights of a free-born Englishman whose premises were being invaded and defied him with a clothes prop and a spade. He was entitled to do that unless the sanitary inspector had a right to enter . . . In the opinion of this court, the appellant now succeeds because the sanitary inspector had not done that which the statute required him to do before he had a right of entry."

Similarly, if a citizen is served with a notice requiring payment of a sum of money under some statutory provision, he is normally entitled to wait until he is sued for recovery of the money and then plead some flaw (if there is one) in the notice which will render him not liable for payment.[19] However, self help may not always be justified. In particular, if statute has provided a special remedy for a breach of statutory duty (for example, the right to ask a Minister to take default action against a local authority who have failed to house a family of homeless persons, under s. 36 (1) of the National Assistance Act, 1948), a person aggrieved should pursue that remedy and not "take the law into his own hands" (by squatting in an empty house).[20]

Perhaps every citizen is not sufficiently confident of his legal rights against the administration to defy them with a clothes prop or a spade, or to wait to be sued, but in practice it is common enough for the substantive or procedural validity of byelaws, regulations or executive action to be raised as a defence in criminal proceedings taken to enforce administrative decisions. This form of judicial review is not always recognised for what it is, but in practice the fact that ultimately the administration must look to the courts to enforce their decrees, will often provide a very effective check against arbitrary action. A public official in this country usually has a healthy respect for the courts, and the abuse or excessive use of power is comparatively rare.

6. CONCLUSION

Enough, it is hoped, has been said in this Chapter to show that the citizen wishing to seek the aid of the courts to quash a decision of the administration must be able to show:

(1) that his grievance is of a kind that the courts will recognise, because for example, a judicial decision was arrived at otherwise than in accordance with the principles of natural justice;

---

[18] [1952] 2 All E.R. 76, at p. 77.

[19] As in *Agricultural, Horticultural and Forestry Training Board* v. *Kent,* [1970] 1 All E.R. 304; [1970] 2 W.L.R. 426, where the Court of Appeal held that the Training Board could not recover sums allegedly due under an industrial training levy scheme, because the defendant had not been advised of his rights of appeal afforded to him by the state.

[20] *Southwark London Borough* v. *Williams,* [1971] 2 All E.R. 175; [1971] Ch. 734.

(2) that the courts will provide a remedy appropriate to the nature of his grievance;

(3) that the remedy that would otherwise normally be available, has not expressly or by necessary implication been excluded in the particular circumstances by the terms of a statute; and

(4) that he is entitled to be a plaintiff in the proceedings selected; *i.e.*, that he has sufficient *locus standi*.[1]

The redress of the grievances of an individual through the medium of the courts of law is a complicated matter; perhaps the most serious criticism that can be made of our legal system in this respect is that it may be extremely difficult for a humble citizen to be able to decide whether the courts will in his case give him the redress he seeks. Legal aid and legal advice at State expense[2] have removed the financial difficulty for some citizens, but the uncertainty of the law and its many complications, remains. Many pleas have been made for a resolution of these complications; one of these is a suggestion that an administrative decision should be declared to be a nullity only if the agency has purported to act beyond the area of its authority[3]; adoption of such an attractively simple principle would not, however, it is thought obviate all opportunity for legal argument. Professor Mitchell, on the other hand,[4] would extend the jurisdiction of the courts to supervise the administration, similar to the French *droit administratif*.[5]

---

[1] As to the problems of *locus standi* generally, see S. M. Thio *Locus Standi and Judicial Review*.

[2] Legal Aid and Advice Act, 1949; Legal Aid Acts, 1960 and 1964; Legal Advice and Assistance Act, 1972.

[3] Millward, "Judicial Review of Administrative Authority in Canada", (1961), 39 Can. B. Rev. 351.

[4] See, for example, his articles, "The Causes and Effects of the Absence of a System of Public Law in the United Kingdom" [1965] P.L. 95, and "The State of Public Law in the United Kingdom" (1966) 15 I.C.L.Q. 133; the theme, as he himself observes, runs through his book, *Constitutional Law*.

[5] For other suggestions as to reform, see Chapter V, *ante*, p. 107.

CHAPTER VII

REDRESS THROUGH THE ADMINISTRATION—TRIBUNALS AND INQUIRIES GENERALLY

1. INTRODUCTION

The complexities of modern civilisation, industrialisation of the community, and the abandonment in government of the principles of *laissez faire,* have led to ever increasing encroachment by the State on the liberties of the individual in the interest of the community, although this is not always opposed to the interests of the individual. One aspect of the Welfare State in post-war Britain has been the dispensation of benefits by state agencies—the redistribution of the country's wealth by legislation and executive action instead of by the "natural" forces of a free economy. In such an environment, opportunities for dispute between the administration and individual citizens are considerable. Many of these disputes are comparatively trivial or repetitive and most turn on questions of fact, often of a technical kind. Clearly, if all were referred to the ordinary courts of law, those courts would soon become choked with business. In many of these disputes the point at issue or the individual's grievance is not merely a question of fact or of law; questions of policy also have to be considered. The dispute may raise issues of public interest or even of conflicting public interests.[1] Proceedings before the Courts are expensive, though not so expensive as is sometimes alleged, and it may be considered in the public interest that a determination should be obtained cheaply. Consequently, in modern legislation, where it is anticipated that a dispute may arise between government agencies or between a government agency and a private individual, provision is often made for that dispute to be heard and determined, not by the ordinary courts of law, but before an administrative tribunal or by a Minister after the holding of an inquiry. Indeed the device has become so popular that it seems there are nearly 2,000 established tribunals of various kinds subject to the supervision of the Council on Tribunals operating in England and Wales at the present time, and many more not subject to the Council's jurisdiction—and this takes no account of the many inquiries. Tribunals may have a wide jurisdiction and a permanent existence or may be constituted *ad hoc* for a particular dispute or class of disputes, and the general principles to be applied in determining matters brought before them may be laid down in general standards formulated in the statute, or each tribunal may be left to determine matters brought before it as it thinks fit.[2]

[1] Such, for example, as arose a few years ago as to whether an atomic energy establishment should be erected at Dungeness in Kent, or whether the site should be preserved as a nature reserve. Use of the land by a private landowner did not come into the question as to which was more in the national interest—birds or electric power.

There are many different circumstances in which an individual may have a right to bring his grievance before an administrative tribunal or inquiry of some kind at the present day. Thus, tribunals have been set up to determine disputed claims for national insurance benefits or for family allowances,[3] to adjudicate upon applications for licences for public service vehicles,[4] to hear objections to assessments for rating,[5] and to determine appeals from tribunals that hear such objections initially,[6] and to determine questions arising out of government controls over employment, such as the terms and conditions of employment and redundancy payments. Inquiries may be directed to consider objections to compulsory purchase orders made by a local authority or by a Government Department,[7] to hear an appeal against refusal by a local planning authority to grant planning permission to carry out development on land[8] or to investigate a railway or aircraft accident.[9] Further, in these cases there is no standard code laid down which must be followed by all kinds of tribunals and inquiries; whether a code of procedure must be followed in a particular instance depends primarily on the constituent statute and any regulations made thereunder by the appropriate Government Department, and also to a lesser extent, on the degree of judicial review (if any) to which the particular tribunal or inquiry may be subject. The Franks Committee recommended that existing tribunals should be regarded as machinery provided by Parliament for the settlement of disputes rather than as part of the machinery of the administration.[10] This recommendation has not been fully implemented,[11] but it is of course true that a tribunal does not always merit the epithet "administrative", in the sense that it is concerned only with considerations of policy and need not observe the principles of natural justice. Nevertheless tribunals of the type hereafter to be discussed are often thought of as being *part* of the administration and are generally so described.

In this Chapter it is intended first to attempt to classify administrative tribunals and inquiries (which are discussed in more detail in the next Chapter), and then to consider such practice rules as may be in existence and also to discuss the Franks Report and the extent to which their recommendations have been implemented.

---

[2] *Post*, p. 204.

[3] Family Allowances Act, 1965, and National Insurance Act, 1965, as amended by the Social Security Act, 1973, *post*, p. 247.

[4] Road Traffic Act, 1960, *post*, p. 256.

[5] General Rate Act, 1967 and the Lands Tribunal Act, 1949, *post*, p. 241.

[6] Such appeals may be heard by further tribunals, as in the case of the valuation courts, or by a Minister of the Crown, as in the case of the National Health Service (*post*, p. 253), and there may or may not be an appeal to the courts of law.

[7] Acquisition of Land (Authorisation Procedure) Act, 1946; Housing Act, 1957; *post*, p. 229.

[8] Town and Country Planning Act, 1971, s. 36, *post*, p. 235.

[9] Regulation of Railways Act, 1871, s. 7; Civil Aviation Act, 1949, s. 10, as amended by s. 23 of the Civil Aviation Act, 1968.

[10] Report, para. 40. As to the circumstances in which the Franks Committee was constituted, see *ante*, p. 24.

[11] Members of tribunals, for example, are still appointed by a Minister, not by the Lord Chancellor, although the Council on Tribunals may make recommendations to the appropriate Minister; Tribunals and Inquiries Act, 1971, s. 5.

2. CLASSIFICATION OF TRIBUNALS AND INQUIRIES

First it should be emphasised that there is in the English legal system no clear mark of distinction between a court of law and a tribunal. Both will have a permanent existence, neither being convened *ad hoc* to determine one matter, and both will hear and determine a dispute. A court—a court of *law*—is, however, normally a body which has historically and formally been so regarded, whereas a tribunal will have some special statutory origin.[12] Courts will be presided over by the "ordinary" judges; the president of a tribunal will not necessarily be a lawyer, and often[13] he will not be a judge. In the course of his judgment in the Court of Appeal in *R.* v. *Local Government Board*,[14] BRETT, L.J., suggested that it was normally only courts of law that were entrusted with "the power of imposing an obligation upon individuals", but whereas this may be one test of ascertaining the nature of a judicial decision, it is not a satisfactory criterion for the nature of a "court", as indeed appears from that case, where it was recognised that Parliament had conferred a similar power on the Board under the statute in question. The Rules of the Supreme Court, the County Court Rules or the Magistrates' Courts Act, 1952 (or other relevant codes), as well as the accepted rules of evidence will govern proceedings before a court; similar,[15] or different, rules may or may not[16] govern the proceedings of a tribunal. Sometimes it is clear that a newly established body is to be a "court"; sometimes it will be clear it is to be a tribunal. The Restrictive Practices Court is a court because it is expressly stated in the constituent statute[17] to be a "superior court of record"; the Lands Tribunal is equally clearly *not* a court, because the constituent statute has provided that it shall be a "tribunal".[18] In practice proceedings before these two bodies, having very diverse jurisdiction, is not dissimilar. Whether a body is a court or a tribunal is therefore primarily a matter of statute law; there are few if any clear distinguishing marks dividing the two.

Next the distinction between a "tribunal" and an "inquiry" must be considered. Neither expression is defined in any statute, but it is submitted that for an investigating agency to be properly described as a "tribunal", it must be constituted under statutory authority, it must have a regular or permanent existence, and also a defined jurisdiction within which it is required to exercise its powers to hear and determine

---

12 The old prerogative of the Crown to establish new courts was one of the major issues in the seventeenth-century struggles between King and Parliament, and was destroyed by 16 Car. 1 c. 10: Holdsworth, *History of English Law*, Vol. I, p. 515. Thenceforth new courts or tribunals could be established only under statute.

13 Tribunals convened under the Tribunals of Inquiry (Evidence) Act, 1921, have, on several occasions, been presided over by a judge of the High Court.

14 (1882), 10 Q.B.D. 309, at p. 321.

15 *E.g.*, the Lands Tribunals Rules, 1963, S.I., 1963, No. 483.

16 Many tribunals are not subject to any detailed procedural rules.

17 Restrictive Trade Practices Act, 1956, s. 2 (3). The National Industrial Relations Court has the same status: Industrial Relations Act, 1971, s. 99 and Schedule 3, para. 13.

18 Lands Tribunal Act, 1949, s. 1.

disputes.[19] The word also suggests that each inquiry or sitting should be presided over by at least two persons, but this is not always the case with administrative tribunals—for example, the Lands Tribunal often consists of but a single member taken from a panel of adjudicators. In ordinary language also a tribunal connotes something similar to or approaching a judicial body. An "inquiry", on the other hand is an investigating agency constituted specifically (in this context under statutory authority, but not necessarily in pursuance of a statutory requirement) to inquire into a particular matter, and it may have few analogies with a court of law. In general, a tribunal will come to conclusions and be responsible therefor, but an inquiry may or may not arrive at any conclusions, and will often be required only to make a report or recommendations to some other government agency (for example, a Minister of the Crown) so as to enable that agency the better to come to a conclusion on the matter.[20] In the case of a tribunal, an individual (often a "person aggrieved") will normally have a statutory right to request his complaint to be heard and determined by the tribunal. In the case of an inquiry the individual's statutory right will most frequently be a right to appeal to a Minister, the statute then providing that the Minister shall convene an inquiry to hear the matter and report to him thereon so that he may make a decision.[1]

Under the Town and Country Planning Act, 1971, the "person appointed" by the Secretary of State (the "inspector") to hold an inquiry into an appeal against a refusal of planning permission may in certain circumstances determine the matter himself, but he will do so "for and on behalf of" the Secretary of State, and the Secretary of State may always call in a particular appeal to be determined by himself.[2] The Town and Country Planning (Amendment) Act, 1972, has introduced a novel procedure for the determination of objections to structure plans. Instead of holding a formal inquiry, the Secretary of State may order the holding of an "examination in public" of such matters affecting the Secretary's consideration of the plan as he considers ought to be examined; which will not necessarily include the

---

[19] *Ad hoc* tribunals established under the Tribunals of Inquiry (Evidence) Act, 1921, are a specialised exception (see *post*, p. 199).

[20] Professor H. W. R. Wade ("The Council on Tribunals", [1960] P.L. 351 at p. 352) has suggested that "Tribunals are concerned with objective decisions, reached by applying rules to facts, rather than with decisions of policy. . . . The case with inquiries is altogether different. Here we have decisions of policy, where the responsibility must be borne by a Minister responsible to Parliament." This is as clear a distinction between the two as is possible, but it should be remembered that the "rules" applied by tribunals may have been influenced by or drafted as a result of policy decisions. Inquiries are not always by any means exclusively concerned with policy, especially those which are fact finding. In the Second Report of the Council on Tribunals it is said (para 11), "Tribunals represent a compromise between the needs of good administration and the demands of justice. They have grown into a supplementary legal system of enormous extent." An interesting examination of the English inquiry procedure has been published in France: *L'Enquête Publique en Angleterre*, by Jean-Luc Boussard (1969).

[1] "Tribunals, generally speaking, exercise an independent jurisdiction: they decide particular cases by applying rules and regulations and sometimes by using their own discretion. Inquiries, on the other hand, form part of the process by which a Minister exercises his discretion—a discretion for which he is answerable to Parliament": Second Report of the Council on Tribunals, para. 12.

[2] See Act of 1971, Schedule 9.

subject matter of all the objections.[3] This public examination is not an inquiry at all in the general sense; it is *sui generis*.[4]

The distinction between tribunals and inquiries is rather descriptive than precise. The only precise classification seems to be one based on legal status; that is examined first and then we consider another possible classification based on the subject matter falling within the jurisdiction of the tribunal or inquiry.

(A) Classification according to legal status.—The Tribunals and Inquiries Act, 1971,[5] does not formally classify tribunals and inquiries, but its provisions suggest that the following classes are known to English administrative law:

(i) *Tribunals to which the Act applies.*—This class includes those tribunals listed in the First Schedule to the Act, and those which may since have been added thereto by statutory instrument made by the Lord Chancellor under section 13 of the Act[6] or by subsequent legislation.[7] The Council on Tribunals[8] is required by section 1 (1) (a) of the Act to keep under review the constitution and working of these specified tribunals, and from time to time to report on their constitution and working, and no power of a Minister to make, approve, confirm or concur in any procedural rules for any such tribunal is to be exercisable except after consultation with the Council (*ibid.*, s. 10); there is also a restriction on the power of a Minister to remove any member of such a tribunal from office (*ibid.*, s. 8). Apart from these provisions, however, not all the sections of the Act apply to all the tribunals; thus, section 7 (selection of chairmen of tribunals) is very limited in its application, and section 13 (providing for appeals to the High Court on points of law) applies to eleven only out of the fifty or so different types of tribunals listed in the First Schedule.

(ii) *Other tribunals.*—These could be described only by a list; that is, those tribunals to which the 1971 Act does not apply. In order that the class may be clearly delimited, it is first necessary to define "tribunal"; as mentioned above, some assistance can be gleaned from statute but this is not conclusive, and we can only fall back on the description used earlier, namely, that a tribunal must have a regular or permanent existence with a defined jurisdiction.[9]

---

[3] These public examinations are statutory inquiries by statute, for the purpose only of making them subject to the supervision of the Council on Tribunals: 1972 Act, s. 3 (1), amending s. 9 (6) of the 1971 Act.

[4] Act of 1972, s. 3, amending s. 9 of the Act of 1971.

[5] The Act of 1971 is a consolidating measure, replacing the Acts of the same name of 1958 and 1966.

[6] See Appendix to this Chapter, *post*, p. 225.

[7] As in the case of the Controller of Plant Variety Rights and the Plant Variety Rights Tribunal (Plant Varieties and Seeds Act 1964, s. 12 (1)).

[8] *Post*, p. 201.

[9] Appeals may lie in these cases from their decisions to tribunals which are listed in the Schedule to the Tribunals and Inquiries Act, 1971. A recently constituted tribunal which is not subject to the supervision of the Council on Tribunals, although procedural rules have to be approved by the Lord Chancellor, is the Disciplinary Committee established by the Hearing Aid Council Act, 1968 (see in particular s. 10 thereof and the Hearing Aid Council Disciplinary Committee (Procedure) Rules Approval Instrument, 1971 (S. I., 1971, No. 754). Another example is the licensing authority (a body of Ministers) established by the Medicines Act, 1968.

(iii) *Statutory inquiries.*—This expression is defined in section 19 (1) of the Tribunals and Inquiries Act, 1971,[10] as including inquiries of two different kinds, namely,

(a) "an inquiry or hearing held or to be held in pursuance of a duty imposed by any statutory provision, . . ."

and the supervision of the Council on Tribunals applies only to those statutory inquiries, as so defined, which are held by or on behalf of a Minister (a term which includes a "Board presided over by a Minister:" *ibid.*; see sections 1 (1) (c) and 12).

(b) "an enquiry or hearing, or an enquiry or hearing of a class, designated for the purposes of this section,"

by an order made by the Lord Chancellor or the Secretary of State for Scotland, in respect of any such inquiry or hearing (or class) held by or on behalf of a Minister and held or to be held in pursuance of a *power* (as distinct from a duty) conferred by any statutory provision. Any such order must be made by statutory instrument, which is subject to the negative resolution procedure. Regulations were made in 1967, under the (now repealed) Tribunals and Inquiries Act, 1966, applying the Acts to a very long list of inquiries.[11] These regulations were made just in time to enable the Council on Tribunals to make a special report on the Stansted Airport affair.[12] Certain inquiries under the Town and Country Planning Act, 1971 (including those where the inspector is empowered to decide) have also expressly been made[13] subject to the Council's supervision.

Perhaps the most important of the many kinds of inquiries that fall within para. (a) above are those constituted to inquire into and report upon objections to compulsory purchase orders and upon appeals against refusals of planning permission by a local planning authority.[14] Under Schedule 9 of the Town and Country Planning Act, 1971, some appeals to the Secretary of State under the Act are now determined on his behalf by the inspector appointed to conduct the inquiry.[15] This class of case is thus difficult to classify. In that the inspector makes the decision (albeit in the name of the Secretary of State) he appears to be acting as a tribunal; but the proceedings are still described as an inquiry and it is expressly made subject to the supervision of the Council on Tribunals as if it were a statutory inquiry.[16] The same observations apply to an inquiry held by a person appointed by a local planning authority to hear objections to a local plan under Part II of the Town and Country Planning Act, 1971, except that in such a case the inspector does not determine the matter.[17]

---

[10] Replacing s. 14 (1) of the Tribunals and Inquiries Act, 1958, as amended by the Act of the same name of 1966.

[11] Tribunals and Inquiries (Discretionary Inquiries) Order 1967 (S.I., 1967, No. 451).

[12] Annual Report of the Council on Tribunals for 1967, para. 8 and Appendix A.

[13] See 1971 Act, Schedule 9 (local plans), Schedule 9, para. 7 (inspectors) and 49 (5) (inquiries held by a Planning Inquiry Commission). The Act does not, however, apply to public examinations held in respect of structure plans under the Town and Country Planning (Amendment) Act, 1972 (*ante*, p. 196).

[14] Town and Country Planning Act, 1971, s. 36; *post*, p. 235.

[15] 1971 Act, Schedule 9, and the Town and Country Planning (Determination of Appeals by appointed persons) (Prescribed Classes) Regulations 1970, S.I. 1970 No. 1454.

[16] 1971 Act, Schedule 9, para. 7. [17] *Ibid.*, s. 13 (1).

(iv) *Other inquiries.*—Other inquiries, which in our system of classification are not tribunals, but which are held pursuant to statutory authority, will not come within the previous class (unless expressly brought within it by order made under the Act), for one or more of the following reasons:

(a) Because the inquiry is not held "by or on behalf of a Minister". Examples of such inquiries are those carried out by the Boundary Commission under the House of Commons (Redistribution of Seats) Act, 1958, or any local inquiries held by a Local Government Boundary Commission or by a district council with respect to a review of local government areas, under section 61 of the Local Government Act, 1972.

(b) Because the particular inquiry is not held pursuant to a *duty* imposed by statute on the Minister holding the inquiry, but held pursuant to a *power* vested in him by statute in that behalf. Examples of inquiries falling within this class are those held by the Secretary of State to inquire into a railway or aircraft accident,[18] or to inquire into an application by a local authority for consent to raise a loan for the purposes of proposed capital expenditure.[19] It is important to note that the power to make rules under section 11 of the 1971 Act can apply only to statutory inquiries as defined, or as extended by order and not to this class.

(v) *Tribunals of inquiry.*—Tribunals constituted by resolution of both Houses of Parliament under the Tribunals of Inquiry (Evidence) Act, 1921, do not fall conveniently into this general classification. A tribunal of this kind is constituted in particular circumstances to inquire into a definite matter described in the Resolution as of "urgent public importance", and it is not held by or on behalf of any Minister of the Crown, nor is it constituted in pursuance of any statutory duty.[20] These special tribunals are not affected by the provisions of the Tribunals and Inquiries Act, 1971, but the Act of 1921 gives to any tribunal constituted thereunder powers to enforce the attendance and examination on oath of witnesses, the production of documents and the issuing of a commission or request to examine witnesses abroad; the same Act also regulates admission of the public to proceedings before the tribunal, and provides for the representation of persons "appearing to be interested" before the tribunal by counsel or solicitor. These tribunals give rise to special difficulties of their own. They have the powers of the High Court and usually consist

---

[18] Regulation of Railways Act, 1871, s. 7; Civil Aviation Act, 1949, s. 10 (as amended).

[19] The requirement that the consent of the Secretary of State shall be obtained as a condition of the exercise by a local authority of their power to borrow money on mortgage is contained in s. 172 and Schedule 13 of the Local Government Act, 1972, and the provisions regulating the holding of an inquiry into an application for such consent are contained in s. 250, *ibid.* (a section which is incorporated into a number of statutes dealing with local government, such as the National Parks and Access to the Countryside Act, 1949); as to this general question, see *post*, p. 425.

[20] The Report of the Royal Commission on Tribunals of Enquiry (Cmnd. 1321, 1966) recommended that this procedure should be used only in relation to circumstances "which occasion a nationwide crisis of confidence".

of a small number of persons, presided over by a High Court Judge.[1] Their procedure is investigatory and inquisitorial rather than in accordance with the more normal accusatory pattern of tribunals in this country, in which the issues before the tribunal are to some extent defined, and any person concerned knows the case he has to meet. In a Tribunal of Inquiry (of which eighteen have been convened since the passing of the Act of 1921[2]), the issues before the Tribunal may not appear until some time after the first investigations have been made; it may be discovered at a comparatively late stage in the proceedings that a certain individual is or may be involved, and not until that stage will it be possible for him to be legally represented or to present his version of the facts before the Tribunal. Because of their quite exceptional nature, however, these Tribunals of Inquiry cannot be fitted logically into any scheme of classification of tribunals and inquiries.

A further factor might be utilised as affording some measure of legal classification, namely whether a particular tribunal or inquiry is concerned solely with the determination of a dispute or disputes between private individuals. The latter may be considered more properly to belong to the sphere of private rather than administrative law, but in cases where there is some element of public interest (although it is just as much a matter of public interest that justice should be done between man and man), statutes have on occasion entrusted administrative tribunals with jurisdiction to determine disputes between individuals to which no government agency is a party. Fortunately perhaps for the continued existence of English law in its traditional form, there are not many examples of this jurisprudential curiosity. The most important are the rent assessment committees established under the Rent Act, 1965, and the less active furnished houses rent tribunals; one head of the jurisdiction of the Lands Tribunal is to determine applications for the discharge and modification of restrictive covenants under section 84 of the Law of Property Act, 1925, as amended by the Act of 1969.[3]

In this Chapter we are not concerned with "domestic" tribunals or inquiries, nor are we discussing the discretionary powers of local authorities or other government agencies to decide matters of policy as part of their ordinary administrative or executive functions. A local authority, for example, may decide on questions of ordinary management of its housing estates, such as whether a tenant shall be permitted to take a lodger into the house or erect a television aerial, without holding an inquiry or constituting a tribunal, and a Minister of the Crown will similarly decide whether or not to confirm a byelaw submitted to him under statutory authority by a local authority or a public utility undertaking, without holding any inquiry (unless, possibly, he has received

---

[1] The Report of 1966 (see p. 199, note 20) includes a recommendation that the Act of 1921 should be amended so as to provide that the Chairman of a tribunal must be a person holding high judicial office, but this has not yet been implemented.

[2] See Report, Appendix C; to this list must be added the Aberfan inquiry of 1966–67, the Northern Ireland disturbances inquiry set up in 1969, under corresponding Northern Ireland legislation and the 1971 inquiry into the Vehicle and General Insurance Co.

[3] And see also their jurisdiction under the Rights of Light Act, 1959; *post*, p. 234.

objections to the proposed byelaw). Domestic inquiries, convened by professional bodies or by trade or employers' unions, are discussed later.[4]

(B) Classification according to subject matter.—Owing to the great variety of subjects dealt with by tribunals (a term which we propose henceforth to use as including, except where the context otherwise requires, inquiries), any classification according to subject matter is liable to be incomplete, or otherwise to be so general as to have no real significance. However, in Chapter VIII, there will be found an attempt at classification according to subject matter of the more important tribunals operating in this country. Sir Carleton Allen has commented on a few more in his *Administrative Jurisdiction*,[5] the pamphlet *Rule of Law* has[6] a useful table at the end, and Vandyk's *Tribunals and Inquiries* provides an almost complete list, but new tribunals have been created since the book was published.

3. THE COUNCIL ON TRIBUNALS

One of the most important recommendations of the Franks Committee[7] was the setting up of a "Council on Tribunals", which should, according to that Committee, be:

> "A standing body, the advice of which would be sought whenever it was proposed to establish a new type of tribunal, and which would also keep under review the constitution and procedure of existing tribunals."

This recommendation was accepted and implemented by the Tribunals and Inquiries Act, 1958, one Council being established for the whole of the United Kingdom, having a special Committee for Scotland.[8] The Council is an advisory and consultative body only, having itself no adjudicatory or executive powers and it is in no sense a super-tribunal, nor a court of appeal from tribunals. Its duties are now set out in section 1 of the Tribunals and Inquiries Act, 1971, (replacing the Act of 1958) as follows:

> "(*a*) to keep under review the constitution and working of the tribunals specified in Schedule 1 to this Act . . . and, from time to time, to report on their constitution and working;
>
> (*b*) to consider and report on such particular matters as may be referred to the Council under this Act with respect to tribunals other than the ordinary courts of law, whether or not specified in Schedule 1 to this Act, or any such tribunal;
>
> (*c*) to consider and report on such matters as may be referred as aforesaid, or as the Council may determine to be of special importance, with respect to administrative procedures involving, or which may involve, the holding by or on behalf of a Minister of a statutory inquiry, or any such procedure."

---

[4] See Chapter VIII, *post*, p. 266.

[5] [1956] P.L. 13.

[6] Published in 1955 by the Inns of Court Conservative and Unionist Society.

[7] Report, para. 128 and see *ante*, p. 24.

[8] The Franks Committee recommended that there should be two Councils, one for England and Wales and one for Scotland. The provisions made by the Act for a separate Scottish Committee amount to almost the same thing; see now Tribunals and Inquiries Act, 1971, s. 1. For an evaluation of the work of the Council on Tribunals, see article by the present author at [1965] P.L. 231.

The tribunals specified in Schedule 1 may be added to from time to time by order made by the Lord Chancellor under section 15 (1) of the Act.[9] The Council must be consulted by the appropriate rule-making authority before any procedural rules are made for any tribunal specified in Schedule 1 to the Act or for any statutory inquiry held by or on behalf of a Minister.[10] The Council must also be consulted before any of the tribunals specified in the Schedule, or any statutory inquiry, is exempted by the Lord Chancellor from the general requirement to give reasons for its decisions, under section 12 (6) of the Act: a power that has not been frequently exercised.[11] Further, the Council may make general, but not specific, recommendations to the appropriate appointing Minister about membership of scheduled tribunals.[12]

The Council publish Reports of its working annually,[13] which outline the nature of the Council's functions. It is a "watch-dog" for the public, but none the less is not the equivalent of an "Ombudsman"[14]; its functions are not executive or investigatory in character, and the members of the Council must look to the public

> "in large measure to inform us of matters requiring to be watched".[15]

The publicity attaching to the issue of these Reports showed clearly, however, that it would be difficult for any Government to ignore indefinitely any firm recommendations for reform made by the Council. As a guide star, the Council follow the Franks Committee's principles of "openness, fairness and impartiality",[16] and apply them to particular cases as they arise. On at least two occasions where disquiet had been expressed over the conduct of inquiry proceedings, the Council made a

---

[9] See, for example, the Mental Health Review Tribunals (Tribunals and Inquiries (Mental Health Review Tribunals) Order 1960, S.I. 1960 No. 810), the tribunal constituted under the Finance Act, 1960, and the Bookmakers' Levy Appeal Tribunals constituted under the Betting Levy Act, 1961 (now the Betting, Gaming and Lotteries Act 1963). The Council have expressed a desire to be consulted in this respect *before* the relevant legislation is introduced by the Government and this is now generally recognised by the Government of the day; see Annual Report of the Council for 1971/2, para. 24.

[10] See Tribunals and Inquiries Act, 1971, ss. 10 and 11.

[11] See below, p. 204, and the Tribunals and Inquiries (Revenue Tribunals) Order, 1959 (S.I., 1959, No. 452), extended to include the tribunal established by s. 28 of the Finance Act, 1960, by the Tribunals and Inquiries (Revenue Tribunals) Order, 1961 (S.I., 1961, No. 152). This matter is also referred to in the Second Report of the Council on Tribunals, at p. 18.

[12] 1971 Act, s. 5.

[13] See Reports of the Council on Tribunals for 1959 to 1971.

[14] See, for example, Professor Hurwitz' article at [1958] P.L. 236, and *ante*, p. 98. The investigation of individual complaints is a feature of the work of the Council on Tribunals; it is said in their Second Report (at p. 7), "Within this field [that of tribunals and inquiries] it is our task to act as a watch-dog for the ordinary citizen and to see that he gets fair play". In recent years the number of complaints investigated by the Council has fallen off considerably; in 1969/70 there were only 88 complaints from members of the public (Annual Report of the 1969/70, para. 22), and the Annual Reports for 1970/71 and 1971/72 give no figures and make no references to complaints. The Parliamentary Commissioner for Administration is a member *ex officio* of the Council on Tribunals (see Chapter V, *ante*, p. 90) and there is considerable liaison between the two (see Report of the Council for 1968, at p. 1).

[15] First Report, para. 128.

[16] *Post*, p. 205.

special investigation and reported on the matter, recommending improvements in the procedure to meet the dissatisfaction.[17]

The Council consists of not more than fifteen nor less than ten members (*plus* the Parliamentary Commissioner for Administration), who are appointed by the Lord Chancellor, and except the Chairman they are not remunerated for their work; the office in London is staffed by a very small number of lawyers and clerical assistants. The Council meet monthly, but a great deal of their work of consultation and the giving of advice to Government Departments is informal, members of the Council from time to time visit particular sittings of tribunals subject to the supervision of the Council,[18] and other members may on occasion investigate complaints received from members of the public.

The most successful of the work undertaken by the Council has undoubtedly been that connected with the drafting of rules of procedure for the various tribunals. Sometimes these rules have been incorporated at least in part in the statute itself,[19] and in other instances the rules are to be found in a statutory instrument, frequently the result of many consultations between the Council and its officers, Government Departments, and interested bodies.[20] As a general observation, it may be said that the Council's views have always been received appreciatively by Government Departments concerned, although there have been a few cases of disagreement with them.[1]

Professor Street, in his Hamlyn Lectures, *Justice in the Welfare State*, has been critical of the functions of the Council on Tribunals, pointing out that their activities have been principally concerned with the "procedural" aspects of the working of tribunals:

> "Far and away the most important questions are the kinds of decisions [a tribunal] is making and, whether it has the appropriate powers and scope. This is not the Council's business, and it is nobody else's" (p. 63).

Before leaving the Council on Tribunals, it may be of value to glance

---

[17] The "Chalkpit Affair": see report printed at [1962] J.P.L. 315 and footnote 4, p. 221, below. The second case was the Packington Estate (Islington) planning appeal, which was debated in the House of Commons in March, 1966; see the accounts at [1966] J.P.L. 205, and [1966] P.L.1. In the Stansted Airport affair (Report of the Council for 1967, Appendix A), there had been no effective public inquiry and the Council issued a special Report to the Lord Chancellor.

[18] Members of the Council are all part-time and therefore but few visits are made each year. Moreover, the Council sometimes experiences difficulty, as the relevant procedural rules do not always entitle the members of the Council to attend sittings of a tribunal subject to the Council's supervision as of right; see *Report* for 1964, at para. 21. When the Tribunals and Inquiries Act 1966 was passing through the House of Lords, an attempt was made to include a clause giving such a right to attend in the case of the betting levy appeal tribunal, but the clause was struck out on third reading. Section 6 of the 1971 Act conferring such a right in respect of appeals to the Secretary of State against a decision of a district auditor has now been repealed as being no longer relevant in respect of the audit procedure of the Local Government Act, 1972: see Chapter XV, *post*, p. 427.

[19] As in the case with the Tribunal established under the Plant Varieties and Seeds Act 1964; see Schedule 4 thereto.

[20] A good example of this was the Town and Country Planning Appeals (Inquiry Procedure) Rules, 1962 (S.I., 1962, No. 1425). For a fuller account of the work of the Council on Tribunals, see article by the present author at [1965] P.L. 321.

[1] Report for 1964, paras 32–34, and footnote 17, *ante*.

at its nearest equivalent across the Atlantic, the (Federal) Administrative Conference of the United States.[2] This is a permanent Federal agency established by Act of Congress in 1968, and it consists of a paid Chairman appointed by the President of the U.S., a Council (unpaid) of 10 persons, also appointed by the President, and some 80 members, representing the Ministries and Federal Agencies and including (as to 40 per cent of their number) lawyers and persons in public life. The main statutory responsibility of the Conference is to study and make recommendations for improvement of procedures in all Federal agency functions which involve "the determination of the rights, privileges, and obligations of private persons through rule making, adjudication, licensing or investigation". It carries out these responsibilities through (at present) 10 Committees, which are advised by lawyers and the Chairman of the Conference, and they make recommendations for adoption by the General Assembly of the Conference; if adopted, these are still, of course, only recommendations, but so far as relevant they will normally be accepted by the several Agencies.[3] Like the Council on Tribunals, the Conference does not interfere with particular agency decisions, nor is it an "Ombudsman", but on occasion it will investigate citizen complaints about agency procedures.

4. GENERAL PRINCIPLES

The traditional attitude of the courts towards subordinate jurisdictions, first towards the local justices of the peace, in both their criminal and administrative capacities,[4] and later towards administrative tribunals and inquiries of various kinds, has been to confine supervision to matters of jurisdiction, which has meant for the most part the application of the doctrine of *ultra vires*,[5] and to maintain only a sketchy and haphazard control over procedure, directed exclusively to ensuring that the principles of "natural justice", as understood in the specialised sense of freedom from bias and *audi alteram partem*, were duly observed; but even then there was no obligation on an administrative tribunal to observe those principles in the same manner as would be adopted by an "ordinary" court of law.[6] By the twentieth century, however, it had become clear that this attitude did not go far enough. As already explained, the Donoughmore Committee[7] endeavoured to draw a distinction between "judicial decisions", which in their view should normally be entrusted to the courts of law (and would probably have included the type of jurisdiction at present entrusted, for example, to the Lands

[2] On this institution, see article by the Chairman (Mr. Jerre S. Williams), "Problems confronting the administrative conference" (1968), Ad. Law Rev. 21:11 N, and note at [1970] P.L. 110.

[3] The Chairman of the Conference has the responsibility of working with the agencies so as to persuade them to accept the conference's recommendations: *ibid.*, p. 16. The Report of the Conference for 1971–72 shows a considerable measure of implementation of the Conference's recommendations by the several Federal Agencies.

[4] See, for example, *The History of Local Government in England*, by Redlich and Hirst, Vol. I (ed. Keith-Lucas), at p. 35.

[5] See Chapter VI, *ante*, p. 133.

[6] *R.* v. *Local Government Board*, v. *Arlidge*, [1915] A.C.120; *ante*, p. 115.

[7] Report of the Committee on Ministers' Powers, 1932, Cmd. 4060.

Tribunal), and "quasi-judicial" decisions, which "fall naturally to Ministers themselves". The Committee could see little room for administrative tribunals in an ideal organisation; there were not as many tribunals in existence in 1932 as there are today, but the Committee recognised that on occasion Parliament might consider "it necessary to depart from the normal course", and entrust judicial functions to some body other than the courts; in such a case, in the Committee's view, the judicial functions involved should be entrusted to a Ministerial Tribunal rather than to a Minister personally.[8] This part of the Donoughmore Committee's recommendations and observations has not received much favour, and the distinction between judicial and quasi-judicial functions seems to be without any practical significance. In 1955, the Franks Committee was set up to

> "consider and make recommendations on the constitution and working of tribunals other than the ordinary courts of law . . ."

and in the early part of their report, this Committee said[9]:

> "Administration must not only be efficient in the sense that the objectives of policy are securely attained without delay. It must also satisfy the general body of citizens that it is proceeding with reasonable regard to the balance between the public interest which it promotes and the private interest which it disturbs."

The principles of natural justice were not sufficient to achieve these objectives, and therefore the Committee identified three "general and closely linked characteristics" which they thought should mark the special procedures of the various administrative tribunals. These characteristics the Committee called "openness, fairness and impartiality".[10] The citizen must be able to feel that he has had a proper and fair chance to state his case, and that his case has been heard before an impartial judge or judges; such an atmosphere could not be engendered at a secret hearing, and it is therefore equally important that as much as possible of the proceedings (making due allowance for personal and private matters where publicity would cause hardship, or possibly involve a breach of national security) should be conducted in public.[11] In spite of the diversities of tribunals and their procedures, they have in recent years acquired a reasonably high reputation for fair dealing, largely due to the high quality of members (often legally unqualified) of tribunals,[12] and of course also to the watchful guidance of the Council on Tribunals.

---

[8] The Donoughmore Committee in several other respects anticipated the recommendations of the Franks Committee (*post*). Thus, they recommended that the parties to a dispute should be given the opportunity of stating their case and of knowing the case they have to meet, that every Tribunal exercising a judicial function should give reasons for its decision which should be made available to the parties, that inspectors' reports should be published, and that "any party aggrieved by the judicial decision of a Minister or Ministerial Tribunal should have an absolute right to appeal to the High Court of Justice on any question of law", although there should be no appeal on any issue of fact.

[9] Franks Report, para. 21.

[10] *Ibid*, para. 23.

[11] There is a most useful summary of the action taken by way of implementation of the recommendations of the Franks Committee in the Report of the Council on Tribunals for 1963, at p. 28.

[12] This has been remarked on by many foreign observers, especially the Americans. It is also significant that in the course of a radio interview on January 13, 1970, a representative of a London gaming club could say, with reference to a recent refusal of a certificate by the Gaming Board for his club, that "we would like a right of appeal to a tribunal, because that is democracy".

There is no standard code of procedure applicable to all tribunals; because of the variety of their jurisdiction it is probably not practicable for any such code to be devised.[13] However, the Council on Tribunals have gradually worked out a few principles that they seek to have included in all procedural rules.[14] A tendency towards the concentration of tribunals has some effect of standardising procedure.[15] It is now proposed to examine the three "characteristics" of the Franks Committee and to see how they work out in practice, in relation both to particular tribunals, and generally, first considering the various aspects of tribunal procedure, and then showing the extent to which the several recommendations of the Committee have been implemented.

(1) Organisation of Tribunals.—When a new tribunal is constituted at the present time, it is rare for a small number of persons to be able to determine all the matters falling within the jurisdiction of the tribunal.[16] It is more common for the enabling legislation to make provision for a number of "tribunals" to be established, or for the constitution of a number of separate panels of "the Tribunal". Thus, there are a number of separate mental health review tribunals and of valuation courts sitting independently in different parts of the country. On the other hand, there is a President of Industrial Tribunals, a Chief National Insurance Commissioner and a Chief Adjudicator under the Immigration Act, 1971. In such cases, where tribunals are organised in accordance with what may be described as a "Presidential system", one (normally full-time) member of the tribunal(s) is *primus inter pares*, as it were; he is responsible for a general oversight of the working of the tribunals for the assignment of chairmen of panels and the arrangement of work loads, and he will in most cases periodically convene meetings of panel chairmen in order to discuss matters of common interest. Where there is no person so appointed, the separate tribunals tend to operate in isolation from each other.[17]

Tribunals are usually staffed (as respects clerks and assistants) by a Government Department, such as Social Security or the Environment, who second civil servants from the Department for a period of duty with a tribunal. The staff of valuation courts are, however, employed by the panels themselves and they are not civil servants. Seconded staff tend not to be of the highest calibre whilst there is no satisfactory career structure for the staff of local valuation courts. Premises also

---

[13] *Post*, page 210.

[14] See article by the present writer at [1965] P.L. 321, especially at p. 335.

[15] To be seen, for example, in the extended jurisdiction of the Lands Tribunal and of the industrial tribunals (*post*, pp. 234 and 262). The merger of the industrial injuries tribunals with the national insurance tribunals by the National Insurance Act, 1966 (Chapter VIII, *post*, p. 247) is another step in the same direction. The rent assessment committees and the furnished houses rent tribunals should certainly be merged (*post*, p. 245). It would perhaps not be inappropriate to amalgamate the industrial tribunals with the National Insurance Commissioners, and perhaps also (if the Board were put on a statutory basis) the Criminal Injuries Compensation Board (Chapter VIII, *post*, p. 243).

[16] A recent exception is the Immigration Appeal Tribunal.

[17] As to the Presidential system, see the Annual Report for 1971/2 of the Council on Tribunals, para. 17.

are normally provided by the "parent" central Departments. These matters at times tend to become somewhat haphazard, and it might be preferable for there to be a "Tribunals Service", responsible for the staffing and accommodation of all tribunals, integrated perhaps with the courts and brought under the supervision of the Lord Chancellor's Department.[18] There could perhaps also be some rationalisation of the areas served by the different tribunals and in the large cities premises could be specially provided (and properly equipped) suitable for sittings of all tribunals in the area.[19]

(2) Appointment of members.—Various principles can be taken into consideration when members of a particular tribunal have to be appointed. Who should be chosen; who should appoint? Should members be nominated by independent bodies, such as local authorities, or by interested bodies, such as trades unions or employers' federations? In some cases members are selected for a particular tribunal or for each sitting thereof, by a Departmental Minister, from a panel nominated by various bodies; in yet other cases, the panel may be chosen by the Lord Chancellor, the nearest equivalent in this country to a Minister of Justice, and the one Minister who is expected to be independent of the Executive, although he is a member of the Cabinet.[20] Again, should the Chairman of the tribunal be a trained lawyer, and should the method by which he is appointed be different from that adopted for other members? Should the Chairman be consulted (as is done with several public corporations) over the appointment of the other members? Should the Chairman and members, or the Chairman alone, be paid for their services? The English system of government has relied very much in the past on the services of intelligent amateurs, members of Parliament, members of local authorities, local magistrates, the jury. Inroads have had to be made on this voluntary system in recent years. Members of Parliament have had to be paid salaries, which, however, even now are not comparable with the salaries paid to the members of many Continental legislatures. Members of local authorities and jurors can claim expenses and allowances, and it has been suggested that senior members of large authorities (such as the G.L.C.,[1]) should be paid salaries. If the voluntary system is relied on too heavily for the staffing of administrative tribunals, the supply of intelligent and experienced men and women prepared and able to give their time—and money—in the service of the country in this and other ways, may be exhausted.

In general principle, the Franks Committee recommended that all Chairmen should be appointed by the Lord Chancellor. This practice was, before the publication of the Report, already followed in a few cases, and in such cases it is customary for the Lord Chancellor's Department to obtain the views of the Department most concerned before making a particular appointment. General adoption of this suggestion

---

[18] If such an integration were effected, however, it would be essential to preserve the informal atmosphere that is an essential characteristic of most tribunals.

[19] On these and related matters, see *Administrative tribunals;* by R. E. Wraith and others (1973).

[20] Chapter I, *ante*, p. 13.

[1] Chapter XIII, *post*, p. 368.

would perhaps have resulted in greater public confidence in the independence of tribunals so staffed. The Lord Chancellor is at present responsible for judicial and magisterial appointments, and the public might be justified in thinking that he would be less partial in his choice than would a Minister responsible for the efficient running of a service which might come under review by one of the tribunals concerned. But the purpose of tribunals is not to obtain a trial in accordance with legal principles alone; policy must at times influence the decision and in some cases an intelligent and experienced expert may be preferable as a member to a layman or lawyer. Consequently this recommendation of the Franks Committee has not been fully implemented, although the Act of 1971 provides[2] that in the case of those tribunals listed in the section[3] the chairman (either the chairman *eo nomine*, or the chairman appointed to act for a particular sitting) shall be selected by the Minister responsible, from a panel of persons appointed by the Lord Chancellor.

Members of tribunals should, said the Committee, be appointed by the Council on Tribunals.[4] This recommendation was not accepted, but section 5 of the 1971 Act provides that the Council on Tribunals may make to the "appropriate Minister" (*i.e.*, the Minister who has power under the existing law to make appointments to membership of tribunals) general recommendations as to the making of appointments to membership of tribunals listed in Schedule 1 to the Act,[5] and the Minister must have regard to any such recommendations. In practice it is understood that such recommendations are not often made, although the Council on Tribunals was consulted by the Lord Chancellor as to the staffing of agricultural land tribunals.[6] No indications were given by the Franks Committee of the type of persons who should be selected, either as Chairmen or ordinary Members of tribunals, except that it was said that

> "all chairmen of tribunals exercising appellate functions should have legal qualifications; chairmen of tribunals of first instance should ordinarily have legal qualifications".[7]

This principle was already applied by several of the constituent statutes[8]; it has been expressly implemented by the 1958 and 1971 Acts only by the provisions of section 9 of the 1971 Act, which requires the chairman or deputy chairman of the appellate tribunal constituted under the National Service Act, 1948, or an umpire or deputy umpire appointed under section 41 (4) of the same Act, to be a barrister or solicitor of at least ten years' standing.[9]

Almost as important as the method adopted for appointment to membership, are the powers given by statute for dismissal of members of tribunals. Obviously, if members are too easily capable of being

---

[2] See s. 7 thereof.

[3] This list may be added to by statutory instrument made by the Lord Chancellor under s. 10 (2) of the Act.

[4] As to this body see *ante*, p. 201.

[5] And see s. 10 (1).

[6] See Garner, "The Council on Tribunals" [1965] P.L. 321, at p. 340.

[7] Report, paras. 55, 58.

[8] For example, in the case of the Transport Tribunal.

[9] See also para. 7 of Schedule 5 to the Immigration Act, 1971, relating to the Immigration Appeal Tribunal.

dismissed by an executive Minister, there will appear to be danger of their following too readily departmental policy in their decisions. The Franks Committee therefore recommended that responsibility for dismissal should rest exclusively with the Lord Chancellor. This principle has been accepted in section 8 of the 1971 Act, which provides that no power (given by a constituent statute[10]) of a Minister of the Crown—other than the Lord Chancellor—to terminate a person's membership of any tribunal specified in Schedule 1 to the Act,[11] shall be exercisable except with the consent of the Lord Chancellor.

As a general rule, the Committee were of the opinion that tribunal service should not be whole-time or salaried:

> "Such a change would, we think, impair many valuable features of the system."[12]

Nevertheless they thought some important appointments ought to be remunerated, such as members of the Lands Tribunal, and (presumably) the Chairman of the Area Traffic Commissioners or of the Transport Tribunal. In 1971 the Council on Tribunals appointed out that "the proportion of women serving on the various types of tribunals was remarkably low."[13] All tribunals should of course be supplied with adequate professional staff. The Committee considered a suggestion that tribunal staffs ought not to be supplied from the executive departments, on the argument that this practice is responsible for a feeling in the minds of some people that the tribunals are dependent on and influenced by the Departments, but this suggestion was rejected, as it was considered that there would not be enough appointments to create an independent corps of tribunal clerks and staff.[14] The Committee did, however, recommend (para. 61) that the duties of the clerk should be confined to secretarial matters and the giving of advice only when requested, and that he should not as a matter of course retire with the members of the tribunal when they came to consider their decision.[15] On these matters there has as yet been no legislation and this may well be a subject on which the Council on Tribunals will make recommendations.

(3) Venue.—It will be of considerable interest to citizens having recourse to a tribunal to know where the sitting will be held. In this respect, administrative tribunals have always considered the public interest and have taken care to ensure that proper notice is given of

---

[10] Many of the enabling statutes empower the appropriate Minister to dismiss a member of a tribunal at will.

[11] Which may be added to: s. 15 (5). There is an exception in certain cases: s. 8 (2).

[12] Para. 57. The Committee did not expand this observation; presumably they had in mind the traditional preference of the Englishman to be "tried by his peers".

[13] Annual Report for 1971/72, para. 87.

[14] *Ante*, p. 206.

[15] As is the general principle in magistrates' courts. In practice the members of a tribunal often remain in the "court", the parties and members of the public being asked to retire. In most cases (*e.g.*, national insurance local tribunals, mental health review tribunals, etc.) it is then customary for the clerk to remain with the members of the tribunal while they deliberate their decision. Justice is thus not always seen to be done, but as the clerk is often little more than a secretary, he may not be in a position to influence the tribunal, even if he should wish to do so.

their sittings to all persons interested, and also that those sittings are held in places reasonably convenient to the parties. Most of the established tribunals either sit in divisions based on local centres (as do the Agricultural Land Tribunals), or they are peripatetic; holding their sittings in convenient places where the business arises (as do the fourteen panels of Traffic Commissioners, and the Lands Tribunal). Some tribunals are organised on a local basis, having comparatively small areas of jurisdiction (such as the rent assessment committees), and it is customary for statutory inquiries to be held locally. Tribunals often meet in the local or other offices of the executive department with which their jurisdiction is concerned; some adverse criticism was made of this practice to the Franks Committee, but they did not consider the location of premises was a major point of principle.[16] In practice, it would seem preferable for some neutral building, such as a local town hall, county court or magistrates' court room to be utilised where possible. The Council on Tribunals have from time to time drawn attention to unsatisfactory accommodation provided for particular tribunals, but add that in almost every case steps have been taken to improve the accommodation.[17] In the American Administrative Procedure Act, 1946, it is provided (section 5 (a)) that any person entitled to notice of an agency hearing shall be

> "timely informed of (1) the time, place and nature thereof; (2) the legal authority and jurisdiction under which the hearing is to be held, and (3) the matters of fact and law asserted. . . . In fixing the times and places for hearings, due regard shall be had for the convenience and necessity of the parties or their representatives."

There may be no need for a similar statutory provision in this country at present, but the general principles should invariably be applied, as they usually are in practice.

(4) Procedure before the hearing.—It is obviously important that the citizen should be made fully aware of the case he has to meet (and, of course, of his right to appeal to or appear before the tribunal in question). "What is needed", says the Franks Committee[18]:

> "is that the citizen should receive in good time beforehand a document setting out the main points of the opposing case".

This recommendation has not yet been implemented in general legislation; indeed it is scarcely a matter for legislation, but it has been covered in procedural rules made by the appropriate Minister for particular tribunals. The Minister has to consult with the Council on Tribunals on such matters,[19] who are always anxious to ensure that this point in particular is covered by the rules. No code has yet been made applying to statutory inquiries generally, but the point is covered in the planning appeal and compulsory purchase procedure rules, and

---

16 Report, para. 66.
17 Second Report, para. 35.
18 Report, para. 72.
19 1971 Act, s. 10.

consultation is required in respect of procedure rules that apply to statutory inquiries.[20]

(5) Procedure at the hearing.—As a general rule, the Franks Committee were of the opinion that procedure should be adopted to suit the particular tribunal; the general object should be "to combine an orderly procedure with an informal atmosphere" (para. 64). It has on occasion been suggested that a standard code of procedure should be enacted, which would apply to all administrative tribunals. As the then Attorney-General said in the House of Commons, however,

> "it would not be practicable to standardise the procedure of all administrative tribunals because their circumstances differ so widely."[1]

Administrative tribunals are not—and never have been—expected to carry out their investigations in all respects in manner similar to the ordinary courts of law, provided they follow the principles of natural justice,[2] but they must of course observe the provisions of any procedural rules applied to them. Where such rules have been made, unfortunately these are not always simple or clear to understand.[3] The following special points require detailed comment.

(a) *Public hearings.*—The principle of openness seems to suggest that all hearings should be held in public. The Franks Committee were satisfied that this should be the normal rule, except that a hearing should be private where considerations of national security would be involved, where intimate personal or financial circumstances would have to be disclosed (for example, hearings before the Income Tax Commissioners, or where a medical examination of an individual would be necessary), or in the case of a preliminary hearing involving professional capacity and reputation. The old adage governing the criminal courts of this country, that "it is as important that justice should be seen to be done as it is that it should be done", is not perhaps completely relevant to an administrative tribunal where the issues may not be as important as a criminal trial, but the parties concerned will not have as much confidence in the impartiality of the proceedings if they know that the Press and the public have no right to find out what is going on. From the point of view of the administration itself also, publicity may enable their point of view to become generally known to the public,[4] and possibly the need for further hearings thereby avoided. Secrecy can rarely be necessary;

---

[20] Tribunals and Inquiries Act, 1971, s. 11. As to planning and compulsory purchase inquiries, see Chapter VIII, and for the compulsory purchase and planning inquiries rules, footnote 12 on p. 219, *post*. Much the same effect has been achieved in relation to other inquiries by Circular 9/58 of the Ministry of Housing and Local Government.

[1] Hansard, 16th June 1965, col. 85, where a list of procedural rules is given. The Public and Administrative Law Reform Committee of New Zealand also consider "it would be impossible to force all administrative tribunals into one single detailed procedural mould": Third Report, para. 65; Sixth Report, para. 3.

[2] See, *e.g.*, *Board of Education* v. *Rice*, [1911] A.C. 179 and Chapter VI, *ante*, p. 117.

[3] See Report of Council on Tribunals for 1964, para. 11.

[4] See article by D. R. Mandelker in [1960] P.L. 256, at p. 268, dealing with planning appeals, where he points out the need for general planning principles to be explained in Ministry decisions.

the official who is afraid of the Press is usually either mistaken or inefficient, or has something to hide. A related point is the requirement that the case an applicant before a tribunal will have to meet is made known to him before the hearing. This is safeguarded in most of the special procedural rules applicable to particular tribunals.[5]

(b) *Legal representation.*—The Franks Committee "had no hesitation" in recommending[6] that the right of a citizen appearing before a tribunal to be able to call upon the services of a legal representative, should be curtailed only in the most exceptional circumstances. In the United States a denial of the right to legal representation before an agency hearing would amount to a breach of the "due process" clause of the Constitution,[7] and this is confirmed in section 6 (a) of the American Administrative Procedure Act, 1946. In this country, until recently, there were several instances where the procedural codes applicable to certain tribunals denied the citizen any right to be represented by a lawyer, under the mistaken idea that the compulsory exclusion of lawyers would simplify the proceedings. As a consequence of the Franks Report, most of these exceptional cases have now been abandoned,[8] and in the case of appeals to an adjudicator or the Immigration Appeal Tribunal under the Immigration Act, 1971, it is expressly provided in the statute[9] that rules of procedure made by the Secretary of State must provide "that any appellant shall have the right to be legally represented".

(c) *Legal Aid.*—Closely allied to the question of legal representation before a tribunal is the further consideration whether individual citizens should be able to call upon the services of the national legal aid scheme introduced by the Legal Aid and Advice Act, 1949, both for representation at the hearing and for advice at an earlier stage. The Franks Committee were of opinion that the system should be extended to the more important, and especially the appellate, tribunals, but this recommendation has not yet been implemented. This question is, of course, bound up with the national economy but it is under consideration by the Council on Tribunals and other official bodies.[10] The question is particularly important in relation to mental health review tribunals (where, *ex hypothesi*, the applicant will often be peculiarly in need of

[5] See, *e.g.*, the Mental Health Review Tribunal Rules, 1960 (S.I. 1960 No. 1139), rules 5–7, and at planning appeal and compulsory purchase inquiries (Ch. VIII, *post*, pp. 219 and 239).

[6] Report, para. 87.

[7] Fifth Amendment: "No person shall be . . . deprived of life, liberty or property, without due process of law; . . ."

[8] Note especially the tribunals dealing with National Insurance and National Service; *post*, pp. 247 and 260. The ban on legal representation still exists in the case of tribunals appointed to investigate complaints against practitioners under the National Health Service (Service Committees and Tribunal) Regulations, 1956, reg. 5 (1), proviso. This is justified by the "strong likelihood that if legal representation were permitted it would be the practitioners who would avail themselves of it, so that complainants would be deterred from coming forward" (Second Report of the Council on Tribunals, paras. 42 and 44).

[9] Immigration Act, 1971, s. 22 (3).

[10] Annual Report of the Council on Tribunals for 1971/72, para. 98; more recently (summer 1973) the matter was being considered by the Lord Chancellor's Legal Aid Advisory Committee.

professional advice) and such major tribunals as the Lands Tribunal. It has also been suggested that assistance should be available for surveyor's advice before rent assessment committees.[11] The £25 legal advice scheme introduced by the Legal Advice and Assistance Act, 1972, should benefit would be appellants before tribunals,[12] although this scheme does not extend to legal representation at a hearing.

(d) *Oaths, etc.*—Should a tribunal have power to administer an oath to witnesses giving evidence, and to issue subpoenas requiring the attendance of such witnesses? The Franks Committee regarded administration of an oath as an open question, suggesting that tribunals should be given such a power, to be used only in exceptional cases at the discretion of the tribunal. As we have seen, some tribunals (*e.g.*, the Transport Tribunal and Tribunals of Inquiry under the Act of 1921) already possess this power. The power to administer an oath is not perhaps so important at the present time when most witnesses are reasonably educated, as it was when the oath was administered to impress on the witness the importance and solemnity of the occasion. If the penalties of perjury were extended to all false evidence given before tribunals, the power to administer an oath would not be necessary. The Committee thought it desirable that all tribunals should be empowered to issue a subpoena at their discretion,[13] but the Council on Tribunals did not agree with this opinion, as a party before a tribunal would be able to obtain a Crown Office subpoena, and the Council considered that the power to obtain a subpoena should remain the responsibility of the parties and not become that of the tribunal.[14]

(e) *Evidence.*—On this subject the Franks Committee[15] were of the opinion that it would be a mistake to introduce the strict rules of evidence applied in the courts. In practice hearsay evidence is frequently admitted before a tribunal, and officials are permitted to give evidence as to matters of opinion, and to produce statistics and other material, without any regard to the "best evidence" rule, whether or not the parties agree (as would be the case in civil litigation).[16] Informality of this kind does not often lead to injustice for, as the Committee observe, the presence of a legally qualified chairman should enable the tribunal to attach proper weight to evidence adduced before them. In the U.S.A., however, the proceedings before an agency hearing may be set aside on review by the courts if it can be shown that the conclusions were (*inter alia*) "unsupported by substantial evidence[17];" the tribunal must there-

---

[11] A voluntary pilot scheme has been running in London, and another has been introduced in Glasgow; Annual Report for 1968, para. 30.

[12] "Tribunal" is not defined for the purposes of the 1972 Act, but s. 17 of the 1949 Act (and the two Acts are to be read together) provides that "tribunal" is to include an arbitrator or umpire. It is therefore reasonably clear that the 1972 Act is not confined to statutory tribunals listed in the Tribunals and Inquiries Act, 1971, and may even include domestic tribunals.

[13] Report, paras. 92, 93.

[14] Second Report, paras. 76–82, and see Report for 1964, para. 28 (8) and (9).

[15] Report, para. 90.

[16] This is particularly relevant in connection with documents; see, *e.g.*, *Macdonnell* v. *Evans* (1852), 21 L.J.C.P. 141.

[17] Administrative Procedure Act, 1946 (American), s. 10 (e), *post. p.* 460.

fore have regard to the weight of the evidence, and on review a court will consider the whole record.[18]

(f) *Costs.*—In the courts of law, costs usually "follow the event"; this is also true in most cases before the Lands Tribunal, and certain other tribunals have power to award costs to a successful party. The subject of costs before inquiries is discussed below, page 222.

(6) Privilege.—An incidental question which may occasionally arise in connection with tribunal hearings, is whether absolute or qualified privilege applies to those proceedings, so as to operate as a bar to an action for defamation.

> "It is necessary, in a matter of this kind, to consider—the constitution and functions and the procedure of the tribunal which falls to be considered, as to whether the rule of absolute privilege applies,"

said HODSON, L.J., when this matter was fully considered in relation to the Disciplinary Committee established under the Solicitors Act, 1957, in the case of *Addis* v. *Crocker*.[19] In that case several contentions were raised in course of argument as to whether absolute privilege should apply, which were answered as follows:

(i) The proceedings were held in private. In reply, HODSON, L.J., said (at p. 636):

> "... in my opinion it is not maintainable, as a matter of law, that the fact that this tribunal is directed by its rules to hear in private and to give its findings and order publicly—and only its findings and order publicly—destroys the right to claim absolute privilege."

(ii) The constitution of the tribunal, established by Act of Parliament, "spoke for itself"; it could administer an oath to witnesses, and their attendance could be enforced by subpoena. The tribunal therefore exercised judicial functions, not administrative functions. As HODSON, L.J., said: (*ibid.*):

> "This is not comparable with a meeting concerned with the issue of licences."

It was also considered material that there was a right of appeal from the Committee to the High Court.

(iii) Irregularity as to matters of detail in the particular proceedings could not destroy the privilege.

Nevertheless, it is by no means clear that absolute privilege will be applied to the proceedings (and the decision was held in *Addis* v. *Crocker* to be "part of" the proceedings for this purpose) of all administrative tribunals. PEARCE, L.J., said in the same case (at p. 638):

> "... the privilege is extended to tribunals which act judicially in a manner similar to courts of justice, but not to merely administrative tribunals."

Where the line is to be drawn does not appear.

---

[18] Schwartz, *An Introduction to American Administrative Law*, at p. 188 and *Universal Camera Corporation* v. *National Labor Relations Board*, 340 U.S. 474, (1951).

[19] [1961] 2 All E.R. 629; [1961] 1 Q.B. 11; and see *Royal Aquarium and Summer and Winter Garden Society* v. *Parkinson*, [1892] 1 Q.B. 431.

Similar arguments were applied to a case involving the Bar Council,[20] although here privilege did not extend to a letter sent before the Council was seised of a matter.

A related problem is that of the privilege of witnesses giving evidence before an administrative tribunal; this has not been clarified, but the Council on Tribunals are of the opinion that there was no evidence of any practical need for an extension of absolute privilege.[21]

A fair and accurate report of the proceedings at a sitting of

> "any commission, tribunal or committee or person appointed for the purposes of any inquiry by Act of Parliament, by Her Majesty or by a Minister of the Crown,"

or of

> "any person appointed by a local authority to hold a local inquiry in pursuance of any Act of Parliament,"

is entitled to *qualified* privilege, unless the defendant has been requested to publish an explanation or contradiction and has refused or neglected to do so.[1] This will certainly apply to most tribunals and to statutory inquiries, and probably to other inquiries directed to be held by a Minister. The tribunal, inquiry or other body in question must, however, be open to the public for this special defence to be available.

(7) Decisions.—Decisions should normally be notified to the parties by the Clerk (or possibly by the Chairman) to the tribunal to the parties in writing, and reasons should be given therefor. The requirement as to reasons is of the first importance (see below, page 217) and the Council on Tribunals will normally endeavour to secure the inclusion of such a requirement in procedural rules (in addition to the general statutory requirement of s. 12 of the 1971 Act).

(8) Appeals.—Appeals from administrative tribunals was one of the matters under discussion at the time when the Franks Committee was constituted. Many writers had discussed the matter and propounded improvements, in particular that there should be an Administrative Division of the High Court, or alternatively, an Administrative Court of Appeal within the existing judicial structure, to which an appeal should lie, on fact or law, from any decision of an administrative tribunal.[2] Professor Robson had suggested there should be an appellate tribunal outside the framework of the ordinary courts, which would provide formal machinery for the redress of grievances in cases of maladministration. The French system of a separate *droit administratif*, presided over by one superior court, was also canvassed by some writers, but this

---

[20] *Lincoln* v. *Daniels*, [1961] 3 All E.R. 740; [1962] 1 Q.B. 237; the fact that the Bar Council derived its authority from the Benchers of the four Inns who themselves derived their authority from the sovereign as the fountain of justice, was not material as constituting any distinction from *Addis* v. *Crocker* (*ante*), where the Disciplinary Committee derived its authority from statute.

[21] The Franks Committee had suggested there was a case for its extension (Report, para. 82); see Second Report of the Council on Tribunals, paras. 67–75.

[1] Defamation Act, 1952, s. 7.

[2] See, for example, *Rule of Law*, published by the Inns of Court Conservative and Unionist Society in 1956, and observations in Chapter V, *ante*, p. 107.

was generally thought to be too great a breach with tradition, and not a solution acceptable to the majority in this country.

The Franks Committee expressed the general view that[3]

> "The existence of a right of appeal is salutary and makes for right adjudication".

Their eventual recommendations on this subject may be summarised:

(a) There should be an appeal on fact, law and merits from a tribunal of first instance to an appellate tribunal.[4] This recommendation has not been adopted in terms but is applied in practice in some cases (for example, from the local valuation courts in rating cases to the Lands Tribunal, and from the licensing authority to the Transport Tribunal in goods vehicle licensing). Whether or not such an appeal is necessary turns on the status of the particular tribunal of first instance. It would not be suggested, for instance, that there ought to be an appeal by way of re-hearing from the Lands Tribunal even when sitting as a court of first instance,[5] but appeals from the local insurance officer to the local appeals tribunal in industrial insurance,[6] are clearly desirable.

(b) As a matter of principle appeal on the merits should not lie from a tribunal to a Minister.[7] This recommendation is almost more honoured in the breach than the observance (for example, in the National Health Service, and from the Traffic Commissioners to the Secretary of State for the Environment in cases of road service licences for passenger service vehicles). The principle is perhaps more easily justified in logic than in practice. A Minister is in theory more likely to be guided by policy than a tribunal of persons appointed by him, but in practice Ministerial jurisdiction will be exercised on the advice of a person appointed by him and there will be little to choose in degree of impartiality between the local tribunal and the expert departmental inspector.

(c) An appeal on a point of law should lie to the courts from a tribunal decision, except from a decision of the National Insurance Commissioner, or Supplementary Benefits Appeal Tribunals.[8] This recommendation has been implemented by section 13 of the Act of 1971, which provides for an appeal in point of law, at the instance of any party who is dissatisfied, to the High Court from any of the tribunals listed in the subsection, by way of case stated. This section applies to most of the more important of the tribunals listed in the First Schedule, and these may be supplemented by order made by the Lord Chancellor under section

---

[3] Report, para. 104.
[4] *Ibid.*, paras. 105–6.
[5] As it does when hearing an application for discharge or modification of restrictive covenants, under s. 184 of the Law of Property Act, 1925 as amended by the Law of Property Act, 1969; there is of course an appeal on a point of law to the Court of Appeal.
[6] Chapter VIII, *post*, p. 247.
[7] Report, para. 105.
[8] Report, paras. 107–12; "The machinery should be simple, cheap and expeditious."

15 (3) of the 1971 Act, or restricted by order under s. 15 (5) (b), *ibid.*[9] An appeal also lies to the High Court from a decision of the Secretary of State for the Environment under section 36 of the Town and Country Planning Act, 1971 (or of an inspector determining the appeal on behalf of the Secretary of State under the Ninth Schedule), or from a decision on an appeal to him against an enforcement notice.[10]

(d) No statute should contain words purporting to oust the remedies by way of *certiorari*, prohibition and *mandamus*.[11] This recommendation by way of putting into statutory form the doctrine of *Re Gilmore*,[12] was implemented by section 11 of the Act of 1958 (now s. 14 of the 1971 Act) discussed in detail elsewhere.[13] What is perhaps more important is the other recommendation of the Franks Committee, to the effect that decisions of tribunals should be reasoned and as full as possible.[14] In view of the general principle that *certiorari* (or prohibition) will lie in respect of an "error on the face of the record",[15] what goes on the record is of the first importance for the effectiveness of judicial review. If no reasons are given for a decision, there will be no error on the face of the record, and therefore there may be no grounds for review by way of *certiorari*. This recommendation also was implemented in the 1958 Act, and s. 12 of the 1971 Act now requires every tribunal specified in the First Schedule, and every Minister coming to a decision after the holding by him or on his behalf of a statutory inquiry, to give reasons for the decision on request[16]; the only grounds on which the tribunal or Minister may refuse to state such reasons, are national security, or because the disclosure of reasons would be contrary to the interests of any person primarily concerned. The section also does not apply to a decision of a Minister in connection with a scheme or order of "a legislative and not an executive character".[17] It is further provided in subsection (5) of the same section that any such reasons

> "shall be taken to form part of the decision and accordingly to be incorporated in the record".

---

[9] Thus, provision was made for an appeal to lie to the High Court on a point of law from a decision of an adjudicator appointed under s. 13 of the National Insurance Act, 1959 (Tribunals and Inquiries (National Insurance Adjudicator) Order, 1959, S.I. 1959 No. 1267 now replaced by the Act of 1971) and from a decision of a person appointed to hear appeals from decisions of the Director of Aviation Safety relating to air operators' certificates (Tribunals and Inquiries (Air Operators' Certificates) Order, 1961, S.I. 1961 No. 153). Express statutory provision is made for an appeal to lie on a point of law from the Plant Variety Rights Tribunal, by s. 10 (2) of the Plant Varieties and Seeds Act, 1964.

[10] Town and Country Planning Act, 1971, ss. 245 and 246.

[11] Report, para. 117.

[12] [1957] 1 Q.B. 574.

[13] Chapter VI, *ante* p. 157.

[14] Report, para. 98.

[15] Chapter VI, *ante*, p. 145.

[16] On an appeal to the courts, where this is permitted by statute (as in a planning case), it is apparently open for the court to order the Minister to state his reasons under s. 12, where he has not already done so, without the necessity for separate *mandamus* proceedings; see *per* Lord DENNING, M.R., in *Earl Iveagh* v. *Minister of Housing and Local Government*, [1963] 3 All E.R. 817, at p. 820; [1964] 1 Q.B. 395, at p. 410.

[17] 1971 Act, s. 12 (2). The exception is reminiscent of the provision in reg. 2 (1) of the Statutory Instruments Regulations, 1947 (Chapter IV, *ante*, p. 62).

In practice this section may not prove to be as satisfactory as it seems,[18] for its provisions do not require that the reasons given shall necessarily be comprehensive.[19]

(9) Defects of tribunal procedure.—What then are the commonest defects of our administrative tribunals as they exist at present? First, one could argue that the lack of a system leads to complication and therefore a lack of comprehension on the part of the ordinary public. There are so many tribunals sitting in different places, at different times, and each subjected to different procedural rules, that it needs an expert to say when—or whether—there may be a remedy. Professor Street in his Hamlyn Lectures for 1968[20] emphasises the complexities of the law administered by many tribunals,[1] and suggests that some body should be charged with the overall responsibility of continuous review of the law operated by the several tribunals.

The informality of procedure before tribunals, desirable as it may be from most points of view, may give rise to appearances of injustice.[2] The rule that tribunals (and inquiries) may not lay down "rules of thumb" which they will follow in subsequent decisions,[3] has been criticised as bringing unnecessary uncertainty into their proceedings.[4] The requirement of having to give reasons for decisions should be made of universal application, and there may be a need to examine further the position and functions of the clerk to a tribunal; in what circumstances should he be allowed to be present during the conclusion of a hearing when the tribunal is deliberating its decision?[5] Legal advice and legal aid for representation before tribunals, is another matter that merits the consideration currently being given to it.[6]

(10) Statutory inquiries.—It remains to consider a few points that apply particularly to statutory inquiries (as above defined).[7]

(a) *Hearings.*—In some statutes provision is made for the Minister to convene an inquiry or a hearing "before a person appointed by him for the purpose".[8] In practice the distinctive features of the "hearing" procedure are that s. 250 of the Local Government Act, 1972 will not

---

[18] If full reasons are not given the purpose of the section will be virtually destroyed. This is particularly relevant in planning decisions: see article cited *ante*, at [1960] P.L. 256.

[19] In *Givaudan & Co., Ltd.* v. *Minister of Housing and Local Government*, [1966] 3 All E.R. 696, an appeal to the courts against a refusal of planning permission was allowed because the reasons given were unintelligible. A similar line was taken by the Court of Appeal in *R.* v. *Industrial Injuries Commissioner, ex parte Howarth* (1968), 4 K.I.R. 621.

[20] *Justice in the Welfare State.*

[1] In particular in relation to notices to quit and the rent assessment committees.

[2] See, for example, a complaint about a local valuation court discussed in the Annual Report of the Council on Tribunals for 1967, at p. 22.

[3] See *R.* v. *London County Council, ex parte Corrie*, [1918] 1 K.B. 68, and Chapter 1, *ante*, p. 26.

[4] See *Administrative Justice*, by H. J. Elcock (1969), Chapter I.

[5] *Ante*, p. 209.

[6] *Ante*, p. 212.

[7] *Ante*, p. 197. As to inquiries generally, see *Public Inquiries as an Instrument of Government*, by Wraith and Lamb, and as to large scale inquiries, "Public Inquiries and Large-Scale Development", by H. R. Burroughs [1970] P.L. 224.

[8] Acquisition of Land (Authorisation Procedure) Act, 1946, 1st. sched., para. 4 (2); Town and Country Planning Act, 1971, s. 36 (4), both of which provide an alternative to a local inquiry (see also 1971 Act, s. 282 (1)).

apply thereto; therefore, there is no general power to award costs, and the proceedings will usually be in private. It is also possible in such case for an actual hearing to be dispensed with completely, and for the Minister to decide on the written representations of the parties, provided they agree.[9]

(b) *Inspectors.*—A local inquiry or a "hearing" will be presided over by a "person appointed by the Secretary of State", commonly referred to as an "inspector", although the term does not appear in the statutes. The Franks Committee heard a considerable volume of evidence on this subject, aimed at the introduction of a special cadre of inspectors, independent of the executive departments to which they are at present attached. The Committee, whilst recognising the preference of some Departments for independent inspectors appointed *ad hoc* (from outside the Department, as in the case of appeals from the Traffic Commissioners), were of the opinion that

> "the main body of inspectors should be placed under the control of the Lord Chancellor, but inspectors may be kept in contact with policy developments in the Departments responsible".[10]

After the publication of the Report, the Government made it clear that they could not accept this recommendation, which therefore has not been implemented. A separate hierarchy of inspectors as contemplated by the Franks Report would, however, give some further assurance of the impartiality that the authors of the Report thought desirable. Inspectors belonging to a Department are obviously influenced by Departmental policy, and although the civil service trade unions are a safeguard against arbitrary dismissals of individuals, an inspector paid by a Department cannot manifestly seem as independent as he probably is in practice.[11]

(c) *Procedure.*—The observations of the Franks Committee on the procedure to be observed by statutory inquiries closely follow those relating to tribunals, and statutory effect has been given to them by s. 11 of the Tribunals and Inquiries Act, 1971 (replacing an earlier provision).

Rules have been made by the Lord Chancellor in consultation with the Council on Tribunals, under the predecessor to section 11 of the Act of 1971, which apply to planning appeal and compulsory purchase order inquiries only,[12] whereby it is provided that at least forty-two days' notice must be given of the date, time and place fixed for the holding of an inquiry, and also the local planning or acquiring authority (as the case may be) must give at least twenty-eight days' notice of the

---

[9] And in some cases under the Town and Country Planning Act, 1971, the inspector will decide on behalf of the Minister; Chapter VIII, *post*, p. 227.

[10] Report, paras. 303–4.

[11] It was said in the Report of the Council on Tribunals for 1961 (para. 70) that the employment of independent inspectors in special cases was to be re-considered.

[12] Town and Country Planning Appeals (Inquiries Procedure) Rules, 1969, S.I. 1969 No. 1092, Town and Country Planning (Appeals) (Determination by Appointed Persons) (Inquiries Procedure) Rules 1968, S.I. 1968 No. 1952, and the Compulsory Purchase by Local Authorities (Inquiries Procedure) Rules, 1962 (S.I. 1962 No. 1424) and see Chapter VIII, *post*, p. 238.

substance of their case to the appellants or objectors.[13] On a planning appeal the applicant may similarly be requested by the Secretary of State to furnish a written statement of the substance of his case on which he intends to rely at the inquiry.[14] These Rules do not, however, apply to other kinds of statutory inquiries, but as they were made (as required by the statute) in consultation with the Council on Tribunals, it seems probable that Government Departments will follow these general principles in other cases.[15]

(d) *Inspectors' reports.*—It has long been established that a party to proceedings before a statutory inquiry has no right to see a copy of the report of the inspector who conducted the inquiry, nor will the courts insist on such a report being produced.[16] The Franks Committee considered this matter, and came to the

"general conclusion that the right course is to publish the inspector's report".[17]

This recommendation has not yet been expressed in as many words in any statute, but the Minister of Housing and Local Government (now the Secretary of State for the Environment) has said[18] that his department will make available to any party to such proceedings a copy of the inspector's report, on request made to him in writing within one month of the giving of the decision,[19] and the Rules made under the predecessor to section 11 of the 1971 Act above referred to, expressly require this action to be taken. At this stage the report may be useless legally, as the Minister's decision will have already been taken; it is submitted that the report could not be regarded as being part of "the record", such that it could be examined on *certiorari*. However, the contents of a report may on occasion afford grounds for an appeal,[20] by reason

---

[13] Similar provisions are contained in the Mental Health Review Tribunal Rules, 1960 (S.I. 1960 No. 1139).

[14] S.I. 1965 No. 473, rule 6 (6); there is no similar provision applying to compulsory purchase inquiries.

[15] Action implementing the Franks Report had already been taken by the Ministry of Housing and Local Government, in Circular 9/58 of that Ministry; this is now *pro tanto* displaced by the Rules. Similar rules have now been made for a number of other statutory inquiries; see the Gas (Underground Storage) (Inquiries Procedure) Rules, 1966, S.I. 1966 No. 1375, the Electricity (Compulsory Wayleaves) (Hearing Procedure) Rules, 1967, S.I. 1967 No. 450, the Compulsory Purchase by Ministers (Inquiries Procedure) Rules, 1967, S.I. 1967 No. 720, and the Pipe-Lines (Inquiries Procedure) Rules, 1967, S.I. 1967 No. 1769. All of these follow the pattern of the Planning Rules, and they have all been made after consultation with the Council on Tribunals. In the case of procedural regulations made by the (former) Minister of Transport under the Docks and Harbours Act, 1966, no prior consultation with the Council on Tribunals is necessary, because they are not made by the Lord Chancellor. Nevertheless, two sets of regulations so made (Licensing of Port Employers (Inquiries Procedure) Regulations, 1967, S.I. 1967 No. 449, and the Ports Welfare Amenities (Inquiries Procedure) Regulations, 1968, S.I. 1968 No. 1062) follow the same pattern.

[16] *Denby (William) & Son* v. *Minister of Health*, [1936] 1 K.B. 337.

[17] Report, para. 343.

[18] Circular 9/58 of that Ministry (*supra*). As the procedure laid down in this Circular covers slum clearance as well as planning appeals and compulsory purchase order inquiries (the latter two of which are now regulated by the Rules, above), and similar action was taken by the Minister of Education (see Circular 2/60 of that Ministry), most inquiries have been provided for.

[19] Made by the Secretary of State or (in some 80% of all planning appeals) by the inspector himself under Schedule 9 to the Town and Country Planning Act, 1971, (*ante*, p. 238).

[20] See, for example, *Lord Luke K.G. of Pavenham* v. *Minister of Housing and Local Government*, [1967] 2 All E.R. 1066; [1968] 1 Q.B. 172.

of the requirement in the procedural rules (introduced after the *Chalk-pit* affair below) relating to planning appeals; that if the Minister proposes to disagree with the findings of fact of his inspector, he must allow the parties an opportunity of asking for the inquiry to be re-opened. It may also prove possible to take extra-legal action, based on the contents of the report, such as making representations to a Member of Parliament.[21]

It has always been reasonably clear that a Minister is not obliged to agree with recommendations (as distinct from findings of fact) contained in an Inspector's report, and in *Nelsovil, Ltd.* v. *Minister of Housing and Local Government*[1] it was emphasised that the Minister is bound to form his own independent view, giving such weight as he thinks proper to the recommendations of his inspector.

In the U.S.A., federal agency hearings must be conducted by specially appointed officers of the agency concerned, known as examiners, who have certain security of tenure and independence of the agency. The examiner who holds the hearing must initially decide the case and make a recommended or tentative decision which will then be notified to the parties, and they will have an opportunity to submit further observations involving possibly, a further hearing.[2] This practice of a hearing into a hearing would seem unnecessary in this country, but in the U.S.A. the idea of "due process of law"[3] governs administrative as well as civil and criminal procedure. On the other hand the present system in this country is far from perfect. The Minister may not agree with the recommendations of his inspector and the parties may have no opportunity of making any further effective representations if his decision is at variance with the inspector's recommendations.[4]

---

[21] There are interesting observations on the form of an Inspector's report in the Report of the Council on Tribunals for 1964, at paras. 86 and 87.

[1] [1962] 1 All E.R. 423.

[2] Administrative Procedure Act, 1946 (American), ss. 8 and 11, and see *Morgan* v. *United States*, 298 U.S. 468, (1936).

[3] See note 7 on p. 212 above.

[4] Difficult problems may arise where the Minister disagrees with his inspector's recommendations; if there has been no error of law, the appellant may have no remedy, but he will often have a sense of grievance. This was brought to the fore in the famous "Chalk-pit" case in 1961 (see notes at [1961] P.L. 121, and [1962] J.P.L. 315). In this case, a neighbouring landowner had given evidence in support of the planning authority at a local inquiry into a planning appeal, suggesting that the decision of the authority should be upheld and planning permission for the development in question be refused. The inspector reported in favour of refusal, but the Minister consulted the Minister of Agriculture, Fisheries and Food, whose officers supplied certain technical information which was not available at the inquiry, and as a consequence of this the appeal was allowed and planning permission was granted. The landowner appealed to the court, but it was held that he had no *locus standi*: *Buxton* v. *Minister of Housing and Local Government*, [1960] 3 All E.R. 408; [1961] 1 Q.B. 278 (*ante*, p. 177). He then complained to (*inter alia*) the Lord Chancellor, who referred the matter to the Council on Tribunals. They reported in April, 1962, recommending that (a) where the Minister differs from his inspector on a finding of fact, he should give the parties at the inquiry an opportunity of commenting thereon (*cf.* the American practice, above), and (b) if there is fresh evidence, expert advice or a fresh issue, the inquiry should be reopened. In a case where the Inquiries Procedure Rules (above, footnote 12 on p. 219) apply, this suggested procedure has been implemented. In any such case where the Minister in future differs from his inspector on a finding of fact, or after the close of the inquiry receives any new evidence (including expert opinion on a matter of fact) or takes into consideration any new issue of fact (not being a matter of Government policy), he may not come to a decision at variance with a

(e) *Costs.*—In 1964, at the request of the Lord Chancellor, the Council on Tribunals reported specially on the subject of costs at statutory inquiries.[5] Under the existing law the Minister convening an inquiry can make an order as to the costs of the parties only at a public inquiry to which section 250 of the Local Government Act, 1972 (replacing a similar provision in the 1933 Act) applies; this section does apply to many important inquiries, including those into objections to compulsory purchase orders and also to planning appeals, but it does not apply to all statutory inquiries, or to any "hearings". The Council on Tribunals recommended in the first place that the power to award costs should be extended to all hearings and inquiries; no amending legislation had yet been introduced to cover this point. They also recommended that as a matter of practice costs should normally be awarded against a party behaving unreasonably, vexatiously or frivolously. This recommendation will in future be acted on by Ministers concerned,[6] as will the further recommendation that a successful objector[7] should be allowed his costs in a case of a compulsory purchase or slum clearance order affecting his land. Costs will not normally be awarded to unsuccessful objectors in such cases, nor will they be awarded to successful appellants in planning appeals (except where the planning authority has acted unreasonably, etc.).

This decision to accept the major recommendations of the Council on Tribunals has gone some way to meet the objections of those who argue that in this matter of administrative control over land use in particular, the individual should be entitled to defend his rights at the community's expense. Until the principle that costs shall follow the event has been applied to all inquiries, however, the apparent injustice remains.

(f) *Appeals.*—No special recommendations were made by the Committee on the subject of appeals from statutory inquiries, but provision is now made for appeals to the High Court (on the grounds of lack of *vires*, or of material fault in procedure, alone) in a number of such cases arising under the Town and Country Planning Act, 1971, by Part XII thereof, replacing similar provisions contained in earlier statutes. Provision had also previously been made for appeals against compulsory purchase orders under the Acquisition of Land (Authorisation Procedure) Act, 1946,[8] and the Housing Act, 1957, Part III,[9] and also in respect of certain orders made under the National Parks and Access to the Countryside Act, 1949.[10] In all these cases any appeal to the High Court must be exercised within six weeks of the

---

recommendation of the inspector without giving persons who had appeared at the inquiry an opportunity of making written representations within 21 days; moreover, if the Minister has received new evidence or taken into consideration any new issue of fact, any such person may within 21 days ask for the inquiry to be reopened, and the Minister must accede to that request.

[5] Cmnd. 2471.

[6] See Circular 73/65 of the Ministry of Housing and Local Government.

[7] Provided he is "qualified"; *i.e.*, entitled under the relevant legislation to object.

[8] 1946 Act, Schedule 1, para. 15.

[9] 1957 Act, Schedule 4.

[10] 1949 Act, Schedule 1, para. 8, and see also the Seventh Schedule of the Highways Act, 1959.

date of the order, etc., appealed against, and the Court will not allow an extension of that time in any circumstances whatsoever.[11]

(g) *Decisions.*—Decisions must be notified to the persons concerned, and reasons must be given on request for those decisions[12]; an incidental matter that received the attention of the Franks Committee is the publication of reports of decisions of Ministers after statutory inquiries. This is done regularly in the case of appeals against planning decisions to the Secretary of State under section 36 of the Town and Country Planning Act, 1971, and also in the case of decisions made in connection with social security benefits.[13] The Committee doubted the advantages of this new body of "case law", pointing out that cases differ because of the changing background of policy.[14]

(h) *The position of third parties.*—Some inquiry proceedings may affect—or seem to affect—the interests of persons other than the parties before the inquiry. In particular, this may be the case on a planning appeal or a compulsory purchase inquiry; a neighbouring landowner may be almost as vitally affected by the subject matter of the inquiry as the appellant or the person whose interest in the land is being acquired (the "statutory objector", as he is called in the rules relating to these inquiries).[15] This factor is recognised to some extent in the case of planning appeal inquiries, as any person on whom the Secretary of State has directed that notice of the inquiry shall be served, is entitled to appear,[16] and in practice the inspector allows any member of the public present at the inquiry who wishes to address him, to do so. Also, before a planning appeal or a compulsory purchase inquiry commences, any "person interested" may inspect the planning or acquiring authority's "statement of reasons".[17]

However, an interested third party is not a "party aggrieved" in a legal sense,[18] and therefore he cannot appeal to the courts from the decision of the Secretary of State, nor, unless he had appeared at the inquiry and asked to be notified of that decision, is he entitled to a copy of the inspector's report.[19]

The "Chalkpit affair"[20] drew attention to this matter, and the Council on Tribunals issued a special report in July 1962,[1] in which they recom-

---

[11] *Smith* v. *East Elloe R.D.C.*, [1956] 1 All E.R. 855; [1956] A.C. 736, and *ante*, p. 158.

[12] *Ante*, p. 146.

[13] *Post*, Chapter VIII, p. 251.

[14] Report, para. 354. The relationship between policy and precedent in connection with planning appeals is considered in an article by Professor Mandelker at [1960] P.L. 256, and see also Chapter I, *ante*, p. 26.

[15] Compulsory Purchase by Local Authorities (Inquiries Procedure) Rules, 1962 (S.I. 1962 No. 1424, made under s. 7A of the Tribunals and Inquiries Act, 1958). As to inquiries into planning appeals, see the similar Town and Country Planning (Inquiries Procedure) Rules 1969 (S.I. 1969 No. 1092), and footnote 12, *ante*, p. 219.

[16] Planning Inquiries Rules (*ante*), rule 7 (1) (g).

[17] Compulsory Purchase Rules, rule 4 (7); Planning Inquiries Rules, rule 6 (5).

[18] *Ante*, p. 151, and *Buxton* v. *Minister of Housing and Local Government*, [1960] 3 All E.R. 408; [1961] 1 Q.B. 278, which was one of the early moves in the "Chalkpit affair" (*ante*, p. 221).

[19] Compulsory Purchase Inquiries Rules, rule 10; Planning Inquiries Rules, rule 13.

[20] See footnote on p. 221, *ante*.

[1] Cmd. Paper 1787. This was the first occasion on which the Council issued a special report on a specific point, as distinct from their annual reports.

mended that the Minister should give a public assurance that third parties would in such cases be given the benefit of the procedure laid down in the various Inquiries Rules,[2] and in particular that they should be allowed to make further representations or ask for the reopening of the inquiry, in any case where new evidence or expert advice is brought in after the close of the inquiry[3]; this privilege should not, in the opinion of the Council, be limited to those whose legal rights are infringed. However, in the House of Lords on July 23, 1962,[4] the Lord Chancellor refused to accept this recommendation fully, and limited its acceptance to those whose legal rights were infringed, expressing the view:

> "It would not be satisfactory to put themselves [*i.e.*, Her Majesty's Government] in a position of conferring new legal rights by administrative assurance on a class of people who had not been clearly defined either in the Act or by subordinate legislation."

---

[2] Footnotes 12 on p. 219, and 15 on p. 220, *ante*.
[3] *Ante*, p. 221.
[4] *The Times*, July 24, 1962.

TRIBUNALS SUBJECT TO THE SUPERVISION OF THE COUNCIL ON TRIBUNALS[1]

(A) Those originally listed in the First Schedule to the Tribunals and Inquiries Act, 1958

Agricultural Land Tribunals.
Arbitrators appointed under the Agricultural Holdings Act, 1948.
Children's voluntary homes appeal tribunals (Children Act, 1948).
Independent Schools Tribunals.
Committees appointed under s. 27 of the Forestry Act, 1967.
The Lands Tribunal.
Milk and Dairies tribunals.
Mines and Quarries tribunals.
Appeal tribunals constituted under the Ministry of Social Security Act, 1966.
The National Health Service appeal tribunal.
A National Insurance Commissioner, National Insurance local tribunals and medical appeal tribunals.
Military Service (Hardship) Committees, Reinstatement Committees, appellate tribunals and umpires under the National Service Act, 1948.
Persons nominated under s. 21 (2) of the Nurses Act, 1957.
The Comptroller-General of patents, designs and trade marks.
Pensions Appeals Tribunals and police and fire service pensions appeals tribunals.
The Performing Right Tribunal.
The Prevention of Fraud (Investments) Tribunal of Inquiry.
Furnished houses rent tribunals.
General and Special Commissioners of Income Tax, and the Board of Referees.
The Traffic Commissioners, and the Licensing Authority for Goods Vehicles.
The Transport Tribunal.
The Wireless Telegraphy Tribunal (Act of 1949, s. 9).

(B) Additional Tribunals added by order or statute and now appearing in Schedule 1 to the Tribunals and Inquiries Act, 1971 or subsequently added thereto

Adjudicators appointed under s. 74 of the National Insurance Act, 1965.
Mental Health Review Tribunals.
Air Transport Licensing Board.
The tribunal appointed for the purposes of Chapter I of Part XVII of the Income and Corporation Taxes Act, 1970 ("dividend stripping").
Persons appointed to hear appeals relating to Air Operator's Certificates.
The Betting Levy Appeal Tribunal.
Persons appointed to hear appeals from magistrates' courts committees relating to the indemnification of justices and their clerks.
The Controller of Plant Variety Rights and the Plant Variety Rights Tribunal.
The tribunal of appeal constituted under the London Building Acts (Amendment) Act, 1939.

---

[1] As at July 1972; those exclusively under the supervision of the Scottish Committee are omitted.

Pensions appeal tribunals established under the War Pensions (Administrative Provisions) Act, 1919.
Industrial tribunals.
Rent assessment committees.
Local valuation courts for rating.
The Iron and Steel Arbitration Tribunal.
The Commons Commissioners appointed under the Commons Registration Act, 1965.
Adjudicators established by the Immigration Appeals Act, 1969, and continued in office by the Immigration Act, 1971.
The Immigration Appeal Tribunal.
The Civil Aviation Authority constituted under s. 1 of the Civil Aviation Act, 1971.[2]
Value Added Tax Tribunals constituted under the Finance Act, 1972.[3]
Misuse of Drugs Tribunals constituted under the Misuse of Drugs Act, 1971.[4]
Family Practitioner Committees constituted under the National Health Service Reorganisation Act, 1973.

---

[2] This tribunal is not listed in the Tribunals and Inquiries Act, 1971, but it was placed under the Council's supervision by s. 5 (3) of the Civil Aviation Act, 1971. The Authority commenced operating on April 1, 1972, and took over the functions of the Air Transport Licensing Board, and also those of persons appointed to hear appeals relating to Air Operators' Certificates. On this, see Annual Report of the Council on Tribunals for 1971/72, at paras. 51–58.

[3] These tribunals are under the supervision of the Council by virtue of the Tribunals and Inquiries (Value Added Tax Tribunals) Order, 1972, S.I. 1972 No. 1210, made under the Tribunals and Inquiries Act, 1971, s. 15.

[4] As above, by virtue of the Tribunals and Inquiries (Misuse of Drugs) Order, 1973, S.I. 1973 No. 1600, made under the same powers.

CHAPTER VIII

REDRESS THROUGH THE ADMINISTRATION—PARTICULAR TRIBUNALS AND INQUIRIES

1. INTRODUCTION

In this Chapter it is proposed to consider a few of the more important tribunals and inquiries exercising administrative jurisdiction in some measure, and in discussing the various bodies it may be necessary to say something about the special branches of law that they respectively apply.[1]

In time of war it has become necessary to bring many matters within the purview of the administration of the country, including exchange control and the supply, marketing and rationing of commodities; in addition the administration may take powers to deprive an individual of his liberty in circumstances where he indulges in conduct which it is considered may hinder the war effort.[2] In peace time, however, even in a modern collectivist society, the administration does not assume such wide powers. Perhaps the most important control of the freedom of the individual exercisable by the administration at the present time is that over the private use of land; after that come the various controls imposed in consequence of those modern social conditions named compendiously "The Welfare State". All these, and other forms of control, involve administrative tribunals of various kinds, whose objects are, ostensibly at least, to redress grievances occasioned by the practical working of the particular control; the tribunals are, however, "built in", as it were, into the particular control, and they can operate only within their individual fields and can administer only the special policy principles laid down, by statute or by the appropriate Central Department, as an integral part of the control.

Some of these tribunals and inquiries will therefore be here considered with reference to the controls with which they are concerned.

2. THE CONTROL OF LAND USE

Property lawyers in this country are accustomed to saying that the fee simple is the largest estate in land known to the law, in that it is capable of subsisting in perpetuity; and it is often added to this remark

[1] No attempt has here been made to make an exhaustive catalogue of all the tribunals in existence at the present time. Some of the more interesting have been picked out for consideration, in the hope that the reader may feel encouraged to make a more detailed study of their procedure, or perhaps to examine the rules applicable to other tribunals. Details vary with tribunals but there are many problems common to all, as discussed in the last Chapter.

[2] Such as the Defence of the Realm Regulations of the 1914–18 War, and reg. 18B of the Defence (General) Regulations, 1939, construed widely in such cases as *R.* v. *Halliday*, [1917] A.C.260, and *Liversidge* v. *Anderson*, [1941] 3 All E.R. 338, [1942] A.C.206.

that the owner of a fee simple may do as he likes with his own, subject only to the common law maxim, *sic utere tuo ut alienum non laedas*. Traditionally, this has been a matter exclusively of private law, but in recent times, the State has gradually become more concerned in the ownership and use made of land. Thus, under the Commons Registration Act 1965, a special machinery has been set up under which private rights to the use of commons may be registered by local authorities, and in disputed cases or cases of difficulty, the matter may be referred to a Commons Commissioner appointed by the Lord Chancellor under s. 17 of the Act.[3] The Commons Commissioners are barristers or solicitors of not less than seven years standing; they are not expressly called tribunals but they are subject to the supervision of the Council on Tribunals,[4] and any person aggrieved by a decision of a Commons Commissioner may require him to state a case for the decision of the High Court.

Much more frequent, however, are the instances where the statute book has provided for some form of administrative control over how land is used by a private individual. There are so many of these, exercisable by central government, local or other agencies, that it may seem appropriate to describe a fee simple as that estate which gives the maximum enjoyment of the land that may at any one time be permitted by the Government. These various kinds of control over the use of land may be considered under several headings.

A. Compulsory acquisition.—Clearly the most important of the diverse controls over land use is the power of "eminent domain",[5] or, as it is inaccurately known in this country, "compulsory purchase"—the right to acquire under statutory authority the ownership (or, in some cases, some lesser interest[6]) in a parcel of land without or against the consent of the owner in the public interest for some specific purpose stated in the enabling statute. There are now very many statutes that confer such a power; a current textbook lists over a hundred sections conferring powers of compulsory acquisition on various public bodies.[7] In the course of the process of compulsory acquisition there are four separate legal stages, namely, a power to acquire, specific authority to acquire the particular piece of land desired, assessment of the compensation that the acquiring authority are required to pay, and finally, the vesting of the legal estate in the land in the acquiring authority. The

---

[3] There is a Chief Commissioner in London and other Commissioners in provincial centres.

[4] Tribunals and Inquiries (Commons Commissioners) Order, 1970, now replaced by the Tribunals and Inquiries Act, 1971.

[5] "The power which the government exerts when it takes private property for public use is called the power of eminent domain": *The Constitution and what it means To-day*, by Professor E. S. Corwin, 11th Edn., at p. 221. This expression involves the idea that the Crown or the State as sovereign is taking for its own use that which was originally its own; the Crown "owns" all the land in England. In Australia, where tracts of land were originally granted by the Crown to colonists, the word "resumption" is used.

[6] For example, a "Compulsory rights order", under s. 4 of the Opencast Coal Act, 1958, or a "Public path creation order" under s. 28 of the Highways Act, 1959.

[7] *Encyclopedia of Compulsory Purchase and Compensation;* Appendices I and II to the *General Statement*.

procedure governing these stages has now been standardised,[8] and each will be described briefly.

(i) *Power to acquire.*—The acquiring authority, whether a local authority, a Government Department or a statutory corporation, must first be able to show that they (or that a class of authorities to which they belong) have been given power by statute to acquire land compulsorily[9] for the particular purposes for which the land which it is desired to acquire, is required. Thus, a district council are authorised to acquire land for housing purposes by the provisions of Part V of the Housing Act, 1957, but a county council are not similarly so authorised, and if a county council should wish to acquire land for the purpose of building a house for a police officer, they would have to be able to point to some other enabling statute, such as the Police Act, 1946.[10]

(ii) *Authority to acquire the particular land.*—Statutory *power* to acquire land in general for the specific purpose is not alone sufficient; the acquiring authority must also be able to show that they have legal sanction for the particular acquisition desired. This is what is most commonly known as "compulsory purchase procedure", and is the process whereby the general power is applied with Ministerial sanction, given under powers delegated by statute, to acquire the particular land. The procedure is now standardised for nearly all cases by the Acquisition of Land (Authorisation Procedure) Act, 1946, and is discussed in more detail below. In some cases there is yet a further procedural stage to be gone through, after the confirmation of the compulsory purchase order by the appropriate Minister. Under the 1946 Act, an order will be subject to the special parliamentary procedure of the Statutory Orders (Special Procedure) Acts, 1945 and 1965,[11] in a few cases, for example where the land to be acquired is part of a common or is the property of another local authority.

(iii) *Assessment of the compensation payable.*—Although there are many circumstances in which a private landowner may find his land taken from him without his consent, by the procedure of compulsory acquisition, Parliament, in granting such powers of compulsory acquisition, has always taken care to ensure that compensation is paid in respect thereof.[12] If the landowner does not accept the amount offered by the

---

[8] By several different codes, as mentioned below. When canals were being built in the late eighteenth century, and later in the early days of the railways, on each occasion a company was formed which needed powers of compulsory acquisition, and the enabling private Act had to contain detailed provisions on all the four headings given in the text. The codes referred to now obviate this; all that is needed is the power to acquire and a general procedure is prescribed for the other stages.

[9] In some instances, a local or private Act may be obtained, giving authority for the acquisition of a particular piece of land—the opportunity for objectors to require a local inquiry is then afforded in the course of the normal private Bill procedure. Perhaps the widest powers now contained in the statute book are those conferred by s. 112 of the Town and Country Planning Act, 1971.

[10] *Hazeldine* v. *Minister of Housing and Local Government*, [1959] 3 All E.R. 693.

[11] *Ante*, Chapter III, page 46.

[12] There is of course no constitutional reason why Parliament should not in future authorise the compulsory acquisition of land without making any provision at all for compensation. In the U.S.A., however, the Fifth Amendment to the Constitution provides that no private property may be taken for public use without just compensation.

acquiring authority in accordance with the statutory terms currently in force,[13] or if he refuses to proceed in the matter, or to lodge any claim, the question of the amount of compensation that should properly be paid may be referred (by either party) to the Lands Tribunal (discussed below). For this stage, the procedure is standardised by the Lands Tribunal Act, 1949, and rules made thereunder, and the principles on which compensation is to be assessed are regulated by the Land Compensation Acts 1961 and 1973, replacing the Acquisition of Land (Assessment of Compensation) Act 1919, and also the relevant provisions of the Town and Country Planning Act, 1971.

(iv) *Acquisition of legal title.*—Having been authorised to acquire the particular land, and compensation having been agreed or left to be determined by the Lands Tribunal, it remains for the acquiring authority to obtain legal title. Where the "vendor" is agreeable, this need not cause any difficulty, but clearly there must be some machinery provided for the case where the owner resists to the last and refuses to make title or to execute a conveyance or transfer of his land. This machinery is provided for by the Compulsory Purchase Act 1965 (a consolidating statute replacing, for most purposes, the Lands Clauses Consolidation Act, 1845), and is initiated by the service of a notice to treat by the acquiring authority, which also constitutes the first step towards assessment of compensation. Once notice to treat has been served, the acquiring authority may follow this with a further notice which, on the expiration of fourteen days, will enable them to enter on the land, subject to their paying interest at the current prescribed rate on the compensation money as from the date of actual entry.[14] After service of a notice to treat normal conveyancing procedure must be followed, or, in the case of a recalcitrant owner, the acquiring authority may execute a deed poll vesting all the estate of the owner (or owners) on whom they have served notice to treat, in themselves.[15]

In the course of this procedure, there are two stages at which a hearing may have to be held, before an inspector appointed by a Minister, or before the Lands Tribunal. The first step in the authorisation procedure[16] is the making of a compulsory purchase order by the acquiring authority, which must be in the prescribed form.[17] The order then has to be advertised locally, a copy must be served on all the owners of any land affected,

---

[13] There is a very useful table of the different terms on which compensation has been payable under statutory authority at different times, in Corfield on *Compensation*, (1959), at p. 120.

[14] Compulsory Purchase Act 1965, s. 11. There are corresponding provisions in the Housing Act, 1957, applicable to acquisitions under Part III thereof.

[15] In such a case the purchase of compensation money must be paid into court: see Compulsory Purchase Act 1965, s. 9. This procedure may now be cut short by the general vesting declaration of the Town and Country Planning Act, 1971.

[16] The procedure of the Acquisition of Land (Authorisation Procedure) Act, 1946, applies to any compulsory acquisition by a local authority, or by the Secretary of State for the Environment acting as highway authority, under any general statute, except Part III of the Housing Act, 1957, and the Light Railways Act, 1896 and 1912 (the latter being now virtually obsolete).

[17] See the Compulsory Purchase of Land Regulations, 1949 (S.I. 1949 No. 507), made under the 1946 Act.

and the order itself must be submitted for confirmation to the appropriate government department (most frequently the Secretary of State for the Environment). An opportunity must be given for objections to be made to the confirming authority, and if any such are received and not withdrawn (and do not refer only to the amount of the compensation payable), the confirming authority are under a statutory duty to hold a public inquiry or a hearing before a person appointed by the Secretary of State for the purpose; such an inquiry or hearing is, of course, a statutory inquiry for the purposes of the Tribunals and Inquiries Act, 1971, but the power to issue a subpoena or make an award of costs does not apply to a hearing.[18] The procedure is informal, although it is now governed by the Compulsory Purchase by Local Authorities (Inquiries Procedure) Rules, 1962.[19]

At least forty-two days' notice in writing of the date, time and place fixed by the Minister for the holding of the inquiry or hearing must be given to every "statutory objector". Then the acquiring authority, having received from the Secretary of State a notification of the "substance" of each objection received by him from an objector, must, not later than twenty-eight days before the date of the inquiry, serve on each statutory objector a written statement of their reasons for making the order, and must also supply a copy of the statement to the Secretary of State. A list of documents, maps and plans (if any) on which the acquiring authority intend to rely must accompany the statement, and any statutory objector must be given a reasonable opportunity to inspect and, where practicable, to take copies of any such documents. The inspector may at the inquiry allow the acquiring authority to alter or add to the reasons given in their statement, but in any such case he must, if necessary by adjourning the inquiry, give every statutory objector an adequate opportunity of considering any fresh reason or document, and he may make a recommendation in his report to the Secretary of State as to payment of any additional costs occasioned by such an adjournment.[20] There is thus a reasonable chance that the objector will be properly informed of the case he has to meet before he enters the inquiry room.

At the inquiry or hearing, the acquiring authority will be entitled to state their case first (unless, with the consent of the authority, the inspector otherwise determines), they being the party who are requiring the Secretary of State to take some action, namely, to confirm the order for compulsory acquisition.[1] The authority will then call their wit-

---

[18] Section 250 of the Local Government Act, 1972, from which this power is derived, is applied to inquiries only by s. 5 of the Acquisition of Land (Authorisation Procedure) Act, 1946.

[19] S.I. 1962 No. 1424 made under the predecessor to s. 11 of the Tribunals and Inquiries Act, 1971; see also the Compulsory Purchase by Ministers (Inquiries Procedure) Rules, 1967; S.I., 1967, No. 720.

[20] Rules of 1962, rule 7 (5). As to costs, see Chapter VII, *ante*, p. 193.

[1] Compare the procedure on an appeal to the Secretary of State against a refusal of planning permission (*post*, p. 235).

nesses,[2] who will be open to cross-examination by or on behalf of the objectors, and to re-examination by the acquiring authority's advocate. Each objector will then be allowed to state his case in turn, either personally or by counsel, solicitor or any other person,[3] and to call his witnesses (who may include representatives of a Government Department[4]) who will themselves be subject to cross-examination and re-examination. The acquiring authority's advocate will then have a right to make a closing speech, and the inquiry will finally be closed by the inspector. He may decide, or be asked by the parties, to inspect the site, and in that event the acquiring authority's representatives and any statutory objectors will be entitled to accompany him.[5] The inspector, an officer of the Secretary of State,[6] will make his report to him, but the inspector is not responsible for making any decision in the matter,[7] although his report will make recommendations and may disclose his private opinions. In some cases at this stage the order will be subject to special parliamentary procedure under the Statutory Orders (Special Procedure) Acts, 1945 and 1965.[8] This merely imposes an extra step that has to be taken; whether or not this applies, the Secretary of State must next decide and in due course will write to the parties, either confirming the order in its original form, confirming it with modifications, or refusing to confirm it, and he will give reasons for the decision. In coming to his decision, the Secretary of State must have considered the inspector's report, but he is not obliged to accept the report, or to adopt any of the recommendations contained therein. The decision must

---

[2] Where evidence is required to be given by witnesses from Government Departments, this often caused difficulties (see Franks Report, paras. 314–20). However, in the case of compulsory purchase orders and planning appeals (S.I. 1962, No. 1424 and S.I. 1969, No. 1092), rules have made provision for this matter. The appellant or objector may in a relevant case apply before the inquiry commences, for a representative of the government department concerned to be made available at the inquiry. A representative will then be called at the inquiry, and give evidence and be subject to cross-examination to the same extent as other witnesses, except that the inspector is required to disallow "any questions which in his opinion are directed to the merits of Government policy".

[3] Rules of 1962, rule 5.

[4] *Ibid.*, rule 6, and see note 2, *ante*.

[5] Rules of 1962, rule 8.

[6] The Secretary of State for the Environment maintains a corps of inspectors, most of whom are qualified surveyors, architects or planners (few are lawyers), whose job it is to conduct these and similar inquiries. It was one of the recommendations of the Franks Committee (Report, para. 303–4) that the main body of these inspectors should be placed under the general control of the Lord Chancellor, whilst being kept in contact with policy developments in the Departments as much as possible. Her Majesty's Government made it clear that they could not accept this recommendation, and therefore it was not provided for in the Tribunals and Inquiries Act, 1958, when most of the other recommendations of the Franks Committee were implemented (and see Chapter VII, *ante*, p. 219).

[7] The inspector will make recommendations to the Secretary of State, and a copy of his report must be made available to the parties on request (see text, below), but the inspector is not required to prepare a draft decision available to the parties for their comments, as is the case under the American Administrative Procedure Act, 1946 (see Appendix 1, *post*, p. 460).

[8] See Chapter III, *ante*, p. 46, and the Acquisition of Land (Authorisation Procedure) Act, 1946, Schedule 1, Part III.

either be accompanied by a copy of the inspector's report, or by a summary of his conclusions and recommendations. A copy of the report itself must be made available to any person entitled to be notified of the decision, within one month of the decision, on written request to the Secretary of State.[9]

The order, when confirmed (with or without modifications) will be subject to a reference to the High Court by any party aggrieved, within six weeks of the date on which notice of confirmation is published in local newspapers; after that date, the validity of the order cannot be questioned in any legal proceedings whatsoever.[10] On any such reference, the High Court may quash the order if it is *ultra vires*, or if the interests of the applicant have been substantially prejudiced by some procedural error.[11] If no objections are made to a compulsory purchase order, or if all objections made are withdrawn, or if the only outstanding objections relate exclusively to the amount of compensation payable, the Secretary of State may confirm the order without holding any inquiry or hearing, as he will usually do in practice.

In law the decision on a compulsory purchase order (or on a planning appeal) is that of "the Minister", and he is responsible for the decision taken in his name in two respects:

(a) *Legally*.—This means little more than that if the validity of the decision is challenged in the courts, the legal department of the Department will handle the case, litigation will be conducted in the name of the Department, and the Department will pay any costs awarded against them by the court.

(b) *Politically*.—This means that the Secretary of State may have to defend the decision in the unlikely event of it being questioned in the House of Commons.

In practice, however, the decision is taken by a civil servant in the name of the Secretary of State (even the decision letter is not often signed by him). The civil servant so entrusted with the decision making power is rarely in a grade higher than that of principal; Professor K. C. Davis has claimed[12] that only five per cent of all planning appeals (which, as we shall see,[13] follow a very similar procedure) get as high in the ministerial hierarchy as an assistant secretary. It is, therefore, more than a little unreal to talk of "the Secretary of State", or even of one of his subordinate Ministers deciding these cases.

At a later stage of the compulsory acquisition procedure, there may be a hearing before the Lands Tribunal, which has the duty of determining the amount of the compensation payable in a disputed case. The

---

[9] Rules of 1962, rule 10.

[10] See also Chapter VI, *ante*, p. 158, and *Smith* v. *East Elloe R.D.C.*, [1956] 1 All E.R. 855, [1956] A.C. 736. Reference has not been made in the text to the powers of the Service Departments in the matter of compulsory acquisition of land. These were adversely criticised in the Franks Report, as previously no provision was made for objections or local inquiries. These faults were rectified by the Land Powers (Defence) Act, 1958, which makes provision for a procedure whereby a Service Department may acquire temporary rights over land for the purpose of manoeuvres or for training. Questions as to compensation that may arise under this Act fall to be determined by the Lands Tribunal.

[11] Acquisition of Land (Authorisation Procedure) Act, 1946, First Schedule, para. 15.

[12] See article at [1962] P.L. 140.

[13] *Post*, p. 236.

Lands Tribunal is not an *ad hoc* body, like an inspector appointed by a Department, convened to hear one matter only, but is permanent, having been constituted under the Lands Tribunal Act, 1949, and possessing a permanent office and secretariat in London. It is in many ways a model administrative tribunal, the embodiment of all that a good tribunal operating under the "Rule of Law" should be. Its procedure is prescribed in considerable detail in Rules,[14] but it remains reasonably informal. The forms prescribed for use are comparatively simple, and the fees moderate. The tribunal sits where its business is to be found, and consequently parties and witnesses are not necessarily faced with the expense and trouble of travelling to London. Members of the tribunal are chosen by the Lord Chancellor from lawyers and qualified surveyors,[15] the member or members constituting the tribunal for any particular hearing being selected according to the nature of the problems involved. There is a right of appeal on a point of law from a decision of the Tribunal to the Court of Appeal, at the instance of either party. As a consequence, the Lands Tribunal shares much of the respect traditionally accorded to the High Court, and except for its limited jurisdiction, is the nearest thing we have in this country to an administrative court. The Franks Committee could find nothing wrong with the Tribunal, and made no recommendations about it, except to suggest a minor extension of its jurisdiction.[16]

The present jurisdiction of the Lands Tribunal may be summarised as follows:

(i) Assessment of compensation for compulsory acquisition (*ante*), and in certain other matters, such as under Part VII of the Town and Country Planning Act, 1971, and in some cases of disputed compensation under the Highways Act, 1959.[17]

(ii) Hearing appeals from local valuation courts in matters concerning disputed assessments of land and buildings for rating (see below).

(iii) Determination of applications for the variation, modification or discharge of restrictive covenants under section 84 of the Law of Property Act, 1925 (as amended by the Law of Property Act, 1969), and giving directions as to notices under the Rights of Light Act, 1959. Both these headings of jurisdiction really concern matters of private law, and it is perhaps surprising that they should have been entrusted to an administrative tribunal, as there is no specialised governmental interest in either of these matters. The jurisdiction over restrictive covenants was taken over by the tribunal when it was created in 1949, from the Official Arbitrators, who were also formerly responsible for settling questions of disputed compensation on compulsory acquisition, and the fact that the jurisdiction of the 1959

---

[14] Lands Tribunal Rules, 1963, S.I., 1963, No. 483.

[15] Lands Tribunal Act, 1949, s.2. The first President of the Tribunal was a former Chief Justice of Palestine.

[16] See para. 159 of the Report.

[17] See s. 266 of the 1959 Act.

Act was entrusted to the tribunal instead of to the county courts[18] is some measure of the confidence shown by Parliament in this tribunal.

B. Town and country planning.—If compulsory acquisition is the most sweeping control exercised by a government agency over the private ownership of land, the controls exercised under the Town and Country Planning Act, 1971 (consolidating the corresponding provisions in earlier legislation commencing in 1947), are certainly the most ubiquitous. No person may carry out "development", which is defined[19] as meaning the

> "carrying out of building, engineering, mining or other operations in, on, over or under land, or the making of any material change in the use of any buildings or other land,"

without the prior consent of the local planning authority, and in giving or withholding that consent the authority have the widest possible discretion.[20] Admittedly, this rule is tempered in some measure by the provisions of the Town and Country Planning General Development Order,[1] under which certain types of development are granted permission "automatically"[2] but in the face of this control it is difficult to argue that an Englishman's house is entitled any longer to be called "his castle". Certainly the right to raise the ramparts against an invader belongs not to the lord of the keep, but to the local planning authority!

In the course of administering this vast field of detailed control, the law has made provision for a number of statutory inquiries to be convened as required in a variety of circumstances. The most important both in consequence and frequency, are the inquiries convened by the Secretary of State, held by an inspector appointed by him to investigate appeals, under section 36 of the Town and Country Planning Act, 1971, against refusal by a local planning authority of permission to carry out development, or against imposition of conditions in a grant of such planning permission. Statutory inquiries may also arise under various other provisions of the 1971 Act:

(i) Into objections to a local plan (part of a development plan) when this is under consideration by the local planning authority.[3]

---

[18] It was originally intended that appeals against rating valuations should lie from local valuation courts to the county courts, and it was so provided in the Local Government Act, 1948; but those provisions were amended before they came into operation, so that appeals now lie to the Lands Tribunal.

[19] Town and Country Planning Act, 1971, s. 290 (1) and s. 22.

[20] They may "grant permission either unconditionally or subject to such conditions as they think fit, or may refuse permission": Town and Country Planning Act, 1971, s. 29 (1).

[1] S.I. 1973, No. 31.

[2] Subject to exclusion in particular cases, and for special reason, by the making of "Directions", which need the confirmation of the Secretary of State, under article 4 of the General Development Order.

[3] See Town and Country Planning Act, 1971, s. 13. In this case the inspector will be appointed by the local authority, not by the Secretary of State. In the case of objections to a structure plan the Secretary of State will hold an "examination in public" of important issues: Town and Country Planning Act, 1972, s. 3; *ante*, p. 196.

(ii) Into objections to an order requiring revocation or modification of an existing planning permission[4] or an order providing for the discontinuance of an existing use.[5] In such a case an order is made by the local planning authority under the relevant section, which has to be submitted to the Secretary of State for confirmation before coming into effect.

(iii) Where an application for planning permission has been called in by the Secretary of State for determination by him.[6]

(iv) Where an appeal is made to the Secretary of State against refusal by the local planning authority of consent to display an advertisement, or against conditions imposed by them in a consent issued for that purpose.[7]

(v) On the making of a tree preservation order[8] made by the local planning authority, but which does not come into operation unless and until it has been confirmed by the Secretary of State.

(vi) On a refusal of listed building consent and certain other matters connected with buildings of special architectural or historic interest.[9]

(vii) On the refusal by the local planning authority of consent to fell trees or woodland which are the subject of a tree preservation order, there is customarily a right of appeal to the Secretary of State given by the order itself.[10]

(viii) On the service of an enforcement notice under section 87 of the Town and Country Planning Act, 1971 an appeal lies on a variety of grounds to the Secretary of State.[11] An enforcement notice may be served where development has taken place without planning permission having been obtained (either expressly or by virtue of a development order[12]), or where a condition or limitation to which a planning permission is subject, has not been observed.[13] A similar right of appeal to the Secretary of State lies on the service of a listed building enforcement notice,[14] but if a similar notice is served in relation to the cleaning up of waste land, the appeal lies to the local magistrates.[15]

---

[4] Town and Country Planning Act, 1971, s. 45.
[5] *Ibid.*, s. 51.
[6] *Ibid.*, s. 35.
[7] *Ibid.*, s. 63, and also Town and Country Planning (Control of Advertisements) Regulations, 1969; these appeals will often be determined on written representations, without a formal enquiry.
[8] Town and Country Planning Act, 1971, s. 60.
[9] Town and Country Planning Act, 1971, Part IV.
[10] Town and Country Planning (Tree Preservation Order) Regulations, 1969, S.I. 1969 No. 17.
[11] Town and Country Planning Act, 1971, s. 94.
[12] Such as the General Development Order, 1973; or a special order under s. 24 (2) of the Act of 1971.
[13] Town and Country Planning Act, 1971, s. 87.
[14] *Ibid.*, s. 97.
[15] *Ibid.*, s. 105.

(ix) On the making by the appropriate local authority of a public path creation order or a public path diversion order,[16] or an order providing for public access to open country.[17]

(x) On the making of an order designating land as being the site of a new town.[18]

(xi) On the refusal by a local planning authority of a certificate of appropriate alternative development, or against the imposition of conditions contained in such a certificate.[19]

(xii) On a refusal of an application for an established use certificate.[20]

This list does not purport to be complete, but there are enough examples to give some indication of the extent of planning control and the variety of occasions on which the Secretary of State may decide (or be required) to hold a public inquiry, or possibly a hearing. In all these cases the procedure will be very similar to that applicable to an inquiry into the objections to a compulsory purchase order, described above, except that the party who will have the right to begin (and therefore also the right to make the closing speech) will be the party requesting the Secretary of State to take the action provided for in the statute; in the case of an appeal against a refusal of planning permission, this will therefore be the appellant. The Compulsory Purchase Inquiry Rules (above) will not apply to these inquiries, but in the case of appeals against the refusal of planning permission (or against conditions contained therein) "called in" inquiries (para (iii) above) and inquiries into tree preservation orders and building preservation orders, a very similar set of Rules apply.[1]

In these cases, the inspector will often inspect the site after the conclusion of the inquiry, and where the Rules apply, he must do so if he is so requested by the parties, and they must be given the opportunity of accompanying him. Several weeks after the inquiry the inspector will submit a report to the Secretary of State. The Secretary of State (or an official on his behalf) will then after consideration make a decision, which will not necessarily conform with the recommendations contained in the report.[2] The report will be made available to the parties on

---

16 Highways Act, 1959, ss. 28, 110 and 111, and Schedule 7. See also Acquisition of Land (Authorisation Procedure) Act, 1946, s. 3.

17 National Parks and Access to the Countryside Act, 1949, s. 65, and First Schedule.

18 Section 1 and the First Schedule to the New Towns Act 1965, replacing corresponding provisions in the New Towns Act, 1946. The Government had stated in 1959 that they did not propose to use the powers of this Act to create any further new towns, but in 1964 a site was designated for the housing of "overspill" from Merseyside, and another was designated early in 1963 at Dawley in Shropshire to house population from the West Midlands. In the late 1960s further towns, on a larger scale, were designated at Peterborough, Northampton and Milton Keynes. Twenty-three towns are established or in course of development in different parts of England and Wales, most of them in the Home Counties.

19 Land Compensation Act, 1961, ss. 17 and 18.

20 Town and Country Planning Act, 1971, ss. 94 and 95.

1 Town and Country Planning Appeals (Inquiries Procedure) Rules, 1969, S.I. 1969 No. 1092.

2 The Minister is expected to consider the matter and come to his own conclusion: *Nelsovil* v. *Minister of Housing and Local Government*, [1962] 1 All E.R. 423; [1962] 1 W. L. R. 404. But he is obliged to consider only the facts before him—including the report of the inquiry—*Rhodes* v. *Minister of Housing and Local Government*, [1963] 1 All E.R. 300; [1963] 1 W.L.R. 208.

request in writing to the Secretary of State, and the decision itself must be supported by reasons. Where the Rules apply, detailed provision is made for these matters; in other cases, the the same principles are normally followed in practice.

In some cases listed in schedule 9 of the Town and Country Planning Act, 1971 and regulations made thereunder,[3] the inspector will determine the matter and make the decision on behalf of the Secretary of State, without reference to him (or to anyone else). This procedure,[4] whereby an inspector becomes in all but name a tribunal, was introduced in order to speed up planning appeals, and at the time when the proposal was under discussion it was pointed out that in the great majority of cases the Secretary of State accepts his inspector's recommendations, so why not let him decide?

In most of the cases mentioned, any person aggrieved by the decision (and in a case where an inspector has decided, the decision for this purpose is still the decision of the Secretary of State, for which the Secretary of State is responsible) will be able to appeal to the High Court within six weeks of the decision, on the ground either that the procedure of the Act and regulations made thereunder has not been complied with, or that the order is *ultra vires*.[5] On the expiration of the six weeks, however, the decision cannot be called into question in any legal proceedings whatsoever.[6] In the case of an appeal against an enforcement notice, again a further appeal lies to the High Court on a point of law.[7] Further, in one case, namely, where the Secretary of State has given a decision on appeal to him, or on reference under section 35 (1) of the 1971 Act, to the effect that particular proposed operations or changes of use involve development or require planning permission [8] there is a right of appeal to the High Court from the decision on a procedural error or a complaint of *ultra vires*, by virtue of section 245 of the Town and Country Planning Act, 1971.

Planning appeals are by far the most common in point of numbers of all statutory inquiries at the present time. The procedure is reasonably satisfactory in most respects, except for the long delays that occur. In February, 1966, the Minister of Housing and Local Government stated in the House of Commons[9] that over 13,000 appeals had been received in 1965, and that there were at that time some 8,500 appeals in his Department awaiting determinations. The average time taken between

---

[3] Town and Country Planning (Determination of Appeals by Appointed Persons) (Prescribed Classes) Regulations, 1972, S.I. 1972 No. 1652.

[4] The procedure followed by the inspector in such a case is very similar to that followed in the normal case where the Secretary of State "personally" decides; in both cases the inspector writes a report which will be made available to the parties on request. See the Town and Country Planning (Determination by Appointed Persons) (Inquiries Procedure) Rules, 1968, S.I. 1968 No. 1952.

[5] Town and Country Planning Act, 1971, s. 245. This is similar to the procedure whereby the validity of a compulsory purchase order may be challenged under the Acquisition of Land (Authorisation Procedure) Act, 1946 (*ante*, p. 233). No person other than a "party aggrieved" may appeal under this procedure: *Buxton* v. *Minister of Housing and Local Government*, [1960] 3 All E.R. 408; [1961] 1 Q.B. 278.

[6] See also Chapter VI, *ante*, p. 158.

[7] Town and Country Planning Act, 1971, s. 246.

[8] *Ibid.*, s. 53.

[9] *Hansard* for 22nd February, 1966, col. 52.

receipt and decision was stated to be 44 weeks for appeals which go to inquiry and 32 weeks for those settled on written representations. It is not surprising, therefore, that local authorities have been asked to encourage appellants to agree to their appeals being settled on written representations,[10] but this clearly cannot always be done. The provisions enabling a decision to be taken by the inspector (now covering some 70 *per cent* of all appeals) have improved but there remain a number of inquiries where the decision still has to be referred by the inspector to the Department.

In cases where there are considerations of national or regional importance or where there are technical or scientific aspects of some proposed development of an "unfamiliar" character,[11] the Secretary of State may refer a planning appeal to a specially constituted Planning Inquiry Commission consisting of a chairman and 2–4 other members appointed by the Minister.[12] This body is then required to investigate the proposal, carry out research if necessary and in most cases to hold a local inquiry[13]; it must then report to the Minister who will make a decision on the matter. This new "high level" kind of inquiry is clearly designed to deal with such matters as proposals for a third London Airport, and others that raise public controversy.

C. Housing.—The construction and management of houses under the Housing Act, 1957 (and its predecessors in title) has not given rise to any need for the institution of special administrative tribunals,[14] but the special branch of housing law known as "slum clearance", has occasioned a considerable crop of litigation concerned with judicial review of procedure before statutory inquiries.

Part II of the Housing Act, 1957 (as amended by subsequent Housing Acts), empowers local authorities[15] to deal with individual unsuitable houses, by way either of requiring their repair, demolition, or cessation of use as dwellings (closing orders), according to the particular circumstances, and appeals lie from their decisions[16] in such matters to the local county court. Part III of the Act, however, provides for a different type of procedure. This Part is concerned with groups of unfit housing, "clearance areas", and under these provisions the authority may deal with any number of houses and other buildings.[17] If a clearance

---

[10] Circular 32/65 of the Ministry.

[11] Town and Country Planning Act, 1971, ss. 47 and 48.

[12] *Ibid.*, s. 47 (2). Notice of the making of a reference to a Commission must be published in accordance with the Town and Country Planning (Planning Inquiry Commissions) Regulations, 1968 (S.I., 1968, No. 1911), made under s. 49 (2), *ibid.*

[13] Any such inquiry will be a statutory inquiry for the purposes of the Tribunals and Inquiries Act, 1971: 1971 Act, s. 49 (5).

[14] The review by the courts of action taken by a local authority in exercising their powers of management, either by way of fixing "reasonable" rents, or of obtaining possession of premises, is really a special branch of the general subject of review of administrative acts of government agencies: see Chapter VI, *ante*, p. 161. As to rent tribunals generally, see *post*, p. 243.

[15] *I.e.*, district councils; Chapter XVI, *post*, p. 448.

[16] In particular, as to whether in an individual case, the house is or is not "fit for human habitation", applying the standards of s. 4 (1) of the Housing Act, 1957.

[17] Buildings other than houses can be included in a clearance area only on the grounds of bad arrangement: Housing Act, 1957, s. 42.

order is made under this procedure, whereby the local authority may require the area to be cleared of all buildings, the order has to be confirmed by the Secretary of State for the Environment before becoming operative, and if any objections are made to the order (and not withdrawn), the Secretary of State will hold a local inquiry before one of his inspectors appointed for the purpose. Again the procedure will follow closely that applicable to an inquiry into objections to a compulsory purchase order; in these cases the local authority, as the party asking the Secretary of State to confirm their order, will open the proceedings. Where objections are lodged against a clearance order, the statute requires the local authority to give notice in writing to the objectors, at least fourteen days before the holding of the inquiry, of the grounds on which they base their claim that the particular house is unfit for human habitation and has therefore been included in the clearance order.[18] Similarly, if the Secretary of State confirms a clearance order, he must, on the request of any objector, state in writing his grounds for deciding that a particular house is so unfit. As in the case of a compulsory purchase order,[19] a person aggrieved may appeal to the High Court within six weeks of the making of a clearance order, on the grounds either that the procedure of the Act has not been complied with (and that he has been prejudiced as a consequence thereof), or that the order is *ultra vires*, but the validity of the order may not be called into question in any other legal proceedings whatsoever.

As an alternative to the making of a clearance order, the local authority may decide to secure clearance of all buildings within a clearance area by themselves purchasing those buildings either by agreement or compulsorily; similarly under an alternative slum clearance procedure, by way of declaring a general improvement area,[20] the authority will be empowered to acquire any property in the area. In the case of the clearance area, the compulsory acquisition authorisation procedure will not follow that prescribed in the Acquisition of Land (Authorisation Procedure) Act, 1946,[1] but will be governed by Part III of the Housing Act, 1957. The two procedures are, however, very similar,[2] the main difference being the different forms which have to be used.[3]

Local authorities also now possess elaborate powers to control the use and management of houses in multiple occupation under the Housing Acts, 1961, 1964 and 1969, and provision is made for appeals to lie against decisions taken under these statutes, sometimes to the local magistrates, and sometimes to the county court.

---

[18] Housing Act, 1957, Schedule 5, para. 5 (3). A similar provision applies to a compulsory purchase order made under Part III of this Act: *ibid.*, Schedule 3, para. 3 (5).

[19] *Ante*, p. 233.

[20] This must be confined to "predominantly residential areas": Housing Act, 1969, s. 28.

[1] *Ante*, p. 229.

[2] The provisions of the Acquisition of Land (Authorisation Procedure) Act, 1946, were in fact modelled on those now contained in Part III of the Housing Act, 1957, as the latter were originally contained in Part III of the Housing Act, 1936.

[3] The Housing (Prescribed Forms) Regulations, 1972, S.I. 1972 No. 228, apply in this case, in lieu of the Compulsory Purchase of Land Regulations, 1949.

D. Valuation for rating.—Under this heading, the subject matter deals rather with taxation than with governmental control of land use. Until 1948, the valuation for rating of land, or "hereditaments" as the taxable units are described in this branch of the law,[4] was the concern of local government, the decisions being made by special committees of local valuation authorities, with appeals to the ordinary courts on points of law.[5] Under the Local Government Act, 1948, as immediately amended by the Lands Tribunal Act, 1949,[6] however, the initial decisions on rating valuation matters are taken by local valuation officers, who are administrative officials of the Board of Inland Revenue. This switch in responsibility for rating valuation from local authorities to a central department was made in the interests of national uniformity. Before 1949 similar premises would often be differently valued in different, though sometimes neighbouring, local authority areas. In this context uniformity was considered to be more important in the national interest than local control. Under the modern law appeals lie from the decisions of local valuation officers to the local valuation courts.

These courts are constituted in accordance with schemes prepared by local authorities, with the approval of the Secretary of State for the Environment, and their members are unqualified unpaid volunteers, having a paid staff of officials to act as clerks. The members chosen are often magistrates, members of local authorities, retired professional men, etc., and they are paid travelling and subsistence expenses. Proceedings are informal, but follow the outline of those before a court of law. Professional advocates and other advisers are permitted to address the court, although the appellant ratepayer often appears in person, and the valuation officer, though not normally a lawyer, will usually conduct his own case. The rating authority also is entitled to appear as a party, and will be represented more often by a member of its finance staff than by a lawyer. Decisions are not announced in court, but communicated subsequently to the parties in writing, and reasons are given for most complicated decisions.[7]

An appeal lies from the decision of a local valuation court, on a matter of valuation, fact or law, to the Lands Tribunal, and from a decision of that Tribunal, as in other matters, an appeal lies on a point of law to the Court of Appeal.

There are many local valuation courts throughout the country; the Franks Committee was not able to find much wrong with the procedure before them, although it was recommended[8] that members of a local valuation court who were also members of a local authority should not

---

[4] As to the meaning of "hereditament", see Chapter XIV, *post*, p. 408.

[5] Appeals lay in the first instance to the local courts of quarter sessions, and from them a further appeal could be taken by way of case stated to the High Court (but no further).

[6] Lands Tribunal Act, 1949, s. 1 (3) (e). The relevant provisions of the L.G.A., 1948 are now repealed and replaced, with other provisions of rating law, by the General Rate Act, 1967.

[7] In practice of course, most decisions are purely factual, and reasons will not then be given. Sometimes, however, complicated questions of law may arise, such as (before 1963) whether or not a particular hereditament was entitled to industrial "de-rating".

[8] See Report, para. 156. In para. 155 it is also recommended that "action should be taken to reduce the numbers of representatives of local authorities".

sit to hear and determine cases arising in the area of the local authority of which they were members. This recommendation has not been given legal form, but is observed in practice in many courts at the present time.[9] In 1965 the local valuation courts were for the first time made subject to the supervision of the Council on Tribunals, by an order made by the Lord Chancellor under s. 10 (1) of the Tribunals and Inquiries Act, 1958.[10]

These are one series of tribunals that at first thought have a jurisdiction which might safely have been entrusted to the courts of law, as they are concerned with technical matters and the application of an artificial standard, the rent a "hypothetical tenant" could reasonably be expected to pay. In practice the tribunals justify themselves by their cheap and relatively speedy procedure,[11] and by the presence of lay adjudicators. Before the passing of the 1948 Act, the work of the tribunals was performed by the local authority assessment committees which, in spite of their name and constitution, were treated by the courts as being semi-judicial bodies subject to review by prerogative writs.[12]

E. Agriculture.—The state regulation of the use of agricultural land was acclaimed in 1947 as being, together with the Town and Country Planning Act of the same year, a revolution in land holding.[13] Under the Agriculture Act, 1947, the Minister of Agriculture and Fisheries was given wide powers to give directions to a farmer as to how he was to cultivate his land, even including the power to dispossess a recalcitrant farmer who was not observing the principles of "good husbandry", and also to prevent a landlord from ejecting his tenant after notice to quit from an agricultural tenancy without the Minister's consent. Many of these Ministerial powers were delegated to local agricultural executive committees (consisting of representatives appointed by the Minister, by the local authority and by local farming interests), and from their decisions appeals lay to special tribunals. The powers to regulate cultivation were abolished by the Agriculture Act, 1958, and the agriculture executive committees were abolished by the Agriculture (Miscellaneous Provisions) Act, 1972.

The duty of adjudicating between landlord and tenant as to whether a notice to quit an agricultural holding should be allowed to take effect in law, is vested in the Agricultural Land Tribunals, of which there are fourteen, one for each "province", or region of the country. This jurisdiction, being the settlement of disputes between private individuals, might have been entrusted to the county courts or possibly the magistrates. However, the justification for the institution of a separate

---

[9] In some cases, where the panel area coincides with the area of a single local authority, it is virtually impossible to apply the recommendation, as at least half the members of the panel are serving members of local authorities.

[10] Tribunals and Inquiries (Local Valuation Courts and Valuation Appeal Committees) Order 1965, S.I., 1965, No. 2190, which also applied to "appeal committees" in Scotland; see now Tribunals and Inquiries Act, 1971, Schedule 1, items 27 and 44.

[11] There were complaints after the passing of the Rating and Valuation (Miscellaneous Provisions) Act, 1955, of heavy arrears lists in valuation courts, but this was rather the result of changes in the law than any maladministration of the courts. By 1960 these arrears were down to manageable proportions.

[12] As will be seen from many leading cases on rating law decided before 1949.

[13] See in particular "The Twilight of Landowning" in 12 Conv. N.S., at p. 3, and other notes and articles in the same volume by the late Professor Harold Potter.

hierarchy of administrative tribunals lies in the requirement that these tribunals must decide whether a notice to quit may be served in accordance with the general principles of "good husbandry",[14] and must therefore have regard not only to the interests of the parties to the dispute, but also to general agricultural policy. Before the passing of the Agriculture Act of 1958, the local committees (and the Tribunals on appeal therefrom) were concerned also with making supervision orders and giving directions under section 12 of the Agriculture Act, 1947, but that section has now been repealed. The Agricultural Land Tribunals did not escape criticism by the Franks Committee—in fact a judicial decision in which it was held that the courts were virtually powerless to intervene, was one of the contributory causes of the setting up of that Committee.[15]

The members of these tribunals are now appointed by the Lord Chancellor,[16] and an appeal lies from their decisions on a point of law to the High Court.[17] Further, the power given to the Minister of Agriculture by section 73 of the Agriculture Act, 1947, to make procedural rules for the Tribunals was transferred by the Act of 1958 to the Lord Chancellor.[18] Agricultural Land Tribunals are listed in Schedule 1 to the Tribunals and Inquiries Act, 1971, and many of the sections thereof apply thereto.

In certain circumstances Parliament has accorded to the owner of agricultural land a greater protection against compulsory acquisition than applies in the normal case, for if the Minister of Agriculture, Fisheries and Food makes a compulsory purchase order under the provisions of the Agriculture Act, 1947,[19] objections are referred in the first instance to the local Agricultural Land Tribunal before the order becomes effective[20]; there is then an opportunity for the validity of the order to be tested before the High Court within six weeks of its coming into effect in the ordinary way.[1]

F. Rent tribunals.[2]—Under the Furnished Houses (Rent Control) Act, 1946 (now replaced by Part VI of the Rent Act, 1968), rent tribunals were set up in many parts of the country[3] and entrusted with

---

[14] Agricultural Holdings Act, 1948, s. 25.

[15] *Wollett* v. *Minister of Agriculture and Fisheries*, [1954] 3 All E.R. 529; [1955] 1 Q.B. 103.

[16] The chairmen of these tribunals were appointed by the Lord Chancellor under the original provisions of the Agriculture Act, 1947 (Schedule 9, para. 14). The method of appointment and selection of the other members criticised in *Woollett's* case has since been improved by the Agriculture (Miscellaneous Provisions) Act, 1954.

[17] Agriculture (Miscellaneous Provisions) Act, 1954, s. 6.

[18] Rules have been made under this provision: Agricultural Land Tribunals and Notices to Quit Order, 1959, S.I. 1959 No. 81.

[19] This provision does not, of course, apply to the compulsory acquisition of agricultural land under some other statutory provision.

[20] Agriculture Act, 1947, Schedule 9.

[1] This is a procedure similar to that applicable to compulsory purchase orders made under the Acquisition of Land (Authorisation Procedure) Act, 1946 (*ante*, p. 233). It was this procedure which brought *Woollett's* case (*ante*) before the court.

[2] For very interesting comments on these tribunals, see Professor H. Street's Hamlyn Lectures, *Justice in the Welfare State* (esp. Chapter 2).

[3] The Act provided for a somewhat strange "adoptive" procedure, whereby a local authority had to pass a resolution stating that it was expedient that the provisions of

jurisdiction in certain disputes under the Act between landlord and tenant of furnished dwelling accommodation. Contracts for the letting of such accommodation can be referred to the local tribunal by either of the parties thereto, or by the local authority, and it was (and is) the task of the tribunal on any such reference to determine what should be a reasonable rent for the facilities stipulated for in the particular contract before them. The local authority are given power to refer particular contracts[4] to the local rent tribunal so that they may keep check on the general level of rents for furnished houses in their district. In practice the power was regarded by some local authorities as too socialistic, and it was used but comparatively rarely. This subject again appears at first thought a matter of private law which could well have been entrusted to the ordinary courts, but as with the Agriculture Act, Parliament created this special series of tribunals, with the object of giving them the widest possible discretion to decide what was a "reasonable" rent in the circumstances of each particular contract, without reference to any rules of law; thereby introducing some element of public policy (especially in the light of the then acute housing shortage). The jurisdiction of the tribunals was increased by the Landlord and Tenant (Rent Control) Act, 1949, which enabled them to fix a standard rent for particular premises for the purposes of the Rent Acts, in respect of unfurnished lettings to which no standard rent applied: but the substantial easing of rent control by the Rent Act, 1957, and the comparative improvement in the housing situation in recent years, has reduced the number of references coming before these tribunals, although their jurisdiction remains unrestricted.

At the busiest period of their existence, from about 1947–1953, the rent tribunals were the subject of considerable criticism in legal and political circles, by reason of the informality of their procedure, their extensive powers, and the fact that their decisions were not open to appeal, on points of either fact or law. Many attempts were made, not all unsuccessful, to obtain a judicial review of decisions by means of the prerogative orders[5] but this was not completely satisfactory.[6] The provisions in Schedule 10 of the Rent Act, 1968 (replacing those in the Act of 1946) regarding the constitution and procedure of furnished houses rent tribunals are of the scantiest, and give the Secretary of State for the Environment the widest possible powers in the selection of members and chairmen of tribunals, none of whom need be legally qualified. Apart from a formal power given to the Secretary of State to pay the chairmen and members,[7] and to appoint and pay a clerk and other staff

---

the Act should extend to their district, and the Minister of Health (now the Secretary of State for the Environment) then made an order extending the Act accordingly. The Act was rapidly and widely adopted.

[4] See, for example, *R.* v. *Furnished Houses Rent Tribunal for Paddington and St. Marylebone, ex parte Kendal Hotels, Ltd.*, [1947] 1 All E.R. 448.

[5] *R.* v. *Rent Tribunal for Paddington North and St. Marylebone, ex parte Perry*, [1955] 3 All E.R. 391; [1956] 1 Q.B. 229.

[6] Procedure by way of *certiorari* can never amount to an appeal on merits, and the order granted cannot revise the order made at first instance. See Chapter VI, *ante*, p. 180.

[7] Rent Act, 1968, Schedule 10. The Act is supplemented by the Furnished Houses (Rent Control) Regulations, 1946 (S.R. & O. 1946, No. 781) which give a party a right

(again not necessarily legally qualified), the statute makes no provision for any procedural rules to govern the business of tribunals. In the event, each tribunal conducts its own business as it thinks best, admitting or not admitting hearsay evidence, or copies of documents, etc., according to no prescribed rules.

The members of rent tribunals are chosen by the Secretary of State from a wide field, many of them having had experience in local government; in general their members are competent, and are drawn from persons having much the same standing as the members of the local valuation courts for rating (*ante*), and the magisterial bench.[8] The great difference has been, until the coming into effect of the Tribunals and Inquiries Act, 1958, that their decisions were not subject to appeal, either to the courts or to any superior administrative tribunal, or even to a Minister of the Crown. Under the Act of 1958, however, rent tribunals have been included in the list of tribunals in respect of which any party in proceedings may appeal on a point of law to the High Court. They are also included in the list of tribunals in respect of which there must be consultation with the Council on Tribunals before procedural rules are made.[9]

The Rent Act, 1965 created a fresh crop of administrative tribunals. Under Part II of the Act[10] provision was made for the registration with rent officers[11] of the rent payable under a "regulated tenancy" of a dwelling-house, and also for the issue of certificates of "fair rent" in respect of such tenancies. There is a "rent assessment committee" for each registration area[12] under the Act, and if either the landlord or the tenant objects to a decision of the rent officer, the objection is referred to the committee for their determination. The committees are therefore really administrative tribunals, and they have been brought within the supervision of the Council on Tribunals[13]; an appeal lies from a decision of a committee on a point of law to the High Court.[14]

---

to be represented before a tribunal by counsel, a solicitor or "any other representative", and provide that the decision of a tribunal is to be a majority one, but otherwise contain few procedural provisions of consequence.

[8] In 1950 it was said: "There is extraordinary variation in the standard of personnel between tribunals, and there are tribunals where, perhaps owing to their ignorance of procedure, a landlord's case may receive scant justice": *Administrative Tribunals at Work*, ed. Pollard, at p. 68.

[9] Tribunals and Inquiries Act, 1971, s. 10 (1) and Schedule 1. No such rules have yet been made. Rent Tribunals were given a special detailed examination by the Council on Tribunals in 1960–1: see Annual Reports for 1961, paras 40–54, and 1962, paras 40–50.

[10] This Part of the Act may be (and was) brought into force on different days for different registration areas: 1965 Act, s. 21 (1).

[11] A rent officer or officers must be appointed for each registration area by the clerk to the local authority in accordance with a scheme made by the Minister after consultation with the local authority (Rent Act, 1968, s. 40). Rent officers are paid by the local authority in accordance with Treasury scales and for superannuation purposes they are deemed to be local government officers, but they can be dismissed only by the proper officer of the local authority on the direction or with the consent of the Minister (*ibid.*, s. 40 (2)).

[12] This coincides with the areas of county councils, or in London, with the areas of the London boroughs and the City: *ibid.*, s. 39.

[13] Tribunals and Inquiries (Rent Assessment Committees) Order, 1965 (S.I., 1965, No. 2151), art. 3, made under s. 10 (1) of the Tribunals and Inquiries Act, 1958; see now Act of 1971, Schedule 1, item 28 (b).

[14] *Ibid.*, art. 4.

By Schedule 5 of the Rent Act, 1968, replacing similar provisions in the Act of 1965, the Secretary of State for the Environment is required to draw up panels of persons to act as chairmen and members of the committees, "some" of whom are appointed by him and some by the Lord Chancellor; each panel is to have a president and vice-presidents appointed from the members appointed by the Lord Chancellor. The president and vice-president are responsible for administrative arrangements; when a committee convenes to determine a case, it consists of a chairman (who must be the president, a vice-president or one other of the members of the panel appointed by the Lord Chancellor) and "one or two" other members.[15] Procedural rules have been made regulating the conduct of business before these committees.[16]

For the most part the Lord Chancellor has appointed lawyers as presidents of panels, but there is no requirement in the Act that the chairman of a committee must be a lawyer. Clerks and other officers may be appointed, but again there is no statutory requirement as to qualifications. It is at first sight surprising that the existing furnished houses rent tribunals were not given this jurisdiction under the 1965 Act, or that the two sets of tribunals were not merged by the consolidating Rent Act, 1968, but the 1946 Act tribunals have not had a completely fortunate history, and they would have required reorganisation to undertake a new task of the magnitude contemplated under the 1965 Act. In practice there is considerable overlapping of membership of the two sets of tribunals, and they share the same office staff.

The Housing Finance Act, 1972, has complicated the question of rent tribunals still further, as section 51 of that Act provides that the panel of persons drawn up for an area to constitute a rent assessment committee shall also constitute a "rent scrutiny board" for the purposes of that Act, but the Secretary of State may appoint additional members solely to act as members of a scrutiny board. These boards have the duty of considering all provisional assessments of the "fair rent" of council houses made by a local authority (or a new town development corporation), and they must either confirm the rent as a fair rent, or substitute some other rent for the provisional assessment. Tenants have a right to make representations about provisional assessments to the local authority, but not to the scrutiny board, nor is there any right to a hearing before the board. The boards have not been brought within the supervision of the Council on Tribunals, although rent assessment committees are subject to that supervision.

Although there is overlapping membership, the rent scrutiny boards are somewhat different in concept from the assessment committees, but there seems very little logical reason why the assessment committees should not be combined with the rent tribunals and possibly also with the local valuation courts.

---

[15] Exceptionally a chairman may be authorised by the president of the panel to sit alone, with the consent of the parties: 1965 Act, Schedule 2, art. 6. It was announced in 1966 that membership of the furnished houses rent tribunals was to be integrated with that of the rent assessment committees.

[16] Rent Assessment Committees (England and Wales) Regulations, 1971, S.I. 1971 No. 1065.

3. PERSONAL WELFARE

It has been a natural consequence of the growth of the "Welfare State" during the post-war years, that a large body of administrative law and practice should have arisen dealing with the settlement of questions relating to the dispensation of state benefits in differing circumstances. Parliament has deliberately and consciously provided that as many as possible of these questions should be decided by administrative tribunals, in preference to the ordinary courts of law. Thus, in the course of the debate on the Bill that became the National Health Service Act, 1946, the late Mr. Aneurin Bevan said:

> "How can a judge of the High Court better decide than the executive council whether a doctor has been an efficient servant of the service? How can he decide that? What particular merit has a High Court Judge over these persons with all their experience?"[17]

Later in the same debate, Mr. Bevan went on to talk of the "judicial sabotage of Socialist legislation", and it was within that context that much of this legislation was initially enacted. The State now provides a national health service, makes special provision for the welfare of children and young people, provides an education service and a free legal aid and advice service (available within prescribed income limits), operates national health and industrial injuries insurance schemes and interferes with the personal life of the citizen for his own good in many other ways unthought of by the *laissez faire* school of the nineteenth century. To operate these many different services, many administrative tribunals have been established, and it is therefore proposed here to consider some of the more important.

A. National insurance.—This branch of the law, which might be termed the keystone of the Welfare State, consists of two main statutes, the National Insurance Act, 1965 (replacing an earlier Act of 1946 and as amended by the Social Security Act, 1973) and the Family Allowances Act, 1965 (also replacing an earlier Act, in this instance, of 1945) which have set up a hierarchy of tribunals to settle questions arising in the course of the administration of these State benefits, adapting and amplifying the procedure that obtained under pre-war Unemployment Insurance Acts. Claims for insurance benefit under this statute are determined in the first instance by local officers appointed by the Secretary of State for Social Services, and appeals from their decisions lie at the instance of aggrieved claimants to local

---

[17] See Hansard No. 25 for 19–25 July 1946, col. 1983. This idea that the ordinary courts of law are apt to hinder any administrative task of importance or complexity is by no means a new one. So great a lawyer as Lord NOTTINGHAM expressed a similar view in declining jurisdiction for the Court of Chancery on any appeal from the special jurisdiction entrusted to the Lord Mayor and Court of Aldermen by 19 Car. II c. 8., after the Great Fire of London to settle boundaries and rents and to compose differences: see Volume 73 of the Selden Society's publications, at pp. cxii–cxiii.

tribunals, the members[1] of which are appointed by the Secretary of State. From decisions of the local tribunals, appeals lie to the National Insurance Commissioner, at the instance of either the applicant or the Department, and on such an appeal there is a complete re-hearing of the case. There is then no further right of appeal to the courts of law, but the Commissioner is of course subject to an order of *certiorari* on the grounds of error of law on the face of the record.[2]

There is at present a single Chief National Insurance Commissioner and eight Commissioners; each of them is appointed by the Crown, and each must be a barrister of not less than ten years' standing.[3] An appeal will normally be heard by a single Commissioner but in a case of exceptional difficulty a tribunal of three Commissioners may be convened; the Chief Commissioner is simply the senior member among his colleagues, and there is no question of a right of appeal from a Commissioner's decision to the Chief Commissioner. The Commissioners are stationed in London, but they may also sit in Cardiff and in Edinburgh.

Procedure before a Commissioner tends to be formalised,[4] but not nearly so much so as before a court of law. Selected decisions of the Commissioners in previous cases are printed and published, and where relevant they are cited as if they were precedents.[5] Before the local tribunals, which often meet in offices of the Department, the procedure is much less formal, the "court room" often being furnished more like an office than a court. As a general rule the principles of openness, fairness and impartiality are observed at both levels; originally legal representation was not permitted at local tribunals, but this is no longer the case and an applicant may be represented by counsel, solicitor, a trade union representative (most commonly) or by any other person.[6]

Both the local tribunals and the Commissioners are listed in Schedule 1 to the Tribunals and Inquiries Act, 1971, and so are subjected to the supervision of the Council on Tribunals.[7]

In addition certain questions arising under the national insurance

---

[1] Each tribunal consists of three members, a person appointed by the Secretary of State to act as chairman (who will normally be a lawyer), an employers' representative, and a person representing employed persons, and the actual tribunals are constituted by the Secretary of State: National Insurance Act, 1965, s. 77. The chairman has to be selected from a panel of persons approved by the Lord Chancellor: Tribunals and Inquiries Act, 1971, s. 7 (1) and (3).

[2] Chapter VI, *ante*, p. 142.

[3] Social Security Act, 1973, s. 87; there may be as many Commissioners as Her Majesty may think fit. Previously separate appointments were made (of the same individuals in practice) under the national insurance and the industrial injuries insurance legislation respectively.

[4] There is no indefeasible right to an oral hearing before the Commissioner but in practice one is granted except in the most trivial cases: see the National Insurance (Determination of Claims and Questions) (No. 2) Regulations, 1967 (S.I., 1965, No. 1570).

[5] In practice the Chief Commissioner decides which decisions shall be so published.

[6] Determination of Claims and Questions Regulations, regulations 9 (4) (local tribunals) and 11 (4) (Commissioner's hearings).

[7] Procedural rules can therefore be made only after consultation with the Council on Tribunals. Therefore in 1967 when it was found that the consolidation of existing procedural rules by the National Insurance (Determination of Claims and Questions) Regulations, 1967 (S.I., 1967, No. 1168) had been made without prior consultation with the Council on Tribunals, those Regulations were cancelled and new Regulations (No. 2 Regulations above referred to) were made after such consultation had been carried out; see also para. 43 of the Annual Report of the Council on Tribunals for 1967.

scheme (and industrial injuries hereafter described) are reserved by the Act and Regulations for the decision of the Secretary of State,[8] who may make his own arrangements (unrestricted by statute) for a person appointed by him to hold a public or private inquiry into the matter to be determined, and to report to the Secretary thereon, thereby leaving the actual decision to the Secretary or (more probably) to some officer in his department. These inquiries have not yet been listed as a "statutory inquiry"[9] and therefore they are not subject to the supervision of the Council on Tribunals; the only safeguard against the Secretary of State acting arbitrarily in such a matter is the provision that an appeal lies from his decision to the High Court on a point of law.[10] In practice of course an aggrieved claimant may wish to have a review of questions of both fact and law; to this he will not be entitled.

B. Industrial injuries insurance.—The present system of State insurance against industrial injuries was introduced by the National Insurance (Industrial Injuries) Act, 1946 (now replaced by the consolidating Act of the same title of 1965), which took the place of the former scheme of workmen's compensation. This had been in force since a statute of 1897, and was a great advance on many systems applicable in other western countries, but it had given rise to a great deal of complicated and expensive litigation in the courts. Questions that fall in practice to be decided in this field are related to injury, disablement, incapacity or death arising in the course of a workman's employment, and although these might seem to be matters admirably suited for determination by the courts of law, practical experience has unfortunately proved that in our modern industrial society there are so many of these claims that bulk alone makes it difficult for all the business to be handled by the courts. Moreover, these cases often take the form of proceedings by an employee against a large public company with considerable resources and little to lose by appealing to the courts on technical points. Therefore, on the grounds of both expedition and cheapness to litigants, the reference of such matters to administrative tribunals was seen by 1946 to have become a necessity, especially as from that date it was also accepted that compensation under the industrial injuries scheme would be borne by national funds.

A hierarchy of tribunals was therefore established by the 1946 Act; until 1966 these were separate from but similar to, the tribunals established for national insurance already described. However, by the National Insurance Act, 1966, the two systems of tribunals were merged, and claimants for industrial injuries benefits in disputed cases proceed in precisely the same manner and to the same tribunals as claimants for disputed insurance benefits (as above described).[11]

---

[8] These are listed in ss. 84 and 85 of the Social Security Act, 1973, and s. 35 of the National Insurance (Industrial Injuries) Act, 1965.

[9] They are not included in the Tribunals and Inquiries (Discretionary Inquiries) Order, 1967 (S.I., 1967, No. 451); *ante*, p. 198.

[10] National Insurance Act, 1965, s. 65 (1) and (3).

[11] There are however separate procedural rules, namely, the National Insurance (Industrial Injuries) (Determination of Claims and Questions) (No. 2) Regulations, 1967 (S.I., 1967, No. 1571).

Certain medical questions arising on a claim for disablement benefit must be referred not to the local tribunals, but to a medical board[12] consisting of two or more registered medical practitioners appointed by the Secretary of State.[13] A dissatisfied claimant may appeal from a decision of a medical board to a medical appeal tribunal constituted under section 38 of the National Insurance (Industrial Injuries) Act, 1965, the members of which are appointed by the Secretary of State.[14] From the medical appeal tribunal a further appeal lies with leave of the tribunal or the Commissioner, to the National Insurance Commissioner, on the ground that the decision of the tribunal was erroneous in point of law,[15] a procedural step which was introduced in 1959 as a direct result of the recommendations in the Franks Report.[16]

Medical appeal tribunals also are listed in the Schedule to the Tribunals and Inquiries Act, 1971; it seems that they are entitled to use their own expert knowledge in addition to or apart from such evidence as may be adduced at the hearing before them.[17]

As mentioned above (para. A) some questions are reserved for determination by the Secretary of State.[18]

C. Family allowances.—Questions as to rights to allowances under the Family Allowances Act, 1965 are determined by the same procedure[19] and tribunals as for national insurance and industrial injuries insurance as above described.

D. Criminal injuries.—The Criminal Injuries Compensation Board is an unusual form of tribunal, in that it was constituted in August 1964 under the Royal Prerogative, and it has not yet been given any statutory basis. Its object is to recommend to the Home Secretary that compensation should be paid *ex gratia* to persons who are injured as a result of crimes of violence. Normally an application is investigated by a single member of the Board (without any hearing), but if the applicant is not prepared to accept the member's award (or if he does not accept a refusal of his application), the applicant is given an opportunity of a formal hearing before three members of the Board, of whom the member who originally investigated the case may not be one. At this hearing the applicant may be represented by counsel or a solicitor, and the Secretary to the Board will present the opposing case.

---

[12] See s. 37 of the National Insurance (Industrial Injuries) Act, 1965, s. 39 (3) *ibid.*, and the Schedule 2 to the National Insurance (Industrial Injuries) (Prescribed Diseases) Regulations, 1959 (S.I. 1959 No. 467).

[13] Exceptionally the matter may be referred to a single medical practitioner; 1965 Act, s. 41.

[14] The members are two registered medical practitioners and a person appointed to act as chairman; the latter must be selected from a panel of persons approved by the Lord Chancellor: Tribunals and Inquiries Act, 1971, s. 7 (1) and (3).

[15] National Insurance (Industrial Injuries) Act, 1965, s. 42.

[16] See para. 174 thereof.

[17] *R.* v. *Medical Appeal Tribunal* (*North Midland Region*), *ex parte Hubble* [1958] 2 All E.R. 374; [1958] 2 Q.B. 228.

[18] *Ante*, p. 248.

[19] The procedure, though very similar, is regulated by a separate set of regulations, the Family Allowances (Determination of Claims and Questions) (No. 2) Regulations, 1967 (S.I., 1967, No. 1572).

No provision is made for any appeal from a decision of three members, and as the Board is not working under statute, it was thought that a prerogative order would not lie. It is, however, clear that *certiorari* will lie to correct a decision of the Board which is wrong in law (or, presumably, if natural justice has not been observed).[20] The Board is not subject to the supervision of the Council on Tribunals; reports of decisions of the Board are, however, regularly issued and noted in the legal press.[1]

E. Social security benefits.—These benefits, which before 1966 were termed "National Assistance", are aimed at the prevention of poverty, and have a respectable history originating in the Poor Relief Act of 1601. The benefits available in case of need under the National Assistance Act, 1948, are now under the general supervision of the Supplementary Benefits Commission, a corporate body appointed by the Secretary of State under the authority of the statute, and enjoying a considerable degree of independence.[2] The functions of the former National Assistance Board (now the Commission)[3] were inherited directly from the poor law unions, the boards of guardians, and, more recently, the poor law authorities under the Poor Law Act, 1930, but their powers under the Act of 1948 are much wider than were those of the former authorities, and the distribution of social security benefits to any person "whose resources are insufficient to meet his requirements" is now carried out in accordance with general principles laid down in the statute, and the element of charity never totally absent from the old poor law has disappeared. The Supplementary Benefits Commission is responsible for determination in the first instance by the Department's local officers of questions as to entitlement arising under the Act. An appeal lies from the decision of a local officer at the instance of a dissatisfied claimant to a local tribunal having jurisdiction where the applicant resides.[4]

These local tribunals are listed in Schedule 1 to the Tribunals and Inquiries Act, 1971, and are therefore subject to the general supervision of the Council on Tribunals. Members of the tribunals are appointed by the Secretary of State for Social Services, but chairmen must be selected from a panel chosen by the Lord Chancellor.[5] There is no provision for any appeal from a decision of a local tribunal, it being provided by section 14 (4) of the National Assistance Act, 1948, that

"any decision of the Tribunal shall be conclusive for all purposes";

but there may be a reference on a point of law to the High Court.[6]

The Commission, which is required to report annually to Parliament, is independent of the Secretary of State, and besides determining entitlement to benefit, it decides whether to take proceedings for the recovery

[20] *R.* v. *Criminal Injuries Compensation Board, ex parte Lain*, [1967] 2 All E.R. 770; [1967] 2 Q.B. 864.

[1] For a general description of the work of the Board, see an article by the present author at [1967] P.L. 323.

[2] As to public corporations generally, see Chapter X, *post*, p. 317.

[3] The changes were made by the Ministry of Social Security Act, 1966.

[4] National Assistance Act, 1948, s. 14, s. 53 and Schedule 5, para. 2, as amended by Schedule 3 to the Ministry of Social Security Act, 1966.

[5] Tribunals and Inquiries Act, 1971, s. 7 (1) and (3).

[6] 1948 Act, s. 14 (3).

of benefit from "liable" relatives; it also assists the Secretary of State in the formulation of policy (for example, in such matters as priorities for research), and it proffers advice on a variety of topics. The Commission is also responsible for investigating the resources of persons applying for legal aid in civil proceedings.

F. Children and education.—In most circumstances questions involving welfare of children and young persons are the concern of courts of law, the matters that fall to be determined being entrusted to local magistrates, or forming part of the traditional jurisdiction of the Chancery Division (now the Family Division) as the guardian of infants. Adoption, legitimation and related matters, being concerned either with the liberty of the subject or questions of personal status, are clearly subjects which should not be entrusted to administrative tribunals. Nevertheless, administration of the state education system and the supervision of foster parents, etc., have been treated as matters in which the State has a special interest. For example, a voluntary children's home has to be registered by the Home Secretary under the Children Act, 1948. In any case where an application for registration of such a home is refused, or it is proposed to remove a home from the register, the applicant or the person carrying on the home may ask the Home Secretary to refer the matter to the appeal tribunal constituted under the provisions of the First Schedule to the Act of 1948. This tribunal has for members at least three "impartial persons", being a chairman selected from a "legal panel" appointed by the Lord Chancellor, and two other members selected from a "welfare panel", appointed by the Lord President of the Council. These tribunals are listed in Schedule 1 to the Tribunals and Inquiries Act, 1971, and consequently are subject to the general supervision of the Council on Tribunals; further, by section 13 of that Act, an appeal lies from a decision of the tribunal to the High Court on a point of law.

Under section 72 of the Education Act, 1944, the Secretary of State for Education and Science[7] may serve a notice of complaint as to the procedure, conduct, etc., of an independent school (*i.e.*, a school not maintained by the local education authority). If such a notice is not accepted, it will be referred for determination to the Independent Schools Tribunal, which is somewhat similarly constituted to the Children Act Tribunal, and consists of three members taken from a "legal panel" appointed by the Lord Chancellor, and an "educational panel" appointed by the Lord President of the Council (and not, it should be noted, by the Secretary of State, the executive Minister concerned)—in each case, members selected must be "impartial persons".[8] This Tribunal also is scheduled to the Tribunals and Inquiries Act, 1971, and an appeal will lie from a decision of the Tribunal to the High Court under section 13 of the Act on a point of law. No appeal lies, however, to any court, tribunal or Minister on the merits; a point which has been mentioned in one of the Reports of the Council on Tribunals.[9]

---

[7] Formerly the Minister of Education.
[8] Education Act, 1944, Schedule 6, para. 4.
[9] Third Report, para. 31.

G. National health service.—The nationalisation of the health services by the National Health Service Act, 1946, might almost be described as the keystone of the structure of the Welfare State. The administration of the service was overhauled by the National Health Service Reorganisation Act, 1973, but this did not affect the tribunals established above the local level. As was perhaps inevitable, the original scheme of the Act of 1946 involved the creation of several elaborate series of administrative tribunals, most of which are concerned with questions of discipline and management of the staff of the service. In the manning of these tribunals professional men, themselves employed in the service, and civil servants play a substantial part. This is a distinctive feature of the tribunals described in this section, for in other cases administrative tribunals constituted since the war are manned, for the most part (and apart from the special cases where provision is made for a member, or a chairman, to be legally qualified) by volunteers who are not making the work a career. Local magistrates, members of local authorities, trade unionists, and representatives of employers' federations, form the great bulk of tribunal membership in the ordinary way, but this observation is not true of the national health service tribunals.

The several tribunals include the following:

(i) *Local committees.*—The personal health services functions of the national health service.[10] are administered locally by Family Practitioner Committees constituted by the Area Health Authority for the area, and the area of the Authority corresponds with that of the local county council. It is the duty of a Family Practitioner Committee (whose members are appointed by a number of bodies, including the Area Health Authority and the local authority) to perform functions prescribed by the Secretary of State relating to the provision of general medical, dental, pharmaceutical and ophthalmic services within their area, under the provisions of Part I of the 1973 Act. These Committees are essentially executive and administrative bodies; they have no judicial or quasi-judicial functions, and they are not in themselves tribunals in any real sense. They are responsible also for disciplinary arrangements concerning practitioners, including the receipt of complaints on professional matters from members of the public. These complaints are heard in private[11] by the Committee or by an officer to

---

[10] The national health service, as established by the National Health Service Act, 1946, had three distinct branches; the Executive Councils, the local health authorities and the hospitals, administered by hospital boards and hospital management committees. In addition, the local sanitary authorities were responsible for public hygiene, sanitation and prevention of disease. This "fragmentation" of the service, one of its most unsatisfactory features, was overcome by the National Health Service Reorganisation Act, 1973. Public health services remain with the newly reorganised county and district councils, but all other health functions (including school medical and dental services and, except in London, the ambulance service) are now the responsibility of the Secretary of State, which functions he carries out through an hierarchy of new bodies (all of which have corporate status), known as Regional Health Authorities, Area Health Authorities, Family Practitioner Committees and special health authorities.

[11] The Acts of 1946 and 1973 do not guarantee the complainant (or the practitioner complained of) any right of representation before the committee by counsel or solicitor, but he may be "assisted by some other person".

whom the duty has been made exercisable by regulations.[12] An appeal lies from a decision of the Family Practitioner Committee to the Secretary of State at the instance of either party; in such a case the Secretary of State will appoint a person to hear the parties and report to him on the matter; the decision of the Secretary of State will be final. Once again we are reminded of the recommendation of the Franks Committee[13] that an appeal ought not to lie from a tribunal to a single Minister.

(ii) *Mental Health Review Tribunals.*—Tribunals consisting of lawyers, doctors and other persons have been constituted for each Regional Health Authority by the Lord Chancellor under the Mental Health Act, 1959,[14] for the purpose of reviewing, on the application of the Secretary of State, the patient, or his nearest relatives, the case of any person liable to be detained under the Act as suffering from mental illness or disorder.[15] Rules[16] as to the procedure before these Tribunals have been made by the Lord Chancellor in consultation with the Council on Tribunals, as required by the 1959 Act; indeed, this is a case where a statute passed after the Tribunals and Inquiries Act, 1958, implements all the relevant recommendations of the Franks Report.[17]

(iii) *The National Health Service Tribunal.*—The National Health Service Tribunal was constituted under section 42 of the National Health Service Act, 1946, and consists of a chairman (who must be a barrister or a solicitor of not less than ten years' standing, appointed by the Lord Chancellor), a member appointed by the Secretary of State in consultation with the Association of Area Health Authorities, and a practitioner member appointed by the Secretary of State from a panel. The Tribunal may hold inquiries only into allegations that the continued inclusion of the name of a particular person in the appropriate list of practitioners would be prejudicial to the efficiency of the services.[1] If the Tribunal finds a case proved in a particular instance, it must direct that the name in question be deleted from the list. Matters may come before the Tribunal on a reference from an Area Health Authority, or from an individual complainant. An appeal lies from a decision of the Tribunal to the Secretary of State at the instance of the respondent alone and not of the complainant or the Area Health Authority.

(iv) *The Secretary of State.* The Secretary of State may himself initiate investigations before the appropriate Area Health Authority or

---

[12] National Health Service Reorganisation Act, 1973, s. 7 (3) and (5).

[13] Report, para. 105.

[14] Mental Health Act, 1959, s. 3 (as amended) and Schedule 1, and Mental Health Act, 1959 (Commencement No. 2) Order, 1960 (S.I. 1960 No. 1159).

[15] As to the powers of these Tribunals, see s. 123 of the 1959 Act.

[16] Mental Health Review Tribunal Rules, 1960 (S.I. 1960 No. 1139).

[17] The tribunals were brought under the supervision of the Council on Tribunals by the Tribunals and Inquiries (Mental Health Review Tribunals) Order, 1960 (S.I. 1960 No. 810). The working of these tribunals was considered in detail by the Council on Tribunals: see their Report for 1963, paras. 27–45. For one of the few cases in which there was an appeal by case stated from a mental health review tribunal, see *Re V.E.*, [1972] 3 All E.R. 373; [1973] Q.B. 452.

[1] 1946 Act, s. 43 (3).

Family Practitioner Committee into such matters as excessive prescribing, certification, and, in the case of general medical and dental practitioners, record keeping. Sir Carleton Allen[2] summarised the appellate jurisdiction of the Minister of Health (as he then was) under this complicated system of tribunals (as since revised):

(a) From the Medical Practices Committee—a special body appointed by the Secretary of State to hear references from Area Health Authorities about certain service requirements and disputes between practitioners;

(b) From Area Health Authorities on all but the "gravest charges" (which appeals lie in the first instance to the National Health Service Tribunal);

(c) From the Tribunal, on complaints which may involve deletion from the appropriate list[3];

(d) From Family Practitioner Committees on matters concerning more or less technical breaches of conditions of service by practitioners;

(e) Certain "arbitral" function in disputes with Area Health Authorities, such as, for example, between a local authority and an Area Health Authority (not now likely to arise often).

Family Practitioner Committees and the National Health Service Tribunal are listed in Schedule 1 to the Tribunals and Inquiries Act, 1971 (as amended by the Act of 1973), and may therefore be subjected in procedural matters to the general supervision of the Council on Tribunals. The outstanding feature of administrative jurisdiction under this Act is, however, the wide powers of the Secretary of State. Having established an apparently independent Tribunal of some standing, Parliament in this instance did not see fit to give it either a wide jurisdiction or conclusive appellate powers, both of these features being reserved for the Secretary of State, from whose decisions no provision is made for any further appeal. There are also no statutory provisions regulating the manner in which the Secretary of State may conduct appeals nor is he required to hold any inquiry before coming to a decision in particular cases.[4] In some cases the Secretary of State may ask

---

[2] "Administrative Jurisdiction", [1956] P.L. 13, at p. 17.

[3] It should be noted that deletion of the name of a practitioner from the appropriate list, though of the gravest possible consequences professionally to the practitioner concerned, is not the same thing as striking off from the medical (or dental) register, which would disqualify the practitioner from practising at all, whether within or outside the National Health Service. Striking off from the medical or dental register is treated as a "domestic" matter, and the appropriate proceedings are taken (under statutory powers) before the General Medical (or Dental) Council, and are no concern of the Secretary of State or of any of the administrative agencies of the National Health Service. As to domestic tribunals, see *post*, p. 266.

[4] In practice, the Secretary of State appoints two or three persons *ad hoc*, one of whom is a lawyer of standing, to hear an appeal and to report to him thereon: see Franks Report, para. 188. He has a general power to hold an inquiry in "any case where he deems it advisable to do so in connection with any matter arising under this Act or the Act of 1973", by s. 70 of the National Health Service Act, 1946 (as amended), and any such inquiry is made a "statutory inquiry", and so subject to the supervision of the Council on Tribunals, by the Tribunals and Inquiries (Discretionary Inquiries) Order, 1967 (S.I., 1967, No. 451), made under the Tribunals and Inquiries Act, 1966; see Chapter VII, *ante*, p. 198.

a Regional Health Authority to hold an inquiry; in such event, the inquiries, not being held by or on behalf of a Minister, would not be "statutory inquiries" and so not within the jurisdiction of the Council on Tribunals.[5]

The Franks Committee recognised the special position of the former Executive Councils as primarily administrative bodies, but recommended[6] that the Tribunal should in general sit in public, and that the right of appeal from the Tribunal to the Minister should be abolished. It could no doubt be suggested that more drastic improvements should be made in this elaborate structure, but, as the Franks Committee pointed out,[7] this hierarchy of tribunals is essentially a means of discipline of practitioners employed in a national service and forms part of their terms and conditions of service with the State. They are therefore predominantly administrative in character and closely connected with the Secretary of State. The tribunals are not really designed to provide a means whereby dissatisfied patients may obtain redress of grievances, as the common law obligations of a doctor towards his patient still remain, even in the National Health Service. Even the Health Service Commissioner (*ante*, p. 107) is not concerned with professional matters of this kind. In most cases lawyers are not permitted to appear before these Committees; the Council on Tribunals has considered this apparent anomaly but has agreed with it, as legal representation might mean that a patient was placed in an unfair position as compared with the doctor against whose conduct he was complaining.[8]

4. TRANSPORT

The provision of means of communication has become so important a subject in a modern society that the State has been compelled to intervene to ensure efficiency. The supervision and licensing of drivers of public transport vehicles and, to a limited extent, the control of road vehicle services, and also the regulation of charges made in respect of all forms of transport, have become a normal feature of our economy. An elaborate system of administration has been established for this purpose, having its own hierarchies of administrative tribunals, which will be described in outline. There are three different classes of tribunals to be discussed, none of which were the subject of much comment by the Franks Committee.[9]

(a) Traffic Commissioners.—A body of Traffic Commissioners (which from 1947 to 1957 were known by the clumsy title of the "Licensing Authority for Public Service Vehicles") has been established for each of the ten traffic areas in England and Wales. The Commissioners at

[5] For a criticism of a case where this action was taken, see Annual Report of the Council on Tribunals for 1968, at paras. 48–52.

[6] Report, para. 203.

[7] *Ibid.*, paras. 191–2.

[8] Second Report, paras. 41 and 44.

[9] Report, paras. 229–32. No evidence seems to have been forthcoming critical of the procedure. The Traffic Commissioners had a short time previously been subjected to a special investigation by the "Thesiger Committee", as a consequence of which certain minor improvements of procedure had been effected.

present owe their constitution to section 120 of the Road Traffic Act, 1960, and in each case the tribunal consists of three members. One of the Commissioners is appointed by the Minister from a panel of persons nominated by county councils in the traffic area, and another is appointed by the Minister from a panel of persons nominated by local authorities within the traffic area (*ibid.*, s. 121). The third Commissioner is a person whom the Secretary of State may appoint as chairman, who is paid a salary and required to devote the whole of his time to his office. The first two members, normally members of the local authorities by whom they have been nominated, are "amateurs" and do not receive salaries. The Commissioners are listed in Schedule 1 to the Tribunals and Inquiries Act, 1971, and their procedure is therefore subject to the general supervision of the Council on Tribunals. Section 153 of the Road Traffic Act, 1960, requires them to hold public sittings for most matters which they have to determine, and these must be arranged at such places as appear to them convenient. At least two Commissioners must be present at each sitting; in practice it is normal for three Commissioners to sit. Their jurisdiction may be summarised as follows.

(i) The refusal, suspension or revocation of a grant of a public service vehicle licence for a particular vehicle[10];

(ii) The grant or refusal of a road service licence giving permission for the provision of a road service by means of duly licensed public service vehicles and the variation of conditions in existing licences.[11] This is in practice by far the widest head of the Commissioners' jurisdiction, and the one in which they get most contested cases, as a road service licence may amount to the grant of a monopoly to operate a service over the specified route. The discretion of the Commissioners to grant or withhold a licence in a particular case is restricted by a list of matters specified in the section to which they are required to have regard; in particular, they must ensure that fares charged are reasonable, and that the services are provided in the public interest;

(iii) Backings of road service licences already granted, for application to other traffic areas[12];

(iv) Issue, suspension, revocation or refusal of licences to individuals to drive or act as a conductor of a public service vehicle.[13]

The form of licences and their issue are regulated by Ministerial Regulations made under the Act,[14] but these do not affect the procedure to be followed before the Commissioners. Persons already providing transport facilities who may be affected by an application for a road service licence, and any local authorities concerned, have a right to make

10 Road Traffic Act, 1960, s. 127.
11 *Ibid.*, s. 135.
12 *Ibid.*, ss. 135 and 137.
13 *Ibid.*, s. 144.
14 Public Service Vehicles (Licences and Certificates) Regulations, 1952 (S.I. 1952 No. 900), as amended.

representations as to the issue or modification, etc., of such a licence,[15] and it is customary for the Commissioners to allow them (and any other party concerned) to appear either personally or by counsel or solicitor. Procedure on an application (as mentioned above, normally heard in public) resembles that before a court of law, but witnesses are not sworn, and strict proof is not always required of statistical and other facts placed in argument before the Commissioners.

Any person aggrieved by the refusal or grant of a road service licence or the imposition of conditions therein, or a local authority who had appeared before the Commissioners, may appeal to the Secretary of State (formerly the Minister of Transport) under section 143 of the 1960 Act. On such an appeal the Secretary of State customarily appoints a single barrister to hold a local inquiry into the matter and to report thereon. The Secretary of State may make such order as he thinks fit on such an appeal provided the order comes within the terms of his appellate jurisdiction,[16] and his order will not be subject to any further appeal. The Franks Committee recommended[17] that this procedure should either be replaced by a right of appeal to the Transport Tribunal (as in the case of goods vehicles—see below), or that there should be a further right of appeal from the decision of the Secretary of State to the court, on a point of law.

Appeals lie from the decisions of the Traffic Commissioners to the local magistrates on questions concerned with drivers' and conductors' licences for public service vehicles.[18]

For the sake of completeness, it should be noted that the licensing of hackney carriages, and of drivers of such vehicles, is a matter for the district council, under the Town Police Clauses Act, 1847 as amended by the Local Government Act, 1972.[19] Persons aggrieved by the decision of the local authority thereunder have a right of appeal to a Crown Court, but there are no provisions in the statute as to how this statutory discretion is to be exercised by the local authority. It is, however, clear that some form of judicial review may be taken against the local authority if the discretion is not exercised at all, or if bias appears in their decision.[20]

(b) The Licensing Authority for Goods Vehicles.—There is a separate Authority set up by the Transport Act, 1968, Part V (replacing earlier legislation), for each of the ten traffic areas, consisting of the Chairman (or Deputy Chairman), sitting alone, of the Traffic Commissioners for the area.[1] When adjudicating as licensing authority for goods vehicles, the Commissioner follows much the same procedure as is applied to or by the Traffic Commissioners themselves. In this capacity he has jurisdiction to grant or refuse licences for users of goods vehicles

---

[15] Act of 1960, s. 135.
[16] *R.* v. *Minister of Transport, ex parte Upminster Services, Ltd.*, [1934] 1 K.B. 277.
[17] Report, para. 231.
[18] Road Traffic Act, 1960, s. 145.
[19] This licensing function is now exercisable by all district councils: 1972 Act, s. 179 (3).
[20] *R.* v. *Weymouth Corpn., ex parte Teletax, Ltd.*, [1947] 1 All E.R. 779; [1947] K.B. 583.
[1] Transport Act, 1968, s. 59.

to hold operators' licences and also special authorisations for the use of large goods vehicles.[2]

When deciding an application the licensing authority has to pay attention to the requirements of the appropriate section,[3] but if these requirements are met he must grant the application. His decisions are also subject to appeal as mentioned below.

(c) The Transport Tribunal.—This body has a lengthy and complicated statutory history. It was given in the Donoughmore Report as an instance where there was the "smallest departure" from the normal course, of leaving "judicial tasks" to His Majesty's Judges.[4] Originally, obligations imposed by statute on railway companies had been enforced by the Court of Common Pleas, and then the Railway and Canal Commission was established in 1873 and 1888, which was a Court of record and was presided over by a High Court Judge. The powers of the Commission in respect of rates and charges were transferred in 1921 to the Railway Rates Tribunal,[5] whose procedure was governed by rules approved by the Lord Chancellor. The Railway Rates Tribunal was itself re-constituted and re-named the Transport Tribunal by the Transport Act, 1947,[6] and the Railway and Canal Commission was abolished. The present Tribunal has five permanent members, appointed by Her Majesty on the joint recommendation of the Lord Chancellor and the Secretary of State. One of these members, who is the President, must be an experienced lawyer, one must be experienced in commercial affairs, two members must be experienced in transport business, and the fifth must be a person experienced in financial matters or economics.[7] In addition, other persons chosen by the Secretary of State for the Environment from a panel appointed by the Lord Chancellor, the Home Secretary and the Secretary of State, may be invited to assist the Tribunal from time to time.[8] This tribunal is described by the Act of 1921 as being a "court", but it is not a court of record in the legal sense, although it has all the powers of the High Court to summon and administer oaths to witnesses, etc.[9] The Tribunal (which is listed in Schedule I to the Tribunals and Inquiries Act, 1971) sits in two Divisions as follows[10]:

(a) The Railway Rates Division,[11] which has power to make orders

---

[2] In the exercise of his functions he must act "under the general directions" of the Minister, which apparently do not necessarily have to be published: 1968 Act, s. 59 (2).

[3] 1968 Act, s. 64 (operators' licences) and s. 74 (special authorisations). In the latter case a licence must be granted if there are no valid objections.

[4] Donoughmore Report, p. 84.

[5] Railways Act, 1921, s. 20 (1).

[6] Transport Act, 1947, s. 72 and Transport Act, 1962, s. 57 and Tenth Schedule.

[7] Transport Act, 1962, s. 57 (1).

[8] Transport Act, 1962, Tenth Schedule, para. 6.

[9] *Ibid.*, para. 10.

[10] Transport Act, 1962, s. 57 (2), which very considerably reduced the jurisdiction of the Tribunal; and Railway and Canal Traffic Act, 1888, s. 17. Only one appeal has in fact been brought from the Transport Tribunal: see *Merchandise Transport, Ltd.* v. *British Transport Commission*, [1961] 3 All E.R. 495; [1962] 2 Q.B. 173.

[11] The former jurisdiction over fares in London was abolished by the Transport (London) Act, 1969, s. 27.

relating to charges for the carriage of mail, armed forces and the police.[12]

(b) The Road Haulage Appeals Division, which will hear appeals from the Traffic Commissioners in their capacity as Licensing Authority for Goods Vehicles, but *not* in respect of the licensing of public service vehicles.[13]

Procedural rules have been made for the Tribunal by the Secretary of State under powers formerly given by the Transport Act, 1947[14]; in practice the Tribunal is conducted in manner very similar to a court of law, the parties normally being represented by counsel, and the proceedings being conducted in public. An appeal lies from a decision of the Tribunal to the Court of Appeal on a point of law.[15] Any proposal to increase transport charges invariably attracts public attention and protest, and the Secretary of State may appear before the Tribunal in the public interest to ensure that the applicant Board can prove their case. The Franks Committee received no evidence critical of or adverse to the conduct of proceedings of this Tribunal, but it is not a typical example of an administrative tribunal.

(d) Area transport users consultative committees.—These committees, which are concerned only with railways, are perhaps technically not tribunals, but proceedings before them in connection with the closure of branch lines resemble very closely normal tribunal procedure. They are further discussed in Chapter X, below, page 337.

5. INDUSTRY AND EMPLOYMENT

A. National Service.

During war-time the liberty of the subject was interfered with to the extent of the imposition of compulsory military service; although the courts have traditionally been the custodians of civil liberties, the complicated administrative machinery needed to operate this policy was entrusted to the supervision of several different kinds of administrative tribunals. Even in peace time these powers survived for many years, although with the ending of compulsory national service they became obsolete. The machinery was, however, an important example of modern administrative law in action, and the several tribunals are described briefly below. The constituent statute was the National Service Act, 1948, which established three groups of tribunals classified according to their jurisdiction.

(a) Postponement of military service.—When an individual was called up for national service, he could apply to the Minister of National

---

[12] Under the Transport Act, 1953 and the Post Office Act, 1953, now very rare in practice.

[13] Transport Act, 1968, s. 70 (operators' licences); s. 80 (special authorisations).

[14] Transport Tribunal Rules, 1965, S.I. 1965 No. 1687 as amended by S.I. 1970 No. 491; the Tribunal now has power to make its own rules under para. 11 of the Schedule 10 of the Transport Act, 1962.

[15] 1962 Act, Schedule 10, para. 15; no such appeal may lie upon "a question of fact or *locus standi*": *ibid.*

Service for a "postponement certificate", postponing the date of his service. If the Minister did not grant a certificate forthwith, the application would be referred to the local Military Service (Hardship) Committee under section 12 of the Act. These committees consisted of a chairman and two members selected by the Minister from a panel chosen for the purposes of the local tribunals set up under the National Insurance Act, 1946.[16] An appeal lay at the instance of either party from a decision of the committee to an umpire (or deputy umpire) appointed by the Minister, who sat with two assessors, also appointed by the Minister.[17]

(b) Conscientious objectors.—Any person called up for national service who claimed to be a conscientious objector, was entitled to have his claim heard before a specially constituted local tribunal, consisting of four members selected by the Minister from a panel of six (who had to be "impartial persons") and two of whom were appointed by the Minister after consultation with organs representative of workers,[18] with a chairman who was a county court judge or a barrister of at least seven years' standing. An appeal lay from the decision of any such tribunal to an appellate tribunal consisting of two persons chosen from a panel of four (also selected by the Minister, and again two were appointed after consultation with workers' organisations), together with a chairman appointed by the Lord Chancellor, who had to be a barrister or solicitor of at least ten years' standing.[19]

(c) Reinstatement in civil employment.—On the completion of national service, an individual had certain rights to be reinstated in his former civilian employment, and disputes arising in connection therewith were referred under the Act to yet a third series of tribunals, known as local reinstatement committees. These consisted of three persons, a chairman, a person chosen from a panel nominated to represent employers and also a person chosen from a panel nominated to represent employed persons, all of whom were appointed by the Minister. In addition, the members of the committee could have the assistance of assessors (appointed by the Minister) with expert knowledge, but no right to vote when the committee came to make their decision.[1] An appeal lay from a decision of a committee to the umpire (or deputy umpire) appointed under section 41 (4) of the Act; that appointment was made by Her Majesty, and the person appointed had to be[2] a barrister or solicitor of not less than ten years' standing.

---

[16] *Ante*, p. 247.

[17] National Service Act, 1948, s. 13. If the decision of the committee was unanimous, an appeal will lie only with the leave of the umpire (*ibid.*); the Franks Committee recommended (see para. 216) that this restriction on the right of appeal should be removed.

[18] Act of 1948, Schedule 4. There were seven of these local tribunals altogether. At the end of their active life, an article in *The Times* (December 13, 1960) expressed the opinion that "it is fair to say that the local tribunals have in general worked well and properly and the suggestion that they might not be entirely impartial was effectively quashed, when, under the Tribunals and Inquiries Act, 1958, they were removed from the aegis of the Ministry of Labour".

[19] Tribunals and Inquiries Act, 1971, s. 9.

[1] Act of 1948, s. 41.

[2] Tribunals and Inquiries Act, 1971, s. 9.

Procedure.—The procedure before these three sets of tribunals, both at first instance and on appeal, was similar; at first parties appearing at first instance were forbidden legal representation,[3] but this was altered as a consequence of the Franks Report, and representation was allowed by counsel, solicitor, trade union representative, or a friend or relative.[4] All tribunals might take evidence on oath, but in general proceedings were informal; indeed the Franks Committee seemed to consider that proceedings before some of the conscientious objectors local tribunals were *too* informal.[5] All these tribunals (both original and appellate) are still listed in the Schedule to the Tribunals and Inquiries Act, 1971, and so were subject to the general supervision of the Council on Tribunals.

B. Employment.

A series of tribunals were set under the Industrial Training Act 1964 which are known as "industrial tribunals". At first they had jurisdiction under the 1964 Act only to determine appeals by persons assessed to a levy made by an industrial training board towards meeting its expenses (1964 Act, s. 12). Since these tribunals were originally constituted, however, their jurisdiction has been greatly expanded to include the following:

(i) Rights to redundancy payments or claims against the redundancy fund, under the Redundancy Payments Act, 1965 (see s. 46 thereof);

(ii) References as to particulars of terms of a contract of employment (s. 8 of the Contracts of Employment Act, 1972);

(iii) References for the determination of compensation claimed for loss of office under a variety of statutes;

(iv) Certain disputes arising under the Selective Employment Payments Act, 1966 (see s. 7 (5) thereof) (now repealed);

(v) Disputes as to the meaning of "dock work" under section 51 of the Docks and Harbours Act, 1966;

(vi) Disputes as to "equal pay" for women, when the Equal Pay Act, 1970 is fully in force[6];

(vii) Complaints by employees against employers under s. 106 of the Industrial Relations Act, 1971, in particular as to trade union membership, etc. (see s. 5), and allegations of unfair dismissal (s. 22).

Ministerial regulations have been made providing for the procedure to be observed before these tribunals[7]; they are subject to the supervision of the Council on Tribunals,[8] and an appeal lies from a tribunal decision on a point of law to the High Court.[9] The President of the Tribunal

[3] National Service (Miscellaneous) Regulations, 1948, S.I. 1948 No. 2683, reg. 23.
[4] National Service (Miscellaneous) Amendment Regulations, 1958, S.I. 1958 No. 661.
[5] Report, paras. 217–19.
[6] As at present provided (by s. 9 (1) of the Act), on December 29, 1975.
[7] Industrial Tribunals (England and Wales) Regulations, 1965 (S.I., 1965, No. 1101).
[8] Tribunals and Inquiries (Industrial Tribunals) Order, 1965 (S.I., 1965, No. 1403); in their Report for 1965, the Council on Tribunals welcomed this "Concentration of jurisdiction in fewer and stronger tribunals": para. 17. See now 1971 Act, item 10.
[9] Tribunals and Inquiries Act, 1971, s. 13 (1).

selects tribunals to hear cases consisting of three persons from a panel of lawyers who are to act as chairmen, and panels of employers' members and workers' members respectively; lawyer and lay members are remunerated for their services. In addition to the President there are full-time regional chairmen at Birmingham, Manchester, Leeds and Newcastle, who are paid substantial salaries. Decisions of the tribunals are published from time to time in a series known as the "Industrial Reports", issued by H.M.S.O. In 1971/2 there were some 9,000 cases before industrial tribunals sitting in various centres in the country.[10] By reason of the changes brought about by the Industrial Relations Act, 1971, these numbers will no doubt increase very considerably, but there were difficulties in the constitution of tribunals in 1971/2, owing to the withdrawal of a substantial number of members from the panel of employed persons serving as members of the tribunals.[11]

The Industrial Relations Court, established by the Act of 1971 is, as its name suggests, not a tribunal but is a "superior court of record".[12]

6. IMMIGRATION OF ALIENS

Hitherto it has always been held that an alien has no legal right to be admitted to this country, and that the Home Secretary has an absolute discretion to refuse him permission to enter; a discretion, with the exercise of which the courts will not interfere. An alien has no right to enter the United Kingdom without leave, and having entered an alien has no right to have the time extended, and therefore there was no question of the Home Secretary being required to observe natural justice in exercising his discretion.[13] This is no longer the law by virtue of the Immigration Act, 1971. This Act perpetuates a hierarchy of tribunals originally constituted by the Immigration Appeals Act, 1969, to hear appeals by persons excluded from entry to the United Kingdom, or against conditions imposed on entry to the U.K., or against directions as to destination contained in a deportation order.[14] These appeals against a decision of an immigration officer will lie in the first instance to an Adjudicator, a person appointed by the Home Secretary who is not required to have any specialised qualifications, but who must not be or remain a member of the House of Commons.[15]

Any party (*i.e.*, the original appellant or the immigration officer) to an appeal to an Adjudicator, may then appeal from a decision (sometimes

---

[10] Report of the Council on Tribunals for 1971/2, p. 32; there were a further 886 hearings in Scotland (*ibid.*, p. 37).

[11] *Ibid.*, para. 75.

[12] 1971 Act, Schedule 3, para. 13.

[13] *Schmidt* v. *Secretary of State*, [1969] 1 All E.R. 904; [1969] 2 Ch. 149; *R.* v. *Leman Street Police Station Inspector, ex parte Venicoff*, [1920] 3 K.B. 72; *R.* v. *Brixton Prison Governor, ex parte Soblen*, [1962] 3 All E.R. 641; [1963] 2 Q.B. 243, and *ante*, p. 167; but the proceedings must be "fair": *Re K. (H.) (an infant)*, [1967] 1 All E.R. 226; [1967] 2 Q.B. 617.

[14] See Act of 1971, ss. 13 (1) and (2), 14, 15, 16 and 17 (1). There is no right of appeal if the Secretary of State certifies that he personally has directed that the appellant is not to be given a right of entry on the ground that his exclusion is "conducive to the public good": see ss. 13 (5), 14 (3) and 15 (3). This exclusion of a right to appeal was clearly intended to cover cases similar to the "Rudi Dutschke" case: see Hepple, (1971) 34 M.L.R. 501.

[15] 1971 Act, Schedule 5, para. 4.

from outside the U.K.), to the Immigration Appeal Tribunal,[16] and the Home Secretary may refer a case back to the Adjudicator or the Tribunal.[17] The members of this Tribunal are appointed by the Lord Chancellor and the president and such other members as the Lord Chancellor may determine, must be chosen from barristers, advocates or solicitors, of not less than seven years' standing; at least three members of the Tribunal are required to sit at each hearing.[18] Rules of procedure have been prepared governing the procedure before Adjudicators and the Tribunal,[19] and both the Adjudicators and the Tribunal are subject to the supervision of the Council on Tribunals.[20]

There is no express right of appeal to the courts from a decision of the Tribunal, but presumably the decisions of the Tribunal could be quashed by *certiorari* in a proper case.[21]

7. REVENUE

This heading includes some of the oldest administrative tribunals and also a group of the newest. In the former category are the General and Special Commissioners, originally constituted for the administration of the land tax; in the latter the V.A.T. (Value Added Tax) Tribunals established by the Finance Act, 1972.

The General Commissioners are appointed by the Lord Chancellor.[1] They are arranged in divisions whose boundaries are fixed from time to time by regulations made by the Lord Chancellor. Each panel of Commissioners serves one division and is staffed by a clerk appointed by them (who is often a local practising solicitor). There are no prescribed qualifications for appointment as a General Commissioner; in practice they are often local magistrates.

The principal jurisdiction of the General Commissioners is to hear and determine appeals by taxpayers against assessments made by local inspectors to income tax.[2] Proceedings before the General Commissioners must be held in private,[3] but they are informal and are not regulated by detailed statutory rules of procedure.[4] The Special Commissioners are all civil servants appointed by the Treasury and they sit only in London.[5] Their jurisdiction coincides with that of the General Com-

[16] 1971 Act, s. 20.

[17] *Ibid.*, s. 21.

[18] *Ibid.*, Schedule 5, para. 12.

[19] Immigration Appeals (Procedure) Rules, 1972 (S.I. 1972 No. 1684).

[20] Tribunals and Inquiries (Immigration Appeals) Order, 1970, now replaced by the Tribunals and Inquiries Act, 1971, Schedule 1, item 8.

[21] For an example where an application for *certiorari* was considered on its merits, see *R.* v. *Immigration Appeal Tribunal, ex parte Joyles*, [1972] 3 All E.R. 213, [1972] 1 W.L.R. 1390. A *certiorari* will also, it seems, lie against an Adjudicator: *R.* v. *Immigration Appeals Adjudicator, ex parte Khan*, [1972] 3 All E.R. 297; [1972] 1 W.L.R. 1058.

[1] Taxes Management Act, 1970, s. 1 (2). Their full title is "Commissioners for the general purposes of the income tax." They are paid travelling and subsistence allowances, but no salary. They must retire at the age of 75.

[2] Taxes Management Act, 1970, Part V.

[3] The procedure is set out—very much in outline—in ss. 50–52 of the Taxes Management Act, 1970.

[4] There is a quorum for proceedings before the General Commissioners of at least two Commissioners and in practice it is customary for only two to sit (Act of 1970, s. 44 (5)), but in the case of the Special Commissioners a single Commissioner may in certain limited circumstances, determine the case (*ibid.*, s. 45).

[5] Taxes Management Act, 1970, s. 4.

missioners, except that they also hear appeals on surtax and other special matters. Certain income tax appeals lie only to the Special Commissioners, and the taxpayer may elect to bring the appeal before them instead of the General Commissioners.[6] Proceedings before the Special Commissioners also are not regulated by any prescribed rules, but it is customary for hearings (again in private) to be conducted in a formal manner, and for accountants and sometimes solicitors and counsel to be instructed.[7] Appeal lies from the General or Special Commissioners by case stated on a point of law (including the misreception of evidence,[8] to the High Court,[9] but subject thereto a determination of the Commissioners is "final and conclusive".[10] The Commissioners have no power to award costs to a successful litigant, and legal aid is not available for proceedings before them.

Each panel of the General Commissioners constitutes a separate tribunal with no machinery providing for co-ordination and the Special Commissioners do not exercise any supervision over them. The V.A.T. Tribunals on the other hand are organised on a presidential system.[11] The President of these Tribunals is appointed by the Lord Chancellor and must be a barrister or solicitor of at least ten years' standing. Each tribunal, when determining an appeal, consists of a chairman alone or a chairman with one or two members. The chairman of a panel is appointed by the Lord Chancellor and other members by the Treasury; no qualifications are specified for panel chairmen or for the other members. The V.A.T. tribunals have an extensive jurisdiction to determine appeals against decisions of the Commissioners of Customs and Excise on such matters are the grant or refusal of registration for V.A.T. and as to the amount of tax chargeable on the supply of goods or services, etc.[12] Rules of procedure regulating the conduct of these tribunals have been made by the Commissioners of Customs and Excise,[13] and the tribunals have been brought within s. 13 of the Tribunals and Inquiries Act, 1971,[14] so that a right of appeal lies to the High Court on a point of law.

A third kind of revenue tribunal is the special tribunal established under s. 28 of the Finance Act, 1960, sometimes known as the "Dividend stripping" tribunal.[15] An inspector is seized with special powers to set aside transactions made by persons who have endeavoured to arrange their affairs so as to avoid tax liability; the taxpayer then has a right to appeal to the tribunal. If he is unsuccessful, an assessment to tax will normally follow against which he can appeal to the Commissioners.

---

[6] *Ibid.*, s. 31 (4).
[7] Ss. 50–52 *ibid.*, apply.
[8] See, for example, *Cooksey and Bibbey* v. *Rednall* (1949), 30 Tax Cas. 514.
[9] Taxes Management Act, 1970, s. 56.
[10] *Ibid.*, s. 46 (2).
[11] Finance Act, 1972, s. 40 and Schedule 6. It is for the President to establish the number of tribunals required: *ibid.*, para. 4.
[12] Finance Act 1972, s. 40.
[13] Value Added Tax Tribunals Rules, 1972, S.I. 1972 No. 1344.
[14] By the Tribunals and Inquiries (Value Added Tax Tribunals) Order, 1972, S.I. 1972 No. 1210.
[15] See now ss. 460 and 163 of the Income and Corporation Taxes Act, 1970.

The procedure of the tribunal is not regulated by rules but it has on two separate occasions been the subject of scrutiny by the House of Lords. In each case[16] the court held that, provided the tribunal acted "fairly", it was not necessary (in view of the preliminary nature of the proceedings) for the principles of natural justice to be observed.

All of these tribunals are subject to the supervision of the Council on Tribunals.

8. INFORMAL BODIES

In addition to the types of tribunal or inquiry above discussed which have all been given legal status of some kind by statute, a number of central government departments have in recent years developed informal procedures whereby an aggrieved citizen may have some measure of redress. Sometimes this may be little more than a reference of the complainant to an officer of a higher grade in the same department, much as a waiter would refer the dissatisfied customer to the maître d'hôtel.[17] Sometimes departmental arrangements are made for a procedure more closely approximating an "appeal"; thus, patients dissatisfied with a decision of an Area Health Authority may be able to refer their complaint to the local Community Health Council or the Health Commissioner.[18] Arrangements of this kind, however, lack statutory authority, and are not binding on the departments.

9. DOMESTIC TRIBUNALS

(a) Introduction.—We have discussed the several cases where an individual may be entitled to appeal to a tribunal established by statute, in search of redress of his grievance, and also the extent to which these tribunals are subject to control by the courts of law.[19] In this section it is proposed to deal with certain less formal tribunals that may be set up voluntarily (normally under a contractural relationship) or more rarely by statute, for the purpose of regulating the affairs of a particular group of persons. Such are tribunals established by the members of any association of individuals, either *ad hoc* or generally for the purpose of settling disputes within the association itself. Thus, a trade union may establish a membership or disciplinary committee; so may a federation of employers, a private members' club or a professional organisation, and such a committee may be given the right, as between the members of the association, to hear and determine a variety of different disputes, such as whether an individual shall be admitted to or permitted to remain in membership of the association, or whether he is in breach of one of the association's rules.

---

[16] *Wiseman* v. *Bornemann*, [1969] 3 All E.R. 275; [1971] A.C. 297. *Pearlberg* v. *Varty*, [1972] 2 All E.R. 6; [1972] 1 W.L.R. 534.

[17] Arrangements of this kind have been standardised in a few central government departments, notably in the Board of Trade and the Post Office (see *Justice* Report at pp. 22–3, and *ante*, p. 98).

[18] National Health Service Reorganisation Act, 1973.

[19] And see article by Professor Mitchell at (1955/6), 2 A.L.R. 80.

These decisions may be of vital importance to the individual concerned. A workman who is excluded from his trade union may lose his right to work, with all that that implies in our modern society[20]; exclusion from his club may seem almost as serious to a prosperous London business man, and the decisions of such bodies as the Disciplinary Committee of the Law Society[1] and of the General Medical Council[2] may well be of crucial importance to those concerned. It is therefore our purpose to examine the extent to which tribunals of this kind are subject to control by the courts of law, and the grounds on which judicial review may be available in such cases.[3]

(b) The grounds of judicial review.—In the first place, many of the tribunals regulating the conduct of members of professions are not true domestic tribunals, in that they have been constituted under statute or possibly by the prerogative (as in the case of some Universities), and therefore—except in so far as express provision for appeals may have been made in the constituent statute[4]—there is no question but that the usual judicial remedies of an action for a declaration or *certiorari* will be available if there has in any particular case been a breach of the principles of "natural justice", or if the tribunal has acted *ultra vires.*[5] Where the tribunal may truly be described as "domestic", and owes its origin purely to a voluntary association of individuals, it is not always so easy to appreciate the grounds on which there can be any judicial review. It is clear on the one hand that if the rules of the association have been broken, the courts have jurisdiction. This is because the domestic tribunal in question owes its origin to a contract—the contract formed when the individual concerned joined the association and thereby agreed to abide by the rules of the association, in consideration of his being accorded the privileges of membership as declared in those same rules. Therefore a member of a trade union may obtain an injunction from the courts restraining a breach of the union rules,[6] or seek a declaration to the effect that a decision of a union committee was contrary to the rules of the union.[7] *Certiorari, mandamus* and prohibition may lie against bodies not established by statute, but they must be at least of a public character; this seems in practice that they must have been established either by statute or under the Royal Prerogative.[8]

---

[20] See Lord McDermott, *Protection from Power under English Law,* Chapter 7.

[1] Solicitors Act, 1957, ss. 46–9.

[2] Medical Act, 1956, s. 33.

[3] On the subject generally, see article by Morris, L. J., "The Courts and Domestic Tribunals", (1953), 69 L.Q.R. 318.

[4] See for example, Solicitors Act, 1957, s. 49. *Certiorari* would formerly lie against the General Medical Council if they had not made "due inquiry" into a particular case: *General Council of Medical Education* v. *Spackman,* [1943] 2 All E.R. 337; [1943] A.C. 627; but now provision is made by s. 36 of the Medical Act, 1956, for an appeal to lie to the Judical Committee of the Privy Council: *Fox* v. *G.M.C.,* [1960] 3 All E.R. 225; [1960] 1 W.L.R. 1017.

[5] Cf., Chapter VI, *ante,* p. 133.

[6] *Bonsor* v. *Musicians' Union,* [1955] 3 All E.R. 518, [1956] A.C. 104.

[7] *Andrews* v. *Mitchell,* [1905] A.C. 78. Proceedings of this kind will now normally be replaced by proceedings under the Industrial Relations Act, 1971.

[8] *R.* v. *Criminal Injuries Compensation Board, ex parte Lain,* [1967] 2 All E.R. 770; [1967] 2 Q.B. 864 and *ante,* p. 250.

It was formerly contended[9] that the courts had a right to quash a decision of a domestic tribunal that had been arrived at in manner contrary to the principles of natural justice, only where the complainant could show that a property right had been interfered with. Therefore, if the member of the voluntary association had to pay a subscription, either on joining the association, or annually, it was agreed that the courts would have jurisdiction to interfere with a decision of a tribunal that would have the effect of depriving him unfairly of that proprietary right, however trivial it might be. This concept was not satisfactory, as the "right to work" may be far more valuable than any proprietary right to a share of the funds of a trade union or club. By the middle of the present century, however, without any apparent change in the method of approach, the courts were recognising that the jurisdiction of a domestic tribunal was founded essentially on contract. It was also gradually established that whereas the parties were *prima facie* bound by the rules of the association which they had joined, and to which they must therefore be implied to have assented, those rules would not be construed in such a manner as to enable the domestic tribunal to disregard the principles of natural justice in coming to its decisions.[10] In the leading case of *Lee* v. *Showman's Guild of Great Britain*,[11] DENNING, L.J., went even further than this[12]:

> "Although the jurisdiction of a domestic tribunal is founded on contract, express or implied, nevertheless the parties are not free to make any contract they like. There are important limitations imposed by public policy. The tribunal must, for instance, observe the principles of natural justice. They must give the man notice of the charge and a reasonable opportunity of meeting it. Any stipulation to the contrary would be invalid. They cannot stipulate for a power to condemn a man unheard. . . . Another limitation arises out of the well-known principle that parties cannot by contract oust the ordinary courts of their jurisdiction. . . . They can, of course, agree to leave questions of law, as well as questions of fact, to the decision of the domestic tribunal. They can, indeed, make the tribunal the final arbiter on questions of fact, but they cannot make it the final arbiter on questions of law. They cannot prevent its decisions being examined by the courts. If parties should seek, by agreement, to take the law out of the hands of the courts and into the hands of a private tribunal, without any recourse at all to the courts in the case of error of law, then the agreement is to that extent contrary to public policy and void."[13]

Whereas the parties may by contract decide to make a committee or tribunal the final arbiter on questions of fact, they cannot prevent its decisions on questions of law being examined in the courts.[14]

This rule that the courts will not enforce a contract which is contrary to public policy is of course a well-known principle of the ordinary law of contract. In an administrative law context it will normally be applied in the form of a failure to observe "natural justice", but in this context of a domestic tribunal, it may take other forms, as in *Eastham* v. *Newcastle United Football Club, Ltd.*,[15] where the complaint was that the contract in question was in unreasonable restraint of trade.

---

9 See Lloyd, "Disciplinary Powers of Professional Bodies", at 13 M.L.R. 281.

10 *Russell* v. *Duke of Norfolk*, [1949] 1 All E.R. 109.

11 [1952] 1 All E.R. 1175; [1952] 2 Q.B. 329.

12 *Ibid.*, at pp. 1180–1.

13 *Cf.* the learned judge's explanation of the term "final" in *Re Gilmore's Application*, *ante*, p. 155.

14 See also *Baker* v. *Jones*, [1954] 2 All E.R. 553.

15 [1963] 3 All E.R. 139; [1964] Ch. 413.

If a breach of natural justice can be established it is clear that a member of a trade union or similar body who is ejected from membership has a right (apart from the provisions of the Industrial Relations Act, 1971, as to which see *post*, p. 270) to have the decision of the domestic tribunal declared to be void by the court. Lord DENNING said in *Annamunthodo* v. *Oilfield Workers' Trade Union*[16]:

> "[Counsel] did suggest that a man could not complain of a failure of natural justice unless he could show that he had been prejudiced by it. Their Lordships cannot accept that suggestion. If a domestic tribunal fails to act in accordance with natural justice, the person affected by their decision can always seek redress in the courts."

The cases in which this principle has been applied to different kinds of domestic tribunals are considered below.

(c) Kinds of tribunals.—It is not proposed to list all the various domestic tribunals that actually exist. It is only practicable to classify such tribunals under several very general headings based on the types of parent association by which they may be set up. There is of course no limit to the types or numbers of tribunals that could be so constituted. Perhaps "tribunal" may itself be too formal or magnificent a word to apply to a body that may often be no more than an *ad hoc* committee charged with investigating an allegation against an individual member of the association, or requested to determine whether such a person shall be allowed into or dismissed from membership of the association. For want of a better word, however, we are so using it in this context.

(1) *Trade Unions.*[17]—Trade unions are probably the most important of the various kinds of voluntary association; although they are not usually incorporated they are accorded by the law some of the normal attributes of legal personality. The relationship between a trade union and its members must, however, depend on contract and the terms of the contract will *prima facie* be binding on the parties. In *Maclean* v. *Workers' Union,*[18] MAUGHAM, J., said[19]:

> "If, for instance, there was a clearly expressed rule stating that a member might be expelled by a defined body without calling upon the member in question to explain his conduct, I see no reason for supposing that the courts would interfere with such a rule on the ground of public policy."

By 1952, however, the general acceptance by the unions of the "closed shop" principle had shown that membership of a trade union was a valuable and essential right, the loss of which might deprive an individual of his right to work. Therefore, in *Lee* v. *Showman's Guild of Great Britain,*[20] DENNING, L.J., in the passage quoted above[1] disapproved of the views of MAUGHAM, J., in the earlier case. If rules of a trade union provide for expulsion by a procedure which flouts the principles of natural

---

[16] [1961] 3 All E.R. 621, at p. 625; [1961] A.C. 945, at p. 956.

[17] On this subject generally, see Rideout, *The Right to Membership of a Trade Union* (1963).

[18] [1929] 1 Ch. 602.

[19] *Ibid.*, at p. 623; but see STAMP, J., in *Hiles* v. *Amalgamated Society of Woodworkers*, [1967] 3 All E.R. 70, at p. 77.

[20] [1952] 1 All E.R. 1175; [1952] 2 Q.B. 329.

[1] *Ante*, p. 268.

justice, it seems that the courts would intervene at common law[2]; on the other hand, the rules will be so construed, if possible, that they require the principles of natural justice to be observed.[3] If a member has been wrongfully expelled from a trade union (*i.e.*, otherwise than in accordance with the rules of the union or in a manner contrary to the principles of natural justice), he may sue for damages for breach of contract,[4] and he may also claim damages if members of the union conspire together with a view to expelling him from membership.[5] However, an applicant for membership of a union has no remedy if he is refused permission to join, even if he is not given an opportunity of being heard on his application.[6]

The Industrial Relations Act, 1971, has not, it seems, changed this branch of the law, but it has created a new remedy open to a member of an "organisation of workers",[7] who may complain of an "unfair industrial practice" to the National Industrial Relations Court if he is subjected to any disciplinary action by the organisation otherwise than in accordance with procedures detailed in section 65 (8) of the Act, which very closely resemble the common law rules of natural justice. It is also an unfair industrial practice if anyone is excluded from membership of such an organisation "by way of any arbitrary or unreasonable discrimination".[8] In future no doubt these remedies will be used in preference to the more expensive common law procedure.

Friendly societies are in much the same position at common law; in *Andrews* v. *Mitchell.*[9] it was held by the House of Lords that a power to expel a member who committed a breach of the society's rules did not confer a power to expel a member summarily; he must be given notice of his alleged offence and an opportunity of expressing his views on the matter.

(2) *Employers' federations.*—Here there can be no question of the loss of a right to work if an individual is excluded from membership of the federation, but such exclusion may have other consequences almost as serious. Thus, in *Byrne* v. *Kinematograph Renters Society, Ltd.*,[10] the trade association were able to prevent a cinema proprietor from obtaining any supplies of films and so drove him out of business. No contract was established in that case, and therefore no remedy was available from the courts by way of an action for damages, for an injunction or for a declaration for violation of the rules of natural justice in the conduct of an inquiry by a "domestic tribunal".

---

[2] *Annamunthodo* v. *Oilfield Workers' Trade Union*, [1961] 3 All E.R. 621; [1961] A.C. 945; if the rules of the trade union provide for an internal remedy of appeal the complainant must seek that remedy before he comes to the courts: *White* v. *Kuzych*, [1951] 2 All E.R. 435; [1951] A.C. 585.

[3] See, *e.g.*, *Lawlor* v. *Union of Post Office Workers*, [1965] 1 All E.R. 353; [1965] Ch. 712.

[4] *Bonsor* v. *Musicians' Union*, [1955] 3 All E.R. 518.

[5] *Huntley* v. *Thornton*, [1957] 1 All E.R. 234.

[6] *Faramus* v. *Film Artists' Association*, [1964] 1 All E.R. 25; see *per* Lord EVERSHED, at p. 28, and Lord PEARCE, at p. 33.

[7] This includes, but is not confined to, a registered trade union.

[8] Industrial Relations Act, 1971, s. 65 (2).

[9] [1905] A.C. 78.

[10] [1958] 2 All E.R. 579.

(3) *Private clubs.*—The leading case on these more informal institutions is *Dawkins* v. *Antrobus*,[11] where it was held that the courts would not interfere with the decision of the members of a club professing to act under their rules, unless it could be shown either that the rules were contrary to natural justice, or that what had been done was contrary to the rules of the club, or that there had been *mala fides* or malice in coming to a decision.[12] As the action taken by the club committee in excluding the plaintiff from membership in that case was done *bona fide*, the court declined to grant the injunction asked for. JAMES, L.J., in the Court of Appeal,[13] observed:

> "We have no right to sit as a court of appeal upon the decisions of the members of a club duly assembled."

In *Young* v. *Ladies Imperial Club*,[14] however, it was established that the rules of the club had not been correctly observed, and therefore the court granted a declaration to the effect that a decision of the club committee was invalid.

(4) *Professional bodies.*—These are commonly regulated by statute; thus, express provision is made for solicitors, doctors, dentists and nurses.[15] In *Weinberger* v. *Inglis*[16] the courts were asked to intervene in a case concerning the Stock Exchange, a private association whose rules were not regulated by statute. An applicant for admission to the Exchange who was duly qualified was refused admission because he was of German descent. However, the courts declined to intervene, as it was admitted that there had been no denial of natural justice. Lord ATKINSON said[17]:

> "If any charge be made against a man on the ground that he did some act or filled some character, then before he can be found guilty of that act, or be found to have filled that character, he must, according to natural justice, get notice of the charge, and be afforded an opportunity of defending himself, but having had that opportunity, if the matter charged be proved, what those in authority may determine to do to him or his interest because of the fact so established is a subject on which he has no right whatever to be heard."

In other words, in the type of case here considered, the person "aggrieved" has only a right to a fair hearing, and not a right to have his case tried *de novo* by the courts.

In some cases concerning professional bodies it may not be possible to establish any contractual relationship, such as exists between a trade union and its members. Thus, in *Davis* v. *Carew-Pole*,[18] which involved the National Hunt Rules, the stewards of the National Hunt Committee found that the plaintiff had offended against the rules, and he was

---

[11] (1881), 17 Ch.D. 615.

[12] Much the same principle was applied to a Parliamentary Constituency Labour Party (an unincorporated association) by MEGARRY, J., in *John* v. *Rees*, [1969] 2 All E.R. 274; [1970] Ch. 345.

[13] In *Dawkins* v. *Antrobus* (*ante*), at p. 628.

[14] [1920] 2 K.B. 523.

[15] As to these, see Miller, "The Disciplinary Jurisdiction of Professional Tribunals", (1962), 25 M.L.R. 531.

[16] [1919] A.C. 606. This case could have been decided on the same basis as *Faramus* v. *Film Artistes' Association*, in that it concerned an application for membership.

[17] *Ibid.*, at p. 631.

[18] [1956] 2 All E.R. 524.

therefore declared to be a "disqualified person", which would have had serious consequences to the plaintiff in his business as livery stable keeper. The learned judge (PILCHER, J.), was of the opinion[19] that an action would lie in such circumstances for a declaration and/or an injunction, if the defendants had made a wrong decision (quite apart from any breach of natural justice), even although he was not in a contractual relationship with them. In *Byrne* v. *Kinematograph Renters Society, Ltd..*,[1] Harman, J., expressed the view that *Davis* v. *Carew-Pole* (and the earlier case of *Abbott* v. *Sullivan*)[2] could have been based on contract; but this could, said Lord DENNING, M.R., in *Nagle* v. *Feilden,*[3] only be done by inventing a fictitious contract,[4] and with respect, one is obliged to agree with this view. *Nagle* v. *Feilden,*[3] came before the Court of Appeal on an interlocutory application, and therefore the substantive law was not fully argued, but in giving judgment, Lord Denning brushed aside the need for a contract as a basis for the intervention of the courts where there has been a breach of the principles of natural justice:

> "Just as the courts will intervene to protect [a man's] rights of property, so they will also intervene to protect his right to work,"[4]

and Salmon, L.J., made observations to the same effect. In this case the appellant asked for a declaration to the effect that the Stewards of the Jockey Club were acting against public policy in refusing her a licence as a trainer, in pursuance of a general unwritten practice of the stewards not to grant licences to women. The defendants applied for the proceedings to be struck out because no cause of action had been shown; the Court of Appeal held that there was an arguable case.

(5) *Universities.*—These bodies are in an anomalous position, being created either by charter under the Royal Prerogative or under statute but with whom members (staff and students, in different senses) enter into contractual relationships. Staff are clearly governed by the terms of their contracts of employment,[5] but it is not clear whether a student's status is entirely dependent on contract, as University regulations made under statute or prerogative authority are binding on him apart from any question of contract. In *R.* v. *Aston University Senate, ex parte Roffey,*[6] the Divisional Court held that the appropriate disciplinary body of the University was obliged to observe the principles of natural justice and to give a student a fair hearing before sending him down, even where the University regulations made no provision for such a

---

[19] Following in particular the dissenting judgment of DENNING, L.J., in *Abbott* v. *Sullivan,* [1952] 1 All E.R. 226, at p. 231; [1952] 1 K.B. 189.

[1] [1958] 2 All E.R. 579, at p. 596.

[2] [1952] 1 All E.R. 226; [1952] 1 K.B. 189.

[3] [1966] 1 All E.R. 689.

[4] *Ibid.*, at p. 694.

[5] *Vidyodaya University of Ceylon* v. *Silva,* [1964] 3 All E.R. 865; *ante*, p. 118.

[6] [1969] 2 All E.R. 964; [1969] 2 Q.B. 538.

hearing.[7] Professor H. W. R. Wade suggests that the court was proceeding on a contractual basis,[8] but this is not clear, and it seems strange that *certiorari* should have been considered appropriate (although on the facts it was not granted) to redress a breach of contract.

In *Glynn* v. *Keele University*[9] the remedy asked for was an injunction, so the question of statutory or contractual duty was not relevant; here it was held that the Vice-Chancellor had certain powers of internal discipline outwith the jurisdiction of the court to review, but in a serious matter (such as when he proposed to exclude a student from residential accommodation at the University) he must act in accordance with natural justice. Nevertheless, the remedy was a discretionary one and as the applicant in this case had (as the court found) suffered no injustice, the remedy was refused.[10]

(d) Summary.—The result of these somewhat unsatisfactory cases therefore seems to be that the courts will (by an appropriate remedy) review a decision of a domestic tribunal (apart from any relevant statutory provisions) where:

(a) the action amounts to enforcing the terms of a contract, in so far as those terms are not contrary to public policy; *or* where

(b) there has been a breach of the principles of natural justice, *either* in a case where the parties are already in a contractual relationship, *or* in a case where as a consequence of such a breach, the complainant has been deprived of his "right to work", whatever this latter expression may mean.[11]

---

[7] See also *Brighton Corpn.* v. *Parry* (1972), 116 Sol. Jo. 483, where it was held on the facts that natural justice *had* been observed.

[8] (1969), 85 L.Q.R. 468; Professor Wade argues convincingly that *certiorari* is not concerned with breaches of contract, but *Lain's case* showed (*ante*, p. 179) that this order will lie to public bodies that have no statutory origin. Why should it not be accepted that a public body, such as a university, established by charter (whether or not issued under a statutory power) should be required to observe natural justice; the charter could be presumed to have been granted on those terms? Perhaps the visitorial jurisdiction within the University should have been exhausted first, in accordance with the principle of *Barraclough* v. *Brown* (*ante*, p. 170); see *Herring* v. *Templeman*, [1973] 2 All E.R. 581, (on appeal, [1973] 3 All E.R. 569), and Mr. J. W. Bridge's article, "Keeping Peace in the Universities", (1970) 86 L.Q.R. 531, at p. 539.

[9] [1971] 2 All E.R. 89; [1971] 1 W.L.R. 487.

[10] Contrast the views of Lord DENNING (not discussed in this case) in *Annamunthodo* v. *Oilfield Workers, Trade Union* (*ante*, p. 269).

[11] There is an obvious conflict between *Faramus* v. *Film Artistes' Association* (*ante*) and *Nagle* v. *Feilden*, if the latter case were decided in substance as suggested by Lord DENNING. Faramus was just as effectively deprived of his "right to work" as was Miss Nagle in the latter case.

CHAPTER IX

ADMINISTRATIVE AUTHORITIES IN LITIGATION

1. INTRODUCTION

In this Chapter it is proposed to deal with such special rules as there may be governing the conduct of legal proceedings taken by or on behalf of the Crown as plaintiff or against the Crown as defendant, and also proceedings taken by or against other agencies of the administration; we shall also consider the circumstances in which such proceedings may be instituted. In one sense, the judicial control of the administration must involve administrative agencies in litigation, and in Chapter VI we emphasised that aspect. Here it is proposed to emphasise the proceedings themselves and any special rules applicable thereto.

First we shall be particularly concerned with the Crown, which in this context means its personified form as a corporation sole,[1] or "The Administration", rather than the person of the Sovereign,[2] and certainly not the Government for the time being in power.[3] "The Government" in the latter sense may have initiated the litigation or the act complained of by a plaintiff, but the courts are concerned with legal concepts and not with political or social ideas. The discussion will deal therefore with the extent to which the Crown may be made liable in civil proceedings in the courts, and also with the special immunities and privileges that can be claimed by the Crown in litigation. As administrative law is concerned with all types of administrative authorities and agencies, this Chapter will deal also with litigation involving the other agencies, whether or not they may be regarded in law as "emanations of the Crown".[4] Criminal proceedings are not our concern, for although the Crown is a party in such proceedings as prosecutor, that branch of the

---

[1] See Maitland, "The Crown as Corporation", Coll. Papers, III, 244.

[2] It is provided in s. 40 (1) of the Crown Proceedings Act, 1947, that "Nothing in this Act shall apply to proceedings by or against, or authorise proceedings in tort to be brought against, His Majesty in His personal capacity".

[3] Legal proceedings in which the Crown is a party are not affected by a dissolution of Parliament or a change in Her Majesty's Ministers.

[4] This expression has been used by some writers to describe government departments or statutory corporations acting on behalf of the Crown. It has been said that the expression first appears in *Gilbert* v. *Trinity House Corpn.* (1886), 17 Q.B.D. 795 (see per DENNING, L.J., in *Tamlin* v. *Hannaford,* [1949] 2 All E.R. 327, at p. 328; [1950] 1 K.B. 18), but its use was severely criticised in the Privy Council case of *International Ry. Co.* v. *Niagara Parks Commission,* [1941] 2 All E.R. 456; [1941] A.C. 328, *per* LUXMORE, L.J., at p. 462, where he said: "Their Lordships are unable to appreciate the precise meaning intended to be attributed to this phrase by the courts below. If it is intended to refer to the Commission in some capacity other than that of agent or servant, it is impossible to ascertain from the judgments delivered what the legal significance of that capacity may be. The word 'emanation' is hardly applicable to a person or body having a corporate capacity. . . . Their Lordships are of the opinion that it would avoid obscurity in the future if the words 'agent or servant' were used in preference to the inappropriate and undefined word 'emanation'."

law is customarily considered separately and not as part of administrative law, although it may properly be classified as a part of public law.

2. CROWN LIABILITY

In this country it cannot be claimed that traditionally the Government is, in the eye of the law, an "honest man", as might be said about the administration in France[5]; in fact, the contrary is almost the case. No considerations of moral right and wrong come into the question of Crown liability, for what is done in the name of the Sovereign cannot be contrary to the common law—"The King can do no wrong". This highly artificial theory had its origins in feudalism, this country being "the most highly feudalised country in Europe".[6] Under feudalism it was unthinkable that the King should be capable of being sued in the courts, as all the courts in the country were his courts, either personally or by grant from him, and this procedural immunity of the King as feudal overlord acquired the significance of a basic constitutional principle. In the political sphere, the principle is fundamental to the origins of the Cabinet system—because the King could do no wrong, it followed that when the administration of the day was badly conducted, it was not the King who was at fault, but his Ministers who must have given him faulty advice; Ministerial responsibility was then the natural development. In its legal aspect, however, no similar development of this principle was allowed and the feudal concept became a fundamental rule of law, to the effect that not only the Sovereign in his or her personal capacity, but also the Crown could not be sued in the courts. This *lacuna* in the common law, as it was described by the Donoughmore Committee in 1932,[7] was incapable of any rational justification, even by such critics of other more logical systems as the late Professor Dicey,[8] and particularly was this the case when the courts insisted on applying the principle strictly.[9] Thus the practice grew up, in an attempt to mitigate the doctrine, that a Crown servant who was sued in respect of a tort that he had committed "in the course of his employment" as such, and in respect of which he was personally liable, could rely on an *ex gratia* indemnity from the Crown; but when this practice was extended by the device of the nominated defendant, whereby the Department concerned would "find" a defendant who could be sued, on the understanding that the Crown would stand behind him and indemnify him against damages, the courts protested and the House of Lords refused to tolerate such a "palpable

---

[5] See Hamson, *Executive Discretion and Judicial Control, passim*, and in particular at p. 214, where it is said that "In France it was a part of the executive itself which developed a public conscience . . . which adopted the remarkable faith that an adequate administration must respect the rights of *l'administré* himself. . . ."

[6] This part of the famous Maitland paradox was true in that every parcel of land in England was subject to the feudal system.

[7] Cmd. 4060, at p. 112.

[8] The whole subject of Crown immunity was scarcely dealt with in his *Law of the Constitution* (see 10th Edn., at pp. 24–6), and no attempt was made either to criticise it or justify it.

[9] The remedy by way of a declaration was sometimes used before the passing of the 1947 Act, as in *Dyson* v. *A.G.*, [1911] 1 K.B. 410, but this remedy would not lie in cases where a petition of right (see below) would have been available in a case of contract: *Bombay and Persia Steam Navigation Co.* v. *MacLay*, [1920] 3 K.B. 402.

fiction".[10] The device of the nominated defendant suggested that the issues before the court were really issues between the plaintiff and the Crown, whereas actually the court had to decide the case as between the parties before them, and they had nothing to do with the fact that the Crown stood behind the defendant.

Adams v. *Naylor,* the case referred to, was decided in 1946, and the discussion that followed this decision was the final spark which set alight an accumulating pile of argument on the subject of Crown immunity generally. The result was the Crown Proceedings Act, 1947,[11] which became law on January 1, 1948.[12] This statute deals with the question of Crown proceedings under the general categories of liability in contract and liability in tort.

(a) Actions against the Crown for breach of contract.—The immunity of the Crown from process had not, at least during the nineteenth century, been applied so rigidly in actions for breach of contract, as it was in tort. A procedure had been developed, whereby the subject wishing to sue the Crown commenced proceedings by way of a "petition of right"; this petition (requesting the Crown to do right in the matter) was referred to the Attorney-General, who would in all normal cases give his *fiat,* although, at least in theory, he might refuse to allow the matter to proceed, without giving any reasons. The proceedings then went for trial in the ordinary way, the Crown submitting to the jurisdiction of the Court as a matter of grace. The procedure itself was rationalised somewhat by the Petitions of Right Act, 1860, and shortly afterwards, *Feather* v. *R.*[13] established that proceedings by way of petition of right would lie for the recovery of land and incorporeal hereditaments, for the recovery of chattels and of money due under a contract or for services rendered, for damages for breach of contract, and for compensation for property taken by the Crown.[14]

The Act of 1947 abolished this old-fashioned and artificial procedure,[15] but retained in force the law behind it, for by section 1 the Act provides:

> "Where any person has a claim against the Crown after the commencement of this Act, and, if this Act had not been passed, the claim might have been enforced, subject to the grant of His Majesty's fiat, by petition of right, or might have been enforced by a proceeding provided by any statutory provision repealed by this Act, then, subject to the provisions of this Act, the claim may be enforced as of right, and without the fiat of His Majesty, by proceedings taken against the Crown for that purpose in accordance with the provisions of this Act."

In contract and allied matters, the Crown can therefore be sued in those circumstances in which a petition of right could have been brought

---

[10] *Adams* v. *Naylor,* [1946] 2 All E.R. 241; [1946] A.C. 543. In this case Viscount SIMON observed (at p. 244): "The courts before whom such a case as this comes have to decide it as between the parties before them and have nothing to do with the fact that the Crown stands behind the defendant. For the plaintiffs to succeed, apart from the statute, they must prove that the defendant himself owes a duty of care to the plaintiffs and has failed in discharging that duty."

[11] Following the Federal Tort Claims Act, 1946, of the Federal legislature of the U.S.A.

[12] Crown Proceedings Act, 1947 (Commencement) Order, 1947, S.R. & O. 1947 No. 2527, made under s. 54 (2) of the Act.

[13] (1865), 6 B. & S. 257.

[14] *A.-G.* v. *De Keyser's Royal Hotel, Ltd.,* [1920] A.C. 508.

[15] Crown Proceedings Act, 1947, Schedule 1, para. 2. This does not apply, however, to proceedings by way of petition of right under the Colonial Stock Act, 1877; see *Franklin v. R.,* [1973] 3 All E.R. 869.

before 1948. As a general rule this means that the Crown is liable for breach of contract in circumstances where any other defendant would be liable according to the ordinary law. However, the following special defences or arguments had been raised in connection with proceedings by way of petition of right during the nineteenth and twentieth centuries, and may therefore still be important even since the coming into operation of the Act of 1947:

(i) It has been suggested that proceedings cannot be brought against the Crown for breach of contract where enforcement of the contract would have the effect of acting as a fetter on the Royal Prerogative. Put in another way, it is argued that the executive, in the interests of the nation, must in certain (undefined) circumstances retain the right to change its mind and may not be hindered by contractual obligations. This theory is said to have originated in *Rederiaktiebolaget Amphitrite* v. *R.*[16] where an arrangement entered into between the Swedish owners of a ship and the British Legation at Stockholm, was subsequently repudiated by the home Government. The Legation had given an undertaking that the ship would be cleared on arrival in England (under the special war-time conditions then prevailing) if she carried more than 60 per cent approved goods as cargo. The ship on arrival in England (on the second occasion), having sailed in reliance on this assurance, was then detained by the Government. Proceedings on a petition of right based on breach of contract were unsuccessful, and it was held that an expression of intention to act in a particular manner made on behalf of the Crown could not be made binding on the Government. The reasoning in this case has not been applied expressly in any subsequent cases in this country[17] and the alleged principle of "executive necessity" as a special defence for the Crown in such proceedings has been doubted by many writers. The decision can be explained on the grounds, first, that the case arose out of exceptional war-time conditions,[18] and second and more important, that the Crown did not intend to make a binding promise, but only expressed its future intentions, which in the event were subsequently altered. In such circumstances there could be no contract at all, as was said by DENNING, J. (as he then was), in *Robertson* v. *Minister of Pensions*[19] (to which we return later on another point[20]). In the same case the learned judge also said (*ibid.*, at p. 770), in reply to the argument that the *Amphitrite* case was an authority for executive necessity being recognised as a special defence in breach of contract:

> "In my opinion the defence of executive necessity is of limited scope. It only avails the Crown where there is an implied term to the effect, or that is the true meaning of the contract."

This argument is not, however, convincing, for there was an express clause in this "contract", and it is difficult to imply a term into a

---

16 [1921] 3 K.B. 500; on this topic, see the careful analysis in *The Contracts of Public Authorities*, by J. D. B. Mitchell, at pp. 27 *et seq.*

17 But see the Rhodesian case of *Waterfalls Town Management Board* v. *Minister of Housing*, [1956] R. & N. 691, where the argument of the *Amphitrite* case was followed *obiter*.

18 There is little justification in the judgment for this view: see Mitchell, *op. cit.*, p. 55.

19 [1948] 2 All E.R. 767; [1949] 1 K.B. 227.

20 Below, p. 293.

contract contradictory to an express term.[1] The absence of any intention to enter into contractual relations is perhaps a better explanation of the *Amphitrite* decision.

In a later case[2] the Crown had leased certain property for twenty-five years, and during the continuance of the lease another Crown department had requisitioned the premises under emergency powers; it was argued on behalf of the tenant that the requisitioning amounted to a breach of the covenant for quiet enjoyment implied in the lease. It was held by the Court of Appeal that no such covenant should be implied which would limit the Crown's future proper exercise of its powers and duties under statute. However, the effect of an express covenant in such a case was left undecided and the general principle of the effect of executive powers exercised under the prerogative (and not derived from statute) was not relevant. In *Reilly* v. *R.*,[3] a barrister who had a contract of employment for a particular purpose with the Government of Canada was not allowed to recover damages when the office was abolished by statute. This decision could be used as an illustration of the so-called *Amphitrite* principle, in that a contract cannot operate as a fetter on the freedom of the executive to introduce legislation in Parliament, but this was not the basis of the decision and the Judicial Committee based their conclusions on the simple principle that[4]:

> "If further performance of a contract becomes impossible by legislation having that effect the contract is discharged."

It is therefore by no means clear that the doctrine of "executive necessity" as a defence to an action for breach of contract by the Crown is acceptable at the present time, unless it is specifically made a term of the contract.

(ii) Contracts of employment with the Crown seem to be in a special position[5]; even an express term in a contract of service with a servant of the Crown cannot oust the Crown's common law right to dismiss the servant at pleasure, without giving rise to any action for breach of contract.[6]

> "Even if the Secretary of State purported to contract with the claimant, he could not in my opinion limit the powers of the Crown to dismiss at pleasure."[7]

This seems to mean that the prerogative in this respect can never be cut down otherwise than under the clear terms of a statute, however valiantly the civil servant plaintiff endeavours to establish some special exception from the general rule in the particular case.

---

[1] See Professor Hogg's interesting discussion of this problem in his comparative study, *Liability of the Crown*, at p. 129 *et seq.* He suggests that the Crown should be entitled to "break" a contract (in the sense that no injunction or other remedy should lie so as to prevent its breach, but that in such a case the Crown should be liable to pay damages to any party injured.

[2] *Crown Lands Commissioners* v. *Page*, [1960] 2 All E.R. 726; [1960] 2 Q.B. 274.

[3] [1934] A.C. 176.

[4] *Ibid.*, at p. 180.

[5] See also Chapter II, *ante*, p. 36.

[6] *Riordan* v. *War Office*, [1959] 3 All E.R. 552; [1959] 1 W.L.R. 1046.

[7] *Per* Lord GODDARD, in *Terrell* v. *Secretary of State for the Colonies*, [1953] 2 All E.R. 490, at p. 496; [1953] 2 Q.B. 482; *ante*, p. 36.

(iii) It is also sometimes argued[8] that the Crown cannot by contract become liable for the payment of money without Parliamentary sanction—a principle said to have been established by *Churchward* v. *R.*[9] It is doubtful whether such an artificial principle would be accepted by the courts today unless a term to that effect could be read into the contract in the particular case.[10]

(iv) The power of the Crown to bind itself by contractual obligations seems also to be incapable of being fettered in a respect common to all governmental agencies vested with discretionary powers under statute or (in the case of the Crown) by virtue of the Royal Prerogative. If a public body has been entrusted with powers and duties expressly or implicitly conferred for specific public purposes, that body cannot divest itself of its discretion by contractual obligations[11]; in other words, a government agency cannot bind itself by contract to exercise a statutory discretion in favour of (or against) a particular person. Thus, in *Wm. Cory & Son* v. *City of London*,[12] it was sought to imply into a contract made by the City of London a term which would have had the effect of preventing that Corporation from subsequently making certain public health byelaws which they were under a statutory duty to make (though possibly not in the particular form chosen); it was held that no such term could be implied into the contract and that if the contract had contained an express term to the like effect, it would have been *ultra vires* the Corporation, and therefore void. It seems that the principle applies also to the Crown[13] although this is not a logical explanation of the *Amphitrite* case.[14]

(v) Further, the Crown cannot be sued in order to recover money received by or on behalf of the Crown from a foreign power under treaty rights, or as "reparations" as a consequence of warlike operations, whereby injuries have been sustained by or occasioned to the claimant, either alone or in common with others of Her Majesty's subjects. If a subject considers he may be one of the persons so injured, his claim for redress against the Crown or to recover some part of the moneys which the Crown has so received, is not one which will be recognised by the courts, as an action will lie neither in tort nor on any contractual concept; a petition of right would not have lain before 1948, and therefore no action in contract can now be brought against the Crown in respect

---

[8] See, *e.g.*, Appendix to Dicey's *Law of the Constitution*, 9th Edn., at p. 528, and Anson, *Law and Custom of the Constitution*, 4th Edn., Vol. II, Part II, at p. 184.

[9] (1865), L.R., 1 Q.B. 173.

[10] See Mitchell, *op. cit.*, at pp. 71–2.

[11] See *ante*, p. 277, and *post*, p. 294. The general principle was accepted without argument in *re Staines U.D.C.'s Agreement, Triggs* v. *Staines U.D.C.*, [1968] 2 All E.R. 1; [1969] 1 Ch. 10.

[12] [1951] 2 All E.R. 85; [1951] 2 K.B. 476, and see also the planning case of *Southend-on-Sea Corpn.* v. *Hodgson*, [1961] 2 All E.R. 46; [1962] 1 Q.B. 416.

[13] As is suggested by *Birkdale District Electric Supply Co.* v. *Southport Corpn.*, [1926] A.C. 355 and confirmed in *Crown Lands* v. *Page* (*ante*).

[14] Another example of the same principle is to be seen in the town and county planning case of *Stringer* v. *Minister of Housing and Local Government*, [1971] 1 All E.R. 65; [1970] 1 W.L.R. 1281. See also Mitchell, *op. cit.*, p. 57, and Hogg, *op. cit.*, p. 136.

thereof: *Rustomjee* v. *R.*[15] In these circumstances, an aggrieved subject must be content with such other remedies as may be open to him, *e.g.*, by representations in Parliament or under the Foreign Compensation Acts, 1950 and 1969.

By the nature of things, a contract with the Crown will be entered into on behalf of the Crown by a Crown servant, except in the occasional case where the Sovereign may enter into a contract in her personal capacity. A Crown servant acting within the scope of his authority will make the Crown liable, even if he acts in his own name,[16] and such a servant will not normally be personally liable on the contract even if he has warranted mistakenly that he had authority to enter into the contract in question.[17] A Crown servant who enters into a contract on behalf of the Crown will, however, make himself liable on the contract if he expressly so provides or the circumstances are such that the court will infer an intention to be bound.[18]

Subject to the foregoing[19] however, there is no special law relating to Government contracts in this country; their interpretation and enforceability is governed by the ordinary rules of the law of contract as between subjects. Here the concept of the "administrative contract" is unknown. In France, on the other hand, where such matters would normally fall to be litigated before the local administrative courts or the *Conseil d'État*, special considerations of what an English lawyer would call "public policy" are applied to the implementation of the terms of the contract in particular circumstances. Thus, in a case decided in 1916[20] a commercial company had entered into a contract with the local commune for the supply of gas, at a prescribed maximum price. As a consequence of the outbreak of war and the occupation of the French coalfields by the enemy, the cost of producing the gas very greatly increased, and the company could not afford to sell gas within the prescribed maximum price, without going into liquidation. The *Conseil d'État* held that the commune had to indemnify the company against their increased costs, as otherwise there would have been no public gas supplies at all, which would have resulted in "disastrous consequences for the inhabitants" of the commune. This doctrine of an implied term (*imprévision*) in an administrative contract is unknown to English law—perhaps because matters of vital public concern, such as the supply of gas or electricity, are not left entirely to private contracts, but are regulated to a greater or lesser extent, especially in times of emergency, by statute. It is really somewhat anomalous that the relationship between (for example) a gas or electricity consumer and the Board responsible for supply should appear to be governed by the private law of contract. In practice, the consumer has to accept the

---

[15] See Mitchell, *op. cit.*, p. 57.

[16] (1876), 2 Q.B.D. 69.

[17] *Gidley* v. *Lord Palmerston* (1822), 3 Brod. & B. 275.

[18] *Macbeath* v. *Haldimand* (1786), 1 Term Rep. 172, and see Chapter II, *ante*, p. 36. *International Ry. Co.* v. *Niagara Parks Commission*, [1941] 2 All E.R. 456; [1941] A.C. 328; *Samuel Bros. Ltd.* v. *Whetherly*, [1908] 1 K.B. 184.

[19] And subject to a few special rules about contracts to which a local authority are a party; see *post*, p. 283.

[20] *Gaz de Bordeaux*, discussed in Waline, *Droit Administratif*, 8th Edn., at p. 216, and see Brown and Garner, *French Administrative Law*, 2nd Edn. Chapter VIII.

standard form of contract, and in many respects he will be subjected to regulations made under statutory authority, which will in some measure regulate his legal liabilities as soon as he has "voluntarily" entered into the contract to (*e.g.*) take a supply of electricity from the Board.[1]

(b) Liability of the Crown in quasi-contract.—The Crown Proceedings Act, 1947, is silent on the liability of the Crown in proceedings in quasi-contract, and therefore the extent of such liability can be measured only by reference to the extent of liability before the Act, by the procedure by way of petition of right. It seems clear that money paid to the Crown under a mistake of fact[2] was recoverable by way of petition of right, and so was money paid under improper pressure, as, for example, where a fee or a licence duty was demanded by a Government Department without any or sufficient statutory sanction.[3] It also seems to follow from *Feather* v. *R.*[4] that a petition of right could have been brought against the Crown to recover money held to the plaintiff's use, and in *A.-G.* v. *De Keyser's Royal Hotel, Ltd.*[5] Viscount DUNEDIN went so far as to say that a petition of right could be brought whenever "in consequence of what has been legally done any resulting obligation emerges", although he was there discussing a case involving the recovery of compensation, and not one of quasi-contract. It would seem therefore that a petition of right would have lain to recover money on a *quantum meruit* (in circumstances where such a claim could be made out in accordance with ordinary common law principles),[6] and that proceedings could now be taken against the Crown in respect of any of the accepted headings of quasi-contractual liability.[7] Proceedings in detinue, normally classified as lying in tort, have been treated in the Courts in this context as if they lay in quasi-contract and therefore

---

[1] Whereas there is but little "special" law of administrative contracts in our legal system, it is clear that a great deal of practice has grown up regulating the placing and terms of government contracts: see *Government Contracts*, bu Volin Turpin (1972).

[2] Money paid under mistake of law is not recoverable, in accordance with the normal rules of the law of quasi-contract. As to the recovery of income tax payments made in mistake of the taxpayer's true position in law, specific provision is made for recovery over a period of six years, by s. 43 of the Taxes Management Act, 1970; and see also *Holborn Viaduct Land Co.* v. *R.* (1887), 52 J.P. 341.

[3] *Brocklebank, Ltd.* v. *R.*, [1925] 1 K.B. 52.

[4] (1865), 6 B. & S. 257.

[5] [1920] A.C. 508, at p. 530; [1920] All E.R. Rep. 80, at p. 88.

[6] See, for example, *Sir Lindsay Parkinson & Co.* v. *Commissioners of Works and Public Buildings*, [1950] 1 All E.R. 208; [1949] 2 K.B. 632. An action in *quantum meruit* was successful against the Crown in the Privy Council case of *R.* v. *Doutrê* (1884), 9 App. Cas. 745.

[7] *Anglo-Saxon Petroleum Co.* v. *Damant*, [1947] 2 All E.R. 465; [1947] K.B. 794, suggests that only the headings of liability listed in *Feather* v. *R.* (*ante*) can be recognised as circumstances in which a petition of right would lie before 1948 and that the Crown could not be made liable in other cases of quasi-contract. In *Feather's case*, it was said that "the only cases in which the petition of right is open to the subject are, where the land or goods or money of a subject have found their way into the possession of the Crown, and the purpose of the petition is to obtain restitution, or if restitution cannot be given, compensation in money or where the claim arises out of a contract, as for goods supplied to the Crown or to the public service". The point was *obiter* only in the *Anglo-Saxon case* and the more general remarks in *De Keyser's case* (*ante*) do not seem to have been cited to the court, and they are not referred to in the judgment. It is submitted that the words quoted from *Feather* v. *R.*, should not now be interpreted as restricting the circumstances in which a petition of right would have lain before 1948.

property wrongfully withheld from a subject by the Crown was held to be recoverable on a petition of right.[8]

(c) Liability of the Crown in tort.—The freedom of the Crown from liability in tort was an application of the principle that "the King can do no wrong"; in fact, if the Crown were liable in tort, the principle would have seemed meaningless.[9] Conditions of modern civilisation and methods of government made the continued application of the old feudal doctrine intolerable, and therefore section 2 of the Crown Proceedings Act, 1947, provided that:

> "(1) Subject to the provisions of this Act, the Crown shall be subject to all those liabilities in tort to which, if it were a private person of full age and capacity, it would be subject:—
>
> (a) in respect of torts committed by its servants or agents;
>
> (b) in respect of any breach of those duties which a person owes to his servants or agents at common law by reason of being their employer; and
>
> (c) in respect of any breach of the duties attaching at common law to the ownership, occupation, possession or control of property;
>
> Provided that no proceedings shall lie against the Crown by virtue of paragraph (a) of this subsection in respect of any act or omission of a servant or agent of the Crown unless the act or omission would apart from the provisions of this Act have given rise to a cause of action in tort against that servant or agent or his estate."

There are therefore now (with breach of statutory duty, mentioned below) four grounds of tortious liability in respect of which the Crown may be made liable. This subsection covers:

(i) Vicarious liability; liability for any tort committed by a Crown servant or agent in circumstances where any other employer would be liable. This of course will include liability for the acts of an independent contractor;

(ii) Employer's liability in respect of torts suffered by the servant or agent at common law; and

(iii) Liability for dangerous premises or dangerous things.

The Act does not affect provisions in other statutes (except in so far as they may be amended by the 1947 Act) which enable certain Ministers of the Crown to sue or be sued in their own name, either in contract or in tort, or indeed in respect of any other head of legal liability, and if a government department can be sued in its own name under the provisions of some statute (*e.g.*, if the servant is an incorporated Department, such as the former Minister of Health[10]), it seems that proceedings in tort would not also lie against the Crown.[11]

---

[8] *A.-G.* v. *De Keyser's Royal Hotel* (*ante*).

[9] See, *e.g.*, *Tobin* v. *R.* (1863), 14 C.B.N.S. 505.

[10] See National Health Service Act, 1946, s. 6 and Ministry of Health Act, 1919. Since the passing of the 1946 Act, the former hospital management committees have been made liable in tort in respect of matters arising out of the administration of the hospitals. Presumably a similar liability will apply to the Area Health Authorities established by the National Health Service Reorganisation Act, 1973; see *post*, p. 323.

[11] A department of the central government may be liable for its own torts in circumstances (if these can be imagined) where it is not acting as Crown agent or servant; see

In order that the Crown may be made liable under this subsection, there must have been a cause of action at common law against the servant or agent. This means that the defences that are open to a Crown servant when sued in respect of some act committed in the course of his employment by the Crown,[12] can be used by the Crown itself when sued under the present section. Thus, the defence of "Act of State" can be used by the Crown—but this must not be equated in any sense to a doctrine of "executive necessity", as will be found in certain other legal systems.[13] "Act of State" in English law has only a very limited application as a defence, as it must arise out of some act performed in the course of relations with another State, or with subjects of another State not within allegiance to the Crown (*i.e.*, outside the realm).[14] The defence of Act of State may also be pleaded in answer to a claim arising out of treaty rights,[15] and neither the Crown nor an officer of the Crown can be sued by any person who is not a British subject in respect of any injuries inflicted outside the realm. Act of State is, however, no defence as against a British subject or person within the Crown's allegiance.[16] It has also been held that detention of an enemy alien within the realm is an act of state in respect of which no action will lie, and no proceedings can be brought by way of *habeas corpus*.[17] The power to deport an alien is similarly not justiciable by the courts, but this depends on the terms of the statute and there is now a right of appeal against an order made by the Secretary of State to the Immigration Appeal Tribunal.[18]

Liability of the Crown in respect of the acts of an agent, an "independent contractor", to use the term commonly employed in the law of tort, causes no difficulty: the Crown is liable on the same grounds as any other principal. In other cases the person by whose hand the tort was committed must be an agent or servant of the Crown.

> "It may be that the grant of any substantial independent discretion takes an officer out of the category of servants of the Crown".[19]

Even if the actual tortfeasor is shown to be a Crown servant or agent the Crown is not necessarily liable in respect of his acts or omissions. The Crown will be so liable only if the particular "officer"[20] is one who

---

the remarks made in *Mackenzie-Kennedy* v. *Air Council*, [1927] 2 K.B. 517, where the theory was accepted, but the claim was unsuccessful on the facts. Section 2 (3) of the 1947 Act seems to contemplate that this may still be possible.

[12] The liability of civil servants for breach of contract is discussed, *ante*, p. 36.

[13] In particular, it is narrower than the "acte de gouvernement" of the French *droit administratif*.

[14] See, for example, the well-known case of *Buron* v. *Denman* (1848), 2 Exch. 167.

[15] *Rustomjee* v. *R.* (*ante*).

[16] "I am of opinion that a British subject—at least if he is also a citizen of the United Kingdom and colonies—can never be deprived of his legal right to redress by any assertion by the Crown or decision of the court that the acts of which he complains were acts of state": *per* Lord REID in *A.-G.* v. *Nissan*, [1969] 1 All E.R. 629, at p. 639.

[17] *R.* v. *Bottrill, ex parte Kuechenmeister*, [1947] K.B. 41.

[18] *R.* v. *Leman Street Police Station Inspector, ex parte Venicoff*, [1920] 3 K.B. 72; *R.* v. *Brixton Prison (Governor), ex parte Soblen*, [1962] 3 All E.R. 641; [1963] 2 Q.B. 243; Immigration Act, 1971, s. 15, and *ante*, p. 263.

[19] *Per* Lord REID in *Bank voor Handel en Sheepvaart N.V.* v. *Administrator of Hungarian Property*, [1954] 1 All E.R. 969; [1954] A.C. 584, at p. 616.

[20] A term which is defined in s. 38 (2) of the 1947 Act, and includes a Minister of the Crown.

was appointed by the Crown directly or indirectly, and was paid at the material time in respect of his duties wholly out of the Consolidated Fund, the Road Fund, or some other fund certified by the Treasury for the purposes of the section.[1] This provision is not really of great importance in the case of a civil servant, as all Central Government expenditure must be met from the Consolidated Fund in the ordinary way, under the authority of statute. It certainly does not mean that the salary of the particular officer concerned must be charged direct on the Consolidated Fund, as are the salaries of the Judges of the Supreme Court.[2] The real importance of the provision is, however, that it excludes from any question of Crown liability action taken by the officers or servants of a statutory corporation, such as the British Railways Board,[3] even if the particular corporation concerned is acting as agent for the Crown.[4] The subsection also has the effect of confirming the principle that the Crown will not be held liable for the torts of police officers who are paid out of local funds.[5] We shall see later that the police paymasters, the local authorities, also are not directly responsible in tort for the acts of officers paid by them, although the chief constables are now so responsible.[6] There is nothing in the statute increasing the liability of individual Crown servants, and therefore the rule that a superior civil servant is not liable for the torts of a junior in his Department, as both are equally servants of the Crown and the senior is in no sense the employer of the junior, is still good law.[7] The restrictive effect of section 2 (6) applies only to torts within section 2, and not, for example, to liability under section 3. This latter section makes special provision in respect of liability of the Crown for breaches of patent rights, infringements of registered trade marks or infringements of copyright.

The Crown Proceedings Act, 1947 does not abridge the prerogative or statutory powers of the Crown[8] nor does it make Her Majesty liable to be sued in tort in Her private capacity,[9] but it is also provided[10] that the Crown will be liable in respect of a breach of a statutory duty, as it would be subject "if it were a private person of full age and capacity",[11] *provided* the duty is one which is binding on persons other than the Crown or Crown officers alone. The statutory duty must also be one which gives

---

[1] Section 2 (6) of the 1947 Act.
[2] See Chapter II, *ante*, p. 40.
[3] *Tamlin* v. *Hannaford*, [1949] 2 All E.R. 327; [1950] 1 K.B. 18.
[4] Such as, for example, the Area Health Authorities, which may be required by a Regional Health Authority to perform such functions as that authority may direct; and the Regional Health Authority is required to perform, on behalf of the Secretary of State, such functions as he may direct: National Health Service Reorganisation Act, 1973, s. 7.
[5] Special provisions are made for the Metropolitan Police Force, the Receiver being specially constituted by statute.
[6] *Fisher* v. *Oldham Corpn.*, [1930] 2 K.B. 364, and Chapter XVI, *post*, p. 442.
[7] *Bainbridge* v. *Postmaster General*, [1906] 1 K.B. 178.
[8] 1947 Act, s. 11.
[9] The Crown Proceedings Act, 1947, s. 40 (1).
[10] *Ibid.*, s. 2 (2).
[11] Does this provision extend the Crown liability under statutes which are not expressly made binding on the Crown? It could be argued that this subsection is wide enough to overrule the normal presumption in favour of the Crown.

rise to an action in tort in accordance with the ordinary principles of the law of tort,

> "while discharging or purporting to discharge any responsibilities of a judicial nature vested in him, or any responsibilities which he has in connection with the execution of judicial process".[12]

The expression "responsibilities of a judicial nature" is not defined in this subsection, and therefore it is not at once clear whether it protects the Crown from proceedings arising out of the acts of members of administrative tribunals paid and appointed by or on behalf of the Crown, such as the Lands Tribunals or the Transport Tribunal. In *Royal Aquarium and Summer and Winter Garden Socy.* v. *Parkinson*[13] the Court had to consider whether proceedings at a meeting of a committee of the London County Council convened to determine what music and dancing licences should be granted (a jurisdiction transferred by the Local Government Act, 1888, from the local justices to the County Council), were "judicial proceedings", so that absolute privilege could be claimed in respect of remarks made thereat in proceedings taken for defamation. LOPES, L.J., said (at p. 452):

> "The word 'judicial' has two meanings. It may refer to the discharge of duties exercisable by a judge or justices in court, or to administrative duties which need not be performed in court, but in respect of which it is necessary to bring to bear a judicial mind—that is, a mind to determine what is fair and just in respect of the matters under consideration. Justices, for instance, act judicially when administering the law in court, and they also act judicially when determining in their private room what is right and fair in some administrative matter before them, as, for instance, levying a rate."

Nothing but administrative business was transferred by the statute to the Council in this case, and applications for licences did not have to be determined judicially; therefore it was held that the proceedings were not an occasion to which absolute privilege would apply.

Following this reasoning, it seems that proceedings before the Lands Tribunal or the Transport Tribunal might be "judicial proceedings" within the present subsection, and so might proceedings before other administrative tribunals, or even before statutory inquiries[14]; therefore the section probably extends Crown immunity to such proceedings. It also seems that administrative tribunals or inquiries may be judicial proceedings in respect of which absolute privilege would attach in a case of defamation; in *Addis* v. *Crocker*,[15] GORMAN, J., cited Lord ESHER, M.R., in the *Royal Aquarium* case (*ante*), who said:

> "The privilege applies wherever there is an authorised inquiry which, though not before a court of justice, is before a tribunal which has similar attributes;"

and held that privilege attached to the proceedings of the disciplinary

---

[12] *Ibid.*, s. 2(5).
[13] [1892] 1 Q.B. 431.
[14] See Chapter VII, *ante*, p. 197.
[15] [1959] 2 All E.R. 773, [1960] 1 Q.B. 87; affirmed, [1960] 2 All E.R. 629; [1961] 1 Q.B. 11, and see Chapter VII, *ante*, p. 214.

committee of the Law Society constituted under section 46 of the Solicitors Act, 1957. However, a tribunal may be regarded as acting judicially for one purpose and not for another, and therefore a decision on what is "judicial" for the purposes of *certiorari* or prohibition will not necessarily be conclusive on the question of Crown privilege.[16] It is, however, clear that the Crown will not be liable for the ministerial acts of those judges who are not Crown servants (*e.g.*, unpaid magistrates or stipendiary magistrates).

Section 9 of the 1947 Act made special provision for limited liability only of the Crown in respect of registered inland postal packets and excluded liability altogether in connection with ordinary letters and parcels. However, the Post Office is now no longer a department of the Central government but an independent public corporation, although a similar exclusion of liability in tort has been given to the Post Office in its new guise.[17]

Section 10 of the 1947 Act makes special provision for members of the Armed Forces of the Crown. By this section it is provided that a member of the Armed Forces cannot sue the Crown *or* another member of those Forces in respect of torts occasioned whilst on service, in so far as they relate to personal injuries or death. In such a case the appropriate Minister must certify that the duty in the course of which the injury was sustained was one which would be recognised as being attributable to service for the purposes of an award of compensation under Royal Warrant or some other similar provision. If these conditions are satisfied, the Crown will not be liable, even if it eventually appears that, under the terms of the Royal Warrant no compensation or pension is payable in the particular circumstances.[18] In this respect the privileges of the Crown have been widened, not restricted, by the Act of 1947, for it is not even possible to sue the individual member of the Armed Forces responsible for the injury.[19]

Section 10—and indeed any of the provisions of the Act—does not affect

> ". . . any proceedings of the Crown otherwise than in right of His Majesty's Government in the United Kingdom."[20]

Further, by section 30 (2), it is provided that nothing in the Act shall operate to prejudice the right of the Crown to rely on the law relating to the limitation of time for bringing proceedings against public authorities. This is a reference to the former provisions of the Public Authorities Protection Act, 1893, and of the Limitation Act, 1939, which prescribed short periods of limitation for such proceedings, but the subsection is now virtually of no effect, as the general law on the subject has been amended by the Law Reform (Limitation of Actions, &c.) Act,

---

[16] See Professor de Smith, *Judicial Review of Administrative Action*, 3rd Edn., especially at p. 65, where it is suggested (footnote) that "Judicial" as used in s. 2 (5) will be construed widely.

[17] Post Office Act, 1969, s. 29.

[18] *Adams* v. *War Office*, [1955] 3 All E.R. 245; [1955] 1 W.L.R. 1116.

[19] See Hanbury at (1952), 68 L.Q.R. 178.

[20] 1947 Act, s. 40 (2) (c).

1954 (which expressly binds the Crown: see s. 5 (a) thereof), and which puts public authorities on the same level as private individuals in this matter.

If a particular action in tort cannot be brought within one or other of the headings of liability provided for in the Act of 1947, those proceedings cannot be brought against the Crown, although it may be possible to make a Government Department the defendant in its own right by virtue of some special statute, and not as agent or employee for the Crown. Liability may attach to the Crown under section 2 (2) of the 1947 Act in relation to dangerous premises, although such liability cannot exceed the limitations of section 2 (2). The Crown is expressly bound by the Law Reform (Limitation of Actions, &c.) Act, 1954, but as there is no mention of the Crown in the Defamation Act, 1952, it seems that that Act does not bind the Crown or affect the liability of the Crown in respect of defamatory words spoken by a servant of the Crown acting in the course of his employment as such.[1]

All the ordinary defences in tort are open to the Crown, and the Crown is entitled to indemnity and contribution from a joint tortfeasor; the provisions of the Law Reform (Contributory Negligence) Act, 1945, are also binding on the Crown (1947 Act, section 4). The Crown is also bound by the Law Reform (Personal Injuries) Act, 1948, and therefore it cannot use the old common law defence of common employment. However, subject to the 1947 Act, the principle that "The King can do no wrong", is still part of the law of England, and section 2 has restored the old adage to its original meaning, in that the Sovereign in Her personal capacity is now completely free from liability in tort.

3. PROCEEDINGS AGAINST THE CROWN

In cases where the Crown may be sued under one or other heading of liability by virtue of the Act of 1947, process may be taken out against one of several Departments, as shown on a list published from time to time by the Treasury under section 17 of the Act; if no Department on that list is appropriate in the particular circumstances, or if the party commencing the proceedings has a "reasonable doubt" whether any and if so which of the listed Departments is appropriate, process may be taken against the Attorney-General.[2]

There are a number of special rules applicable to Crown proceedings, some of which are contained in the Act of 1947, and others are the result of the common law. These may be summarised as follows:

(i) Prerogative orders of *mandamus*, *certiorari* or prohibition will not lie against the Crown, as the Crown cannot sue itself. Similarly, the Court will not grant an injunction against the Crown, nor against a Minister of the Crown when he is carrying out functions conferred on

---

[1] See Treitel, "Crown Proceedings: some Recent Developments" [1957] P.L. 321, extracts from which will be found in Yardley, *A Source Book of English Administrative Law*, 2nd edn. at pp. 323 *et seq.* The Contracts of Employment Act, 1972, also does not bind the Crown.

[2] 1947 Act, s. 17 (1).

him by statute as a representative or as an officer of the Crown.[3] On the other hand, in *Harper* v. *Secretary of State for the Home Department*[4] the Court of Appeal considered an application for an injunction to restrain the Home Secretary from presenting for her Majesty's approval a scheme which the lower court had held to be *ultra vires*. In the court below in *Harper's* case, an injunction had apparently (see *Merricks*' case, at p. 455) been granted against the Home Secretary acting in a personal capacity; it is difficult to understand this reasoning, but the Court of Appeal discharged the injunction on the ground that the scheme was not *ultra vires*, whilst doubting the power to grant an injunction against an officer of the Crown. Where a discretion is conferred on a Minister of the Crown *eo nomine*, there is no difficulty; thus, in *Padfield* v. *Minister of Agriculture, Fisheries and Food*,[5] a *mandamus* was granted against the Minister directing him to exercise a discretion vested in him by statute, in such a way as not to frustrate the objects of the statute.

There is no doubt that the court may make a declaration in proceedings brought against the Crown; this is expressly provided for in section 21 (1) of the 1947 Act. However, this does not mean that in circumstances where, in such proceedings between subjects, the court could grant an interlocutory injunction, it could in similar proceedings brought against the Crown grant an interlocutory declaration.[6] No execution or enforcement of a judgment will lie against the Crown.[7]

(ii) A statute does not bind the Crown unless a clear intention to that effect appears from the statute itself or from the express terms of the Crown Proceedings Act, 1947. This general principle of the common law is preserved by the Crown Proceedings Act, 1947, for by section 40 (2) (f) thereof it is provided:

> "Nothing in this Act shall . . . affect any rules of evidence or any presumption relating to the extent to which the Crown is bound by any Act of Parliament."

The general rule was first to be found, according to the editor of Maxwell,[8] in *Willion* v. *Berkley*.[9] On the other hand, where statute covers the same ground as an existing rule of the prerogative, it must be assumed that it was intended that the statute should abridge the prerogative to that extent.[10] By way of modern examples of the general rule, it has been held that Crown property is not subject to the provisions of the Rent Acts,[11] and that Crown property is not bound to contribute to a private

[3] *Per* UPJOHN, J., in *Merricks* v. *Heathcoat-Amory and the Minister of Agriculture, Fisheries and Food*, [1955] 2 All E.R. 453, at p. 456; [1955] Ch. 567. Certainly an injunction would not be granted to interfere with the due process of the prerogative: see *R.* v. *Treasury Lords Commissioners* (1872), L.R., 7 Q.B. 387.

[4] [1955] 1 All E.R. 331; [1955] Ch. 238.

[5] [1968] 1 All E.R. 694; [1968] A.C. 997, and see Chapter VI, *ante*, p. 136.

[6] *Underhill* v. *Minister of Food*, [1950] 1 All E.R. 591.

[7] Street, *Governmental Liability*, p. 182.

[8] *Interpretation of Statutes*, 11th Edn., p. 129.

[9] (1561), 1 Plowd. 227. "The King is not generally bound by all statutes in general words unless he is specially named." See also *A.-G.* v. *Donaldson* (1842), 11 L.J. Exch. 338.

[10] This, of course, was the principle applied in *A.-G.* v. *De Keyser's Royal Hotel, Ltd.*, [1920] A.C. 508; [1920] All E.R. Rep. 80, at p. 88.

[11] *London County Territorial & Auxiliary Forces Association* v. *Nichols*, [1948] 2 All E.R. 432; [1949] 1 K.B. 35, and *Wirral Estates, Ltd.* v. *Shaw*, [1932] 2 K.B. 247, but on this point see now s. 4 of the Rent Act, 1968. Hospitals are occupied by Area Health Authorities on the instructions of the Regional Health Authorities and the Secretary of

street works scheme.[12] Many modern administrative statutes make special provision for Crown property, it being assumed that apart therefrom the Crown shall not be bound thereby.[13]

(iii) By common law the Crown has the right of choice of venue, and can always require proceedings to be transferred into the Queen's Bench Division. This privilege is not of any great moment under modern conditions, nor would it often be claimed.

(iv) A limited "privilege" can be claimed in respect of documents; the court can in the public interest refuse to order the production of documents in the course of legal proceedings, whether or not the Crown is a party in those proceedings and whether the proceedings are civil[14] or criminal. The Crown therefore need not in such a case respond to a *subpoena duces tecum*, and it can resist a summons for discovery of documents in the course of litigation, as in either event the legal process may be met by a certificate of the appropriate Minister asking for the court to intervene. This certificate must be signed by the political head of the department of the public service involved; this is a function which strictly cannot be delegated to a civil servant,[15] as the Minister will be personally responsible to Parliament. Formerly the certificate claimed Crown immunity and was accepted without investigation by the court, but this has now been changed, as appears below.

A similar claim can be made in respect of evidence as to facts, although the court will not normally support a claim that a particular witness should not be allowed to give evidence at all. In *Duncan* v. *Cammell Laird & Co., Ltd.* (see *post*), Viscount SIMON, L.C., said:[16]

> "The present opinion is concerned only with the production of documents, but it seems to me that the same principle must also apply to the exclusion of verbal evidence which, if given, would jeopardise the interests of the community."[17]

The decision to claim privilege in the particular case is that of the Minister, but the decision whether or not an order for disclosure should be granted is a matter for the court. The leading case on the subject was, until 1968, *Duncan* v. *Cammell Laird & Co., Ltd.*,[18] which

State on behalf of the Crown, and they are therefore "occupied for the public services of the Crown", and so are exempt from the controls of the Public Health Act, 1936, relating to the commission of public nuisances, in particular the emission of smoke; *Nottingham No. 1 Area Hospital Management Committee* v. *Owen*, [1957] 3 All E.R. 358; [1958] 1 Q.B. 50 (and see now the similar provisions in the Clean Air Act, 1956).

[12] *Hornsey U.D.C.* v. *Hennell*, [1902] 2 K.B. 73.

[13] See, for example, s. 22 of the Clean Air Act, 1956, applying special restrictions on Crown premises instead of the substantive provisions of the statute. "Crown Premises" is defined in some detail, the provisions of the section being also applied to premises occupied for the service of a "visiting force" under the Visiting Forces Act, 1952. In the Highways Act, 1959, certain sections only are said to "bind the Crown": see s. 287 thereof.

[14] *Ellis* v. *Home Office*, [1953] 2 All E.R. 149; [1953] 2 Q.B. 135.

[15] *Gain* v. *Gain*. [1962] 1 All E.R. 63; [1961] 1 W.L.R. 1469.

[16] [1942] 1 All E.R. 587, at p. 595.

[17] This was followed in *Broome* v. *Broome* (*Edmundson cited*), [1955] 1 All E.R. 201; [1955] P. 190, and applied in *Gain* v. *Gain* (*ante*, at p. 64), where WRANGHAM, J., was pressed to permit a witness to give oral evidence as to the contents of documents in respect of which privilege was claimed: "If it jeopardises the interests of the community to disclose the documents it must equally jeopardise the interests of the community to allow oral evidence which explicitly or implicitly discloses the contents of those documents".

[18] [1942] 1 All E.R. 587; [1942] A.C. 624.

concerned proceedings arising out of the loss of the submarine *Thetis* in Liverpool Bay just before the outbreak of the last war. In order to establish liability against the Government contractors, the plaintiffs asked for production of certain documents, including the contract and blueprints for the construction of the vessel; the Crown claimed privilege. It was held by the House of Lords that such an objection, when formally and validly taken, must be accepted by the court as conclusive, and that the court is not entitled to see the papers in question to ascertain whether the claim of privilege is or is not justified. Viscount SIMON also pointed out (at p. 595):

> "The withholding of documents on the ground that their publication would be contrary to the public interest, is not properly to be regarded as a branch of the law of privilege connected with discovery. 'Crown privilege' is for this reason not a happy expression. Privilege, in relation to discovery, is for the protection of the litigant and could be waived by him. The rule that the interest of the State must not be put in jeopardy by producing documents which would injure it is a principle to be observed in administering justice, quite unconnected with the interests or claims of the particular parties in litigation, and, indeed, is a rule upon which the judge should, if necessary, insist, even though no objection is taken at all."

For some thirty years the Courts interpreted *Duncan* v. *Cammell Laird* as establishing the principle that they must accept a Ministerial certificate claiming privilege, although the courts have always considered themselves entitled to ensure that the Minister himself (or his Parliamentary secretary) had directed his mind to the matter[19] and also that the certificate was in due form.[20] If privilege is claimed in respect of a class of documents, and not just for a single document, the Minister must describe the nature of the class and the reason why the documents should not be disclosed.[1]

This principle that the court could not go behind a Ministerial certificate claiming Crown "privilege" had been taken further in *Auten* v. *Rayner*,[2] in which the court refused to listen to an allegation that the Minister concerned was influenced by a personal bias, or might have been so influenced, in deciding to grant a certificate. The argument of *Ross-Clunis* v. *Papadopoullos*,[3] to the effect that judicial review will be permitted to ascertain whether there are any grounds at all on which a reasonable Minister could have been satisfied in the circumstances,[4] might have been used to support an action for a declaration to the effect that a particular certificate claiming "privilege" was void, but the same argument could certainly not be used to support an application for *certiorari* to quash a Ministerial certificate in such a case, as the process of issuing a certificate is an executive and not a judicial act.[5]

---

[19] *Re Grosvenor Hotel* (*London*) *Ltd.* (*No.* 1), [1963] 3 All E.R. 426; the judge is entitled in his discretion to adjourn the case to enable the Minister to comply with this requirement: *ibid.* (on appeal) [1964] 1 All E.R. 92; [1964] Ch. 464.

[20] The document must be specified with sufficient particularity: *Merricks* v. *Nott-Bower*, [1964] 1 All E.R. 717; [1965] 1 Q.B. 57.

[1] *Per* Lord DENNING, M.R., in *Re Grosvenor Hotel* (*London*) *Ltd.* (*No.* 2), [1964] 3 All E.R. 354, at p. 362; [1965] Ch. 1210, at p. 1233.

[2] [1958] 3 All E.R. 566; [1958] 1 W.L.R. 1300.

[3] [1958] 2 All E.R. 23; [1958] 1 W.L.R. 546.

[4] Chapter VI, *ante*, p. 163.

[5] See *Duncan's* case, *ante*, and Chapter VI, *ante*, p. 179.

However, in *Conway* v. *Rimmer*,[6] the House of Lords decided that the broad interpretation of *Duncan* v. *Cammell Laird* was wrong, and that the court could overrule a Minister's certificate claiming privilege, at least where the certificate was made on the ground that the document is one of a class that ought not to be produced; although it seems that in a few instances the nature of the documents themselves may be such that production ought to be withheld.[7] In this case a former police officer sued a senior officer in the force for malicious prosecution; it was a material part of his case to prove what had been said about him by the senior officer in certain probationary reports made when the plaintiff was a police officer. The Home Office claimed privilege for this class of document, but the House of Lords held that it was the duty of the courts to examine the documents in question (without their being shown to the parties) and decide whether or not the claim was justified:

> "On the one side there is the public interest to be protected; on the other side of the scales is the interest of the subject who legitimately wants production of some documents, which he believes will support his own or defeat his adversary's case. Both are matters of public interest, for it is also in the public interest that justice should be done between litigating parties by production of all documents which are relevant and for which privilege cannot be claimed under the ordinary rules. They must be weighed in the balance one against the other."[8]

This judgment has now been put into statutory form, for the provisions of the Administration of Justice Act, 1970,[9] enabling a court to order disclosure of documents, etc., apply specifically to the Crown, except that no such order may be made if the court considers "that compliance with the order, if made, would be likely to be injurious to the public interest."[10]

It is clear, therefore, that in relation to all classes of documents, it is a matter for the court to decide whether or not to grant disclosure against the Crown or a public body. It only remains to discuss the circumstances in which an order is likely to be refused. Under the old law, it was argued[11] that there were two different classes of circumstances in which a claim of Crown privilege is justified. First, where the security of the State was involved; these were the circumstances of *Duncan* v. *Cammell Laird, Ltd.* (*ante*), as it was obviously a matter of State security in time of war that blueprints on which the design of many submarines then in service was based should not be disclosed to the enemy. In the second place, Crown privilege has been justified in circumstances where a report has been made by one Crown servant to another in the course of his duties. In such circumstances, it was

---

6 [1968] 1 All E.R. 874; [1968] A.C. 910.

7 Such for example as Cabinet papers: see speech of Lord HODSON at p. 902.

8 *Per* Lord UPJOHN, at p. 914; typical of all the speeches of their Lordships in this case.

9 Administration of Justice Act, 1970, ss. 31–34.

10 *Ibid.*, s. 35.

11 These arguments are clearly put forward in the judgment of Lord NORMAND in the House of Lords in the Scots case of *Glasgow Corpn.* v. *Central Land Board*, 1956 S.L.T. 41 at p. 42. One of the factors persuading the House of Lords in *Conway* v. *Rimmer* to take the line they did, was that this course had already been adopted in Scotland and several Commonwealth jurisdictions.

argued, the report should be treated as confidential if it was prepared under conditions in which the officer making the report expected it to be so treated (for example, where a senior civil servant has made a report on the personal health, conduct or abilities of another); if the report were subsequently to become the subject of examination in a court of law its confidential nature would be destroyed, and in future cases no civil servant would be prepared to write frank and full reports, in case they might subsequently have to be produced in litigation, to the great detriment of the public service of the Crown. It was this latter type of document that was in issue in *Conway* v. *Rimmer*; indeed it can be contended that *Duncan* v. *Cammell Laird* is still good law so far as single documents are concerned where a certificate is given on the grounds of State security.

It had frequently been pointed out before *Conway* v. *Rimmer* that there might be grave risk of injustice if Crown privilege were claimed too freely or lightly. As DEVLIN, J., said in *Ellis* v. *Home Office*,[12] in a case where a claim of Crown privilege was upheld:

> "But before I leave this case I must express, as I have expressed during the hearing of the case, my uneasy feeling that justice may not have been done because the material before me was not complete, and something more than an uneasy feeling that, whether justice has been done or not, it certainly will not appear to have been done."[13]

To a limited extent, the defects of the strict doctrine of Crown privilege had been officially recognised even before *Conway* v. *Rimmer*, and on two occasions the Government of the day stated that privilege would not be claimed in certain defined circumstances. It was announced by the Lord Chancellor in 1956 that H.M. Government would in future not claim Crown privilege in certain circumstances.[14] A somewhat similar statement was made in 1962[15] with regard to the production in civil cases of statements made to the police, which is of course of particular relevance in "running down" actions.

Exemption from disclosure under the 1970 Act could now be claimed "in the public interest" by any public authority, and not only by the Crown or a central government department acting on behalf of the Crown. Formerly, a local authority exercising emergency powers to requisition premises on behalf of the Crown, was held not entitled to claim Crown privilege,[16] but in a recent case, exemption from disclosure

---

[12] [1953] 2 All E.R. 149; [1953] 2 Q.B. 135.

[13] Other cases concerning the law as it stood before *Conway* v. *Rimmer* are: *Broome* v. *Broome* (*Edmundson cited*), [1955] 1 All E.R. 201; [1955] P. 190; *Re Grosvenor Hotel* (*London*) *Ltd.* (*No.* 1), [1963] 3 All E.R. 426; [1964] Ch. 464; on appeal, [1964] 1 All E.R. 92; [1964] Ch. at p. 475; *Merricks* v. *Nott-Bower*, [1964] 1 All E.R. 717; [1965] 1 Q.B. 57; *Re Grosvenor Hotel* (*London*) *Ltd.* (*No.* 2), [1964] 3 All E.R. 354; [1965] Ch. 1210; *Wednesbury Corpn.* v. *Minister of Housing and Local Government*, [1965] 1 All E.R. 186; [1965] 1 W.L.R. 261. For articles, see 79 L.Q.R. 37, 153, 487; 80 L.Q.R. 24, 156 and [1963] P.L. 405.

[14] 197 H.L. Deb. 741–8, June 6, 1956, and see [1956] P.L. 275.

[15] H.L. Deb., Vol. 237, No. 46, col. 1191.

[16] *Blackpool Corpn.* v. *Locker*, [1948] 1 All E.R. 85; [1948] 1 K.B. 349, in which a local government officer acting under delegated emergency powers on behalf of a central government department was not permitted to claim Crown privilege in respect of documents which it was desired to withhold from production.

was granted to a statutory corporation.[17] Police documents have on several occasions been treated as Crown documents in respect of which privilege may be claimed (on the certificate of the Home Secretary) as was done in *Conway* v. *Rimmer* (*ante*).

(v) An agent of the Crown is not personally liable on any contract entered into by him on behalf of the Crown, and therefore a civil servant cannot be held liable in damages for breach of a warranty of authority in any matter in which he is acting as a Crown agent or servant.[18] This was a principle of the common law and it does not seem to have been affected in any way by the Crown Proceedings Act, 1947.

(vi) It has been suggested that the Crown is not bound by the doctrine of estoppel. Estoppel is a rule whereby a party is precluded from denying the existence of some state of facts which he had previously asserted and on which the other party has relied or is entitled to rely. In this sense the Crown is bound by estoppel.[19] The rule most commonly arises in practice from a representation of fact, made fraudulently or innocently, but which subsequently turns out to be untrue; it may be used as a defence and not as a cause of action. In order that an estoppel may arise, the representation must be clear and unambiguous, there must be an intention that the injured party should act thereon, and there must be a detriment suffered by the party acting thereon as a natural consequence thereof.[20] Estoppel is said to be a rule of evidence and not of law. The principle may be extended to cover statements as to future intention, so that

> "if a man gives a promise or assurance which he intends to be binding on him and to be acted on by the person to whom it is given, then, once it is acted on he is bound by it".[1]

This latter rule, it seems, binds the Crown as it does any other person who may be affected and so may a true estoppel. The doctrine cannot, however, operate so as to override the clear words of a statute, nor does it apply to criminal proceedings.[2] So far as the terms of a statute are concerned, where it is (for example) provided that a certain operation may not be undertaken legally without a licence being first obtained from the appropriate Government Department, an assurance given to an individual by an official in the Department concerned to the effect that no such licence would be necessary in the particular circumstances, could not have the effect of overriding the statute or of legalising the particular operation in the absence of a licence. These were the

---

17 Documents belonging to the Gaming Board, but abstracted improperly from their files, were entitled to privilege when this was claimed in the public interest: *Rogers* v. *Secretary of State for the Home Department*, [1972] 2 All E.R. 1057; [1973] A.C. 388.

18 *Dunn* v. *Macdonald*, [1897] 1 Q.B. 555; *ante*, p. 39.

19 *A.-G. to Prince of Wales* v. *Collom*, [1916] 2 K.B. 193.

20 *Freeman* v. *Cooke* (1848), 2 Exch. 654; *Re Lewis, Lewis* v. *Lewis*, [1904] 2 Ch. 656.

1 *Per* DENNING, J. in *Robertson* v. *Minister of Pensions*, [1948] 2 All E.R. 767, at p. 770; [1949] 1 K.B. 227, at p. 231, referring to his own decision in *Central London Property Trust, Ltd.* v. *High Trees House, Ltd.*, [1947] K.B. 130.

2 *Lund* v. *Thompson*, [1958] 3 All E.R. 356; [1959] 1 Q.B. 283; the Crown cannot be estopped from taking criminal proceedings simply by virtue of a statement to the effect that no proceedings would be taken.

facts and decision of *Howell* v. *Falmouth Boat Construction Co.*,[3] where the House of Lords expressly repudiated a suggestion made by DENNING, L.J., in the Court of Appeal to the effect that it was a rule of law that:

> "Whenever government officers in their dealings with a subject, take on themselves to assume authority in a matter with which the subject is concerned, is entitled to rely on their having the authority which they assume."[4]

Similarly, a local authority or other governmental agency acting under statutory powers cannot utilise the doctrine of estoppel in such a manner as to use a false statement as to the extent of their statutory powers, and thereby obtain powers in excess of those given to them by the statute.[5] The distinction between *Robertson's* case,[6] where a statement made by one Government Department as to the entitlement of the plaintiff to a pension (in circumstances where that department no longer had any jurisdiction) was held to be binding on another department concerned, and the *Falmouth Boat Construction* case seems to be that in the former case the representation on which the plaintiff relied was as to a matter of fact (the plaintiff would not have been able to bring an action to recover his pension, and the proceedings were by way of appeal from a decision of the Pensions Appeal Tribunal), but in the latter case the representation was as to a matter of law, to which the doctrine of estoppel cannot apply.

It is clear that the doctrine of estoppel cannot be used against (or in favour of) the administration

> "so as to give *de facto* validity to *ultra vires* administrative acts".[7]

Faulty advice on a matter of law given by a Crown servant[8] cannot be allowed to alter the legal position, even to the detriment of the Crown or any other government agency, such as a local authority,[9] but similar faulty advice as to the nature of future executive action may be held binding on the Crown (apart from criminal proceedings),[10] and may prevent an authority from pleading a technical point in legal proceedings.[11]

---

[3] [1951] 2 All E.R. 278; [1951] A.C. 837, and see also *Jackson Stansfield & Sons* v. *Butterworth*, [1948] 2 All E.R. 558.

[4] [1950] 1 All E.R. 538, at p. 542; [1950] 2 K.B. 16, at p. 25.

[5] *Canterbury Corpn.* v. *Cooper* (1909), 100 L.T. 597, and *Rhyl U.D.C.* v. *Rhyl Amusements, Ltd.*, [1959] 1 All E.R. 257; [1959] 1 W.L.R. 465. In *Ministry of Agriculture and Fisheries* v. *Hunkin* (unreported, but cited in *Ministry of Agriculture* v. *Matthews*, [1949] 2 All E.R. 724, at p. 729); [1950] 1 K.B. 148, Lord GREENE, M.R., said "The power given to an authority under a statute is limited to the four corners of the power given. It would entirely destroy the whole doctrine of *ultra vires* if it was possible for the donee of a statutory power to extend his power by effecting an estoppel."

[6] *Ante*, p. 277.

[7] Schwartz, *An Introduction to American Administrative Law*, at p. 233.

[8] The same principle was applied in the United States in *Federal Crop Insurance Corpn.* v. *Merrill* 332 U.S. 380 (1947), cited by Schwartz, *op. cit.* at p. 232.

[9] See *Southend-on-Sea Corpn.* v. *Hodgson*, [1961] 2 All E.R. 46; [1962] 1 Q.B. 416, where an opinion of an officer of the local authority as to the legal position of the defendant was held to be no bar to the authority taking an opposite view.

[10] As in *Re War Damage Act 1943, Re 56, Denton Road, Twickenham, Middlesex*, [1952] 2 All E.R. 799.

[11] *Re L(A.C.)* (*an infant*), [1971] 3 All E.R. 743, where a local authority had led a party to child care proceedings to assume that a written objection to a resolution of the local authority was not necessary. Actually the statute required such a notice to be given within a prescribed time; the court held that in these circumstances the local authority would be estopped from alleging that no written objection had been issued in time. See also *Lever (Finance), Ltd.* v. *Westminster Corporation*, [1970] 3 All E.R. 496.

(vii) The Crown cannot normally sue itself; but this does not mean that proceedings cannot be brought on behalf of the Crown in the right of one of Her Majesty's Governments in the Commonwealth against the Crown in the right of another of such governments.[12]

(viii) Special rules apply to proceedings against the Crown instituted in a County Court.[13] The plaint note, which is the originating process in all county court proceedings, does not have to specify any date of hearing, and a summons is not issued until the Crown has had an opportunity of considering whether the particulars accompanying the plaint note contain sufficient details. The summary County Court procedure by way of a default action cannot be brought against the Crown.

(ix) Finally it may be worth noting that the effect of the legal aid scheme under the Legal Aid and Advice Act, 1949, has been to remove the financial deterrent from the commencement of proceedings against the Crown. Litigants may be able to obtain a legal aid certificate, and are no longer intimidated by the extent of the financial recourses of their potential adversary.

4. PROCEEDINGS INSTITUTED BY THE CROWN

Except for the Crown's privilege as to choice of venue and the other procedural matters above discussed, the Crown as plaintiff is in much the same position as any other litigant—save, of course, for its financial resources. It has been suggested that the Crown cannot sustain an action for damages *per quod servitium amisit* (*i.e.*, on the grounds that the defendant has by his conduct injured the plaintiff's servant and so deprived the plaintiff of his services), because there is no contract of service between the Crown and its employees (military or civilian), but this does not seem correct reasoning, in view of such cases as *Terrell* v. *Secretary of State for the Colonies*,[14] from which it is reasonably clear that there is a contract between the Crown and its employees, though subject to a clause that the servant shall be dismissable at pleasure.[15] In the leading case of *A.-G. for New South Wales* v. *Perpetual Trustee Co.*,[16] which arose out of injuries sustained by a police constable, whereby the Crown became liable to pay the injured constable a pension, it was held by the Privy Council that the action *per quod servitium amisit* would not lie, as it had originated in the context of domestic relations and could not now be extended to "public relations". Further, in *Inland Revenue Commissioners* v. *Hambrook*,[17] a case arising out of injuries sustained by a civil servant as a consequence whereof the Crown had paid him *ex gratia* a matter of some nine months' sick pay, it was held that the action would not lie at the suit of the Crown because the

---

[12] See such cases as *Dominion of Canada* v. *Province of Ontario*, [1910] A.C. 637 and Jennings, *Constitutional Laws of the British Commonwealth*, 1957 Edn., Vol. I, at p. 22.
[13] Crown Proceedings Act, 1947, s. 15; and see the County Court (Crown Proceedings) Rules, 1947 (C.C. Rules, Order 46, r. 13).
[14] [1953] 2 All E.R. 490; [1953] 2 Q.B. 482, and see Chapter II, p. 36.
[15] *Riordan* v. *War Office*, [1959] 3 All E.R. 552; [1959] 1 W.L.R. 1046.
[16] [1955] 1 All E.R. 846; [1955] A.C. 457.
[17] [1956] 1 All E.R. 807.

relationship between the Crown and the civil servant (as with the police constable in the *New South Wales* case) was not the ordinary one of master and domestic servant. Moreover, damage was essential to the cause of action and an act of grace did not amount to damage in law in respect of which the Crown could recover.

5. PROCEEDINGS BY AND AGAINST LOCAL AUTHORITIES

As a general principle of English law, it may be said that a local authority is an independent legal person, as capable of suing and being sued as any other person, and that no special rules apply to legal proceedings in which a local authority may be involved. Since the passing of the Law Reform (Limitation of Actions, &c.) Act, 1954, this statement is more nearly completely correct, as that statute abolished the special limitation periods that could previously have been pleaded in legal proceedings by any "public authority".[18] However, a local authority may have certain special defences in proceedings in tort, and some formal rules apply to contracts made by local authorities. Further, where a local authority has recourse to the courts (usually the magistrates' courts—in which case the proceedings are criminal in form) in order to enforce its administrative decisions, standard procedural rules have to be observed, which do not apply in other contexts.

We shall therefore deal now with the special features of proceedings in which local authorities may be engaged.

(a) Proceedings in tort.—It was sometimes contended[19] that as local authorities, being creatures of statute, were subject to the doctrine of *ultra vires*—in other words, that they could not do anything for which they had no express or implied statutory authority[20]—they could not be liable in tort arising out of any act that was *ultra vires*. It is certainly in the public interest that the *ultra vires* principle should not be allowed to provide a defence in proceedings in tort, as this could logically amount to a complete defence against all claims. Even if the argument were confined to *ultra vires* acts that were not in themselves tortious, such as the operation of a public transport undertaking without express statutory powers,[1] such a defence would cause considerable injustice in practice. Logically, if a corporation has no powers to enter into a contract or carry out certain work, its employees cannot commit a tort so as to make the corporation liable, in carrying out an act which is *ultra vires* the corporation. The defence was, however, decisively rejected in *Campbell* v. *Paddington Corpn.*,[2] in which it was held that the

[18] A considerable amount of case law, now fortunately obsolete, had grown up dealing with the nature of the circumstances in which a public authority could plead a special limitation period.

[19] See Professor Goodhart at 2 Camb. L.J. 350, and the learned editor of Salmond's *Torts, contra*; 16th Edn., at p. 439.

[20] See *post*.

[1] As in *A.-G.* v. *Leicester Corpn.*, [1943] 1 All E.R. 146; [1943] Ch. 86.

[2] [1911] 1 K.B. 869. Even if a particular act of the local authority is *ultra vires*, it is still their act, and they cannot thereby escape responsibility for the action of their servants or agents in the execution of their instructions. A local authority may be liable in negligence or for breach of statutory duty, although negligent acts or acts committed in breach of a statutory duty are strictly *ultra vires*; see, *e.g.*, *Hesketh* v. *Liverpool Corpn.*, [1940] 4 All E.R. 429.

defendant Council was liable in damages in respect of injuries caused by the erection of a stand in the road (for the purpose of viewing King Edward VII's funeral procession), an act which the Council had no legal power to carry out. As a necessary corollary to the general principle, the law holds a local authority liable for the torts of its employees and servants in accordance with the usual rules of the law of master and servant. This is so even if the employee in question is a professional man, as in the case of a doctor employed (before the passing of the National Health Service Act, 1946) in a hospital operated by a local authority.[3] If, on the other hand, the employee has independent statutory duties vested in him by virtue of his office, the local authority will not be liable in respect of his torts just because they may be his paymasters; this in particular applies to police officers, for whom the local police authority are not responsible in tort.[4] By virtue of the authority's vicarious liability for the acts of its servants or agents, a local authority has been held liable for defamation[5] and even false imprisonment.[6] Criminal proceedings may lie against a local authority,[7] although quite clearly it could not be said that the authority had statutory permission to commit a crime. Certain special defences may properly be raised, in appropriate cases, by a local authority against whom proceedings are taken in tort, as follows:

(i) *Statutory authority.*—The plea of statutory authority may be used as a defence in proceedings for nuisance or trespass, but the local or other public authority setting up such a defence must be able to show that the statute confers more than a mere power to carry out a certain function; the statute must go so far as to authorise, if not to require, the function to be carried out in the particular manner complained of.[8] In *Metropolitan Asylum District* v. *Hill*,[9] a local authority had statutory authority to erect a smallpox hospital, and this was pleaded as a defence in proceedings brought on the allegation that the erection of the hospital in the situation proposed would cause a nuisance. It was held that the statute merely authorised the erection of a hospital, not the erection of the particular hospital on the site chosen; it was therefore to be implied that the power given by the statute must be exercised in such a manner

---

[3] *Gold* v. *Essex County Council*, [1942] 2 All E.R. 237; [1942] 2 K.B. 932.

[4] *Fisher* v. *Oldham Corpn.*, [1930] 2 K.B. 364 but see now, *post*, p. 443. An inspector appointed under the Diseases of Animals Acts is in a similar position as regards his employing local authority: *Stanbury* v. *Exeter Corpn.*, [1905] 2 K.B. 838. There is, however, no similar provision applying to public health or other inspectors employed by a local authority.

[5] *De Buse* v. *McCarty and Stepney B.C.*, [1942] 1 All E.R. 19. A local authority is also capable of being a plaintiff in proceedings for defamation: see *Bognor Regis U.D.C.* v. *Campion*, [1972] 2 All E.R. 61; [1972] 2 Q.B. 169.

[6] *Percy* v. *Glasgow Corpn.*, [1922] 2 A.C. 299.

[7] Such as proceedings for a statutory nuisance, taken at the instance of another local authority: *R.* v. *Epping* (*Waltham Abbey*) *Justices, ex parte Burlinson*, [1947] 2 All E.R. 537; [1948] K.B. 79.

[8] If a statute, for example, empowers a railway to be built on a prescribed line, no action in nuisance in respect of the vibrations and noise, etc., thereby caused can lie, as these consequences are unavoidable: see *Hammersmith and City Rail. Co.* v. *Brand* (1869), L.R. 4 M.L. 171.

[9] (1881), 6 App. Cas. 193; for a modern application of the principle, see the Canadian case of *B.C. Pea Growers* v. *City of Portage La Prairie* (1964), 49 D.L.R. (2d) 91.

as not to cause a nuisance.[10] Further, a statutory power must be exercised without negligence, and if the public authority concerned exercises its statutory powers negligently, the defence of statutory authority will be of no avail.[11]

It is convenient to comment here also on the action for damages for breach of a statutory duty. In order that a local or public authority may be held liable in such circumstances, the statute must impose a duty as distinct from a mere power, there must be no other remedy open to the plaintiff, and the plaintiff must have suffered injury as a consequence of the breach, and he must also be the victim of the particular mischief which the statute was designed to prevent. Thus, if a local authority has a permissive power conferred on it by statute, no action will lie against it if it fails or refuses to exercise that power. In a case where a catchment board had a statutory power to repair a breach in a river wall, it was held to be not liable in damages arising out of its failure to exercise that power.[12] However, it seems that once a local authority has chosen to exercise a power (for example, to inspect work in progress to ascertain whether it complies with the Building Regulations), it must proceed to act without negligence.[13] This principle has been explained another way by Lord DENNING, when he observed[14] that not all the functions of a local authority can be divided into two categories, powers and duties. "There is a middle term. It is *control*." His Lordship then went on to explain that where a statute gives a local authority control over some activity carried out by a private individual (such as building work), this carries with it a duty to exercise that control without negligence. If negligence can nevertheless be proved against the authority, they will be liable to any person suffering injury in consequence.[15]

If there is some other remedy open to the plaintiff, such as an appeal to the Minister in a case where a local authority fails to provide a public sewer in accordance with its duties under section 14 of the Public Health Act, 1936, again an action will not lie, it being assumed that the statute intended the special remedy provided to be exclusive.[16] Where a duty is expressly created by statute and a criminal sanction is imposed for a breach of that duty, the courts will not normally grant a plaintiff who claims he has suffered as a consequence of the breach of the

---

[10] See also such cases as *Rapier* v. *London Tramways Co.*, [1893] 2 Ch. 588, and *Farnworth* v. *Manchester Corpn.*, [1929] 1 K.B. 533, at p. 561.

[11] *Geddis* v. *Bann Reservoir Proprietors* (1878), 3 App. Cas. 430; *Fisher* v. *Ruislip-Northwood U.D.C.*, [1945] K.B. 584.

[12] *East Suffolk Rivers Catchment Board* v. *Kent*, [1940] 4 All E.R. 527; [1941] A.C. 74.

[13] See *per* SACHS, L.J. in *Dutton* v. *Bognor Regis United Building Co., Ltd.*, [1972] 1 All E.R. 462, at p. 480. This doctrine was not applied in relation to legislative or quasi-judicial functions (for example on a grant of planning permission which subsequently was declared void) of a local authority by the Supreme Court of Canada in *Welbridge Holdings, Ltd.* v. *Metropolitan Corporation of Greater Winnipeg* (1972), 22 D.L.R. (3d) 407.

[14] In the same case, at p. 470.

[15] As in the *Bognor Regis* case (*ante*), where a purchaser of a house was able to recover damages from the local authority when he could prove that their building inspector in the course of exercising the Council's powers under the Building Regulations, had failed to detect that the house was being erected on a former rubbish tip. As a consequence the house subsided some years later.

[16] *Pasmore* v. *Oswaldtwistle U.D.C.*, [1898] A.C. 387, and see Chapter VI, *ante*, p. 159.

duty, a remedy by way of damages: the ruling principle seems to be the intention of the statute. Thus, in *Keating* v. *Elvan Reinforced Concrete Co., Ltd.*,[17] the Court of Appeal refused to allow a civil action for damages for breach of a statutory duty[18] to fence and guard a street in which a local authority's contractors were carrying out repairs. The object of the Act of 1950, said Lord PEARSON (at p. 143)

> "is to regulate the relations between undertakers who exercise statutory powers to break up streets and highway authorities and other authorities who are, by virtue of their functions, concerned with the way in which those operations are carried out by the undertakers."

Sometimes of course the statute may itself provide for a civil remedy[19]; exceptionally,[20] the court may be prepared to find an "intention" in the statute to allow a civil action for damages for breach of the duty.[1]

In most cases the defendant in proceedings on a statute will be a local authority, but the action is not confined to those cases, and the Crown, or a Government Department, may be made responsible in a proper case.[2]

(ii) *Nonfeasance.*—It can be said that a local authority will not be liable in respect of acts of nonfeasance (as distinct from acts of misfeasance or malfeasance) but this is true only in so far as cause for complaint arises from failure to exercise a statutory *power*; if the statute provides that an authority *may* take a certain action, no proceedings can be brought against it by a person who suffers damage as a consequence of the failure to exercise that power, although, as we have seen, if the power is exercised, and the authority is guilty of negligence, an action may lie against it. In the normal case of a local authority failing to carry out a statutory *duty*, it will as mentioned above, be liable.

In the solitary example of the highway authority, however, nonfeasance used to be a defence even where the complaint was based on a breach of the statutory duty to maintain a highway, where the highway was maintainable at the public expense.[3] This anomaly in the law was the result of the principle that liability for the repair of highways rested on the "inhabitants at large", as it was considered too

---

[17] [1968] 2 All E.R. 139; [1968] 1 W.L.R. 722.

[18] Under the Public Utilities Street Works Act, 1950.

[19] Possibly by way of appeal to a Minister, as under s. 322 of the Public Health Act, 1936.

[20] As in *Monk* v. *Warbey*, [1935] 1 K.B. 75; see Salmond on *Torts*, 16th Edn., at p. 246.

[1] Another example of a case where an action was refused is *Watt* v. *Kesteven County Council*, [1954] 3 All E.R. 441; [1954] 3 W.L.R. 729, where parents of a school boy were not allowed to raise a civil action for a declaration against the local education authority on the ground that they were in breach of their statutory duty under the Education Act, 1944, to have regard to the wishes of the parents in relation to pupils' education (in the outcome it was not established that there was any breach of duty). Contrast, however, *Ministry of Housing and Local Government* v. *Sharp*, [1969] 3 All E.R. 225; [1969] 3 W.L.R. 1020 where the negligence of a local land charges registrar was held to be actionable at the suit of an incumbrancer (the Ministry, who had registered a charge which was not disclosed) because such a plaintiff was within the class of persons that the statute was designed to protect.

[2] *Darling* v. *A.-G.*, [1950] 2 All E.R. 793; Crown Proceedings Act, 1947, s. 2 (2).

[3] Highways Act, 1959, s. 44 (1).

onerous a duty to make them responsible for every hole in a highway, where they had not actually caused the defect.[4] This special defence applied only to a highway authority acting as such, and could never be pleaded by the highway authority when it had actually done work in the highway, or in respect of some object in the highway which it had allowed to fall into disrepair but which had originally been placed there under some powers other than as highway authority, such for example, as a traffic stud put in the carriageway for the purpose of giving directions to traffic,[5] a refuge erected for the convenience of foot passengers,[6] or a sewer grating constructed not as part of the drainage of the highway,[7] but as part of a main sewer lying under some part of the highway.[8] Therefore it was held that where a highway authority had diverted a stream passing under a highway and had failed to provide a grid as it should have done, as a consequence whereof the plaintiff's land was flooded some 30 years later, the authority was liable in damages and no question of the nonfeasance defence could arise.[9] In another case, however,[10] where the highway authority had carried out works to improve the drainage of the highway, and it appeared that the works done were inadequate and the plaintiff was injured as a consequence of road flooding, the authority was held not liable as the works it had carried out had been executed properly. It was not responsible for having failed to do all that could have been done and the defence of nonfeasance was successful.

This special defence of nonfeasance has now been abolished, but a highway authority (including the Secretary of State when acting as such) can plead special defences listed in s. 1 (3) of the Highways (Miscellaneous Provisions) Act, 1961,[11] in proceedings taken against the authority for damages, based on a failure by the authority to carry out their statutory duty under section 44 of the Highways Act, 1959, to keep in repair any highway maintainable at the public expense, which by virtue of section 38 of the 1959 Act is vested in the authority. These defences will not, however, be open to the authority in cases where they are not acting as highway authority.

(b) Contractual liability.—A local authority cannot enter into an *ultra vires* contract; if a contract entered into by a local authority is *ultra vires*, it will be void *ab initio* and the authority cannot be made liable in damages for its breach.[12] Further, a public authority cannot make use of the doctrine of estoppel so as to clothe itself with powers

---

[4] *Russell* v. *Men of Devon* (1788), 2 Term Rep. 667. The principle was preserved, for a time, in s. 298 of the Highways Act, 1959, but see below.

[5] *Skilton* v. *Epsom and Ewell U.D.C.*, [1936] 2 All E.R. 50; [1937] 1 K.B. 112.

[6] *Polkinghorn* v. *Lambeth B.C.*, [1938] 1 All E.R. 339.

[7] *Winslowe* v. *Bushey U.D.C.* (1908), 72 J.P. 259.

[8] If, however, the grating were part of the highway itself, having been constructed with the object of draining the highway, then nonfeasance could be pleaded as a defence: *Thompson* v. *Brighton Corpn.*, [1894] 1 Q.B. 332.

[9] *Pemberton* v. *Bright*, [1960] 1 All E.R. 792; [1960] 1 W.L.R. 436.

[10] *Burton* v. *West Suffolk County Council*, [1960] 2 All E.R. 26; [1960] 2 Q.B. 72.

[11] For an interpretation of these defences, see *Littler* v. *Liverpool Corpn.*, [1968] 2 All E.R. 343, *Burnside* v. *Emerson*, [1968] 3 All E.R. 741; [1968] 1 W.L.R. 1490, and *Rider* v. *Rider*, [1973] 1 All E.R. 294; [1973] Q.B. 505.

[12] *Rhyl U.D.C.* v. *Rhyl Amusements, Ltd.*, [1959] 1 All E.R. 257; [1959] 1 W.L.R. 465.

in excess of those vested in it by statute.[13] In consequence of these two principles an authority could repudiate a lease into which it had no powers to enter.[14] There is also a general principle, binding on local authorities as well as the Crown and public authorities generally, that where statute has conferred a discretionary power, the authority cannot divest itself of that power by contract.[15] In other respects, a local authority is subject to the normal rules of the law of contract as is any ordinary individual.

As a general rule at common law, however, a local authority (in common with other corporations) would not be liable on a contract unless the contract was under the seal of the authority. This rule was altered by the Corporate Bodies' Contracts Act, 1960, which provides that a local authority or other corporate body (not being a company incorporated under the Companies Act) should be bound by any contract which the law requires to be in writing or evidenced by writing (*e.g.*, a contract for the sale of land under section 40 of the Law of Property Act, 1925), or which may be by parol, provided the contract is signed or made (as the case may be) by an officer or agent acting or purporting to act on their behalf. This statute makes very little substantive change in the law, its effects being mainly procedural. A party contracting with a local authority is not concerned to ensure that standing orders are complied with[16]; therefore an officer of a local authority acting under ostensible authority[17] may bind his employers contrary to their express instructions. In addition there were exceptions to the common law rule which are not affected by the Act of 1960:

(a) A contract entered into verbally or in writing only can be ratified subsequently under seal;

(b) The authority could appoint an agent under seal, who was then enabled to enter into a contract which would bind the authority, although that contract might not itself be under seal[1];

(c) As regards third parties, a contract could always, and still can, be enforced against a local authority if it has been partly performed by the plaintiff[2];

(d) Contracts of trivial importance, or daily occurrence or urgent necessity did not need to be under seal (or in writing) to be enforceable;

---

[13] As to doctrine of estoppel, see *ante*, p. 293.

[14] *Canterbury Corpn.* v. *Cooper* (1909), 73 J.P. 225; *Rhyl* case (*ante*).

[15] *Ante*, pp. 279, 293.

[16] Local Government Act, 1972, s. 135 (4).

[17] "Once an agent is clothed with ostensible authority, no private instructions prevent his acts within the scope of that authority from binding his principal": *National Bolivian Navigation Co.* v. *Wilson* (1880), 5 App. Cas. 176, at p. 209, cited in Cheshire & Fifoot, *Law of Contract*, 8th Edn., at p. 478.

[1] The authority could not, however, avoid the necessity for a seal by drafting their standing orders appropriately and then merely complying with those standing orders: *A. R. Wright & Son* v. *Romford Corpn.*, [1956] 3 All E.R. 785; [1957] 1 Q.B. 431. This has, of course, been altered by the Act of 1960.

[2] *Lawford* v. *Billericay R.D.C.*, [1903] 1 K.B. 772.

(e) It is customary for a local authority to make provision for the preparation and sealing of contracts by standing orders made under section 135 of the Local Government Act, 1972, but these are of internal effect only[3]; if standing orders are not observed, this will not of itself affect the validity of the contract so far as other parties are concerned.[4]

As a general principle, the employees of a local authority are in a normal contractual relationship with their employer[5]; formerly some senior officers were in a specially privileged position in that they could not be dismissed by their employing local authority without the consent of the Secretary of State, but these provisions have been repealed by the Local Government Act, 1972.[6]

(c) The doctrine of *ultra vires*.—Reference has been made earlier in this Chapter to the doctrine of *ultra vires*. This doctrine applies to every legal person created by statute—to trading corporations, commercial companies, public corporations and local authorities—and stated briefly, amounts to a general principle that a creature of statute has only such powers as Parliament may have chosen to confer on it.[7] As we have seen, the principle is of great importance in the law of contract, as an *ultra vires* contract is void *ab initio*, and it may be said to be the basis of judicial control over the acts of administrative authorities, as it operates to limit their functions. Thus, an action for a declaration will lie against a corporation in respect of the *ultra vires* use of public funds, by any person interested in those funds,[8] and it has even been said that a local authority must act as a trustee of its funds for the benefit of its ratepayers.[9] The limit of a local authority's statutory powers may be ascertained by the procedure of an action for a declaration, as in the case where an authority wanted to operate a municipal laundry, which was held to be *ultra vires*,[10] and in another case where another

[3] Though made under statutory authority, they do not take legal effect as byelaws, and they do not require any confirmation by a Minister. Standing orders are rules of procedure for the internal government of the particular authority; if those relating to contracts are not complied with, and the authority has lost money or some financial advantage as a consequence thereof, the matter may be the subject of a report, or possibly a disallowance (see Chapter XV, *post*, p. 427) by the district auditor, assuming that the particular authority's accounts are subject to district audit.

[4] L.G.A. 1972, s. 135 (4) and *Royal British Bank* v. *Turquand* (1856), 6 E. & B. 327, a case on company law, the effect of which applies equally to local authorities.

[5] Certain statutes prior to 1933 had provided that local authorities employed their staffs "at pleasure", and therefore in *Brown* v. *Dagenham U.D.C.*, [1929] 1 K.B. 737, it was held that a local authority could dismiss their clerk without notice. But this was changed by the 1933 Act. Under the Local Government Act 1972, s. 112 (2), any officer holds office on "such reasonable terms and conditions . . . as the authority appointing him think fit".

[6] See, *e.g.*, Local Government Act, 1933, s. 100 (1).

[7] See also Chapter VI, *ante*, p. 133.

[8] *Prescott* v. *Birmingham Corpn.*, [1954] 3 All E.R. 698; [1955] Ch. 210, where a ratepayer successfully applied for a declaration against a local authority to the effect that they had no statutory powers to introduce a special scheme of concessionary travel to old people on the vehicles belonging to the local authority's road transport undertaking. See also "Judicial Control of the Spending Powers of Local Authorities," at (1956), 72 L.Q.R. 237.

[9] *A.-G.* v. *Aspinall* (1837), 2 My. & Cr. 613, a case which has lost some of its effect as a consequence of recent statutes (see *post*).

[10] *A.-G.* v. *Fulham Corpn.*, [1921] 1 Ch. 440.

authority wanted to operate a municipal printing establishment, which was held to be incidental to their normal functions of a local authority, and was therefore *intra vires*.[11]

Section 137 of the Local Government Act, 1972,[12] has to some extent made a breach in the *ultra vires* doctrine in its application to local authorities. By this section, any local authority[13] may incur expenditure for any purpose which "in their opinion is in the interests of their area or any part of it or all or some of its inhabitants", provided there is no existing statutory authority (whether or not subject to Departmental approval) for that item of expenditure. A specific resolution must be passed authorising each item or items of expenditure and each authority may not spend more than the product of a rate of 2p in the pound[14] each year under this section. The section is thus of limited application, but when it is used, it would seem that there is very little opportunity of control over the local authority's discretion by either the district auditor[15] or the courts. Possibly, by analogy with *Ross-Clunis* v. *Papadopoullos*,[16] the court might be persuaded to declare particular expenditure to be *ultra vires*, on the ground that no local authority could conceivably have formulated the honest opinion that the expenditure in question was in the interests of the area or its inhabitants, but clearly it would have to be a most exceptional case to be able to establish such an argument.

Corporations were formerly[17] brought into existence by exercise of the royal prerogative without recourse to Parliament, and it has been argued that the ancient municipal corporations, not being the creatures of statute,[18] were entitled to the benefit of the common law principle that an artificial person created by virtue of the royal prerogative could in law do anything that a normal person might do,[19] except in so far as they were forbidden so to act by statute, and that they were therefore not restricted by the *ultra vires* doctrine. There was some justification for this view in relation to those chartered boroughs created before 1835. However, these have all been abolished by the Local Government Act, 1972, and any Royal Charters creating the style of borough (outside London) after April 1, 1974, will be issued under the statute.[20] London boroughs issued with charters after 1965 are in the same position, these charters having been created under the London Government

---

[11] *A.-G.* v. *Smethwick Corpn.*, [1932] 1 Ch. 562.

[12] Re-enacting, in slightly wider form, s. 6 of the Local Government (Financial Provisions) Act, 1963.

[13] Including a parish or community council, but *not* a parish meeting.

[14] Or such other amount as may be fixed by order made by the Secretary of State.

[15] *Post*, p. 427.

[16] [1958] 2 All E.R. 23; Chapter VI, *ante*, p. 163.

[17] The only modern examples of a public chartered corporation, other than a local authority, are such bodies as the Universities, the Arts Council of Great Britain and the British Broadcasting Corporation.

[18] The argument applied only to corporations created by virtue of the Royal Prerogative, prior to the passing of the Municipal Corporations Act, 1835. Since that date, all new municipal corporations were created under the authority of statute, although they may have been granted a royal charter. For further argument, see the third edition of this book, at p. 286.

[19] *Sutton Hospital* case (1612), 10 Co. Rep. 23a.

[20] Local Government Act, 1972, s. 245.

Act, 1963. The *ultra vires* doctrine now clearly applies to all local authorities and the "Maud" Committee on "Management of Local Government"[1] were of the opinion that the doctrine "has a deleterious effect on local government because of the narrowness of the legislation governing local authorities' activities".[2] This legalistic background certainly does at times discourage enterprise and handicap development, and the Committee therefore recommended that local authorities should be given a "general competence" to do

> "whatever in their opinion is in the interests of their area or its inhabitants, subject to their not encroaching on the duties of other governmental bodies and to appropriate safeguards for the protection of public and private interests."

This would have amounted in effect to an extension of the principle in what is now section 137 of the 1972 Act,[3] but it would not have amounted to an abolition of the *ultra vires* doctrine, as the authorities would still have had to work within their statutes; indeed, it is difficult to appreciate how the *ultra vires* doctrine could be abolished without destroying the supremacy of Parliament. The safeguards referred to in the Committee's recommendation "for public and private interests", would, we suspect, prove difficult to define with any precision, and this may well be a disadvantage in any further reforming legislation. However, apart from section 137, a power to give rate fund moneys to charity and to provide for disasters, the legislature in 1972 did not accept the views of "little Maud".

(d) Prerogative orders.—Proceedings by way of prerogative orders, and other supervisory proceedings such as actions for a declaration or injunction, are dealt with elsewhere in this book.[4]

6. LOCAL AUTHORITY PROCEEDINGS

Under this heading we deal with rules of procedure, and a few kinds of proceedings specially applicable to local authorities, having already dealt with special rules of legal liability applicable to such authorities.

Many statutes confer on local authorities[5] powers to secure enforcement with certain standards, imposed in the interests of the public. The Housing Act, 1957, for example, requires the housing authority to take certain action in respect of a house which is not "fit for human habitation" in accordance with certain specified requirements[6]; the Public Health Act, 1936, imposes a duty on the local authority to take

---

1 H.M.S.O., 1967; this is the Committee sometimes irreverently described as "little Maud", which preceded the Royal Commission Report known as "Redcliffe-Maud". By the time the latter Report appeared Sir John Maud of the Committee had become Lord Redcliffe-Maud of the Commission. See Chapter XIII *post*, p. 400.

2 *Report*, paras 283–286.

3 *Ante*, p. 303.

4 See Chapter VI, *ante*, p. 171 *et seq*.

5 As to the kinds of local authorities, see Chapter XI, *post*, p. 360.

6 See Housing Act, 1957, s. 4 (1).

action where premises within the authority's district are "in such a condition as to be prejudicial to health or a nuisance",[7] and also requires the authority to take action to ensure that the sanitary accommodation provided for a building shall be "sufficient", and that "satisfactory provision" shall be made for drainage.[8] The Food and Drugs Act, 1955, empowers a local authority to take proceedings in respect of any food which is intended for but is "unfit" for human consumption,[9] and the Offices, Shops and Railway Premises Act, 1963, enables (*inter alia*) the local authority to require that "suitable and sufficient" sanitary accommodation shall be provided for the employees at any office or shop in their district[10]; the Factories Act, 1961, requires the occupier of a factory to keep the walls of his factory in a "state of cleanliness",[11] and there are many other examples in the statute book of the enforcement of statutory standards through the agency of local authorities.

There is no procedure common to all these statutes, but most follow a common pattern, or one of a few variants therefrom.

(a) In the first place, it is normally made the express duty of the local authority to enforce the particular standard in question. In most cases, the statute leaves it to the authority to decide for itself what steps it will take, if any, to ascertain when the standards should be enforced—when, for example, food is being sold that is unfit for human consumption, or whether a particular shop has insufficient sanitary accommodation; but in some cases the statute imposes on the local authority the duty of inspecting its district and finding out cases where the standards are not observed, for example, to carry out a review of housing conditions.[12] These statutory duties—those of taking action in appropriate circumstances, and those of carrying out inspections—are probably duties of imperfect obligation, in that no one is enabled to take proceedings in the courts to compel their execution. Presumably an individual able to show that he had suffered damage as a consequence of the duty not having been performed would be able to sue the authority for a breach of statutory duty, but the circumstances in which such an action could arise are very improbable.[13]

---

[7] 1936 Act, s. 92. The expression "prejudicial to health or a nuisance" is not defined in the Act, except that (by s. 343 (1)) "prejudicial to health" means "injurious, or likely to cause injury, to health". The expression must also be construed within the general context of public health: *Pilling* v. *Abergele U.D.C.*, [1950] 1 All E.R. 76; [1950] 1 K.B. 636.

[8] Public Health Act, 1936, ss. 44 and 39.

[9] Food and Drugs Act, 1955, ss. 8 and 109.

[10] Offices, Shops and Railway Premises Act, 1963, s. 9.

[11] Factories Act, 1961, s. 1; without prejudice to the generality of this provision, the section goes on to describe particular standards that must also be complied with, and regulations have been made going into further details for particular kinds of factories (Factories (Cleanliness of Walls and Ceilings) Order, 1960, S.I. 1960 No. 1794).

[12] Housing Act, 1969, s. 70.

[13] If an individual has suffered damage as a consequence of the failure of the regional water authority (who have succeeded to the local authority: Water Act, 1973) adequately to sewer the district (as is required by s. 14 of the Public Health Act, 1936), he may complain to the Secretary of State for the Environment under s. 322 of the Public Health Act, 1936; *ante*, p. 169.

(b) Where the appropriate official of the local authority has discovered a case, either as the consequence of a complaint from a member of the public, or as the result of his own observation on inspection, in which the statutory standards are not being observed, he will first report to the local authority. Usually this report need not follow any particular form, but in the case of an unfit house, an officer may decide to make an official representation,[14] which by the statute is required to be in writing. On receiving such a report, the local authority (or a committee of the authority to whom power may have been delegated by the authority[15]) will consider the matter. The process of coming to a decision must be undertaken by the members of the local authority (or of the committee), unless the power to come to a decision has been delegated to an officer[16]; and where an officer has acted on his own initiative, it seems that the local authority may adopt his action and validate it retrospectively.[17]

(c) The decision so taken by the local authority will normally be to serve a notice on the person concerned, requiring him to comply with the prescribed standards; in some cases, however, the statute authorises commencement of criminal proceedings forthwith (without any prior warning, although in most circumstances, it is customary first to issue an informal warning, and in one instance at least the statute requires such a warning to be sent).[18] Where a notice has to be served, the officer responsible will prepare it; it must be in writing, and must in some cases follow a prescribed form.[19] In this branch of the law the precise details of procedure must be strictly observed, and the penalty for error will be invalidity *ab initio*. Thus, if there is a right of appeal against the notice, this must be stated,[20] and the notice must be signed by an officer who has been authorised by his local authority to sign, either generally or specially.[1] Where the notice requires work to be executed, the requirements of the notice must be clearly stated, only the minimum necessary to secure compliance with the standard must be specified, and a reasonable time must be stated within which the works required are to be completed.[2]

---

[14] Housing Act, 1957, s. 157 (5).

[15] Under s. 101 of the Local Government Act, 1972; Chapter XIII, *post*, p. 395.

[16] This was formerly not possible in the absence of express statutory authority: see *St. Leonard's Vestry* v. *Holmes* (1885), 50 J.P. 132, and *cf. Allingham* v. *Minister of Agriculture and Fisheries*, [1948] 1 All E.R. 780; but now such authority exists, under s. 101 of the Local Government Act, 1972.

[17] *Firth* v. *Staines*, [1897] 2 Q.B. 70; *Warwick R.D.C.* v. *Miller-Mead*, [1962] 1 All E.R. 212; [1962] Ch. 441.

[18] Clean Air Act, 1956, s. 30.

[19] See, for example, the Housing (Prescribed Forms) Regulations, 1972 (S.I., 1972, No. 228), which prescribe the forms to be used in connection with most of the controls of the Housing Acts, 1957 to 1969. If the statute requires a particular form to be signed by a specified officer of the authority, the form will be invalid if it is signed by some other officer: *Becker* v. *Crosby Corpn.*, [1952] 1 All E.R. 1350.

[20] *Rayner* v. *Stepney Corpn.*, [1911] 2 Ch. 312.

[1] Sometimes (see, *e.g.*, s. 284 of the Public Health Act, 1936) the statute may authorise particular officers of the local authority to sign particular notices: and see footnote 19.

[2] This of course will be a question of fact: *Ryall* v. *Cubitt Heath*, [1922] 1 K.B. 275.

(d) Where the requirements of a notice are not complied with, the statute may give the local authority power to act in default. In these cases, the authority must be sure that the time prescribed by the notice for compliance has expired, and they may carry out only the minimum works necessary for compliance with the terms of the notice. The statute normally provides, in cases where it confers such default powers,[3] a right for the local authority to recover their expenses reasonably incurred in so acting in default; sometimes the statute also provides that a share of the local authority's general overhead expenses may be added to those actually incurred,[4] but in any case, the authority must be reasonably economical in carrying out the work, and should (for example) normally accept the lowest tender received in any case where they decide to carry out the work by a contractor instead of by their own labour. The statute normally enables the authority to add interest at a prescribed rate[5] to any sum so recoverable from the person originally liable to comply with the terms of the notice, and this interest will run from the date of the demand.[6] These expenses are normally made recoverable as a civil debt summarily before the local magistrates,[7] or alternatively before the ordinary civil courts. Proceedings before the magistrates must be commenced within six months of the date of demand,[8] but this time limit does not apply to proceedings before the county court or High Court.[9] There is, however, in most cases,[10] no time limit within which the original demand must be served, and therefore if the right to take proceedings on a demand has become statute barred, the authority may wait until the property concerned is sold, and then serve a demand on the new "owner".[11] Statutes often provide that expenses incurred as a consequence of taking action in default of compliance with a statutory notice, shall be a charge on the land; such a charge should be registered as a local land charge under the Land Charges Act, 1925, and the local authority will then have all the remedies of a mortgagee in possession under the Law of Property Act, 1925,[12] and their charge will rank in priority to all other prior charges (including rent charges) affecting the property.[13]

(e) As an alternative to requiring the service of a notice, the statute may empower the local authority to prosecute an offender who has not

---

[3] As, for example, in many sections of the Public Health Act, 1936, and s. 9 (repair of unfit houses) of the Housing Act, 1957.

[4] These may not exceed 5 per cent in the case of the Public Health Act, 1936: s. 292 thereof.

[5] The rate, prescribed by Regulations, is at present 7 per cent; see, *e.g.*, Public Health (Rate of Interest) Order, 1968, S.I., 1968, No. 231.

[6] See, *e.g.*, Public Health Act, 1936, s. 291.

[7] Magistrates' Courts Act, 1952, s. 50.

[8] *Ibid.*, s. 104.

[9] *Blackburn Corpn.* v. *Sanderson*, [1902] 1 K.B. 794.

[10] The normal expression in the statute is to the effect that the local authority may "from time to time recover from the owner for the time being": see, *e.g.*, Highways Act, 1959, s. 181 (1), and *Dennerley* v. *Prestwich U.D.C.*, [1930] 1 K.B. 334.

[11] *Dennerley* v. *Prestwich U.D.C.* (*ante*).

[12] The provisions of s. 101 of the Law of Property Act, 1925, will be applied as the result of ss. 15 (2) and 11 of the Land Charges Act, 1925 and s. 4 of the Land Charges Act, 1972.

[13] *Paddington Borough Council* v. *Finucane*, [1928] Ch. 567; *Bristol Corpn.* v. *Virgin*, [1928] 2 K.B. 622.

complied with the particular statutory standard; in some cases the authority may be empowered to bring a prosecution as well as serve a statutory notice,[14] and in yet others, a prosecution may be brought (possibly as well as taking default action) in respect of a failure to comply with a statutory notice in due time.[15]

Where it is decided by the local authority[16] to prosecute in any such case, the information must be laid by an officer of the authority[17] authorised so to act either generally or specially.[18] The case may be taken (before the magistrates) by any member or officer of the local authority authorised by them so to act, whether or not a solicitor or counsel.[19] An appeal will normally lie from the decision of the local magistrates, either on a point of law by way of case stated to the Queen's Bench Division of the High Court,[20] or by way of re-hearing at the instance of a party aggrieved to the Crown Court; the local authority will not themselves be a "party aggrieved" in this sense if they lose a criminal prosecution brought by them, even if they have been ordered to pay the costs of the defence.[1]

(f) In exercising these powers, the local authority may need to exercise also certain ancillary powers. Thus, the statute giving the substantive power also customarily empowers a local authority to serve a notice on the occupier of property requesting information to be furnished as to the identity of the owner or owners of that property, under pain of prosecution for an offence if the information is withheld.[2] Also the statute in most cases will empower the duly authorised officers of the local authority to effect forceable entry on property where this becomes necessary for them to carry out their statutory functions (*e.g.*, for the purpose of inspecting a house under the Housing Act, 1957 (*ante*), or so as to carry out works which the owner of the premises may have been

---

[14] As, for example, under s. 290 (6) of the Public Health Act, 1936, which procedural section is applied to many of the substantive sections of the same Act and of the Public Health Act, 1961.

[15] Public Health Act, 1936, s. 94 (2) (nuisance abatement notices).

[16] Formerly this decision could not be delegated to an officer, and if an officer of the authority commenced legal proceedings on his own initiative, costs could not be given against the local authority if the proceedings were to fail. However, proceedings could always be taken by an officer where there is no statutory restriction on the commencement of proceedings (see, *e.g.*, *Snodgrass* v. *Topping* (1952), 116 J.P. 332), but in a number of local government statutes, and the Public Health Act, 1936, in particular (see s. 298), it is provided that "proceedings in respect of an offence created by or under this Act shall not, without the written consent of the Attorney-General, be taken by any person other than a party aggrieved, or a council or a body whose function it is to enforce the provisions or byelaws in question . . .". It seems that in view of the wording of s. 101 of the Local Government Act, 1972, this function of an authority, like all others, may be delegated to an officer.

[17] Or one of their members: Local Government Act, 1972, s. 223.

[18] *Bob Keats, Ltd.* v. *Farrant*, [1951] 1 All E.R. 899.

[19] Local Government Act, 1972, s. 223.

[20] Magistrates' Courts Act, 1952, s. 87.

[1] *Ealing Borough Council* v. *Jones*, [1959] 1 All E.R. 286; [1959] 1 Q.B. 384. *R.* v. *Dorset Sessions Appeals Committee, ex parte Weymouth Corpn.*, [1960] 2 All E.R. 410; [1960] 2 Q.B. 230; Chapter VI, *ante*, p. 176.

[2] Public Health Act, 1936, s. 277; Housing Act, 1957, s. 169; Highways Act, 1959, s. 259; Town and Country Planning Act, 1971, s. 284.

required to execute and in respect of which he is in default). The procedure enabling them to effect entry is highly technical; a 24-hour notice has first to be served, and then if the local authority's officers meet with obstruction, they have to obtain a magistrate's warrant.[3] The occupier of a dwelling house is entitled to resist entry made otherwise than strictly in accordance with the terms of the statute[4]; any entry otherwise effected is a trespass, and the officers concerned are trespassers *ab initio*,[5] being liable for everything they may have done on the premises since entry was first effected. This right to resist an illegal entry is of fundamental importance, for in any proceedings that may follow (*e.g.*, for trespass) or in criminal proceedings under the statute for obstruction,[6] the legal validity of the whole of the local authority's proceedings may be considered, thereby providing a manner in which the courts may review the action of the local authority.[7]

(g) In most cases where a local authority are empowered to serve a notice on an individual requiring him to take certain action, the statute confers on the individual recipient a right to appeal against the notice. Normally such an appeal will lie to the local magistrates,[8] but in some cases direct to the Crown Court,[9] sometimes to the county court,[10] and in at least one case the only appeal provided is to the Secretary of State for the Environment.[11] On such an appeal, the matter may be at large, but in some cases the statute limits the ground on which a party may appeal[12]; in cases where such a right of appeal is allowed by the statute, it is often provided that if no appeal is in fact made, or where an appeal is made on grounds specified in the statute, matters which could have been grounds for such an appeal may not be raised in subsequent proceedings (*e.g.*, in proceedings brought to recover the expenses of the local authority incurred by acting in default of compliance with the notice.[13])

(h) Frequently in this context, the local authority will have to decide who is to be the recipient of a notice, or the identity of the person who must be made the defendant in criminal proceedings. Sometimes

---

[3] See, for example, Public Health Act, 1936, s. 287.

[4] *Stroud* v. *Bradbury*, [1952] 2 All E.R. 76; Chapter VI, *ante*, p. 191.

[5] *Six Carpenters' Case* (1610), 8 Co. Rep. 146a.

[6] Most statutes of the type we are here considering contain a provision making it an offence to obstruct any person (usually an officer of the local authority) acting in the execution of the Act, as is done, for example, by s. 288 of the Public Health Act, 1936. Obstruction for this purpose must be "wilful", but it need not amount to actual violence. The test seems to be that the defendant must have intended to prevent the execution of the powers given by the Act: see *e.g.*, *Betts* v. *Stevens*, [1910] 1 K.B. 1, and *Eaton* v. *Cobb*, [1950] 1 All E.R. 1016.

[7] See Chapter VI, *ante*, pp. 138 and 190.

[8] As under s. 290 (3) of the Public Health Act, 1936.

[9] As under s. 59 (3) of the Highways Act, 1959; and see Courts Act, 1971.

[10] As in the case of s. 20 (1) of the Housing Act, 1957.

[11] As under s. 193 (5) of the Highways Act, 1959, and see also s. 207 (1), *ibid*. In the case of appeals against enforcement notices under the Town and Country Planning Act, 1971, appeals lie to the Secretary of State for the Environment and from his decisions thereon to the High Court on a point of law: see s. 246 of that Act.

[12] See, for example, s. 290 (3) of the Public Health Act, 1936.

[13] See s. 37 (1) of the Housing Act, 1957.

the statute enables the authority to serve the notice on or take the proceedings against the person responsible,[14] or the occupier of premises,[15] but in many cases the recipient of the notice or summons is required to be the "owner". This expression is usually defined in the enabling statute, most frequently by reference to the person in receipt of a "rack-rent", or the person who would be entitled to such a rent if the property were in fact let at a rack-rent,[16] rack-rent being in its turn defined as meaning

> "a rent which is not less than two-thirds of the rent at which the property might reasonably be expected to let from year to year, free from all usual tenant's rates and taxes, and tithe rentcharge (if any), and deducting therefrom the probable annual average cost of the repairs, insurance and other expenses (if any) necessary to maintain the same in a state to command such rent".[17]

If the "wrong" person is chosen as the recipient of a notice or the defendant in proceedings, any subsequent proceedings will fail, even if the local authority acted in reliance on information given by that person himself: see *Courtney-Southan* v. *Crawley U.D.C.*[18]

(i) In other proceedings, the statute may require a certain activity to be licensed or registered as a condition of it being carried on or continued. Thus, almost the whole of the law of town and country planning may be described in these terms. Planning permission, in the form of a licence, must be obtained from the local authority before any development (not falling within one or other of the specially exempt classes[19]) is carried out "in, on, over or under" any land[20] and permission similarly has to be obtained for the display of an advertisement.[1] When the statute empowers a local authority to grant such a licence, it may give them a wide discretion (as in the case of town and country planning), or it may impose restrictions that must be observed in the exercise of their discretion whether or not to grant a licence in a particular case[2]; there may or may not be an appeal against the local authority's decision to refuse a licence, and a licence may be granted unconditionally or subject to conditions.[3] As an alternative, in some circumstances, the

---

[14] Public Health Act, 1936, s. 93, but note the proviso.

[15] Such an option is given by, for example, s. 39 of the Public Health Act, 1936. In the case of an enforcement notice served under s. 87 of the Town and Country Planning Act, 1971, the notice has to be served on *both* the owner *and* the occupier of the premises to which the notice relates.

[16] Public Health Act, 1936, s. 343 (1), but contrast the definition in s. 188 (1) of the Housing Act, 1957, and see article by the present writer at (1957) 21 Conv. (N.S.) 141.

[17] Public Health Act, 1936, s. 343 (1).

[18] [1967] 2 All E.R. 246; [1967] 2 Q.B. 930.

[19] For example, under the General Development Order, 1973, S.I. 1973, No. 31, made under s. 23 of the Town and Country Planning Act, 1971.

[20] See definition of "development" in s. 22 (1) of the Town and Country Planning Act, 1971.

[1] Under the Town and Country Planning (Control of Advertisements) Regulations, 1969, S.I., 1969, No. 1532, made under s. 63 of the Town and Country Planning Act, 1971.

[2] As in the case of a licence for a moveable dwelling under s. 269 of the Public Health Act, 1936 (see *Pilling* v. *Abergele U.D.C.*, [1950] 1 All E.R. 76; [1950] 1 K.B. 636). Under Part I of the Caravan Sites and Control of Development Act, 1960, the statute limits the type of conditions that may be imposed: s. 4, and see s. 5 (6).

[3] See, for example, the Milk and Dairies (General) Regulations, 1959 (S.I., 1959, No. 277), made under the Food and Drugs Act, 1955.

statute may require a particular activity to be registered with the local authority; this normally means that if the prescribed standards are satisfied, the local authority will have no discretion, and will be legally bound to register a person on application[4]; sometimes a fee may be charged for registration, sometimes not.[5]

(j) Local authorities may also be concerned in proceedings for an injunction to prevent the infringement of some right of the public in which they are concerned; such as a public nuisance affecting the health of the district or the continued flouting of a byelaw or local Act in force in the local authority's area.[6] In these circumstances the Attorney-General should[7] be joined as a party, but it seems clear that the authority are entitled to commence the proceedings; they will have sufficient *locus standi.*

7. THE PUBLIC CORPORATIONS IN THE COURTS

The nature of statutory corporations and their powers is discussed in the next Chapter[8]; we are here concerned only with their position in litigation. In general terms, a statutory corporation is in no different position from that of any other litigant before the courts; a corporation cannot now plead a special period of limitation, either by virtue of some particular statute[9] or because of its status as a "public authority",[10] and the constituent statute does not customarily provide for such a

---

[4] Sometimes the registration authority are given powers of entry, as in the case of premises suspected of being used as a scrap metal store under s. 6 (2) of the Scrap Metal Dealers Act 1964; a police constable has similar powers of entry on registered premises, under s. 6 (1), *ibid.*

[5] A fee of £1 may be charged under the Rag Flock and Other Filling Materials Act, 1951, and see also para. 9 of Schedule 7 to the Betting, Gaming and Lotteries Act 1963 (small lotteries). If there is no express statutory authority for a fee, the registering (or licensing) authority have no power to charge a fee as a condition of issuing a registration certificate or a licence (see, for example, *Brocklebank* v. *R.*, [1925] 1 K.B. 52). This principle is of particular importance in planning law, as by reason thereof it has been held by the Secretary of State on appeal to him that a similar condition imposed in a planning permission was invalid; see Selected Appeal Decisions (Bulletins issued by the Minister of Housing and Local Government, and published by H.M.S.O.), II/17, and V/5.

[6] *A.-G.* v. *P.Y.A. Quarries, Ltd.*, [1957] 1 All E.R. 894; [1957] 2 Q.B. 169; *A.-G.* v. *Harris*, [1960] 3 All E.R. 207; [1961] 1 Q.B. 74, and cf. *A.-G.* v. *Melville Construction Co.* (1968), 112 Sol. Jo. 725 (concerning the breach of a tree preservation order).

[7] Under s. 100 of the Public Health Act, 1936, the local authority may apply for an injunction in their own name, where they are satisfied that summary proceedings for the abatement of a statutory nuisance will be inadequate. In *Warwickshire County Council* v. *British Railways Board*, [1969] 3 All E.R. 631; [1969] 1 W.L.R. 1117, Lord DENNING expressed the opinion *obiter* that the consent of the Attorney-General was not necessary where the local authority act under s. 276 of the Local Government Act, 1933 (see now s. 222 of the 1972 Act), which empowered them to take proceedings where they deem it expedient "for the promotion or protection of the interests of the inhabitants of their area"; but this opinion was not followed by GOFF, J., in *Prestatyn U.D.C.* v. *Prestatyn Raceway, Ltd.*, [1969] 3 All E.R. 1573.

[8] Chapter X, *post*, p. 317.

[9] Such, for example, as s. 11 of the Transport Act, 1947, repealed by s. 1 (c) of the Law Reform (Limitation of Actions, &c.) Act, 1954.

[10] Under the Public Authorities Protection Act, 1893, and s. 21 of the Limitation Act, 1939, both repealed by s. 1 of the Law Reform (Limitation of Actions &c.) Act, 1954.

corporation to have any other special privileges; the normal provision is merely that:

> "The Council shall be a body corporate with perpetual succession and a common seal."[11]

The only questions that arise in this context are the circumstances in which a statutory corporation may be entitled to Crown immunity, the extent to which it may plead statutory authority as a defence, and the liability of these corporations in *mandamus* or similar proceedings.

(a) Crown immunity.—The question whether a particular statutory corporation is entitled to Crown immunity (in so far as this still exists) depends on the terms of the constituent statute and in particular whether that statute has provided that the corporation shall be a Crown servant. With such problems is bound up the question whether the corporation is entitled to claim Crown privilege in litigation.[12] There is a distinction here between Ministers of the Crown or Government Departments and statutory bodies acting (or required to act) for and on behalf of the Crown on the one side, and independent authorities set up by statute, subject maybe to control to some degree by a Government Department, but not expressed to act for or on behalf of the Crown. The first class, "emanations of the Crown", to use a much criticised expression of DAY, J.,[13] are entitled to claim Crown privilege and Crown immunity; the second class are not so entitled. Where the borderline falls, has normally to be determined in relation to the particular constituent statute of the statutory body in question. The question must be considered in relation to some of the more important of the statutory corporations.

(i) The former British Transport Commission, and consequently the Railways Executive, and the other Executives, which were "nothing more nor less than agents of the Commission"[14] were clearly not agents of the Crown.

> "In the eye of the law the Commission is its own master and is answerable as fully as any other person or corporation. It is not the Crown and has none of the immunities or privileges of the Crown. Its servants are not civil servants, and its property is not Crown property. It is as much bound by Acts of Parliament as any other subject of the King. It is, of course, a public authority and its purposes, no doubt, are public purposes, but it is not a government department nor do its powers fall within the province of government."[15]

The four Boards set up by the Transport Act, 1962, seem to be in the same position in this respect as the former Commission,[16] and the

---

[11] Harbours Act, 1964, Schedule 1, para. 1. Since the doctrine of mortmain was abolished by the Charities Act, 1960, reference to "licences in mortmain", to be found in earlier statutes, is no longer necessary.

[12] *Ante*, p. 287.

[13] In *Gilbert* v. *Trinity House Corpn.* (1886), 17 Q.B.D. 795, at p. 801, and see *ante*, p. 289; and see DIPLOCK, L. J., in *B.B.C.* v. *Johns*, [1964] 1 All E.R. 923, at p. 943; [1965] Ch. 32, at p. 82 and below.

[14] *Tamlin* v. *Hannaford*, [1949] 2 All E.R. 327, at p. 329; [1950] 1 K.B. 18.

[15] *Ibid.*, *per* DENNING, L.J.

[16] Transport Act, 1962, s. 1.

"new authorities" established by the Transport Act, 1968, are expressly declared *not* to be servants or agents of the Crown.[17]

(ii) The Central Land Board, set up under the Town and Country Planning Act, 1947, and now dissolved[18] was an agent of the Crown, as it was required to exercise its functions "on behalf of the Crown"[19]; it was, therefore, entitled in a proper case to claim Crown privilege in litigation.[20] The Countryside Commission is probably in the same position.[1]

(iii) The Regional Health Authorities, Area Health Authorities, Special Health Authorities and the Family Practitioner Committees, constituted under the National Health Service Reorganisation Act, 1973, replacing similar bodies under the National Health Service Act, 1946, are all corporations by statute, and they are required to carry out the administration of the health service hospitals subject to the control and on behalf of the Secretary of State. The Secretary of State in turn, a corporation sole in his own right,[2] is the owner of the hospitals, which he can use for any of his functions under the Acts of 1946 and 1963.[3] All property vested in the Secretary of State must be held "in trust for His Majesty for the purposes of the [Ministry of Health]."[4] It was held, therefore,[5] that hospital premises were "occupied for the public service of the Crown" for the purposes of section 106 of the Public Health Act, 1936.[6] Section 13 of the National Health Service Act, 1946, made hospital boards and hospital management committees expressly liable in tort and contract,[7] but this section has been repealed by the National Health Service Reorganisation Act, 1973. It seems, therefore, that, unlike their predecessors, the hospital management committees, the new regional and area health authorities will be able to use Crown immunities, in so far as these are preserved under the Crown Proceedings Act, 1947.[8]

---

[17] Transport Act, 1968, s. 52 (5), and Chapter X, *post*, p. 303.

[18] The functions of the Board were transferred to the Minister of Housing and Local Government (now the Secretary of State for the Environment) on the dissolution of the Board by the Central Land Board (Dissolution and Transfer of Functions) Order, 1959 (S.I. 1959 No. 530), made under s. 63 of the Town and Country Planning Act, 1954.

[19] Town and Country Planning Act, 1947, s. 3 (3).

[20] *Glasgow Corpn.* v. *Central Land Board*, 1956 S.L.T. 41; *Conway* v. *Rimmer* (*ante*, p. 291).

[1] National Parks and Access to the Countryside Act, 1949, s. 2 (5), Countryside Act, 1968, s. 1.

[2] Ministry of Health Act, 1919, s. 7 (3).

[3] National Health Service Act, 1946, s. 6, (4), left unrepealed by the National Health Service Reorganisation Act, 1973.

[4] Ministry of Health Act, 1919, s. 7 (3).

[5] *Nottingham No. 1 Area Hospital Management Committee* v. *Owen*, [1957] 3 All E.R. 358; [1958] 1 Q.B. 50.

[6] See now Clean Air Act, 1956, s. 22. On the other hand the management committee or board of governors of a teaching hospital are the "occupiers" of the hospital for the purposes of the Landlord and Tenant Act, 1954, and not the Minister: *Hills (Patents), Ltd.* v. *Governors of University College Hospital*, [1955] 3 All E.R. 365; [1956] 1 Q.B. 90.

[7] See, *e.g.*, *Bullard* v. *Croydon Hospital Group Management Committee*, [1953] 1 All E.R. 596; [1953] 1 Q.B. 511.

[8] But not as to documents; see 1973 Act, Schedule 1, para. 15 (2).

(iv) The "commercial" corporations—the British Gas Corporation, the electricity boards and the air corporations—are certainly not Crown servants; they are not expressed to be so in their constituent statutes, and they are financially independent, if not self-supporting. The Atomic Energy Authority, in spite of the close control that is exercisable over its functions by the Secretary of State for Education and Science, would seem not to be a servant or agent of the Crown[9]; the Independent Broadcasting Authority is expressly excluded from claiming immunity,[10] as is the British Airports Authority.[11]

(v) The British Broadcasting Corporation is in a somewhat different position, in that it is incorporated by Royal Charter, but in *B.B.C.* v. *Johns*,[12] where it was argued that the B.B.C. was entitled to Crown immunity, and therefore to exemption from liability to income tax, it was held that Crown immunity did not apply. In the course of his judgment in the Court of Appeal, DANCKWERTS, L.J., said[13]:

> "The fact that the B.B.C. was incorporated by royal charter is not a conclusive factor. . . . It appears to me that the B.B.C. was deliberately incorporated in the form in which it was created, because it was thought to be in the public interest that broadcasting should not be conducted by a government agency or as a government function."

Where the public corporation is created by some foreign state, the question may then arise whether it is entitled to immunity from legal process in this country on the ground that is "part" of the foreign Government. A government corporation is entitled to immunity even if its functions are of a commercial character,[14] and so was a corporation whose objects were to assist, promote, encourage and advance the industrial development, prosperity and economic welfare of the Province of New Brunswick; this was described by Lord DENNING, M.R., as the "alter ego" of the Government of New Brunswick.[15]

(b) Statutory authority.—The circumstances in which statutory authority may be pleaded as a defence by a statutory corporation, and the general principles governing that defence, are the same as those applicable to a local authority, *mutatis mutandis*.[16] Similarly, if the statutory corporation in question were to exceed its statutory powers, the principle and consequences of the doctrine of *ultra vires* would apply, except that in practice the statutory powers of these corporations seem to be drawn in very wide terms, and it would consequently be difficult to establish an actual case of an *ultra vires* act.[17]

---

[9] It is not so treated in its constituent statute, the Atomic Energy Authority Act, 1954.

[10] Independent Broadcasting Authority Act, 1973, s. 2 (4).

[11] Airports Authority Act, 1965, s. 1 (7).

[12] [1964] 1 All E.R. 923; [1965] Ch. 32.

[13] *Ibid.*, at pp. 937–8.

[14] *Baccus S.R.L.* v. *Servicio Nacional del Trigo*, [1957] 1 Q.B. 438.

[15] *Mellenger* v. *New Brunswick Development Corpn.*, [1971] 2 All E.R. 593; [1971] 1 W.L.R. 604.

[16] *Ante*, p. 297.

[17] See, for example, the extent of the powers given to the Atomic Energy Authority by the Acts, of 1954, especially s. 2 (2) (d) thereof, empowering the Authority to "do all such things . . . as appear to the Authority necessary or expedient for the exercise of the foregoing powers". The High Court at least examined the powers of the British Railways Board and found the Board was acting *intra vires*, in *Charles Roberts & Co., Ltd.* v. *British Railways Board*, [1964] 3 All E.R. 651; [1965] 1 W.L.R. 396.

(c) Breach of statutory duty.—In many cases the constituent statute imposes express duties on a statutory corporation. For example, by the Electricity Act, 1957 (s. 2 (5)), it is made the duty (*inter alia*) of the Central Electricity Generating Board to

> "develop and maintain an efficient, co-ordinated and economical system of supply of electricity in bulk for all parts of England and Wales".

It is difficult to visualise circumstances in which a private individual would be able to sue the Board for damages in respect of an alleged breach of such a wide duty, and also be able to show that he (the plaintiff), being one of a class of persons whom the statute was designed to benefit, had suffered actual damage as a consequence of the breach of the duty.[18] In a different field, however, the "regulatory" commissions, such as the General Dental Council (a statutory corporation set up under the Dentists Act, 1956), are given a number of statutory duties, and in their case, the courts will be able to exercise powers of enforcement by application of the normal principles of judicial review.[19]

It is also doubtful whether the courts would be able to grant an order of *mandamus* to enforce the execution of a statutory duty by a public corporation in circumstances such as section 2 (5) of the Electricity Act, 1957 (*ante*).[20] Where there is some other remedy, *mandamus* will not lie,[21] but in many of these cases there is no question of any alternative remedy—it is a matter of *mandamus* or a denial of "justice". On the other hand, *mandamus* is a discretionary remedy, and the courts may be of the opinion that it was the intention of the statute to impose duties of imperfect obligation only, and to leave enforcement to Parliament. The question might be looked at from another point of view as being an example of the distinction between matters of policy, which is the concern of the politicians and of Parliament, and questions of law which alone are the concern of the courts. The difficulty here of course in this context is that Parliament also may have virtually no control. There has as yet been no litigant bold enough to ask for an order of *mandamus* against a public corporation,[1] and it is perhaps doubtful whether he would achieve much by so doing.

As pointed out by Professor Robson,[2] statute has in some cases formulated the powers of a statutory corporation in subjective terms,

---

[18] See *ante*, p. 297.

[19] And see Chapter VI, *ante*, p. 111.

[20] And compare s. 12 (3) of the Independent Broadcasting Authority Act, 1973, (replacing earlier legislation to the same effect) whereby the Independent Broadcasting Authority are required to "do all that they can to secure . . . that there is adequate competition to supply programmes between a number of programme contractors . .". These duties are as vague from the point of view of enforcement against the corporations, as are their powers when it comes to a question of *ultra vires*, as above mentioned. Nevertheless, the Court of Appeal was prepared to require the Authority to carry out their duty under s. 4 (1) (a) of the 1973 Act (as it now is) to ensure that the programmes broadcast do not offend against good taste or decency: see *A.-G.* v. *Independent Broadcasting Authority*, [1973] 1 All E.R. 689; [1973] Q.B. 629.

[21] See, *e.g.*, *R.* v. *Dunsheath, ex parte Meredith*, [1950] 2 All E.R. 741; [1951] 1 K.B. 127, one of the few cases reported on *mandamus* proceedings in the last twenty years or so that did not deal with the criminal jurisdiction of local magistrates.

[1] Or in a case arising out of a section of a statute imposing a duty on a Minister of the Crown to take steps to ensure a national policy for some particular service; see, *e.g.*, Water Act, 1945, s. 1.

[2] *Nationalised Industry and Public Ownership* (1960), at p. 71.

empowering them to be the judges of the extent of those powers.[3] In such cases the doctrine of *ultra vires* ceases to have any meaning, by whatever legal machinery it is sought to be invoked. The typical section of an enabling statute stating that the statutory corporation in question shall have no power to commit an unlawful act[4] does not really take the matter any further, as the *ultra vires* doctrine is not concerned with acts which are already prohibited by the ordinary criminal or civil law; further, as Professor Robson pertinently asks,[5] what is the correct legal position if a Minister acting within his very widely drawn legal powers, gives directions to a statutory corporation to commit an "unlawful act"?

---

[3] For example, the National Coal Board are empowered to do anything "which in their opinion is calculated to facilitate the proper discharge of their duties": Coal Industry Nationalisation Act, 1946, s. 1 (3); Robson, *op. cit.*, p. 71, and *cf.* footnote 20 on p. 315, *ante*.

[4] For example, Gas Act, 1948, s. 1 (9).

[5] *Op. cit.*, p. 72.

CHAPTER X

THE PUBLIC CORPORATIONS

1. INTRODUCTION

We have now considered what is normally understood by the term "central government"; local government will be dealt with in the Chapters that follow: it remains to discuss the third and newest form of government agency, the public corporation.[1]

Government in the days before the industrial revolution in this country was traditionally a matter of protecting the realm against the King's enemies from without, and of maintaining internal order, the latter being achieved somewhat inadequately by the minimum possible number of officials and administrative agencies; local government was almost exclusively in the control of the local justices of the peace.[2] On occasion, however, a particular problem would arise demanding the setting up of some kind of special administrative machinery. The Council of the North and the Council of Wales were the answer of the early Tudors to the menaces from across the borders of their kingdom; and when the drainage of Romney Marsh, the Fens and of other areas became a necessity, a semi-military organisation was abandoned in favour of purely civilian Commissioners of Sewers.[3] These Commissioners had several features in common with the modern public corporations, in that they were established by statute for the purpose of carrying out a limited range of functions and a particular administrative task, and, moreover, in order to carry out that task, they were given considerable independence of the central government. They were controlled primarily (like their contemporaries, the justices of the peace) through and by the superior courts of law, especially the Court of King's Bench, and they were themselves regarded rather as courts of law than as public corporations or local authorities in any modern sense. Indeed, at that time, the idea of corporate personality had not been developed, and a Tudor lawyer would have seen no point in ascribing personality to a commission of private gentlemen subject to control by the prerogative writs of *certiorari*, *mandamus* and prohibition.

Nevertheless, the germ of the idea that a special administrative task

---

[1] On this topic generally, see Hood Phillips, *Constitutional and Administrative Law* (5th Edn.), Chapter 27 and literature listed on p. 472 thereof. For a comparative analytical treatment of public corporations in many Western countries, see *Government Enterprise* (ed. Friedmann and Garner), 1970.

[2] In particular, in the counties outside the boroughs.

[3] At first *ac hoc* Commissions were issued by virtue of the royal prerogative, then from 1427 onwards Commissioners of Sewers were established by statute, empowered to issue ordinances and to supervise their execution almost in the modern fashion: Holdsworth, *History of English Law*, Vol. X, pp. 196 *et seq.*

needed a special administrative authority to carry it out lived on. With the development of more sophisticated juristic concepts, the *ad hoc* authority was created, having a separate corporate personality. Many such authorities were brought into being in the nineteenth century under various private Acts of Parliament, such as the improvement commissioners, the paving commissioners, the boards of health and the poor law boards (and later the school boards), established for many urban areas. Those survivors from Victorian days, the Mersey Docks and Harbour Board and the Metropolitan Water Board, like the *ad hoc* authorities, were nearer to the modern corporations than were the earlier Commissioners.

All these various bodies, however, were entrusted with statutory functions to be exercisable only over a defined, comparatively restricted local area. The urge towards nationalisation of many public undertakings recognised and implemented by the Socialist Government that came into power at the end of the Second World War, made development of some new form of administrative machinery essential. Comparative independence of Treasury and Whitehall control, and of party politics, seemed to be essential if commercial enterprise was to have any scope at all under public ownership. The precedents were to hand,[4] and therefore the modern form of public corporation was adopted to administer the newly "nationalised industries", and also to play its part in managing some of the agencies of the "Welfare State" (in particular the hospitals), which formed the other part of the Government's "reconstruction" programme. The new agencies were therefore given separate corporate existence and limited functions, but responsibility for those functions extended over the whole country, or over a wide area thereof, much greater than that which could conveniently be administered by a single all-purpose local authority. The modern public corporation is really a compromise between nationalisation and private enterprise; the institution is essentially an instrument devised for administering some particular enterprise in the public interest. The other outstanding feature of the public corporation is its independence—legally virtually complete—of the central government, while carrying on an enterprise of national importance. In some cases the idea of a commercial enterprise is to the fore—this is obvious in the case of the gas and electricity corporations, for example; in the case of other corporations such as the Countryside Commission, the emphasis is on regulation, but even here the idea of public enterprise is not totally absent, the purpose of the corporation being to further "national parks" and the proper use of the countryside.

No statute or court has ever attempted or been asked to define the expression "public corporation", but it is desirable that a description should at least be attempted. The essential characteristics may perhaps be listed as follows:

(a) the corporation must, as the name implies, have a separate cor-

---

[4] The London Passenger Transport Board, established in 1934, furnished a more recent precedent.

porate personality, conferred either by statute or by charter issued under the royal prerogative[5];

(b) the corporation must by its constituent statute or charter be entrusted with a limited range of functions of a governmental character, exercisable over a defined but normally extensive area, or in some cases over the country as a whole;

(c) the corporation must in law be independent of the central government, capable of being sued in its own name; in a few cases it may be a Crown servant[6] but normally it is independent of the central government for most practical purposes, except general policy.

In addition, there are a number of bodies of a somewhat anomalous character which satisfy the two last named of these characteristics but which are not legal persons in law, either because the constituent statute has not so provided, or because a Royal Charter has not been issued. Such are the Law Commission[7] and formerly the Race Relations Board,[8] to give examples of recently created agencies.[9]

2. THE CORPORATIONS

Any attempt at logical classification of the public corporations as they at present exist (which does not amount to a mere list) is almost as vain as an attempt at a precise definition, but such a task at least provides a means of describing them. They fall naturally into three large and somewhat ill-assorted groups.

(a) Commercial undertakings.—This group includes the corporations managing the great public utilities which were taken into public ownership and control for the most part during the years immediately succeeding the Second World War, and they are sometimes referred to as "the nationalised industries". The group therefore includes:

(i) *Electricity.*—The Central Electricity Generating Board, the Central Electricity Council and the twelve Area Electricity Boards.[10]

(ii) *Gas.*—The former Gas Council and the Area Gas Boards, now replaced by the British Gas Corporation.[11]

(iii) *Coal.*—The National Coal Board.[12]

---

[5] The only modern corporations that we are here considering that have been created by charter are the British Broadcasting Corporation and the Nature Conservancy. The Bank of England was created by Charter in 1694.

[6] Sometimes a corporation may be required so to act on occasion, as may be the case with the Sugar Board.

[7] Law Commissions Act 1965.

[8] Race Relations Act 1965; now a corporate body by the Act of 1968.

[9] The Criminal Injuries Compensation Board is another example; this body (primarily a tribunal) is a creature of the Royal Prerogative, not being referred to in the statute book. It obtains its revenue from the general Vote of the Home Office: see Chapter VIII, *ante*, p. 250.

[10] Electricity Acts of 1947 and 1957; there are two further Boards in Scotland.

[11] Gas Act, 1948, as amended by the Gas Act, 1972.

[12] Coal Act, 1938; Coal Industry (Nationalisation) Act, 1946; Coal Industry Act, 1949.

(iv) *Surface Transport.*—On the nationalisation of the railways in 1947, the Transport Act of that year established the British Transport Commission and six subordinate Executives, all of which were public corporations but which could act only as agents for and on the instructions of the British Transport Commission.[13] The Transport Act, 1962, made drastic alterations in this organisation. The British Transport Commission was dissolved, its assets and responsibilities being divided between four Boards, the British Railways Board, the London Transport Board, the British Transport Docks Board, and the British Waterways Board.[14] In addition, the Railways Board was required to set up a number of Regional Railway Boards[15] to share between them responsibility, on behalf of the British Railways Board, but these were in turn abolished by the Transport Act, 1968. The 1968 Act also established the National Freight Corporation and the Freight Integration Council (the latter *not* having corporate status). The Council have[16] the duty of integrating the work of the railways, the Docks Board, the Waterways Board, the Freight Corporation, the National Bus Company, the Scottish Group, under the general directions of the Secretary of State for the Environment, and the Post Office (under the general directions of the Minister for Posts and Telecommunications).

(v) *Broadcasting and Communications.*—The Independent Broadcasting Authority (formerly the Independent Television Authority, but so re-named by the Sound Broadcasting Act, 1972), and the British Broadcasting Corporation are not really of equal status, as the I.B.A. was originally established as the Independent Television Authority by the Television Act, 1954,[17] and is legally independent of but subject to general directions from the Minister of Posts and Telecommunications. The B.B.C. was established by charter in 1927, the charter being renewable periodically (at present at ten year intervals), and a licence to broadcast programmes is granted by the Minister to the Corporation, in which power is reserved to the Minister enabling him to give instructions prohibiting the Corporation from broadcasting specified matter.[18] The Post Office was established as a public corporation by the Post Office Act, 1969, and given the responsibility of providing postal and telecommunications services, and also a "giro" system; the National Savings Bank was, by the same Act, made the responsibility of the Treasury.

---

[13] Transport Act, 1947, s. 5; the Executives were later abolished by the Transport Act, 1953.

[14] Transport Act, 1962, s. 1 (1). This Board has been left unaffected by the re-organisation of water generally by the Water Act, 1973.

[15] *Ibid.*, s. 2 (2).

[16] 1968 Act, s. 6.

[17] See now Independent Broadcasting Authority Act, 1973.

[18] Wireless Telegraphy Act, 1949; Television Act, 1954; see now the consolidating Independent Broadcasting Authority Act, 1973.

(vi) *Atomic Energy.*—The Atomic Energy Authority.[19]

(vii) *Air Transport.*—The Civil Aviation Authority (responsible for the regulation and licensing of civil aircraft),[20] the British Airways Board (responsible for providing air transport services and controlling the British Overseas Airways Corporation and the British European Airways Corporation)[1] and also the British Airports Authority, responsible for management of aerodromes at Heathrow, Gatwick Stansted and Prestwick.[2]

In this group, the functions carried on by the particular corporations are really commercial businesses, and because of the nature of the work undertaken, the managing body resembles the board of directors of a public company. It is usually, but not necessarily, contemplated in the constituent statute that such a corporation shall be financially self-supporting, although the national exchequer provides a reserve against insolvency, unless Parliament subsequently decides the corporation must be put into liquidation.[3] The enterprise in question is usually (but not invariably, as in the case of British Airways) a monopoly, and therefore the corporation is expected (often expressly required, by the constituent statute) to conduct its affairs in the public interest, and not exclusively for profit, as in private industry. It is claimed by the supporters of this kind of State business that the elimination of competition favours efficiency and obviates waste and extravagant advertising. The device of the public corporation is of particular value in this context as it allows some measure of commercial enterprise and control in management by persons of practical experience, while avoiding the detailed Parliamentary and Treasury control which would be inseparable from direct administration by the central government. It was apparently this latter argument that persuaded H.M. Government to convert the Post Office into a public corporation.

In the special case of road passenger transport and road haulage, Parliament has seen fit to use a different kind of machinery. Prior to nationalisation of the railways in 1947, the railway companies had obtained substantial shareholdings—in many cases all the shares—in local omnibus companies, and the partial nationalisation of road haulage under the Transport Act, 1947 took the form of acquiring the shares in private companies. No formal organisation for the administration of these holdings was made under the 1947 Act, but the Transport Act, 1962 established a public corporation known as the Transport Holding Company,[4] which was expressly required to hold and manage these securities in public transport companies, as if it were "a company engaged in a commercial enterprise". The directors of the company were appointed by the Minister of Transport, and the Minister had wide

[19] Atomic Energy Authority Act, 1954.
[20] Civil Aviation Act, 1971.
[1] *Ibid.*, replacing the Air Corporations Act, 1949. BOAC and BEA are dissolved as of April 1st, 1974, Air Corporations (dissolution) Order 1973, S.I. 1973 No. 2175
[2] Airports Authority Act 1965, s. 1.
[3] As in the case of the British Transport Commission (*ante*).
[4] Transport Act, 1962, s. 29 (1) and (6).

power to give directions to the Company and even could by order extend or vary the objects and powers of the Company.[5]

In practice, the Minister gave very few directions and these related normally to such financial matters as investment policy, but of course the directors of the Company frequently consulted with representatives of the Ministry. Below the Company was a vast structure of companies, each incorporated under the Companies Acts, in most of which all the shares were held by the Holding Company,[6] and these companies themselves were grouped for management purposes. Thus, the road passenger companies were split regionally between six "Tilling" Groups and a Scottish group (39 separate companies in all), and there were also 21 companies in which the Holding Company owned substantial (but not controlling) holdings. Similarly, in road haulage there were over 30 companies organised in five groups, as well as two shipping companies and companies operating travel agencies (in particular Thos. Cook & Son, Ltd). The relationship between the Holding Company and these commercial companies was not regulated by the Act of 1962, as it depended entirely on company law. The Holding Company appointed all the directors, which they were entitled to do by virtue of their shareholdings, and in making certain of the most important appointments they consulted with the Ministry in accordance with an "understanding" (*not* a formal direction) to that effect. In choosing directors the Holding Company were concerned to secure efficient management, and usually individuals were chosen who were experienced in the transport industry.

This structure was reorganised by the Transport Act, 1968 which provided for the eventual dissolution of the Transport Holding Company. All the securities held by the Holding Company in omnibus companies (listed in Schedule 7) were transferred to a new public corporation, the National Bus Company, except those relating to Scotland which were transferred to another new public corporation, known as the Scottish Transport Group (see s. 28 (2)). So far as transport of goods by road is concerned, the assets of the Holding Company (such as British Road Services Ltd. and Pickfords) relating thereto are transferred to yet another new public corporation, the National Freight Corporation (s. 4 and Sched. 3). All the boards and new authorities are required to act in carrying on their statutory activities "as if they were a company engaged in a commercial enterprise" (s. 134 (2)), and none of the new authorities are to be regarded as the servant or agent of the Crown (s. 52 (5)). In practice it seems that these bodies will operate in a manner very similar to that followed by the Transport Holding Company. This elaborate story was taken one stage further by the Transport Holding Company Act, 1972, under which the Secretary of State obtained power to give directions to the Holding Company to sell off

---

[5] *Ibid.*, s. 29 (4) and (9).

[6] For the list of holdings as at the date of the Act, see 1962 Act, Fourth Schedule, Part IV, lists A and B. Since 1962, more holdings were acquired, especially in road haulage (see Annual Reports of the Transport Holding Company, submitted to Parliament under s. 29 (16) of the Act).

any portion or portions of its assets; the first directions given under the Act concerned the sale of the shares in Thos. Cook & Son, Ltd.

In addition, the Minister of Transport was enabled by the Act of 1968 to set up in areas specified by him, passenger transport authorities and passenger transport executives,[7] which between them carry on all road passenger undertakings in the area and these authorities thereupon acquire the assets of local authority and commercial bus companies operating in the area. In the metropolitan counties established by the Local Government Act, 1972,[8] the county councils become passenger transport authorities and a separate passenger executive will be established in parallel with them for each metropolitan county.[9]

It might be assumed that this elaborate structure had been invented for the purpose of concealing "nationalisation" from the public; but this would be false. The system has grown as a result of history and was not consciously created in the first place. Detailed public control over the operation of the various companies is certainly remote as a consequence, but at least the machinery was justified by the quite substantial profit that the Holding Company was able to hand over to the Exchequer each year.

(b) Managerial bodies administering public services.—This group includes those public corporations which have been established to undertake the control of some institution or series of institutions which are not commercial in nature, but which are sufficiently specialised to merit direct administration apart from the established organs of central or local government. In this group are the Regional Health Authorities,[10] their agents the Area Health Authorities, and any still existing governors of teaching hospitals,[11] and also the new town development corporations[12] and the New Towns Commission.[13] The National Ports Council[14] is a newcomer to this group; their principal duties include the formulation of a national plan for the development and improvement of harbours. The Housing Corporation was set up by the Housing Act 1964[15] to assist housing societies to provide new housing, and the Water Resources Board[16] was a research body constituted primarily to give advice on matters of water conservation. The Tourist Boards established by the Act of 1969,[17] may perhaps be included in this group, in that they are expected to make schemes for the furtherance of tourism and may make grants or loans for the provision

---

[7] An Executive is to be deemed to be a local authority for superannuation purposes (Schedule 4, Part II, para. 5) but is a body corporate by virtue of s. 9 (1) (b) of the Act. An Authority may be given corporate status by order made by the Secretary of State under s. 9 and Schedule 4, Part III, para. 2.

[8] *Post*, Chapter XI, p. 360, and Chapter XVI, p. 455.

[9] Local Government Act, 1972, s. 202.

[10] National Health Service Reorganisation Act, 1973, s. 5.

[11] *Ibid.*, s. 15.

[12] New Towns Act, 1946; New Towns Act 1965.

[13] New Towns Acts, 1959 and 1965.

[14] Harbours Act 1964, s. 1, and Schedule 1, para. 1.

[15] Section 1 and Schedule 1, para. 1.

[16] Water Resources Act 1963, s. 13 and Schedule 6, para. 1, dissolved by the Water Act, 1973, and replace by the National Water Council.

[17] The Boards are the British Tourist Authority, the English Tourist Board, the Scottish Tourist Board and the Wales Tourist Board; Development of Tourism Act, 1969.

of new hotels. Another newcomer is the British Library Board, established to manage the newly-created British Library, which is to be "a national centre for reference study and bibliographical and other information services . . .".[18] Corporations in this group are not expected to be economically self-supporting, and in consequence, they are financially and in many other respects subject to detailed control by the central government.

(c) Regulatory bodies.—In this group are to be found a number of corporations entrusted with the regulation and furtherance of particular defined social policies. They are usually much "closer" to the Central Government than are the corporations in the other groups, in that they are more susceptible to detailed directions from a Minister; indeed, they are sometimes little more than a specialised branch of a Central Department. Thus, the Location of Offices Bureau, designed to encourage the moving of offices away from London, could have been constituted as a section of the Department of the Environment; instead it is a public corporation, established by statutory instrument made under a 20 year old statute.[19] The Eggs Authority[20] might well have been established as a Government sub-Department; so might the National Radiological Protection Board, especially as its statutory functions may be increased by directions given by "the Health Ministers".[1] The Hairdressing Council,[2] and the Hearing Aid Council,[3] the Horserace Betting Levy Board[4] and the White Fish Authority[5] are perhaps a little further removed from central government. So was the Land Commission,[6] the Countryside Commission[7] and the Nature Conservancy (established under Royal Charter in 1949). A very specialised example of a public corporation established to execute a defined section of Government policy of great political and national importance, was the former National Board for Prices and Incomes, established by Royal Warrant in April 1965, but put on a statutory basis as a corporation by the Prices and Incomes Act, 1966.[8] The Counter-Inflation Act, 1973, created new statutory corporations having much the same functions, but possessing novel titles, namely, the two "Agencies" to be known as the Price Commission and the Pay Board, which may subsequently be amalgamated into a single Agency, by Order in Council.[9] Of considerable importance is the Commission on Industrial Relations, established by the Industrial Relations Act, 1971, and so is the Monopolies and Mergers

[18] British Library Act, 1972, s. 1.
[19] Location of Offices Bureau Order, 1963 (S.I., 1963, No. 792), made under s. 8 of the Minister of Town and Country Planning Act 1943.
[20] Agriculture Act, 1970.
[1] Radiological Protection Act, 1970.
[2] Hairdressers (Registration) Act, 1964, s. 1, and Schedule 1, para. 6.
[3] Hearing Aid Council Act, 1968.
[4] Betting, Gaming and Lotteries Act, 1963, s. 24.
[5] Sea Fish Industry Act, 1970; the Herring Fish Industry Board has similar functions.
[6] Land Commission Act, 1967, s. 1 and Schedule 1; the Commission was dissolved by the Land Commission Dissolution Act, 1971.
[7] Formerly the National Parks Commission, established by the National Parks and Access to the Countryside Act, 1949. Its title was changed by the Countryside Act, 1968.
[8] Section 1 and Schedule 1 (since repealed).
[9] Act of 1973, s. 1; for constitution, see Schedule 1.

Commission, re-constituted by the Fair Trading Act, 1973. The Local Employment Act, 1972 established three new corporations (one each for England, Scotland and Wales) to manage industrial estates vested in them by the Secretary of State for Trade and Industry. The Decimal Currency Board is another example of a corporation given a very definite piece of work to do; the creating statute[10] even contains provision for the "death" in duecourse of the Board which it creates. The Medicines Commission will, it is anticipated, have a more permanent existence (see Medicines Act, 1968).

This class of public corporations, which is not susceptible of precise delimitation, has been growing very rapidly in recent years. The problems of control[11] are not always as acute in this class as they are with others, as many of these corporations are visualised by their "parents" (the Government of the day) as a specialised instrument to perform some defined task, and therefore the legal powers and duties of the corporation are more precisely defined.

3. GENERAL FEATURES OF PUBLIC CORPORATIONS

Every public corporation is different in detail as to its constitution and powers, but there are a number of features common to all or to most corporations.[12]

(a) *As to constitution.*—The constitution of no two public corporations is identical. Each, however, has a governing body established by the constituent statute or charter, consisting of a chairman and a defined number of members.[13] A power to appoint the chairman, a vice-chairman and the members, to prescribe their tenure of office, and to dismiss from or terminate an office is also usually provided for by statute, and is often entrusted to a Minister of the Central Government. Sometimes the Minister is restricted by the statute in his choice of members; sometimes he is required to consult with outside bodies (such as local authorities) before making appointments; more often he is unfettered in his choice. In most cases where members of a public corporation are paid a salary, they are disqualified from becoming Members of the House of Commons.[14] Consequently a Member of Parliament

---

[10] Decimal Currency Act, 1967.

[11] *Post*, p. 327.

[12] See table, *post*, p. 342.

[13] In some cases the size of the governing body is left to the discretion of the appointing Minister (this is so with the Regional Health Authorities), and sometimes he may be able to vary the size of the Board (in the case of the National Radiological Protection Board, after consultation with the existing members: Radiological Protection Act, 1970, s. 2 (2)).

[14] See Parts II and III of Schedule 1 to the House of Commons Disqualification Act, 1957. All members of those corporations and other bodies which are listed in Part II are disqualified from being members of the House of Commons; Part III similarly lists particular offices to which disqualification also attaches. When a new corporation is brought into existence by statute it is customary to include in the statute a provision adding the corporation to the bodies in Part II: see, for example, Water Resources Act 1963, Schedule 6, para. 4; Medicines Act, 1968, s 2 (6). However, this is not always done: see Hairdressers (Registration) Act, 1964. The Nature Conservancy, Rural Development Boards, the Meat and Livestock Commission and the Hearing Aid Council, are the only corporations listed in the table given on p. 342, *post*, which do not appear in either Part II or Part III of the Schedule to the 1957 Act (as amended). Chairmen in receipt of remuneration only are included in Part III in so far as the health service cor-

appointed as a member of such a public corporation must resign his seat in the House. There is no corresponding restriction on membership of the House of Lords. Too great a freedom conferred on a Minister in this matter may of course lead to charges of nepotism or favouritism or of making appointments on political grounds, but at least a Minister is answerable for any such acts to Parliament. It is also customary to provide in the constituent statute for cases where a member of the governing body of the corporation has a financial interest in a matter with which the corporation is concerned.[15] In many cases the statute will provide for a salary to be paid to the chairman of a corporation, and in most cases to the members also.

(b) *As to finance.*—It is normal practice in the statutes for a public corporation to be required to keep its own separate accounts, to have these audited by qualified auditors,[16] and to cause the accounts and a copy of any report thereon made by the auditors to be published annually, together with a general report of the activities of the corporation; in many cases the accounts and report have to be presented to Parliament. The nationalised industries are, in general, expected to pay their way "taking one year with another",[17] but other corporations are entirely or mainly dependent on grants from the national exchequer. In the case of the corporations that are now managing businesses formerly in private ownership, interest may have to be paid on stock granted to former shareholders, and the rate of interest to be paid is regulated by Ministerial directions issued from time to time under statutory authority.[18] The "non-commercial" corporations, such as the Countryside Commission, will normally be subject to audit by the Comptroller and Auditor-General.[19]

(c) *As to status.*—Some public corporations are expressly required by their constituent statutes to act for and on behalf of the Crown[20]; others can act only on the directions of a specific Minister,[1] whilst others, and these include all the corporations in our first class above mentioned as controlling undertakings, are legally independent. The latter are therefore not Crown servants and are not entitled to claim Crown privilege or immunity in litigation.[2] Although the National Radio-

porations are concerned: see National Health Service Reorganisation Act, 1973, Schedule 4, para. 77.

[15] See the elaborate provisions added to the Act of 1957 by s. 4 and the Schedule to the Air Corporations Act, 1969, and compare the position in local government; *post*, p. 378.

[16] See, for example, Airports Authority Act, 1965, s. 8 (2).

[17] White Paper on *The Financial and Economic Obligations of the Nationalised Industries*, Cmd. 1337, dated April 1961; see para. 5 thereof.

[18] See, for example, directions given by the Minister of Fuel and Power to the former Area Gas Boards on April 20, 1949, April 28, 1950 and July 30, 1953, under the Gas Act, 1948, Schedule 2, Part II, para. 5 (Reports of the Gas Council, 1948–50 at p. 102, 1950–1 at p. 84, and 1952–3 at p. 85).

[19] *Cf.* the system of audit of accounts of local authorities; Chapter XV, *post*, p. 426.

[20] For example, the former Central Land Board; Town and Country Planning Act, 1947, s. 3 (3).

[1] Such as Area Health Authorities: National Health Service Reorganisation Act, 1973, s. 7.

[2] *Tamlin* v. *Hannaford*, [1949] 2 All E.R. 327; [1950] 1 K.B. 18, and see Chapter IX, *ante*, p. 274. In some cases it is expressly provided that a corporation is not to be regarded as the servant or agent of the Crown: see, for example, Transport Act, 1962, s. 30, and Transport Act, 1968, s. 52 (5) and (in relation to the Commission on Industrial Relations), Industrial Relations Act, 1971, Schedule 3, para. 31 (2).

logical Protection Board is expressly declared not to be a servant or agent of the Crown,[3] any land occupied by the Board is to be deemed to be occupied by or on behalf of the Crown for public purposes.[4]

4. CONTROLS OVER PUBLIC CORPORATIONS

(a) Judicial control.—The ordinary means of judicial control over the activities of any government agency apply equally, at least in theory, to a public corporation; indeed the jurisdiction of the courts over a public corporation is the same as it is over any private or public company, except that the powers of the former depend on the terms of a special statute while the powers of a company will depend on the terms of its memorandum of association.[5] In many cases, however, the statutory powers of a public corporation are so widely drawn that it becomes virtually impossible even to visualise circumstances in which any court could hold any particular act of such a corporation to be *ultra vires*. Where duties are imposed on a corporation by statute these also are often so vaguely drawn that it would be impracticable to obtain a *mandamus* against the corporation or to sue the corporation in an action for breach of statutory duty. Thus, by section 2 (1) of the Atomic Energy Act, 1946, and section 1 (1) of the Radioactive Substances Act, 1948, the Atomic Energy Authority[6] is empowered to produce, use and dispose of atomic energy, to carry out research and

> "to do such things as may seem to them necessary and expedient for the exercise of the foregoing powers".

Air services provided by the British European Airways Corporation and the British Overseas Airways Corporation must be provided "at reasonable charges",[7] but it is doubtful whether any court could be persuaded to avoid a contract made with the Corporation on the ground that the charges were not "reasonable". The Central Electricity Generating Board are under a statutory duty[8]

> "to develop and maintain an efficient, co-ordinated and economical supply of electricity":

but this also seems to be a duty of imperfect obligation, in the sense that it is unenforceable in a court of law. Many other examples of a like kind will be found on perusal of the statute book. It is also by no means clear whether the power to commence proceedings to restrain a public corporation from acting *ultra vires* is confined to a person "aggrieved" by any such act (as in *Smith* v. *London Transport Executive, ante*). Can, for example, the responsible Minister himself take such proceedings?

---

[3] Radiological Protection Act, 1970, s. 2 (9).
[4] *Ibid.*, s. 2 (4).
[5] *Smith* v. *London Transport Executive*, [1951] 1 All E.R. 667; [1951] A.C. 555.
[6] Established by the Atomic Energy Authority Act, 1954.
[7] Air Corporations Act, 1949, s. 1; these two corporations are now subject to control by the British Airways Board, which may give them directions: Civil Aviation Act, 1971, s. 38.
[8] Electricity Act, 1957, s. 2 (5).

There are no "shareholders", who can bring themselves within the company law rule of *Burland* v. *Earle*,[9] but who can invoke the jurisdiction of the Attorney-General in such cases?

On the other hand, public corporations may sue and are liable to be sued as are any other legal persons. The usual statutory provision is that the corporation "shall be a body corporate with perpetual succession"[10] and legal proceedings must then be taken by or against the corporation in its corporate name. The corporation will be liable for the wrongful acts of its servants or agents in accordance with the ordinary principles of the law of agency and vicarious liability.[11] Where a statute refers to a "person", this will normally include a public corporation.[12] Where a corporation has been created as part of a scheme of nationalisation of a particular industry, the corporation will normally inherit the privileges and obligations of the companies or other bodies whom they have succeeded, and the constituent statute will make provision accordingly.[13] In some cases the statute may expressly provide that a corporation shall be liable to be sued,[14] but this is unusual. Crown privilege will not apply to a corporation[15] unless and except in so far as it may be required to act for or on behalf of the Crown, and in such a case privilege may be applied by the statute.[16] Formerly, following the precedent set for local authorities by the Public Authorities Protection Act, 1893,[17] constituent statutes made provision for favourable periods of limitation to apply to actions against public corporations,[18] but now, by the Law Reform (Limitation of Actions &c.) Act, 1954, these special periods have been abolished, and a public corporation—and a local authority for that matter—stands in this respect in the same position as any other litigant. The constituent statute will also often provide that the corporation in question shall have power to hold land "without licence in mortmain"; this has been no longer necessary since the abolition of the doctrine of mortmain by section 38 of the Charities Act, 1960, and every corporation now has power to hold land. Express statutory power is, however, still necessary if the corporation wishes to acquire land compulsorily.

---

[9] [1902] A.C. 83.

[10] For example, Independent Broadcasting Authority Act, 1973, Schedule 1, para. 3 (1); Atomic Energy Authority Act, 1954, Schedule 1, para. 1. Sometimes the words "and a common seal" are added; see, *e.g.*, Transport Act, 1968, s. 9 (1) (b).

[11] See, for example, *Barnett* v. *Chelsea and Kensington Hospital Management Committee*, [1968] 1 All E.R. 1068.

[12] Interpretation Act, 1889, s. 12.

[13] Coal Industry Nationalisation Act, 1946, ss. 5–9, and 49; Gas Act, 1948, Part II.

[14] National Health Service Act, 1946, s. 13 (now repealed). Nevertheless, a hospital is premises "occupied for the public service of the Crown", and therefore in public health and related legislation (*e.g.*, the Clean Air Act, 1956), a health service corporation in which the hospital is vested may have a special defence available to them: see *Nottingham Area No. 1 Hospital Management Committee* v. *Owen*, [1957] 3 All E.R. 358; [1958] 1 Q.B. 50.

[15] The constituent statute sometimes expressly so provides; Electricity Act, 1957, s. 38.

[16] As in the case of the Sugar Board; Sugar Act, 1956, s. 3 (4).

[17] As amended by the Limitation Act, 1939, under which a special limitation period of twelve months (formerly six months) was provided for.

[18] See, for example, Coal Industry Nationalisation Act, 1946, s. 49, New Towns Act, 1946, s. 17, and Gas Act, 1948, s. 14, all repealed (with similar provisions in other statutes) by the Act of 1954 referred to in the text.

(b) Ministerial control.—Public corporations are not normally servants of a Minister of the Crown, but this is the position of the Regional Health Authorities established by the National Health Service Reorganisation Act, 1973, which are required to carry out their functions as may be directed "on behalf of" the Secretary of State.[19] In the normal case, however, public corporations are independent of the Central Government, though it is customary for the constituent statute to provide that a Minister of the Crown shall be entitled to give directions, of a more or less general character (according to the terms of the statute) to a public corporation operating within that Minister's field of interest. Thus, the Secretary of State for Education and Science has power to give the Atomic Energy Authority

> "such directions as he may think fit, and the Authority shall comply with any directions so given".[20]

This power is not really so wide as at first appears, as such directions may be given only after consultation with the Authority, and the Secretary of State

> "shall not regard it as his duty to intervene in detail in the conduct by the Authority of their affairs unless in his opinion overriding national interests so require".[1]

The Secretary of State for Trade and Industry may after consultation with the Gas Corporation,[1] give directions of a general nature to them[2]; and many other similar examples could be given.

In practice few directions are given,[3] and those few have related most frequently to financial matters, such as the rate of interest to be paid by the British Gas Corporation or by Electricity Boards to holders of stock given to them as compensation on nationalisation of the industry. Nevertheless, this power to issue directions is important—the Minister is given by Parliament a right to exercise ultimate control in the national interest if he chooses to do so. Clearly, in the interests of efficient management of any nationalised industry there should be as little interference from Whitehall as possible. The Independent Broadcasting Authority affords a specialised example of the degree of control exercisable by a Minister. Under section 23 of the Independent Broadcasting Authority Act, 1973, the Minister of Posts and Telecommunications (formerly the Postmaster-General) has power to make regulations as to the grant of broadcasting facilities in respect of sporting and other events of national interest and he can exercise detailed control over technical processes used by the Authority, by notice served under section 22 of the 1973 Act; further, any Minister may give directions as

---

[19] National Health Service Reorganisation Act 1973, s. 7.

[20] Atomic Energy Authority Act, 1954, s. 3 (2).

[1] *Ibid.*, s. 3 (3). This is customary in most of these statutory provisions enabling a Minister to give directions; it is also usually stipulated that before giving such a direction, the Minister must consult with the corporation.

[2] Gas Act, 1972, s. 7 (1).

[3] But see *ante*, p. 326. In sixteen Reports of the former British Electricity Authority, the Central Electricity Authority, the Central Electricity Generating Board and the Electricity Council, covering the period from 1947 to 1961, there are references to only nine directions given by the Minister, and these related exclusively to financial matters, and three of those related exclusively to the form in which accounts were to be kept; as to the former Transport Holding Company, see *ante*, page 322.

to particular broadcasts (*ibid.*).[4] Control is perhaps even closer over the British Broadcasting Corporation, for in this case the Corporation is permitted to operate only under the terms of a licence, which is granted for a limited period (at present ten years) and the terms of the licence are customarily debated in Parliament when it is due for renewal. New town development corporations also may be, and are in practice, subject to detailed directions from the Secretary of State for the Environment instructing them to exercise, or not to exercise, their functions in a particular manner, and they also have to obtain the consent of the Secretary of State in a number of matters.[5]

A Minister may also be empowered by the constituent statute to make regulations affecting the manner in which a corporation may conduct their functions. It is common form for the statute setting up a corporation to empower the Minister to make regulations as to the method of appointment and dismissal of members,[6] how the corporation is to conduct its business, declarations of financial interest of members, etc.,[7] and in some instances a Minister may be empowered to make regulations of a more general nature which affect the corporation as if it were a private company or private individual subjected to governmental control. Thus, the Secretary of State may make regulations under section 26 of the Gas Act, 1972, as to standards of gas pressure and purity, etc., which will affect the operation of an undertaking carried on by the British Gas Corporation.

It is sometimes argued that the responsible Minister retains the most effective means of control over the activities of a public corporation by virtue of his powers to appoint and to dismiss the individual members of the corporation. The terms of appointment of a member can often be discovered only from the appointment letter itself, but in the Post Office Act, 1969, a provision appears requiring the Minister to "lay before each House of Parliament a statement of the term for which [a member] has been appointed" (Schedule 1, para. 2 (2)). The power of appointment is invariably vested in a Minister, or nominally in Her Majesty, who will of course accept advice on such a matter, and the constituent statute rarely restricts the Minister's choice of members to any significant extent, but sometimes persons to be appointed as

[4] On November 20, 1962, the P.M.G. directed that the I.T.A. (the fore-runner to the present I.B.A.) should not in future issue "magazine programmes".

[5] In the course of a debate in the House of Commons on July 13, 1962, the Parliamentary Secretary to the Ministry of Housing and Local Government revealed that his Minister was contemplating giving a direction under the New Towns Act, 1946, to the Welwyn Garden City and Hatfield New Town Development Corporation requiring the Corporation to modify the terms on which the Corporation granted long leases of dwelling-houses; the corporation included in these leases a clause to the effect that "except with the previous consent of the corporation, the premises should be used as a single private dwelling house for occupation by one family", and the expression "family" was defined with some precision. In the Minister's view this seemed "to fetter the right of the individual to invite whom he wished to live in his own house", and in this the Minister apparently had the support of the House. (*The Times*, July 14, 1962.)

[6] In some cases detailed provision for these matters is made in the constituent statute itself (as, for example, in the Gas Act, 1972, and the Electricity Acts, 1947 and 1957).

[7] Provisions as to this matter are rarely as elaborate as ss. 94–98 of the Local Government Act, 1972, relating to local authorities, but these provisions (see Chapter XII, *post*, p. 378) were obviously used as a precedent. In some cases the Minister is required to avoid persons having a substantial financial interest in the particular industry, when appointing members of the corporation (see, *e.g.*, Sugar Act, 1956, s. 2 (6)).

members are required to be chosen from specified professions or groups of people qualified in some specified manner; in addition it is becoming increasingly common to require a Minister to appoint the Chairman of the body first, and then to require him to consult with the Chairman in selecting the other members.[8] In some cases the term of office of a member of a corporation is specified in the statute,[9] in others this is left to be determined by the Minister.[10] There is often a power given to the Minister to declare an office held by a member to be vacant if the member is absent from meetings for a specified period,[11] if he is adjudged a bankrupt or makes a composition or arrangement with his creditors, is incapacitated by infirmity of mind or body,

> "or is otherwise unsuited to continue to discharge his duties;"[12]

the latter case amounts, of course, to a power of removal vested in the Minister without any precise cause shown. In practice this power of removal is very rarely exercised, and any such exercise could be questioned in Parliament; in one instance specific power to terminate an office by notice is conferred by the statute, and if this power is exercised, a copy of the notice must be laid before Parliament.[13] In another case,[14] no provision at all is made for dismissal of members of the Board, but they are appointed for periods of three years only.

Generally it would be expected that a Minister would appoint as head of an important public corporation, a person whose political thinking was in accord with that of the Government of the day. But Lord Robens remained at the National Coal Board for a considerable time under administrations from both principal parties, and the Conservative Government appointed as Chairman of British Railways in 1971 a former Labour Minister of Transport (Mr. Richard Marsh).

Undoubtedly, however, very close Ministerial control is maintained in those circumstances where the particular corporation is dependent on the central government for finance. This is true in the case of the Atomic Energy Authority, the Regional and Area Health Authorities, the new towns development corporations, and such corporations as the Countryside Commission. The British Transport Commission also was dependent on annual subventions from the government, until it got into such financial difficulties that Parliament itself had to carry out a scheme of reconstruction.[15] Even where a corporation is normally financially self-supporting, as in the gas or electricity industry, it will have to obtain the approval of the appropriate Minister to the raising of capital; it will similarly have to obtain Ministerial consent in any case

---

[8] See, for example, Post Office Act, 1969, s. 6 (3).

[9] See, for example, the powers of the Minister of Posts and Telecommunications in relation to the members of the Independent Broadcasting Authority: Television Act, 1954, s. 1 (4).

[10] The Minister may in such a case, when appointing a Member, reserve power to himself to dismiss the member on notice.

[11] Compare Local Government Act, 1972, s. 85 (Chapter XII, *post*, p. 378).

[12] See, for example, the Countryside Commission and the Commission for the New Towns. In the case of the Post Office, the form of words is "otherwise unable or unfit to discharge the functions of a member": Post Office Act, 1969, Schedule 1, para. 5.

[13] Independent Broadcasting Authority Act, 1973, Schedule 1, para. 1 (6).

[14] Public Health Laboratory Service Act, 1960, Schedule.

[15] Transport Act, 1962.

where it is seeking to acquire land compulsorily. In these respects the control of the appropriate Government Department over a public corporation is similar to the controls exercisable by central departments over the activities of a local authority.[16]

It is invariably made a requirement in the constituent statute or charter that a report and accounts shall be sent annually to the appropriate Minister, and he is required to lay a copy before both Houses of Parliament. It is also often provided that the corporation shall provide information as to its activities at the request of the Minister, either generally or as to particular matters. Such provisions as these, whilst not providing in themselves for any direct governmental control, at least ensure that a Minister will have the means of informing himself about the corporation's activities, without which any attempts at control would tend to become futile; they further give an opportunity for matters concerning the corporation to be raised in Parliament (see below).

In practice, Ministerial control over matters of policy in a particular nationalised industry goes much further than an account of the formal means of control would suggest. The members of the governing body of the corporation will know the Minister and his senior civil servants personally, and many opportunities will arise for the Minister's views to be made known to the management of the corporation. It is because of these close but undefinable links that the formal control powers, by way of the issue of directions, or the dismissal of members, are rarely exercised. This is particularly true of the National Freight Corporation and the National Bus Company (*ante*, p. 322), in respect of which the Minister's legal powers of control seem to be very largely confined to the appointment of the directors. Actually a very close working liaison exists between the boards of these bodies and the staff of the Ministry.

(c) Parliamentary control.—The whole *raison d'être* of establishing a public corporation for a particular administrative task or undertaking, instead of entrusting it to a Minister of the Crown assisted by civil servants, is to free the task in question from the possibilities of detailed scrutiny by individual members of Parliament and by the Treasury, which is the characteristic accompaniment of Ministerial responsibility. Nevertheless, the functions carried on by the public corporations are of public concern and are performed in the public interest, and Members of Parliament may on occasion wish to exercise some measure of control over these seemingly unruly children of the statute book. Such controls (in the form of debates or discussion) as may be exercisable by Parliament in practice, arise as follows:

(i) *The constituent statute.*—All the public corporations—with the exception of those few established by Royal Charter[17]—owe their existence to Parliament and it is a matter for Parliament in the constituent statute to define the powers of the corporation and the degree of independence it is to be allowed to enjoy. If a corporation is exercising too

---

[16] Chapter XV, *post*, p. 422.

[17] The Bank of England, the British Broadcasting Corporation, and the Nature Conservancy.

great a measure of freedom it can be brought to heel by a revisionary statute, or can be abolished by the same means; what Parliament has made it can also destroy. This is not, however, a type of control that can frequently be employed, nor is a private member likely to succeed in obtaining either Parliamentary time or support for new legislation on such a topic. However, the constitution of a particular corporation may require amendment from time to time, and the consequent Bill may provide the opportunity for a general debate on the affairs of the corporation.[18]

(ii) *Debates.*—Occasions for a debate on the affairs of a public corporation will arise on motions of supply, when a vote may be included for financial assistance to the corporation. This may give rise to comments in the House of Commons on any matter concerning the corporation, but again the opportunity will but seldom arise. Sometimes there may also be an opportunity for a debate on the reception of the Annual Report and Accounts of a particular corporation.

(iii) *Questions.*—This is the traditional method by which individual Members may seek from responsible Ministers redress of the grievances of their constituents. Questions raising matters under the control of bodies or persons for which Ministers of the Crown are not responsible, such as public corporations or local authorities, are not, however, admissible as there is no one in Parliament who can be called upon to answer.[19] Sometimes a question about the affairs of a public corporation may nevertheless be accepted and answered; obviously if the question is directed to a matter within the responsibility of a Minister, it will be in order, and this would apply to a question as to the nature or effect of a direction given by the Minister to a public corporation under a statutory power. In some circumstances where the question merely seeks information, the Minister may be prepared to accept it[20] and reply that "he has been informed by the [Board] to the effect that . . .". Questions aimed at the conduct by a corporation of its affairs will not, however, normally be accepted by a Minister; in one case, Mr. John Hay said of the British Transport Commission:

> "It is a commercial undertaking engaged in a commercial enterprise, and we [the Government] do not propose to interfere with its commercial judgment in the matter."[1]

The House of Commons, it has been said, is not a meeting of the shareholders of a public corporation, nor are the Ministers of the Crown in the position of directors of the corporation.[2] The whole subject of Questions raises two separate issues, first whether the particular question is in order under the Rules of the House, and second whether the Minister concerned is prepared to give an answer.[3] An unsatisfactory answer to a

---

[18] As was, for example, the case when the Gas Act, 1972, was passing through Parliament.

[19] Erskine May, *Parliamentary Practice*, 18th Edn., at p. 325.

[20] *Parliament at Work*, by Hanson and Wiseman, at p. 87.

[1] *Parliament at Work*, at p. 92.

[2] On this matter generally, see *Parliamentary Reform, 1933–1960* (Hansard Society) at p. 132.

[3] On "questions" generally, see Chapter IV in *Parliament and Public Ownership*, by A. H. Hanson.

Question may lead to an adjournment debate, but this will be confined to half an hour only of Parliamentary time.

With the exception of the Decimal Currency Board, and the Intervention Board for Agricultural Produce (Chapter V, *ante*, p. 101), the public Corporations are not within the jurisdiction of the Parliamentary Commissioner for Administration, nor will the Commissioners for Local Administration cover the corporations.[4] The National Health Service Reorganisation Act, 1973, however, does make provision for separate Health Commissioners for England and for Wales (at present both offices are held by the Parliamentary Commissioner; see *ante*, p. 107).

(iv) *Select committee.*—In 1956, the House of Commons established a Select Committee having as its terms of reference:

"to examine the Reports and Accounts of the Nationalised Industries".

This of course gave the Committee what were potentially very wide terms of reference. As has been explained, however, by one of the Chairmen of the Committee,[5] it was not intended that the Committee should act as an auditor or "grand inquisitor" into the affairs of the Corporations.[6] Primarily they are concerned to investigate whether the particular industry is efficiently managed, and in their investigations (assisted by a minimum of technical staff), the Committee have concerned themselves with such matters as the control of capital investment, and the attitude adopted by the managers of the corporation towards the question whether they are providing a public service or a commercial undertaking.

Since 1956 the Committee has produced several interesting and valuable reports. Most of these reports make detailed suggestions or observations as to the work of a particular corporation; thus, the Committee has expressed disappointment at the slow rate of progress of the National Coal Board in making briquettes from small naturally smoky coal,[7] and in connection with the railways, the Committee said that if Government subsidies were to be paid, they should be paid openly and for specific services.[8] In arriving at their recommendations the Committee examine the reports and accounts of the particular public corporation, and then take evidence from members or servants of the corporation and from elsewhere. Their proceedings have become in fact a thoroughgoing investigation of the general operation of the corporation in question. The Committee is, however, small in number (not more than twelve persons), its personnel may change from year to year, and it has no time to report on more than one or two industries each year.

---

[4] Chapter V, *ante*, p. 98. In this respect Britain is not out of step with the home of the Ombudsman, as the Swedish *Justitieombudsman* has no jurisdiction over the State-owned monopoly companies which are the nearest Swedish equivalent to English public corporations: see *Government Enterprise* (Stevens, 1970), Chapter 9.

[5] Sir Toby Low, in an article "The Select Committee on Nationalised Industries", at (1962) 40 Public Administration, at p. 1.

[6] Andrew Shonfield, in his "Modern Capitalism", makes some interesting criticisms of this attitude; see in particular at pp. 392–3.

[7] "Report from the Select Committee on the Nationalised Industries" (February 20, 1962), commenting on an earlier Report on the National Coal Board; see para. 43.

[8] Report of the Select Committee on "British Railways" (July 11, 1960), at para. 425.

In September 1968 the Committee published a long report on Ministerial Control of the Nationalised Industries in which it was suggested that a single Minister should be made responsible for overall co-ordination of the activities of the nationalised industries, but this was not implemented.[9]

(d) Control by the public.—Apart from the legal and parliamentary controls already discussed, it is important to consider also such machinery as there may be to enable public opinion to influence the manner in which a public corporation conducts its affairs. This is of particular importance in this branch of public administration, because the influence of the elected representative, so important in local government, is almost[10] totally absent. Indirectly, in some instances where the particular corporation is required or expected to be financially self-supporting, the need to obtain revenue from the public as consumers must have some influence. In some sectors there may be competition with private business (as in the case of the airway corporations), or even with other public corporations (as between gas and electricity), and in such cases the interests of the consumer cannot be totally ignored. Where the corporation is carrying on a public utility service, however, it is usually a near or complete monopoly and the profit motive may then become comparatively unimportant; in other sectors, such as the hospitals, the element of commercial enterprise is completely absent. However, in several of the monopoly undertakings, there are elements of the public interest, and the corporation cannot conduct its affairs solely with a view to making a profit or even covering expenses. Thus, the railways may be expected to continue to operate unremunerative services, the National Coal Board may be expected to produce smokeless fuels on uneconomic terms in the interests of alleviating air pollution, and the electricity boards may be expected to supply electricity in rural areas on favourable terms in the interests of agriculture.

These and similar considerations may be of great importance, and Parliament has therefore made provision for two different means of representation of the "consumer" or public interest, applicable to certain of the public corporations discussed in this Chapter.

(i) *Consumer or "Consultative" Councils.*—These are bodies established under the authority of the statute constituting the corporations concerned with the object of enabling "consumers" to ventilate their grievances, or make their views known to the corporations. The outstanding examples of consumer councils are to be found in the electricity and gas industries. By the Electricity Act, 1947, a consumer council is established for the area covered by each electricity board. Membership of each consumer council is drawn from persons nominated by local

---

[9] For a criticism of this report, see the chapter (IV) by Professor Robson in *Government Enterprise* (1970).

[10] Even where members of local authorities are invited to serve on a public corporation, they are not elected to the particular office, and they rarely consider themselves responsible to the electorate in such an office. The constituent statute does not usually provide that a member of a public corporation shall resign or lose his office if he ceases to be a member of the local authority which nominated him.

authorities,[11] and other organisations in the area, but the appointments are made by the Minister and there is no system of election. The area Consumer Council is staffed by persons employed by the area electricity board, the chairman of the council is a member of the area board, and the offices of the council are invariably in the same premises as the area of the board. Meetings of the area consumer councils are normally, but need not be, open to the public and the press, and many consumer councils have established divisional committees, inviting persons not on the council itself to serve on the committees; but it is still very doubtful whether members of the public generally have any great interest in or knowledge of the affairs of the electricity or gas consumer councils. The councils are entitled to make representations to their area boards, but there have been very few occasions when alterations of policy decisions have resulted. Tariff questions have on occasion been raised, as for example where it seemed to a consumer council that a particular tariff was operating unfairly against a particular consumer or group of consumers, and on a few such occasions modifications in the tariff have been made by the Board as a result, but it is by no means certain that the modification was due to the representations made by the consumer council, as distinct from the pressure that would in any event have been brought to bear on the Board by the particular group of consumers concerned. Housewives or other individuals with a grievance are encouraged officially to complain to a consumer council, but they may well be ignorant of its existence. Press reports of meetings of these bodies are rarely interesting, and as the staff of a consumer council are employed by the area board, there is not always any desire on their part to drive home a particular complaint or to seek to obtain a complete answer to a question. At the local divisional committee level, the meetings do serve to confront local managers with such zealous advocates of the consumer interest as representatives from local authorities, and they provide a forum for the aggrieved householder. The Council or committee will usually be able to obtain a reasoned answer to a complaint—often in circumstances where the answer should have been given at the initial raising of the complaint in the showroom. If a question of "policy" is raised, however, the consumer councils are usually powerless. The friendly and close relations that often exist between an Area Board and its Consumer Council may, whilst desirable from many points of view, militate against any real improvements or modifications in policy being achieved.[12] It is by no means clear that the Consumer Council are really able to justify their continued existence in the administrative machinery of the gas and electricity industries.

---

[11] It has been suggested that the true reason for the establishment of the consultative councils was to pacify those local authorities who lost their own electricity or gas undertakings on nationalisation.

[12] Members of the Central Electricity Authority addressed several joint meetings of consumer councils in 1954 (6th Report, para. 77), and in most reports of the former Gas Council, some comment such as the following appeared (15th Report, page 46): "There has grown up a sense of confidence and co-operation between the Councils and the Area Boards real enough to enable criticism to be perfectly frank without disturbing the good feeling between them."

Until 1972, there was a precisely similar arrangement for the gas industry, but the Gas Act, 1972, by abolishing the area boards, had to make fresh provision for consumer councils.[13] This it has done by establishing a National Gas Consumers' Council, and a number of Regional Gas Consumers' Councils. Initially there is to be a Regional Council for each of the areas of the former gas boards, but the constitution of Regional Councils may be varied by directions given by the Secretary of State. The National Council is to consist of the (paid) Chairmen of the Regional Councils and such other persons (not exceeding 30 in total, including the chairmen) as the Secretary of State may appoint. The Regional Councils may themselves appoint local committees. The comments (above) about the electricity bodies will, it seems, apply equally to these new Gas Consumers' Councils; their success will depend very largely on the measure of publicity and public attention they are able to attract.

In the coal industry, there are two advisory councils for the whole country,[14] and there are a number of area transport users consultative committees[15]; there is also an Air Transport Advisory Council. These bodies are required to submit annual reports to Parliament, but apart from this, they seem to attract little public attention or serve any very useful purpose. Members of the public with an individual grievance in practice rarely have the time or energy to seek out a body of this kind.

The Post Office Act, 1969 established "users councils" for Scotland, Wales and Monmouthshire, and for Northern Ireland, and also one for the British Islands.[16] The Minister of Posts and Telecommunications and the Post Office may refer for consideration and report, any matter relating to the services of the Post Office, to the appropriate Users' Council, and each Users' Council have the duty of considering representations made by a "user" of services provided by the Post Office, and also other matters relating to such services. Each User Council is also required to report annually to the Minister and a copy of these reports has to be laid before both Houses of Parliament. Chairmen and members of the Councils are to be appointed by the Minister and the Chairman of the National Council (for the whole of the British Islands) may not be a member of the House of Commons.

Advisory Committees have also been set up for railway transport. The proposed closure of a branch railway line may sometimes arouse public interest; representations may in such a case be made to the relevant area transport users consultative committee, who may then decide to hold a public sitting.[17] Proceedings on such an occasion often resemble an arbitration rather than a consultation, although the latter is the true nature of the proceedings, for the committee are endeavouring to discover the views of the travelling public in order the better to advise the

---

[13] See Gas Act, 1972, ss. 9, 10 and 11, with Schedule 3.
[14] The Domestic Coal Consumers Council and the Industrial Coal Consumers Council.
[15] Transport Act, 1962, s. 56.
[16] Post Office Act, 1969, s. 14.
[17] They are not, however, a statutory inquiry, and so are not subject to the supervision of the Council on Tribunals: see *Hansard* for March 9, 1964, col. 4.

Minister, who may not proceed with the closure until he has received their report. In recent years it has seemed that these committees have proved their value, as on several occasions the Minister has refused to make a closure order after receiving a report from the committee. Reports had been made in no less than 161 cases during 1964 (Report of the Central Transport Consultative Committee for 1964).[18]

In the case of air transport there are six regional committees, the Edinburgh Airport Users Consultative Committee, an Advisory Council for the Channel Islands, and an Airports Board for the Isle of Man, that must be consulted in appropriate cases by the Air Transport Licensing Board, before granting, revoking or suspending a licence for air services.[19]

There is an elaborate system of consumer control provided for the national health service by the National Health Service Reorganisation Act, 1973. Apart from the right to complain to the Health Commissioner (*ante*, p. 107), a member of the public may make representations to the local Community Health Council (an unincorporated body), which will normally cover the area of an Area Health Authority (in itself co-terminous with the area of a county council). It is the duty of these Councils "to represent the interests in the health service of the public in the district".[20] In addition there are joint consultative committees, to provide co-ordination between Area Health Authorities and county and district councils.[1]

(ii) *Membership*.—In other cases, Parliament has arranged for members of certain of the public corporations to be nominated by local authorities and other bodies interested in the functions of the particular corporation. This is in particular a feature of the authorities in the National Health Service; Area Health Authorities must include members appointed by local authorities, and a similar rule applies to Family Practitioner Committees. These authorities must also include representatives of the several medical, etc., professions.[2] Members of Consumer Councils are appointed by the Minister concerned, but it is usually provided that he must consult with or receive nominations from local authorities or other bodies concerned.[3] It is also common for the constituent statute to provide that some at least of the members of a particular corporation should be selected from persons qualified in

---

[18] A correspondent in *The Times* (January 20, 1966) has suggested that the present procedure for rail closures is too complicated. Not only does the Secretary of State have to wait for a report from the local consultative committee, but also the licensing authority for public service vehicles must consider any proposal for new public road services, and the economic planning boards established by the Department of Economic Affairs have to be consulted. Where the statutory procedure is not fully observed, the courts may be able to intervene: see *Warwickshire County Council* v. *British Railways Board*, [1969] 3 All E.R. 631; [1969] 1 W.L.R. 1117.

[19] These committees are established under s. 2 (7) of the Airports Authority Act, 1965.

[20] National Health Service Reorganisation Act, 1973, s. 9.

[1] *Ibid.*, s. 10.

[2] National Health Service Reorganisation Act, 1973, Schedule 1.

[3] Gas Act, 1972, s. 9 (4); Electricity Act, 1947 (as amended by Schedule 1 to the Electricity Act, 1957), s. 7 (2); Post Office Act, 1969, s. 64 (4).

some specified respect in the particular industry concerned.[4] Such statutory devices as these are not necessarily effective in ensuring that the views of the public are made known to the managing body of the corporation.

The road passenger transport undertakings are in a special position here. Because in form the undertakings are still operated by independent companies (except those run by passenger transport authorities or local authorities in the larger towns), consumer councils were presumably thought to be inappropriate. The control of the National Bus Company and the former Transport Holding Company (above, p. 322) is used to ensure efficiency; the public interest element is represented, somewhat spasmodically, by the Traffic Commissioners.[5] When granting a licence, the Commissioners must have regard, *inter alia*, to the public interest.[6]

5. MISCELLANEOUS BODIES

As well as the generally accepted public corporations "properly so called" which have been discussed hitherto in this Chapter, there are many anomalous bodies having corporate personality, owing their origin and status to a statute, and exercising some measure of governmental functions, but which, due mainly to their specialised nature and restricted functions, are not commonly described as "public corporations". Such are the various joint boards constituted under many different statutes, usually as a result of Ministerial intervention, each charged with the performance of a single defined function, which may in other areas be exercised by a local authority. In such cases the particular function is entrusted to an *ad hoc* joint board, in order that the particular service may be administered over an area wider than that of a single local authority; in this category fall, for example, a few joint planning boards constituted under the Town and Country Planning Act, 1971 and its predecessors, to act as local planning authorities for some of the areas of the national parks, and a few united health districts.[7] Combined police authorities which are by statute made bodies corporate,[8] provide another example. Somewhat similar in constitution are the regional water authorities constituted under the Water Act, 1973, and the inland drainage boards constituted under the Land Drainage Act, 1930, whose areas often cut across those of the local authorities. The water authorities are the more powerful successors of the former river authorities, being responsible not only for the prevention of river

---

[4] See, for example, Transport Act, 1962, s. 1 (4) (London Transport Board). In the Gas Act, 1972, it is provided that, in choosing members of the British Gas Corporation, the Secretary of State is to have "regard to the desirability of having members who are familiar with the special requirements and circumstances of particular regions and areas" (s. 1 (2)).

[5] Chapter VIII, *ante*, p. 256.

[6] Road Traffic Act, 1960, s. 135.

[7] Public Health Act, 1936, s. 6.

[8] Police Act 1964, s. 3 (1).

pollution, but also for water supply and the provision of sewers and sewage disposal. These bodies are independent of direct central government control, except that the members are in most cases appointed by the Secretary of State, but usually he will make appointments from nominations submitted to him by local authorities in the area. They may be said to be much nearer in status and the nature of their functions to local authorities than to the ordinary public corporations.[9]

There are also many other bodies whose status is difficult to define juristically. Agricultural marketing boards established by schemes made under the Agricultural Marketing Act, 1958, are bodies corporate, as are development councils for particular industries, which may be established by orders made by a Minister under the Industrial Organisation and Development Act, 1947. However, wages councils constituted by a Minister[10] for a particular trade or industry are not corporate bodies, nor are many of the advisory bodies set up under statute, such as the Clean Air Advisory Council,[11] the Council on Tribunals,[12] the Building Regulations Advisory Committee,[13] and the Consumer Protection Advisory Committee.[14] The Poisons Board, in spite of its title and formal constitution,[15] is not a corporation and is merely an advisory committee. These bodies, as many of their names suggest, have no executive functions, being established merely so that they may advise and inform the Minister concerned on topics coming within their several fields of interest.

We have already referred to the device used in the Transport Act, 1962, whereby ordinary commercial companies are virtually nationalised, whilst being allowed to continue as independent legal persons under the Companies Acts. A similar device was employed in the case of Cable and Wireless Ltd., all the shares in which were compulsorily acquired by H.M. Government under the Cable and Wireless Act, 1946; considerable shares are also owned by the Treasury in a few other commercial companies.[16] In all these cases the directors are appointed by the Government (normally by the Treasury), by virtue of the holding in the company. These holdings are often regarded primarily as an investment; in the case of Cable and Wireless, Ltd. and the transport undertakings, the share holdings are regarded primarily as a means of control and management.

6. CONCLUSION

The most disturbing problem in connection with public corporations, especially those responsible for the management of the nationalised industries, is undoubtedly that of control. A powerful corporation,

---

[9] See also, Chapter XI, *post*, p. 367.

[10] Under s. 1 of the Wages Councils Act, 1945.

[11] Clean Air Act, 1956, s. 22.

[12] Tribunals and Inquiries Act, 1971, s. 1; on this subject generally, see Chapter VII, *ante*, p. 201.

[13] Public Health Act, 1961, s. 9.

[14] Fair Trading Act, 1973, s. 3.

[15] Poisons Act, 1972, Schedule 1.

[16] A complete list of Government holdings in industrial companies (other than transport) was published in *The Times* on January 26, 1966. The crisis over Rolls Royce in 1970–1 led to the Rolls Royce Purchase Act, 1971, under which the Treasury was empowered to purchase the shares of the company.

having great financial resources, employing many personnel and possessing monopolistic powers conferred by statute, should be answerable in some measure to the elected representatives of the nation and to the courts of law. The Industrial Reorganisation Corporation,[17] for example, by exercise of its controls over mergers and its powers to assist particular industries by grants or loans, could have had a very considerable influence over the development of the economy. In many respects controls over such corporations seem tenuous and ineffective. On the other hand, any large-scale commercial enterprise must be allowed freedom to carry on research, to experiment, and even on occasion to make mistakes. Indeed, the justification for the constitutional device of the public corporation has been said to be so as to secure freedom from civil service (and particularly Treasury) controls, and from the influence of party politics.[18] It is one of the modern problems of public administration, how these conflicting objectives can be reconciled.

In the Appendix will be found a table giving particulars of most of the more important public corporations, in which the information given concentrates on the points discussed in this Chapter.

---

[17] Established by the Industrial Reorganisation Corporation Act, 1966; see chapter by T. C. Daintith in *Government Enterprise*. The Corporation was, however, dissolved by the Industry Act, 1971.

[18] These problems are fully considered, in relation both to the United Kingdom and to many other countries in *Government Enterprise* and other literature there cited.

APPENDIX TO CHAPTER X

THE PUBLIC CORPORATIONS

Serial No.	Service and Corporation	Constituent Statute[1]	Managing Body			Degree of Independence		Principal Functions
			Number of Members	By whom Appointed	Special Features	Ministerial Directions	Public Relations Organisation	
1	2	3	4	5	6	7	8	9
1.	*Agriculture* (a) Eggs Authority	Agriculture Act, 1970.	Chairman, deputy and 12–14 members (s. 2 (2)).	Minister of Agriculture, Fisheries and Food and Ministers for Scotland, Wales and Northern Ireland.	Members may be paid; Members must be chosen after consultation with specified organisations and representative of particular interests (s. 2 (2)).	Ministers may give directions of general character after consultation with the Authority, in the public interest (s. 19).	None.	General duty of improving the marketing of eggs (s. 2 (2) and ss. 3–11).
	(b) Rural Development Boards.	Agriculture Act, 1967.	Chairman, deputy Chairman and 4–10 other members (Sched. 5, Part II, para. 1).	Minister of Agriculture, etc., and the Secretary of State for Scotland.	Members may be paid; may be M.P.s. Members to be chosen from persons having experience or knowledge of agriculture or forestry. Board to be established by Ministerial order after enquiry, and may be dissolved by him (Sched. 5, Part I).	No power to give directions but Board must consult with Forestry Commission (s. 46 (3)).	None.	Established for a specified area; they must apply special measures of the Act for meeting problems of development as rural areas of hills and upland: ss. 45 and 46.
	(c) Meat and Livestock Commission.	Agriculture Act, 1967.	Chairman and deputy Chairman and not more than 8 other members	Minister of Agriculture, etc., and Secretary of State for Scot-	Members must be paid and may receive compensation on ceasing to be	Commission must perform functions conferred on them by Ministers;	None.	Commission have general duty of promoting greater efficiency in the livestock industry and the

					may be M.P.s.	Commission (s. 4); Commission may delegate to any of the three statutory committees (s. 2). Minister may give directions of a general character after consultation (s. 20).		ducts industry (s. 1 (1)), and also many specific functions (see Part I). Ministers must appoint three Committees (s. 2).
2.	*Air* (a) British Airways Board.	Civil Aviation Act, 1971.	8–15 members (s. 37).	Secretary of State for Trade and Industry.[2]	Provision of air transport services; supervision of B.E.A. and B.O.A.C. Not a servant of the Crown: s. 37 (4).	Secretary of State may give directions of general character or specific directions as to particular matters after consultation with Board (s. 40).	None	See col. 6.
	(b) British European Airway Corporation. (c) British Overseas Airways Corporation.	Air Corporations Acts, 1949 to 1967; Civil Aviation Act, 1971.	Chairman, Deputy Chairman, and 3–9 other members (1949, s. 2).	Secretary of State for Trade and Industry; he may terminate office of member who is "unable or unfit".	Each member must be paid.	Secretary of State may give directions "Of a general character in relation to matters appearing to him to affect the national interest"—*after* consultation (s. 5), and see s. 8 of 1966 Act.	Air Transport Advisory Council: Civil Aviation Act, 1949, s. 12.	"To provide air transport services and to carry out all other forms of aerial work, in any part of the world" (s. 3). Either corporation may be dissolved by order of the Secretary of State (1971 Act, s. 57).

APPENDIX TO CHAPTER X

Serial No.	Service and Corporation	Constituent Statute	Managing Body			Degree of Independence		Principal Functions
			Number of Members	By whom Appointed	Special Features	Ministerial Directions	Public Relations Organisation	
1	2	3	4	5	6	7	8	9
	Air—cont. (d) Civil Aviation Authority.	Civil Aviation Act, 1971.	6–12 members (s. 1).	Secretary of State for Trade and Industry.	Not a servant of the Crown: s. 1 (4).	Secretary of State may give "guidance" to Authority also directions in time of emergency (s. 4 (1)) and, in consultation with the Authority, more general directions (s. 4 (3)).	Consultative Committees have been established (see p. *338*).	To secure that British airlines provide air transport services (s. 3), and to this end to provide a licensing system, etc. (s. 2).
	(e) British Airports Authority.	Airports Authority Act, 1965.	Do.	Minister of Aviation; Minister may terminate office of member who is "unable or unfit" to act.	Members are paid.	Minister may give directions of general character which appear to him to affect the national interest; after consultation (s. 2 (6)).	None.	Manage the aerodromes at Gatwick, Heathrow, Stansted and Prestwick; *not* to provide navigation services except with consent of Minister (s. 2).
3.	*Atomic Energy* United Kingdom Atomic Energy Authority.	Atomic Energy Act, 1946; Radioactive Substances Act, 1948; *Atomic Energy Authority Act, 1954*.	Chairman and 7–15 members (s. 1 (2) as amended by A.E.A. Act, 1959, s. 1).	Secretary of State for Education and Science.[3]	Each member must be paid; 5 of the members must hold certain qualifications.	Minister has wide general powers, but not on matters of detail;[4] effective financial control.[5]	None.[6]	Activities under s. 2 (1) of 1946 Act and s. 1 (1) of 1948 Act, and also see list in s. 2 (2) of 1954 Act.

4.	*Broadcasting and Communications* (a) British Broadcasting Corporation.	Chartered Corporation; Licence and Charter renewable from time to time.[7]	Chairman, Deputy and 7 Governors.	Her Majesty in Council.	All governors are part-time; executive head is the Director-General.	Any Minister may require B.B.C. to refrain from sending specified matter.[8]	B.B.C. carries out internal arrangements for "listener research".	B.B.C. operates under licence from Minister, granted under Wireless Telegraphy Act, 1949.
	(b) Cable and Wireless, Ltd.	Public Company; all shares transferred to public ownership by Cable and Wireless Act, 1946.	Has the constitution and status of an ordinary public company, unaffected by the nationalisation statute.					
	(c) Independent Broadcasting Authority.	Television Act, 1964; reconstituted by *Independent Broadcasting Authority Act, 1973*.	Chairman, Deputy and 5 or more members (s. 1 (1)); Sched. 1.	Minister of Posts and Telecommunications; he may terminate office of a member by notice: Sched. 1.	Members must be paid; three of them must have regional interests: Sched. 1.	Minister may give directions ss. 22 and 28; regulations may be made as to advertising (ss. 8–9 and Sched. 2.	I.B.A. may appoint advisory committees: s. 9.	"To provide television and local sound broadcasting services of high quality", additional to those of the B.B.C.: s. 2 (1).
	(d) Post Office.	Post Office Act, 1969.	Chairman and 3 (or 6)–12 members: s. 6 (1). Members must have had experience: s. 6 (4).	Minister of Posts and Telecommunications.	Members must be paid: Sched. 1, para. 4.	Minister may after consultation give directions of general character in national interest: s. 11 (1). He may direct P.O. to do work for a government department: s. 12.	User Councils established by s. 14—a National Council and three "Country Councils."[10]	To provide postal and telecommunications services and also a banking "giro" system (s. 7).
5.	*Coal* National Coal Board.	Coal Act, 1938; *Coal Industry (Nationalisation) Act, 1946*; Coal Industry Act, 1949.	Chairman and 8–11 members (s. 2 (2)).	Minister of Power.	Members must be paid; must be selected from qualified persons (s. 2 (3)).	Minister may give directions of a general character, on matters appearing to affect the national interest: s. 3; *after* consultation.	Industrial Coal Users and Domestic Coal Users Consumers' Councils.	Working and getting coal; securing efficient development of coal-mining industry; making supplies of coal available (s. 1).

APPENDIX TO CHAPTER X

Serial No.	Service and Corporation	Constituent Statute	Managing Body			Degree of Independence		Principal Functions
			Number of Members	By whom Appointed	Special Features	Ministerial Directions	Public Relations Organisation	
1	2	3	4	5	6	7	8	9
6.	*Commonwealth* Commonwealth Development Corporation.	Overseas Resources Development Acts, *1948* and 1959, Commonwealth Development Act, 1963.	Chairman, Deputy and 4–10 members (s. 1 (2)).	Secretary of State for Foreign and Commonwealth Affairs.	Members must be paid; must be selected from qualified persons (s. 1 (3)).	Minister may give directions of a general character in matters appearing to him to concern the public interest: s. 10 (1).	None,[6] but local interests must be consulted (s. 8), and the Corporation must consult with employees (s. 9).	Long list of enterprises in s. 3. May be added to by order with consent of Treasury.
7.	*Electricity* (a) Central Electricity Generating Board.	Electricity Act, 1957.	Chairman and 7–9 members (s. 2 (2)), one of whom is to be Deputy Chairman (s. 2 (4)).	Secretary of State for Trade and Industry	Members must be chosen from qualified persons (s. 2 (3)).	—	None.[6]	May give directions to Area Boards and must co-ordinate distribution of electricity; may generate and acquire supplies of electricity; s. 1 (5), and general powers in s. 1 (7).
	(b) Electricity Council.	Electricity Acts, 1947 and *1957*.	Chairman, 2 Deputies, 3 members, 3 members of the Generating Board, Chairmen of the Area Boards.	Secretary of State for Trade and Industry (only Chairman and Deputies).	Unusual interlocking membership with Area Boards; members paid.	"Such directions of a general nature as seem to be in the national interest": s. 8 (1), may be given by the Minister.	None.[6]	Advise the Minister; promote and assist maintenance and development by Area Boards of "an efficient, co-ordinated and economical system of electricity supply" (s. 3 (4)).

	(c) Area Boards (12 in number plus two in Scotland).	Electricity Acts, *1947* and 1957.	Chairman and 5–7 members (s. 3 (3)(a)); one may be Deputy.	Secretary of State for Trade and Industry	Members must be chosen from qualified persons.	Do.	Consumer Council attached to each Area Board.	Acquire bulk electricity; carry out efficient and economical distribution in area.
8.	*Finance and Industry* (a) Bank of England.	Chartered Corporation; Bank of England Act, 1946.	Governor, Deputy Governor and 16 Directors.	Her Majesty on the advice of the Prime Minister.	Governor and Deputy hold office for 5 years; they may be reappointed.	Treasury may give directions in the public interest, after consultation with the Governor.	None.[6]	Not defined by statute.
	(b) Decimal Currency Board.	Decimal Currency Act, 1967.	Chairman and 6–13 other members (s. 4).	Treasury.	Members may be paid salaries or fees and allowances (Sched. 3, para. 8). Treasury may provide by order for dissolution of the Board: s. 6 (1).	Treasury may give "directions of a general character": p. 5 (2).	None.	"To facilitate the transition from the existing currency and coinage to the new currency and coinage": s. 5 (1).
9.	*Fisheries* (a) Herring Industry Board.	Sea Fish Industry Act, 1970.	Chairman and others at discretion of Ministers (s. 29).	Minister of Agriculture, Fisheries and Food, and Secretaries of State for Scotland and Wales.	Provision may be made for election of members: s. 29 (3).	Ministers may revise or modify the Board's scheme; and may give directions of general character (s. 29 (5)).	Ministers must appoint a consumers' committee and a committee of investigation: s. 32. Also a Herring Industry Advisory Council s. 30.	Board required to make scheme for industry, and to keep generally under review matters relating to the industry.
	(b) White Fish Authority.	Sea Fish Industry Act, 1970.	Chairman, Deputy and such members as Ministers may determine (s. 1 (2)).	Do.	Special Scottish Committee (s. 2).	Ministers may give general directions, in the national interest, *after* consultation; any such directions must normally be published (s. 4 (2)).	White Fish Industry Advisory Council: s. 3.	Reorganising, developing and regulating the industry (and see s. 5). Authority must act as agent of *any* Minister if so required: s. 4 (4).

APPENDIX TO CHAPTER X

Serial No.	Service and Corporation	Constituent Statute	Managing Body			Degree of Independence		Principal Functions
			Number of Members	By whom Appointed	Special Features	Ministerial Directions	Public Relations Organisation	
1	2	3	4	5	6	7	8	9
10.	*Forestry* Forestry Commission.	Forestry Acts, *1945* and 1951.	Chairman and 9 Commissioners (s. 1 (1)).	Her Majesty, by warrant under the Sign Manual.	Some Commissioners must have specified knowledge and experience: s. 1 (2). Commissioners must be paid.	Commissioners must comply with such directions as may be given to them by the Minister of Agriculture, Fisheries and Food and the Secretary of State for Scotland: s. 2.	None.[6]	They have the "general duty" of "promoting the interests of forestry, the development of afforestation, and the production and supply of timber" Forestry Act, 1919, s. 3 (1).
11.	*Gas* British Gas Corporation.	Gas Act, 1972.	Chairman and 10–20 members.	Secretary of State for Trade and Industry.	Members must be paid; some members must have regional interests (s. 1 (2)).	Directions of a general character may be given, after consultation in the national interest (s. 7 (1)).	National Gas Consumers' Council and Regional Councils (s. 9).	To develop and maintain an efficient, co-ordinated and economical system of gas supply for G.B., etc. (s. 2).
12.	*National Health Service*[11] (a) Regional Health Authorities.	National Health Service Reorganisation Act, 1973.	Chairman and such other members as Secretary of State thinks fit Sched., 1, (para. 1).	Secretary of State for Health and Social Services	Members must include certain qualified persons.	Functions must be carried on subject to and in accordance with Secretary of State's regulations and directions and on his behalf.	None.[6]	To exercise such functions relating to the health service as the Secretary of State may direct and on his behalf: s. 7 (1).

(b) Area Health Authorities.	Do.	Chairman and such other members as the Regional Authority Board thinks fit (Sched. 1, para. 2).	Appropriate Regional Health Authority.	The Authority must consult local authorities and other bodies when making appointments.	The Authorities are required to act subject to any regulations or directions given by the Regional Authority.	There is a Community Health Council for the area of each Area Authority (s. 9).	To exercise such of the functions exercisable by the Regional Authority as the latter may direct: s. 7 (2).
(c) Boards of Governors of Hospitals (see 1973 Act, Sched. 2).	Do.	Do. (3rd Sched., Part III).	Secretary of State.	Nominations must be made by University, teaching staff, etc.	As for Regional Authorities, *supra*.	None.	"Generally to manage and hospital on behalf of the Minister."
(d) Family Practitioner Committees.	Do.	30 members.	Area Health Authorities, local authority and other bodies (Sched. 1, para. 6).		To preform prescribed functions (s. 7 (3)).	None.	Concerned with the provision of medical, dental, ophthalmic and pharmaceutical services in the area.
(e) Hearing Aid Council.	Heating Aid Council Act, 1968.	Chairman and 11 other members chosen from specified classes of persons (Sched. para. 1).	Secretary of State for Trade and Industry.	No provision for payment of members; members may be M.P.s as schedule to 1957 Act *not* extended. Period of office of members: 4 years (Sched. para. 2 (1)).	None; but in some cases approval of Board of Trade must be obtained: s. 1 (4).	None.	General function of securing adequate standards of competence and conduct among persons engaged in dispensing hearing aids: s. 1 (1).
(f) Medicines Commission.	Medicines Act, 1968.	Not less than eight, of whom one is to be appointed Chairman (s. 2 (2) (4)).	Secretary of State; Ministers for Scotland and Northern Ireland, Minister of Agriculture, Fisheries and Food, and Minister of Agriculture for Northern Ireland.	Members must be chosen from specified classes, after consultation (s. 2 (2) (3)). Members may be paid: Sched. 1, para. 5.	None.	None.	To give advice to the Ministers relating to medicinal products when they consider it expedient or when requested (s. 3 (1)). Committees may be established by Ministerial orders (s). 4).

APPENDIX TO CHAPTER X

Serial No.	Service and Corporation	Constituent Statute	Managing Body			Degree of Independence		Principal Functions
			Number of Members	By whom Appointed	Special Features	Ministerial Directions	Public Relations Organisation	
1	2	3	4	5	6	7	8	9
	National Health Service—cont. (g) National Radiological Protection Board.	Radiological Protection Act, 1970.	Chairman and 7–9 members (This number may be altered by Secretary of State.)	Secretary of State for Social Services and Ministers for Scotland, Wales and Northern Ireland.	Land occupied by Board to be deemed to be Crown property but Board is not servant of the Crown (s. 2).	Board assumes functions given by Ministers: p. 1 (3); must comply with directions given by Ministers after consultation with A.E.A. and M.R.C. (s. 1 (7)).	Advisory Committee (s. 4)	Research, information collection, etc. about radiation hazards (s. 1 (1)).
13.	*Housing* Housing Corporation.	Housing Act, 1964.	Chairman, Deputy Chairman and not more than seven members (Sched. 1, para. 2).	Minister of Housing and Local Government and Secretary of State for Scotland.	Members may be paid remuneration and allowances; no prescribed qualifications for members.	Minister may give directions of general nature (no reference to public interest or consultation): s. 1 (2). Minister's consent is often necessary (s. 3 (1), 3 (3), 4 (2) etc.).	None; but they have express duty to publicise aims and principles of housing societies (s. 1 (1)).	"To promote and assist the development of housing societies," etc. (s. 1 (1)).
14.	*Iron and Steel* National Steel Corporation.[12]	Iron and Steel Act, 1967.	Chairman and 7–20 other members; one member may be appointed Deputy Chairman.[13]	Secretary of State for Trade and Industry.[14]	Members must have had "wide experience of and shown capacity in" one or more of 6 listed topics (s. 1 (3)).	May give directions to Board as to compilation of statistics and forecasts (s. 6).	None.[6]	To carry on any iron and steel activities, to sell iron and steel products and to carry on the activities of any publicly owned company as authorised by the Minister (s. 2).

15.	*National Parks, etc.* (a) Countryside Commission.	Countryside Act, 1968; National Parks and Access to the Countryside Act, 1949.	Chairman, Deputy and as many members as the Minister may determine: 1949, s. 2 (1).[15]	Secretary of State for the Environment.[16]	Chairman, Deputy and members are paid; office of member may be terminated if Minister considers member is "unable or unfit".[17]	May give directions of a general character as appears to the Minister to be expedient: 1949, s. 3 (1).[18] Functions are exercisable "on behalf of the Crown": 1949, s. 2 (5).	None,[6] but local authorities may be invited to nominate members of a local planning board established for a particular National Park.	"The preservation and enhancement of natural beauty, particularly in National Parks, and the encouragement, provision or improvement of facilities for persons resorting to National Parks" (s. 1) of 1969 Act, and see s. 1 (2) of 1968 Act.
	(b) Nature Conservancy.	Chartered Corporation.[19]	12–18 members, 6 of whom retire every year (all are eligible for re-appointment).	The Committee of the Privy Council appointed for the organisation and development of agricultural research.[20]	Members may be paid honoraria, with the consent of the Treasury.	The Conservancy is responsible to and must comply with any directions given by the Privy Council Committee; the Treasury *may* make grants to the Conservancy.[21]	None.[6]	Establishing, maintaining and managing nature reserves, and accepting such functions and powers as may be specifically delegated to them by statute.[22]
16.	*Race Relations* Race Relations Board.	Race Relations Act, 1968.[23]	Chairman and not more than 11 other members (s. 14 (27)).	Secretary of State.	Members are to be paid: Sched. 1, para. 4.	No provision for directions.	Board must appoint conciliation committees: s. 14 (5).	The Board has the function of securing compliance with the provisions of Part I of the Act and the resolution of differences arising out of any of those provisions: s. 14 (1).

APPENDIX TO CHAPTER X

Serial No.	Service and Corporation	Constituent Statute	Managing Body			Degree of Independence		Principal Functions
			Number of Members	By whom Appointed	Special Features	Ministerial Directions	Public Relations Organisation	
1	2	3	4	5	6	7	8	9
17.	*Sugar* Sugar Board.	Sugar Act, 1956.	Chairman, not more than 4 other members (s. 2 (1)).	Minister of Agriculture, Fisheries and Food.	Not more than 3 members to be whole-time; members not to have "substantial financial interest" in sugar industry; to be appointed in consultation with Chairman.	Board may be directed to buy or sell sugar as agent for the Minister.[24]	None.[6]	To deal in Commonwealth sugar pursuant to Government agreements, or under the direction of the Minister.
18.	*Tourism* The British Tourist Authority, The English Tourist Board, the Scottish Tourist Board and the Wales Tourist Board.	Development of Tourism Act, 1969.	British Authority: Chairman and not more than 5 other members; others, Chairman and not more than 6 (s. 1).	Secretary of State for Trade and Industry.	No qualifications specified for members; Board members are to be paid (1st Sched., para. 6).	Schemes made by the B.T.A. are subject to confirmation by the Board of Trade; Board of Trade or Secretary of State may after consultation with a Board give directions "of a general character" (s. 19 (1)).	No special arrangements but the Boards are primarily concerned with publicity.	To encourage tourist (s. 2) amenities and facilities (s. 2); the B.T.A. may make schemes for assistance for tourist projects (s. 3); any Board may subject to approval by Board of Trade carry out particular tourist projects (s. 4) and make grants for new hotels, etc. (Part II); any Board may also administer scheme of registration of hotel accommodation (s. 17).

19.	*Town and Country Planning* (a) New Town Development Corporations.[25]	New Towns Act, 1965.	Chairman, Deputy and not more than 7 other members (s. 2).	Secretary of State for the Environment.[16]	Secretary of State must consult with local authorities concerned as to membership; must have regard to desirability of one or more members with local knowledge.	Secretary of State may give directions restricting exercise of powers, or requiring powers to be exercised in manner specified (s. 4).[26]	None.[6]	"To secure the laying out and development of the new town in accordance with" proposals approved by the Secretary of State.
	(b) The Commission for the New Towns.[27]	New Towns Act, 1965.	Chairman, Deputy and not more than 13 other members (9th Sched., para. 1 (1)).	Do.	Members may be paid; a member may be removed if he is "unable, unfit or unsuitable".	Secretary of State may give directions but he must have regard to the purpose for which any particular new town was developed: s. 37 (2).[28]	None.[6]	To take over, hold, manage and turn to account the property previously vested in a new town development corporation.
	(c) The Location of Offices Bureau.	Town and Country Planning Act, 1943; S.I., 1963, No. 792.	Chairman, Deputy Chairman and not more than two members.	Do.	Members may be paid remuneration and allowances.	Bureau must comply with such directions of a general character as may be given by the Secretary of State	None.	To assist the Secretary of State and to encourage the decentralisation and diversion of office employment from congested areas in central London.

APPENDIX TO CHAPTER X

Serial No.	Service and Corporation	Constituent Statute	Managing Body			Degree of Independence		Principal Functions
			Number of Members	By whom Appointed	Special Features	Ministerial Directions	Public Relations Organisation	
1	2	3	4	5	6	7	8	9
20.	*Transport*[29] (a) British Railways Board;	Transport Act, 1962.	(a) Chairman, 2 Vice-chairmen, 10–16 members;	Secretary of State for Trade and Industry.	Members must be paid; persons selected as members must hold certain qualifications (s. 1). [This applies to corporations (a)–(g) inclusive.]	Secretary of State may give directions of a general character on matters which appear to him to affect the national interest, after consultation (s. 27).[30] He may also give directions requisite on any recommendation of the Freight Integration Council (which is not a body corporate): 1968 Act, s. 6 (1).	Central Transport Consultative Committee and Area Transport Users Consultative Committees (s. 56).	(a) To provide railway services: 1962, s. 3 (1);
	(b) London Transport Board.	Do.	(b) Chairman, Vice-chairman, 4–9 members;	Do.				(b) To provide an adequate and properly co-ordinated system of passenger transport for London: 1962, s. 7 (1);
	(c) British Transport Docks Board;	Do.	(c) Chairman, Vice-chairman, 4–9 members;	Do.				(c) To provide port facilities: 1962, s. 9 (1);
	(d) British Waterways Board.		(d) Chairman, Vice-chairman, 4–9 members (s. 1).	Do.				(d) To provide services and facilities on inland waterways: 1962, s. 10.
	(e) National Freight Corporation.	Do.	(e) Chairman, 6–12 other members.	Do.				(e) To provide properly integrated services for carriage of goods by road and rail (1968, s. 1).
	(f) National Bus Company.[31]	Do.	(f) Chairman, 5–10 other members.	Do.				(f) To co-operate with the local Executives, and otherwise to carry passengers by road, vessel or hovercraft in England and Wales.

	Transport cont. (g) Scottish Transport Group.	Transport Act, 1968.	(g) Chairman, 5–10 other members.	Secretary of State.	[*see* above]	[*see* above]	[*see* above]	(g) To co-operate with the local Executives, and otherwise to carry passengers by road, vessel or hovercraft in Scotland.
	(h) The National Ports Council.	Harbours Act, 1964.	Chairman and 7–11 members; one to be Deputy Chairman (s. 2).	Do.	Council to pay members remuneration and allowances.	Minister may after consultation direct Council to promote research (s. 3 (2)); Minister must consult council on several occasions (s. 9 (6), 12 (1), 13 (1), etc.).	None.	Must formulate and keep under review a national plan for the development of harbours in Great Britain, etc. (s. 1 (1)).
21.	*Water* National Water Council.[32]	Water Act, 1973.	Chairmen of the Regional Authorities and up to 10 other members (s. 4).	Secretary of State for the Environment and the Minister of Agriculture, Fisheries and Food.	Minister may pay members remuneration and allowances (Sched. 3).	Ministers may give directions of general nature after consultation with the Council (s. 4 (9)).	None.	To advise any Minister; to promote and assist efficient performance by water authorities of their functions, etc. (s. 4 (5)).

[1] Where more than one statute is cited in this column, the principal statute is printed in italics. References under each entry to sections refer to that statute in each instance.

[2] Acting by the Minister for Aerospace.

[3] Formerly the Lord President of the Council; later the Minister for Science.

[4] See text above, p. 329.

[5] The Authority may be paid such sums as the Minister may determine, subject to the consent of the Treasury. The Authority has in addition some independent income from the sale of atomic energy, but this is not sufficient to meet its expenditure.

[6] This merely indicates that no statutory or formal provision is made.

[7] The first Royal Charter was granted on 1st January 1927; it was renewed in 1964 for a period of 12 years, expiring on 31st July 1976.

[8] Under clause 15 (4) of the Licence; it is also provided that the Corporation may not derive income from advertising. By the Charter the Corporation is specifically required to be a non-profit making organisation.

[9] A copy of any such notice must be laid before each House of Parliament: *ibid.*

[10] There is no "Country Council" for England.

[11] The total number of Regional and Area Health Authorities depends on regulations made by the Secretary of State under the 1973 Act.

[12] Replacing the Iron and Steel Board, arrangements for whose dissolution are contained in the 1967 Act.

[13] By virtue of s. 1 (8) of the Iron and Steel Act, 1949, "revived" by s. 1 (6) of the 1967 Act.

[14] Originally the Minister of Supply; see S.I. 1955 No. 876 and S.I. 1957 No. 95.

[15] At present there are nine members.

[16] Originally the Minister of Town and Country Planning; see S.I. 1951 No. 142 and S.I. 1951 No. 1900.

[17] National Parks and Access to the Countryside (National Parks Commission) Regulations 1949, S.I. 1949 No. 2361, reg. 2 (i).

[18] Any direction so given must be made public; s. 3 (2).

[19] Royal Charter dated 23rd March, 1949.

[20] This Committee was first established in 1930, and now consists of the Lord President of the Council, the Minister of Agriculture, Fisheries and Food, the Home Secretary, the Secretary of State for Scotland, the Secretary of State for Education and Science and the Secretary of State for Foreign and Commonwealth Affairs.

[21] National Parks and Access to the Countryside Act, 1949, s. 96.

[22] *Ibid.*, Part III in particular.

[23] This Board existed under the Race Relations Act, 1965, but until the coming into operation of the 1968 Act, it had no corporate status.

[24] Where the Board so acts it is an agent of the Crown; s. 3 (3).

[25] There are at present twenty-six in England and Wales.

[26] In addition, the development corporations are dependent for finance on the Secretary of State, who has power to make advances to them, subject to the approval of the Treasury; 1965 Act, s. 42. The consent of the Secretary of State is required to certain transactions such as the compulsory acquisition of interests in land. In practice Departmental control over the new town development corporations is considerable: see note 5 on p. 330, *ante*.

[27] This is a single corporation, constituted to take over the property of the development corporations as the development of the several towns becomes virtually complete.

[28] The Commission, like the development corporations, is dependent for its finances on advances made by the Secretary of State with the consent of the Treasury; 1965 Act, s. 42.

[29] Under the Acts of 1962 and 1968; the former arrangements are here ignored. The "new authorities" (items (e), (f) and (g)) owe their corporate status to the incorporation of relevant provisions of the 1962 Act into the Act of 1968: see Sched. 1, para. 6 thereof. In addition, the 1968 Act empowers the Secretary of State to constitute in particular areas Passenger Transport Executives and Passenger Transport Authorities (all of which will be corporate bodies). When the Secretary of State "sees fit by order so to direct", there will be yet another corporate body, the Channel Tunnel Planning Council (1968 Act, s. 143).

[30] A Board may also be authorised by the Secretary of State under the 1962 Act to acquire land compulsorily (s. 15); the Secretary of State has to approve of borrowings by a Board (s. 19), and the Treasury may issue guarantees (s. 21).

[31] The former Transport Holding Company was dissolved under the 1968 Act and replaced by the Bus Company and the Scottish Group.

[32] Replacing the former Water Resources Board, and with somewhat wider functions.

CHAPTER XI

LOCAL AUTHORITIES

1. INTRODUCTION

In the Chapters that follow we are dealing with those organs of the executive outside the central government that are concerned with local government. In the second Report of the Local Government Manpower Committee[1] it was said that local authorities in this country are responsible bodies competent to discharge their own functions, exercising their responsibilities in their own right. The Committee (consisting of representatives of both the central Government and local authorities), made this observation in the course of a survey of the growing elaboration of central control over the detailed work of local authorities,[2] but it also brings out clearly the essential feature of English local government, which is both "local" *and* "government", within its own sphere; English local authorities are not mere local organs of a central government, as in many Continental countries.[3] Each local authority has a separate independent existence, and power to take decisions and make mistakes within the extent of the powers entrusted to it by the general law. The central government exercises a considerable control over the manner in which an authority may carry on its affairs, but local authorities remain independent entities and in no sense organs of the central Government.[4]

This independence of local authorities is the result of history, and of the history of towns in particular, which through the centuries secured privileges from the king or intermediate overlords; first freedom from internal taxes and then rights to appoint their own justices and to exemption from the jurisdiction of the county magistrates. When the new authorities were created in the nineteenth century they were known at first as poor law unions,[5] which were duplicated by the sanitary boards. Later they became urban and rural district councils,[6] but the municipal corporations, as the towns were then called,[7] formed the

---

[1] Cmd. Paper 8421 (1951).

[2] *Post*, Chapter XV, *post*, p. 442.

[3] Local Government in England and Wales grew not from de-centralisation but from the "democratisation" of the conduct of local affairs; see *Le Local Government en Grande Bretagne*, by Roger Garreau (Paris), a perceptive account of the English system by a Continental writer.

[4] With the exception of emergency powers, such as food rationing, entrusted to local authorities as agents of the Central Government during the war of 1939–45.

[5] Created by the Poor Law Amendment Act, 1834.

[6] Constituted under the Local Government Act, 1894, and replacing the urban and rural sanitary districts of nineteenth-century Public Health Acts. Hereafter in these footnotes the expression "Local Government Act" will be abbreviated to "L.G.A.".

[7] After their constitutions had been reformed by the Municipal Corporations Act, 1835. On the history of local government generally, see *The History of Local Government in England*, by Redlich and Hurst (ed. Keith-Lucas, 1959).

pattern for their constitution. The characteristics[8] of an English local authority are as follows:

(a) The authority is always a separate person in law. This refers to the concept of personality—the principle whereby the law alone can decide what natural or "artificial" persons shall be accorded the badge of legal personality. At the present day every natural person is a person in law,[9] and the law also recognises groups of persons or individuals organised in a particular manner as having legal personality, these being known sometimes as "artificial" persons.[10] Incorporation—the conferment by the law of the badge of personality—may be effected by statute or by the Crown by virtue of the prerogative (by means of a document known as a charter). Both kinds of incorporation were before 1974 to be found in local government—now all local authorities are statutory corporations, but before 1974 some[11] were common law corporations by charter. The difference between the two kinds is not of great importance,[12] the main point being that all local authorities are persons in law.

(b) The local authority must have governmental powers over a defined local area, although the authority may not possess all the local government powers exercisable in respect of that area.

(c) The authority must be financed, at least in part, by rates drawn from the inhabitants of the area over which it governs.

(d) The authority itself must be controlled by representatives elected directly[13] on an adult franchise by the inhabitants of the area which it governs.

(e) The local authority must be able to exercise over its area a number of governmental functions (the exact number and nature of the functions depend primarily on the kind of particular authority and to some extent on its size and resources), but those functions can be conferred only by statute.

Applying these tests, it becomes obvious that a local committee set up by a Central Department to advise the Minister, cannot be a local authority, nor can a branch of a Government Department concerned

---

[8] The expression "local authority" is defined in many administrative statutes, normally by the provision of a list of the bodies that are to fall within the expression, as explained below. These characteristics apply to all local authorities, as they were, and are, before and after the reorganisation of 1974.

[9] This was not always the case; in the Middle Ages monks and outlaws were "dead" in law.

[10] A corporation is logically no more an artificial person than is a human being, as both depend for their status of personality on the law. The common law also ascribes personality to certain offices, known as "corporations sole", such as the bishop of a diocese or the former Minister of Health (see Ministry of Health Act, 1919, s. 7 (3)), but all local authorities are "corporations aggregate" having a number of corporators. Local authorities generally are now incorporated in the name of the Council.

[11] The ancient municipal corporations, *i.e.*, those in existence in 1835 and allowed to remain in existence by being scheduled to the Municipal Corporations Act, 1835. New boroughs created since that date were brought into existence by Royal Charter issued not under the Prerogative, but under an express statutory power, and the status of borough may now be conferred on a district council by Royal Charter issued under s. 245 of the L.G.A., 1972, and in London under s. 1 (2) of the London Government Act, 1963.

[12] As to the effect on the doctrine of *ultra vires*, see Chapter IX, *ante*, p. 302.

[13] The L.G.A., 1972, has abolished the office of alderman in all cases.

with a particular area. Area electricity boards are not local authorities, as they draw no part of their finances from local rates, and neither have they any wide range of powers, being *ad hoc* authorities. There are, however, certain special kinds of authorities which are not local authorities properly so called, but which have a number of the characteristics of a local authority; to these we return later.[14]

2. THE KINDS OF LOCAL AUTHORITIES

The Local Government Act, 1972,[15] reorganising local government and repealing the Act of the same title of 1933, divides the whole of England (outside London) into administrative counties and districts. All districts are of the same single kind, although some may be given the special name and status of "borough", by Royal Charter issued under the Act,[16] but the districts so favoured will have no special functions, although they may succeed to certain dignities.[17] Those parts of districts that were, under the Act of 1933, "rural" districts, are further sub-divided into parishes,[18] which may or may not have a parish council, and may in some cases resolve to take upon themselves the status of "town".[19] In six conurbations[20] the counties are styled "metropolitan counties", and the districts "metropolitan districts", and in these cases the division of functions as between counties and districts is somewhat different from the situation in other parts of the country (for which, see below). Similar provision is made for Wales,[1] except that here the parishes are known as "communities", and there are no conurbations.

Each of these local government areas (except some parishes, as explained below) has a governing body known as a council, and each council has been entrusted by Parliament with some—a few or many—local government functions to be exercised in its area. Over the whole country, including London[2] and Wales, there is now "two tier" or—where there is a parish or community—"three tier" local government, and all local government functions are shared out between the county council and the district council; but in the areas having "three tier" local government, the same powers have to be shared between three local authorities, the county council, the council and the parish council, or parish meeting, or the community council or community meeting (as the case may be[3]). The sharing out of powers is effected by Parliament; there is no question of the county council and the district councils in the county coming together and agreeing on a sharing of the powers avail-

[14] *Post*, p. 367.
[15] See s. 1 thereof; the Act came into force on April 1, 1974.
[16] See s. 245 thereof.
[17] Such as the appointment of ceremonial officers, the ownership of civic plate, etc.
[18] New parishes may be created in urban areas: L.G.A., 1972, Schedule 1, Part V. Parishes are known as "communities" in Wales.
[19] L.G.A., 1972, s. 245 (6); this status carries with it no additional functions. The chairman of the parish Council will have the title of "town mayor".
[20] Namely, Greater Manchester, Merseyside, South Yorkshire, Tyne and Wear, West Midlands and West Yorkshire; L.G.A., 1972, Schedule 1, Part I.
[1] *Ibid.*, Part II.
[2] For London, see *post*, p. 368. By "London" in this context is meant the area governed by the Greater London Council.
[3] As to the different kinds of parishes, see *post*, p. 365.

able,[4] and in no sense are the authorities of the higher rank—the county councils or the district councils in relation to their parishes—in any general supervisory position over the authorites "below" them; Parliament has regarded two or three tier local government rather as a partnership than as a hierarchy of greater and lesser authorities. The system may be shown diagrammatically thus:

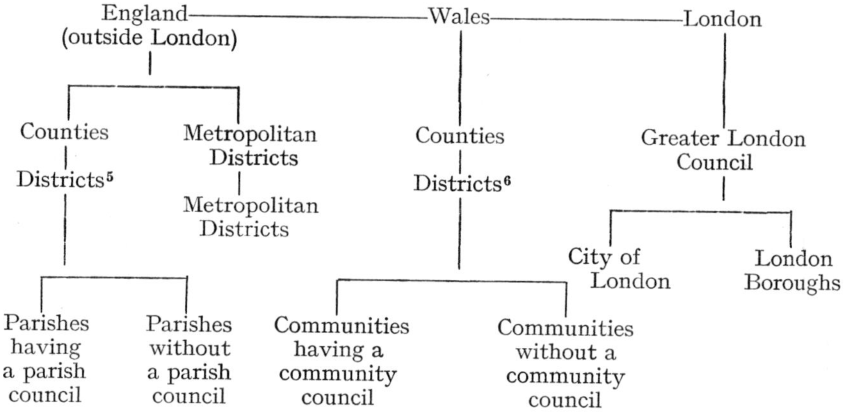

We shall return to local government functions later, but it is important to appreciate the relative importance of the types of authorities and this can be done only by understanding the range and variety of local government functions entrusted to them by Parliament. Thus, under three tier local government the more important functions are divided as follows:

County Councils	District Councils	Parishes (Communities in Wales)
All highways except trunk roads and bridges[7]	Abatement of nuisances and public health generally[12]	Allotments
Education and libraries[8]	Housing	Footpaths
Town and county planning[9]	Entertainments and publicity	Mortuary
Personal social services[8]	Refuse collection	Open spaces and recreation grounds
Fire[10]	Cemeteries	Burial grounds
Police[10]	Markets	Bus shelters
Museums and art galleries	Factories and offices[13]	
Youth employment[8]	Rating	
Food and drugs, and other consumer protection services	Town and country planning[9]	
Parks and open spaces[9]	Recreation[9]	
Refuse disposal[11]		
Small holdings		

For footnotes see page 362.

Where there is no parish, the district will exercise the parish functions listed above. Pre-1974 parishes in England will for the most part (subject to the "divided parishes" listed in Part IV of Schedule 1 to the 1972 Act) continue in existence, and new parishes in former urban districts or boroughs may be constituted by the Boundary Commission.[14] In Wales there are communities everywhere, so three tier government is general.

There are no metropolitan areas in Wales. In the metropolitan areas in England, the counties have less functions than they have elsewhere, personal health services and education in particular are the responsibility of the metropolitan district councils. Each metropolitan county is also a passenger transport area,[15] but in other counties the county council will be responsible for the development of policies which will promote "the provision of a co-ordinated and efficient system of public transport" for the county.[16]

It should also be appreciated that the Local Government Act, 1972, gives the widest possible facility for agency or delegation arrangements between one local authority and another, either of equal status, or as between district and county,[17] and joint committees of two or more authorities also may be established.[18]

3. THE CONSTITUTION OF LOCAL AUTHORITIES

Each local authority has a governing body in all cases except certain parishes and communities consisting of a council, most of whose members are directly elected by the local electorate. The constitutions of the several kinds of authorities under the 1972 Act are similar, but will be considered separately. The pattern of the former "municipal corporation" created by the Acts of that name of 1835 and 1882 still survives in fundamentals. Separate sections of the Act apply to England and to Wales respectively, but the provisions are very similar, and references below are given to the English provisions only.

---

[4] There is, however, a certain amount of give and take by use of the device of delegation; see below, p. 370.

[5] Not all districts have parishes (see p. 365).

[6] *All* districts have communities.

[7] Trunk roads and bridges over trunk roads are the responsibility of the Department of the Environment. District councils may claim maintenance powers for urban roads footpaths and bridlepaths.

[8] In metropolitan areas, these are the responsibility of the metropolitan districts, *not* the counties.

[9] This function is shared between the counties and districts.

[10] These services are often administered by special amalgamated authorities.

[11] A district council function in Wales.

[12] Sewerage and sewage disposal is now the concern of the water authorities, as is water supply.

[13] In so far as these are the concern of local authorities.

[14] L.G.A., 1972, Schedule 1, Part V.

[15] *Ibid.*, s. 202.

[16] *Ibid.*, s. 203.

[17] *Ibid.*, s. 101 (1); *post*, p.

[18] *Ibid.*, s. 102.

(a) Principal Councils.—So far as constitution alone is concerned there is no difference between a county and a district; both are corporations and both are described as "principal councils" in the 1972 Act. There is also no difference from the point of view of constitution *or* functions between a district and a borough or a city. A district council may present a petition to Her Majesty the Queen for the grant of a charter[19]; if this is acceded to, the district will be entitled to the style and title of a "borough". If the district includes within its area a district formerly possessing some special style (such as "city", "Royal Borough", "Royal town", "Regis", etc.), the charter may permit that special style to be retained for the post-1974 district.[20] But these special titles *per se* confer no additional governmental functions.

The council of a district consists of the chairman ("mayor" if the district is a "borough" or "city") and councillors, and the council is a corporate body.[1]

(i) *The Chairman.* The chairman (or mayor) is elected annually at the meeting of the Council held during March, April or May[2] by the members of the council present at the meeting (by a majority vote[3]), from among the councillors.[4] He will hold office until his successor becomes entitled to act as chairman,[5] but his term of office will normally be one year; if he is still a member of the council he may be re-elected. The election of Chairman must be the first item of business transacted at the council's annual meeting.[6] The chairman of a principal council may be paid such allowances "as the council think reasonable"[7]

The chairman when present, must preside over meetings of the council[8]; he therefore has the ordinary common law powers of a chairman of a meeting, designed to keep order and to ensure that standing orders are complied with.[9] He may call a meeting of the council at any time, and must do so if a requisition for that purpose is presented to him, signed by five members of the council.[10] In the event of an equality of votes he has a second or casting vote at meetings,[11] and he will probably (according to the terms of the particular council's standing orders) be an *ex officio* member of most or all the committees of the council.

---

19 *Ibid.*, s. 245 (1).
20 *Ibid.*, s. 245 (2).
1 *Ibid.*, s. 2 (3).
2 In an election year this date is fixed; in every fourth year, when there is no election of councillors, the date is fixed by the council: L.G.A., 1972, Schedule 12, Part I, para. 1.
3 *Ibid.*, para. 39.
4 *Ibid.*, s. 3 (1). Under the pre-1974 law, the mayor of a borough need not have been a member of the council, but this provision has been changed.
5 L.G.A., 1972, s. 3 (2).
6 *Ibid.*, s. 4 (1).
7 *Ibid.*, s. 3 (5).
8 L.G.A., 1972, Schedule 12, Part I, para. 5 (1).
9 As to standing orders, see Chapter XIII, *post*, p. 397.
10 L.G.A., 1972. Schedule 5, Part I, para. 3.
11 *Ibid.*, Part VI, para. 39 (2).

During his year of office the chairman or mayor is now no longer, *ex officio* a justice of the peace as the Justices of the Peace Act, 1968 provides that only persons appointed by name to the commission of the peace for an area shall be justices of the peace.[12] Apart from certain minor functions in connection with elections, the chairman has no special legal functions. Ceremonially, however, the chairman of a district council is entitled to precedence in all places in the district, subject only to Her Majesty's royal prerogative.[13] In matters of precedence therefore the chairman should yield only to the sovereign, members of the Royal Family and the Lord Lieutenant of the County.

The mayor of a city has as such no special title, but in some cities the mayor may be entitled to be called "Lord Mayor", and in the cases of London, York and Cardiff alone in England and Wales, the Lord Mayor is entitled to the further prefix "Right Honourable". None of these titles has any legal effect on the functions of either their holder or the council of which he is the head.

(ii) *The Vice-Chairman.*—Every principal council must appoint one of its members to be vice-chairman.[14] The vice-chairman has all the powers of the chairman if for any reason the chairman is unable to act or his office is vacant, and he may be paid an allowance by the council. He holds office until immediately after the election of a new chairman at the next annual meeting of the council.

(iii) *Aldermen.*—This ancient office has been abolished by the Local Government Act, 1972, even in London, where the office was preserved by the London Government Act, 1963. However any principal council may confer the title of "honorary alderman" on a past member of the council (L.G.A., 1972, s. 249).

(iv) *The Councillors.*—Councillors are elected every first, second and third year in a four year cycle[15] by the local government electors of the district or county, and each councillor holds office for a period of four years, one-third of the total number retiring every election year.[16] There is no prescribed number of councillors for councils generally, but the precise number for each county and district will be determined in accordance with the number of wards, the boundaries of which are fixed by the Secretary of State (in the event of changes after receiving proposals from the Boundary Commission.[17])

(v) *Sheriffs.*—Before 1974, twenty-one boroughs[18] had the right or privilege of appointing their own sheriff, and it was normal for a member of a council to be so appointed. This did not add to the membership of

---

12 1968 Act, s. 1. Special provision is made for the Lord Mayor and aldermen of the City of London.

13 L.G.A., 1972, s. 3 (4).

14 *Ibid.*, s. 5.

15 L.G.A., 1972, s. 7. A non-metropolitan district council may decide for a system of whole council elections once every four years: *ibid.*, s. 7 (4).

16 *Ibid.*

17 *Ibid.*; as to the Boundary Commissioners for England and for Wales, see *post*, Chapter XIII, p. 405.

18 See *Civic Ceremonial*, 2nd Edn., at p. 91, by the present author.

the council, as the person appointed could remain a member as sheriff, his duties being mainly ceremonial in nature, and his executive duties were performed by a permanent official known as the Under-Sheriff (often a local solicitor). The right to appoint a local sheriff by a district council may be granted by a charter according the title of borough to a district.[19] Each county will have a high sheriff,[20] who need not be a member of the county council and will not become a member by virtue of his office.

(b) Parishes in England.—Every rural district before 1974 was divided into a number of civil parishes, the boundaries of which did not necessarily coincide with those of the corresponding (if any) ecclesiastical parishes. These continue (in some instances with modifications of boundaries) in existence after 1974, and new parishes may be established in former urban areas. There are now two kinds of parishes for the purposes of local government.

(i) *Parishes having a parish council.*—These are parishes where a separate parish council has been established; *i.e.*, where the parish was a rural borough in March 31, 1974, where on that date the parish was co-extensive with a rural district, or where the parish is listed in Parts IV or V of Schedule 1 to the 1972 Act, or if the district council has subsequently established a parish council.[1] The district council must so act if the number of local government electors in the parish is 200 or upwards and must do so in a case of a parish having between 150 and 200 electors if the parish meeting so resolve.[2]

If the parish has at least 150 electors the district council *may* establish a parish council[3]; if the parish has less than 150 electors the parish meeting may apply for the council to be dissolved, and the district council may then so order.[4] With the consent of the parish meetings, parishes also may be grouped by order made by the district council.[5]

A parish council is similar in constitution to a district council; it has a chairman elected by the council from the councillors, and the council may also appoint one of their members to be vice-chairman.[6] The chairman holds office for a year; councillors hold office for three years and retire simultaneously every third year.[7] A parish council must consist of not less than five members, as may be fixed from time to time by the district council.[8] The body corporate in a parish having a separate parish council is the council.[9]

(ii) *Parishes not having a separate parish council.*—If a parish has no separate parish council, the chairman of the parish meeting and the

---

[19] L.G.A., 1972, s. 246.
[20] *Ibid.*, s. 219. High sheriffs are appointed each year by Her Majesty.
[1] L.G.A., 1972, s. 9 (4).
[2] *Ibid.*, s. 9 (2).
[3] *Ibid.*, s. 9 (3).
[4] *Ibid.*, s. 10.
[5] *Ibid.*, s. 11.
[6] *Ibid.*, s. 15.
[7] *Ibid.*, s. 16 (3).
[8] *Ibid.*, s. 16 (1).
[9] *Ibid.*, s. 14 (2).

"proper officer" (*i.e.*, an officer appointed in that behalf) of the district council are a body corporate by the name of "the Parish Trustees" of the parish.[10]

Every parish must have a parish meeting, whether or not it also has a parish council. The meeting consists of all the local government electors of the parish[11]—or such of them as may choose to come (there is no quorum prescribed by statute for such a meeting.) A parish meeting must be called at least once every year[12] and at their "annual assembly" they must choose a chairman.[13] Parish meetings are the most democratic form of local government in this country, but their powers are small, especially where the parish has a separate parish council.[14] In the normal case decisions are taken by a majority of those present at the meeting and voting on the question, but a poll may be demanded at the meeting on any question arising (whether or not it has been put to the vote); such a poll must be taken by ballot either if the person presiding at the meeting consents, or if the poll is demanded by not less than ten, or one-third, of the local government electors present at the meeting, whichever is the less.[15]

(iii) *Towns*.—These are not really a separate kind of local government unit, but under s. 245 of the L.G.A., 1972, any parish council (or, in Wales, a community council), may resolve that the parish shall have the status of a "town". The chairman and vice-chairman of the parish council are then known as the town mayor and deputy town mayor respectively, and the parish meeting is known as a town meeting. The enhanced dignity, however, gives no added functions whatever to the parish so named.

(c) **Communities in Wales.**—In Wales the lowest tier authority is known as a community, and there are communities throughout the country. Some communities have a separate council, others do not, and there is always a community meeting. *Mutatis mutandis* the rules as to parishes as above described are the same as those for communities, but they are contained in a separate set of sections in the 1972 Act,[16] and the community not having a separate council does not have the benefit of incorporation.[17]

---

10 *Ibid.*, s. 13 (3).
11 *Ibid.*, s. 13 (1).
12 *Ibid.*, Schedule 12, para. 14. If there is no parish council the parish meeting must assemble at least twice in every year: *ibid.*
13 *Ibid.*, s. 15 (10).
14 Some matters can, however, only be determined by a vote of the parish meeting, even where the parish has a separate parish council. The parish meeting is in quite different form from the town's meeting of the New England States in the U.S.A., where every year the "town warrant" has to be passed in town meeting, settling the general pattern for the town's administration for the ensuring year; there is no question of a parish meeting settling an annual "programme".
15 L.G.A., 1972, Schedule 12, para. 18.
16 Sections 27–37 and Schedule 12, Parts IV and V.
17 See s. 32.

4. SPECIAL AUTHORITIES

In addition to the local authorities properly so called as described above there are also a number of *ad hoc* authorities which possess most of the characteristics of a local authority[18], except that of being governed by directly elected local representatives. These are the "joint boards" that may be set up under a number of statutes[19] to administer one specified service over a defined local area. They are bodies corporate and can therefore be constituted only under statutory authority, which usually means that they are brought into being by an order made by the appropriate Minister, but in some cases they may owe their origin to a special local Act power. Joint boards may be constituted to administer a port health district[20] or education services for the area of two or more councils,[1] or town and county planning functions[2] for two or more authorities, and combined police authorities may be established under the Police Act, 1964.[3] A joint board has power to precept for its revenues on local authorities within its area, and the majority of its members will normally consist of representatives from the councils of those local authorities, but these members are appointed by the appropriate Minister and are not directly elected to serve as such. Water authorities[4] are technically not "joint" boards, as the initiative in creating a joint board normally[5] comes from the constituent local authorities, and a water authority's area will normally cut across the boundaries of many local authorities; but in other respects such an authority is very similar to a joint board; it is certainly an *ad hoc* authority, being entrusted with a specified range of functions, and constituted by the Secretary of State under statutory authority. The water authorities, replacing the former river authorities, are large corporations with a number of functions; in particular, by their constituent statute, the Water Act, 1973, they have taken over the sewerage functions of local authorities.

Joint boards must be distinguished from joint committees, which may be constituted by any two or more local authorities acting in concert.[6] A joint committee will have only such powers as may be entrusted to it by its constituent authorities, it will not be a body corporate, and it will have no power to precept for or levy a rate or to borrow money[7]; it will have to look for its finances to its constituent

---

[18] *Ante*, p. 359.

[19] A list will be found in Chapter XI of *Local Government Areas*, by J. H. Morris (1960). To these should be added the combined police authorities under the Police Act 1964.

[20] Public Health Act, 1936, s. 2.

[1] Education Act, 1944, s. 6, and Schedule 1, Part I.

[2] Town and Country Planning Act, 1971, s. 1 (2); this device has been used for the administration of planning in the Peak National Park.

[3] Under the terms of an amalgamation scheme made by the Home Secretary; such an authority is a body corporate: 1964 Act, s. 3 (1).

[4] Constituted under the Water Act, 1973.

[5] The appropriate Minister may, however, have compulsory powers under the statute.

[6] L.G.A., 1972, s. 102 (1).

[7] *Ibid.*, s. 101 (6).

authorities.[8] On the other hand, the members of joint committee will be members of the constituent authorities, chosen by them.

5. LONDON GOVERNMENT

Local government within the area administered by the Greater London Council is different from that applicable to the rest of the country in two respects. First, the local authorities in the area are themselves differently organised, and second, some of the local government law applicable to "Inner London" is contained in a separate series of statutes, and is different in points of detail. The "Greater London" area is very much greater than the area formerly administered by the London County Council, as "London Government" was extended into the Home Counties by the London Government Act 1963,[9] which came fully into force on April 1, 1965.

Within "London" as it is understood in law,[10] local government is organised as a two tier structure, consisting of the Greater London Council on the one hand and on the other 32 London Boroughs, the City of London, the Middle Temple and the Inner Temple.[11] In addition there are a number of *ad hoc* authorities administering services which, outside London, are often the concern of local authorities. These are the Port of London Authority, the Thames Conservancy, the London Transport Board,[12] and the Metropolitan Police.[13]

The reforms made by the 1963 Act were of the first importance, although details may be open to criticism. Whilst the whole of the London "region" was not brought within the G.L.C. area, that area does much more nearly represent "London" as its inhabitants know it than the old L.C.C. area. The G.L.C. is one of the largest local authorities in the world, having a population of about 8 million, a rateable value of over £635 million and an area of 620 square miles.

(a) Greater London Council.—This is constituted similarly to a county council outside London, and there are now no aldermen, this office in London (as elsewhere) having been abolished by the Local

---

[8] Any functions may be delegated to a joint committee by the constituent local authorities, except the power of levying or issuing a precept for a rate, or of borrowing money: *ibid.*

[9] Whilst not all the recommendations were accepted *in toto*, this Act was passed as a consequence of the Report of the Royal Commission on Local Government in Greater London, 1957–60, Cmd. 1164.

[10] There are, of course, many different "Londons", even in an administrative sense; see Report of the Royal Commission (*ante*), Chapter IV. Each of the *ad hoc* authorities has its own administrative area, different from each other, and themselves differing from, the area of the Greater London Council.

[11] London Government Act 1963, ss. 1 and 2. The two Temples are strictly a third tier within the City of Westminster.

[12] Concerned not only with railways, but also with road passenger transport: see Transport Act, 1962, s. 7.

[13] Under the direct administration of the Home Secretary, the Metropolitan Police is responsible for the whole of the G.L.C. area (*except* the City of London).

Government Act, 1972.[14] The functions of the G.L.C. are less than those of a normal county council; they are responsible for main drainage, for traffic and for fire and ambulance services, but they have no education (see below), welfare or health services; housing they exercise in common with the London Borough Councils. The G.L.C. is responsible for the preparation of a development plan, but the London Boroughs are responsible for development control under the town and country planning legislation.

(b) London Borough Councils.—These are similar to the extra-London district councils, having a mayor and councillors, and there are now no aldermen.[15] They have most of the functions of a metropolitan district council outside London, but as the G.L.C. have a few unusual functions, they have correspondingly less. They are responsible for development control, health and welfare, refuse collection (but not disposal, which is the concern of the G.L.C.), libraries, local parks (the large open spaces such as Kenwood are administered by the G.L.C.) and they are the rating authorities. The Royal Commission Report and the Act visualises the Boroughs as the "primary units" of local government, and each has a population (1961) on average of approximately 250,000, so their resources are considerable. They replaced 101 local authorities of varying size and status.[16]

(c) The City of London.—The constitution of the City is quite different (except that it is presided over by the Lord Mayor[17]) from that of any other local authority in the country. There is very little said about the City in the London Government Act, 1963 or in the Local Government Act, 1972, and its constitution has not been affected thereby; even its powers, which resemble those of a London Borough, have been only very slightly reduced. The corporate body is the "Mayor and Commonalty and Citizens of the City of London", and the governing body consists of three "courts":

(i) The Court of Common Hall—consisting of the Lord Mayor, the two sheriffs, the 26 aldermen, and the liverymen of the City Companies.

(ii) The Court of Aldermen—consisting of the aldermen, who are elected for life.

(iii) The Court of Common Council—consisting of the Lord Mayor, the aldermen, and 159 common councilmen, elected annually.

The City Corporation has somewhat larger functions than those of a metropolitan district council; it has its own police force and is the port health authority.

(d) The Temples.—The Middle Temple and the Inner Temple are, technically,[18] separate local authorities, but almost the only local govern-

---

[14] L.G.A., 1972, Schedule 2, para. 1; this will not become effective until 1976: see *ibid.*, para. 9.

[15] This will not become effective until 1977: L.G.A., 1972, Schedule 2, para. 9.

[16] For general observations, see article by the present writer, "London Government and its Reform", at [1961] P.L. 256.

[17] *Ante*, p. 363.

[18] London Government Act, 1963, s. 2.

ment services for which they are responsible are the lighting of the Inns, maintenance of roads and pavements and the collection of rates, for which the City Council issue a precept.

(e) Education.—In the case of Inner London (the area formerly administered by the London County Council), the G.L.C. are the education authority, but they are required to act through a special committee on which each Inner London borough is represented. In the remainder of London ("outer London") the education service is administered by the London Boroughs in that area.[19]

6. RELATIONS BETWEEN AUTHORITIES

Under two or three tier local government, the several kinds of authorities are regarded by Parliament as standing in an informal partnership, as sharing local government functions between them in their respective areas. Local government cannot in practice be administered in watertight compartments, and there are therefore devices provided for by statute to ease difficulties and complexities of administration. These are:

(a) *Joint boards.*—The joint boards are *ad hoc* authorities constituted to administer particular services under statutory authority. These have already been discussed.[20]

(b) *Joint committees.*—The joint committees are constituted by two or more authorities acting in concert; these again have already been discussed.

(c) *Delegation.*—This concept, borrowed from the law of agency, enables one local authority to clothe another authority with one or more of its functions, so that the delegate may act as its agent. The device may be employed only where statutory authority exists therefor, for every local authority has been entrusted with a discretion by Parliament to exercise governmental functions within its powers, and that discretion can be entrusted to another only in circumstances where a statute permits.

Until 1972 Parliament was comparatively ungenerous in the powers it gave local authorities to effect delegation agreements. As a consequence, however, of a number of reports that preceded the reorganisation statute of 1972,[1] the Act of that year adopts a fundamentally different attitude. By section 101, it is provided that any local authority may arrange for the discharge of any of their functions by a committee, a sub-committee,[2] an officer,[3] or by any other local authority. A county may, therefore, delegate to a district (or *vice versa*), one district may delegate to another, and a parish or community may delegate to another, or a district may delegate to a parish (or a community).[4] The Minister also may make compulsory arrangements for the discharge

---

[19] *Ibid.*, s. 30.

[20] *Ante*, p. 367.

[1] "Mallaby" and "Maud" in particular; *post*, p. 383.

[2] For delegation to committees, see *post*, p. 395.

[3] For delegation to officers, see *post*, p. 385.

[4] A parish meeting may delegate to a committee: L.G.A., 1972, s. 108.

of a county function by a district council, for a limited period from 1974.[5] Officers may be "lent" by one local authority to another,[6] and one local authority may obtain goods and services in bulk on behalf of other authorities.[7] Furthermore, district councils may be required to perform sewerage (but not sewage disposal) functions on behalf of the water authority.[8]

Delegation agreements or arrangements of this kind do not, however, apply to:

(a) the levying, or issuing a precept for a rate, or the borrowing of money[9];

(b) functions under the Diseases of Animals Act, 1950[10]; and

(c) functions for which the local authority are required by law to appoint a committee.[11]

Delegation is a popular administrative device, although the Royal Commission on London Government described it as "papering over the cracks" in the administration of local government; the delegating authority retains control, while the delegate is allowed a certain measure of power in running the service or operating the control to which delegations refers. Supervisory powers do not remain in the delegating authority *per se*; the extent to which they can interfere with the manner in which delegation is exercised by the delegate depends on the terms of the delegation agreement.[12] In spite of the principle *delegatus non potest delegare* (which though a rule of the law of trusts, applies to the delegation of administrative functions),[13] it appears that a function delegated by one authority to another must become the function of the delegate sufficiently to permit them in turn to delegate that function to a committee of their number under section 101 of the Local Government Act, 1972.[14]

(d) *Informal relations.*—Quite apart from the law, it has become a feature of modern local government for the several kinds of authorities to meet together in associations. These bodies hold conferences and periodic meetings where ideas are exchanged, formally and informally, and the members of the association discuss matters which in their view need legislative reform or other attention from the central government. It has become customary for Ministers of the Crown to consult with members of local authority associations before promoting new legislation or exercising powers of delegated legislation; the associations also, in manner similar to the trade unions, frequently put forward and urge on the Government the sectional interests of their members. This practice was most noticeable in the course of the protracted discussions on the

[5] *Ibid.*, s. 110. This is designed to ease the process of changeover consequent on the coming into operation of the 1972 Act on April 1, 1974.
[6] L.G.A., 1972, s. 113.
[7] Local Authorities (Goods and Services) Act, 1970.
[8] Water Act, 1973, s. 15.
[9] L.G.A., 1972, s. 101 (6).
[10] *Ibid.*, s. 101 (7).
[11] *Ibid.*, s. 101 (9) and (10).
[12] *Huth* v. *Clarke* (1890), 25 Q.B.D. 391.
[13] See, *e.g.*, *Cook* v. *Ward* (1877), 2 C.P.D. 255.
[14] *Joyner* v. *Guildford Corpn.* (1954), 5 P. & C.R. 30 (a county court decision).

reorganisation of local government that preceded and finally resulted in the Local Government Act, 1958.[15] The strength of the local authority associations has perhaps at times tended to exacerbate feelings of friction between the several classes of authorities, but in the sphere of obtaining or recommending reforms of detailed law and administrative methods they have proved invaluable.

As a consequence of the reorganisation of local government under the Act of 1972 the local authorities have had to re-group themselves and form new associations. Thus, the most powerful of the associations pre-1974, the Association of Municipal Corporations, has been dissolved, and the Association of Municipal Authorities and the Association of District Councils have been formed to take its place. The Association of County Councils continues for the present, with revised membership. In 1973 and 1974 discussions were pending on proposals to form a federation of the Associations but this has not met with general agreement. There are also associations of local authorities (in some cases with other than local authority members), such as the Association of Health and Pleasure Resorts and the Housing and Town Planning Council.

The local authority associations in recent years have combined to form agencies for special purposes of common interest such as the Local Government Training Board (formed as a limited company) and the Local Authorities Management Services and Computer Committee. There is also an international body, the International Association of Local Authorities. Local government officers also have formed associations to protect and discuss matters of special interest; these include SOLACE (the Society of Local Authority Chief Executives) replacing the former prestigious Society of Town Clerks.

7. THE ACQUISITION OF FUNCTIONS BY LOCAL AUTHORITIES

The conferment of new functions on local authorities or the re-allocation of existing functions between authorities is of course a matter for Parliament, but there are a number of steps that a particular authority may take to enlarge its field of activities or to acquire new functions:

(a) *The exercise of discretionary functions.*—Many of the normal local authority functions, such as the emptying of dustbins or the maintenance of highways, are mandatory duties which the authority is required by law or can be required by a Minister to undertake, but other services are optional or "permissive", in that the statutory powers are there, bus a local authority cannot be compelled to exercise them. Such are the provision of entertainments,[16] the making of advances for the purchase of houses by private individuals[17] and the making of grants to assist youth clubs,[18] or house improvements.[19]

(b) *Adoptive Acts.*—Some Acts are on the statute book, but do not

[15] See Chapter XIII, *post*, p. 402.
[16] Under L.G.A., 1972, s. 145.
[17] Under the Housing (Financial Provisions) Act, 1958, s. 43.
[18] Under the Physical Training and Recreation Act, 1937.
[19] Housing Act, 1969, s. 1.

apply to the area of any particular local authority area unless and until the council thereof has passed a resolution and observed any other procedural requirements specified in the Act, "adopting" its provisions; such are several provisions of the Public Health Acts Amendment Act, 1907, and in a slightly different sense[20] Part VI of the Rent Act, 1968, referring to furnished lettings and section 17 of the General Rate Act, 1967, relating to the rating of unoccupied property. A somewhat similar device, known as "Clauses Acts", which needed adoption by a special Act, was often used in the nineteenth century, but this has now become obsolete.

(c) *Local Acts.*—At a further stage, an enterprising local authority may not be satisfied with discretionary functions and adoptive Acts but may wish to exercise new powers, such as to operate a municipal savings bank[1] or a laundry[2]; where no statutory powers exist for such functions, the authority will have to promote a Bill in Parliament to obtain a local Act. There is power to do this by machinery laid down in the Local Government Act, 1972.[3]

(d) *Byelaws, etc.*—An authority may also acquire new powers for itself by making byelaws[4] or a compulsory purchase order for the acquisition of a piece of land[5]; in both of these cases, the authority will require express statutory powers justifying their action, which will also require confirmation by the appropriate Minister. Similarly, the making of a development plan under the Town and Country Planning Act, 1971 will—when confirmed by the Secretary of State—have the effect of conferring new powers on the planning authority, and so will the making of a tree preservation order under the same Act,[6] within a much smaller compass.

(e) *Delegation.*—As we have already seen, a local authority may acquire new functions not in their own right, but by the "leave and licence" of some other local authority, most commonly the county council. Joint boards and joint committees normally acquire their functions by this means, sometimes as a result of Ministerial direction, and sometimes by agreement between authorities.

---

[20] In that this Act does not confer any substantial powers on the local authority itself, but "adoption" by Ministerial order has the effect of extending the provisions of Part VI to the area.

[1] As was done by the City of Birmingham many years ago.

[2] See *A.-G.* v. *Fulham Corpn.*, [1921] 1 Ch. 440.

[3] L.G.A., 1972, s. 239; and see Chapter III, *ante*. p. 45.

[4] Chapter IV, *ante*, p. 80.

[5] Chapter VIII, *ante*, p. 228.

[6] 1971 Act, s. 60.

CHAPTER XII

THE MEMBERS AND OFFICERS OF LOCAL AUTHORITIES

1. INTRODUCTION

The theoretical relationship between members, the elected representatives, of local authorities and their employees, the local government officers, at least is reasonably clear. The elected representative is a part-time amateur elected on a wide franchise by the local inhabitants, whilst the officer is a full-time salaried employee, often possessing specialist qualifications appointed by and answerable only to the elected representatives. A member is concerned with the formulation of policy, whilst it is the function of the officer to proffer advice, to guide and assist the member to formulate policy and to execute that policy when duly formulated, and also generally to administer the business and everyday affairs of the authority. As we have already seen, however,[1] the line between policy and administration cannot be precisely defined, and many senior local government officers are as much concerned in practice with policy-making as they are with its execution, and their responsibilities are increasing and widening as a consequence of current local government reforms. First, however, we must consider how individuals become members of a local authority, the special rules of law applicable to them, *qua* members, and also the law relating to local government officers. In the next Chapter the organisation of local authorities will be considered, which will involve an outline of the committee system as at present known in English local government.

2. ELECTIONS

Before 1974 there were two distinct forms of election in local government, direct election by the electorate, who are those having the local government franchise, and indirect election by members of the particular local authority. The latter, whereby members of the former borough and county councils elected "alderman" has now been abolished by the Local Government Act, 1972. The election of the chairman of a county district parish or community council is of a different kind, as only an existing member of the council concerned may be so elected.

A. Election of councillors

(1) *The Franchise.*—The local government franchise is basically the same as the parliamentary franchise, in that every person of voting age (18 years)[2] resident in the area of the local authority on the qualifying

[1] See Chapter I, *ante*, p. 4.
[2] Representation of the People Act, 1969, s. 1.

date[3] is entitled to be included in the register of electors, and so is entitled to vote. In addition peers of the realm can vote in local government elections, but the former qualification of an occupier (owner or tenant) of land or premises in the area having a yearly value of not less than £10 has been abolished.[4] A person cannot be resident in more than one place, and therefore no one can now vote for more than one local authority membership.

(2) *Nominations.*—The first step in any local government (or parliamentary) election is the publication of the notice of election by the proper officer to the local authority concerned. A candidate must then obtain a nomination paper, signed by a proposer and a seconder and by eight assentors, all of whom must be local government electors for the area of the authority, and lodge this at the local authority's offices, accompanied by a consent to the nomination signed by himself and stating his qualifications to be a councillor,[5] before noon on the day fixed by law[6] for the reception of nomination papers. The returning officer[7] then adjudicates upon the validity of the nomination papers, and declares them valid or void, as the case may be; a notice has to be published to that effect. If there are more valid nominations than there are councillors to be elected, there has to be a poll; if not, those persons duly nominated are declared elected unopposed on the morning of the day on which the poll would have been held. If less candidates are validly nominated than the number of vacancies, any retiring councillors for vacancies not so filled remain in office.

(3) *The poll.*—If there is a poll in any particular election, notice thereof must be given by the returning officer. Arrangements are made for persons who have applied (on grounds recognised by law[8]) before nomination day to vote by post, ballot papers being sent to them some few days before polling day. At the poll itself elaborate precautions are taken to ensure the secrecy of voting, to prevent the personation of an elector by some other person, and to prevent corrupt and illegal practices.[9] Thus, the ballot box must be shown empty to those present at

---

[3] October 10, in every year; the register comes into force on the ensuing February 16; Electoral Registers Act, 1949, s. 1, as amended by s. 1 of the Electoral Registers Act, 1953.

[4] Representation of the People Act, 1969, s. 15.

[5] The candidate must be aged at least 21 and a British subject, and must also be able to satisfy one of the following qualifications:

(a) inclusion in the register of local government electors for the area; *or*

(b) residence within the area of the authority during the whole period of twelve months preceding the election; *or*

(c) a principal or only place of work during that twelve months, within the area; *or*

(d) occupation as owner or tenant of land or premises within the area during the whole of that twelve months.

He must also not be *disqualified* from being elected or being a councillor (see below). In the case of a parish, residence within three miles of the parish boundary is a sufficient qualification: L.G.A., 1972, s. 79.

[6] See Representation of the People Act, 1949.

[7] He will be an officer of the council appointed by them in the case of county and district council elections, or an officer of the district council in the case of parish or community council elections: L.G.A., 1972, s. 41.

[8] *E.g.*, on the grounds of illness, unavoidable absence from the neighbourhood on the day of poll, etc.

[9] In the case of a *corrupt* practice, the prosecution must be able to prove, so as to secure a conviction, an intention to commit the offence on the part of the accused; in the case of an *illegal* practice the statutory prohibition is absolute. The proof of corrupt and illegal practices may invalidate an election (see *post*).

the polling station at the commencement of the poll, each ballot paper must be marked with a secret mark prior to issue, all staff engaged in the conduct of the election and candidates and agents must make a statutory declaration undertaking to preserve secrecy, and no one may disclose how or whether any person has or has not voted in any particular election. After the close of poll, the votes cast are counted, and the candidate who has obtained the highest number of votes[10] is declared elected by the returning officer.

(4) *The result.*—The result of a poll must be duly published, and before a newly elected councillor acts in that capacity he must make a statutory declaration of acceptance of office.[11]

A duly elected candidate, however, as well as being qualified to be a councillor,[12] must not be disqualified,[13] *i.e.*, he must not hold any paid office with that local authority,[14] he must not have been adjudged a bankrupt or made a composition or arrangement with his creditors, he must not within the previous five years have been surcharged by a district auditor to an amount exceeding £500, or have been disqualified, under Part VIII of the 1972 Act,[15] and also he must not be disqualified on the ground of his having committed a corrupt or illegal practice at elections;[16] a coroner is disqualified from being elected to the council of the area for which he serves.

B. Elections of the Chairman of a Principal Council.—The election of a chairman of a county or district council, or of the Greater London Council or a London Borough Council (whether or not he is entitled to be designated "Mayor" or "Lord Mayor"), must be the first business at the annual meeting of the council[17]; all members of the council, except an outgoing chairman who is (otherwise) no longer a member of the council,[18] are entitled to vote, and the voting is usually by show of hands, the decision being taken by a majority vote in the ordinary way. There is no need for a formal nomination, but speeches in support of a particular candidate are customary in most councils; at the annual meeting the decision is often unanimous, as the members, in order to preserve the dignity of the office, may have informally selected the person they are prepared to support at an earlier private meeting. Any member of the council may be elected as chairman. Before acting as such, a newly elected chairman must make a statutory declaration of

---

10 If an equal number of votes are cast for two or more candidates for the same vacancy the returning officer must determine the result by lot.

11 L.G.A., 1972, s. 83.

12 These are the same requirements as those qualifying a person to be elected; see *ante*, p. 375.

13 L.G.A., 1972, s. 80.

14 For an interesting interpretation of this provision, see *Boyd* v. *Easington R.D.C.*, [1963] 3 All E.R. 747; [1963] 1 W.L.R. 1281.

15 See Chapter XV, *post*, p. 427. The reference to a £500 surcharge can relate only to pre-1974 events.

16 Above, p. 375.

17 1972 Act, s. 4 (1); for Wales see s. 23 (1), and for London, Schedule 2, para. 3 (1).

18 *Ibid.*, s. 4 (2), s. 23 (2) and Schedule 2, para. 3 (2).

acceptance of office,[19] and it was formerly customary to require him to take the judicial oath and the oath of allegiance.[1]

If a retiring chairman (and any chairman holds office until his successor is entitled to act) wishes to stand as a candidate for a further term of office, it seems that he cannot remain in the chair, as no man may act as returning officer in his own election. On the other hand, the statute[2] provides that the chairman, if present, shall preside at any meeting of the council; in these circumstances, therefore, it seems desirable that an outgoing chairman seeking re-election should leave the council chamber during the election[3]; in a close election this will deprive the chairman of the opportunity of voting for himself, whereas any opponent will not be similarly disfranchised. If a salary attaches to the office,[4] this does *not* mean that a candidate for office has a pecuniary interest in the matter that has to be disclosed.[5]

C. Vice-Chairman.—A vice-chairman of a county, of the Greater London Council, a parish or a community council, is chosen by majority vote of the council at a council meeting. In the case of parishes and communities the appointment is optional; in other cases it is mandatory.[6] In the case of a London Borough the mayor may appoint a member of the council to be deputy mayor.[7]

D. Disputed elections.—The validity of any election may be questioned by means of an election petition presented to the Queen's Bench Division either by four or more voters or by a candidate. This is then referred to an election court consisting of a commissioner appointed by the Q.B.D.; an appeal lies from him to the Q.B.D. by case stated.[8] County courts also have limited jurisdiction in some matters; a judge may for example in certain circumstances order an inspection of the counted ballot papers.[9]

3. THE LAW RELATING TO COUNCILLORS

A number of the provisions of the Local Government Act, 1972 and related legislation are concerned with the rights, powers, privileges and duties of councillors, as such.

A member of a council can resign his office in one way only by writing signed by him and delivered to the proper officer[10] of the council of

---

[19] *Ibid.*, s. 83.

[1] This is now not necessary, as the chairman (or mayor) is no longer an *ex officio* justice of the peace: Justices of the Peace Act, 1968.

[2] L.G.A., Schedule 2, para. 5.

[3] *Re Wolverhampton Borough Council Aldermanic Election*, [1961] 3 All E.R. 446.

[4] Under s. 3 (5), s. 22 (5), Schedule 2, para. 2 (4) of the L.G.A., 1972.

[5] See now s. 94 (5) of the L.G.A., 1972, clarifying the law on this point.

[6] L.G.A., 1972, ss. 5 and 24. In the case of the Greater London Council, a vice-chairman *may* be appointed, and the council may also appoint a deputy chairman: 1972 Act, Schedule 2, para. 4.

[7] *Ibid.*, para. 5.

[8] Representation of the People Act, 1949, ss. 112–137.

[9] As in *McWhirter* v. *Platten*, [1969] 1 All E.R. 172; [1970] 1 Q.B. 508.

[10] This is an expression defined by s. 270 (3) of the 1972 Act as meaning an officer appointed by the authority for the particular purpose. It has been introduced by the 1972 Act because of the abolition of any obligation on a local authority under the statute to appoint an officer as "town clerk" or "clerk to the authority", or a "treasurer", etc.

which he is a member, or in the case of a parish or community councillor, to the chairman of the council, and in the case of a chairman of a parish or community council or parish meeting, to the council or meeting.[11] Once a notice of resignation has been so delivered and received it cannot be withdrawn, as it takes immediate effect.[12]

The Local Government Act, 1972, contains complicated provisions for the holding of elections to fill casual vacancies; in general a casual vacancy need not be filled if the term of office to which the vacancy relates has less than six months to run,[13] but this does not apply in the case of a vacancy in the office of a chairman.[14]

Members of local authorities are not entitled to any salaries or wages for their services to the public; they may, however, claim certain allowances to cover travelling expenses and subsistence whilst attending meetings of the local authority or its committees or on other "approved duties", and also an attendance allowance fixed by the authority in respect of the performance of an "approved duty". If a councillor is not entitled to an attendance allowance, he may claim a financial loss allowance if he has lost salary or wages or incurred some special expenditure (such as, for example, a self-employed shopkeeper who may have to hire a special assistant for periods when he is away) as a consequence of performing the approved duty. Allowances may also be paid to members in respect of their attendance at conferences and certain meetings outside the authority's area.[15] In addition, allowances may be paid to chairmen and vice-chairmen.[16]

Where a member of a local authority has a pecuniary (*i.e.*, financial) interest, whether direct or indirect, in any contract, proposed contract or other matter, and is present at a meeting of the authority where the contract or other matter is under consideration, he must as soon as practicable after the commencement of the meeting disclose the fact of his interest, and not take part in the consideration or discussion of, or vote on any question with respect to the contract or other matter.[17] Several points arise in connection with this important provision:

(a) What is an interest?—The interest in question must, however slight, be a financial one, but the interest of a councillor's spouse is his own interest if known to him, and the two parties to the marriage are living together, and must be disclosed.[18] Special provision is also made for company directors and partners having an interest in a company or partnership.[19] The interest need be indirect only for it to be brought

[11] L.G.A., 1972, s. 84.
[12] *R.* v. *Wigan Corpn.* (1885), 14 Q.B.D. 908. At one time a fine had to be paid: Municipal Corporations Act, 1882, s. 36.
[13] L.G.A., 1972, s. 89 (3).
[14] *Ibid.*, s. 88. If a member of a local authority does not attend any meeting for a period of six months, he ceases to be a member, unless his absence is excused by resolution of the council: *ibid.*, s. 85.
[15] See L.G.A., 1972, ss. 173, 174 and 175.
[16] *Ibid.*, s. 3 (5), 22 (5), 15 (5), 34 (5), Schedule 2, para. 2 (4) (chairmen), and ss. 5 (4), 24 (4), Schedule 2, para. 5 (4). In the Greater London Council an allowance may be paid both to the vice-chairman *and* the deputy chairman (Schedule 2, para. 4 (4)). There is no provision in the Act for the payment of an allowance to the vice-chairman (as such) of a parish or community council.
[17] L.G.A., 1972, s. 94.
[18] *Ibid.*, s. 95 (3)
[19] *Ibid.*, s. 95 (1).

within the section; a councillor has an indirect interest in a matter if he is a partner of a person, or a member of a company, who or which has a direct pecuniary interest, and "matter" is to be understood widely and is not limited to those "matters" which are *eiusdem generis* as "contracts or proposed contracts". Thus, in *Rands* v. *Oldroyd*[20] a councillor was a director of a firm of contractors which had resolved not to undertake any contracts with the council while the director remained a member thereof. When the councillor voted on a question coming before the council as to whether particular construction work should be put out to tender or be undertaken by the council's own labour force, he was held to have committed an offence under this provision, having voted on a matter in which his company had a direct financial interest, for the company's resolution could have been rescinded at any time. The way in which a councillor votes on a matter in which he has an interest is not material; he will offend against the section equally if he votes *against* his financial interest as if he votes to his own financial advantage.[21] However, a member is not to be treated as having an interest in a contract or other matter by reason only of an interest "which is so remote or insignificant that it cannot reasonably be regarded as likely to influence a member" in the consideration or discussion or voting on the matter in question.[22] This provision (introduced in 1964) certainly eased the situation of *Rands* v. *Oldroyd* somewhat, but it should be appreciated that the test of remoteness or insignificance is an objective one; it is not sufficient for a member to claim that *he* would not be influenced. The test which would be applied by the court is whether it is reasonable that *any* member should be influenced by the particular interest.

(b) Exemptions.—Section 94 does not apply, if the councillor might be said to have an interest in a matter simply as a ratepayer or inhabitant of the area, or only as a consumer of water or a passenger on a municipal transport undertaking.[1] Further, if he has shares in a company or society to an amount not exceeding £1000, or 1/100th of the total issued share capital of the company (whichever is the less) such an indirect interest is ignored for the purposes of the section.[2]

(c) Action to be taken.—When the section applies, the member must disclose his interest as soon as practicable, which apparently means, where the item appears on the agenda, at the commencement of the meeting, or in any other case as soon as the item in question is raised. The section applies to council and committee and joint committee meetings[3] and the details of any disclosure should be recorded in the minutes of the meeting, and also in a special book kept by the proper officer of the authority for the purposes of the section.[4] A member may

[20] [1958] 3 All E.R. 344; [1959] 1 Q.B. 204.

[21] *Brown* v. *D.P.P.*, [1956] 2 All E.R. 189; [1956] 2 Q.B. 369; the earlier cases on the subject are summarised in *Everett* v. *Griffiths*, [1924] 1 K. B. 941.

[22] L.G.A., 1972, s. 97 (5).

[1] L.G.A., 1972, s. 97 (4).

[2] *Ibid.*, s. 97 (6).

[3] L.G.A., 1972, s. 105.

[4] L.G.A., 1972, s. 96 (2); this book is required to be open to inspection by the members.

give a general notice of his interest in the affairs of a particular firm or company, etc.,[5] and this will then be a sufficient disclosure of such interest, but he will still of course have to refrain from speaking or voting on any particular matter in which that firm or company is or may be concerned. Standing orders of the particular local authority may supplement the provisions of the section by requiring any member having an interest to leave the room in which the meeting of the council (or committee) is held during the discussion and voting on the particular matter unless the council (or committee) by resolution invite him to remain in the room in any particular instance.[6]

(d) Dispensations.—The Secretary of State (or the district council, in the case of a parish or community council) may remove any disability —either from speaking or voting or both—imposed on any individual member under this section in any case where, (i) the number of members of the local authority so disabled at any one time would be so great a proportion of the whole as to impede the transaction of business, *or* (ii) it appears that it is in the interests of the inhabitants of the area that the disability should be removed.[7]

In practice in most cases an application for a dispensation under this subsection is made by the proper officer of the authority acting on the instructions of the council; but the Secretary of State will at times grant a dispensation where the application is made by or on behalf of the particular member or members concerned. The Secretary of State will readily grant a limited dispensation from the disability to speak, but a very special case has to be made out for him to grant a dispensation permitting an "interested" member or members to vote on the matter. The existence of an "interest" does not preclude a member from discussing or voting on the question whether or not application shall be made for such a dispensation.[8] Sometimes a general dispensation is given by Departmental Circular, as has been done in connection with certain housing matters in relation to councillors who are tenants of houses owned by the authority.

(e) Failure to comply with the section.—Any person who fails to comply with the provisions of the section will be liable on conviction in proceedings commenced by or on behalf of the Director of Public Prosecutions, to a fine not exceeding £200, unless he can prove that he did not know that the matter in which he had an interest was the subject of consideration at the meeting.[9] Perhaps it would also be a defence for him to establish that he did not know that he had the interest in question, and that it was not reasonable that he should have had that knowledge. It is the duty of any officer of the authority who is a solicitor, as an officer of the Court, to report to the Director of Public Prosecutions any case of a breach of the section that comes to his notice. It seems to be

---

[5] *Ibid.*, s. 96 (1).
[6] These Standing Orders are made under the authority of L.G.A., 1972, s. 94 (4).
[7] L.G.A., 1972, s. 97.
[8] *Ibid.*, s. 94 (3).
[9] *Ibid.*, s. 94 (2) and (3).

the general opinion that if a member votes on a matter in which he has an interest in defiance or disregard of the section, this will not invalidate the decision of the council, even if his vote can be shown to have been the deciding factor.[10]

(f) Interest of officers.—An officer having a direct or indirect pecuniary interest in a matter before the council also must give written notice to the council of the fact of his interest.[11] A member of a local authority may not while he is a member, or for 12 months after he ceases to be a member, hold any paid office under the authority (other than the office of chairman, or vice-chairman).[12]

(g) General observations.—Section 94 is a difficult section to operate in practice, and is liable to cause bad feeling between members and between a member and lawyers employed as officers by the authority. Members often ask for advice on the application of the section to the member's personal circumstances, but such advice should charily be given, as the officer is employed to advise the council, and not invididual members. If a general notice has been given by a member, the officer may remind him of that fact when a particular matter comes before the committee or council, but otherwise the initiative of disclosure should come from the member himself and not from an officer or the chairman.

It seems clear that this section, designed to prevent corruption in local government, does not totally exclude the principle of the common law that a governmental agency must be free from bias, and must not be "judge in its own cause". When the authority is acting quasi-judicially, it seems that its decision may be quashed by the courts if bias can be proved to have influenced the decision.[13]

4. OFFICERS

As a general rule a local authority may appoint such officers as they think necessary for the proper discharge of the functions of the council[14]; there is, however, a saving in the 1972 Act for certain statutory provisions which require that specific officers *must* be appointed. Thus, an education authority must appoint an education officer, and a weights

[10] This is almost certainly true where the decision of the local authority has no element of a judicial or quasi-judicial nature, although it may be logical to argue that a vote given by a person prohibited from voting is in law not a vote at all. A decision of a bench of magistrates will be quashed if it is shown that one of the deciding magistrates had an interest in the matter: *R.* v. *Barnsley Licensing Justices, ex parte Barnsley and District Licensed Victuallers' Association,* [1959] 2 All E.R. 635; [1959] 2 Q.B. 276, and this principle applies also to a local authority acting under a statute confirming a discretion which has to be exercised in a judicial manner: *R.* v. *Hendon R.D.C., ex parte Chorley,* [1933] 2 K.B. 696; see also *R.* v. *Weymouth Corpn., ex parte Teletax,* [1947] 1 All E.R. 779; [1947] K.B. 583, and *ante,* p. 124. If a member declares an interest and then insists on voting in breach of a section, it seems that in these circumstances the vote is a nullity, and this was virtually the position under the Municipal Corporations Act, 1882, s. 22 (see *Nell* v. *Longbottom,* [1894] 1 Q.B. 767).

[11] L.G.A., 1972, s. 117.

[12] *Ibid.,* s. 116.

[13] *R.* v. *Hendon R.D.C., ex parte Chorley* (note 10, *ante*), in which the effect of s. 22 of the Municipal Corporations Act, 1882 (which corresponded to s. 76) was ignored; and see *ante,* p. 122.

[14] L.G.A., 1972, s. 112; an authority may also employ officers so as to lend them to another local authority: see *ibid.,* s. 113.

and measures authority must appoint inspectors of weights and measures.[15] There is, however, now no statutory obligation on any local authority to appoint a clerk, a treasurer, a medical officer or a public health inspector, though there is no provision prohibiting the appointment of any of these officers. The 1972 Act, when referring to functions to be performed by officers, is in each case content to refer to the "proper officer"; *i.e.*, the particular officer appointed by his local authority to perform that specific function.[16] All these officers are the employees of the respective councils by whom they are appointed and there is no "national" local government service, as there is one civil service. On the other hand certain provisions apply assuring them reasonable terms and conditions of employment:

(a) A few officers can be appointed only with the consent of a Minister of the Crown.[1]

(b) The superannuation or pension rights of local government officers are now assured by a complicated statutory code[2] administered by local authorities under the supervision of the Secretary of State for the Environment, and provision is made for these rights to be preserved if a local government officer transfers his employment from one local authority to another or from a local authority to some other form of public employment, such as the civil service or a public corporation.

(c) There is no special law applicable to local government officers as there is to civil servants, their terms of employment depending on their particular service contracts.[3]

(d) In practice a code of service conditions and salary scales is laid down for local government officers generally throughout the country by a National and a number of Provincial Joint Councils, consisting of equal numbers of representatives of local authorities and of local government officers. These conditions of service and the decisions on disputes of the National Joint Council, have no legal effect but in practice they are honoured by both sides. There are similar codes applying to Chief Officers.

The relationship between officers—and more particularly chief officers—and the elected representatives who are the members of the local authority by whom they are employed, is not easy to define. Each officer is an employee of the local authority and not of any particular member or members of that authority, and he can be given instructions

---

[15] For the complete list, see L.G.A., 1972, s. 112 (4).

[16] *Ibid.*, s. 270 (3).

[1] Chief education officers; they also can be dismissed only with the consent of the Secretary of State for Education and Science (Education Act, 1944, s. 88). Police authorities may call upon chief constables, deputy chief constables and assistant chief constables to retire in the interests of efficiency, but they may do so only with the approval of the Home Secretary: Police Act, 1964, ss. 5 (4) and 6 (5). See also Chapter XV, *post*, p. 433.

[2] See the Local Government (Superannuation) Acts, 1937 and 1953 and the Superannuation Act, 1972.

[3] But their terms and conditions of service must be reasonable: L.G.A., 1972, s. 112 (2). The Industrial Relations Act, 1971, prohibiting "unfair dismissal", also applies.

only by the authority itself or by a committee of the authority acting on its behalf. The authority concerns itself with policy while the officers are concerned with the execution and implementation of policy decisions arrived at by the local authority. On the other hand, in the course of the process of policy making, the officer's advice, legal, technical, financial or general, as the case may be, will often be asked for and also often volunteered, especially in committee. Indeed, it is in committee that the "officer–member" relationship which often approximates more to a partnership than to that of master and servant, comes most into operation. In the informal atmosphere of a committee room where the press and public are not present, where the rules of debate are not applicable, and where officers can speak as freely—or almost as freely—as members, there is ample opportunity for an able officer to express his views on the matter before the committee and to advise them as to the course of action. Because of wide experience, from posts with other authorities, or from long service with the one authority, as well as his technical knowledge and skill, a chief officer will often take a prominent part in the process of formulating policy, although of course he will have no voice when the formal vote is finally taken. The person occupying the position of chief executive officer (sometimes described as the clerk) to the authority is in a specially strong position in this respect; he may be a solicitor, by tradition and according to his terms of service, he is the senior of the authority's chief officers (*primus inter pares*,[4] not commanding officer), the adviser of the chairman on all ceremonial matters, and he (or his representative) will attend *all* meetings of the council and of its committees. He is thus in a unique position to co-ordinate the advice to be given to the council, and although much will depend on personalities, with many authorities his reputation and influence is very high indeed.

In recent years as the result of several reports[5] on management in local government, many authorities no longer appoint as their senior officer a clerk or town clerk *eo nomine*. Their senior official is more commonly designated "chief executive officer", and his principal tasks will be to co-ordinate the work of the authority, to act as leader of the officers of the authority, and as principal adviser to the council on matters of general policy. As a chief officer, at a somewhat lower level, there will normally be an officer whose task it is to perform the functions of clerk (*i.e.*, as secretary) and possibly as legal adviser to the authority. In some councils the posts of chief executive and clerk are

---

[4] "First among equals." Above all, the chief executive officer is—or should be—responsible for a general oversight of the council's administration, while each of the other chief officers is the executive officer of his own department. Often he is also establishment officer, or at least the chief adviser on staff and establishment questions, and he may be responsible for any organisation and methods organisation operated by the particular local authority. Formerly the town clerk performed many of the functions of the modern chief executive officer, and indeed in many towns it is still true to say the C.E.O. is but the old town clerk with a new name.

[5] In particular, "Staffing of Local Government" (the "Mallaby" Report) H.M.S.O., 1967; "Management of Local Government" (the "Maud" Report), H.M.S.O., 1967, and the "New Local Authorities: management and structure" (the "Bains" Report), H.M.S.O., 1972.

held by the same person: yet other councils may not see the need to appoint a chief executive, but at the time of writing this is rapidly becoming rare. The old title of town clerk will probably be retained by those district councils that obtain borough status.

In an unreported case[6] in 1944 Lord CALDECOTT, C.J., said,

> "The office of Town Clerk is an important part of the machinery of local government. He may be said to stand between the Borough Council and the ratepayers. He is there to assist by his advice and action the conduct of public affairs in the Borough, and if there is a disposition on the part of any member of the Council to ride roughshod over his opinions, the question must at once arise as to whether it is not his duty forthwith to resign his office or at any rate, to do what he thinks right and await the consequences."

However, this case concerned questions of illegal and improper payments out of the rate fund, and it is clear that this view should not be read as justifying an officer in pursuing his own views on matters of policy contrary to the declared decisions of the Council. In the course of his Report on his Inquiry into the affairs of Bognor Regis in 1965,[7] Mr. Ramsay Willis, Q.C. (now Willis, J.) said (at p. 66),

> "In my view, he [the Clerk] is the employee of his Council and it is to them that his primary loyalty and duty lie and it is to them that he is answerable for his actions. In the course of advising his Council there is clearly no objection to a clerk telling them that he considers their proposals to be wrong and, if he thinks fit, submitting his views to them in writing. I consider, however, that he should express his opinion in a manner that will not embarrass his Council and that once his view is known to them he should leave them to come to their own decision. It is the duty of Councillors to formulate the policy for the local authority and they are directly answerable for their actions to the ratepayers at the polls."

Put in another way, the relationship between councillors and officers has been well described by Dr. Herman Finer in his *English Local Government*[8]:

> "The standard of living and social well-being of the world today is, as never before, crucially dependent upon the application of exact knowledge to its policy-making, its activities, its indescribably intricate and interlaced human inter-relationships, its organisation and its apparatus. This is contributed by the professional official. On the other hand, the councillors have the opportunity of permeating the expert with the will of the community; they let the official know both what the public will not stand and what it insists upon having. The expert himself has the occupational disease of the expert, the incapacity to see his own enthusiasm in due proportion to all the other enthusiasms and interests which constitute the total character of government and humanity. It is the committee's business to introduce and impose the sense of proportion after hearing what science has to say."

As we have said, this relationship has been changing recently. With the introduction of the concept of the chief executive officer, very much larger authorities with more functions, and also the extensive power given to any authority by section 101 of the Local Government Act,

---

[6] *Re Hurle-Hobbs, ex parte Riley* (the "Finsbury case"); see Hurle-Hobbs on *The Law Relating to District Audit*, and Headrick, *The Town Clerk in English Local Government* (1962), at p. 45.

[7] Unfortunate disputes had arisen between the members of the Bognor Regis U.D.C. and their clerk; Mr. Willis was appointed to hold the inquiry by the Minister of Housing and Local Government and the Council, acting jointly.

[8] Third Edition, at p. 231.

1972, to delegate any of their functions to an officer, the power and influence of chief officers and of the Chief Executive in particular, must be considerably enhanced. It is not likely that the delegation power will be widely used to enable officers to decide questions of major policy, but it should be used to empower officers to decide the more routine and detailed issues so that councillors will no longer consider it to be their function (as some had considered in the past) to supervise the detailed running of administrative departments.

The chief executive officer of a large city or county comes near to the position of a managing director of a large commercial company. He will have control of modern computer and statistical services, and an organisation and methods team, and will be responsible for work studies; it is contemplated in the "Bains" Report[9] that he will not necessarily be a lawyer, or a member of any particular (or any) profession. Most departments in the modern authorities are no longer arranged in accordance with a splintered committee structure (Parks, Housing, Highways, etc.), but on a broad functional basis (Finance, Technical Services, Social Services, etc.), each with a Director in charge and subordinate specialist and technical services.

All officers of a local authority must act under the Council's directions, but the authority will be liable in tort in accordance with the ordinary principles of vicarious liability for their acts within the course of their employment.[10] An officer, whether or not he has the express instructions or authority of the council, and even if he is acting contrary to the provisions of standing orders, may none the less incur a contractual liability on behalf of his council if he is acting within his ostensible authority, in accordance with the ordinary law of agency.[11] A treasurer or financial officer to an authority, however, is apparently in a special position; he is a servant of the local authority, but all payments to and out of the general rate fund will be paid to and by him, and he stands in a fiduciary relationship to the ratepayers as a body. He cannot plead the orders of the council as an excuse for an unlawful act, such as payment out of the general rate fund of moneys in circumstances not authorised by law.[12] Moreover, if a chief or other officer gives false or misleading advice to his local authority whereby rate fund moneys are lost or misapplied, the item of account may be disallowed by the district auditor.[13]

In a few cases an officer of a local authority has always had a right or duty to take action on his own initiative. This applies to an inspector appointed under the Diseases of Animals Act, 1950, when acting on behalf of the Ministry of Agriculture, Fisheries and Food (as he may be

---

[9] See footnote 5, *ante*, p. 383.

[10] See, for example, *Ormerod* v. *Rochdale Corpn.* (1898), 62 J.P. 153.

[11] "No private instructions prevent his [the agent's] acts within the scope of his ostensible authority from binding his principal." *National Bolivian Navigation Co.* v. *Wilson* (1880), 5 App. Cas. 176, *per* Lord BLACKBURN. The opportunities for this doctrine to be applied have arisen more frequently in local government as a consequence of the abolition of a need for a seal on contracts, under the Corporate Bodies' Contracts Act, 1960 (*ante*, p. 301). Superior orders would of course be no defence to an officer sued in tort.

[12] *A.-G.* v. *De Winton*, [1906] 2 Ch. 106.

[13] See Chapter XV, *post*, p. 428.

required to do[14]) and to a public health inspector under certain sanitary provisions of the Public Health Acts.[15] However, in other cases, an officer will have no authority to act on his own initiative; he must first obtain the instructions of his local authority unless delegated powers have been expressly vested in him by his local authority under s. 101 of the Local Government Act, 1972. Except where this has been done, any purported delegation would offend against the principle *delegatus non potest delegare*,[16] although in practice and on many occasions an officer will assume the authority of the council to act in a particular case, especially if it is one of emergency. In such cases, however, the officer will be responsible personally if the council refuses to confirm his action retrospectively.[17] Under the modern law, it seems that most local authorities will delegate routine decisions to their officers,[18] the only difficulty in practice, in cases involving litigation (where, for example, an officer has started criminal proceedings in his authority's name), will be to prove that the function in question was within the exact terms of the delegation.

An officer is a servant or employee of the council and not of a senior officer in his department, or even of a committee of the council. Therefore an officer employed in the fire department or the public health department, for example, is bound by the instructions of the fire or public health committee only in so far as the particular committee is acting with the authority of the council delegated to them for the purpose. *A fortiori*, an officer is not entitled to act on the instructions of an individual member of a committee or even of the chairman, and he cannot properly be criticised if he refuses to accept instructions from such an individual. On the other hand between committee meetings consultation between an officer and the chairman of the appropriate committee should be regular and normal, and often a chief officer will obtain "his" chairman's approval to some course of action that he is obliged to take in advance of obtaining formal committee approval. Responsibility to the council (normally through the appropriate committee) for the operation of a department is that of the chief officer, not the chairman of the committee, and the latter has no right to interfere with the chief officer's work or to give orders to subordinates or inspect premises in the absence or without the knowledge of the departmental chief officer.[19]

---

14 See ss. 73 and 59 (5) of the Act of 1950, and *Stanbury* v. *Exeter Corpn.*, [1905] 2 K.B. 838, where it was held that in these circumstances the local authority were not liable in respect of action taken by an inspector employed by them acting under the statute.

15 See in particular several sections of the Public Health Act, 1961. Similar powers are vested in a medical officer of health in respect of infected milk under the Milk and Dairies Regulations. 1959.

16 *Allingham* v. *Minister of Agriculture and Fisheries*, [1948] 1 All E.R. 780, and *ante*, p. 141.

17 If the authority eventually ratify the act of one of their officers this will normally be effective: *Firth* v. *Staines*, [1897] 2 Q.B. 70; *Warwick R.D.C.* v. *Miller-Mead*, [1962] 1 All E.R. 212; [1962] Ch. 441.

18 Especially in planning matters; the power to delegate given by s. 101 was here anticipated by s. 64 of the Town and Country Planning Act, 1968.

19 These matters are usually provided for in the local authority's standing orders.

Assignment of particular duties to the several officers of a local authority is very largely a matter for the particular employing authority's own discretion. A "proper officer" must be appointed to act as returning officer in elections,[20] and as registrar of local land charges,[1] and a "proper officer" must also be appointed to have custody of documents and records,[2] and to maintain the freemen's rolls.[3] Proper arrangements for receipt of moneys paid to the local authority and the issue of moneys payable by them must be carried out,[4] but there is no express reference in the Local Government Act, 1972, to any person being required to act as "treasurer". In practice such an officer will be necessary, the same being true of public health inspectors. Most of the functions of the former medical officers of health will be carried out by the "community physicians" appointed under the National Health Service. Generally, the statute has been content to leave a wide discretion with local authorities, subject only to the terms of the several service agreements that have been negotiated by the officers' associations with the representatives of local authorities.

To quote Dr. Finer again:

> "The modern administrative official contributes three things at least which no other agency of government can give: they are expertness, permanency, and the guarantee of impartial advice and execution".[5]

5. CENTRAL AND LOCAL GOVERNMENT COMPARED

In spite of some similarities, in that both exercise a range of governmental functions over a specified area, there are really more differences than similarities between a local authority and Parliament. A local council cannot be dissolved before the expiration of its legal term of office; the chairman of the council does not have to enjoy or maintain the confidence of the council as does the Prime Minister in the House of Commons, and it is not necessary that the chairmen of committees should all share the same political views, as do Her Majesty's Ministers at any one time. Whereas a council may be organised internally in party political groups, this has no legal significance, and there is no question of the "Cabinet", the leaders of the political party "in power" having to resign if they fail to secure a majority on a particular vote, although it may be customary for a chairman who has lost the confidence of his committee to resign from that office (but not to resign his seat on the council). Further, the chairman of a committee is not in the same position as a Cabinet Minister, as he is not the executive head of a Department nor is he responsible to the council for the conduct of any Department; such matters are the concern of the chief officer. Similarly, a local government officer is not in the same position as a civil servant. As will appear from comments elsewhere in this book[6]

---

[20] L.G.A., 1972, s. 41.
[1] *Ibid.*, s. 212.
[2] *Ibid.*, s. 225.
[3] *Ibid.*, s. 248.
[4] *Ibid.*, s. 148.
[5] *English Local Government*, 3rd Edn., at p. 273.
[6] Chapter II, *ante*, p. 36.

on the legal status of a civil servant, that status is peculiar to him, but a local government officer is legally, *vis à vis* his employers (and the outside world), in a position similar to that of the employee of any private employer; in particular the provisions of the Industrial Relations Act, 1971, about (*inter alia*) "unfair dismissal", apply to him. However, his conditions of service are guarded as are those of a civil servant by Whitley Council machinery, and his superannuation rights are provided for by statute. He is not required to take orders from any single elected representative, but his identity will be generally known and he will rarely be anonymous as is often the case with a civil servant, except those in the very highest grades. A local government officer will admit to some individuality in his dealings with the public; he will act on the council's instructions, but will at times express a personal view, or admit that he may be prepared to recommend "his" council to take a certain course of action. The civil servant, on the other hand, will hide behind the person of his Minister, and will aver in correspondence that he is "directed" by the Minister to take the action specified, even where the decision has in fact been taken by himself.

The relationship between an officer of a local authority and the elected representatives will be much closer in local government than the corresponding relationship can ever be in the central government. Members and officers meet at committee and council meetings several times a month, and senior officers are responsible (normally through the Chief Executive Officer) to the council as a whole for the conduct of their departments, whilst at the centre the Minister stands between the civil servants and the ordinary Members of Parliament. Further, officers from different departments in local government meet one another frequently, whilst the civil service is more impersonal, and its departments are often insulated from one another. Local government officers consider it their duty to advise all members of their local authority on the same basis, regardless of any question as to whether they belong to the political party that may happen at the time to have majority support on the Council. A civil servant on the other hand considers himself as the adviser of the government of the day, and he is not available to members of the opposition. However, in both local and central government, there is the same strong tradition that the professional officer must be loyal to the elected representatives whatever may be their political views.

So far as the functions of government are concerned, local authorities are involved almost exclusively in administration, as they are primarily a branch of the executive, whilst preserving their independence and within closely defined statutory limits they are empowered to make policy decisions. From a legal standpoint, their "judicial" decisions are few, but in arriving at conclusions on matters of policy, they are subject to correction or review by the courts if they exceed their powers or (perhaps) if they are guilty of bad faith in exercising those powers.[7] Their legislative functions again are few, being confined to such powers as may have been given them by statute to make byelaws for specific purposes.[8]

[7] Chapter VI, *ante*, p. 47.
[8] Chapter IV, *ante*, p. 80.

On the other hand, as organs of government, local authorities are much nearer in the range and nature of their functions, and also in the degree of freedom which they enjoy from outside control, to the agencies of the central government, than they are to the statutory corporations.[9]

6. THE PREVENTION OF CORRUPTION

Fortunately for the healthy administration of this country, Ministers of the Crown, civil servants, local government officers, members of local authorities and other public officers are remarkably free from the taint of corruption.[10] That this is true is largely due to the general atmosphere of public opinion; an official of intelligence could, given sufficient determination, circumvent the provisions of most laws designed against corruption. Nevertheless, there are provisions of the criminal law dealing with the subject; they are not exclusively concerned with local government officers or even only with local government, but for convenience we consider them in this context.

The leading statute is the Public Bodies Corrupt Practices Act, 1889. This contains two substantive provisions creating offences:

(a) *The soliciting of bribes by an officer* (*section 1* (*1*)):

> "Every person who shall by himself or by or in conjunction with any other person, corruptly solicit or receive, or agree to receive, for himself, or for any other person, any gift, loan, fee, reward, or advantage whatever, as an inducement to, or reward for, or otherwise on account of any member, officer, or servant of a public body as in this Act defined, doing or forbearing to do anything in respect of any matter or transaction whatsoever, actual or proposed, in which the said public body is concerned, shall be guilty of a misdemeanour."

(b) *The offering of bribes* (*section 1* (*2*))

> "Every person who shall by himself or by or in conjunction with any other person corruptly give, promise, or offer any gift, loan, fee, reward, or advantage whatsoever to any person, whether for the benefit of that person or of another person, as an inducement to or reward for or otherwise on account of any member, officer, or servant of any public body as in this Act defined, doing or forbearing to do anything in respect of any matter or transaction whatsoever, actual or proposed, in which such public body as aforesaid is concerned, shall be guilty of a misdemeanour."

Two points need to be explained in connection with the two offences thus somewhat verbosely created:

(a) "*Corruptly.*"—If money or consideration is given or offered to an officer or member of a public body by or from some person holding or seeking to obtain a contract from the public body concerned, the money, etc., is to be deemed to have been given and received corruptly unless the contrary is proved; the onus in such circumstances is on the defence to rebut this presumption. If the offeror of a bribe intends the public servant or officer to enter into a corrupt bargain, he will be guilty of an offence under the Act, even if he (the offeror) had no intention of carrying out the transaction.[11]

---

[9] Chapter X, *ante*, p. 317.

[10] For a somewhat contrary view, see *Local Government Corruption and Public Confidence*, by Regan and Morris, at [1969] P.L. 132. As to local "Ombudsmen", see Chapter V, *ante*, p. 104.

[11] *R.* v. *Smith*, [1960] 1 All E.R. 256; [1960] 2 Q.B. 423.

(b) *Persons to whom the section applies.*—It will be noted from the terms of the section that it applies to both members and officers of any "public body"; this expression was defined in some detail by section 7 of the 1889 Act by reference to various types of local authorities, but the definition was widened by section 4 of the Prevention of Corruption Act, 1916, to include as well as the local authorities of the 1889 Act, "local and public authorities of all descriptions". Ministers of the Crown, civil servants and others acting on behalf of Her Majesty are therefore not brought within this Act, although the members or servants of joint boards and joint committees are within its provisions. In *R.* v. *Newbould*,[12] it was held that the expression "local and public authorities" must be construed within the limits indicated by an application of the *eiusdem generis* rule, and that therefore the National Coal Board was not a "public body" for the purposes of this statute. Neither would the airways corporations[13] nor the health service authorities[14] be public bodies, but in section 1 (1) of the Transport Act, 1947, it was expressly declared that the British Transport Commission was to be a "public body". Similarly, the four Boards which replaced the Commission under the Transport Act, 1962, are described in the statute as "public authorities" (see section 1 (1)), which presumably attracts the protection of the 1916 Act. Crown servants (in the widest sense) are subject to the very similar provisions of the Prevention of Corruption Act, 1906, which prohibits the acceptance by or offering to any kind of agent (including a commercial agent acting for a private individual and including any person acting for another[15]) of a bribe with an intention to corrupt; the special meaning of "corrupt" contained in the 1916 Act applies as it does to the provisions of the 1889 Act. No proceedings may be taken under the 1906 Act without the consent of the Attorney or Solicitor General.[16]

There is also a common law misdemeanour of "misbehaviour in a public office", which apparently would include behaviour which amounts to oppression, extortion, corruption or bribery, partiality, and acting fraudulently.[17]

These provisions, with the rules about "interest" in local government[18] and those in relation to judges,[19] are, with the exception of the law of conspiracy the total of English law on corruption, although there are also elaborate and detailed provisions prohibiting corrupt and illegal practices at elections.

---

12 [1962] 1 All E.R. 693.

13 Under the Civil Aviation Act, 1949; Chapter X, *ante*, p. 302.

14 Under the National Health Service Reorganisation Act, 1973, Chapter X, *ante*, p. 338.

15 In Scotland it has been held that this section applies to a police constable acting in the execution of his duty. Although the constable is not employed by the chief constable he acts on his behalf and so is an agent within the meaning of the 1906 Act: *Graham* v. *Hart*, 1908 S.C.(J.) 26.

16 1906 Act, s. 2.

17 For a recent example of a prosecution, see *R.* v. *Llewellyn-Jones*, [1967] 3 All E.R. 225; [1968] 1 Q.B. 429.

18 *Ante*, p. 378.

19 Here reliance is placed on the common law and the rules of "natural justice"; as to magistrates, see, for example, *R.* v. *Lancashire Justices* (1906), 75 L.J.K.B. 198.

CHAPTER XIII

THE ORGANISATION OF LOCAL AUTHORITIES

1. COUNCIL MEETINGS

In the eyes of the public, the meeting of the council, held[1] in many cases monthly or even more often, is the occasion when the local authority come to their conclusions and make their decisions. Except in so far as functions may have been delegated to committees,[2] this is, of course, true also in law, for decisions can be taken only by or with the authority of the council on a majority vote at a properly convened meeting at which at least a quorum of the members is present.[3] Nevertheless in practice the real process of arriving at a decision, based on reports and advice of officers, is done in committee, where discussion can be free, unaffected by any considerations of not divulging financial or other "secrets" to the public, and also where, being removed from the public gaze, party political opinions tend to be less forcefully expressed or persisted in. The normal procedure at council meetings therefore consists in reception of reports of proceedings at the several committees of the council and the taking of decisions thereon by the council either by way of accepting or rejecting (or amending) the various committees' recommendations.

Under the Public Bodies (Admission to Meetings) Act, 1960, it is provided that any meeting of a local authority or other public body to which the Act applies (as listed in the Schedule to the Act, which includes all local authorities, parish meetings, education committees, regional hospital boards, etc.)[4] shall be open to the public. When a meeting is so open, at least three clear days' public notice of the meeting must be given[5]; any newspaper is entitled on request to a copy of the agenda and any reports to be received at the meetings, and members of the public and representatives of newspapers cannot normally be excluded.[6] However, the authority may at any meeting by resolution exclude the public (and the press),

---

[1] There must be one meeting every year, but the council may themselves decide how many other meetings are necessary: L.G.A., 1972, Schedule 12, para. 1 (1), 2, 7, 23, and 24. A parish council must hold at least three further meetings each year: *ibid.*, para. 8.

[2] *Post*, p. 393.

[3] L.G.A., 1972, Schedule 12, para. 39.

[4] Or of a committee which the local authority is required to appoint: L.G.A., 1972, s. 100.

[5] This does not override the provisions of Schedule 12 of the L.G.A., 1972, which is to the like effect. The 1960 Act is wider in its operation than that of 1972, as it applies to bodies other than local authorities.

[6] Subject to the right to exclude individuals for disorderly conduct or misbehaviour: s. 1 (8) of the Act of 1960.

"whenever publicity would be prejudicial to the public interest by reason of the confidential nature of the business to be transacted or for other special reasons stated in the resolution and arising from the nature of that business or of the proceedings" (*ibid.*, s. 1 (2)).

The need to receive reports from officers, etc., may be treated as a "special reason" within this provision (s. 1 (3)).

The Act applies to any case where a council resolves itself into committee,[7] as it does to the council itself and it also applies to any committee of the authority whose members consist of or include all members of the body.[8] It does not, however, apply to a committee of a local authority acting under delegated powers,[9] although it had been suggested in the course of discussions when the Bill was going through Parliament that it should so apply. There is no reason, of course, why a local authority (or any other public body for that matter) should not decide to admit the press to meetings of committees either generally, or to those acting under powers delegated by the Council.

The publication of any defamatory matter contained in an agenda or other accompanying papers by issue to the public at a meeting or to a newspaper before the meeting, is to be treated as a privileged occasion for the purpose of the law of libel, and hence will not be actionable unless it is proved that the publication was made with malice.[10]

The Act of 1960 was passed as a result of considerable agitation; previously the law governing admission of the public to council meetings was contained in the Local Authorities (Admission of the Press to Meetings) Act, 1908, which was thought unsatisfactory, partly because it guaranteed no rights to representatives of the Press as such: this Act has been repealed by the Act of 1960, which does not really, however, go very much further than the 1908 Act because the Press can still be excluded by resolution, as above explained, and the old evil of the Council which decides everything in committees consisting of a majority of their members, remains.

By the Local Government Act, 1972, a council meeting must be duly convened by a summons given or sent at least three clear days before the meeting to each member of the council; this summons must specify all the business proposed to be transacted at the meeting[11] and the agenda may not include the item "any other business".[12] A notice to the like effect must be published at the offices of the council. The statute also makes provision for the summoning of special meetings of the council by its chairman or on the requisition of a limited number of members of the council.[13]

The procedure at council meetings will be comparatively formal—especially with the large post-1974 authorities. Standing orders will

---

[7] S. 1 (6).
[8] S. 2 (1).
[9] *Post*, p. 393; and see footnote 4, *ante*, p. 391.
[10] S. 1 (5); thereby modifying to that extent the decision in *De Buse* v. *McCarty and Stepney B.C.*, [1942] 1 All E.R. 19; [1942] 1 K.B. 156.
[11] L.G.A., 1933, Schedule 12.
[12] It is specifially provided in the Schedule that no business other than that specified in the summons to the meeting may be transacted at any council meeting except as a matter of urgency.
[13] L.G.A., 1972, Schedule 12.

normally regulate such matters as the length of speeches, prohibit the moving of motions without notice, and prevent a member from speaking more than once in the same debate. Officers will not speak at council meetings, unless their advice is specifically requested by the chairman, and any such requests for advice will usually be addressed to the C.E.O., who may himself obtain the information required from a technical officer.

The statutes are singularly silent about procedure at council meetings. It is provided that questions coming before a local authority are to be decided by a majority of those members present and voting, that a record is to be made of the members present, and that minutes must be kept.[14] In other respects the statute is content to leave the regulation of meetings to the council's own standing orders. A chairman of any meeting held on private premises (*i.e.*, premises not open to the public) has a right to order the expulsion of a member of the public who is causing a disturbance, the smallest possible degree of force being used,[15] and this right has been preserved by the Public Bodies (Admission to Meetings) Act, 1960.[16] As a general rule, however, a member of a local authority can be expelled from a meeting which he is entitled to attend, only in accordance with standing orders, which must themselves be *intra vires*.[17]

2. THE COMMITTEE SYSTEM

As mentioned above, every local authority comes to its decisions in committee meetings rather than in council; indeed most local authorities adopt a standing order to the effect that no matter shall be decided by the council until it has been considered and reported upon by the appropriate committee. Any local authority may appoint a committee to advise them on any matter relating to the discharge of their functions,[18] or the local authority may arrange for the discharge of any of their functions (other than the levying or issuing a precept for, a rate or borrowing money[19]) by a committee or a sub-committee,[20] and the number of members of a committee and their term of office must be fixed by the council. Persons who are not members of the local authority may be co-opted by the authority to serve on any committee, other than a finance committee, provided that at least two-thirds of the members of every committee are members of the local authority.[1] This principle of co-option is used in many cases where the advice of outside members is considered helpful,[2] such as schoolmasters or clergymen on the library committee, ladies experienced in voluntary work on the social services committee, etc. Any person who is not disqualified from being

---

14 L.G.A., 1972, Schedule 12, Part VI.
15 See *e.g.*, *Marshall* v. *Tinnelly* (1937), 81 Sol. Jo. 903.
16 1960 Act, s. 1 (8).
17 *Vaughan* v. *Hampson* (1875), 33 L.T. 15.
18 L.G.A., 1972, s. 102 (1) and (4).
19 *Ibid.*, s. 101 (6).
20 *Ibid.*, s. 101 (1). They may also delegate to another local authority (*ante*, p. 370) or to an officer (*ante*, p. 385).
1 *Ibid.*, s. 102 (3).
2 It is also used to provide interlocking membership between local authorities; thus a county council health committee may appoint an area sub-committee consisting in part of members of district councils in the area.

a member of the local authority may be co-opted to a committee[3]; a co-opted member need not therefore be qualified to be a member, and may be (for example) of less than full age.[4]

There are several different ways of classifying committees, none of which has any important legal significance, but the several classes provide an effective means of describing the operation of the committee system as it works in modern English local government:

(a) *Standing and special committees.*—Standing committees are those which are constituted for the whole of a council's year and entrusted with a range of functions, the extent of the range varying according to the nature of the authority and the volume of business involved. Such are the housing, public health and fire brigade committees. Special committees, sometimes described as "*ad hoc* committees", are those which are constituted on a special occasion or for a special purpose, and which are entrusted with one particular matter or matters to investigate and report; when a special committee has reported it becomes *functus officii*. Such would be a committee appointed by a council to investigate a particular proposal, such as a major development scheme, or an alleged case of maladministration in one of the departments of the council; the majority of a local authority's committees are of the "standing" type.

(b) *Functional and service committees.*—Every local authority recognises this division between kinds of committees in practice, though it is not always clearly defined. By a functional, or a departmental committee, is meant one which is seised with the general supervision of a defined range of a council's functions, such as the housing or the parks committee; there will normally be a department under a chief officer primarily responsible for the administration of the same range of functions. By a service committee is meant a committee concerned with a certain aspect or aspects of the council's work as it affects all the functions of the council and all its departments. Such are the finance committee, the establishment committee (concerned with all staff matters[5]) and the law and parliamentary committee. In most local authorities the service committees are regarded as the most important; the senior members of the council are usually members and standing orders will normally provide (for example) that a functional (or "spending") committee may not incur or recommend expenditure on behalf of the council unless the proposal has first been sanctioned by the finance committee either generally in the annual estimates or specially on a particular occasion. Similarly, it is usual for standing orders to provide that even specialist committees, such as the transport committee or the entertainments committee, may not recommend the alteration of the gradings of officers or the establishment of a department without the consent of the establishment committee. These service committees also help to coordinate the work of the council as a whole by ensuring that the finances

---

[3] L.G.A., 1972, s. 104.
[4] See, *ibid.*, s. 79.
[5] This refers to officers only; it is customary in local government to distinguish between "officers", and "servants" or "workmen".

are kept properly balanced as between committees and the salary grading of comparable officers kept uniform in the several departments.

(c) *Statutory committees.*—In a few cases a local authority may be required by law to appoint a committee for particular purpose. These are now listed in s. 101 (9) of the Local Government Act, 1972, and include the social services committees required under the Local Authority Social Services Act, 1970. In these cases the statute also normally provides that the authority may act only on the recommendation or report of the committee, although this does not mean that the council are obliged to accept any such recommendation.

(d) *Joint committees.*—These have already been discussed.[6]

(e) *Executive and advisory committees.*—This classification of committees runs across the other classifications discussed above. Any committee may be entrusted by the council with the power of making decisions on behalf of the council; the only functions that may not be so delegated to a committee are those of "levying, or issuing a precept for, a rate, or borrowing money".[7] If there is no such delegation the committee will be advisory only and none of its recommendations will have any legal effect unless and until they have been accepted (either in their original form, or modified) by the council at a council meeting. A committee may of course be partly executive and partly advisory; it will then normally submit a report to the council meeting in two parts, distinguishing between its delegated and its advisory functions. Executive committees are now very common; indeed without the device of delegation, reasonable expedition in the despatch of business would be virtually impossible. Where a committee is acting within delegated powers, any decision so taken cannot be varied or cancelled by the council; members can only express their disapproval of any such decision. An executive committee that no longer had the confidence of the council could be dissolved by the council, but the council would still be bound by the decisions taken by that committee before its dissolution.[8] Nevertheless although decisions of a committee acting under delegated powers bind the council, minutes of such a committee are not minutes "of the council".[9]

Procedure in committee meetings will normally be much less formal than that at meetings of the council. Standing orders as to the moving of motions, length of speeches, etc., will not usually apply, and the advice of officers will (or should) be freely and frequently requested and proffered. A committee is the creature of the council and it is entirely subject to the council for such powers as it may possess, and if the council has laid down any procedural rules these must be observed.

---

[6] Chapter XI, *ante*, p. 367.

[7] L.G.A., 1972, s. 101 (6). This power is wide enough to overcome the principle *delegatus non potest delegare*: see Chapter VI, *ante*, p. 141. Powers delegated to a local authority can it seems themselves be delegated to a committee by the delegate authority (*ante*, p. 371). If a committee of a local authority acting under delegated powers from the Council wishes to delegate some power to a sub-committee of their number, authority so to sub-delegate would have to be obtained from the Council, but the council may delegate direct to a sub-committee.

[8] *Battelley* v. *Finsbury Corpn.* (1958), 56 L.G.R. 165.

[9] *Wilson* v. *Evans*, [1962] 1 All E.R. 247, and Chapter XV, *post*, p. 437.

Most councils permit their standing committees to choose their own chairmen, but some require committees to submit the person selected as chairman to the whole council for confirmation. There is no law regulating the size of a committee, but a committee consisting of a majority of the members of the council is generally thought to be undesirable, in that it may be tempted to "steam roller" its proposals through the council.[10]

The question is sometimes raised whether a committee can consist of one member of the Council only; this becomes important if it is desired to delegate a power to decide a particular matter or matters to an individual member (for example during the summer recess), as there is power under s. 101 (1) of the Local Government Act, 1972 only to delegate to a "committee, a sub-committee or an officer". In the company law case of *Re Scottish Petroleum Co.*,[11] a company had power by its articles to delegate to "committees consisting of members of their body", and it was expressly provided that the plural number included the singular; it was held that delegation to a single member was valid. In the Local Government Act, 1972, the plural also includes the singular, unless the contrary intention appears,[12] but s. 101 (1) makes no reference to a committee "of members", as in the case referred to, and it is submitted that there is sufficient evidence of a contrary intention[13] to prevent the word "committee" from being interpreted in any sense other than the ordinary one of meaning a body of persons of at least two in number.

So far we have described the ordinary or "traditional" structure of committees within a local authority. In 1967, the Maud Committee on Management of Local Government recommended that local authorities

> "should adopt the guiding principle that issues are dealt with at the lowest level consistent with the nature of the problem," although
> "the ultimate direction and control of the affairs of the authority [should] be with the members."[14]

The Bains Report,[15] a few years later, said:

> "[Officers] must be allowed to advise on policy formulation and take decisions within a policy framework laid down by the members either in Council or in committee. They are skilled men, trained specifically for the work of a local authority and should be given responsibility and authority accordingly."

Therefore, there should be considerable delegation to committees and to officers, a recommendation made possible by the 1972 Act.[16]

The Maud Report had made drastic suggestions for the alteration of the committee structure, including the establishment of a small management board for each local authority.[17] This did not, however,

---

[10] A meeting of a committee consisting of all the members of the council must be open to the public: above, p. 391.

[11] (1882), 51 L.J. Ch. 841.

[12] Interpretation Act, 1889, s. 1 (1) (b).

[13] See, for instance, s. 103 (5), which opens with the words "Every [not *each*] member of a committee appointed under this section . . ."

[14] Report, para. 152.

[15] "The new local authorities—management and structure" (1972), para. 3, 37.

[16] Section 101 thereof in particular.

[17] Maud Report, para. 158.

prove popular, and Bains was content to recommend that each local authority should establish a Policy and Resources Committee, to provide co-ordinated advice to the council in the setting of its plans, objectives and priorities.[18]

3. STANDING ORDERS

Minutes of the proceedings of every meeting of a local authority and of every committee thereof must be drawn up and entered in a book kept for the purpose, and the minutes must be signed by the person presiding at the next ensuing meeting of the authority or committee; any minute purporting to be so signed is receivable in evidence in legal proceedings without further proof.[19] Apart from this and similar requirements[1] of statute, any local authority may make such standing orders as it chooses for the regulation of its proceedings and business,[2] and it *must* make orders with respect to contracts made by the authority or its committees.[3] Standing orders do not have the effect of law; they merely regulate the order of proceedings as between the several members of the authority, and there can be no criminal sanction for the non-observance of a standing order.[4] Consequently, although the former Minister of Housing and Local Government prepared a set of Model Standing Orders,[5] there is no provision for a Minister to consent to or approve standing orders, as is the case with byelaws. Standing orders, or financial regulations, which are of the same legal status, will in most cases provide for matters such as the following:

(a) Procedure at council meetings (except in so far as this is regulated by statute, for standing orders can, naturally, never override or modify a statutory provision);

(b) The respective powers and duties and the constitution of the several committees of the local authority;

(c) Procedure for the declaration of the interest of members in matters brought before the council or a committee[6];

(d) Methods of appointment and procedure for variation of conditions of service of officers employed by the council[7];

---

[18] Bains Report, para. 4, 14.

[19] The book may now be in looseleaf form: L.G.A., 1972, Schedule 12, para. 41.

[1] Such as the provision that matters coming before a local authority shall be decided by a majority of the members present and voting at a meeting; *ibid.*, para. 39.

[2] *Ibid.*, para. 42.

[3] *Ibid.*, s. 135.

[4] Moreover, standing orders must be *intra vires*. Thus, if a standing order required members to wear gowns at council meetings, it seems that an individual member could not be excluded from a meeting (even by resolution of a majority of the council), simply because he refused to wear a gown. Persistent disorder by a councillor is in a different category, for although he may be in breach of standing orders, the chairman of a meeting is at common law given a duty to preserve order, even to the extent of excluding a member if necessary.

[5] Editions of the Models relating to proceedings and business, and to contracts, were issued in 1963 and were adopted by most local authorities.

[6] Chapter XII, *ante*, p. 378, and L.G.A., 1972, ss. 94–98.

[7] The standard conditions of service for officers, negotiated on a national basis, stipulate that such matters may not be discussed in public.

(e) Assignment of duties as between the several departments and chief officers of the council;

(f) Procedure for selection of the chairman of the council preparatory to his election at the annual meeting[8];

(g) Procedure for receipt and payment of moneys, safe custody of cash, certification of accounts and the financial responsibilities of the several chief officers, etc.[9]

(h) The sealing of documents;

(i) Orders of precedence as between the several civic dignitaries on ceremonial occasions such as Royal visits, church parades, etc.;

(j) Advertisements for the entering into, and procedure regulating the execution of contracts, either generally or only those in excess of a specified amount. If these "contracts" standing orders are not complied with, the consequences to the local authority will be internal only, and a failure to comply with a provision of standing orders could not affect the validity of the contract as between the local authority and the other party to the contract.

4. DEPARTMENTAL ORGANISATION

There is no standard organisation for the several departments of local authorities in this country, as there is no standard system for the arrangement of committees. Each local authority can make its own arrangements, this being the natural consequence of the comparative independence of authorities from central control and of the related feature that each local authority employs its own staff, there being no national local government service.[10] In practice, however, local authorities of similar size and status tend to adopt the same or a similar departmental organisation. Thus, each county district council will have a clerk's (or secretary's) department, a chief technical officer's (or surveyor's) department, a treasurer's or finance department and a public health (or chief environmental health officer's) department; other service departments, according to the size and functions of the authority, may include an architect's department and a central purchasing department. "Functional" departments in a large authority may include the education department, the library and museum department, the housing, fire service, transport and parks departments. Except in the very largest local authorities, it is usual for the functional departments to look to the service departments for appropriate technical assistance. Thus, the clerk's department will be responsible for giving legal advice, preparing contracts and other documents, conveyancing and the conduct of legal proceedings, for all the council's departments; the central purchasing department will buy stationery

---

[8] Such orders are not binding, as the election can only take place at a public council meeting, but a selection procedure is followed by many councils so that the election in the public meeting may at least appear to be unanimous.

[9] See ss. 147, 148 of the L.G.A., 1972.

[10] Chapter XII, *ante*, p. 382.

and many other goods in bulk for all departments, and the finance department will be responsible for receiving money, authorising payments, paying staff wages, preparing draft estimates and auditing accounts relating to the whole of the council's business. Each department will normally be under a chief officer, but in some cases a council may designate what would normally be an independent department under another council as a sub-department under the general supervision of a chief officer; thus, in a small town the housing department in charge of a "Director of Housing", a "Housing Manager" or a "Housing Officer" may be a sub-department of the clerk's or the treasurer's, or even the surveyor's department.

The departmental structure need not necessarily follow exactly or even nearly that of the committee structure of the local authority concerned. Thus, a council not large enough to have an independent housing department or parks department, may none the less have a separate housing committee and a parks committee. A county borough may well have a separate public health committee charged with the supervision of the council's functions relating to sanitation and hygiene, and also a social services committee, although all these matters may in their executive aspect be the concern of the health department.

One of the major organisational dangers in any large local authority is disintegration or fragmentation of departments, or even of committees. Too many departments and committees may be set up or constituted and inadequate arrangements made for co-ordination, at chief officer and committee level. In the case of committees, co-ordination should be effected by the policy and resources committee or, failing this, by service committees such as the finance committee and the establishment committee. At officer level, the head of each department will normally be a technical expert, not an administrator (as in the Civil Service); consequently the task of co-ordination (made all the more necessary in view of the "casual, intermittent, part-time nature of the local councillorship" as Dr. Finer points out[11]), falls to the lot of the chief executive officer.[12]

In recent years a practice has been growing up (encouraged by the Bains Report) of grouping departments under a senior Chief Officer. Thus, there may be a Director of Works, responsible for the highways, sewerage, parks, building, architects, planning and possibly other departments; the Director of Cultural Services might be responsible for education, libraries, museums, youth training, entertainments, publicity and tourism, etc. By establishing a small number of "super" Chief Officers, greater departmental co-ordination can thus be achieved. Such an administrative arrangement could be made to fit in conveniently with the "management boards" (*ante*, p. 396), and it also enables a more satisfactory use to be made of modern equipment and techniques, such as computers and critical path analysis.

---

[11] *English Local Government*, 3rd Edn., at p. 241.
[12] Chapter XII, *ante*, p. 383.

5. BOUNDARIES AND FUNCTIONS

(a) *General observations*

Local government in England and Wales, as we knew it immediately before April 1, 1974, was of nineteenth-century origin; the boroughs were reformed by the Municipal Corporations Act, 1835, the county councils and county borough councils were the invention of the Local Government Act, 1888, while urban and rural district councils, one of the consequences of the cholera epidemics and poor law reform, were brought into existence by the Local Government Act, 1894.[13] The pattern of local government having been thus settled, the twentieth century had been very largely occupied in allocating and re-allocating functions as between the different classes of local authorities, and arguing about their geographical areas. Radical change did not come, however, until the Local Government Act, 1972, came into force on April 1, 1974. First, however, it is necessary to trace the story of the movements for reform leading up to 1972.

Functions and areas should be inextricably bound together in any discussion of rearrangement or reform of local government: geography must be related to financial and other resources in drawing a local government map, and the range of functions entrusted to a particular authority must be related to and dependent on both resources and geography. A small market town will not normally be able to afford its own technical college, but if it is a long way from other centres of population, it may properly be allowed to administer its own library service. The administrative boundaries that would best suit one service may well not suit another service; the argument, for instance, that water supply areas should follow watersheds and reflect geological features, and disregard the boundaries of local authorities is the primary justification for the establishment of the new water authorities by the Water Act, 1973. From the point of view of efficiency, boundaries between authorities may be a hindrance to efficient police, or to a lesser extent, fire brigade or ambulance administration. Such arguments pressed to their logical limit would lead to some local government services being administered centrally, and to *ad hoc* areas and authorities being constituted for others; a result which would destroy completely the traditional fabric of local government in this country. The English system has always relied on independent authorities having a range of services to administer, sufficient to attract the voluntary services of members of the public, and with adequate resources to be able to employ efficient and skilled technical staff. The distribution of functions between authorities represents a compromise, not always the best that can be found, between administrative efficiency and localised administration.[14]

---

[13] For the history of local government, see *The History of Local Government in England*, by Redlich and Hirst, 2nd Edn. (1958) by B. Keith-Lucas.

[14] "Twentieth century municipalities are faced with a dilemma. To meet increasingly greater and more complex technical demands the local units should be large enough to maintain an adequate staff and facilities. The units should also be small enough to preserve the local community atmosphere and spirit in which each citizen feels he has

(b) *Reforms of 1930–1950*

Reform—or re-constitution of particular local government services—was an outstanding feature of legislation during the period 1930–1950. Thus, in this period:

(A) The following services were lost to local government altogether:

Passenger road service licensing (Road Traffic Act, 1930)
Trunk roads (Trunk Roads Act, 1936 and 1946)
Hospitals (National Health Service Act, 1946; since reorganised in 1973)
Electricity supply (Electricity Act, 1947)
Public assistance (National Assistance Act, 1948)
Valuation for rating (Local Government Act, 1948)
Gas supply (Gas Act, 1948)
Milk and Dairies—T.T. Herds (Milk and Dairies Regulations, 1949).
River pollution prevention (Rivers (Prevention of Pollution) Act, 1951; Water Resources Act, 1963; Water Act 1973)

(All these services are now administered either by central government agencies or by independent statutory bodies); in addition, in many cases water supply was transferred from local authorities to *ad hoc* boards.

(B) The following services were transferred from county district councils to county councils:

County roads (Local Government Act, 1929)
Elementary education (Education Act, 1944)
Police (some boroughs—Police Act, 1946)
Maternity and child welfare (National Health Service Act, 1946)
Town and country planning (Town and Country Planning Act, 1947)
Fire Brigades (Fire Services Act, 1947)
Magistrates courts and quarter sessions (some boroughs: Justices of the Peace Act, 1949; quarter sessions were abolished and replaced by crown courts by the Courts Act, 1971).

(C) By way of some measure of compensation district councils were given the following new local government functions:

Civic restaurants (Civic Restaurants Act, 1947)
Child Care (Children Acts, 1948–58)
Entertainments (Local Government Act, 1948)
Publicity (Local Government Act, 1948)
Grants for old people's welfare (National Assistance Act, 1948, s. 31) and to encourage sport (Physical Training and Recreation Acts, 1937–1958)
Licensing (pet shops, 1951, rag flock, 1951, gaming, 1956 and 1960)
Smoke Control (Clean Air Act, 1956)
Roadside seats, etc. (Parish Councils Act, 1957).

---

an opportunity to be politically effective": *The Structure of Local Government throughout the World*, published 1961 by the International Union of Local Authorities at The Hague, an excellent comparative study.

The relationship between functions and areas is not always appreciated in discussions on local government reform, although there has been some awareness of the need for periodic reviews of geographical areas: population movements, developing and decaying industries, the growth of traffic problems and the influence of two world wars all have their effects on local authorities and areas.

(c) *Boundary reviews 1945–1958*

Parliament has from time to time made provision for reviews of local government areas. Under the Local Government Acts, 1929 and 1933, county councils were required to undertake periodic reviews of county districts in their areas, and a number of small urban and rural districts were amalgamated by this method during the decade 1929–1939. Then in 1945 a Local Government Boundary Commission was constituted[15] for the purpose of reviewing local government areas throughout the country, but the Commission were given no powers to re-arrange or re-allocate local government functions, and after they had made a report which was too revolutionary for the government to accept, the Boundary Commission was dissolved[16] and the whole matter of local government re-organisation was shelved for another ten years. In the meantime, there were other procedures (rarely used) available on the statute book for the alteration of the boundaries of local authorities or of less important local government areas.

(d) *Local Government Act, 1958*

This Act set up a new Local Government Commission for England and a separate Commission for Wales. This statute recognised that apart from the difficulty of drawing a local government map which would suit all existing local government functions, there were also the special problems of the "conurbations", large areas of urban population where no geographical features separate one local authority area from another, and also of the small ancient boroughs rich in history and traditions but with resources which are often inadequate for the exercise of any considerable range of functions. The problems of re-organisation were therefore handled in the Act of 1958 in the following manner:

(i) *The conurbations.*—London[17] was first dealt with separately, being excluded from the machinery of the Act completely. As a consequence of the Report of a Royal Commission,[18] local government in Greater London was completely reorganised by the London Government Act, 1963.

Outside London, the Act made provision for five special review areas (Tyneside, West Yorkshire, South-East Lancashire, Merseyside and West Midlands[19]) and the Commission was given special powers in respect thereof. Within these areas the Commission were empowered

---

15 Local Government (Boundary Commission) Act, 1945.

16 Local Government (Boundary Commission) (Dissolution) Act, 1949.

17 In this context very much more than the area of the former London County Council was meant by the term "London"; the area covered by the Royal Commission's Report spreads far into the suburbs.

18 Cmnd. Paper 1164; Chapter XI, *ante*, page 368.

19 Compare the six metropolitan areas of the 1972 Act (*post*).

to make recommendations for the alteration of the area of a county or of a county borough, the creation of a new county or county borough, and also for similar action in respect of county districts within the areas.

(ii) *Outside the conurbations.*—Here the Commission were empowered to review and make proposals for alteration of the boundaries of counties and county boroughs only. After these reviews and any consequent alterations had been made it became the responsibility of county councils to review the boundaries of the county districts within their (revised) areas and make proposals for their alteration.

The special problem of the small ancient boroughs was met by provisions of the Act enabling an order to be made for the inclusion of a borough within the boundary of an existing (or newly formed) rural district. The borough then became known as a "rural borough"; it retained its mayor and councillors, its town clerk, its charters and its corporate property, but in other respects it had the status and powers of an ordinary parish council (without any parish meeting).[20]

The Commission made a number of recommendations as to boundary changes in various areas of the country, some of which were implemented (and others rejected[21]). Thus, Luton and Solihull became county boroughs,[1] the West Midlands Special Review Area was parcelled out between five enlarged county boroughs and the City of Birmingham, a number of county boroughs were extended in area,[2] Cambridgeshire and the Isle of Ely were made one county, as were Huntingdon and the Soke of Peterborough,[3] while a new county borough was created at Teesside.[4]

(e) *Boundaries; 1966–1974.*

However, by 1966, views about local government reform were changing, and it was then thought that the piecemeal boundary changes of the 1958 Act were inadequate. In this year the Minister announced the appointment of a Royal Commission,

> "to consider the structure of Local Government in England,[5] outside Greater London,[6] in relation to its existing functions, and to make recommendations",

and in 1967 the two Local Government Commissions were dissolved by the Local Government (Termination of Reviews) Act, 1967. The Royal Commission reported in 1969,[7] making quite revolutionary

---

[20] LG.A., 1958, Schedule 7. The few rural boroughs established before 1972 are now ordinary parishes and may adopt the style of "town" (*ante*, p. 366).

[21] Thus, a proposal for the amalgamation of the County of Rutland with Leicestershire did not succeed.

[1] S.I. 1963, No. 169; S.I. 1963, No. 170.

[2] Northampton (S.I., 1965, No. 250), Coventry (S.I., 1965, No. 222) and Leicester (S.I., 1966, No. 78) (*inter alia*).

[3] S.I., 1964, No. 366. [4] S.I., 1968, No. 526.

[5] A White Paper setting out proposals for Wales was issued in 1967 (Cmd. 3340); a separate Royal Commission was established for Scotland.

[6] London had been reorganised in 1963; Chapter XI, *ante*, p. 368.

[7] Cmnd. 4040; sometimes known as the "Redcliffe-Maud Report", after the Commission's chairman.

recommendations. With the exception of three metropolitan areas[8] they were of the opinion that the whole of England should be administered by 58 "unitary authorities", each possessing almost all the local government functions and a minimum population of 250,000 (many would have a considerably larger population). Above the unitary authorities, there would have been 8 provinces, with elected councils functions (mainly regional planning); below the unitary authorities, the and few existing councils of county boroughs, non-county boroughs, urban districts and parishes[9] would have continued to exist, but with virtually no functions, other than the right to be consulted by the unitary authorities and to express the views of their local inhabitants. In the three metropolitan areas the various local government functions would have been shared between a single "metropolitan authority" for each area, and a few very substantial "metropolitan districts", with existing local councils in an advisory capacity as elsewhere.

These proposals raised considerable controversy, and when, consequent upon the general election of 1970, the Conservative Government undertook to legislate on local government reform, the proposals of the Royal Commission were abandoned. Eventually the Local Government Act, 1972, re-drew the local government map, establishing the pattern described in Chapter XI with six metropolitan areas[10] in England (in addition to Greater London), and 38 other counties, with 8 counties in Wales. Each county has a number of districts, all of equal status, but the metropolitan districts are larger in population and have a few more functions than the other districts.[11] A Boundary Commission was set up to determine and keep under review (for each county) the boundaries of county districts and parishes (and the communities in Wales). The constitutional provisions of the L.G.A., 1933, were all abolished and new (in essentials similar) provisions established, which gave greater freedom to local authorities, in particular in relation to their powers of delegation.[12]

The 1972 Act came into force on April 1, 1974, although the new authorities had been elected a year before. The same date saw the coming into operation of the reorganisation of the national health service,[13] of the reorganisation of river authorities[14] (who, in their new guise as "water authorities" took over sewerage and sewage disposal and also water supply from local authorities) and detailed changes in the financial provisions relating to local government.[15] The same date also saw a substantial change in the law relating to the assessment of compensation for compulsory acquisition of land,[16] and the establishment

---

8 West Midlands, Merseyside and "Selnec" (South East Lancashire and North East Cheshire).

9 Not the rural districts.

10 Greater Manchester, Merseyside, South Yorkshire, Tyne and Wear, West Midlands and West Yorkshire: see L.G.A., 1972, Schedule 1.

11 As to definition of functions, see Chapter XI, *ante*, p. 361. The "provinces" of the Royal Commission Report were abandoned.

12 *Ante*, p. 372.

13 National Health Service Reorganisation Act, 1973.

14 Water Act, 1973; *post*, p. 444.

15 Local Government Bill.

16 Land Compensation Act, 1973.

of commissioners for local administration.[17] All these changes are considered, in so far as they are relevant, in the appropriate passages of this edition.

(f) *Local Government functions and organisation*

Apart from boundaries, although closely concerned with them, is the question of functions. Which authority or class of authority can be entrusted with which functions, and indeed which functions can be entrusted to local government? Some of these questions were solved, partially or completely, by the legislation of 1930–1950 (*ante*); others were solved by the 1972 Act.

The library service had previously been reorganised by the Public Libraries and Museums Act, 1964, weights and measures by the Act of 1963 and police forces were in many cases amalgamated by orders made by the Home Secretary under the Police Act, 1964.

So far as the internal organisation of local authorities is concerned, reforms were suggested by two Committees appointed by the Minister of Housing and Local Government, at the request of the local authority associations. These were taken further by the Bains Report of 1972, which has already been referred to in this and the preceding Chapters.

(g) *Boundaries, etc.—post 1974*

It seems unlikely that the legislature will be persuaded to effect any further alterations to the structure of local government for some years after the upheavals of 1974. But the Act of 1972 recognises that population movements and other causes may make it desirable from time to time to make boundary and other changes in particular areas. Therefore, the Local Government Boundary Commissions for England and Wales respectively,[1] in addition to their tasks of settling district and parish boundaries as at April 1, 1974, have been given the permanent task of reviewing local government areas at intervals of not less than ten years and not more than fifteen years.[2] In addition, they may make proposals for interim changes, and individual authorities may ask the appropriate Commission to carry out a review of their area.[3] Proposals made by the appropriate Commission[4] must be made to the Secretary of State for the Environment, and he may then make an order to give effect to the proposals with or without modifications, or he may decide to make no order.[5] Any such order has to be made by statutory instrument.[6]

When a Commission is carrying out a review of an area, it must ensure that persons who may be "interested"[7] are informed of the proposal and they must consult local authorities affected.[8]

---

[17] Local Government Bill, Part III.

[1] Public corporations, established by Part IV and Schedules 7 and 8 of the 1972 Act.

[2] 1972 Act, ss. 48 and 55.

[3] *Ibid.*

[4] *Ibid.*, ss. 47 and 54.

[5] *Ibid.*, ss. 51 and 58.

[6] *Ibid.*, s. 266 (1).

[7] It is not clear what is meant here; there can be no question of a *legal* interest, in the sense in which the courts have used the term in other contexts; see Chapter VI, *ante*, p. 176.

[8] L.G.A., 1972, s. 60.

District councils have a duty to keep under review the boundaries of parishes or communities within their district, and they may make recommendations for alterations to the appropriate Commission, who must then consider such recommendations.[9] The Commissions, and any district council, have power to hold a local inquiry,[10] but the procedure will not be subject to the supervision of the Council on Tribunals, as such inquiries are not "statutory inquiries".

Alterations in the boundary between England and Wales may be considered by the two Commissions acting jointly.[11]

A county, a district or a London borough may change its name by resolution of the council on which at least two-thirds of the members voting thereon vote in favour.[12] A parish or community name may be changed by the district council at the request of the parish (community) council or (if there is no council) at the request of the parish (community) meeting.[13]

No local authority has power to promote a Bill in Parliament for altering local government boundaries.[14]

---

[9] *Ibid.*, ss. 50 (8) and 55 (2).

[10] *Ibid.*, s. 61; s. 250 (2), (3) and (5) of the Act will apply to any such review. It should be noted that there is no further inquiry before the Secretary of State makes an order giving effect to a Commissioner's proposal, nor is any such order subject to Parliamentary approval.

[11] L.G.A., 1972, s. 62.

[12] *Ibid.*, s. 74; as to Greater London, see s. 77.

[13] *Ibid.*, ss. 75 and 76.

[14] *Ibid.*, s. 70.

CHAPTER XIV

LOCAL GOVERNMENT FINANCE

1. INTRODUCTION

The organisation of local government finance is of particular importance and interest to students of English administrative law, for the following reasons:

(a) Local authorities are truly independent only to the extent that they can control their own finances, and many of the administrative controls exercised by organs of the Central Government over local authorities are in fact financial in character, as will be explained in the next Chapter.[1]

(b) The manner in which local rates are assessed and collected is closely regulated by law and the system has resulted in the constitution of an elaborate hierarchy of administrative tribunals.

(c) The internal working of local authorities has been and is profoundly influenced by financial considerations.

In this Chapter we shall discuss first the several sources of a local authority's revenues, including some comments on the levying and collection of rates, and then we shall describe briefly the methods whereby a local authority exercises control over its expenditure.

The primary source of income of all local authorities is the general rate levied on all immovable (except agricultural) property within the authority's district. Historically income from the authority's own property, such as rents and licence fees, was also of great importance, but this is now financially insignificant. Almost as important as rates are government grants; indeed, many authorities at the present time derive at least a half of their total income from this source.

In recent years many criticisms have been expressed of the local government financial system, mainly based on the argument that local authorities need additional independent sources of income, so that they can be less dependent on the Central Government. The Redcliffe-Maud Royal Commission in effect side stepped the question, by recommending the constitution of large unitary authorities which would, quite apart from any financial reforms, enjoy very considerable resources, and this is in some measure true of the new authorities established by the Local Government Act, 1972. The examination of the subject carried out in 1971[2] showed, however, that new sources of finance would be difficult to find, and that the only satisfactory reform of local government finance was to increase central exchequer grants while leaving local authorities free to decide how much they

---

[1] *Post*, p. 439.

[2] "Green" Paper, "The Future Shape of Local Government Finance", July 1971, Cmnd. 4741.

want to spend. Criticisms of the rating system have, to some extent, been met by the introduction of rent rebates and provisions enabling authorities to rate unoccupied property, both of which are discussed below. We now discuss *seriatim* the three forms of local authority income.

2. LOCAL AUTHORITY INCOME—(I) RATES

Traditionally the primary source of income of a local authority is the local rate; a levy on the occupiers of landed property within the authority's area. The history of rates goes back to the Poor Relief Act of 1601; the modern law has now been consolidated in the General Rate Act, 1967. Rates are a local tax, the amount of which is fixed by the local authority, but the unit on which the rate is levied, the value of each hereditament[3] in the district, is assessed by a department of the Central Government on principles uniform to the whole country.[4] We are proposing therefore to discuss first valuation procedure and principles, and then principles of liability to and the levying of rates.

A. Valuation

(i) *Machinery.*—The valuation of hereditaments for rating purposes is now the responsibility of the Board of Inland Revenue. The local valuation officer is responsible for the initial compilation of the valuation list; he makes a series of proposals to the effect that each particular hereditament should be valued at a specified amount, and then the ratepayers concerned and the local rating authority[5] have a right to object to the proposals. If the local valuation officer does not accept any such objection, the matter is referred to the local valuation court (an administrative tribunal)[6] for determination, subject to an appeal (on law or merits) to the Lands Tribunal and from there to the Court of Appeal (on a point of law alone) and from the Court of Appeal to the House of Lords.

(ii) *Principles.*—The general principle of valuation for rating purposes is that the "gross value" of the hereditament is the annual rent that a tenant holding the property on a tenancy from year to year could reasonably be expected to pay, on the basis that the landlord would be liable for the cost of repairs and insurance and that the tenant would be liable for payment of the usual tenant's rates and taxes. This principle applies to all types of hereditament liable to pay rates whether a particular hereditament is actually let or not[7] and the assessment is not necessarily the actual rent that is being paid at the moment, although this is

[3] A technical expression, bearing little relation to the same word as used in the law of real property, meaning property liable to rating: General Rate Act, 1967, s. 117. The property liable to rating is explained in s. 16, *ibid.*, as consisting of lands, houses, coal mines, other mines, and sporting rights.

[4] Until the passing of the Local Government Act, 1948, valuation was the responsibility of each local authority, and attempts at attaining uniformity of valuation throughout the country were informal and largely unsuccessful.

[5] The district council: see *post*.

[6] *Ante*, Chapter VIII, *ante*, p. 241.

[7] Property which is totally incapable of being let (*e.g.*, a highway or a recreation ground "dedicated" to the public) is therefore not liable to rating.

naturally the best evidence as to what the assessment should be. Special principles, for which there is no statutory authority, but which have on many occasions been accepted by the Courts,[8] have been adopted in practice for arriving at the rent which a "hypothetical tenant" might be expected to pay for some particular hereditament. Thus, the "contractors' method" is used to arrive at a valuation for certain business properties in the computation of which profits and losses of the business are taken into account. Certain types of hereditaments are, or have been, entitled to deductions from the notional rent in arriving at the gross value[9]; in such a case the hereditament is said to be entitled to the benefit of "de-rating". Thus:

(a) Agricultural property, other than dwelling houses, is totally exempt from rating.[10]

(b) Industrial and freight-transport hereditaments were, until the passing of the Rating and Valuation Act, 1959, de-rated to the extent of three-quarters of their rateable value; under the 1959 Act this de-rating provision was reduced to one-half and then by the Rating and Valuation Act, 1961,[11] the concession was totally withdrawn, and rates are now payable on the full assessment of such hereditaments.[12]

(c) Sewers are not rateable, being expressly exempted from liability to rating. Watercourses are similarly exempt, and so are most parks and sheds and huts used for housing invalid chairs or vehicles for disabled persons.[13]

(d) Shops and offices were de-rated to the extent of one-fifth of their assessment, from 1957 to 1963.[14]

(e) Dwelling houses have been specially treated under various statutes. Before 1963,[15] they were assessed as if the valuation had been carried out on 30th June 1939; therefore the valuation was assessed on the basis of what a hypothetical tenant would have paid in rent as at that date (in some cases for a house that was not then in existence!). Under the Rating and Valuation Act, 1959, assessments as from 1st April, 1963 were related to the actual date of valuation. Dwelling houses have, since the financial year 1967–8, been de-rated to an amount of a specified number of pennies in the rate, to be prescribed by Ministerial Regulations.[16]

---

[8] The method of assessing dwelling-houses by calculating a base figure of rent per foot super from the actual rental evidence, was accepted in *R.* v. *Paddington Valuation Officer, ex parte Peachey Property Corpn., Ltd.*, [1965] 2 All E.R. 836; [1966] 1 Q.B. 380; and see article by the present writer at (1966), 110 Sol. Jo. 340.

[9] In addition to these deductions, a "rateable deduction" is made from the gross value of dwelling houses, in accordance with a statutory scale, to arrive at the "rateable value" on which the rates are levied; this deduction is supposed to cover the cost of repairs.

[10] L.G.A., 1929.

[11] S. 1 thereof.

[12] The de-rating of industrial hereditaments had been introduced at the time of the economic depression in 1929.

[13] General Rate Act, 1967, ss. 42–45.

[14] Rating and Valuation Act, 1957.

[15] See Valuation for Rating Act, 1953, and s. 1 of the Rating and Valuation Act, 1957.

[16] General Rate Act, 1967, s. 48, replacing the L.G.A., 1966.

(f) Gas and electricity hereditaments, vested in the several boards, are exempt from rating in the ordinary sense, but a gross sum is agreed for the whole country and this is apportioned as between all the local authorities according to elaborate formulae laid down by statute. Similar provisions apply to railway and canal hereditaments occupied by the Railways Board, the London Board and the British Waterways Board constituted under the Transport Act, 1962.[17]

(g) Crown property is exempt from rating, but in practice the Crown makes *ex gratia* payments to local authorities in lieu of the rates that would otherwise be recoverable.

(h) Charitable properties also are specially treated for rating purposes. The law on this subject has suffered greatly from imprecise and changing legislation in recent years, but the position was to some extent clarified by the Rating and Valuation Act, 1961.[18] Under this Act any hereditament which is occupied by, or by trustees for, a charity (in the accepted legal sense of that term) and wholly or mainly used for charitable purposes, and any hereditament held upon trust for use as an almshouse (an expression which is not defined in the Act), except where the institution is a university or is specified for the purpose by the Secretary of State, is to be entitled to 50 per cent de-rating.[19]

(i) Special provisions apply to the valuation of hereditaments occupied by the National Coal Board, mines, quarries, docks and harbours, and broadcasting stations,[20] county and voluntary schools,[1] and statutory water undertakings.[2]

(iii) *Currency of valuation list.*—Valuation of property is rarely an exact science and this is particularly true of valuation for rating. Although a valuation list is settled nominally once every five years, each list is notionally in force for one rating period only (which may be a period of either six or twelve months) and a decision as to what is the correct valuation of a particular hereditament in one valuation list is not conclusive for subsequent lists.[3] A proposal for the alteration of the current list may be made at any time by the valuation officer, the rating authority, or by the ratepayer, but normally of course there should be some change in circumstances (such as the erection of a garage or the making up of a private road in which the hereditament is situate) justifying any such proposal. In any case where the ratepayer is not prepared to accept the valuation officer's decision, he has (in effect) a right of appeal to a local valuation court.[4]

---

17 General Rate Act, 1967, ss. 32–34; Chapter X, *ante*, p. 320. The Secretary of State will be empowered by the Local Government Bill to use different methods for the rating of these hereditaments.

18 See now General Rate Act, 1967, s. 40, and Schedule 8.

19 The amount of the allowance may be increased by a particular local authority, at their discretion.

20 1967 Act, s. 35. 1 *Ibid.*, s. 30. 2 *Ibid.*, s. 31.

3 *Society of Medical Officers of Health* v. *Hope*, [1960] 1 All E.R. 317; [1960] A.C. 551.

4 See Chapter VIII, *ante*, page 241.

B. Rating.—The occupier of the hereditament is primarily liable for payment of the rates, but in the case of certain small dwelling houses, the rating authority may by resolution make owners liable,[5] or an individual ratepayer of a dwelling house may be granted a discount by the rating authority as a reward for prompt payment[6]; a ratepayer may also agree to pay by instalments.[7] If the property temporarily has no occupier and is not "beneficially occupied",[8] it will be treated as "void" and only half rates will be payable in respect of this period.[9]

The district councils alone are the rating authorities; they are responsible for computing the rate required for the district and for collecting it from the occupiers of hereditaments. The rate is always expressed as a certain sum in the £; for each pound of the assessment of the hereditament the occupier will pay that multiple of the rate. Thus, a house assessed at £50 rateable value will, if the rate has been levied at 75p, pay £37.50 in rates, or £75 if the rate has been levied at £1.50. The amount of the rate required is arrived at first by finding the gross sum of the council's estimated requirements for the financial year in question, and then dividing that by the gross product of a 1p. rate in the area, that figure itself being computed from the sum total of the assessments of all the hereditaments in the districts. The estimated requirements for the year[10] are arrived at as follows:—

		£
	(A) Sum required to meet the Council's own requirements (based on estimates prepared by each of the spending committees of the council, and approved by the council)	x
plus	(B) Sums required by "precepting" authorities. These are, the county council and any parish or community councils in the area[11] and in most cases also various *ad hoc* authorities, such as the water authority (as drainage authority)	y
		$£x+y$

---

[5] General Rate Act, 1967, s. 55. [6] *Ibid.*, s. 51. [7] *Ibid.*, s. 50.

[8] This is a technical expression, as there must be both possession in law and some degree of use and enjoyment of the hereditament, for the same to be liable to rates. An empty house is not fully rateable, but an empty bungalow used as a "show house" on a building estate would be, as it would be in "use": see, *e.g.*, *Bayliss* v. *Chatters*, [1940] 1 All E.R. 620.

[9] Provided the premises have been unoccupied for a period of more than three (or, in the case of a newly erected dwelling-house, six) months: Local Government Act, 1966, ss. 20–22, now replaced by s. 17 and Schedule 1 of the General Rate Act, 1967. These sections are not applicable to a rating area until they have been adopted by the local authority by resolution. Before the 1966 Act came into force unoccupied property was not liable to rates at all. These provisions will be amended in detail by the Local Government Bill.

[10] Rates are normally computed once a year, but an authority may adopt six months as a rating period.

[11] See Local Government Act, 1972, ss. 149 and 150.

		£	
less (C)	Any sums receivable from the Central Government[12]	a	
(D)	Other income (see below)..	b	
(E)	Any sums taken from balances or reserves[13]	c	
		$a+b+c$	
	Net requirements		£ $(x+y)-(a+b+c)$

Rates are payable on demand; a "demand note" (in due form[14]) has to be served by the rating authority on the occupier[15] of each hereditament in respect of which rates are payable, and proceedings may be taken for recovery of the sum due if not paid after the expiration of seven days from the date of service of the demand note. These proceedings may take only the form of a complaint before the local magistrates: a rating authority cannot sue for rates in the High Court or county court. The magistrates may make an order for payment or issue a distress warrant, on the authority of which distraint may be levied on the ratepayer's goods. The magistrates may also issue a warrant for committal of the ratepayer to prison if satisfied that failure to pay the sum demanded has been due to wilful refusal or culpable neglect on the part of the ratepayer.[16] But although an authority may not sue for sums due by way of rates,[17] they can institute bankruptcy proceedings,[18] or proceedings for the liquidation of a limited company[19] for their recovery, and these sums rank as priority debts[20] in any such proceedings. Precepts—the sums required by local authorities other than rating authorities, and in particular by the county councils[1]—are computed by the precepting authority in manner exactly similar to that described above for rates. The authority receiving a precept cannot question it in any way and merely have the duty of providing the money required by the precept.

---

[12] As to grants, see *post*, p. 415.

[13] A local authority is not authorised by statute to include in the requirements on which the rate is computed any sum to build up a reserve: the rate is intended to cover current requirements only, and capital expenditure has to be covered by way of loans (see below). Nevertheless all local authorities may budget for a "working balance"—a sum sufficient to tide them over at the end of a year until the produce of the next year's rate has been received, and in many cases this working balance tends gradually to increase over the years. From time to time also an authority may budget for anticipated expenditure which it does not actually incur, possibly through shortage of labour or changes of policy, and so in this way a reserve or large working balance may be built up. Where this occurs the balance should be reduced with the result that a smaller sum will be required in rates in a subsequent year.

[14] Rate-demands Rules, 1958, S.I. 1958 No. 2198.

[15] Or the owner in certain cases (see *ante*).

[16] Money Payments (Justices Procedure) Act, 1935.

[17] *Liverpool Corpn.* v. *Hope*, [1938] 1 All E.R. 492; [1938] 1 K.B. 751.

[18] *Re McGreavy, ex parte McGreavy* v. *Benfleet U.D.C.*, [1950] 1 All E.R. 442; [1950] Ch. 269.

[19] *Re North Bucks Furniture Depositories, Ltd.*, [1939] 2 All E.R. 549; [1939] Ch. 690.

[20] So far as twelve months' arrears only are concerned.

[1] In practice, it may have to be as large a proportion as two-thirds of the total rates levied by a district council to represent the sum required to meet the county council precept. Some district councils will receive precepts from the county council "above" it in the hierarchy, and from the several parishes or communities in their district below it.

A right of appeal against a rate to the Crown Court (formerly quarter sessions) was given by the Poor Relief Act, 1743,[2] but this right was severely restricted by the Local Government Act, 1948;[3] no appeal will lie in respect of any matter of which relief might have been obtained by a proposal for amendment to the valuation list, an objection to such a proposal, or an appeal against such an objection to a local valuation court. Appeals to the Crown Court will still lie, however, where the grounds of appeal are based on such matters as the procedure for the making of the rate, facts such as non-occupation of a rateable hereditament, or entitlement to exemption from rating.[4] Any person who is aggrieved by a rate or by any neglect, act or thing done or omitted by the rating authority, or any person who has a material objection to the inclusion or exclusion of any person in or from, or to the amount charged to any person in, any rate may appeal; appeal lies to the next sitting of the Crown Court after the making of the rate, and the court may amend the rate in detail or quash it completely. An appeal lies from the Crown Court to the High Court by case stated on a point of law.

An appeal will not lie against a rate on the ground that some of the expenditure for which the rate is levied to provide will be *ultra vires* the authority. An aggrieved ratepayer in such circumstances must take separate proceedings, either by appearing before the district auditor,[5] or by appealing to the courts by an action for a declaration and/or an injunction.[6]

Ratepayers in humble circumstances may now be entitled to claim a rebate, calculated in accordance with an elaborate formula provided for in sections 48 and 49 and the Schedule 9 of the General Rate Act, 1967[7] (to be amended by the Local Government Bill).

3. LOCAL AUTHORITY INCOME—(2) MISCELLANEOUS

Under this heading may be included income from municipal undertakings, such as rents from Council houses, takings from public entertainments, the hiring out of deck chairs in parks or on the seashore, and bus fares in the case of a public transport undertaking operated by the authority. Many municipal undertakings, such as open air swimming pools and burial grounds, are run at a loss; others that are equally necessary in the interests of inhabitants, such as crematoria, public halls and markets, are usually run at a profit. Profits from public undertakings are sometimes used to reduce the rates, but most local authorities use such profits exclusively to improve the service given by

---

[2] Which itself replaced earlier legislation.

[3] See s. 53 thereof, now replaced by s. 7 of the General Rate Act, 1967.

[4] This procedure was used considerably in connection with charities claiming partial exemption from rates under s. 8 of the Rating and Valuation (Miscellaneous Provisions) Act, 1955 (since repealed).

[5] See Chapter XV, *post*, p. 427.

[6] See Chapter VI, *ante*, p. 187.

[7] Replacing provisions introduced in the Rating Act, 1966.

the undertaking, particularly where those contributing to the undertaking are not identical with the general body of ratepayers (as, for example, in the case of a transport undertaking operating partly outside the local authority's area).

Rents from municipal property are another form of miscellaneous income, and this may represent a very substantial annual contribution to the rates. Rents for council houses have to be credited to a special housing revenue account, any balance on which could not be used in aid of rates.

Licence fees must also be included, although these in total never amount to any considerable sum. Express statutory authority for the levying of a fee is required in each instance[8]; statutes in recent years imposing new controls administered by local authorities have usually included a power to make a charge as a condition of the issue of a licence.[9]

Most local authorities impose "fines" for the non-return of library books at the end of the stipulated lending period, and this practice has now been legalised by section 8 of the Public Libraries and Museums Act, 1964.

4. LOCAL AUTHORITY INCOME—(3) GRANTS

For many years local authorities were expected, and in practice did, live "of their own". The income from corporate property was sufficient to meet their modest expenditure, but by the end of the nineteenth century, when new public health and similar duties were thrust upon them by statute, the resultant expenditure was met by the levying of rates.

By the early years of the twentieth century, however, it had become clear that local government would in some measure have to be subsidised from the central exchequer. These subsidies or grants took two forms: firstly a general subvention towards the expenditure of the local authority, not earmarked for any particular purpose, and secondly, particular grants in aid of specific local government services or "approved" expenditure on particular services. Grants in aid were very popular with the central government and with Parliament during the first half of the twentieth century, as they provided a means whereby detailed control could be exercised over the activities of local authorities, and whereby the development of particular services could be encouraged (possibly at the expense of others).

By the 1950's, however, it was considered that this emphasis on grants in aid was undermining the independence of local authorities and increasing the general administrative cost of local government, as technical officers were being duplicated at central and local levels in order to exercise such detailed control. Grants in aid also tended to create a false balance between the several services; locally elected councillors

---

[8] *Liverpool Corpn.* v. *Arthur Maiden, Ltd.*, [1938] 4 All E.R. 200.

[9] *E.g.*, permits for the holding of "amusements with prizes" (Betting, Gaming and Lotteries Act, 1963, and Gaming Act, 1968); Pet Animals Act, 1951; Rag Flock and other Filling Materials Act, 1951; Rent Act, 1957 (Certificates of Disrepair). The Local Government Bill will in many instances, allow the local authority to fix the fee at their discretion.

answerable to the ratepayers, are always mindful of the need to keep the rate burden as low as possible, and consequently are more prepared to spend money on services that attract government grant than on those which are financed entirely from rates. The whole structure of exchequer subsidies for local government was therefore overhauled by the Local Government Act, 1958, the underlying principle of which has been said to be[10]

> "to strengthen the autonomy of local government generally by substituting as far as possible a block grant for specific subsidies for specific purposes where contributions are made by the central government, and so reducing the amount of detailed supervision over local authority expenditure exercised by government departments in the interests of the tax-payer".

Further drastic revisions were made by the Local Government Act, 1966, which to some extent brought back the grants in aid. The net result of the 1958 and 1966 Acts and subsequent legislation is as follows:

(a) Grants in aid.—Most of the grants in aid paid to local authorities immediately prior to the coming into effect of the 1958 Act were withdrawn. The grants so treated are listed in a Schedule of that Act[11] in the designation "relevant expenditure", and the Minister was formerly required to have regard to the grants paid before 1958 in respect of those services when computing the gross amount of the exchequer grant; but under s. 1 of the 1966 Act this can now be ignored (see below).

Some grants in aid of specific services remain, and new ones have been created. The most important of these are:

(i) *Roads.*—The Secretary of State for the Environment makes grants towards approved expenditure incurred on the maintenance and improvement of classified roads, on street lighting[12] and on traffic signs, and also bears the whole cost relating to trunk roads.[13] Most of these are to be revised by the Local Government Bill.

(ii) *Housing.*—For a considerable period after the War of 1914–18, and to a greatly increased extent after the War of 1939–45, substantial government subsidies were paid in respect of each house built by a local authority under the Housing Acts, and approved by the Ministry of Housing and Local Government. Subsidies paid in respect of these

---

[10] Royal Commission on Local Government in Greater London, 1957–60 (Cmd. 1164), para. 266.

[11] Schedule 1, Part I. The list is as follows: Education (except school milk and meals), which formerly was 60 per cent grant aided in respect of all approved expenditure; health services (National Health Service Act, 1946, Part III); fire services (formerly a 50 per cent grant, the service being subject to control by inspection, which remains): child care; town planning (except certain grants for re-development of "blitzed" areas, which grants remain): road safety and school crossing patrols; registration of electors; physical training and recreation; provision of accommodation under the National Assistance Act, 1948.

[12] Local Government Act, 1966, s. 28; the amount of the grant, expressed as a percentage of actual expenditure incurred, varies according to the classification of the road. The classification of each road is determined by the Secretary of State; *ibid.*, s. 27.

[13] The Department is the highway authority in respect of all trunk roads but most of the construction and maintenance work is undertaken by the county councils as agents for the Department.

houses were paid for many years, as they took the form of a lump sum per house each year for a period of sixty years; however, no subsidies were payable in respect of houses built for "general needs" from 1956–61.[14] Annual subsidies of varying amounts were, however, payable in respect of new dwellings erected to meet the needs of persons displaced as a consequence of slum clearance, those erected as a part of a scheme of town development[15] and certain exceptionally expensive forms of development such as one-bedroom dwellings and dwellings erected on expensive sites.[16] By the Housing Act, 1961, subsidies were again made payable in respect of each dwelling erected (without regard to the purpose): the amount of the subsidy varied, however, according to the financial resources of the local authority. A further revision was made by the Housing Subsidies Act, 1967, under which subsidies payable for 60 years were based on the aggregate cost of construction of houses, and special subsidies were made for particular forms of development (such as large blocks of flats, dwellings provided to meet special needs, etc.).

However, the whole scheme of subsidies from the Exchequer and the rents charged by local authorities was drastically changed by the Housing Finance Act, 1972. Subsidies are no longer paid in respect of individual houses, but local authorities are expected to make economic charges by way of rent payable by their tenants, subject to rebates for those tenants not able to pay. Rent allowances are also payable by local authorities to those tenants of privately owned houses who cannot afford to pay the "fair rent". The income so received and the allowances that the authority has had to make are then computed, and grants are made from the Exchequer towards the authority's housing revenue account in accordance with elaborate rules set out in the Act. Obviously rents could not be increased by large amounts in one year, but it is the intention of the Act that ultimately income and expenditure will balance without the need for Exchequer assistance. Government subsidies are still, however, paid in respect of expenditure incurred in the making of improvement grants and standard grants[17] to private individuals by local authorities.

(iii) *Police.*—A 50 per cent grant is payable in respect of all local authority police expenditure approved by the Home Office.

(iv) *Miscellaneous.*—There are a number of miscellaneous items of minor or special local government expenditure which attract grants in aid, such as civil defence approved expenditure, the cost of town planning redevelopment[18] and town development under the 1952 Act, certain expenses arising under the Clean Air Act, 1956,[19] the purchase of land

---

[14] A nominal subsidy of 1*s.* per annum was paid in respect of each such house. Provision was made for this in the statute so that the Minister could increase the amount of the grant without having to obtain amending legislation.

[15] Under the Town Development Act, 1952.

[16] See Housing (Financial Provisions) Act, 1958.

[17] Under the Housing Act, 1969, replacing earlier legislation.

[18] Local Government Act, 1966, s. 7.

[19] See s. 13 of that Act.

for open spaces[20] and the reclamation of derelict land,[1] special expenditure due to substantial numbers of immigrants in the area,[2] expenditure incurred in connection with the administration of justice,[3] and on remedial operations carried out in relation to disused coal tips.[4] Grants may also be made to local authorities which, in the opinion of the Secretary of State, are required to incur expenditure by reason of the existence in an urban area of "special social need" (an expression which is not defined but which is apparently open to interpretation by the Secretary of State[5]).

(b) Rate Support grants.—In place of the grants in aid that were withdrawn under the Act of 1958, the central government made available for distribution to local authorities generally a gross sum, computed by reference to the 1958–59 expenditure on those items (increased by rises in cost and any proved need subsequently to develop the services in question), and this lump sum was distributed to all county boroughs and county councils in the country in accordance with a prescribed formula.

The 1966 Act now provides for an even more complicated system of exchequer grant. These, known as "rate support grants", are made up of three elements (to be revised in matters of detail by the Local Government Bill)[6]:

(i) *The Needs Element.*—Payable to the councils of counties, London boroughs, the Common Council of the City of London and the Greater London Council, and based on population weighted by other factors, including the number of persons under 15 years of age in the population, the number of persons under 5 and over 65, the density of population per acre, and the road mileage per 1,000 persons, etc.

(ii) *The Resources Element.*—Payable to *any* local authority with rate resources lower than the national average in proportion to their population.

(iii) *The Domestic Element.*—Payable to rating authorities only, to compensate them for loss of rates caused by such partial de-rating of dwelling-houses as may be directed by the Minister.

The total sum available for distribution by way of rate support grants is calculated by the Secretary of State with the approval of the Treasury, on no precise prescribed standards[7] (in other words the amount will depend on what sum the Cabinet consider the national economy can afford), and stated in an order which will be subject to the affirmative

---

[20] Local Government Act, 1966, s. 8.

[1] *Ibid.*, s. 9.

[2] *Ibid.*, s. 11.

[3] A list will be found at Appendix VII of Cross, *Local Government Law*; the grants in respect of school milk and meals were withdrawn under s. 14 of the 1966 Act.

[4] Mines and Quarries (Tips) Act, 1969, s. 25.

[5] Local Government Grants (Social Need) Act, 1969: see note at (1969) 32 M.L.R. 672.

[6] See 1966 Act, s. 1 (4) and Schedule 1.

[7] But the Secretary of State is required to consult with "such associations of local authorities as appear to him to be concerned", and to have regard to levels of prices, to fluctuations in demands for services and the need to develop local government services (s. 1 (3)).

resolution procedure in the Commons; any particular order then remains in force for a period specified, not less than two years.[8] The division of this sum between the three elements will then also be prescribed by the Secretary of State in the same order.

(c) General observations.—It may be thought that the grant system as explained above in outline is quite unnecessarily complicated, but it should be appreciated that it has been framed with two objectives in mind. Firstly it was the intention of Parliament that the method of distribution of such central moneys as may be available should be laid down in legislation so that the central executive should retain little discretion[9] and no powers to favour one authority or class of authority at the expense of others. Payment of the rate support grants (as was the case with the general grant under the 1958 Act) is not to be conditional (except in the most general terms, exercisable only in an extreme case[10]) on the particular authority using its money in a manner desired or approved by the central government. Secondly, an attempt has been made in the legislation to provide for as fair a distribution as possible, making allowances for authorities with resources lower than the average. When the Local Government Act, 1958, was passing through Parliament many different groups of local authorities engaged in unseemly wrangles and arguments for larger shares of the "cake", although the Minister pointed out that special claims, if met, would only have the effect of reducing the shares payable to other authorities and could not increase the total size of the "cake" available for distribution.

These two factors reacting on each other can but result in complicated legislation. We can be thankful that the system is not worse or as difficult to understand and to operate as are the systems applicable in some Continental countries.[11] It is unfortunate that local government cannot be financially independent without the need for any subventions from the central government, but it seems unlikely that such a consummation "devoutly to be wished" can be achieved.

5. LOCAL AUTHORITY EXPENDITURE—(1) REVENUE

Unlike income, the law is not concerned to control the detailed expenditure of local authorities, provided they are acting *intra vires*. As all income received by the principal council must be paid into the authority's general rate fund,[12] so all expenditure must be paid out of that fund, under the authority of some statute,[13] and if the authority's accounts are subject to district audit, the district auditor is entitled to

[8] However, there is no legal reason why the total sum so provided for should not be increased during the two year or other period, as was done by the Rate Support Grant (Increase) Order, 1969.

[9] The grants in aid under the 1966 Act are however to some extent at the discretion of the Secretary of State.

[10] 1966 Act, s. 4, and Chapter XV, *post*, p. 431.

[11] As, *e.g.*, in France; see *An Introduction to French Local Government*, by Bryan Chapman, Chapter VI.

[12] L.G.A., 1972, s. 148 (4).

[13] The general but limited power given by s. 137 of the Local Government Act, 1972 (Chapter IX, *ante*, p. 303) is in some measure an exception from the statement in the text.

disallow any payment not authorised by law.[14] Expenditure for which there is a general statutory authority, but which was none the less in the circumstances unreasonable, may similarly be disallowed.[15]

Control over expenditure is exercised by the local authority itself by the following methods:

(a) By the supervision of the finance committee. It is normally provided by the council's standing orders[16] that no expenditure may be incurred unless it has been approved generally,[17] or specially by the finance committee. The effectiveness of this control will depend on the personnel of the finance committee and especially of its chairman; if the committee is prepared to sanction every request from another committee for special expenditure, the control will become meaningless. It should be remembered, however, that the committee is itself responsible to and liable to be overruled by the council; the finance committee should neither approve expenditure uncritically nor disapprove expenditure for policy reasons, unsupported by sound financial considerations. Policy is a matter for the council as a whole, and should not become the preserve of the finance committee.

(b) By scrutiny of accounts. It is usual for standing orders of a local authority to provide for accounts for payment to be scrutinised by members of a sub-committee of the finance committee; this is required not so much so as to ensure that the authority is not incurring illegal expenditure or is not being defrauded—these matters being the concern of the officers in the finance department—but rather to ensure that expenditure is not wasteful and that other committees are using the moneys allocated to them wisely. This is at best a spasmodic control, and it could perhaps be dispensed with safely.[18]

(c) Finally, there is the control exercised over the council's expenditure by its treasurer or financial officer and his department, reinforced by the District or other auditor.[19] The duties of the treasurer and the extent to which he is entitled to scrutinise the accounts and contracts of departmental officers will normally be laid down in standing orders or financial regulations, and he will normally be required to maintain an effective system of permanent internal audit. Dishonesty and peculation is now, fortunately, a rarity in local government in this country; this is due not only to the high standards of the public service but also to the efficient manner in which finance staffs have carried out their duties. The more progressive local authorities have adopted "organisation and methods" and "time and motion" studies in recent years and many local authorities have permanent officials on their staff concerned with such matters.

---

[14] *Post*, Chapter XV, *post*, p. 428.
[15] As in *Roberts* v. *Hopwood*, [1925] A.C. 578, *ibid.*
[16] Chapter XIII, *ante*, p. 397.
[17] In the annual estimates.
[18] Provided proper accounts are kept: Local Government Act, 1972, s. 148 (5).
[19] Chapter XV, *post*, p. 427.

Until comparatively recently, statutes required elaborate machinery to be established for the control of payments out of the general rate fund. A county council could not incur any expenditure exceeding £50 except on an estimate submitted by the finance committee,[20] and payments had to be made in pursuance of an order signed by three members of the finance committee, while cheques had to be countersigned by the clerk of the county council or some other approved person.[1] Similar provisions, with certain exceptions, applied to borough councils.[2] Now however, these requirements have disappeared and the Local Government Act, 1972, is content merely to require that accounts shall be kept.[3]

6. LOCAL AUTHORITY EXPENDITURE—(2) CAPITAL

The cost of all routine expenditure of a local authority such as salaries, wages, maintenance of buildings and the collection of refuse, must be borne out of current revenue, from yearly income. The Local Government Act, 1972, confers on every local authority a general power to borrow money,[4] but this relates to capital purposes only, and current expenditure may not be defrayed by way of a loan, and the sanction of the Secretary of State must be obtained for any proposed loan.[5] The only case where the sanction of the Secretary of State is not required is where a local authority borrow money temporarily for the purpose of defraying expenses pending the receipt of revenues receivable by them, or for the purpose of defraying expenses pending the raising of a loan which they have been authorised to raise.[6] Once the sanction has been obtained to the raising of the loan, the authority may now raise the money how it pleases, in the open money market,[7] from the Public Works Loan Board (at the ruling rate of interest)[8] or by accepting loans from local residents or others, or by the issue of bonds[9]; all moneys borrowed must be charged indifferently on all the revenues of the authority.[10]

The authority's standing orders will normally provide that no committee of the council may recommend that a loan should be raised for a specific purpose until that recommendation has been considered by the finance committee; and it will be remembered that the raising of a

---

[20] L.G.A., 1933, s. 86 (2).
[1] L.G.A. Act, 1933, s. 184.
[2] *Ibid.*, s. 187.
[3] L.G.A., 1972, s. 148 (5).
[4] *Ibid.*, s. 172 and Schedule 13.
[5] *Ibid.*, Schedule 13, para. 1, and see Chapter XV, *post*, p. 425.
[6] *Ibid.*, Schedule 13, para. 10.
[7] Money may be borrowed outside the U.K. only with the consent of the Treasury: L.G.A., 1972, Schedule 13, para. 3.
[8] Under the Local Authorities Loans Act, 1945, all loans raised by local authorities had to be raised with the P.W.L.B., but this control was allowed to lapse at the end of 1952.
[9] L.G.A., 1972, Schedule 13, para. 2.
[10] *Ibid.*, Schedule 13, para. 11. Since the passing of the Trustee Investments Act, 1961, in particular, which makes local authority stock "trustee investments", local authorities generally borrow large sums from small investors.

loan, with the levying of a rate, is a matter which may not be delegated for the decision of a committee or a joint committee.[11]

When a loan has been raised, this will be repayable over a period agreed between the authority and the lender, and approved by the Secretary of State (as sanctioning authority), and therefore repayments of the loan (usually with interest thereon) will be a charge to the revenues of the authority for the period of the loan. Indeed, the repayment of instalments of loan capital and interest charges thereon is often the largest single item in any local authority's annual expenditure.

Apart from external borrowing, a local authority may also borrow from its own internal resources, such as the officers' superannuation fund, but even here the sanction of the Secretary of State to the raising of the loan will be necessary. An authority may also set up a fund to defray capital expenditure, provided not more than specified maximum sums are paid into the fund each year[12]; similar provisions relate to the establishment of a repairs and renewals fund.[13] Further, a local authority may invest capital in authorised securities or in an investment scheme prepared by an association of local authorities and approved by the Treasury, under section 11 of the Trustee Investments Act, 1961.

---

[11] L.G.A., 1972, s. 101 (6), and Chapter XIII, *ante*, p. 395.

[12] *Ibid.*, Schedule 13, paras. 16 and 17. The maximum sum at present is the product of a rate of 5p in the pound.

[13] *Ibid.*

CHAPTER XV

CONTROLS OVER LOCAL AUTHORITIES

1. INTRODUCTION

Local authorities in this country are not mere agents of the central government; they are, as already explained, independent bodies exercising functions conferred on them by statute in their own right.[1] This does not mean, however, that they are completely free agents in the same sense that Parliament is supreme. They are sovereign only within their powers and those powers are capable of being changed at any time by Parliament. They are therefore also subject to the control of the courts by the operation of the *ultra vires* doctrine, which has already been discussed elsewhere.[2] Whether the courts have jurisdiction to intervene in cases where a local authority has acted within its powers, but unfairly or in bad faith is a question open to doubt.[3]

If a local authority is given a discretion by statute to take such action "as it thinks fit", the court will normally expect them to exercise that discretion reasonably in the interest of their ratepayers,[4] and a power given to them by statute for a particular purpose or purposes can be exercised only in execution or furtherance of that purpose or those purposes.[5] However, when the statute gives no indication to the effect that a particular discretion must be exercised "reasonably", or in any particular manner, and there is no financial aspect to which the court can apply the doctrine that a local authority is in the position of trustee of the corporate funds in the interest of the ratepayers,[6] it would seem that the court will not fetter the discretion of the local authority, and will not reverse or modify a decision made on a matter of pure "policy".[7] Thus, where a local authority was entrusted with powers of "general management" of houses vested in them under the Housing Acts, the court would not quash the determination of a tenancy of a council house tenant or review the reasons which prompted the local authority to take that course of action provided it was clear that the tenancy was in fact determined pursuant to this power; *i.e.*, provided the court was satisfied the

---

1 Second Report of the Local Government Manpower Committee, 1951 (Cmd. Paper 8421).

2 See Chapter IX, *ante*, p. 302. The courts exercise control over local authorities by a number of different methods, by orders in the nature of the prerogative writs, actions for declaration, and in criminal or other proceedings instituted by a local authority to implement their policy, as discussed at Chapter IX, *ante*, p. 304.

3 See Chapter VI, *ante* p. 147.

4 *Roberts* v. *Hopwood*, [1925] A.C. 578; *post*, p. 429.

5 *Sydney Municipal Council* v. *Campbell*, [1925] A.C. 338.

6 *A.-G.* v. *Aspinall* (1837), 2 My. & Cr. 613.

7 As to the distinction between matters of "policy" and administration, see Chapter I, *ante*, p. 4.

authority were acting *intra vires*.[8] The courts will intervene so as to prevent a statute from becoming a cloak for fraud,[9] but they will not, on the grounds of an allegation of bad faith alone, ignore the precise terms of a statute, such as a provision to the effect that the validity of an administrative act, for example the making of a compulsory purchase order, may not be questioned in legal proceedings.[10] Powers given to a local authority by statute in unrestricted terms are not subject to control by the courts, except where some element of a financial nature is concerned,[11] or where there is some question of the authority acting outside their powers, so enabling the court to apply the *ultra vires* doctrine.[12] For example, the courts would probably not intervene so as to question the action of a local authority in determining (by proper notice) the tenancy of a council house occupied by a tenant who kept a dog, in execution of a policy adopted by the council in discrimination against dog owners generally. Such an attitude would involve matters of policy, not law, susceptible to correction through the ballot box, not the courts.

The principles of "natural justice", as known to the common law, freedom from bias and *audi alteram partem*, may be applied by the courts as a justification for the review of action taken by a local authority. The second principle, *audi alteram partem*, cannot often be applied, as the authority are rarely in the position of adjudicating in a *lis*, where there are two sides to hear or be heard. Freedom from bias has been given some measure of statutory recognition by sections 94–98 of the Local Government Act, 1972, previously discussed.[13] As there explained, bias on the part of one or more members of a local authority will be accepted by the courts as a justification for invalidating a decision of the authority only where they are acting judicially; but criminal proceedings may be instituted against any individual member so "interested". Special forms of judicial control are exercisable over a local authority's byelaws and these also are discussed elsewhere.[14]

Apart from the control effected by the courts, local authorities are subject to a number of other forms of control over their activities, some of which are precise and provided for by statute, which also depend in some measure on the doctrine of *ultra vires*. Thus, it is clear that an act of a local authority is invalid if the sanction or approval of a Minister of the Crown or some other governmental agency is not obtained, in a case where such sanction or approval is required under the enabling statute. Other controls are more general and indirect, in that if the authority make some unpopular decision their members may lose their seats at the next election, or if their actions are seriously opposed to the policy of the central government, unpleasant consequences may follow

[8] *Shelley* v. *London County Council*, [1948] 2 All E.R. 898; [1949] A.C. 56, explained in *St. Pancras B.C.* v. *Frey*, [1963] 2 All E.R. 124; [1963] 2 Q.B. 586.

[9] *Lazarus Estates, Ltd.* v. *Beasley*, [1956] 1 All E.R. 341; [1956] 1 Q.B. 702.

[10] *Smith* v. *East Elloe R.D.C.*, [1956] 1 All E.R. 855; [1956] A.C. 736.

[11] *Aspinall's case, ante; Prescott* v. *Birmingham Corpn.*, [1954] 3 All E.R. 698; [1955] Ch. 210 also had a financial element.

[12] Section 137 of the Local Government Act, 1972 gives a local authority certain limited spending powers of a very general nature: see Chapter IX, *ante*, page 303.

[13] Chapter XII, *ante*, p. 378.

[14] Chapter IV, *ante*, p. 82.

in the form of a reduction or stoppage of government grants or the taking of default action by a Minister of the Crown, at the expense of the local authority in default. These controls can be classified as administrative and political, and the various forms must now be considered.

2. ADMINISTRATIVE CONTROLS: GENERALLY

Administrative controls have at least one feature in common, in that they are provided for by law and that their ambit, *i.e.*, the area within which they may be operated, is circumscribed by law. They are, however, many and at times far-reaching; in fact the ubiquitousness of the controls that may be exercised by the organs of the central government over the manner in which a local authority exercise their administrative discretions may make a local authority appear (and feel) at times to be a mere department of the central government. Rarely do these controls take the form of naked directives, but the need to obtain Ministerial sanction before a financial loan can be raised, or before a draft order or byelaw made by the local authority acquires any legal effect, has the effect of making a local authority compliant to the Minister's will. This central direction is by no means always exercised from party political motives; often a local authority, a majority of whose members belong to the political party for the time being in power in the central government, will be seriously at variance with the Minister concerned over some local project. Disputes about boundary questions or the broader local government issues (such as the local administration of police forces) have divided politicians of the same party at both local and central levels. These controls are normally exercised rather in the name of efficiency and uniformity than as part of a party political programme, although the implementation of housing policies and more recently education policy, has proved to be an exception. Restrictions on capital expenditure imposed by Treasury controls are also the result of national policy, in which local government is regarded as one of several competitors for such capital as may be nationally available.

Central control of local government is, however, usually justified as being necessary in order to ensure that a minimum standard of efficiency is provided in the several local services. Local independence, it is urged, should not be permitted to such an extent that, for example, the fire service becomes inefficient or corrupt, or that one particular local authority offers a poorer education system than another. The advocates of improved standards for particular services—usually the experts in each service—would deny local authorities the right to make "wrong" decisions. The extent to which this attitude is allowed to influence the legislature, for all administrative controls must in England ultimately depend for their sanctions on legislation,[15] will depend to some extent on current standards and the importance ascribed to the particular service in prevailing public opinion. By the end of the nineteenth

[15] This is one of the results of the legal independence of local authorities in England. In so far as the mayor of a commune in France acts as a representative of the central government, he can be given orders from his superior the prefect. Even in matters of purely local concern the commune may be subject to the "tutelage" of the prefect or the central government. Such administrative sanctions are unknown in England, where ultimate reliance has to be put on the "ordinary" courts of law. A very different picture

century, it had become generally accepted that it was a proper concern of the then Local Government Board to ensure that reasonable sanitary standards were enforced and applied by local sanitary authorities, but there was no central supervision of many local services, such as the antiquated local fire brigades of the day, often still operated on a voluntary basis. The administration of the complicated housing legislation by local authorities is today subjected to most detailed supervision by the central government,[16] but local authorities are to a considerable extent left free to make their own decisions whether to provide many types of amenities for their inhabitants, such as recreation grounds, swimming pools, entertainments, etc.[17] Local government has not yet been put into a strait jacket to the extent that every authority must act or not act, exactly alike.

It is, however, the desire for greater freedom from central government control for local authorities, especially in view of the almost insuperable difficulties in the way of finding new sources of revenue, that was the strongest argument for the creation of large local authorities. The local authorities created by the 1972 Act, although not as substantial as the unitary authorities recommended by the Royal Commission, for the most part enjoy ample resources and are able to deal with central government Ministries on a more equal footing than was often possible in the past.

We must now consider the several types of central administrative control at present operating. They will be considered in three groups, namely, financial controls, "approval" controls, and directory and advisory controls.

3. FINANCIAL CONTROLS

These are by far the most important kind of administrative controls exercised by organs of the central government over the discretion[18] of local authorities. They may be sub-divided as follows.

(a) Applications for loan sanction.—No single local authority has financial resources adequate to finance all its capital expenditure from annual revenue; for major schemes they are obliged to borrow capital money. Indeed it would not be equitable to their present ratepayers if they were to finance such schemes out of revenue, for a policy of "pay as you go" would have the effect of casting the entire cost of a scheme or building which should be of benefit to future generations of ratepayers, on to the pockets of existing ratepayers, to be paid in one or possibly

is to be seen in Sweden, where local authorities have a general competence to administer their own affairs and they are subject to but slight administrative supervision. There is an interesting comparative study in Volume 4 of The Report of the Committee on the Management of Local Government (H.M.S.O., 1967).

[16] Through the medium of subsidies and the need to obtain loans for capital projects.

[17] This kind of freedom is particularly noticeable in connection with the "permissive powers", those conferred on local authorities by statute and which they are under no express duty to exercise. On this subject generally, see Griffith, *Central Departments and Local Authorities* (1966).

[18] "Discretion" is here used in the sense of the power to decide on specific action to be taken, in the course of exercising a particular function entrusted to a local authority by the legislature.

two years only. Section 172 and Schedule 13 of the Local Government Act, 1972, confers on all local authorities a general power to raise a loan for a number of purposes, and incorporates other general borrowing powers, subject in any such case to the consent of the sanctioning authority[19] being obtained.

Before this consent can be obtained the local authority will have to explain its proposals in considerable detail to the government department concerned, and the officers of that department will investigate the matter thoroughly. If the local authority's proposals involve development of any kind, the central officers will need to be assured that other interests (such as public utility undertakings, water authorities, highway authorities, etc.) have been consulted and that, where necessary, planning permission has been obtained for the project. The officials of the Department will investigate the financial aspects of the application, ensuring that the resources available to the local authority are adequate, they will satisfy themselves as to engineering and other technical procedures, often making suggestions on matters of technique or expertise, and they may also be concerned to ensure that general Departmental policy is being followed.[20] Further, if the local authority's proposals seem to be of a kind that may for one reason or another be likely to provoke local opposition, the Secretary of State may decide to hold a public local inquiry,[21] which will have to be advertised in advance and at which members of the public and local organisations will be allowed to make representations or observations. Even if the Secretary of State does not order the holding of a local inquiry, he will in most cases direct one of his inspectors to visit the local authority's offices and investigate the application as fully as possible. By this means the Department concerned may exercise a very considerable control over the activities of a local authority, as the Department may not only insist on the adoption of some particular technique, such as the use of less steel in the construction of a reservoir at a time when steel is nationally in short supply, but also they may prohibit completely, by withholding loan sanction, the adoption of a particular proposal, such as the erection of an incinerator for house refuse, on the ground that the central government (meaning probably in such case, the civil service experts) favour controlled tipping as a means of refuse disposal. This particular control, financial in purpose and statutory in form, is thus often used to enforce Government policy which is not necessarily exclusively financial. This is not to say that the courts would ever be able to intervene, on the argument that the Secretary of State had acted *ultra vires* in refusing to approve a particular application for loan sanction; his discretion is expressed in the statute in the widest possible terms and consequently is not normally capable of review in the courts.

In addition to the control over the raising of a loan, the Treasury

---

[19] In most circumstances the Secretary of State for the Environment.

[20] Sometimes of a most detailed kind. For example, a few years ago the Ministry insisted as a matter of policy that every house erected under the Housing Acts in respect of which a loan sanction was requested, was to be provided with an outside w.c. in addition to that provided within the dwelling.

[21] A public inquiry will usually be convened if the proposal involves the erection of a building, such as a refuse incinerator, which may offend against local amenities.

exercises a further control, under the Borrowing (Control and Guarantees) Act, 1946, over the sources from which local authorities may from time to time be allowed to borrow, and the rates of interest chargeable to local authorities by the Public Works Loan Board. The power given by section 11 of the Trustee Investments Act, 1961, enabling local authorities to combine to form an investment fund, is also subject to Treasury approval. In recent years some local authorities have considered it financially desirable to borrow money from foreign sources, but in order to do so formerly they had to obtain statutory authority by means of a local Bill; now Treasury consent alone is necessary.[22]

(b) Audit.—Since the creation under the influence of Chadwick of the poor law boards of guardians by the Poor Law Amendment Act, 1834,[1] the principle that the accounts of local authorities should be subjected to audit by central government inspectors has been accepted by Parliament. During the present century, until the passing of the L.G.A., 1972, it was the accepted principle in Whitehall that all local authority accounts *ought* to be audited by the district auditors appointed by and responsible to the Secretary of State for the Environment.[2] Although the law allowed certain accounts of borough councils to be audited by professional auditors or by the antiquated system of elected auditors, this was actively discouraged in Whitehall. However, the Act of 1972[3] allows county councils and district councils to choose between district audit and audit by an "approved auditor" (*i.e.* by a qualified provisional auditor approved by the Secretary of State)[4]; district councils may make the choice for parishes or communities within their district, and any such authority may change their mind subsequently. The accounts of the Greater London Council and the London borough Councils are all however, subject to district audit.[5]

Any auditor, "district" or "approved", must, of course, carry out a proper financial check of the accounts; in addition he is expressly required[6] to ensure that regulations made by the Secretary of State as to accounts[7] have been followed, and that proper accounting practices have been observed. He has a right of access to all necessary documents,[8] and any person interested may inspect all books, etc., produced at audit[9]; in addition, a local government elector for the area has a right to question the auditor about the accounts.[10] After the conclusion of the audit, the auditor must send a report on the audit within 14 days to the local authority and this report must be included in the business of the appropriate meeting of the local authority at which the press are present.[11] The powers of district and approved

---

22 L.G.A., 1972, Schedule 13, para. 2 (2).

1 See Redlich and Hurst's *History of Local Government in England*, ed. Keith-Lucas at pp. 103 *et seq.*

2 L.G.A., 1972, s. 156.

3 *Ibid.*, s. 154.

4 *Ibid.*, s. 164.

5 *Ibid.*, s. 154 (2) (b).

6 *Ibid.*, s. 157.

7 *Ibid.*

8 *Ibid.*, s. 158.

9 *Ibid.*, s. 159 (1).

10 *Ibid.*, s. 159 (2).

11 *Ibid.*, s. 160.

auditors respectively in the event of any irregularity appearing on the audit are different, as appears below.

(i) *District Auditors.*—If a district auditor considers that any item of account is "contrary to law", he may apply to the High Court (or, if a small sum only is involved, to the local county court) for a direction to that effect, *unless* the item has been sanctioned by the Secretary of State (see below).[12] On such an application the court may refuse to make the declaration, or, if they do make a declaration, they may order that any person responsible for incurring or authorising the illegal expenditure shall repay it in whole or in part. If any sum so ordered to be repaid exceeds £2,000, the court may order the person concerned (if he is a member of a local authority) to be disqualified from being a member of a local authority for a specified period. An order to repay, or a disqualification order, may not be made if the court is satisfied that the person responsible "acted reasonably or in the belief that the expenditure was authorised by law".[13]

If the district auditor considers that some person has failed to bring into account some sum that should have been so included, or that a loss has been incurred, or deficiency caused by the "wilful misconduct"[14] of any person, the auditor may certify that the sum concerned is due from that person; the sum may then be recovered from that person by the district auditor or by the local authority.[15]

Any local government elector for the area may attend before the district auditor and make objections to any of the accounts.[16] If the district auditor does not then apply for a declaration and the elector is "aggrieved", the elector may require the auditor to state his reasons within a period of six weeks; a similar right is given to any person against whom a certificate has been made by the district auditor to the effect that a sum of money is due from him. In either case a person aggrieved by the auditor's decision may then appeal to the court.[17]

This procedure replaces the former powers[18] of the district auditor to disallow an item of account and surcharge the amount on the person responsible. Except in cases of dishonesty or wilful misconduct, the court has been interposed between the auditor and the person responsible (who may be a member *or* an officer of the local authority[19]).

In practice these powers of the district auditor are very important. They may be exercised in such a manner as to operate as a control over a discretionary power vested in the local authority by statute. Thus,

---

[12] *Ibid.*, s. 161 (1).

[13] *Ibid.*, s. 161 (2) and (3).

[14] The former section included the word "negligence", which was considered in *Pentecost* v. *London District Auditor*, [1951] 2 All E.R. 330; [1951] 2 K.B. 759. A deliberate decision to break the law on the part of members of a local authority amounts to "misconduct": *Asher v. Lacey*, [1973] 3 All E.R. 1008.

[15] L.G.A., 1972, s. 16 1(4). Similarly disqualification will apply if the amount is in excess of £2,000, in any case of wilful misconduct: s. 161 (7).

[16] *Ibid.*, s. 159 (3).

[17] *Ibid.*, s. 161 (5) and (6).

[18] See L.G.A., 1933, s. 226–230.

[19] But cannot be a third party, such as a contractor: *Re a Decision of a District Auditor*, [1947] 2 All E.R. 47; [1947] K.B. 879.

in the famous case of *Roberts* v. *Hopwood*,[20] the relevant statute empowered the local authorities to pay their employees such wages "as they may think fit", there being no indication in the statute as to how this discretion was to be exercised. Nevertheless, when the Poplar Borough Council paid certain of its employees wages in excess of those generally ruling in the locality because it was of opinion that the latter were too low, the district auditor disallowed the excess wages as being unreasonable in the interests of the ratepayers, and therefore contrary to law, and his decision was upheld by the House of Lords on appeal. Again, in *Taylor* v. *Munrow*,[1] the local authority was under a statutory duty to review from time to time the rents charged by landlords of premises which had formerly been held under requisition by the authority and to subsidise tenants out of the general rate fund where it was considered that the increased rents that the landlords were allowed to charge by law would cause hardship to the tenants. The authority decided that all increases in rent of such premises which were permissible under the Rent Act, 1957, should be paid by the Council, its reasons for so deciding being based on a dislike of the political policy underlying the 1957 Act. The district auditor disallowed the consequent payments, on the ground that the local authority must preserve a balance between its duty to the general body of ratepayers and its duty under the statute to the tenants; this balance had not been kept and therefore the payments were contrary to law. These decisions were really based on an application of the doctrine of *ultra vires*; the discretion vested in the local authority by the statute was in each case held to be subject to the implied intention of the statute that the discretion should be exercised reasonably and with due regard to the financial interests of the ratepayers. This aspect of the exercise of the powers of district auditors is considered more fully in Chapter IX.[2]

In any case where a local authority wish to take a certain course of action involving expenditure, and it is clear that they have no legal powers to incur that expenditure, or where the legal position is doubtful, it has become customary for them to ask the Secretary of State for the Environment to sanction the expenditure, under the provision in s. 161 (1) of the 1972 Act.[3] The effect of this sanction, if granted, is that the district auditor will then not be able to apply for a declaration or issue a certificate in respect of any expenditure so sanctioned. The Secretary of State is quite unfettered in the exercise of his discretion to grant sanction; in practice it is often used to permit expenditure on ceremonial matters such as the purchase of robes for members of a borough council or local celebrations at times of national rejoicing.[4] The sanction does not, however, legalise the payment; the legality

---

[20] [1925] A.C. 578; Chapter VI, *ante*, p. 148.

[1] [1960] 1 All E.R. 455; [1960] 1 W.L.R. 151.

[2] *Ante*, pp. 302 *et seq.*

[3] Formerly the proviso to s. 228 (1) of the L.G.A., 1933.

[4] At the time of the coronation of Her present Majesty in 1953, the then Minister gave a general sanction by Circular to all local authorities in respect of any expenditure reasonably incurred in respect of local celebrations.

of expenditure may still be questioned in the courts in proceedings for a declaration[5] or one of the prerogative orders.[6]

This sanction of the Secretary of State under this provision provides an effective central government control over the extraordinary expenditure of local authorities. Over the years a considerable body of precedent has been built up as to the type of expenditure that will, and will not, be sanctioned, and decisions are noted from time to time in the professional press. The control exercised by the auditors themselves is more direct and definite in operation; it is rather that of a watchdog whose duty it is to ensure that the authority keeps within the limits set by Parliament; nevertheless, general advice about administrative and financial methods proffered by district auditors to local authority officers in the course of their audit visits is always carefully considered and often followed, even where there is no question of any irregularity. In this informal way district auditors are able to impose certain minimum standards of accountancy methods and related matters on most local authorities in the country. Moreover, the Secretary of State may at any time direct a district auditor to hold an extraordinary audit of any accounts of a local authority (without their consent)[7]; this is a power which is usually exercised only where there is some reason to suspect peculation or misappropriation of funds.

(ii) *Approved Auditors*.—Where the audit is conducted by an approved auditor the powers to apply for a declaration or issue a certificate do not apply, but if such an auditor considers that any item of account is contrary to law, or that some item has not been brought to account that should have been so included, or if a loss has been incurred or deficiency caused by the wilful misconduct of some person, he is under an express duty forthwith to report the matter to the Secretary of State, who may then consider whether he should order a district auditor to hold an extraordinary audit of the accounts.[8]

(c) Grants.—The general subject of grants has already been considered[9]; it is obvious that when a particular service may be the subject of grants in aid, the control exercisable by the central government department concerned over the local authority receiving the grants will be of the closest. This was at one time particularly noticeable in relation to the education and personal health services, in respect of which grants in aid were paid to the extent of 60 per cent of all approved expenditure. It was indeed the desire to give further freedom to local authorities that led to the withdrawal of these grants and the substitution of an exchequer grant in the Local Government Act, 1958. However, this type of detailed control still exists in relation to highways, where grants in aid may in the case of some classes of roads be as high as 75 per cent of expenditure. In housing also substantial grants are

[5] At common law, outside the Act. See Chapter VI, *ante*, p. 188; Chapter IX, *ante*, p. 304.

[6] Chapter VI, *ante*, p. 177.

[7] Whether the audit has originally been carried out by a district auditor or by an approved auditor.

[8] L.G.A., 1972, s. 162.

[9] Chapter XIV, *ante*, p. 414.

still paid in certain circumstances,[10] and as a consequence the Secretary of State may insist on being satisfied that the quite detailed standards of construction laid down in the Housing Manual and its current amendments are observed.

Following the precedent of earlier statutes, section 4 of the Local Government Act, 1966[11] empowers the Secretary of State to reduce the rate support grant payable to a local authority in any case where the recipient authority has

> "failed to achieve or maintain a reasonable standard in the discharge of any of their functions, regard being had to the standards maintained by other authorities . . ."

If the practice under the corresponding sections in earlier Acts is any guide, it seems unlikely that this section will frequently (if ever) be used; it rather exists *in terrorem*, as a justification for the Secretary of State to require local authorities to maintain certain standards of administration. It may also be regarded as a basic legal authority for the practice of the various government departments to give gratuitous advice to local authorities on many subjects.

The Secretary of State may also make regulations for prescribing standards and general requirements in relation to any local authority function[12]; this again is a provision that has not often been used in practice, except in connection with the education service.

4. "APPROVAL" CONTROLS

Under this heading we are considering a number of administrative controls exercisable by a government department over the discretionary powers of local authorities. They all have a statutory origin, and they all take the form of a consent or approval that has to be obtained from the Central Department before the act of the local authority is complete or legally effective. In this class of control there is no question of any active intervention or meddling by the Central Government in the affairs of the local authority; the initiative is at local level and the local authority is required by statute to obtain paternal approval, as it were, to its projects. The occasions on which approval of this kind may have to be obtained may be considered as follows:

(a) *Compulsory purchase orders, etc.*—Confirmation by the appropriate government department is an integral part of the procedure whereby a local authority may be empowered to acquire a particular parcel of land compulsorily. As a preliminary to the giving (or withholding) of such confirmation, the appropriate Minister (normally the Secretary of State for the Environment) will order the holding of a local inquiry into any objections received by him. The procedure before the inquiry must be "quasi-judicial" in nature,[13] but in coming to his decision the Minister is not bound to follow his inspector's report and he may be governed by questions of policy. Similar to the procedure

---

[10] *Ibid., ante,* p. 415.
[11] This is to be re-enacted in the Local Government Bill.
[12] 1966 Act, s. 4 (2), replacing s. 3 (4) of the Local Government Act, 1958.
[13] Chapter VIII, *ante,* p. 230.

on compulsory purchase orders is the power given to the Minister to confirm (or quash) a variety of other orders and schemes made by local authorities, such as clearance orders under Part III of the Housing Act, 1957, public path orders of various kinds and access orders under the Highways Act, 1959 and the National Parks and Access to the Countryside Act, 1949, and development plans under the Town and Country Planning Act, 1971.

(b) *Schemes.*—A number of statutes require local authorities to prepare schemes for the administration of a particular service, and in these cases the scheme will have to be submitted for the approval of the appropriate Minister. Examples are development schemes under the Education Act, 1944, and schemes for organisation of local valuation courts under the Local Government Act, 1948.[14] In these cases the control of the central department concerned is very real; there are rarely any private interests to be considered (as in the case of orders falling within sub-para. (a) above), and the officials of the Department are therefore free to scrutinise (and usually do) the whole scheme in detail.

(c) *Byelaws.*—The procedure for the making of byelaws under sections 235–238 of the Local Government Act, 1972, has already been described elsewhere,[15] and it will be remembered that confirmation by the appropriate Minister is an essential step in that procedure. In practice this control is exercised very strictly, and a Minister will rarely agree to confirm byelaws which differ from the model series issued by his Department.[16] Local initiative in drafting new byelaws will have to be capable of justification by reference to very special local circumstances, except in the unusual case where no model series have been prepared for the particular byelaw making power.

(d) *Discretionary powers.*—Certain discretionary powers vested by statute in local authorities, incapable of classification, are made exercisable "subject to the approval of the Minister". Such are the powers of a county council to undertake the provision of housing accommodation[17] and a number of certain kinds of land transactions by local authorities,[18] and also the somewhat different powers of the Secretary of State to direct a local authority to cease taking certain action in relation to an emergency or disaster in their area.[19]

---

[14] Schemes for the delegation of a service to another authority are another case where Departmental approval formerly had to be obtained, but this is no longer necessary under s. 101 of the L.G.A., 1972.

[15] Chapter IV, *ante*, p. 80.

[16] This was particularly noticeable in the context of building byelaws under Part II of the Public Health Act, 1936. Indeed these had become so standardised as a consequence of strict Ministerial control, that the change to a series of building regulations made by the Minister and applicable to the whole country, was effected in February 1966 under powers conferred by the Public Health Act, 1961, with scarcely any protests from local authorities.

[17] L.G.A., 1972, s. 194 (2).

[18] *Ibid.*, ss. 121 (1), 122 (3), 123 (2).

[19] *Ibid.*, s. 138 (2). A number of the less important instances where the consent or approval of the Secretary of State has to be obtained under existing legislation will be removed by the Local Government Bill.

In many of these cases it will be found in practice that the officials advising the Minister have devised a series of standards or rules which will be applied in any particular case when approval is sought. If the case falls within these standards or rules, which are of course extra-legal, and their content is often not known to the local authorities concerned, approval will be granted. If approval cannot be obtained, the only remedy open to the local authority is the extra-legal one of making representations to the local Member of Parliament.

(e) *Appointment and dismissal of officers.*—Before 1974, the law provided in several instances[20] for the consent of the appropriate Minister being obtained to the appointment by a local authority of an individual to fill a named post under the employment of the authority. This control remains in relation to certain senior police officers,[1] but it has otherwise been abolished by the Local Government Act, 1972. In general, section 112 of that Act empowers any local authority to appoint "officers as they think necessary", with the proviso that certain named officers (*e.g.*, chief education officers, inspectors of weights and measures, etc.) *must* be appointed.[2] In a few of these cases the persons selected for such appointments must hold qualifications prescribed by the appropriate Minister.[3]

A chief constable may be called on to retire "in the interests of efficiency", by the police authority, but only with the approval of the Secretary of State.[4]

5. DIRECTORY AND ADVISORY CONTROLS

Under this heading we are considering a number of central controls whereby the government agency concerned can give directions and/or advice to local authorities. If directions are ignored, legal consequences will, or may, follow; if procedure prescribed under statutory authority is not followed, for example, the action taken by the authority may in some cases be legally invalidated, and in other cases expenditure may be rendered illegal.[5] If advice contained in a Departmental circular or letter is ignored, however, legal consequences will not often result immediately, but the central department may be able to bring the recalcitrant authority to heel by the exercise of some other control, such as the reduction or withdrawal of a grant in aid or possibly even the rate support grants.[6]

These controls may be considered under the following sub-headings:

---

[20] In relation to chief education officers, in particular: Education Act, 1944, s. 88.

[1] Police Act, 1964: Chapter XVI, *post*, pp. 441 *et seq.*.

[2] See L.G.A., 1972 s. 112 (4).

[3] Weights and Measures Act, 1963, s. 42; Local Authority Social Services Act, 1970, s. 6.

[4] Police Act, 1964, s. 5 (4).

[5] For example, if the procedure prescribed by regulations as to allowances payable to members, made under s. 178 of the L.G.A., 1972, is not followed, payments made may be illegal and be made the subject of an application for a declaration by the district auditor (*ante*, p. 428).

[6] Chapter XIV, *ante*, p. 417.

(a) *Regulations.*—In many instances statutes empower Ministers to prescribe an administrative procedure to be followed in the course of putting the policy of the statute into effect[7]; sometimes this may go so far into detail as to empower the Minister to prescribe a set of forms to be used for certain purposes.[8] In other cases a statute may empower the Minister to fill out the details of the statute, and to prescribe the detailed circumstances in which the general principles of the statute are to apply. These are of course but specialised applications of the normal features of delegated legislation[9] to the context of local government, but it is important to appreciate that by this means detailed orders may be given by the central agency to the local authority. In these cases more than mere advice is involved; the instructions have the force of law.[10]

(b) *Inspection.*—In four services—education, children, police and fire brigades[11]—the appropriate Central Department concerned maintains a body of inspectors whose duties are to visit local authorities throughout the country and to report to their Departments on the respective standards of efficiency. The inspectors of constabulary are linked to the grant in aid system, approval of local expenditure ranking for grant being governed very much by the advice of the inspectors, and this was also the origin of the Education Inspectorate. Since the coming into effect of the Local Government Act, 1958, however, the education service has no longer attracted the substantial grants in aid that were formerly paid, and this justification for the inspectorate no longer exists. Education inspectors therefore have little more than an advisory status, but they maintain a high standard and their advice and suggestions are still listened to with considerable respect.

(c) *Directions.*—In some circumstances, a Minister may be empowered to give directions to a particular local authority, as distinct from powers to make regulations of general effect. Thus, the Secretary of State for the Environment may direct a local planning authority to refer an application for permission to develop land to him for his decision, instead of deciding the application itself.[12] Directions are in a sense a form of subordinate legislation, in that they are made under statutory authority, and they have legal effect, but they are particular, not general in operation, and they will not normally be required to be made by statutory instrument.[13]

---

[7] Sometimes this may be effected by circular letter, and not by formal regulations, as for example, the standards prescribed for the making of improvement grants under the Housing Act, 1969, and for caravan sites under the Caravan Sites and Control of Development Act, 1960, s. 5 (6).

[8] As under the Housing Act, 1957.

[9] See Chapter IV, *ante*, p. 51.

[10] The prices and incomes and the "counter-inflation" legislation had an important impact on the freedom of local authorities, in particular in relation to the rents of Council houses.

[11] District auditors, considered above, might also be considered to be inspectors in the present sense. "Inspectors" appointed to hold local inquiries into compulsory purchase orders, etc., have restricted functions only and are not inspectors in the present sense.

[12] Town and Country Planning Act, 1971, s. 35.

[13] Chapter IV, *ante*, p. 60.

(d) *Circulars.*—Every government department concerned to any extent with the general supervision of a local government service will from time to time proffer general advice by means of circular letters to local authorities. In this way changes in government policy, advice on particular difficulties and information as to technical developments and the results of research[14] are notified to local authorities. Information on a variety of topics and statistical returns[15] are often called for from all or particular kinds of local authorities; rarely are authorities put under any express legal obligation to provide this information[16] but it is normally required for a good reason and furnished with good grace.

The legal background for the type of controls discussed in this paragraph, especially the last mentioned one of giving advice, is in some services to be found in the general words of a statute conferring supervisory duties on the Minister concerned. Thus, section 1 of the Minister of Town and Country Planning Act, 1943 (now repealed) charged that Minister with the duty of

> "securing consistency and continuity in the framing and execution of a national policy with respect to the use and development of land throughout England and Wales".

Section 1 of the Education Act, 1944, confers on the Secretary of State for Education and Science a duty

> "to promote the education of the people of England and Wales and the progressive development of institutions devoted to that purpose, and to secure the effective execution by local authorities under his control and direction of the national policy for providing a varied and comprehensive educational service in every area".

Duties phrased in such vague, if well turned, terms are scarcely capable of enforcement in a court of law,[17] but they afford justification, which perhaps is scarcely needed, for the kind of supervisory action by the central department which at times may be regarded as "meddling" by the recipient local authority. In other cases there is no statutory authority at all justifying the giving of advice.

(e) Default powers.—In the exceptional case, a central department may have recourse to the "big stick" of a default power. These are given to the department concerned in a number of statutes, including the Housing Acts of 1957 and 1958, and the Public Health Act, 1936; in some cases they may be exercised by the Minister *proprio motu*, whilst in others the statute provides machinery whereby a member of the public may complain to the Minister about an alleged default by a local authority[18] and so endeavour to spur him to take default action. In

---

[14] Such as the reports of the Road Research Laboratory, the Building Research Station and the National Water Council.

[15] Especially those of a financial nature—the product of a penny rate, projected capital expenditure of the authority, etc.

[16] But see L.G.A., 1972, s. 230.

[17] Compare the general statutory duties imposed on statutory corporations: Chapter X, *ante*, p. 327.

[18] For example, Public Health Act, 1936, s. 322.

practice these powers are rarely used,[19] but they exist in the background, as it were, to give teeth to the Minister's advice and directions. In spite of the many controls vested by statute in the various government departments, a persistent local authority can if it wishes exercise a considerable degree of autonomy.[20]

6. OTHER ADMINISTRATIVE CONTROLS

Apart from controls exercisable by a Minister over the discretionary powers of local authorities as above described, there are a few cases where a county council may exercise some measure of control over the discretionary powers of district and parish councils within the county.[1] Thus every county council has certain reserve powers in relation to housing, and with the approval of the Secretary of State, they may undertake the provision of housing accommodation within a county district.[2]

A district council has certain administrative functions in relation to parishes or communities within the district. Thus, it may make an order for the grouping of parishes,[3] must provide for the establishment of a parish council for a parish having a population of more than 200,[4] or may dissolve an existing parish council for a parish of a population of less than 150.[5] Where a parish or community council desire to acquire land compulsorily the order may be made (after due inquiry) for them by the district council[6]; a parish or community council may borrow money with the consent of the Secretary of State, but they do not also require the consent of the county or district council.[7] A district council is also responsible for reviewing the boundaries of and electoral arrangements for parishes[8] in the district and making recommendations for the revision thereof to the appropriate Boundary Commission.[9]

---

19 Often there is a political background, as in the case a few years ago, when the Labour-controlled Coventry Corporation refused to carry out their civil defence functions and the Conservative Government of the day exercised their default powers, and carried on a civil defence service for the City by a Commissioner appointed by the Minister. The cost of administering this service was then charged by the Minister to the City's rate fund. The Housing Finance Act, 1972, contains special powers for the Secretary of State to make an order declaring a local authority to be in default in discharging their functions under the Act in the matter of rent rebates and charging fair rents for council houses (*inter alia*). After such an order has been made, the Secretary of State may appoint a Housing Commissioner who will have power to discharge the defaulting local authority's functions at their expense. The Secretary of State may also reduce the payment of any housing subsidies from central government funds to any defaulting authority (see Housing Finance Act, 1972, ss. 95–99).

20 See, for example, Professor Keith-Lucas' interesting historical account of "Poplarism", at [1962] P.L. 52.

1 Normally the relationship between the county council and their district councils is that of an informal partnership, and a district council is in no sense subservient to the county council; Chapter XI, *ante*, p. 370.

2 L'G.A., 1972, s. 194.

3 *Ibid.*, s. 11 (4) and s. 29 (Wales).

4 *Ibid.*, s. 9; there is no precisely similar provision for Wales.

5 *Ibid.*, s. 10; again there is no provision for Wales.

6 *Ibid.*, s. 125.

7 *Ibid.*, Schedule 13.

8 Communities in Wales.

9 L.G.A., 1972, ss. 48 (8) and 57 (4).

7. POLITICAL CONTROLS

As well as judicial and administrative controls, all local authorities are subject, as indeed is the central government itself, to political controls, exercisable by public opinion often expressed through the Press, and ultimately exerted through the medium of the ballot box. Apart from the actual machinery of elections, in order that this form of control may be effective at all, the public must be informed of the conduct of affairs by the local authority. Primarily this is assured through the media of the Press and broadcasting, and Parliament has made certain provisions for ensuring that sources of information shall be available for the Press.[10]

Apart from the powers of the Press, however, there are a number of statutory provisions giving rights to members of the public as such. The more important of these are the following:

(a) The right to attend meetings of the authority and of any committees thereof consisting of all the members of the authority.[11]

(b) The right to inspect accounts, question the auditor and where the audit is conducted by a district auditor, to attend before him and make objections to the accounts.[12]

(c) The right to inspect copies of the minutes of proceedings of the authority, and to make copies thereof or extracts therefrom[13] and to take similar action in relation to orders for payment.[14]

(d) The right to inspect the authority's abstract of accounts and to make a copy or extract thereof.[15] This of course savours rather of "bolting the stable door", as long before the abstract is published all the expenditure to which it relates will have been incurred, but such an inspection may result in objections to the district auditor under s. 159 of the L.G.A., 1972.

(e) The right to inspect registers of various kinds, ranging from the register of planning applications[16] and the register of local land charges[17] to the register of allowances paid to members of the authority.[18]

---

[10] In particular by the Public Bodies (Admission to Meetings) Act, 1960, as amended by s. 100 of the L.G.A., 1972, discussed in Chapter XIII, *ante*, p. 391.

[11] *Ibid.*

[12] L.G.A., 1972, s. 159, *ante*, p. 427.

[13] *Ibid.*, s. 228 (1). "Minutes" of the authority in this context has a restricted meaning, and does not include minutes of the meeting of a committee of the authority, even one acting with delegated powers: *Wilson* v. *Evans*, [1962] 1 All E.R. 247; [1962] 2 Q.B. 383.

[14] *Ibid.*, s. 228 (2).

[15] *Ibid.*, s. 228 (3) and (4).

[16] Town and Country Planning Act, 1971, s. 34 and Town and Country Planning (General Development) Order, 1973 (S.I. 1973 No. 31) art. 17.

[17] Land Charges Act, 1925, s. 15. Inspection will here usually take the form of applying for an official search, but personal searches also are permissible.

[18] Local Government (Members' Allowances) Regulations, 1948 (S.I. 1948 No. 1784), art. 6 (1), made under ss. 113 and 117 of the L.G.A., 1948; and see now s. 178 of the L.G.A., 1972.

(f) The right to inspect various documents that are required by statute to be placed on deposit at the offices of the local authority, such as the statutory statement as to public rights of way under the National Parks and Access to the Countryside Act, 1949, the development plan under the Town and Country Planning Act, 1971, and such documents made by the local authority as draft byelaws, clearance orders under the Housing Act, 1957, and compulsory purchase orders.

In some cases the statute empowers the local authority to make a small charge for allowing the applicant to inspect the document in question; but, unless expressly otherwise so provided, the inspection may be made free of charge.[19] In some cases the right to inspect is conferred on all members of the public or on "persons interested" only, and in other cases only on local government electors for the area.[20]

Control by individual members of Parliament over the activities of local authorities is non-existent. Occasionally a local constituent may write to his Member of Parliament complaining of the action or inaction of his local authority; the most that the Member can do in such a case is to write to the proper officer of the authority concerned and ask for his observations on the matter, and then reply to the constituent accordingly. Similarly, the Secretary of State for the Environment (or any other Minister) will refuse to answer questions in the House of Commons about action taken by or matters concerning a local authority, such matters not being his responsibility. Members of Parliament, no more than Ministers of the Crown or even the Government itself, are not responsible for the acts (or inactivities) of local authorities, who remain independent bodies in their own right, in spite of the many detailed controls exercisable by the various governmental agencies as herein explained. This position will not be affected by the creation of Commissioners for Local Administration,[21] but the establishment of this means of "ventilating grievances" will give members of the public a very valuable means of checking maladministration in local government.

---

[19] L.G.A., 1972, s. 228 (5).

[20] The right is reinforced in the L.G.A., 1972, by a provision making it an offence to obstruct any person entitled, from making a copy, etc., of any document, or from inspecting it; see s. 228 (7). Special provision is made by s. 229, *ibid.*, for the keeping of photographic copies instead of originals.

[21] Chapter V, *ante*, p. 104.

CHAPTER XVI

LOCAL AUTHORITY SERVICES

1. INTRODUCTION

In this Chapter it is intended to outline, as briefly as possible, the more important functions of local authorities. Some indication has already been given of the manner in which these functions are at present divided between the different local authorities,[1] and in this Chapter we are concerned only incidentally with the class of authority responsible for the administration of any particular service. The many functions entrusted by Parliament—for all local government functions must emanate from Parliament[2]—to local authorities defy any logical classification. There are few, if any, functions of government which by their nature must necessarily in any governmental system be administered by independent local bodies. That this is true can be seen from the ease of the transfer of functions between central and local government in recent years[3] and from examples in other countries; in France, for example, roads and bridges are administered by a Central Department, and in parts of the United States local authorities have a wider range of independent functions than they have in this country.

Until the nineteenth century English local government was almost exclusively a matter of maintenance of public order. This in itself was confined to an inefficient police force, the "watch" of Shakespearean fame, a poor law of considerable rigour, and ill-defined and poorly executed duties for the maintenance of highways. In the towns such local government as there was was in the hands of close corporations, many members of whom were corrupt and inefficient, and in the country districts it was administered by the magistrates. Control from the centre was virtually non-existent, depending, as we have seen, almost exclusively on the courts by means of the prerogative writs. The nineteenth century brought the industrial revolution, the break-down of the old poor law and cholera epidemics in the towns. The pre-1974 organisation of boroughs and urban local authorities and later of the county and rural district councils was the result, the principal function of the new authorities being sewerage and sewage disposal; a service which in 1974 was very largely taken out of local government control.[4] As the industrialisation of the country developed, so the need for further controls over private development was gradually appreciated, and further functions were created by statute and entrusted to local govern-

---

[1] See Chapter XI, *ante*, p. 361; as to recent revisions see Chapter XIII, *ante*, p. 405.
[2] This is because local authorities are themselves creatures of Parliament and are subject to the *ultra vires* doctrine.
[3] Chapter XIII, *ante*, p. 401.
[4] Water Act, 1973; *post*, p. 444.

ment; housing and (later) town and country planning and the personal health services in particular.

At the turn of the century, the rise of advanced thinkers in many of the newly created local authorities, the Fabians in the Metropolitan Boroughs[5] and the Liberals in Birmingham in particular, with their desire to raise the standard of living of the "working classes", led to an intensive period of municipal enterprise. Gas, electricity and water supply, tramways, public parks, markets and wash houses became local government functions largely by the initiative of the local authorities themselves, either by obtaining local Acts or by adopting permissive powers given generally in "Clauses Acts" or other statutes. By the middle of the present century, the standard of civilisation demanded better housing and education and a wide range of personal, almost paternal, services characterised by the expression "welfare" (or, more recently, "the social services"), and comprising the care of the sick, the young, the elderly, the mentally ill and the disabled. Voluntary effort has played a great part in the development of these services and the work of the volunteer is still by no means redundant, but social welfare is now to a very considerable extent the responsibility of local government, subject to the general supervision of central Departments.

Like so many others, the present has been said to be an age of transition in local government, and some indication has already been given[6] of present-day problems of local government boundaries and organisation and the recent reforms. As we have said, there is no logical classification of local government functions, but we propose to consider them in an order approximately corresponding to the chronological order in which they were entrusted to local government. We shall therefore start with roads, deal next with police, in the broader sense of public control generally, then consider the sanitary and public hygiene services, town and country planning, the public utility services, and finally the social services and the administration of justice.

2. HIGHWAYS

The quality of a country's roads has always been a measure of its standard of civilisation, from Roman times to the present day, so concerned with trunk roads and "motorways". Traditionally in this country the maintenance of highways—ways over which the law guarantees to all[7] of Her Majesty's subjects a right to pass and repass on their lawful occasions—has been the concern of the "inhabitants at large". Since 1959[8] however, this duty has been placed expressly on the highway authority. The identity of the highway authority for any particular highway depends on the status and location of that highway. Thus, for special roads and trunk roads, the highway authority is the Secretary

---

[5] G. B. Shaw was a member of the St. Marylebone Metropolitan Borough Council for several years at this period.

[6] Chapter XIII, *ante*, p. 400.

[7] In the case of a "special road" however, particular classes of "traffic"—including "animals ridden, led or driven" or "pedestrians"—may be excluded altogether: see Highways Act, 1959, s. 12 and Schedule 4.

[8] Highways Act, 1959, s. 38.

of State for the Environment, their maintenance not being strictly speaking the concern of local government[9]; in other cases the county council (in both metropolitan and non-metropolitan areas) is the highway authority.[10] District councils, however, have powers of maintenance (only) in respect of footpaths, bridleways and urban roads, and additional powers may be delegated to them by the county council.[11]

The highway authority has full powers of management of the surface of the highway; they are in law owners of sufficient of the surface, the "top two spits",[12] and of the air above the surface, to enable them to carry out their duties as highway authority, and they have powers to widen or improve the highway; they may now be liable in an action for damages at the suit of someone injured if they fail to keep the road surface or drains in repair.[13]

Street cleansing is the responsibility of the district council,[14] which is not necessarily the highway authority; street lighting also is now normally the responsibility of the highway authority,[15] and the erection and maintenance of a number of traffic signs is the responsibility (on any class of highway) of the Secretary of State, whilst other signs can be erected only with his approval. The police authority also has some responsibilities in highway and road traffic law, and consequently there is no one authority responsible for "traffic management," or "la circulation", as the French call it, even in relation to one particular road.[16]

3. PUBLIC ORDER

This function, one of the most important of any government, is in this country almost exclusively the concern of local government. It may be considered under several headings.

(a) Police.—The idea of the independence of the local authority police forces from central control has always been regarded in this country as one of the essential guarantees of personal liberty. Apart from the Metropolitan Force, which is responsible for an area almost, but not precisely, corresponding to that of the G.L.C.,[17] and which is directly administered by the Home Office, the responsibility for administration of those forces that have not been amalgamated with other areas, remains

---

[9] The Minister may, and to a considerable extent does in practice, delegate the maintenance of special and trunk roads to county borough and county councils.

[10] L.G.A., 1972, s. 187.

[11] Under the general delegation clause in s. 101, *ibid.*

[12] See the judgment of DENNING, L.J., in *Tithe Redemption Commissioners* v. *Runcorn U.D.C.*, [1954] 1 All E.R. 653; [1954] Ch. 383.

[13] A highway authority was not formerly liable in nonfeasance; Highways Act, 1959, s. 298, but see the Highways (Miscellaneous Provisions) Act, 1961, and Chapter IX, *ante*, p. 299.

[14] See the Protection of the Environment Bill.

[15] Except for footpath lighting, which may be the responsibility of some authority other than the highway authority: Local Government Act, 1966, Part III.

[16] In Greater London, however, this is the responsibility of the G.L.C.

[17] The Metropolitan Police Area excludes the City of London, which retains its separate Force administered by the City Corporation.

with the county councils. This responsibility is not, however, very great in practice, for the police authority cannot give detailed instructions to individual police officers about crimes or prosecutions. Under the Police Act, 1964, the police authority in a county is the police committee, consisting as to two-thirds of its members of members of the county council and as to one third of county magistrates appointed by the Crown Court. Special provision is made in the Act for the combination of police authorities under amalgamation schemes, made on the application of police authorities, or at the initiative of the Home Secretary without any such application.[18] Where there is such a scheme, the police authority for the combined area will be a body corporate; it will consist as to two-thirds of its members of members of the constituent councils, and as to one-third of magistrates for the constituent areas.[19] The police authority is responsible "to secure the maintenance of an adequate and efficient police force for the area",[20] and in particular will be concerned, subject to regulations made by the Home Secretary, with the pay and appointment of members of the force, and the provision of buildings and equipment. In all forces the appointment of the chief constable and deputy chief constable is subject to the approval of the Home Secretary; in practice this is by no means meaningless, and there have been several examples in recent years when local authorities have been unable to obtain the Home Secretary's approval to a proposed appointment.[1] Further, the Home Secretary may require the police authority to call upon their chief constable to retire in the interests of efficiency.[2]

Supervision by the Home Office and H.M. Inspectors of Constabulary is very close, partly because of the 50 per cent grant in aid made by the Government in respect of all approved expenditure. Rates of pay and conditions of service of officers are prescribed in regulations made in consultation with the Police Council.[3]

A police constable in uniform has special powers of arrest, but in general he is in the same legal position as any member of the public whose duty it is to assist in keeping the peace and to apprehend criminals. A police officer is not a servant of the local authority in whose force he serves, and consequently the authority are not responsible at common law for the acts of a police officer committed in the course of his duties of detecting or preventing crime.[4] The Crown also is not responsible, although a constable is in a sense an officer of the Crown, because he is

---

[18] *Ibid.*, s. 21 (1) and (2). The Home Secretary has made a considerable number of such schemes in recent years. Thus, the City of Nottingham force was combined with that of the County of Nottinghamshire; there is a single West Midlands Constabulary, and the Exeter force has been combined with that of Devonshire. There are now only some 40 separate police forces in the country.

[19] *Ibid.*, s. 3.

[20] *Ibid.*, s. 4 (1).

[1] See Chapter XV, *ante*, p. 433. The local police authority has a right to dismiss a Chief Constable in any case of breach of discipline or for other good reason, subject to his right to appeal to the Home Secretary under the Police Regulations; he also has a statutory right to make representations to the local authority: Police Act, 1964, s. 5 (5).

[2] *Ibid.*, s. 29 (1).

[3] *Ibid.*, ss. 33 and 45.

[4] *Fisher* v. *Oldham Corpn.*, [1930] 2 K.B. 364.

not paid directly from the Consolidated Fund.[5] The position was, however, regularised by the Police Act, 1964. By section 48 of that Act the chief constable for the police area was made liable in respect of torts committed by police officers under his direction and control in the performance or purported performance of their functions. If damages are awarded against a chief constable, these must be paid out of the police fund by the police authority, and they are also expressly empowered to pay any damages or costs awarded against an individual police officer.

Other reforms of the police service made by the Police Act, 1964 are not the concern of this book, but the whole statute may be cited as an example of the extent to which the Central Government may exercise control over the functioning of what remains, at least in theory, a local government service.[6]

(b) Fire brigades.—The fire service was not put on a satisfactory legal basis until the passing of the Fire Services Act, 1947, which imposed the duty of maintaining an efficient service on county and county borough councils (confined now, of course, to county councils). Except that there have been no amalgamation schemes, there are many similarities with the police service, in that Home Office supervision is close, approved expenditure attracts government grants, there is a disciplinary code applicable to all brigades made under the authority of statute, and local forces are subject to central inspection. Wide powers are conferred on fire officers to enter premises to extinguish fires or for fire prevention purposes, but firemen may not be used on police duties.

(c) Civil defence.—This service, the "Fourth Arm" as it has been called, is in an anomalous position, in that it is dependent on the Central Government for general direction and policy, but is administered by the "corps authorities", who, under the Civil Defence Act, 1948, are the county councils. In the event of war it is clear that the service would have to be put on a military footing, the local authorities becoming mere agents of the central government.

(d) Weights and measures.—This service, which is often administered in the Public Control Department of a local authority with related matters such as the control of diseases of animals, poisons, fertilisers and feeding stuffs, and the licensing of miscellaneous activities including hackney carriages, riding establishments, scrap metal dealers and gaming,[7] really forms part of the maintenance of public order, and is one of the few minor local government services having a long history. Prosecutions for false weights, adulterated beer and mouldy bread were common in mediaeval times and until quite recent times many ancient boroughs appointed ceremonial officers with quaint names such as

---

[5] See, *e.g.*, *A.-G. for New South Wales* v. *Perpetual Trustee Co.*, [1955] 1 All E.R. 846; [1955] A.C. 457 and Chapter IX, *ante*, p. 284.

[6] See article by D. E. Regan at [1966] P.L. 13.

[7] Small lotteries and "amusements with prizes" under the Betting, Gaming and Lotteries Act, 1963 and the Gaming Act, 1968.

"Aletaster",[8] whose offices were sinecures. Weights and measures duties are now the concern of county councils, but in Wales the Secretary of State may, before April 1, 1974, have designated a district council as the weights and measures authority for that district.[9] The Trade Descriptions Act, 1968, and the Fair Trading Act, 1973 have extended the functions of weights and measures authorities. The administration of the Shops Acts,[10] designed primarily to ensure reasonable hours of work for shop assistants and shopowners, must also be mentioned; but although this legislation dates only from the early years of the present century, much of it is virtually out of date, as trade unions and changes in the habits of the people have made it unnecessary to secure most of the objects of the statutes by legislation.

4. SANITATION AND PUBLIC HYGIENE

Although there are instances of spasmodic attempts by certain of the ancient boroughs to enforce reasonable standards of public health in Tudor times[11] and later, there was really no comprehensive concept of a public health service until the middle of the nineteenth century. The great Public Health Acts, of 1848, 1858, 1872 and 1875, on which the present "principal Act" of 1936 is built, brought not only the modern public health service into being, but also made the creation of efficient local sanitary authorities—the district councils[12]—in the modern pattern essential. "Public health" today comprises a number of detailed functions, most of which are the concern of district councils.

(a) Sewers and sewage disposal.—It was, until 1974, the duty of the local authority to provide such public sewers as may be necessary for the effective draining of their district,[13] and to cleanse and empty[14] all public sewers vested in them, but this duty has now been transferred to the water authorities,[15] in whom also all public sewers are vested. Sewerage and sewage disposal are now, therefore, functions of these new authorities, but the Water Act, 1973, requires a water authority to make arrangements for the discharge of sewerage functions (but not sewage disposal) by the district council on behalf of the water authority. The abatement of nuisances and other purely public health functions

---

[8] The duty of regulating the size of loaves of bread and testing the quality of beer, was imposed on Mayors of boroughs under several statutes in the Middle Ages.

[9] L.G.A., 1972, s. 201. New functions will be conferred on these authorities under the Consumer Credit Bill and (in relation to motor fuel) the Protection of the Environment Bill.

[10] Now consolidated in the Shops Act, 1950.

[11] As, for example, when Shakespeare's father, John was fined by the Corporation for leaving a dungheap outside his house in Henley Street, Stratford-on-Avon (see *Shakespeare*, by Ivor Brown, at p. 41).

[12] Subject to the provisions of the Water Act, 1973.

[13] Public Health Act, 1936, s. 14, as amended.

[14] *Ibid.*, s. 23.

[15] The water authorities, of which there are 10 covering the whole of England and Wales (including the Welsh National Water Development Authority) are large *ad hoc* public corporations established by the Water Act, 1973. They have inherited the river pollution prevention functions of the former river authorities, and in addition to sewerage and sewage disposal, they are responsible for water supply and land drainage, fisheries protection and recreation on rivers, within their areas.

conferred by the Public Health Act, 1936, remain, however, the responsibility of district councils.

As an owner of premises in the district also has a statutory right to cause his drain (or sewer) to be connected with any public sewer, it will be appreciated that in this branch of the law it is important to understand the meaning of "public sewer". Unfortunately the term is not given any precise meaning by the statute[16]; suffice it here to say that a sewer is a conduit, whether artificial or natural (usually, of course, the former) used for the conveyance of soil or surface water (or both) from buildings or paved surfaces[17] from two or more separate premises not within the same curtilage, a conduit serving one premises only being a drain. A sewer vested in a water authority by virtue of section 20 of the Public Health Act, 1936, as amended by the Water Act, 1973, (in the majority of cases because it was constructed by their predecessor local authority) is a public sewer, and is their responsibility.

The water authority cannot legally be compelled to construct new sewers except by complaint made to the Secretary of State[18] but they have statutory powers to construct public sewers through privately owned land, subject to payment of compensation. The district council, as sanitary authority retain a variety of powers[19] to require the abatement of nuisances, the machinery here usually taking the form of a notice requiring the landowner (or occupier) concerned to carry out certain works, followed by a statutory power for the authority to enter on the land in default of compliance with the notice and carry out the work themselves, and then to recover their expenses thereby incurred from the person in default.

Disposal of sewage is a function of the water authority. They have powers to construct sewage works, and they may not cause sewage effluent to flow into a river or watercourse so as to cause pollution; outfalls to the sea are not, however, at present subject to any special control.[20] The prevention of river pollution used to be a function of local authorities, but this also is now the concern of the water authorities.

(b) Refuse collection.—The collection and disposal of refuse by incineration or tipping has become a major problem of urban civilisation and it is one of the more expensive functions of local authorities. In general, the collection of refuse is the responsibility of the district council, but the disposal of refuse and the provision of places for the

---

[16] The nearest attempt at a definition is the catalogue given in s. 20 (1) of the 1936 Act.

[17] Highway drains will not normally be sewers, and conduits designed exclusively as land drains cannot be public sewers (see Public Health Act, 1875, s. 13).

[18] Under s. 322 of the Public Health Act, 1936. They also cannot be sued in the courts on the ground that their failure to carry out their statutory duty to provide an adequate public sewer has caused a private nuisance: *Smeaton* v. *Ilford Corpn.*, [1954] 1 All E.R. 923; [1954] Ch. 450.

[19] Amplified by the Public Health Act, 1961.

[20] At common law there is no right for any person to discharge polluting matter into the sea, and the person responsible may be liable in damages or to an injunction if a nuisance is caused by any such discharge: *Foster* v. *Warblington U.C.*, [1906] 1 K.B. 648. The Rivers (Prevention of Pollution) Act, 1961 imposes controls over discharges to estuaries and certain coastal waters, and the Protection of the Environment Bill will introduce new controls.

deposit of refuse[1] is the responsibility of the G.L.C. and the county councils, except in Wales where this also is a district council function.[2] The enforcement of the Deposit of Poisonous Waste Act, 1972, also is a district council function. Salvage and the sale of by-products can bring in substantial revenue to local authorities, as has been demonstrated over many years by the City of Bradford and other authorities.

(c) Inspection of premises.—The Public Health Act, 1936, and related legislation gives a number of powers to district councils to inspect buildings,[3] shops,[4] factories,[5] inns and refreshment houses,[6] catering premises[7] and offices,[8] to ensure that certain standards of sanitation or hygiene (varying in each case) are observed. The pattern of this legislation, subject to minor variations, is a power of entry, coupled with a power to serve a notice requiring works to be executed, either so as to ensure that sanitary accommodation is provided or that rules of hygiene are observed, followed with the conferment on the local authority of a power either to carry out the works in default and to recover the expenses thereby incurred, or to take proceedings for a penalty in the criminal courts. Often the standard to be imposed, expressed in the statute in some such terms as "suitable and sufficient" or "satisfactory", is left virtually at the discretion of the local authority, although there may be an appeal to the courts, often the local magistrates, against their decisions.

(d) Building control.—Under the Public Health Act, 1936, local sanitary authorities were empowered to make byelaws as to methods of construction, siting, types of materials, etc., to be used in the erection and alteration of buildings, and to enforce the provisions of such byelaws, in the interests of public health and public safety. This power was, however, repealed by the Public Health Act, 1961, and the Minister of Public Buildings and Works[9] was empowered to make "building regulations", effective over the whole country, of similar content to the former Model Series of byelaws; these regulations came into operation on February 1, 1966[10] and are enforceable by district councils. In addition to taking proceedings for breach of the regulations—the normal method of enforcement[11]—local authorities have power to pull down offending work at the expense of the building owner.

---

[1] Civic Amenities Act, 1967; under the Protection of the Environment Bill, disposal authorities will have to prepare a plan for the disposal of waste in their areas.

[2] L.G.A., 1972, Schedule 14.

[3] Public Health Act, 1936, s. 44.

[4] Shops Act, 1950; Offices, Shops and Railway Premises Act, 1963.

[5] Factories Act, 1961, ss. 1–7.

[6] Public Health Act, 1936, s. 89, as amended by the Public Health Act, 1961, s. 80.

[7] Food and Drugs Act, 1955, s. 13 and the Food Hygiene (General) Regulations, 1960, made thereunder.

[8] Offices, Shops and Railway Premises Act 1963.

[9] Responsibility has since been transferred to the Secretary of State for the Environment.

[10] The Building Regulations 1972, S.I. 1972 No. 317, replacing earlier regulations of 1965.

[11] In practice a great deal is effected by persuasion and prosecutions are rare.

These provisions have proved to be of great value in preventing the worst type of "jerry building", and have done much to raise building standards generally; the detailed requirements are phrased in a reasonably flexible form[12] and do not operate so as unduly to cramp novel styles and techniques in the building industry.

(e) Slum clearance.—The law on this important branch of public health is now primarily contained in the Housing Act, 1957, although the nuisance abatement provisions of the Public Health Act, 1936, may in some circumstances be used to deal with the single insanitary house. This subject may be summarised as follows:

(i) Individual unfit houses may be required to be repaired by a notice served under section 9 of the 1957 Act or they may be "represented" as unfit and then (after the persons interested in the house have had an opportunity of being heard before the local authority),[2] the local authority (the district council) must make a demolition order or a closing order in respect thereof. A demolition order requires the owner of the house to demolish it, while the effect of a closing order is to prevent the house from being used for human habitation or for any purpose other than one approved by the local authority.

(ii) Houses in multiple occupation may be dealt with under the Housing Acts of 1961, 1964 and 1969, which empower the local authority to require such a house to be put into repair, or to limit the number of persons or households who may occupy the house. Where other powers prove fruitless, the local authority may take possession of a house in multiple occupation by making a "control order"; ownership will remain in the owner but the local authority will exercise powers of management in respect thereof.[14]

(iii) Areas of unfit houses may be dealt with under Part III of the Housing Act, 1957. Under this procedure the authority may define an area as a "clearance area" and then make a "clearance order", whereby the owners must themselves demolish all the buildings (which need not necessarily all be "houses") in the area, but are enabled to retain the sites and may, subject to certain restrictions, arrange for their redevelopment. Alternatively, the authority may acquire all the land in the clearance area (either compulsorily or by agreement) and then demolish the buildings and redevelop the area as a whole. Larger areas may now be dealt with as general development areas under the Housing Act, 1969, whereby the authority may use a variety of powers in order to secure the rehabilitation of an extensive area.

---

[12] For example, the local authority may, in a particular case, agree to relax or dispense with a provision in the Regulations, and if the authority refuse so to act on an application made by a developer, the developer will be entitled to appeal to the Secretary of State. Decisions on such appeals are published from time to time, and a body of informal "case law" is slowly building up.

[13] A strange type of procedure this, which recurs in a few other local government statutes, whereby the local authority whose officials have decided that the house is unfit, are obliged to give the owner or occupier an opportunity of arguing before them to the effect that the house is not unfit and/or that no action should be taken in respect thereof. This puts into statutory form the decision in *Cooper* v. *Wandsworth Board of Works* (1863), 14 C.B.N.S. 180, Chapter VI, *ante*, p. 118.

[14] Housing Act 1964, s. 73.

(iv) Improvement grants may—and in some cases must[15]—be made by the local authority, with exchequer assistance,[16] towards the cost of improving or converting privately owned dwellings, so as to make the maximum possible use of existing dwellings. As a general rule an owner who wishes to improve his house is expected to apply for a grant.

In all these cases, the general standard of what is an "unfit" house, is determined by the authority, by applying the detailed standards of section 4 of the Housing Act, 1957. Appeals by aggrieved persons against the decisions of a local authority (other than a refusal of an improvement grant) will in most circumstances lie to the local county court, but in the case of a clearance order, the appeal lies to the Secretary of State for the Environment.

(f) Housing.—This is the service on which more public money is at present expended annually than on any other local government service except education, but it is of comparatively recent growth. It started as a result of the need to provide new homes for families replaced by the early slum clearance schemes undertaken at the end of the last century; then the housing shortage after the war of 1914–19 and the more acute conditions prevailing after the war of 1939–45 made it essential for local authorities to build houses for letting to meet general needs, and not only to meet those arising out of slum clearance. The housing service thus consists of two main branches:

(i) *Provision of the houses.*—This involves a complicated series of powers to purchase land and construct houses and flats, roads, and other necessary works (see Part V of the Housing Act, 1957); and

(ii) *Housing management.*—As a consequence of the extensive building schemes of the post-war years, local authorities are now the largest landlords in the country. Management of these vast estates consequently occupies a great deal of the time of members and officers of housing authorities, who may be called upon to decide such questions as the allocation of tenancies to those in greatest need, the rent structure,[17] and the handling of difficult or unsatisfactory tenants. Human problems of this kind make the Housing Committee of most local authorities one of the busiest, and the housing department one of the more important.

(g) Parks and pleasure grounds.—The provision of parks and open spaces by local authorities has always been regarded as a branch of the law of public health,[18] although the management of the many open spaces in the average large city has now become a major service. Besides the provision of open spaces as such, ancillary amenities, such as

---

[15] Where the dwelling lacks all or some of the "standard amenities"—such as a water-closet or a fixed bath or shower in a bathroom—and it is proposed to provide them; see Housing Act, 1969, Part I. Increased grants are payable in "development areas": Housing Acts, 1971 and 1973.

[16] The central government pay 75 per cent of the annual loan charges referable to the grants which have been incurred by a local authority in making improvement or "standard" grants: Housing Act, 1969.

[17] As to the extent to which local authorities are subject to the control of the courts in this matter, see Chapter VI, *ante*, p. 168.

[18] The principal statutory provision on the subject is still s. 164 of the Public Health Act, 1875.

sports grounds, bathing pools (both indoor and outdoor), athletic centres and even golf courses are frequently provided by local authorities. The law on the subject is complicated in matters of detail, and in practice municipal parks and allied amenities rarely, if ever, pay for themselves.

(h) Food and drugs.—Since 1974 the food and drugs authorities throughout the country have been the county councils,[19] but district councils have certain food and drugs functions, some of which are shared with the county council. The most important sections of the Food and Drugs Act, 1955 are penal provisions prohibiting the sale or exposure for sale, etc., of adulterated food or food intended but unfit for human consumption. The Food Hygiene Regulations,[20] prescribe standards of cleanliness and hygiene to be observed by persons handling food, and there are elaborate codes regulating the observance of hygiene at dairies and in the course of handling milk, and requiring the licensing of persons dealing in or distributing milk[1] and regulating the use of "special designations"[2] such as "tuberculin tested" and "pasteurised" in connection with milk. The control of slaughterhouses and knackers' yards is contained in another complicated code,[3] which severely restricts the opening of new slaughterhouses while permitting local authorities to operate public slaughterhouses.

(i) Notifiable diseases.—The control of notifiable diseases[4] by legislation administered by local medical officers of health was one of the most important features of the public health service in the last century. Fortunately today we are not as subject to these scourges, thanks mainly to the basic preventative services of sanitation, housing and clean food. Notification of diseases when they occur, compulsory disinfestation of premises, prohibition on the mixing of infected persons with other members of the public and the closure of public buildings to children[5] are measures still on the statute book and they have to be implemented on occasion, but they are now the responsibility of the appropriate Area Health Authority, under the National Health Service, and are no longer of local authority concern.[6] Compliance with the orders of a medical officer under these provisions may at times cause hardship, and therefore there is a general provision in the statute[7] requiring the Area Health Authority to pay compensation in such cases.

(j) The prevention of river pollution.—This used to be a local authority function but by the Water Act, 1973, (replacing in this respect the Water Resources Act, 1963) it is now thought of as being

---

[19] L.G.A., 1972, s. 198.

[20] *I.e.*, the "General" Regulations (S.I. 1970 No. 1172), the "Docks, Carriers, etc." Regulations (S.I. 1960 No. 1602) and the "Markets, Stalls and Delivery Vehicles" Regulations (S.I. 1966, No. 791.)

[1] Milk and Dairies (General) Regulations, 1959 (S.I. 1959 No. 277).

[2] Milk (Special Designation) Regulations, 1960 (S.I. 1960 No. 1542).

[3] Slaughterhouses Act, 1958, read with the unrepealed sections of Part IV of the Food and Drugs Act, 1955 and regulations made thereunder; these provisions are to be consolidated in the Slaughter-houses Bill.

[4] As defined by s. 47 of the Health Services and Public Health Act, 1968, a definition which can from time to time be expanded by individual health authorities.

[5] Public Health Act, 1961, s. 40.

[6] National Health Service Reorganisation Act, 1973, Schedule 4, para. 2.

[7] Public Health Act, 1936, s. 278.

part of the wider task of water conservation, and is entrusted to the water authorities,[8] which are independent statutory corporations constituted by statute. Many of their members are representatives of local authorities and they precept for their income on county councils in the area. They have effective powers of control over the discharge of trade sewage and other effluents into any watercourse controlled by them. Allied to this function is that of land drainage, which is administered partly by the river authorities, and partly by smaller but similar *ad hoc* bodies known as land drainage boards, operating under the Land Drainage Act, 1930 (as amended).

(k) Coast protection.—Maritime local authorities—district councils having a seaward boundary—may take measures to prevent erosion by the sea, and may make levies towards their expenses on privately owned land that they consider will benefit therefrom[9]; they are also entitled to claim substantial grants towards their approved expenses from the central exchequer, which grants in aid were preserved by the Local Government Act, 1958.

(l) Clean air.—The Clean Air Act, 1956, conferred new powers on local sanitary authorities, empowering them to take legal proceedings in respect of the discharge of dark smoke, or of any smoke at all in an area which, by a complicated administrative machinery, they had declared by order[10] to be a "smoke control area"; these powers were strengthened in matters of detail by the Clean Air Act, 1968. Since 1956 many local authorities in industrial areas have implemented the provisions of the Act energetically and effectively and under the 1968 Act, the Secretary of State is given certain powers to compel a local authority to make smoke control area orders; but the statute law remains defective in that it does not deal with the discharge of sulphur into the atmosphere. Pollution from industrial premises is controlled in some measure by the Alkali Inspectorate of the Department of the Environment.

5. TOWN AND COUNTRY PLANNING

The control of land use, to give another name to this newest of the major local government functions, is little more than sixty years old, the first statute having been passed in 1909.[11] Like housing, the subject grew out of the public health service, it being gradually realised that it was futile to construct sewers and abolish slums if development were allowed which would in a few years become new slums. Town and country planning now applies to the whole country, planning authorities being both the county and the district councils;[12] the distribution

---

[8] See *ante*, p. 444.

[9] Coast Protection Act, 1949. The power to levy coast protection charges on "contributory land" still exists on the statute book, but in Circular 41/62, the Minister of Housing and Local Government expressed the hope that it would not be used in future.

[10] Subject to the Minister's approval: Clean Air Act, 1956, s. 11.

[11] Housing and Town Planning, &c., Act, 1909.

[12] Outside a few areas, in particular in the "national parks" where there are joint planning boards.

of powers between the two classes of authorities is very complicated,[13] but in broad terms, the county is responsible for the preparation of the development plan (especially the structure plan) while the district councils are responsible for the control of development, so far as this does not conflict with the provisions of the development plan. The principal Act is now the Town and Country Planning Act, 1971, a consolidating statute replacing the Act of 1947 and later Acts. This deals with the subject under the following headings:

(a) Development plans.—It is the duty of every planning authority to make a development plan (which when made has to be submitted to the Secretary of State for approval) for their area. This plan will show in more or less detail[14] how the land in the area ought to be used; it will indicate areas which ought to be primarily devoted to certain broad types of use, such as "residential" or "industrial". Land which is already developed will normally be shown as having its existing predominant use, but sometimes, as in the case of a slum neighbourhood, it may be the intention in the future to change that use. The siting of public buildings, open spaces, schools, etc., both existing and projected, will be shown and so also will major roads. The form and content of development plans were radically overhauled by Part I of the Town and Country Planning Act, 1968 (now Part II of the 1971 Act) but these provisions are in force only in those local planning authority areas to which it has been applied by Departmental order. Where these provisions are in force the development plan will consist of a "structure plan" (a written statement supported by maps and diagrams) and a number of "local plans" for selected parts of the local planning authority's area. The making of a plan is a complicated piece of administrative machinery; many public interests, often conflicting, have to be consulted, and private landowners have a right to make objections against a structure plan or a local plan. Objections to a structure plan must be considered by the Secretary of State, who may then order an examination in public of those matters that he considers ought to be so examined.[15] This is a novel procedure designed to expedite consideration of the essential issues but it may mean that an individual landowner or other interested person will have no opportunity of explaining his objection or of testing the weight of any contrary views of the planning authority. The plan will, however, need confirmation by the Secretary of State before it has legal effect, and any person aggrieved by an error of procedure or if the Secretary of State has exceeded his legal powers, will be able to appeal to the court.[16] Objections to a local plan will be heard by a person appointed by the local authority before they confirm the plan (which in this case will not require Departmental

---

[13] See L.G.A., 1972, Schedule 16.

[14] In urban areas the development plan will go into considerable detail. In rural areas, large tracts of countryside will be left uncoloured on the map, indicating that no development of any kind is there contemplated.

[15] Town and Country Planning Act, 1971, s. 9 (3), as amended by the Town and Country Planning (Amendment) Act, 1972.

[16] 1971 Act, s. 242.

confirmation). The development plan relates to the whole of the planning authority's area, indicating where the authority think development ought to take place and showing what they consider to be the optimum use of the land in their area, often, of course, preserving the *status quo*.

(b) Control of development.—Development plans by themselves have little precise legal effect although they may seriously affect the value of particular parcels of land; they merely indicate what the views of the planning authority are, often in very general terms. Although a particular piece of land may be shown on a development plan as being zoned for a particular use, this does not mean that development conforming with that use may be carried out without express planning permission.

The "teeth" of planning law, in its relationship to the private landowner, are to be found in Part III of the 1971 Act. This Part of the Act provides that no "development", an expression which is very widely defined,[17] may, with certain exceptions of a comparatively minor nature,[18] be carried out without the prior permission of the local planning authority. When considering an application for permission to carry out development in a particular case, the planning authority are required to have regard[1] to the provisions of the development plan and to any other material considerations. The contents of the development plan are thus of considerable importance, but they are by no means conclusive; an intending developer cannot in all cases look at the plan and decide for himself that permission will be readily obtainable in his case, and in no circumstances,[2] however clear a case he may appear to have on planning merits, can he legally carry out his development without first applying for permission. The requirement that express permission must be obtained is justified by the fact that the plan is drawn in broad terms, and may not always specify precisely the use intended for each small parcel of land; moreover, the planning authority are concerned with much more than the use of the land and they will be entitled to consider questions such as design, external appearance, access to roads, amenities of the neighbourhood, etc. A development plan is not intended to be rigid or static; it is subject to periodic alteration or revision.

In order that this requirement to obtain planning permission may not be ignored, Parts III, IV and V of the 1971 Act include complicated sections designed to secure enforcement of planning control. If any development that needs planning permission is carried out and that

---

[17] "Development" means "the carrying out of building, engineering, mining or other operations in, on, over or under land, or the making of any material change in the use of any buildings or other land": 1972 Act, s. 22.

[18] In practice these exceptions may be of considerable importance. Some are provided for in s. 22 of the Act itself, by way of restricting the definition of development, and in others the General Development Order, 1973, provides that certain operations and changes of use shall not require express permission, while the Town and Country Planning (Use Classes) Order, 1972, provides that certain changes of use within specified classes shall not amount to development.

[1] But not *exclusive* regard thereto: see *Simpson* v. *Edinburgh Corpn.*, 1961 S.L.T. 17.

[2] Subject to the exceptions above mentioned (see note 18, *ante*).

permission is not obtained, or if a condition[3] or limitation attached to a planning permission is not complied with, the planning authority may serve an "enforcement notice" requiring steps to be taken to discontinue an offending use or to demolish a building erected without permission, etc., under penalty of proceedings being taken or the planning authority taking default action at the expense of the offender. This may be reinforced by a "stop notice", which makes it a criminal offence to carry out or continue any operations on the land specified in the enforcement notice and the stop notice.[4]

The Act also provides[5] for any applicant aggrieved by a refusal of planning permission, by a condition or time limitation attached to a planning permission, or by an enforcement notice, to appeal to the Secretary of State, who then appoints an inspector to preside at a local inquiry and in certain cases to determine the appeal on behalf of the Secretary of State.[6] When the decision is known the applicant (or the planning authority) has a right of appeal on a point of law to the High Court. As well as the main provisions of Part III of the 1971 Act controlling proposed development, there are incidental provisions dealing with specific matters, supplementing the powers of local planning authorities. Thus:

(i) They may order the discontinuance of an "existing use" of land or the removal of existing buildings, in respect of which planning permission has previously been given,[7] or they may revoke a planning permission previously given, in each case on payment of compensation in respect thereof;[8]

(ii) The authority may also exercise a tight control over the display of advertisements, as there is a complete code of law regulating this subject, contained in Regulations made by the Secretary of State under the Act[9];

(iii) Special powers are given to make orders to preserve trees or belts of woodland in the interests of "amenity",[10] to preserve buildings of special architectural or historical interest[11] or to require the tidying up of waste land.[12]

---

[3] The circumstances in which a condition may be void have gradually been worked out in a series of decisions on appeals to the Secretary of State: see also *Pyx Granite Co.* v. *Ministry of Housing and Local Government*, [1959] 3 All E.R. 1; [1960] A.C. 260, *Fawcett* v. *Buckingham County Council*, [1960] 3 All E.R. 503 and *Chertsey U.D.C.* v. *Mixnam's Properties, Ltd.*, [1964] 2 All E.R. 627.

[4] 1971 Act, s. 90.

[5] *Ibid.*, s. 36.

[6] *Ibid.*, Schedule 9; Town and Country Planning (Determination of Appeals by Appointed Persons) (Prescribed Classes) Regulations, 1972, S.I. 1972 No. 1652; as to inquiries generally, see Chapter VIII, *ante*, p. 230, and as to other rights of appeal to the Secretary of State, see list at p. 235.

[7] Or where it is to be deemed to have been given under a General Development Order, or by virtue of pre-1948 planning law.

[8] 1972 Act, ss. 51 and 170, and ss. 45 and 164, respectively.

[9] 1971 Act, s. 63; Town and Country Planning (Control of Advertisements) Regulations, 1969, S.I., 1969 No. 1532. This operates in manner similar to the control of development; indeed, the Regulations are clearly modelled on Part III of the Act.

[10] 1971 Act, s. 60.

[11] *Ibid.*, ss. 54 to 58 and Schedule 11; which together constitute a very extensive code in its own right.

[12] *Ibid.*, s. 65.

Control of development in this wide sense is of course the part of planning administration that most closely affects the individual, as owner or occupier of land, and therefore this is the branch of the subject where the elected representatives can exercise most influence. The preparation of development plans, except in the widest possible general terms, tends to become the province of the expert; but when the contents of the plan have to be applied in the particular case, then the views of the amateur, representing the "man in the street" become of value. No doubt this is the reason why the Local Government Act, 1972, makes provision for the administration of development control to be in most cases the concern of district councils.

(c) Positive planning.—There are also wide powers for the compulsory acquisition of land for planning purposes by a local authority[13] or for their several purposes by statutory undertakers or a Government Department.[14]

In other respects, the operation of a development plan and the administration of Part III of the 1972 Act has tended to be restrictive rather than positive in outlook. However, there are special forms of positive planning that have been undertaken, and are still being undertaken, under other statutes:

(i) Under the National Parks and Access to the Countryside Act, 1949, planning authorities can provide for new public rights of way and rights of public access to open country, and the Secretary of State may establish national parks,[15] areas of outstanding natural beauty, and nature reserves (to be administered by the Nature Conservancy).[16]

(ii) Under the New Towns Act, 1965 (replacing the New Towns Act, 1946), the Secretary of State may establish "new towns" on sites designated by him. The administration of these new towns, is entrusted to development corporations, independent bodies specially constituted for the purpose. When the new towns are established and developed, their administration (apart from the ordinary functions of local government) passes to the Commission for the New Towns, under section 35 of the New Towns Act, 1965 (formerly the New Towns Act, 1959). By way of contrast, the Town Development Act, 1952, provides different machinery[17] for the expansion of existing towns, by moving to them industries and population from overcrowded areas.

(d) Financial provisions.—Interwoven with the substantive planning provisions of the 1947 Act were its financial provisions, designed primarily to secure that in the years of redevelopment that it was anticipated would follow the war, then newly ended, local authorities would be able to purchase land at low prices, at the then "existing use value". This is not the place to trace the vicissitudes in the law that

---

13 This will be the county *or* the county district council.

14 1971 Act, ss. 112 and 113.

15 In a national park the local planning authority (in some cases a joint board) have exceptional powers of control and to provide amenities, etc. Local authorities may establish "country parks" under the Countryside Act, 1968.

16 An independent body incorporated by Royal Charter in 1949: Chapter X, *ante*, p. 324.

17 Not much used until the early 1960s, when the London County Council entered into agreements for the "export" of population and industry into small towns in Hampshire.

have taken place since 1947; at the present time an acquiring authority are required to pay on the compulsory acquisition of land, compensation approximately equivalent to the value of that land in the open market.[18]

6. THE UTILITY SERVICES

These were the great new local government services of the days of municipal enterprise and socialism, in the early years of the present century. Many city and borough councils obtained special powers by local Acts of Parliament to operate gas, electricity and water undertakings, to run trams and other forms of public transport and (later) to open municipal aerodromes. Markets had been under the control of local authorities in many old towns almost from time immemorial; their administration was standardised by the Markets and Fairs Clauses Act, 1847, and the Food and Drugs Acts of 1938 and 1955. At the present day many former municipal undertakings are no longer the concern of local government. Gas and electricity supply and distribution have been "nationalised", and these services are now administered under the general supervision of independent statutory corporations.[19] Until recently, water supply might be the responsibility of a company, or of a local authority operating under a special Act or under the Public Health Act, 1936, but water undertakings are now the responsibility of the water authorities established by the Water Act, 1973.[20]

Minor utilities operated by local authorities include the entertainments undertakings[1] which in some large holiday resorts achieve almost the status of "big business". Local authorities may also operate their own catering services[2]; provide baths and wash-houses[3] and burial grounds, caravan sites,[4] cemeteries and crematoria.[5] Municipal transport is still an important feature of local government in many large cities, but these functions of local authorities in metropolitan areas have been taken over by *ad hoc* local statutory corporations,[6] and non-metropolitan counties are responsible for the co-ordination of public transport in their areas.[7]

---

[18] Town and Country Planning Act, 1959, now replaced by the Land Compensation Acts, 1961 and 1973. The Land Commission Act, 1967 imposed a substantial tax on all new development and any increase in development value, but this was repealed in 1971.

[19] Electricity Act, 1947, and Gas Acts, 1948 and 1972. As to the independent corporations, see Chapter X, *ante*, p. 317.

[20] *Ante*, p. 444.

[1] By s. 145 of the L.G.A., 1972, any local authority may provide for entertainments (such as theatres, orchestras, etc.) or contribute towards their expenses of providing such entertainments, without any limitation on such expenditure.

[2] Civic Restaurants Act, 1947.

[3] Public Health Act, 1936, Part VIII.

[4] Caravan Sites and Control of Development Act, 1960, s. 24; Caravan Sites Act, 1968.

[5] Cremation Act, 1902.

[6] The "passenger transport authorities" and "passenger transport executives" appointed under the Transport Act, 1968. There is an executive for each of the six metropolitan counties established by the L.G.A., 1972 (see s. 202 thereof).

[7] L.G.A., 1972, s. 203.

7. THE PERSONAL SERVICES

(a) Education.—Under this general heading the most important, and certainly the most expensive service, is education. The local administration of this service is entrusted by the Education Act, 1944, as amended by the Local Government Act, 1972, to the counties and, in metropolitan areas, to the metropolitan districts. In London, educacation is administered by the Inner London Education Authority (covering that part of London administered before 1965 by the former London County Council) and by the London borough councils. Former schemes of divisional administration have been abolished by the 1972 Act.[8]

Education is divided by the Act of 1944 into three stages, namely, primary up to the age of about eleven, secondary from the age of eleven to the age when the particular child leaves school, and further education from the school leaving age (as from the school year commencing in the autumn of 1972, sixteen[9]) onwards. Schools are divided into several kinds, and tuition at all schools maintained by the local education authority must be provided free of charge. It is the duty of the local education authority to ensure that there are sufficient schools,

> "to afford for all pupils opportunities for education offering such variety of instruction and training as may be desirable in view of their different ages, abilities and aptitudes."[10]

Subject to special provisions as to religious education[11] it is the duty of the parent, enforceable by the local education authority by means of "school attendance orders",[12] of every child of compulsory school age to cause him to receive efficient full-time education suitable to his age, ability, and aptitude, either by regular attendance at school or otherwise.[13]

(b) Libraries.—This service is now under the general supervision of the Secretary of State for Education and Science,[14] but in other respects libraries have always been regarded in local government (except by some county councils) as being separate from the education service. The operative statute is now the Public Libraries and Museums Act, 1964 as amended by the Local Government Act, 1972,[15] under which any county or district council, or the council of a London borough (or the G.L.C.) may be a library authority. Every non-metropolitan county council and every metropolitan district council must be a library authority; which of the other authorities in a particular case exercises library functions will depend on agreement between the county and district concerned. There is also power for the Secretary of State for Education and Science to establish a joint board.[16]

---

[8] *Ibid.*, s. 192.
[9] Raising of the School Leaving Age Order, 1972 (S.I. 1972 No. 444).
[10] Education Act, 1944, s. 8.
[11] *Ibid.*, ss. 25–30.
[12] *Ibid.*, s. 37.
[13] *Ibid.*, s. 36.
[14] It is his duty to "to superintend and promote the improvement of the public library service provided by local authorities in England and Wales": Public Libraries and Museums Act, 1964, s. 1.
[15] L.G.A., s. 206; there are slightly different arrangements in Wales: see *ibid.*, s. 207.
[16] Public Libraries and Museums Act, 1964, s. 5.

A library authority *may* (this being a permissive, not a mandatory service) provide libraries, museums and art galleries. Premises so provided must be open to the public, free of charge, but authorities now have powers to charge for borrowing articles (*e.g.*, pictures or gramophone records) other than books or pamphlets, and also for failing to return a book or other article before the end of the period for which it was lent.[17]

(c) Health services.—Most of these services (including the ambulance service outside London) are now[18] the responsibility of the Regional and Area Health Authorities under the National Health Service. Still left in local authority administration are, however, the social services (see below), the ambulance service in London, food hygiene and the environmental health services.

(d) Social services.—Closely allied to the personal health services are the social services entrusted by the National Assistance Act, 1948, as amended by the Local Authority Social Services Act, 1970, and the Local Government Act, 1972,[1] to the councils of non-metropolitan counties (who must consult from time to time with district councils in the county), and to the councils of metropolitan districts. Each local authority is required to appoint a director of social services,[2] and to establish a social services committee to assist them in carrying out their functions,[3] which must be carried out under the "general guidance" of the Secretary of State for Social Services. These functions may be briefly summarised as follows:

(i) The provision of residential accommodation for those persons who are in need of care and attention by reason of age, infirmity or other special circumstances.

(ii) The provision of temporary accommodation for those urgently in need because of unforeseen circumstances. This service is really the historical successor of the former "casual ward" in the local workhouse.

(iii) The making of arrangements for the promotion of the welfare of blind, deaf, dumb, crippled and otherwise handicapped persons by providing recreational and training facilities or by giving financial assistance to voluntary organisations devoted to these purposes.

(iv) The local authority have certain duties of registration and inspection of old and disabled person's homes, as they also have under the Mental Health Act, 1959, in respect of homes for mentally disordered persons.

(v) The making of provision for persons who are chronically sick or disabled, under the Chronically Sick and Disabled Persons Act, 1970.

---

[17] *Ibid.*, s. 8.
[18] National Health Service Reorganisation Act, 1973.
[1] L.G.A., 1972, s. 195.
[2] Local Authority Social Services Act, 1970, s. 6.
[3] *Ibid.*, s. 2; there must be delegation of functions to this committee: *ibid.*

(e) The children's service.—This is a comparatively new service created by the Children Act, 1948 (as amended by the Children Act, 1958 and the Local Government Act, 1972), which requires local authorities to take into their care, in cases where it is necessary in the interests of the child's welfare, any child under the age of seventeen who is without parents or guardians, who has been abandoned or lost, or whose parents or guardians are unfit or unable to look after him. When a child comes into the care of a local authority all parental right in respect of that child vest in the local authority until the child is eighteen years of age. Further, a juvenile court may commit a child to the care of the local authority—even without the consent of that authority. Other functions of the children authority relate to child protection, the registration and inspection of "child minders" (or foster-parents), the adoption of children, and the supervision of children and young persons in need of care or protection. These functions are exercised by the local authority responsible for social services, and must be delegated to the social services committee of the authority.[4]

8. THE ADMINISTRATION OF JUSTICE

The administration of civil justice is not the concern of local government, but magistrates' courts are administered, so far as staffing, premises and stationery, etc., is concerned, by magistrates' courts committees constituted under the Justices of the Peace Act, 1949. There must be a separate magistrates' courts committee for each county.[5] There are no longer any courts of quarter sessions, these having been replaced by Crown Courts under the Courts Act, 1971, and all local civil courts of record have been abolished by the Local Government Act, 1972.[6] However, the council of a district that has acquired borough status may appoint a person to be "honorary recorder" of the borough, under s. 54 of the Courts Act, 1971.

Coroners are appointed and paid by each county council and by the Greater London Council and the Common Council of the City of London.[7] Each county council may arrange for the division of the county into coroners' districts.[8]

In addition, each county has a Lord Lieutenant appointed by the Crown, whose duties were originally military but are now almost exclusively ceremonial.[9] Each county has a high sheriff[10]; again primarily a ceremonial officer, as his duties connected with the execution of writs and the summoning of juries are customarily performed by a permanent official known as the under-sheriff,[11] whilst an officer of the

[4] Local Authority Social Services Act, 1970 (as amended): *ante*.

[5] Justices of the Peace Act, 1949, ss. 16–18; as amended by the Local Government Act, 1972.

[6] See s. 221 and Schedule 28.

[7] Local Government Act, 1972, s. 220 (1).

[8] *Ibid.*, s. 220 (4).

[9] *Ibid.*, s. 218.

[10] *Ibid.*, s. 219.

[11] He is a paid official and the post is often held by a local solicitor: Sheriffs Act, 1887, as amended by the Local Government Act, 1972, s. 219.

council will usually be requested to act on his behalf as deputy returning officer for the conduct of parliamentary elections entrusted by statute to the sheriff.

Further, those local authorities which have predecessor authorities who appointed sheriffs (*i.e.*, some 20 or so former boroughs) may continue to appoint to such "offices of dignity".[12] In these cases the sheriff will normally be a member of the council and will have no functions in law, but may on occasion deputise for the Mayor. Some former boroughs appointed an officer known as "High Steward", again with no functions; there is no legal reason why this practice should not be continued where thought desirable.

9. CONCLUSION

This survey "in little", as it were, of the functions of local authorities has perhaps given some indication of the extent of their range. The adage that it is the function of local government to care for the citizen from the cradle (or earlier) to the grave may not be as true as it was a few years ago before many services had been "nationalised", but local government in this country remains a major industry employing very many individuals and calling on the spare time and voluntary effort of many elected and co-opted representatives. The list of functions can never be complete,[13] for they are varied from time to time by general and local Acts of Parliament and a complete compendium of local government law would fill many volumes. The independence of local authorities in this country leads to variety in the range of functions exercised, due to their initiative in obtaining local Acts, or in exercising "permissive" functions (*i.e.*, those which are not made duties by statute), as well as to variety in the standards observed by particular local authorities in exercising those functions. Geography also may add variety, for a seaside resort or an ancient market town will wish to conduct their local government in a manner different from that adopted by a large industrial city.

The essential feature of a modern local authority is that it should possess a wide range of functions. That range should be as wide as practicable, having regard to the authority's area and resources, so that the interest of members may be retained and the authority may be able to recruit to their staff able and efficient officers. The extent to which discretionary powers may be exercised, and the standard of services provided, depend of course on an authority's resources.

---

[12] Local Government Act, 1972, s. 246.

[13] Among those not mentioned above are the operation of ferries (under the authority of a royal charter or a local Act), zoological gardens, and a local telephone service (at Kingston-upon-Hull).

APPENDIX I

THE ADMINISTRATIVE PROCEDURE ACT OF THE U.S.A. (1946) (as amended)

AN ACT to improve the administration of justice by prescribing fair administrative procedure.

Be it enacted by the Senate and House of Representatives of the United States of America in Congress assembled,

TITLE

Sec. 1.—This Act may be cited as the "Administrative Procedure Act".

DEFINITIONS

Sec. 2.—As used in this Act—

(a) *Agency.*—"Agency" means each authority (whether or not within or subject to review by another agency) of the Government of the United States[1] other than Congress, the courts, or the governments of the possessions, Territories, or the District of Columbia. Nothing in this Act shall be construed to repeal delegations of authority as provided by law. Except as to the requirements of section 3, there shall be excluded from the operation of this Act (1) agencies composed of representatives of the parties or of representatives of organizations of the parties to the disputes determined by them, (2) courts martial and military commissions, (3) military or naval authority exercised in the field in time of war or in occupied territory, or (4) functions which by law expire on the termination of present hostilities, within any fixed period thereafter, or before July 1, 1947, and the functions conferred by the following statutes: Selective Training and Service Act of 1940; Contract Settlement Act of 1944; Surplus Property Act of 1944.

(b) *Person and Party.*—"Person" includes individuals, partnerships, corporations, associations, or public or private organizations of any character other than agencies. "Party" includes any person or agency named or admitted as a party, or properly seeking and entitled as of right to be admitted as a party, in any agency proceeding; but nothing herein shall be construed to prevent an agency from admitting any person or agency as a party for limited purposes.

(c) *Rule and rule making.*—"Rule" means the whole or any part of any agency statement of general or particular applicability and future effect designed to implement, interpret, or prescribe law or policy or to describe the organization, procedure, or practice requirements of any agency and includes the approval or prescription for the future of rates, wages, corporate or financial structures or reorganizations thereof, prices, facilities, appliances, services or allowances therefor or of valuations, costs, or accounting, or practices bearing upon any of the foregoing.[2]

---

[1] This expression refers of course only to agencies of the *Federal* government; the statute does not apply to any of the agencies of the several States of the U.S., some of which have passed statutes to a like effect. As to law in the States, see *State Administrative Law*, by F. E. Cooper.

[2] It has been suggested that rate-making ought to be deleted from this definition, so that that process would become adjudication. In practice there has also been considerable argument over the question when does an accepted principle laid down in an agency decision become a "rule" for the purposes of this section; compare the problems in English law which arise when an administrative body exercising a discretion attempts to lay down guide lines as to how it proposes to exercise that discretion; *ante*, p. 26.

"Rule making" means agency process for the formulation, amendment, or repeal of a rule.

(d) *Order and adjudication.*—"Order" means the whole or any part of the final disposition (whether affirmative, negative, injunctive, or declaratory in form) of any agency in any matter other than rule making but including licensing. "Adjudication" means agency process for the formulation of an order.

(e) *License and Licensing.*—"License" includes the whole or part of any agency permit, certificate, approval, registration, charter, membership, statutory exemption or other form of permission. "Licensing" includes agency process respecting the grant, renewal, denial, revocation, suspension, annulment, withdrawal, limitation, amendment, modification, or conditioning of a licence.

(f) *Sanction and relief.*—"Sanction" includes the whole or part of any agency (1) prohibition, requirement, limitation, or other condition affecting the freedom of any person; (2) withholding of relief; (3) imposition of any form of penalty or fine; (4) destruction, taking, seizure, or withholding of property; (5) assessment of damages, reimbursement, restitution, compensation, costs, charges, or fees; (6) requirement, revocation, or suspension of a licence; or (7) taking of other compulsory or restrictive action. "Relief" includes the whole or part of any agency (1) grant of money, assistance, license, authority, exemption, exception, privilege, or remedy; (2) recognition of any claim, right, immunity, privilege, exemption, or exception; or (3) taking of any other action upon the application or petition of, and beneficial to, any person.

(g) *Agency proceeding and action.*—"Agency proceeding" means any agency process as defined in subsections (c), (d), and (e) of this section. "Agency action" includes the whole or part of every agency rule, order, licence, sanction, relief, or the equivalent or denial thereof, or failure to act.

Public Information [3]

Sec. 3.—Every agency shall make available to the public the following information:

(a) *Publication in the Federal Register.*[4]—Every agency shall separately state and currently publish in the Federal Register for the guidance of the public (A) descriptions of its central and field organization and the established places at which, the officers from whom, and the methods whereby, the public may secure information, make submittals or requests, or obtain decisions; (B) statements of the general course and method by which its functions are channeled and determined, including the nature and requirements of all formal and informal procedures available; (C) rules of procedure, descriptions of forms available or the places at which forms may be obtained, and instructions as to the scope and contents of all papers, reports, or examinations; (D) substantive rules of general applicability adopted as authorized by law, and statements of general policy or interpretations of general applicability formulated and adopted by the agency; and (E) every amendment, revision, or repeal of the foregoing. Except to the extent that a person has actual and timely notice of the terms thereof, no person

---

[3] As amended by Public Law 89–487 dated 4th July 1966, effective as from 4th July 1967.

[4] Compare the provisions of the Statutory Instruments Act, 1946, requiring instruments to be numbered, printed and put on sale. The Federal Register is published daily and is somewhat similar in content to the London Gazette, except that it includes the full text of all Presidential proclamations and executive orders, and also other orders, regulations, notices or similar documents promulgated by Federal administrative agencies having general applicability and legal effect. The Register is a modern publication, having been introduced as a consequence of the discovery in the course of proceedings in the Supreme Court in *Panama Refining Co.* v. *Ryan* (1935), 293 U.S. 388, that a Government regulation had been revoked without the accused, Government enforcement officers and the lower courts, being aware of the revocation; see (1934), 48 Harv. L.R. 198. Similar publications of State government regulations are to be found in most of the States.

shall in any manner be required to resort to, or be adversely affected by any matter required to be published in the Federal Register and not so published. For purposes of this subsection, matter which is reasonably available to the class of persons affected thereby shall be deemed published in the Federal Register when incorporated by reference therein with the approval of the Director of the Federal Register.

(b) *Agency opinions and orders.*—Every agency shall, in accordance with published rules, make available for public inspection and copying (A) all final opinions[5] (including concurring and dissenting opinions) and all orders made in the adjudication of cases, (B) those statements of policy and interpretations which have been adopted by the agency and are not published in the Federal Register, and (C) administrative staff manuals and instructions to staff that affect any member of the public, unless such materials are promptly published and copies offered for sale. To the extent required to prevent a clearly unwarranted invasion of personal privacy, an agency may delete identifying details when it makes available or publishes an opinion, statement of policy, interpretation, or staff manual or instruction: *Provided*, That in every case the justification for the deletion must be fully explained in writing. Every agency also shall maintain and make available for public inspection and copying a current index providing identifying information for the public as to any matter which is issued, adopted, or promulgated after the effective date of this Act and which is required by this subsection to be made available or published. No final order, opinion, statement of policy, interpretation, or staff manual or instruction that affects any member of the public may be relied upon, used or cited as precedent by an agency against any private party unless it has been indexed and either made available or published as provided by this subsection or unless that private party shall have actual and timely notice of the terms thereof.

(c) *Agency records.*—Except with respect to the records made available pursuant to subsections (a) and (b), every agency shall upon request for identifiable records made in accordance with published rules stating the time, place, fees to the extent authorized by statute and procedure to be followed, make such records promptly available to any person. Upon complaint, the district court of the United States in the district in which the complainant resides, or has his principal place of business, or in which the agency records are situated shall have jurisdiction to enjoin the agency from the withholding of agency records and to order the production of any agency records improperly withheld from the complainant. In such cases the court shall determine the matter de novo and the burden shall be upon the agency to sustain its action. In the event of noncompliance with the court's order, the district court may punish the responsible officers for contempt. Except as to those causes which the court deems of greater importance, proceedings before the district court as authorized by this subsection shall take precedence on the docket over all other causes and shall be assigned for hearing and trial at the earliest practicable date and expedited in every way.

(d) *Agency proceedings.*—Every agency having more than one member shall keep a record of the final votes of each member in every agency proceeding and such record shall be available for public inspection.

(e) *Exemptions.*—The provisions of this section shall not be applicable to matters that are (1) specifically required by Executive order to be kept secret in the interest of the national defense or foreign policy; (2) related solely to the internal personnel rules and practices of any agency; (3) specifically exempted from disclosure by statute; (4) trade secrets and commercial or financial information obtained from any person and privileged or confidential; (5) interagency or intra-agency memorandums or letters which would not be available by

---

[5] Final opinions of an agency are not of course precedent in any legal sense, but they will tend to be followed in subsequent decisions. This is why the law of 1966 (amending s. 3) required some measure of publicity to be given to opinions, as some agencies are tempted to lay down rules of practice in their opinions, in preference to making "rules" to which the procedure of s. 4 (below) would apply; see footnote 2, above.

law to a private party in litigation with the agency; (6) personnel and medical files and similar files the disclosure of which would constitute a clearly unwarranted invasion of personal privacy; (7) investigatory files compiled for law enforcement purposes except to the extent available by law to a private party; (8) contained in or related to examination, operating, or condition reports prepared by, on behalf of, or for the use of any agency responsible for the regulation or supervision of financial institutions; and (9) geological and geophysical information and data (including maps) concerning wells.

(f) *Limitation of exemptions.*—Nothing in this section authorizes withholding of information or limiting the availability of records to the public except as specifically stated in this section, nor shall this section be authority to withhold information from Congress.

(g) *Private party.*—As used in this section, "private party" means any party other than an agency.

RULE-MAKING[6]

Sec. 4.—Except to the extent that there is involved (1) any military, naval, or foreign affairs function of the United States or (2) any matter relating to agency management or personnel or to public property, loans, grants, benefits, or contracts—

(a) *Notice.*—General notice of proposed rule-making shall be published in the Federal Register (unless all persons subject thereto are named and either personally served or otherwise have actual notice thereof in accordance with law) and shall include (1) a statement of the time, place, and nature of public rule-making proceedings; (2) reference to the authority under which the rule is proposed; and (3) either the terms or substance of the proposed rule or a description of the subjects and issues involved. Except where notice or hearing is required by statute, this sub-section shall not apply to interpretative rules, general statements of policy, rules of agency organization, procedure, or practice, or in any situation in which the agency for good cause finds (and incorporates the finding and a brief statement of the reasons therefor in the rules issued) that notice and public procedure thereon are impracticable, unnecessary, or contrary to the public interest.

(b) *Procedures.*—After notice required by this section, the agency shall afford interested persons an opportunity to participate in the rule-making through submission of written data, views, or arguments with or without opportunity to present the same orally in any manner[7]; and, after consideration of all relevant matter presented, the agency shall incorporate in any rules adopted a concise general statement of their basis and purpose. Where rules are required by statute to be made on the record after opportunity for an agency hearing, the requirements of sections 7 and 8 shall apply in place of the provisions of this subsection.

(c) *Effective dates.*—The required publication or service of any substantive rule (other than one granting or recognizing exemption or relieving restriction or interpretative rules and statements of policy) shall be made not less than thirty days prior to the effective date thereof except as otherwise provided by the agency upon good cause found and published with the rule.

(d) *Petitions.*—Every agency shall accord any interested person the right to petition for the issuance, amendment, or repeal of a rule.

---

[6] This section providing for antecedent publicity for rule-making, "has proved most beneficial in practice": Schwartz and Wade, *Legal Control of Government*, at p. 87.

[7] This principle, that an interested person should have a right to participate in the delegated law-making process, goes much further than the duty to *consult* imposed on a Minister in some modern English statutes (Chapter IV, *ante*, p. 74). According to Professor K. C. Davis, however, it should be recognised as part of the essential principle of an individual's "right to a hearing": see "English Administrative Law—An American View", at [1962] P.L. 151.

Adjudication

Sec. 5.—In every case of adjudication required by statute[8] to be determined on the record after opportunity for an agency hearing, except to the extent that there is involved (1) any matter subject to a subsequent trial of the law and the facts de novo in any court; (2) the selection or tenure of an officer or employee of the United States other than examiners appointed pursuant to section 11; (3) proceedings in which decisions rest solely on inspections, tests, or elections; (4) the conduct of military, naval, or foreign-affairs functions; (5) cases in which an agency is acting as an agent for a court; and (6) the certification of employee representatives—

(a) *Notice*.—Persons entitled to notice of an agency hearing shall be timely informed of (1) the time, place, and nature thereof; (2) the legal authority and jurisdiction under which the hearing is to be held; and (3) the matters of fact and law asserted. In instances in which private persons are the moving parties, other parties to the proceeding shall give prompt notice of issues controverted in fact or law; and in other instances agencies may by rule require responsive pleading. In fixing the times and places for hearings, due regard shall be had for the convenience and necessity of the parties or their representatives.

(b) *Procedure*.[9]—The agency shall afford all interested parties opportunity for (1) the submission and consideration of facts, argument, offers of settlement, or proposals of adjustment where time, the nature of the proceeding, and the public interest permit, and (2) to the extent that the parties are unable so to determine any controversy by consent, hearing, and decision upon notice and in conformity with sections 7 and 8.

(c) *Separation of functions*.—The same officers who preside at the reception of evidence pursuant to section 7 shall make the recommended decision or initial decision required by section 8 except where such officers become unavailable to the agency. Save to the extent required for the disposition of ex parte matters as authorized by law, no such officer shall consult any person or party on any fact in issue unless upon notice and opportunity for all parties to participate; nor shall such officer be responsible to or subject to the supervision or direction of any officer, employee, or agent engaged in the performance of investigative or prosecuting functions for any agency. No officer, employee, or agent engaged in the performance of investigative or prosecuting functions for any agency in any case shall, in that or a factually related case, participate or advise in the decision, recommended decision, or agency review pursuant to section 8 except as witness or counsel in public proceedings. This subsection shall not apply in determining applications for initial licenses or to proceedings involving the validity or application of rates, facilities, or practices of public utilities or carriers; nor shall it be applicable in any manner to the agency or any member or members of the body comprising the agency.

(d) *Declaratory orders*.—The agency is authorized in its sound discretion, with like effect as in the case of other orders, to issue a declaratory order to terminate a controversy or remove uncertainty.

Ancillary Matters

Sec. 6.—Except as otherwise provided in this Act—

(a) *Appearance*.—Any person compelled to appear in person before any agency or representative thereof shall be accorded the right to be accompanied, represented, and advised by counsel or, if permitted by the agency, by other qualified representative. Every party shall be accorded the right to appear in person or by or with counsel or other duly qualified representative in any agency

[8] Of the *Federal* Congress; of course the entire statute applies only to Federal procedures and statutes.

[9] See also s. 7 below.

proceeding. So far as the orderly conduct of public business permits, any interested person may appear before any agency or its responsible officers or employees for the presentation, adjustment, or determination or any issue, request, or controversy in any proceeding (interlocutory, summary, or otherwise) or in connection with any agency function. Every agency shall proceed with reasonable dispatch to conclude any matter presented to it except that due regard shall be had for the convenience and necessity of the parties or their representatives. Nothing herein shall be construed either to grant or to deny to any person who is not a lawyer the right to appear for or represent others before any agency or in any agency proceeding.

(b) *Investigations.*—No process, requirement of a report, inspection, or other investigative act or demand shall be issued, made, or enforced in any manner or for any purpose except as authorized by law. Every person compelled to submit data or evidence shall be entitled to retain or, on payment of lawfully prescribed costs, procure a copy or transcript thereof, except that in a nonpublic investigatory proceeding the witness may for good cause be limited to inspection of the official transcript of his testimony.

(c) *Subpenas.*—Agency subpenas authorized by law shall be issued to any party upon request and, as may be required by rules of procedure, upon a statement or showing of general relevance and reasonable scope of the evidence sought. Upon contest the court shall sustain any such subpena or similar process or demand to the extent that it is found to be in accordance with law and, in any proceeding for enforcement, shall issue an order requiring the appearance of the witness or the production of the evidence or data within a reasonable time under penalty of punishment for contempt in case of contumacious failure to comply.

(d) *Denials.*—Prompt notice shall be given of the denial in whole or in part of any written application, petition, or other request of any interested person made in connection with any agency proceeding. Except in affirming a prior denial or where the denial is self-explanatory, such notice shall be accompanied by a simple statement of procedural or other grounds.

Hearings

Sec. 7.—In hearings which section 4 or 5 requires to be conducted pursuant to this section—

(a) *Presiding officers.*—There shall preside at the taking of evidence (1) the agency, (2) one or more members of the body which comprises the agency, or (3) one or more examiners appointed as provided in this Act; but nothing in this Act shall be deemed to supersede the conduct of specified classes of proceedings in whole or part by or before boards or other officers specially provided for by or designated pursuant to statute. The functions of all presiding officers and of officers participating in decisions in conformity with section 8 shall be conducted in an impartial manner. Any such officer may at any time withdraw if he deems himself disqualified; and, upon the filing in good faith of a timely and sufficient affidavit of personal bias or disqualification of any such officer, the agency shall determine the matter as a part of the record and decision in the case.

(b) *Hearing powers.*—Officers presiding at hearings shall have authority, subject to the published rules of the agency and within its powers, to (1) administer oaths and affirmations, (2) issue subpenas authorized by law, (3) rule upon offers of proof and receive relevant evidence, (4) take or cause depositions to be taken whenever the ends of justice would be served thereby, (5) regulate the course of the hearing, (6) hold conferences for the settlement or simplification of the issues by consent of the parties, (7) dispose of procedural requests or similar matters, (8) make decisions or recommend decisions in conformity with section 8, and (9) take any other action authorized by agency rule consistent with this Act.

(c) *Evidence.*—Except as statutes otherwise provide, the proponent of a rule or order shall have the burden of proof. Any oral or documentary evidence may be received, but every agency shall as a matter of policy provide for the exclusion of irrelevant, immaterial, of unduly repetitious evidence and no sanction shall be imposed or rule or order be issued except upon consideration of the whole record or such portions thereof as may be cited by any party and as supported by and in accordance with the reliable, probative, and substantial evidence. Every party shall have the right to present his case or defense by oral or documentary evidence, to submit rebuttal evidence, and to conduct such cross-examination as may be required for a full and true disclosure of the facts. In rule-making or determining claims for money or benefits or applications for initial licenses any agency may, where the interest of any party will not be prejudiced thereby, adopt procedures for the submission of all or part of the evidence in written form.

(d) *Record.*—The transcript of testimony and exhibits, together with all papers and requests filed in the proceeding, shall constitute the exclusive record for decision in accordance with section 8 and, upon payment of lawfully prescribed costs, shall be made available to the parties. Where any agency decision rests on official notice of a material fact not appearing in the evidence in the record, any party shall on timely request be afforded an opportunity to show the contrary.

Decisions

Sec. 8.—In cases in which a hearing is required to be conducted in conformity with section 7—

(a) *Action by subordinates.*—In cases in which the agency has not presided at the reception of the evidence, the officer who presided (or, in cases not subject to subsection (c) of section 5, any other officer or officers qualified to preside at hearings pursuant to section 7) shall initially decide the case or the agency shall require (in specific cases or by general rule) the entire record to be certified to it for initial decision. Whenever such officers make the initial decision and in the absence of either an appeal to the agency or review upon motion of the agency within time provided by rule, such decision shall without further proceedings then become the decision of the agency. On appeal from or review of the initial decisions of such officers the agency shall, except as it may limit the issues upon notice or by rule, have all the powers which it would have in making the initial decision. Whenever the agency makes the initial decision without having presided at the reception of the evidence, such officers shall first recommend a decision except that in rule-making or determining applications for initial licenses (1) in lieu thereof the agency may issue a tentative decision or any of its responsible officers may recommend a decision or (2) any such procedure may be omitted in any case in which the agency finds upon the record that due and timely execution of its function imperatively and unavoidably so requires.

(b) *Submittals and decisions.*—Prior to each recommended, initial, or tentative decision, or decision upon agency review of the decision of subordinate officers the parties shall be afforded a reasonable opportunity to submit for the consideration of the officers participating in such decisions (1) proposed findings and conclusions, or (2) exceptions to the decisions or recommended decisions of subordinate officers or to tentative agency decisions, and (3) supporting reasons for such exceptions or proposed findings or conclusions. The record shall show the ruling upon each such finding, conclusion, or exception presented. All decisions (including initial recommended, or tentative decisions) shall become a part of the record and include a statement of (1) findings and conclusions, as well as the reasons or basis therefor, upon all the material issues of fact, law, or discretion presented on the record; and (2) the appropriate rule, order, sanction, relief, or denial thereof.

Sanctions and Powers

Sec. 9.—In the exercise of any power or authority—

(a) *In General.*—No sanction shall be imposed or substantive rule or order be issued except within jurisdiction delegated to the agency and as authorized by law.

(b) *Licenses.*—In any case in which application is made for a license required by law the agency, with due regard to the rights or privileges of all the interested parties or adversely affected persons and with reasonable dispatch, shall set and complete any proceedings required to be conducted pursuant to sections 7 and 8 of this Act or other proceedings required by law and shall make its decision. Except in cases of wilfulness or those in which public health, interest or safety requires otherwise, no withdrawal, suspension, revocation, or annulment of any license shall be lawful unless, prior to the institution of agency proceedings therefor, facts or conduct which may warrant such action shall have been called to the attention of the licensee by the agency in writing and the licensee shall have been accorded opportunity to demonstrate or achieve compliance with all lawful requirements. In any case in which the licensee has, in accordance with agency rules, made timely and sufficient application for a renewal or a new license, no license with reference to any activity of a continuing nature shall expire until such application shall have been finally determined by the agency.

Judicial Review

Sec. 10.—Except so far as (1) statutes preclude judicial review or (2) agency action is by law committed to agency discretion—

(a) *Right of review.*[10]—Any person suffering legal wrong because of any agency action, or adversely affected or aggrieved by such action within the meaning of any relevant statute, shall be entitled to judicial review thereof.

(b) *Form and venue of action.*—The form of proceeding for judicial review shall be any special statutory review proceeding relevant to the subject matter in any court specified by statute or, in the absence or inadequacy thereof, any applicable form of legal action (including actions for declaratory judgments or writs or prohibitory of mandatory injunction or habeas corpus) in any court of competent jurisdiction. Agency action shall be subject to judicial review in civil or criminal proceedings for judicial enforcement except to the extent that prior, adequate and exclusive opportunity for such review is provided by law.

(c) *Reviewable acts.*—Every agency action made reviewable by statute and every final agency action for which there is no other adequate remedy in any court shall be subject to judicial review. Any preliminary, procedural, or intermediate agency action or ruling not directly reviewable shall be subject to review upon the review of the final agency action. Except as otherwise expressly required by statute, agency action otherwise final shall be final for the purposes of this subsection whether or not there has been presented or determined any application for a declaratory order, for any form of reconsideration, or (unless the agency otherwise requires by rule and provides that the action meanwhile shall be inoperative) for an appeal to superior agency authority.

(d) *Interim relief.*—Pending judicial review any agency is authorized, where it finds that justice so requires, to postpone the effective date of any action taken by it. Upon such conditions as may be required and to the extent necessary to prevent irreparable injury, every reviewing court (including every court to which a case may be taken on appeal from or upon application for certiorari or other writ to a reviewing court) is authorized to issue all necessary and appropriate process to postpone the effective date of any agency action or to preserve status or rights pending conclusion of the review proceedings.

(e) *Scope of review.*—So far as necessary to decision and where presented the reviewing court shall decide all relevant questions of law, interpret constitutional and statutory provisions, and determine the meaning or applicability of the terms of any agency action. It shall (A) compel agency action unlawfully withheld or

---

[10] This subsection provides a simple procedure for the challenge of administrative action before the courts, by way of a petition for review, of which there is no close parallel in England. The section has been used to compel an agency to provide a hearing in accordance with the "due process" clause of the Constitution: see *Wong Yung Sung* v. *McGrath* (1950), 339 U.S. 33 and Schwartz & Wade, *op. cit.*, at p. 111.

unreasonably delayed; and (B) hold unlawful and set aside agency action, findings, and conclusions found to be (1) arbitrary, capricious, an abuse of discretion, or otherwise not in accordance with law; (2) contrary to constitutional right, power, privilege, or immunity; (3) in excess of statutory jurisdiction, authority, or limitations, or short of statutory right; (4) without observance of procedure required by law; (5) unsupported by substantial evidence[11] in any case subject to the requirements of sections 7 and 8 or otherwise reviewed on the record of an agency hearing provided by statute; or (6) unwarranted by the facts to the extent that the facts are subject to trial de novo by the reviewing court. In making the foregoing determinations the court shall review the whole record or such portions thereof as may be cited by any party, and due account shall be taken of the rule of prejudicial error.

Examiners

Sec. 11.—Subject to the civil-service and other laws to the extent not inconsistent with this Act, there shall be appointed by and for each agency as many qualified and competent examiners as may be necessary for proceedings pursuant to sections 7 and 8, who shall be assigned to cases in rotation so far as practicable and shall perform no duties inconsistent with their duties and responsibilities as examiners. Examiners shall be removable by the agency in which they are employed only for good cause established and determined by the Civil Service Commission (hereinafter called the Commission) after opportunity for hearing and upon the record thereof. Examiners shall receive compensation prescribed by the Commission independently of agency recommendations or ratings and in accordance with the Classification Act of 1923, as amended, except that the provisions of paragraphs (2) and (3) of subsection (b) of section 7 of said Act, as amended, and the provisions of section 9 of said Act, as amended, shall not be applicable. Agencies occasionally or temporarily insufficiently staffed may utilize examiners selected by the Commission from and with the consent of other agencies. For the purposes of this section, the Commission is authorized to make investigations, require reports by agencies, issue reports, including an annual report to the Congress, promulgate rules, appoint such advisory committees as may be deemed necessary, recommend legislation, subpena witnesses or records, and pay witness fees as established for the United States courts.

Construction and Effect

Sec. 12.—Nothing in this Act shall be held to diminish the constitutional rights of any person or to limit or repeal additional requirements imposed by statute or otherwise recognized by law. Except as otherwise required by law, all requirements or privileges relating to evidence or procedure shall apply equally to agencies and persons. If any provision of this Act or the application thereof is held invalid, the remainder of this Act or other applications of such provision shall not be affected. Every agency is granted all authority necessary to comply with the requirements of this Act through the issuance of rules or otherwise. No subsequent legislation shall be held to supersede or modify the provisions of this Act except to the extent that such legislation shall do so expressly. This Act shall take effect three months after its approval except that sections 7 and 8 shall take effect six months after such approval, the requirement of the selection of examiners pursuant to section 11 shall not become effective until one year after such approval, and no procedural requirement shall be mandatory as to any agency proceeding initiated prior to the effective date of such requirement.

---

[11] This important rule introduces, it seems, a test "not of the *rightness* but the *reasonableness* of administrative findings of fact": Schwartz, *An Introduction to American Administrative Law*, at p. 189.

APPENDIX II

BIBLIOGRAPHY ON ADMINISTRATIVE LAW

This does not purport to be a complete list of works, but it is hoped that it will prove to be of assistance to the student wishing to obtain further information on particular topics. References to articles in periodicals are not included in this list, but will be found in the text.

1. General Books

Anson, *Law and Custom of the Constitution* (Oxford).
Bagehot, *The English Constitution* (Oxford).
Brett & Hogg, *Administrative Law Cases and Materials* (Australian) (Law Book Co.).
Dicey, *Law of the Constitution* (Macmillan).
Foulkes, *Introduction to Administrative Law* (Butterworths).
Garner, *Public Control of Land* (Sweet & Maxwell).
Griffith & Street, *Principles of Administrative Law* (Pitman).
Heuston, *Essays in Constitutional Law* (Stevens).
Jennings, *The Law and the Constitution* (U. of London Press).
Marshall, *Constitutional Theory* (Oxford).
Marshall & Moodie, *Some Problems of the Constitution* (Hutchinson).
Mitchell, *Constitutional Law* (W. Green & Sons).
Hood Phillips, *Constitutional and Administrative Law* (Sweet & Maxwell).
Robson, *Justice and Administrative Law* (Stevens).
de Smith, *Constitutional and Administrative Law* (Penguins).
Wade & Phillips, *Constitutional Law* (Longmans).
Wade, *Administrative Law* (Oxford).
Yardley, *A Source Book of English Administrative Law* (Butterworth).

2. Central Government and Legislation

Allen, *Law and Orders* (Stevens).
Allen, *Law in the Making* (Oxford).
Carr, *Concerning English Administrative Law* (Oxford).
Hanson & Wiseman, *Parliament at Work* (Stevens).
Jennings, *Cabinet Government* (Cambridge).
Kersell, *Parliamentary Supervision of Delegated Legislation* (Stevens).
Parliamentary Reform, 1933–1960, The Hansard Society (Cassell).
Morrison, *Government and Parliament* (Oxford).
Sieghart, *Government by Decree* (*A comparative study*) (Stevens).
Stacey, *The British Ombudsman* (Oxford).
Wheare, *Government by Committee* (Oxford).
Wheare, *Maladministration and its Remedies*, Hamlyn Lectures (Stevens).

3. Judicial Review

Denning, *Freedom under the Law*, Hamlyn Lectures (Stevens).
Dowrick, *Justice According to the English Common Lawyers* (Butterworth).
Jackson, *Natural Justice* (Sweet & Maxwell).
Marshall, *Natural Justice* (Stevens).
McDermott, *Protection from Power*, Hamlyn Lectures (Stevens).
McWhinney, *Judicial Review in the English Speaking World* (U. of Toronto Press).
Port, *Administrative Law* (Longmans).
Rubinstein, *Jurisdiction and Illegality* (Oxford).
Schwartz & Wade, *Legal Control of Government* (Oxford).
de Smith, *The Judicial Review of Administrative Action* (Stevens).
Thio, *Locus Standi and Judicial Review* (Singapore U.P.).
Zamir, *The Declaratory Judgment* (Stevens).

4. Administrative Tribunals

Allen, *Administrative Jurisdiction* (Stevens).
Elcock, *Administrative Justice* (Longmans).
Keeton, *Trial by Tribunal* (Museum Press).
Hewart, *The New Despotism* (Ernest Benn).
Pollard, *Administrative Tribunals at Work* (Stevens).
Street, *Justice and the Welfare State*, Hamlyn Lectures (Stevens).
Vandyk, *Tribunals and Inquiries* (Oyez).
Wraith & Lamb, *Public Inquiry as an Instrument of Government* (Allen & Unwin).
Wraith & Hutchesson, *Administrative Tribunals* (Allen & Unwin).

5. Proceedings against Public Authorities

Hogg, *Liability of the Crown* (Law Book Co. of Australia).
Mitchell, *The Contracts of Public Authorities* (Bell).
Street, *Governmental Liability* (Cambridge).
Williams, Glanville, *Crown Proceedings* (Stevens).

6. Local Government

(a) *General*

Buxton, *Local Government* (Penguins, Law & Society).
Cross, *Local Government Law* (Sweet & Maxwell).
Finer, H., *English Local Government* (Methuen).
Griffith, *Central Departments and Local Authorities* (Allen & Unwin).
Hart, *Introduction to the Law of Local Government and Administration* (Butterworths).
Headrick, *The Town Clerk in English Local Government* (Allen & Unwin).
Jackson, *The Machinery of Local Government* (Macmillan).
Jennings, *Principles of Local Government Law* (U. of London Press).
Redlich & Hirst, *The History of Local Government in England* (ed. Keith-Lucas) (Macmillan).
Robson, *Local Government in Crisis* (Allen & Unwin).
Warren, *Municipal Administration* (Pitman).

(b) *Particular topics*

Cross, *Encyclopaedia of Highway Law* (Sweet & Maxwell).
Garner, *Civic Ceremonial* (Shaw & Sons).
Garner, *Law of Sewers and Drains* (Shaw & Sons).
Lumley's *Public Health* (Butterworth).
Heap, *An Outline of Planning Law* (Sweet & Maxwell).
Schofield & Sales, *Housing Law and Practice* (Shaw & Sons).

7. Public Corporations

Government Enterprise: A Comparative Study (ed. Friemann and Garner) (Stevens).
Hanson, *Parliament and Public Ownership* (Cassell).
Robson, *Nationalised Industry and Public Ownership* (George Allen & Unwin).

8. Foreign and Commonwealth Systems

Legrand, *L'Ombudsman Scandinave* [in French: L.G.D.J.].
Rowat, *The Ombudsman* (Allen & Unwin).

Australia

Benjafield & Whitmore, *Australian Administrative Law* (Law Book Co.).
Brett & Hogg, *Administrative Law, Cases and Materials* (Butterworth).
Hogg, *Liability of the Crown* (*ante*).

Canada

Dussault, *Le Contrôle Judiciaire de l'administration au Québec* (University of Laval Press).
Reid, *Administrative Law and Practice* (Butterworth).

France

Brown & Garner, *French Administrative Law* (Butterworth).
Chapman, *An Introduction to French Local Government* (Allen & Unwin).
Hamson, *Executive Discretion and Judicial Control*, Hamlyn Lectures (Stevens).
Schwartz, *French Administrative Law and the Common Law World* (N.Y. University Press).
Waline, *Droit Administratif* (Sirey—Paris).

India

Fazal, *Judicial Control of Administrative Action in India and Pakistan* (Oxford).
Markose, *Judicial Control of Administrative Action in India* (Madras Law Journal).

New Zealand

Paterson, *An Introduction to Administrative Law in New Zealand* (Butterworth).

U.S.A.

Cooper, *State Administrative Law* (Bobbs-Merrill).
Corwin, *The Constitution and What it means Today* (Princeton U. Press).
Davis, *Administrative Law Treatise* (West Publishing Co.).
Davis, *Discretionary Justice* (Louisiana State U.P.).
Parker, *Administrative Law* (Bobbs-Merrill).
Schwartz, *American Constitutional Law* (Cambridge).
Schwartz, *An Introduction to American Administrative Law* (Oceana & Pitman).
Schwartz & Wade, *Legal Control of Government* (Oxford)—a comparative study of judicial control in Britain and the United States.

9. Reports

Donoughmore Committee Report (1932; Cmd. 4060).
Franks Committee Report (1957; Cmd. 218).
Royal Commission on Local Government in Greater London, 1957–60 (1960; Cmd. 1164).
Annual Reports of the Council on Tribunals, 1959–date.
Quarterly and Annual Reports of the Parliamentary Commissioner for Administration, 1968–date.
The Citizen and the Administration (a Report by *Justice*: Stevens, 1961).
The Rule of Law in a Free Society (International Commission of Jurists, 1959).
The Rule of Law (Conservative Political Centre, 1955).
Let Right be Done (Conservative Political Centre, 1966).
The Citizen and his Council (a Report by *Justice*: Stevens, 1969).
Administration under Law (a Report by *Justice*: Stevens, 1971).
Report of the Committee on the Staffing of Local Government ("Mallaby" Committee, H.M.S.O., 1967).
Report of the Committee on the Management of Local Government ("Maud" Committee, H.M.S.O., 1967), Vols. 1 and 4.
Report of the Royal Commission on Local Government in England, 1966–1969 ("Redcliffe-Maud"; Cmnd. 4040).

INDEX

C

O

Q

U

V

W